GARDENS
OF EUROPE

A Traveller's Guide

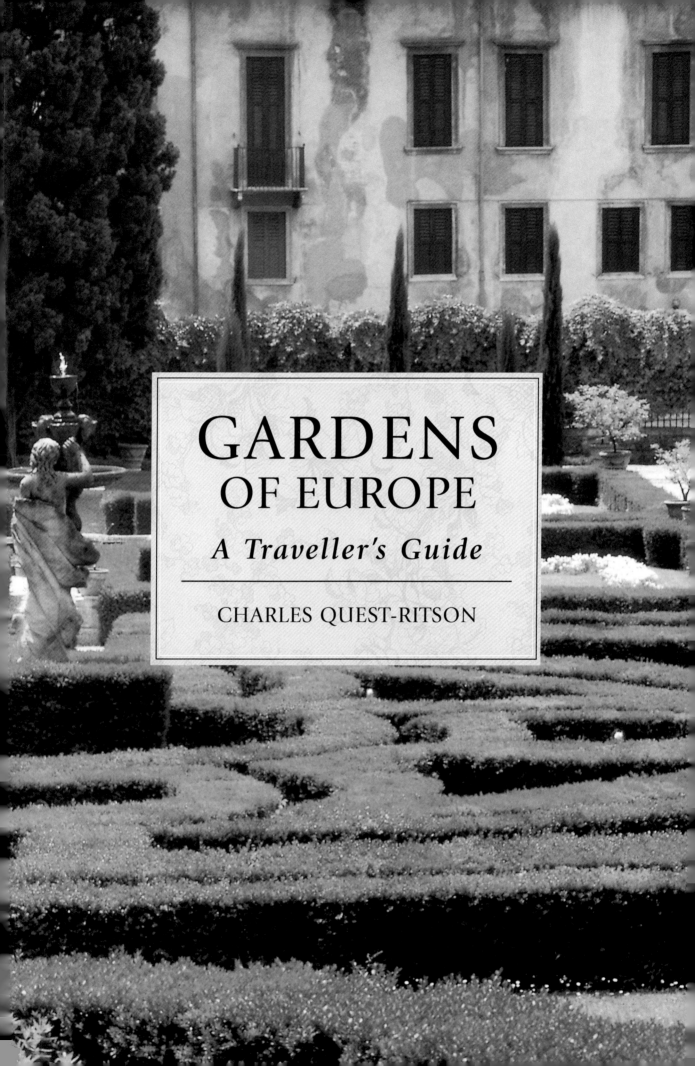

GARDENS
OF EUROPE

A Traveller's Guide

CHARLES QUEST-RITSON

This edition first published
in England in 2007 by
Garden Art Press
an imprint of
Antique Collectors' Club Ltd
Sandy Lane, Old Martlesham
Woodbridge, Suffolk
IP12 4SD, England

Book first published in Australia in 2007 by
Bloomings Books Pty Ltd

ISBN 10: 1 870673 55 7
ISBN 13: 978-1-870673-55-6

British Library Cataloguing-in-Publication Data
A catalogue record for this book is available from
the British Library

Designer: Danie Pout Design
Editor: Judy Brookes
Publisher: Warwick Forge
Printer: Everbest Printing Co Ltd

While every care has been taken to ensure that
information in this book is accurate, much of it
is subject to change and readers are well advised
to confirm opening hours and other details.

The Publisher would be pleased to hear from
anyone wishing to correct information or offer
comment about the gardens that could be included
in a future edition of *Gardens of Europe*. We should
also like to hear from anyone wishing to volunteer
photographs for future editions.
Email: *warwick@bloomings.com.au*

RIGHT: Hidcote Manor, Great Britain
Previous pages
PAGE i: Villa d'Este, Italy
PAGES ii–iii: Giardino Guisti, Italy

Foreword

This is an important book. It is more than fifteen years since any author has attempted a comprehensive survey of European gardens – gardens that all merit a visit. The last full study was published in 1990 before politics swept away boundaries and restrictions in central and eastern Europe.

Charles Quest-Ritson is well known for his scholarly works on gardening topics. He brings his knowledge of history and a fund of botanical expertise to his writing and skilfully covers centuries of change in garden styles, combined with an understanding of the importance today of botanical gardens, arboreta and private plant collections. He also has a gift for garden description, which he employs to full extent in *Gardens of Europe*. His enthusiasm and objectivity will fire the reader to exploration. This book is not only a practical – if bulky – guide for the energetic, it is also eminently readable for the armchair traveller. Indeed, few of us can hope to visit all the distant corners of Europe where his research has taken him.

Since the earliest desert gardens in western civilisation, the development of gardening has depended upon an aesthetic compromise between man's art and nature's promise. Today, the dialogue has altered; nature is threatened and man's role in saving the environment depends on understanding and collation of knowledge. Botanic gardens, originally gardens of 'simples' for medical students, today play a vital role in research and education of the public, whose support they need.

Although this is primarily a guide book, Quest-Ritson traces the nuances of garden history in the different and very

Parc del Laberint, Spain. Light and shade are important elements of formal gardens in Spain and Italy.

Germany has many of Europe's best baroque and landscape gardens, such as Schloßgarten Schwerin.

varied climatic conditions and landscape that prevail on such a large canvas. Rightly he gives the 16th-century Italian renaissance garden pride of place in influencing the subsequent developments of the baroque and rococo gardens in France and the rest of Europe. From Italy we have learnt the principles of design: a geometry with careful alignment, cross-axes, volumes of space and focal points, expanded by the French to control optical illusions and linear perspective.

These ideas were adopted by the royal courts of Europe, their influence spreading to Sweden and St Petersburg, leaving a legacy of authoritarian formality. Many of these gardens still exist today, vividly described in this guide. The 18th-century landscape movement, in which man learned to work with nature rather than against it, originated in England, perhaps not surprisingly since the temperate climate of the British Isles encouraged plantsmanship and a passion for gardening. Instead of geometric patterns, the

new style (rapidly spreading throughout Europe as 'the English garden', in which plants and naturalistic planting became as important as any design formula) has continued in the ascendant, keeping the gardener in touch with nature and plant ecology. The public park is now an essential ingredient of city planning, providing recreational facilities and educating people to environmental issues.

Gardens of Europe is a thoroughly practical guide book and offers opportunities to visit relatively unsung gardens in relatively obscure gardening territories without ignoring the grander sweeps of history and the iconic gardens that set the trends of their day. It has everything to recommend it.

Penelope Hobhouse

Contents

Foreword by Penelope Hobhouse v
Introduction ix
Symbols Key xv
The Great Gardens of Europe xv

Introduction

It has been fun writing this book, and an education, too. As it progressed, I realised that I had probably visited as many leading European gardens as anyone else before me. For the first time, the opening up of central and eastern Europe has made possible what was unthinkable twenty years ago, when Penelope Hobhouse and Patrick Taylor wrote their pioneering book, *The Gardens of Europe* (George Philip, 1990). I owe a debt to their inspiration and help, and to Penelope's enthusiasm for my attempt to update our knowledge of Europe's garden heritage.

The opportunity to visit and revisit so many gardens in the ex-Communist countries has also enabled me to consider Europe's garden heritage as a whole, to make comparisons and to come to conclusions. Many are fairly obvious: England, for example, is the place to see horticultural gardens, France is the great exponent of the baroque, Germany has the best botanic gardens in Europe, and Italy was the crucible of the Renaissance, where 'modern' gardens were first made in about 1500. There is much, too, to admire and enjoy in such countries as Spain, Portugal, Poland and Russia, as well as Scandinavia and central Europe.

But other conclusions are perhaps less obvious: the importance of wealth for the creation of great gardens, the significance of fashion (it enables owners to use their gardens to show off), the importance of continuity for the survival of gardens, and the ill effects of war, impoverishment and social revolution.

GARDENING HISTORY

The history of gardening is the history of taste, fashion and economic progress, as applied, for the most part, to the surroundings of dwellings. Many of the changes over the last 500 years have come from looking to the past for fresh inspiration. Classicism is an outstanding example. Renaissance styles were directly inspired by the writings of the ancients. Archaeological excavations in the period 1500–1750 gave fresh impetus to such architects as Pirro Ligorio in Italy, Le Nôtre in France and William Kent in Britain. So did the discovery and excavation of such sites as Pompeii and Herculaneum from 1750 onwards. Throughout the 19th century the great imperial powers of France, Germany and Great Britain adopted classical splendour as statements of wealth, achievement and national self-esteem.

OPPOSITE: The gardens at Villandry, though less than 100 years old, recall the great renaissance gardens of France.

Schönbrunn, Vienna. Baroque and rococo gardens attained some of their most complex and exquisite forms in Germany and Austria.

Despite the scholarship of mediaeval historians and archaeologists, our knowledge of gardens before 1500 is scant. Modern reconstructions abound, but they are usually over-imaginative, sanitised, romantic, idealised visions. Indeed, very little remains from the 16th century in any part of Europe, except in Italy and Spain, each of which has traces of ancient Roman and Islamic gardens. The year 1660 is a more appropriate starting date for modern garden history, when the Thirty Years War and the English Civil War both ended, and Louis XIV was firmly established on the throne of France. By 1720, all the set-piece statements of monarchical might were in place – Het Loo, Hampton Court, Drottningholm, Peterhof and Versailles. They were shortly followed by a secondary spate of power statements from up-and-coming rulers – Caserta, Sanssouci and Wilanów.

These grand baroque gardens were followed from about 1750 onwards by the landscape style that originated in England at such estates as Stowe and Stourhead and spread quickly throughout the continent. It reached St Petersburg in 1762, when the Empress Catherine the Great converted the grand palace gardens of Tsarskoe Selo to a flowing natural layout, and as far afield by 1785 as the Neapolitan palace of Caserta, whose English garden (with un-English plants) is still the greatest example of the landscape style within the Mediterranean basin.

The landscape style continued to dominate the 19th century, but this was accompanied by a return to formality and, more specifically, to Italianate gardens based on a re-interpretation of the renaissance style. Italianate gardens occur throughout Europe, at such places as Sanssouci in Germany and Shrubland in England, and may even be found in Italy itself in such stunningly beautiful gardens as Villa Durazzo-Pallavicini near Genoa.

The Moorish style developed in Spain from about 1830 as a response to the excavations at Granada; it was boosted towards the end of the century by the

Arts-and-Crafts movement, so that the Arabic style became the dominant Spanish garden idiom that it remains today. Japanese gardens entered European consciousness as a result of the commercial opening up of the archipelago in the 1860s. The Japanese style remains a powerful influence in European gardens today, though most examples are Euro-Japanese hybrids, the result of cross-pollination between oriental originals and European perceptions. The same is true of the short-lived fashion for Chinese gardens in the 18th century. Nevertheless, most European garden history grew out of Europe itself.

Not all styles were widely exported outside their country of origin. The English woodland style, popular between 1880 and 1950 and typified by the Savill and Valley gardens near Windsor, is seldom seen on the mainland of Europe, and the same is true of the 1920s French neo-classicism outside France. The 'new German' 20th-century planting of natural masses of herbaceous plants has not, with few exceptions, been exported successfully to the rest of Europe. There is, however, much to learn from the leading examples within Germany itself, notably the Sichtungsgarten at Weihenstephan, Hermannshof at Weinheim and Gruga-park at Essen.

Many of the wealthy garden owners in the 19th century made extensive collections of plants of every kind, from orchids and cacti to exotic fruits and arboreta. Usually it is only the trees that remain, especially in central and eastern Europe, to remind us of the riches and aspirations of a long-lost social order.

Nowadays, there are so many different trends, fuelled by increased prosperity and aesthetic education, that it is hard to be certain which will, in retrospect, be seen to have dominated the early years of the 21st century. Certainly, the English

passion for gardening with ornamental plants has spread widely throughout Europe, and there has never been more historical re-creation and reconstruction than currently in eastern Germany. There are also experiments in creative ego-trips like Vigeland in Norway and Niki de Saint Phalle's Tarot Garden in Italy, and a widespread rediscovery, especially in France and Germany, of the 19th-century love of large, colourful exotic bedding schemes. It is worth a long journey to see such gardens as Lyon's Parc de la Tête d'Or and Ludwigsburg's Blühendes Barock, where the art is practised with consummate skill.

Political and social history is also reflected in the development of botanic gardens. Padua's was the first, founded in 1545 as a collection of useful herbs. Pharmacology was the driving force behind most of the early botanic gardens, all of them creatures of renaissance learning. During the 17th century they became instruments for the collection

Giardini dei Tarocchi in Italy is Europe's best example of a garden devoted to surrealism.

Pavlovsk Park, Russia. The classical revival contributed much to the elegance of landscape parks and gardens.

and study of plants and, in the 18th century, provided the material for the systematic ordering of the botanical world by such taxonomists as Carl Linnaeus in Uppsala. By the beginning of the 19th century, botanic gardens were statements of national power and imperial ambition. Bavaria's botanic garden at Munich was intended to out-shine the great Prussian example in Berlin. Kew became the instrument for com-mercial plantations of commodity crops like rubber and tea throughout the British Empire. And most botanic gardens nowa-days, though still endowed with great plant collections, see themselves as public amenities and agents for biodiversity.

USING THIS GUIDE

The aim of this book is to supply sufficient detail to enable readers to decide which European gardens to visit and when. The list is not exhaustive, but the gardens are (in my judgement) the best in each country and representative of what that country offers. Thus, there is an emphasis upon historic gardens in Italy, but upon horticultural creations in the Netherlands, because that is where each country's

strength lies. The book as a whole tries to achieve a fair balance between the different kinds of garden, where the principal interest may be historic, artistic, botanic or horticultural. Each of these has subdivisions: a historic garden, for example, may be important for its design, its decoration, its influence, its association with historic events or the strength of its underlying message. It is as well to remember that not all gardens exist to grow plants in; the great layouts of the 17th and 18th centuries were statements of power, not of horticultural dalliance.

Gardens are listed by country (e.g. France, Italy) or region (e.g. Scandinavia) and then roughly according to their geographical position, starting at the top left-hand corner of a map and moving across as if one were reading a book. Thus, for example, the gardens of Germany begin in Schleswig-Holstein and end in Bayern. The number borne by each garden on the relevant map corresponds to its position within the chapter. Almost all the listed gardens are open regularly and equipped to welcome visitors. A few remain open only by appointment, but in these cases permission to visit is readily given. It is essential to check visiting hours and facilities before planning a visit and again before setting out. Most gardens now have dedicated websites that are well kept, up to date and informative.

I have included a good range of botanic gardens and arboreta, because their *raison d'être* when most were founded was the accumulation of collections of living plants, for medicine and study, for economic potential and to inspire awe. Many garden visitors are principally interested in seeing plants well grown, and learning about new plants that they might be able to grow themselves. Botanic gardens are a bottomless fund of inspiration and delight to plantsmen.

The incidence of good gardens is unevenly spread. Do not assume that, because Belgium and Denmark are small countries, their gardens are not of interest. They may be fewer, but their standard is certainly a match in quality for the four big nations (England, France, Germany and Italy). But there are also many more gardens in Britain, France and Germany than in, say, Slovakia or Greece. Here the discrepancy is explained not by size or population, but in terms of history, wealth and culture – Slovakia and Greece lack a patrician culture.

When planning a trip, you should remember that gardens are enormously influenced by climatic, geological and geographical conditions. The western edges of the continent have a mild, maritime climate, while winters in inland eastern Europe are extremely cold. The Mediterranean enjoys cool, damp winters and hot, dry summers, but the high mountain ranges all over the continent support a large indigenous alpine flora adapted to long winters of snow. These factors affect not just the plants that grow in a garden, but also the garden's structure and even its visiting hours. Do not plan to visit alpine gardens or rose gardens in winter. Soil, too, has an effect. The richest alpine gardens are made of plants found naturally on limestone rocks, while the flat, sandy, acidic soils of northern Europe, stretching from Belgium right across to St Petersburg, are perfect for heathers and rhododendrons.

Zámecký Park, Czech Republic. Rare plant collections, extensive glasshouses and seasonal bedding were often flaunted by the wealthy.

The naturalistic planting in Piet Oudolf's garden in the Netherlands is successfully contained by strong architectural features, such as these hedges cut like classical pediments.

Visitors from North America or Australia will know how much the climate and growing conditions differ within those continents. The same is true of Europe. Roses reach their peak of beauty in southern Spain at the end of April, a month later in Tuscany and Paris, at the end of June in England and northern Germany, and not until mid- or late July in Sweden and Finland.

The actual condition of a garden makes a great difference to the pleasure of visiting it. One of the criteria I adopted in making my selection for this book was the current standard of management and maintenance. A few of the gardens are not maintained as well as they were in the past, and these shortcomings are generally mentioned in the text. You should not, however, expect such elevated levels of excellence in poorer countries with recent histories of war and deprivation as in the rich, established democracies of north-west Europe. The fate of the great gardens – and houses too – that were once among the chief jewels of Hungary, the Czech Republic and Poland is still one of the most obvious differences today between 'Eastern' and 'Western' Europe.

How much is retrievable in central and eastern Europe where an aristocratic culture was systematically destroyed or neglected by 40 years of Communism? Not much, I suspect; at least until the countries in question reach a state of economic development where reconstruction becomes an achievable priority. The unification movements that led to the creation of modern Italy and Germany also brought about a loss of variety as the symbols of older political loyalties were allowed to crumble. The Bourbon kings of the Two Sicilies would weep to see the condition today of their La Favorita park outside Palermo, as would the kings of Saxony if they returned to Dresden's Großergarten.

Today Europe is one country: travel within its boundaries is much easier now than twenty years ago and Europeans themselves are more widely travelled. Road, rail and air travel is fast and comfortable, border controls are fewer and less stringent, the Euro has been adopted as the single currency in all major countries except Russia and the United Kingdom, and English has emerged, for better or worse, as the common language in which people from different nations converse.

ACKNOWLEDGEMENTS

I owe a debt of gratitude to the many people who have helped me along the way as I researched, visited and wrote about gardens all over Europe – and most obviously my wife, Brigid, who has had to suffer my long absences from home. But I am even more indebted to my editor, Judy Brookes, and publisher, Warwick Forge: one of the great joys of writing this book has been their enthusiasm, encouragement, tirelessness and willingness to solve problems of substance and detail. And the book is dedicated to John Phillips of Home Covert in England, in whose garden I have learned more about plants over the last 35 years than from any book. Do not look for it within these pages – Home Covert is open too seldom to qualify for inclusion – but it is a measure of what a keen plantsman can achieve in a single lifetime. It has inspired hundreds of garden owners from England and all over the world to become better gardeners themselves; could any man ask for a better legacy?

Charles Quest-Ritson

Charles Quest-Ritson

SYMBOLS KEY

🅿	Parking	🌱	Plants for sale
☕	Café	🎁	Giftshop
🍴	Restaurant	📖	Bookshop
🚾	Toilets	🏠	Open house
♿	Disabled access	🍽	Snacks

The Great Gardens of Europe

For those visitors with limited time, my recommendations for the best gardens in Europe are as follows:

AUSTRIA Alpinum Wien, Schloßpark Belvedere
BELGIUM Arboretum Kalmthout, Serres Royales
DENMARK Botanisk Have Københavns Universitet, Frederiksborg Barokhave
FRANCE Bagatelle, Le Bois des Moutiers, Château de Vaux-le-Vîcomte, Château de Versailles, Château de Villandry, Jardin Alpin du Lautaret, Jardin Exotique de Monte Carlo, Jardin Exotique de Roscoff, Jardin des Plantes de Paris, Jardins de Plantbessin, Jardins de Valloires, Musée Claude Monet, Parc de la Tête d'Or, Villa Ephrussi de Rothschild
GERMANY Berlin Botanischergarten, Europas Rosarium, Frankfurt Palmengarten, Grugapark, Herrenhausen, Hofgarten Veitshöchheim, Insel Mainau, Munich Botanischergarten, Pfaueninsel, Rhododendron Park, Schloß Augustusburg, Schloßgarten Schwetzingen, Schloßpark Sanssouci, Schloßpark Wilhemshöhe, Westfalenpark, Wörlitzer Park
GREAT BRITAIN Bodnant Gardens, Hidcote Manor, Newby Hall, Royal Botanic Garden (Edinburgh), Royal Botanic Gardens (Kew), Savill Garden, Sissinghurst Castle Garden, Stourhead, Tresco Abbey, RHS Garden Wisley
IRELAND Mount Stewart, National Botanic Gardens (Dublin)
ITALY Giardini Boboli, Giardini e Rovine de Ninfa, Giardino Giusti, Isola Bella, La Landriana, Orto Botanico di Palermo, Sacro Bosco di Bomarzo, Villa Carlotta, Villa d'Este, Villa Durazzo-Pallavicini, Villa Gamberaia, Villa Lante, Villa Taranto
THE NETHERLANDS Ada Hofman, Arboretum Trompenburg, Hortus Haren, De Keukenhof, Paleis Het Loo Nationaal Museum
POLAND Nieborów & Arkadia
PORTUGAL Jardim Episcopal, Palácio dos Marquêses da Fronteira, Palácio de Queluz, Quinta da Regaleira
RUSSIA Peterhof, Tsarskoe Selo
SPAIN Alhambra & Generalife, Jardi Botànic Mar i Murtra, Jardins de los Reales Alcázares, Parc Guëll
SWEDEN Drottningholms Slottsparken, Göteborgs Botaniska Trädgård, Norrvikens Trädgårdar

---

FOLLOWING PAGES: Through his writings, the late Christopher Lloyd made the Long Border at Great Dixter the most famous in England.

Gardens of Italy

The gardens of Italy have always been extremely influential. The styles that evolved in classical times were exported as part of Roman civilisation to every corner of the Empire. In renaissance times the gardens of the 1st-century Villa Adriana near Tivoli were much studied, as were the gardens of Pompeii (destroyed in the volcanic eruption of AD 79) in the 18th and 19th centuries.

Even more influential, in the event, were the gardens of the Italian Renaissance, inspired by archaeological remains and the writings of the ancients. The ideas expounded by such humanists as Leon Battista Alberti in *De re aedificatoria* (1452) became the model that every country in Europe copied. It is hard to underestimate the importance of such gardens as Bramante's Corte del Belvedere in Rome (1503) and those of the late 16th century at the Villa Aldobrandini at Frascati. The principles first articulated during the course of the Renaissance are still the basis of garden design today: it was from Italy that we learned the lessons of line, volume, symmetry, cross-axes and focal points. Renaissance masters taught us the importance of unity of style between the garden and house, and between the garden and wider landscape.

As the gardens of Italy evolved into the styles that are now called mannerist, baroque and rococo, so these in turn became the models that were exported abroad. England's greatest exposure to the Italian Renaissance did not begin until early in the 17th century, when the baroque was already well established. Little or nothing in Germany survived the Thirty Years War, so that it is to the grander, late-baroque Italian style that we owe such masterpieces as Wilhelmshöhe in Kassel. It was Italy that inspired such French designers as André le Nôtre to create large gardens of broderie in the early 18th century. Indeed it was in France, Germany and Austria that the baroque and rococo reached their finest expression, often the work of Italian craftsmen called in to advise.

Not until late in the 18th century did a totally different manner of gardening emerge – a non-Italian fashion that would engulf all Europe. The English landscape style penetrated every part of Italy, sweeping away many of the famous old gardens. Just as the Italian Renaissance has left us with Italian gardens in England, so too the landscape movement has given us examples of English gardens in the very different climate of Italy. The *giardino inglese* at the royal palace of Caserta (1790) was the brainchild of Sir

OPPOSITE: Sir Thomas Hanbury laid out the gardens of Giardini Hanbury in an old olive grove running down to the Mediterranean Sea.

William Hamilton, while the English garden at the Villa Borghese in Rome was largely designed by the Scottish painter Jacob More. The fashion for English-style parks continued through to the end of the 19th century and beyond. The phrases *parco inglese* and *prato inglese* still have a distinct meaning in modern Italian usage.

A second wave of English influence came in the 20th century with the modern fashion for gardening with plants. Some of those were made by English emigrants – Villa Taranto at Pallanza and the gardens of Ninfa in Latina are impressive instances – or by English designers like Russell Page. Outstanding examples have now been made by Italians themselves: La Landriana near Rome is a garden of international importance. The English way of using plants for decorative effect is the preferred style of most Italians today.

Italy is a country of many nations. Local traditions are strong. But the differences between gardens in the various regions of Italy are small and largely determined by climate. The rich soils and super-temperate climate of the north Italian lake district bring pro-digious horticultural results. High rainfall induces quick and luxuriant growth. Here are many of the best horticulturists' gardens, remarkable collections of camellias and azaleas, and streets lined with *Magnolia grandiflora*. High up in the Italian mountains, from the Alps to the southern Apennines, are some of Europe's best botanic gardens dedicated to the cultivation of alpines. The Mediterranean littoral allows the development of exotic plant collections: from the Giardini Hanbury near Ventimiglia to the Orto Botanico in Palermo, the coasts of Italy are rich in scientific variety and palm-lined promenades.

It was in Italy that botanic gardens evolved. Padua and Pisa both claim the distinction of founding the first botanic garden for the study of medicinal plants. In fact, there was already a garden of useful medicinal herbs at the Vatican in the 1510s. Botanic gardens continue to flourish as centres of scientific research and conservation, often attached to universities, in every part of Italy. *Botanico* is the word that Italians use to describe any garden made principally for the collection and enjoyment of plants: Professor Fineschi's famous rose garden in Tuscany is a *Roseto botanico*.

Nevertheless, it is the great historic gardens that most visitors come to see. Italy has by far the largest concentration of 16th- and 17th-century gardens in Europe. In Villa Lante at Bagnaia, the Giardini Giusti at Verona or the Villa di Castello near Florence, the importance, influence and contribution that Italian gardens have made to European cultural history is most strongly felt. These are truly great gardens that have been carefully studied and beautifully described by writers and scholars for hundreds of years; they never lose their capacity to amaze, impress and move us with their beauty and creativity. It is here among the box parterres, shaded alleys, fountains and rills that we come closest to under-standing the spirit of the Renaissance and the genius of the Italian people.

The destruction of historic gardens by the landscape movement began to be stemmed in the late 19th century. Rich foreign residents – cultural exiles from England, Germany and the United States – started to restore and re-create the formal gardens that had been lost through neglect or the tyranny of fashion. Restoration is now a passion for Italians themselves; they have the money to do the work and the education and knowledge to do it well. Conservation

The water cascade at La Reggia di Caserta stretches down the hillside for nearly 3 km towards the immense palace of King Ferdinand IV.

bodies like *Fondo per l'ambiente italiano* have set a good example, and public funds are sometimes available to help owners to restore their heritage and keep it in good condition. Gardens are generally better maintained than 20 years ago. Vision and commitment have revived the gardens of Villa Barbarigo at Valsanzibio in the Padovano and the Villa Chigi at Cetinale around Siena. Restoration gallops apace at Villa d'Este in Tivoli and the Vatican gardens in Rome. And, unless they are closed for repairs, almost all the most important and inspirational historic gardens of Italy are now open to the public, whether regularly or by appointment.

When you plan your itinerary, remember that gardens tend to come in clusters and be connected to cultural tourism. Rome, Florence, the Lakes and the Euganean hills are all rich in gardens – and much else – to visit. By the same token, there is little to be found in Calabria or Basilicata; good gardens exist,

but they are seldom accessible. Visiting gardens in Italy is time-consuming. Roads are often inadequate and traffic heavy. Travel is punctuated by unexplained queues and delays. Your journeys between gardens will take longer than you expect. The names of properties often change with the owners. Many people call the Villa Reale at Marlia the Villa Pecci-Blunt, after the family that bought it in 1924. Do not expect lots of colourful flowers. With few exceptions, it is historic importance and beauty that we find in Italian gardens. The same trees appear in most Italian gardens – cedars, taxodiums, trachycarpus palms, liquidambars and planes. Only in the lakeland region does a mild, damp climate combine with rich, acid soil to support a wider range of ornamentals. Roses, camellias, wisteria, oleanders and lagerstroemias are great features of the Italian lakes. There is always much to see and admire as you drive past the region's many sumptuous villas and gardens.

Gardens of Italy

1. Parco Burcina 'Felice Piacenza'
2. Castello Ducale di Agliè
3. Giardino Alpinia
4. Isola Bella
5. Isola Madre
6. Villa San Remigio
7. Villa Taranto
8. Villa Durazzo-Pallavicini
9. Giardino Esotico Pallanca
10. Giardini Hanbury
11. Fondazione André Heller
12. Villa Melzi
13. Villa del Balbianello
14. Villa Carlotta
15. Villa Sommi Picenardi
16. Villa Cipressi
17. Villa Monastero
18. Villa Reale, Monza
19. Villa Cicogna Mozzoni
20. Villa della Porta Bozzolo
21. Castel Trauttmansdorff
22. Villa Emo
23. Orto Botanico di Padova
24. Villa Barbarigo Pizzoni Ardemani
25. Villa Pisani Bolognesi
26. Villa Nazionale Pisani
27. Villa Trento da Schio
28. Giardino di Pojega
29. Parco Sigurtà
30. Giardino Giusti
31. Castello di Duino
32. Castello di Miramare
33. Villa Manin
34. Giardino Storico della Reggia
35. Villa Caprile
36. Villa Imperiale
37. Il Roseto di Cavriglia
38. Villa le Balze
39. Villa della Petraia
40. Giardini Boboli
41. Giardino dei Semplici
42. Villa di Castello
43. Villa la Pietra
44. Villa Pratolino
45. Villa i Tatti
46. Villa Gamberaia
47. Villa Torrigiani
48. Villa Garzoni
49. Palazzo Pfanner
50. Villa Grabau
51. Villa Reale, Marlia
52. Villa Massei
53. Villa Mansi
54. Venzano
55. Orto Botanico di Pisa
56. La Foce
57. Giardino dei Tarocchi
58. Villa Chigi Cetinale
59. Giardini e Rovine di Ninfa
60. Villa Aldobrandini
61. Orto Botanico di Roma
62. Villa Borghese
63. Villa Doria Pamphilj
64. Villa Adriana
65. Villa d'Este
66. La Landriana
67. Giardini del Vaticano
68. Villa Lante
69. Sacro Bosco
70. Villa Farnese
71. Isola Bisentina
72. Castello Ruspoli
73. La Reggia di Caserta
74. La Mortella
75. Chiostro di Santa Chiara
76. Orto Botanico di Napoli
77. Giardini di Pompeii
78. Villa Cimbrone
79. Villa Rufolo
80. Orto Botanico di Catania
81. Villa Imperiale del Casale
82. Taormina Gardens
83. Villa Palagonia
84. Orto Botanico di Palermo
85. Palazzina Cinese & Parco della Favorita
86. Villa Malfitano
87. Orto Botanico di Cagliari

PIEMONTE

1. Parco Burcina 'Felice Piacenza'

13814 Pollone (BI)

The Piacenza Park at Pollone is Italy's best woodland garden – a piece of late Victorian England in the cold foothills of the Piemontese Alps. Felice Piacenza was a passionate plantsman and, for over 50 years, planted rhododendrons and other exotics. He inherited a good collection of mid-19th-century conifers: among the many pines, firs, spruces, cedars, cypresses and thujas are exceptional specimens of redwoods, taxodiums, the umbrella pine (*Pinus pinea*), the Douglas fir (*Pseudotsuga menziesii*) and the Serbian spruce (*Picea omorika*). Piacenza's most impressive additions were extensive areas dedicated to mass plantings of rhododendrons and azaleas (at their peak in May). Beech trees – there are many different cultivars here – are another speciality, as are oaks, chestnuts, maples, *Sorbus* species, birches, Japanese cherries and much else besides. Spring and autumn bulbs carry colour through the year.

The great Italian landscape architect Pietro Porcinai helped to pull the garden together in the 1950s and Felice's son Guido Piacenza has been responsible for very extensive new plantings over the last 25 years. A recent addition is a collection of old Italian apple cultivars – a great Piemontese tradition.

Main entrance by Piazza San Rocco in Pollone ⟦C⟧ 0152 563 007
Open All year daily dawn–dusk
Size 57ha (141ac)
Owner Ente Parco Burcina
⟦P⟧ ⟦WC⟧ ⟦&⟧
⟦W⟧ www.parcoburcina.piemonte.it

2. Castello Ducale di Agliè

10011 Agliè (TO)

Agliè is the best of the many palace gardens around Turin that belonged to the Piemontese rulers who became kings of Italy in 1860. The palace itself resembles a fortress – brick-built, big and brooding. Its gardens are effective, but not extravagant, as befits a people renowned for parsimony and militarism. The terrace behind the castle needs restoration, but leads out from a vast conservatory. Oranges in large pots are put out for the summer. Below is a formal garden, first laid out in 1646 but restored many times since. Beyond is a 19th-century park in the English style, with conifers, red oaks, hornbeams and plane trees The main park, however, is across the road and made on a grander scale. A huge fountain, only intermittently functional, leads you through a wooded landscape and on towards a large lake.

This impressive fountain at Castello Ducale di Agliè was built in the 1760s.

16km N of Torino ⟦C⟧ 0124 330 102
Open All year Tue–Sun 8.30am–7.30pm (earlier in winter)
Size 100ha (247ac)
Owner Soprintendenza per i Beni Architettonici ed il Paesaggio del Piemonte ⟦P⟧ ⟦□⟧ ⟦▦⟧
⟦W⟧ www.ambienteto.arti.beniculturali.it

3. Giardino Alpinia

Via Alpinia, 22
28839 Alpino di Stresa (VB)

If you have ever seen a postcard view of Lake Maggiore with Isola Bella as a small island in the foreground and snowy mountains behind, it was probably taken at Alpinia. The ten-minute cable-car journey up from Stresa and

Over 1000 different plants are grown at Giardino Alpinia – and the views of Lake Maggiore are breathtaking.

the wonderful views are two good reasons for visiting this very interesting garden of alpine plants at 800 m up on the side of Monte Mottarone.

The garden was started on a bare, open site in 1934, with help from the Swiss Correvon family of nurserymen. The acid, silaceous soil supports plants of every sort, even ferns and lichens. There are classics, like edelweiss (*Leontopodium alpinum*) and *Rhododendron ferrugineum*; masses of soldanellas, pulsatillas, gentians and violas; lilies like *Lilium pomponium* and *L. bulbiferum*; crocuses in spring; and *Colchicum autumnale* as the season ends. Plants like *Gentiana lutea* and *Paradisea liliastrum* have naturalised in the meadows. Most are planted, as much for horticultural effect as for botanical interest, in roughly made, raised-up beds of boulders and rocks, filled with gritty soil. There are over 1000 species (the number is still growing), and *Geranium*, *Dianthus* and *Campanula* are particularly well represented.

Best reached by cable-car from Carciano di Stresa █ 032 320 163 **Open** Apr–mid-October daily 9.30am–6pm **Size** 4ha (10ac) **Owner** Consorzio Giardino Alpinia 🅿 🔲 🆆
Ⓦ www.giardinoalpinia.it
@ info@giardinoalpinia.it

4. Isola Bella

28050 Isola Bella (VB)

Isola Bella still fulfils its original purpose – to astound and delight its visitors, as effectively now as 300 years ago. It was built for Prince Vitaliano Borromeo in the 1670s and 1680s and the entire island is taken up by the palace, the garden and their dependencies.

The design was conceived as a whole: it resembles a vast, fantastic galleon with the palace in the bows and the baroque garden at the stern, stepped up on no less than ten terraces. You enter the garden from a small, enclosed yard,

climb some steps, turn a corner, and behold the whole structure tiered up before you, level after level. Each is hung with statues, fountains, finials, balustrades, grottos, rocaille decoration and basins. It would need a superhuman effort of will to resist the temptation to draw near and climb the terraces until you reach the very top. Here, the whole design reveals itself, with a baroque parterre right at the bottom, flanked by four huge conical yew trees, relics of the original planting 300 years ago. There are pools, lawns, rows of lemon trees, decorative bedding schemes and some fine trees, like a vast and ancient liriodendron.

Trees were not part of the original design, and Isola Bella is above all an architectural extravagance. Nevertheless, many exotic plants have been used to show off the exceptional climate of the island – acacias, myrtles, *Camellia reticulata*, and espaliered orange trees, for example, as well as roses, hydrangeas and oleanders to give colour throughout the year.

In Lake Maggiore. Nearest access is Stresa. Ferries run by Navigazione Lago Maggiore
(*see* www.navigazionelaghi.it)
█ 0323 932 483 **Open** Mid-Mar–mid-Oct daily 9am–5.30pm **Size** 3ha (7ac) **Owner** Borromeo family
🔲 🔳 🆆🅲 🔲 🔲
Ⓦ www.borromeoturismo.it
@ *See* website

Isola Bella's 17th-century pool and parterres are best seen from the ship-like terraces above.

Papyrus grows unprotected in the formal pool at Isola Madre.

5. Isola Madre
28050 Isola Madre (VB)

You must visit *both* the Borromean island-gardens – Isola Bella and Isola Madre. They are completely different from each other, though developed by the same family over hundreds of years, and both immaculately maintained.

Isola Bella is architectural and baroque; Isola Madre is an ornamental landscape – a thick, introspective woodland garden with exquisite flowery glades. The approach is fairly formal: you pass a multitude of pots, steps, urns and figures on the climb up the terraces to the palace. Behind it is the largest *Cupressus cashmiriana* in Europe. All around is English-style woodland garden, full of interesting trees and shrubs, many planted 50 years ago with advice from Henry Cocker of Villa Taranto. The trees are oaks and 19th-century conifers: beneath is an enthusiast's collection of tree ferns, huge bamboos, *Acer palmatum* cultivars, mountainous rhododendrons, camellias and azaleas – the garden is really at its best when they flower in early May.

The thick planting means that you feel completely alone in this perfect garden; peacocks and fancy pheasants increase the illusion of being in paradise.

There are occasional views down long walks bordered by camellia hedges to an embarkation point, quay or wharf. As you wait for the boat back, you will notice tender ornamental shrubs, like feijoas and cultivars of *Pittosporum tenuifolium*, trained against the walls. Peer over the rocky edges and you will see beschornerias and yuccas right down to lake level.

In Lake Maggiore. Nearest access points are Pallanza & Baveno. Ferries run by Navigazione Lago Maggiore (*see* www.navigazionelaghi.it)
C 0323 932 483
Open Mid-Mar–mid-Oct daily 9am–5.30pm **Size** 8ha (20ac) **Owner** Borromeo family
🅿 🍴 🚻 ♿ 🏫
W www.borromeoturismo.it
@ *See* website

6. Villa San Remigio
28922 Pallanza (VB)

Villa San Remigio has one of the most dramatic and beautiful of all gardens in the Italian Lakes – complex, luxuriant and theatrical. It was made between 1896 and 1916 by Silvio and Sophie della Valle di Casanova – he a half-English Neapolitan marquess; she his wholly-English cousin.

The house and garden were developed together as a latter-day homage to the Neapolitan baroque (it helps to remember that this was the period when the Arts and Crafts movement was strongest in Italy). The house is at the top of the hill, and the garden falls away in broad terraces on both sides. They are richly decorated with mossy balustrades, pilasters, pots, seats, *putti*, urns, shell-shaped seats, ornamental paving and fine rocaille work on the retaining walls. Fountains, pools, piscinas, statues, columns and ironwork are set off by box hedges, yew obelisks and topiary. The terraces have names like 'The Garden of Happiness' and 'The Garden of Memories'. Armorial motifs and quotations from Latin poets appear in surprising places. A life-sized statue of a near-naked Venus stands on a cushion in a huge pearly shell chariot, hitching up her cloak; she is drawn in triumph by two horses, their hooves transmuted into fins. Camellias, irises, climbing roses and wisteria fill the terraces.

All around is an English-style park of ancient conifers and huge beech trees, with relics of a fine horticulturist's garden of azaleas, rhododendrons, Japanese maples and magnolias. Here, too, is the door in the wall that led through to Villa Taranto next door; only Sophie della Valle di Casanova and her friend Neil McEacharn had keys.

A major restoration program has just begun; meanwhile, Villa San Remigio remains a place of intense, romantic melancholy.

The gardens of Villa San Remigio are a romantic Anglo-Italian fantasy of great beauty and complexity.

Signed in Verbania–Pallanza,
up a narrow, twisting lane
C 0323 503 249 (tourist office)
Open By appointment with tourist
office, Mar–Oct **Size** 8ha (20ac)
Owner Provincia di Verbania **P** **WC**
W www.verbania-turismo.it
@ turismo@comune.verbania.it

7. Villa Taranto

28922 Verbania–Pallanza (VB)

Villa Taranto has the largest collection of plants in Italy. Its maker, Neil McEacharn, reckoned that he had introduced 20 000 different taxa into it – and that at least 90% of those plants had never been grown in Italy before. The trees and shrubs have fared best, and the warm, wet climate of the Italian Lakes has ensured that many are now the tallest specimens in Europe.

McEacharn was a Scot with a fortune (made in Australia) to spend on his hobby when he bought Villa Taranto in 1930. By 1951 it was good enough to be given to the state as the Italian equivalent of the Royal Botanic Gardens at Kew. McEacharn worked closely with his head gardener Henry Cocker, and together they quickly built up an amazing collection, with every plant chosen for its botanical interest but planted to display its horticultural worth. Outstanding specimens include *Quercus palustris*, *Cercidiphyllum japonicum*, *Acer rubrum*, *Eucommia ulmoides* and a very tall, two-trunked *Emmenopterys henryi* (now 25 m high), which was the first to flower in Europe.

The design includes rather minimalist formal areas and, because it is made on a steep slope, required several kilometres of roads and over 8 km of dry-stone walling: 80 men worked on the garden's creation. A large, irregular-shaped pool is filled with sacred lotuses (*Nelumbo nucifera*) flowering in June and July; one of the glasshouses is dedicated to *Victoria amazonica*.

Camellias and magnolias are two specialities, and McEacharn brought some of the rhododendrons from his old garden in Scotland. But Villa Taranto is far from being just another botanic garden. It is a very popular public spectacle, with lots of colour at every season: 80 000 tulip bulbs alone are planted every year. Standards of labelling and maintenance are well above average.

On shore of Lake Maggiore, best
approached from Intra end of Verbania
C 0323 556 667 **Open** Apr–Oct
daily 8.30am–6.30pm **Closes** 5pm
Oct **Size** 40ha (99ac) **Owner** Ente
Giardini Botanici Villa Taranto
P **E** **WC** **&** **Y**
W www.villataranto.it
@ entevillataranto@tin.it

LIGURIA

8. Villa Durazzo-Pallavicini

Via Ignazio Pallavicini, 17
16155 Genova Pegli (GE)

Parco Durazzo-Pallavicini dates from the 1840s. Marchese Ignazio Alessandro Pallavicini employed some 350 workers on its creation over six years. The park is one of Italy's best 19th-century gardens, and represents a very Italian development of the English style – a combination of prodigious buildings, thick woodland and botanical treasures.

The long drive takes you past the botanic garden and a series of attractive 19th-century glasshouses, but it is the sheer size, number and variety of the garden follies behind the palace that is astounding. The recommended route leads you along the Viale Classico and through two enormous neoclassical triumphal arches.

A short climb brings you to the lake, which is the most extraordinary, original and exciting heart of the garden – an irregular body of water boasting a Roman bridge, an

Villa Taranto's pool and formal garden have the only geometric straight lines in this Scottish-style woodland garden.

The juxtaposition of many different styles is one of the extraordinary, opulent charms of the Villa Durazzo-Pallavicini park.

Egyptian obelisk, a Rose Pavilion, a Turkish kiosk and, most dramatically, a Chinese bridge-cum-pagoda on a promontory. At the centre of the lake is a round Doric temple sheltering a statue of Diana, with centaur-tritons rising from the waters to guard her at the four points of the compass.

Nearby is the elegant rococo temple of Flora, its entrance and garden thickly planted with colourful flowers. Other features include a Heroes' Tomb, a battlemented folly, a Swiss Hut, and many grottos and caverns not open to the public. The thick, evergreen woodland incorporates a good collection of ancient camellias, most of them dating from the 1850s. A large *Cinnamomum aromaticum* and a vast *Magnolia grandiflora* stand near the house.

Immediately next to railway station at Pegli ☎ 010 666 864 **Open** All year Tues–Sun 9am–7pm (10am–5pm winter) **Size** 11ha (27ac) **Owner** Comune di Genova
🚻 ♿
@ villapallavicini@astergenova.it

9. Giardino Esotico Pallanca

Via Madonna delle Ruote, 1
18012 Bordighera (IM)

The Pallanca garden was started nearly 100 years ago as the show garden attached to a leading cactus nursery, but has now become a tourist attraction in its own right. Cacti and succulents predominate, though there are also palms, chorisias and strelitzias near the entrance.

The garden occupies a very steep south-facing slope and is one of the best of its type: the nursery is tidy and plants are well grown. They are grouped both botanically and according to their size or shape. Thus, there is a bed devoted to showing Mexican genera – *Astrophytum*, *Mammillaria* and *Ferocactus* – while, a little further up, *Astrophytum* and *Ferocactus* form part of a specimen bed for cultivars that grow in a spiral shape. Opuntias, agaves, aloes and the ever-popular *Echinocactus grusonii*

Cacti and succulents of every kind flourish at Giardino Esotico Pallanca.

grow throughout the garden and bind it together. There are many specimens of exceptional size – a vast *Trichocereus pasacana*, for example – and many rarities among a total of over 3000 taxa.

E of Bordighera, on left just after tunnel that runs behind Grand Hotel del Mar ☎ 0184 266 347 **Open** Daily in season **Size** 1ha (2½ac) **Owner** Pallanca family
🚻 ♿
🌐 www.pallanca.it

10. Giardini Hanbury

18038 La Mortola Inferiore
Ventimiglia-Latte (IM)

The gardens at La Mortola were founded in 1867 by a rich Englishman called Sir Thomas Hanbury. He was a devout Quaker, who wanted to undertake scientific experiments in acclimatisation, and to make a collection of plants that was both useful and instructive.

Hanbury amassed some 4000 different taxa in his spectacular private botanic garden, which he created within the old south-facing olive grove. His special interests, now magnificently mature, included aloes, agaves, cacti, palms, South African bulbs and making a complete collection of citrus cultivars. Queen Victoria came to lunch and was overwhelmed by the garden's beauty. Sir Thomas's son Cecil gave it a horticultural overlay in the 1920s and 1930s to emphasise its harmonies and contrasts of colour and form. He also added Italian elements – avenues, marble staircases, cupolas and scented gardens.

The entrance is right at the top, from which the whole garden appears as an enchanting landscape of palms, cypresses, olives, cycads and Judas trees that stretches right down to the pines by the edge of the sea. Its riches seem endless: banks of South African daisies, soaring agaves and echiums, wisterias, tree peonies, roses, rare tropical fruits, an avenue of the late-

Sir Cecil and Lady Hanbury added many Italianate details to the gardens of Giardini Hanbury during the 1920s and 1930s.

flowering *Salvia leucantha*, and vast patches of naturalised *Scilla peruviana*. Halfway down the hillside, a bridge leads over the remains of the old Roman Via Aurelia. At the bottom stands an old olive press and a copse of beautiful, rugged umbrella pines (*Pinus pinaster*).

The Hanbury Gardens take pride in the number of different plants in flower every year on New Year's Day – as many as 500. But the truth is that they are a treat to visit at any time of the year.

3km from French frontier on Corniche road. 🄲 0184 229 507 **Open** All year daily 9am–7pm (4pm winter), but opens 10am Oct–Mar **Size** 20ha (49ac) **Owner** Italian State. Administered by Università di Genova
Some parking 🄿 🆆🄲
partly accessible to wheelchairs
🅆 www.amicihanbury.com

LOMBARDIA

11. Fondazione André Heller
Via Motta, 2
25083 Gardone Riviera (BS)

This is better known as Giardino Hruska (the Hruska Garden) and is the life work of Arturo Hruska who, between 1910 and 1971, created the largest private rock-garden in Italy.

Vast quantities of dolomitic rock went into building the garden's precipitous mini-mountains and their many different microhabitats. It is not large, but tightly designed with narrow paths, and is very popular with tourists. There are still over 2000 taxa to admire, though the rock faces are rather weedy and many of the Alpine plants have disappeared.

It remains a good garden because there has been much replanting in recent years in a different style – including tender exotics like orchids put out for the summer. The Austrian owner, André Heller, has added sculptures and other installations by such artists as Roy Lichtenstein and Keith Haring.

Town centre; follow signs to Giardino Botanico 🄲 0336 410 877 **Open** 15 Mar–15 Oct daily 9am–6pm **Size** 1ha (2½ac) **Owner** Fondazione André Heller
🄿 🄲 🆆🄲 ♿ 🏠
🅆 www.hellergarden.com
@ info@hellergarden.com

12. Villa Melzi
22021 Bellagio (CO)

Villa Melzi is a landscaped park with an exquisite lakeside setting and lots of horticultural interest. The garden is long and narrow, but space has been well used. It is also very well maintained.

Francesco Melzi d'Eril built the impressive neoclassical house and landscaped the garden in the 1800s; he was a supporter and friend of Napoleon I, who created him chancellor of the kingdom of Italy and Duke of Lodi.

The garden was laid out in the English style – the first in Como – by the Italian architects Canonica and Villoresi, who also worked on the park of Villa Reale at Monza. Features from this period include the Turkish-style kiosk and Gian Battista Comolli's statue of Dante and Beatrice (the inspiration for Liszt's *Dante Sonata*).

Throughout the garden are fragments of sculptures and antique carvings from ancient

Villa Melzi's oriental kiosk provides a reference to Napoleon I's Egyptian campaigns.

Greece, Rome and Egypt: some were gifts from Napoleon. But the garden's greatest feature is an overlay of azaleas and rhododendrons introduced from English nurseries in the 1950s by Duke Tommaso Gallarati-Scotti after a tour of duty as Italian Ambassador in London. Also from this period is the Japanese garden near the entrance, where mature specimens of Japanese maples surround a series of pools. Elsewhere are many fine trees: ginkgos, tulip trees, cypresses, redwoods, camphora, ilex, magnolias, *Pinus montezumae* and an avenue of pollarded plane trees.

The garden is especially enjoyable when the azaleas flower in April and May; afternoon is best for photography, when the light is reflected off the lake and illumines the hillside.

Southern edge of Bellagio village
☎ 0335 813 1417 **Open** Mar–Oct daily 9am–6.30pm **Size** 8ha (20ac) **Owner** Melzi family 🚾 ♿

13. Villa del Balbianello
22016 Lenno (CO)

Villa del Balbianello is a place of rare and ravishing beauty. It was built by Cardinal Angelo Durini towards the end of the 18th century on a rocky promontory on Lake Como. The lack of soil meant that no Italian-style garden was planted, nor an English-style

park. The garden is therefore a modern attempt to bind together the buildings, the trees, the lake and the rocky outcrop.

The highest point is filled by the Cardinal's elegant arched loggia from which glorious views stretch up and down the length of the lake. *Ficus pumila* wraps itself around the pillars of the central colonnade; it is carefully trimmed to give an irregular swagged effect. On the way up are lines of pollarded plane trees, hedges of laurel and parterres of box.

Much of the planting dates from the middle of the 20th century when the villa belonged to Americans General and Mrs Butler Ames. They imported soil and planted azaleas on the steep lawns. Elsewhere are cypresses, palms and cycads, as well as balustrading, urns, vases and statues.

The long walk from Lenno passes through thick natural woodland with anemones, hepaticas and hellebores in spring and cyclamen in autumn. But the approach by boat is easier and much more dramatic.

Pedestrian access (800m) on Tue, weekends & pub hols; otherwise accessible only by boat from Lenno
☎ 034 456 110 **Open** Mid-Mar–Oct daily (except Mon & Wed) 10am–6pm **Closed** 1pm–2pm weekdays **Size** 2ha (5ac) **Owner** FAI (Fondo per l'ambiente italiano)
🅿 🚾 📷 🚽
🅦 www.fondoambiente.it
@ faibalbianello@fondoambiente.it

Villa Carlotta has exotic plants, rich bedding and superb standards of maintenance.

14. Villa Carlotta
Via Regina, 2
22019 Tremezzo (CO)

Villa Carlotta is the most beautiful and romantic German garden in Italy – a treasure house of well-established plants of every kind. Its name is a memorial to Princess Charlotte of Prussia, Duchess of Saxe-Meiningen (1831-55), whose parents gave her the estate in 1850.

The formal garden in front of the house, the grand double staircase, balustrades, fountains and the cascade of the dwarves all date back to the 18th century when the estate belonged to the Marchesi Clerici.

Most of landscaping was undertaken in the latter part of the 19th century, though much of the ornamental planting is more recent. One of the terraces has a pergola of tied-in orange and lemon trees. Roses like 'Mermaid' and 'Pretty Pink' fill some of the retaining walls, alongside trachelospermums and lagerstroemia. There are many camellia hedges around and below the house, typically 8 m high but occasionally taller.

Within the landscaped park are extensive collections of rhododendrons, deciduous azaleas, ancient camellias, palms, eucalyptus, camphor trees, mature conifers, araucarias, bamboos and

The loggia is the central point of Villa del Balbianello's exquisite garden.

Japanese maples. Callistemons, crinums, cordylines, yuccas and erythrinas celebrate the mild climate. A dark valley is filled with tree ferns. Though probably best when the rhododendrons flower in early May, it is a garden with much of interest at every season. Important individual trees include *Picea orientalis*, *Magnolia grandiflora*, *Pseudotsuga menziesii* 'Glauca' and *Cedrus deodara*.

On western shores of Lake Como, 5km S of Menaggio 🄲 034 440 405 **Open** Apr–Sep daily 9am–6pm; Mar & Oct 9am–11.30am & 2–4.30pm **Size** 7ha (17ac) **Owner** Ente Villa Carlotta Parking nearby 🄳 🄵 🆆🅲 🄵 🄵 🆆 www.villacarlotta.it

15. Villa Sommi Picenardi

23887 Olgiate Molgora (LC)

Villa Sommi Picenardi is set in a fine English park, with spacious lawns and meadows rolling down from the front of the house. The trees include a cut-leafed beech (*Fagus sylvatica* 'Aspleniifolia') planted in 1880 and a vast plane tree dating back to about 1810. You would not guess that there is a charming green theatre to one side of the house, planted in the 1930s with hornbeam wings and box-edged stalls – and clever tricks of perspective.

But the jewel of Villa Sommi Picenardi is the secret, hidden garden at the back of the house, best seen from within. No-one knows when (or by whom) it was made, which is a pity because the quality of the workmanship is exceptionally fine and delicate. The late-baroque style suggests that it was made in about 1700. An impressive staircase leads first to a terrace hung with roses and then up a steep staircase to a belvedere. Pots, urns and stately statues are perched on the balustrades. The walls have beautiful patterns in pebbles of different colours, while the central fountain has complicated mosaics and shell-edges to its

The finely worked staircase above the formal garden at Villa Sommi Picenardi is a masterpiece.

pilasters. A small, neat pool with a fountain of bronze sea horses is the centrepiece of the formal garden that links the terraces to the house.

18km S of Lecco 🄲 039 508 333 **Open** By appointment **Size** 15ha (37ac) **Owner** Marchesa Alessandra Sommi Picenardi 🄿 🄵 www.villasommipicenardi.it @ iredae@tin.it

16. Villa Cipressi

Via IV Novembre, 18
22050 Varenna (LC)

Villa Cipressi is an opulent hotel next to Villa Monastero on the shores of Lake Como. Its gardens are very steeply terraced down to the lakeside. Avenues of trachycarpus palms

are underplanted with ceratostigma and aspidistras. Wisterias curl around the iron balustrading and up into the centennial cypresses. The retaining walls are planted with oleanders and lemon-scented verbena. Loquat trees and vast evergreen magnolias give shade. There is a fine variegated beech tree at the southern end.

As with most of Como's gardens, there is nothing very rare here, but the incomparable site, the size of some of the specimens and the sense of luxuriance combine to create an excellent garden.

On Lake Como, near village centre 🄲 0341 830 113 **Open** All times on request **Size** 2ha (5ac) 🄵 🆆🅲 www.hotelvillacipressi.it

The views from Villa Cipressi's terraced garden across Lake Como are beautifully framed by architectural features.

17. Villa Monastero
Via Venini, 128
22050 Varenna (LC)

The garden at Villa Monastero is very long and thin, occupying a splendid site (once a monastery) between the public road and the shore of Lake Como. It was laid out along two main terraces and luxuriantly planted at the start of the 20th century. Its owner was the Austrian Walter Kees, a keen amateur botanist, from whom (as an enemy alien) the property was confiscated in 1918. He planted the garden's many interesting trees: lines of trachycarpus and cypresses, a large number of palms (including *Brahea edulis*, *B. armata* and *Jubaea chilensis*) and the vast *Magnolia grandiflora* by the house, which stretches its branches out over the lake.

The garden buildings are exceptionally charming: an exquisite tiled loggia extends out over the edge of the lake, and a little temple occupies the highest terrace. A retaining wall is planted with a great many different citrus trees, including mandarins, clementines, lemons, kumquats, grapefruits and bergamots. Oleanders, wisteria and climbing roses give colour all year, while the beds around the house are thickly planted with colourful flowers.

Edge of Varenna, just beyond Villa Cipressi ▮ 0341 295 450
Open Apr–Oct daily 9am–7pm
Size 2ha (5ac) **Owner** Istituzione Villa Monastero ▮
▮ www.villamonastero.org

18. Villa Reale
20052 Monza (MI)

The park at Monza claims to be the largest walled park in Europe. It swarms with cyclists, joggers, footballers and children. Within its bounds are chapels,

The modern rose garden at Monza's Villa Reale is nicely set out in front of the old orangery.

a swimming pool, the national motor-racing stadium – and the palace built by the Viceroy Eugène de Beauharnais in 1805. There are good trees to see among the relics of his experimental plantings, but the only part of real horticultural interest is the modern rose garden. This is outside the park, in front of the palace itself, and approached directly from the road. It is handsomely laid out and well maintained. A large section is given to the Italian national rose trials, but it has a good collection of modern roses, especially climbers, Hybrid Teas, groundcover and repeat-flowering shrub roses. The garden reaches its peak during the last week of May and first week of June but, since almost all the roses are repeat-flowering, there is colour right through to late autumn. It has its own website at www.airosa.it and is open 8.30 am – 12 noon and 3 pm – 8 pm daily (except Mon) in May & June. It remains open 8.30 am – 12 noon and 2 pm – 5 pm on weekdays until December, but is closed in August and from January to April.

15km NE of Milan
▮ 039 322 003 **Open** All year daily 7am–8.30pm (7pm in winter)
Size 685ha (1691ac)
Owner City of Monza
▮ ▮ ▮ ▮ ▮
▮ www.comune.monza.mi.it/rd/
la_tua_citta/3222.htm
▮ ammparco@comune.monza.mi.it

The views across Lake Como from Villa Monastero are enhanced by colourful bedding, interesting plants and elegant garden architecture.

19. Villa Cicogna Mozzoni

Viale Cicogna, 8
21050 Bisuschio (VA)

The garden around this renaissance villa is one of the oldest and most charming in northern Italy. It was started by Ascanio Mozzoni in 1560 and continued by his great-grandson Carlo Cicogna Mozzoni 100 years later. Its design was influenced by contemporary gardens that Ascanio had seen in Rome and Florence, and aimed to link the house to the landscape.

A beautiful enclosed garden leads off the entrance courtyard, which has elegant open porticos with very fine frescoed ceilings. Here are two balustraded tanks with fountain statues in the centre, two parterres with small fountains and bright bedding, and a wall set with busts and sculptures. It is an astonishingly harmonious composition. Steps take you to the terrace behind the house, where a water staircase (156 steps) leads up to a four-columned canopy and an English-style woodland garden. A simple green parterre on the other side of the house is surrounded by box hedges and purple cordylines in pots.

The slender arcades of Villa Cicogna Mozzoni are an elegant backdrop to its garden's renaissance design.

A series of balustraded terraces marches up the hillside behind the Villa della Porta Bozzolo.

8km NW of Varese 📞 0332 471 134 **Open** Guided tours only: Apr–Oct Sun & pub hols 9.30am–12 noon & 2.30–7pm, but daily in August (pm only). Office open only mornings; ring to ask when guided tours leave **Size** 18ha (44ac) **Owner** Cicogna Mozzoni family Parking nearby 🚾 🌐 www.villacicognamozzoni.it @ eleopaa@tin.it

20. Villa della Porta Bozzolo

Viale Bozzolo
21030 Casalzuigno (VA)

Visit Casalzuigno when the gardens first open: the morning sun shines brilliantly on the magnificent baroque garden as you climb up the hill towards the gates of Villa della Porta. It is an astounding sight – one of the most beautiful and harmonious of all formal gardens – and quite eclipses the palatial 16th-century house.

The main feature is a staggered and staggering sequence of steep balustraded terraces topped by statues of plump cherubs. The terraces lead up to a grass amphitheatre and a long, straight, watery staircase, which seems to cut vertically through the woodland behind. This is early 18th-century baroque at its most flamboyant. The terrace on which the house sits is the broadest and leads sideways through iron gates along an avenue of lofty, decidu-ous oaks underplanted with hydrangeas. It ends with a tall summerhouse, whose back wall bears an expansive fresco of Apollo and the muses. Other terraces are planted with irises, climbing roses, and fruit trees. Lemon trees in pots line the steps. The facings of the terraces are cut in tufa stonework, which gives a rough but decorative finish and has been used to create charming patterns. The amphitheatre was planted with 500 000 crocuses in 2000; it is said to be the biggest planting of crocuses in Italy. Maintenance is excellent.

10km E of Laveno 📞 0332 624 136 **Open** Mid-Feb–mid-Dec 10am–5pm, but **closes** 6pm Mar–Sep **Closed** Mon, except pub hols **Size** 25ha (62ac) **Owner** FAI (Fondo per l'ambiente italiano) 🅿 🚻 🍴 🚾 📷 🖼 🌐 www.fondoambiente.it/luoghi/ Casalzuigno @ faibozzolo@fondoambiente.it

TRENTINO

21. Castel Trauttmansdorff

Sankt Valentin Strasse
39012 Merano (BZ)

The gardens around Trauttmansdorff castle are very new (they opened in 2001) and very extensive. They have a large educational content aimed at schoolchildren, and something of a political message too – Merano is in Italy's German-speaking alpine region – but are nevertheless interesting and enjoyable to see.

Below the castle, on a steep, south-facing slope, are gardens of Mediterranean plants like ilexes, olives, vines, figs, cypresses and lavender. Elsewhere, the plantings tend to be more geographical: Japanese maples grow alongside rice terraces and tea plantations and there are young woodlands dedicated to trees and shrubs from East Asia and North America. In some cases, the gardens are made in national styles, including a formal Italian garden and English herbaceous borders. The German-style *Bauerngarten* is a statement of local identity.

There is much for children to see and learn from, including question-and-answer pavilions and multimedia shows: concern for the conservation of the natural vegetation, climate change, and human impact are major themes. And the whole enterprise is not just a garden, but seeks to incorporate a variety of creative ideas – artistic, literary, acoustic and electronic. Is this the way forward for 21st-century gardens?

On road to Scena, 3km N of Merano **C** 0473 235 730 **Open** 15Mar–15Nov daily 9am–6pm **Closes** 9pm mid-May–mid-Sep **Size** 12ha (30ac) **Owner** Centro di Sperimentazione agraria e forestale Laimburg
P ⬚ ⬚ WC ⬚ ⬚ ⬚
W www.trauttmansdorff.it
@ botanica@provinz.bz.it

VENETO

22. Villa Emo
Loc. Rivella
35043 Monselice (PD)

Villa Emo is a new garden in the flatlands north of Monselice. The design recalls classical Italian renaissance gardens, but the plantings are generous, in the modern French style. The handsome house was probably designed by Palladio's

Good modern planting, as seen in Villa Emo, is rare in Italy.

pupil Vincenzo Scamozzi and occupies an open, sunny site. Its front façade looks onto a small canal and a young formal garden edged in box. Here, and all around the house, are large quantities of modern roses. The fish ponds at each side have water lilies and long strips of irises along their edges. Behind the house is a large grass enclosure, hedged by privet, containing the heraldic device of the Emo family. English mixed borders fill the beds outside. At the far end, a very long border is planted *à la Giverny*, with strips of irises, bergenias, roses, hemerocallis and sternbergias, to give flowers in succession throughout the year. Elsewhere the visitor can stroll down an avenue of *Magnolia grandiflora*, another of taxodiums and through a collection of young trees.

Signed from SS16 N of Monselice; turn left immediately after canal bridge **C** 0429 781 970 **Open** Apr–Oct Thur–Sat 2–7pm plus 10am–7pm Sun & bank hols **Size** 4ha (10ac) **Owner** Contessa Giuseppina Emo P ⬚
W www.villaemo.it
@ villaemo@villaemo.it

23. Orto Botanico di Padova
Via Orto Botanico, 15
35123 Padova (PD)

History, beauty and interesting plants are all abundantly present in Padua's botanic garden. It was founded in 1545 (which makes it one of the world's oldest) to encourage Venetian research into medicinal plants. It is still a garden for plants and is currently the best maintained and curated in Italy. The plants are well cultivated, too – well grown and well labelled.

Look over the side of the bridge that leads to the entrance and you will see a mass of woody tubercles erupting from the roots of *Taxodium distichum*. Then walk towards the walled garden to an avenue of *Trachycarpus fortunei* under-planted with paeonies. Plants are everywhere, but the design is also striking: a complete circle, 84 m across, encloses a square, and is tricked out with geometrical beds (small, stone-edged, enclosed by iron railings) in which plants are grown for study. The whole garden is surrounded by a high wall with elegant 18th-century gateways at

The approach to the house is the climax of a visit to Villa Barbarigo Pizzoni Ardemani.

the four points of the compass and statues by Antonio Bonazza.

As with all ancient botanic gardens, there are some fine trees: specimens of *Ginkgo biloba* planted in 1750, *Magnolia grandiflora* (1786) and a vast *Cedrus deodara* (1826). The garden also has a number of special collections both in its glasshouses and outside: carnivorous plants; medicinal and poisonous plants; plants of the nearby Euganean hills; plants of the maquis; an alpine collection;

freshwater plants; succulents; and orchids. A total of 6000 different taxa grow within the garden's small compass. In the palm house are the original palms that inspired Goethe's theories on the development of the plant kingdom. But the most awe-inspiring part of a visit is to contemplate how many garden plants were introduced to Europe and first grown in this very garden, among them lilac, tulip trees, sunflowers and the humble potato.

The towers of St Anthony's cathedral project above the buildings of Padua University's botanic faculty in Orto Botanico di Padova.

Just S of city centre
☎ 0498 272 119 **Open** All year daily 9am–1pm & 3–6pm Apr–Oct; Nov–Mar weekdays only **Size** 2.2ha (5½ac) **Owner** L'Università di Padova
🅿 🍴 🆆🅲 ♿ 🏠 ♿
🆆 www.ortobotanico.unipd.it

24. Villa Barbarigo Pizzoni Ardemani

Valsanzibio (PD)

Valsanzibio has the most important baroque garden in the Veneto, quite unaffected by later fashions but continuously restored to a very high standard. It was built in the 1660s by the Venetian procurator Zuane Francesco Barbarigo as an allegory of man's progress towards salvation. Take away this spiritual dimension and you still have an impressive walk up towards his sumptuous house.

You need to imagine that you have arrived by gondola through the system of canals that has brought you from Venice. You moor at the vast, white marble gateway known as Diana's pavilion and tie your boat to the painted poles. From there you climb up the superb sequence (backed by very tall hedges) of fountains, pools, waterworks and statues, which unfold before you.

When you arrive almost at the top (beware the *giochi d'acqua*), a broad grass avenue cuts across the ascent and you realise that you have been climbing only a secondary axis – there, far away to the right, lies the villa itself. Five-metre box hedges, very neatly clipped, lead past the Rabbit Island (an Ancient Roman symbol of divine immanence) and a statue of Time interrupting his flight across space (representing the transcendence of human aspiration). Everywhere are statues, each with a precise symbolism, until you reach the stairs up to the house, rising as if to an altar, where eight allegorical statues extol the garden and its owner. The fountain of divine revelation in front of the house symbolises the final goal of human perfectibility.

Signed from SS16 N of Monselice **[** 0498 059 224 **Open** Mar–Nov daily 10am–1pm & 2pm–dusk **Size** 16ha (40ac) **Owner** Pizzoni Ardemani family **P ⊞ WC ⎞ 🛍** **W** www.valsanzibiogiardino.it **@** info@valsanzibiogiardino.it

25. Villa Pisani Bolognesi

Via Roma, 25
35040 Vescovana (PD)

The gardens of Villa Pisani are a Victorian reinterpretation of the classical Italian

The arch at the centre of Villa Pisani Bolognesi's charming formal garden is topped by a doge's cap.

style. They were made by Evelina Van Millingen, the English wife of Count Almoro Pisani, from 1852 onwards. Villa Pisani's are the only Anglo-Italian gardens made during the years when the Veneto was under Austrian rule.

The formal garden is Italianate, with suggestions of a Turkish influence – Evelina Van Millingen was brought up in Constantinople – and chunky yew topiary at the sides. Over the central fountain is a metal arch (with rambling roses up the side) topped by the Pisani doge's cap. Lemon trees in pots and figurines (herms and naughty dwarfs) surround the box-edged parterre. Roses, paeonies and geraniums in pots give colour throughout the summer and autumn. Beyond

the furthest hedge of clipped yew is an informal garden leading out into a spacious park.

The edges of the park are thickly wooded, with tall magnolias, plane trees, yews and limes underplanted with aucubas and box. The garden buildings include a rock garden, two follies known as the Temple of Baal and the Walls of Jericho, a theatre, and a unique family chapel built in the English Elizabethan style.

NW of Rovigo, 6km from Boara Pisani exit on A13 **[** 0425 920 016 **Open** All year Mon 2pm–sunset & by appointment **Size** 8ha (20ac) **Owner** Scalabrin family **P WC ⎞** **W** www.villapisani.it **@** info@villapisani.it

The building at the end of the water-parterre is the stables of Villa Nazionale Pisani.

26. Villa Nazionale Pisani

Via Doge Pisani, 7
30039 Stra (VE)

Villa Nazionale Pisani is the grandest of the Venetian villas on the Brenta canal, built by the Pisani family in the 17th century and rebuilt 100 years later.

Behind its impressive bulk lies an equally spectacular 18th-century baroque garden. The original formal parterres were replaced early in the 20th century with a rectangular pool, which stretches for most of the way between the palace and the superb stables at the far end. The water serves to reflect the architecture of each and the immensity of the sky between. It also emphasises the monumental scale of the ensemble.

Within the park is a large circular maze, popular with visitors: the circular turret at its centre has a viewing platform served by two spiral staircases. Other features to see and admire include the woodland walks; an ice-house disguised as a volcano (complete with lava flow and statues); a handsome orangery; a wisteria tunnel; a 'coffee house' (effectively, a latter-day banqueting house); and a large collection of citrus trees in pots. Recent restoration has put this garden into top form again.

On Brenta canal 9km E of Padova
049 502 270 **Open** All year
Tue–Sun 9am–7pm (4pm Oct–Mar)
Size 10ha (25ac)
Owner The State

www.beniculturali.it

27. Villa Trento da Schio

Piazza da Schio, 4
36023 Costozza di Longare (VI)

The first view of this imposing baroque garden is very impressive – three broad flights of steps lead up the hillside from terrace to terrace. Sculptures line the ascent and fill the balustrades; many are by Orazio Marinali, whose workshop was on the neighbouring property. Up towards the top, where the steps divide, is a very beautiful statue of Amphitrite. Higher still is Neptune's fountain, with a strapping statue of the sea god. The *limonaia* is reached by a flight of steps with six grotesque dwarves up the sides. The lemon trees in pots fill out the parterres.

The history of the garden's development is poorly documented, but it is clear that almost all its features date from the 18th century, when it belonged to the Trento family. The 19th-century park below the house has some handsome mature trees, most notably several paulownias.

10km SE of Vicenza
0444 555 099 **Open** All year
Tue–Sun 9am–dusk **Size** 2ha (5ac)
Owner da Schio family
www.costozza-villadaschio.it
info@.costozza-villadaschio.it

28. Giardino di Pojega

Villa Rizzardi
Negrar di Valpolicella (VR)

The gardens at Villa Rizzardi are a very late expression of the baroque. They were laid out for Count Antonio Rizzardi in 1783 by the famous Veronese garden architect Luigi Trezza (1752–1823). You can still see the original plans in the library at Verona.

The house is currently let to Miguel Berrocal, the Spanish sculptor, so you enter the garden, from the estate yard, along a hornbeam tunnel high above the formal gardens. You then descend through a garden, with an oval *bassin* at the centre and hedges of box, to the main formal garden, recently restored, at the back of the house.

The magnificent feature that opens out here is a hop-hornbeam walk with hedges 10 m high and 150 m long. They arch over so that only a strip of sky appears at the top, matched by a long, narrow strip of grass below. This avenue leads to a rotunda with

Note the fine statues from the Marinali workshops at Villa Trento da Schio.

The largest 'green theatre' in Italy is at Giardino di Pojega.

a view up to a belvedere built at the highest point of the garden, but the green theatre draws you away to one side. It is much larger and more spacious than the Tuscan ones, with seven terraces of clipped box and stone steps leading up to mythological statues from Greek theatre. A *sacro bosco* of hornbeam, ilex, yew and maple, underplanted with *Trachycarpus fortunei*, surrounds the *tempietto*, built (as a ruin) of tufa, pebbles and pieces of stalactites. The grassy walks are perfumed by wild thyme, mint and marjoram.

Villa Rizzardi is perhaps loveliest in spring when the hop-hornbeams are in new leaf and blue muscari fleck the grass.

20km N of Verona ☎ 0457 210 028 **Open** Apr–Sept Thur 3–7pm **Size** 5.4ha (14ac) **Owner** Az. Agr. Guerrieri Rizzardi
🅿 🚾
🆆 www.guerrieri-rizzardi.it
@ pojega@guerrieri-rizzardi.it

29. Parco Sigurtà
37067 Valéggio sul Mincio (VR)

This vast modern garden was laid out in an informal style with help from Henry Cocker, the English-born director of the Villa Taranto gardens on Lake Maggiore. Work started in 1941 and the garden has been open to the public since 1978. There is a great amount to see in any season, and as the park is very large, you are best advised to hire a golf cart or bicycle at the entrance.

The first features are a line of irises, more than 500 m long, and a wall covered in different cultivars of *Campsis*. Much of the outer area is woodland and there are avenues of cypresses, tree paeonies, catalpas and limes. Very large expanses of closely mown grass occupy the central parts – the finest, neatest, greenest lawns in Italy. Planting is undertaken in large clumps: whole copses are put to lagerstroemias, maples, hydrangeas, hibiscus, forsythias, kerrias or prostrate conifers. The 18 ponds have an excellent collection of water lilies, lotuses, water hyacinths, papyrus and water hibiscus (*Hibiscus coccineus*). Right at the top, an avenue of roses runs straight for 400 m along the crest of the hill towards the castle of Valeggio sul Mincio. The recommended circuit is 7 km, but you will want to deviate, loop back and dally, so allow a lot of time for your visit.

8km SE of Peschiera del Garda ☎ 0456 371 033 **Open** Early Mar–early Nov daily 9am–7pm (last entry 6pm) **Size** 50ha (123ac) **Owner** Sigurtà family 🅿 🍴 🚾 ♿ 🆆 www.sigurta.it @ info@sigurta.it

30. Giardino Giusti
Via Giardino Giusti, 2
37129 Verona

The Giusti garden has a long history. Some of the cypress trees near the entrance are reckoned to date back to the garden's foundation in the late 15th century, but the present layout is due to Agostino Giusti in the 1570s. Goethe praised the garden's position and tall cypresses, while garden historian Sir George Sitwell described it as one of the most important in Italy. It was especially influential towards the end of the 19th century

Parco Sigurtà's vast garden brings a view of the castle of Valeggio sul Mincio into its modern landscape.
OPPOSITE: No garden gives such a good impression of a young baroque layout as this recently restored masterpiece of Giardino Giusti.

when neo-Renaissance garden-makers and restorers were looking for period models.

Recent restoration work enables us to see a renaissance garden as it was in its prime. The entrance is dramatic: you pass through a courtyard behind the palace and a long, straight avenue of majestic cypresses soars up the hillside behind. The view is terminated by a balcony, a grotto carved from the tufa rock, and a grimacing face on the cliffs above. The main garden is off to the side, laid out in gentle terraces with box-edged beds, young cypresses, baroque statues, fountains, parterres and fragments of Roman masonry. This is the part that, more than any other Italian garden, gives us an idea of what renaissance gardens really looked like. The box-edged maze on the other side of the main avenue dates from 1786 and has recently been replanted.

NE side of old city **☎** 0458 034 029 **Open** Daily (except 25 Dec) 9am–8pm (or dusk if earlier) **WC**

FRIULI

31. Castello di Duino
34013 Duino–Aurisina (TS)

Duino Castle is most interesting for its history, its cultural associations (James Joyce and Rainer Maria Rilke

Plants flourish in the dry moat of Castello di Duino.

The formal gardens at Castello di Miramare are a north European dream of Mediterranean perfection.

both stayed here) and the spectacular views from its high headland along the jagged Karstic cliffs. Handsome statues line the driveway. There has been a castle here from at least the 3rd century: a commemorative stone marks a visit by the Emperor Diocletian. The modern formal garden (about the size of a tennis court) has a rectangular pool, fountain, lawns and brightly coloured bedding. Bedding also enlivens the castle moat. Sheer rock is everywhere to be seen: the wonder is that anything grows here at all.

Middle of village, 22km W of Trieste **☎** 040 208 120 **Open** Mar–Oct daily (except Tue) 9.30am–5.30pm plus weekends in winter **Closes** 4.30pm Oct & 4pm winter **Size** 1ha (2½ac) **Owner** Thurn und Taxis family **☎ WC ▯ ▯** **W** www.castellodiduino.it **@** castellodiduino@libero.it

32. Castello di Miramare
Viale Miramare
34014 Trieste

Archduke Maximilian of Hapsburg (the ill-fated Emperor of Mexico) started building Miramare Castle in 1856 on a barren, rocky peninsular. A substantial stone pergola (planted with Banksian roses and wisteria all along its 300-m length) curves around the back of the castle and leads first to the formal gardens and then to the 'swan lake'. The impressive formal gardens – generously filled with colourful bedding and graced with classical statues on very tall plinths – look out to sea. The rather overgrown swan lake acts as a reservoir for the waterworks in the formal gardens. All are surrounded by dense, exotic woodland.

Maximilian had a special interest in experimental forestry and his conifers are now in their prime: sequoias, Monterey cypresses, cedars of Lebanon and araucarias have all grown to a great size. Native umbrella pines, cypresses and holm oaks thicken the woodland, and a valley between the castle and the formal gardens is densely underplanted with trachycarpus palms. The luxuriant plantings and impressive formal gardens are all protected from the bitter Bora wind by shelter-belts of *Pinus nigra* (Austrian pine). The result is a northerner's Mediterranean dream come true: gothic quatrefoils take the place of columns in the garden's balustrading.

At Grignano, 8km NW of Trieste ☎ 040 224 143 **Open** Daily 8am–7pm **Closes** 6pm Mar & Oct, & 5pm in winter **Size** 22ha (54ac) **Owner** Soprintendenza delle Belle Arti di Trieste 🅿 🚻 ♿ 🏛 💻 📷 ₩ www.castello-miramare.it @ info@castello-miramare.it

33. Villa Manin

Piazzale Manin, 10
33030 Passariano di Codroipo (UD)

After years of neglect, the Villa Manin has bounced back as a garden for the display of contemporary sculpture. The original palace and garden (both enormous) were made for the extravagant Manin family – Ludovico Manin was the last Doge of Venice – and rise incongruously from the flat Friuli plain.

The palace has two great, curved arcaded wings and the grass they enclose offers the first taste of what is to come – an abstract arrangement of coloured discs set into the turf. You enter the main gardens through the palace. The formal garden (1715) disappeared in Napoleonic times and the land-scape park was remade in the 1960s. An enormous flat lawn – perhaps 800 m long and 200 m wide – is edged with cedars and oaks. Right at the end are two artificial hills known as Etna

Michael Jackson's cut-out contrasts with the 18th-century grandiosity of Villa Manin.

and Parnassus. The latter has heavy, chunky statues of Apollo, the Muses and Pegasus, while Etna sports Pluto kidnapping Proserpine. The permanent exhibition of modern sculptures and installations, which Villa Manin has started to display since 2004, are spaced out along the lawn and within the woodland. The combination of old and new works rather convincingly.

Passariano is halfway btn Pordenone & Palmanova ☎ 0432 906 509 **Open** Tue–Sun 9.30am–7.30pm summer; 10am–6pm winter **Size** 19ha (47ac) **Owner** Villa Manin Centro d'Arte Contemporanea (as tenants) 🅿 🚻 ♿ (most) 📷 ₩ www.villamanincontemporanea.it @ info@villamanincontemporanea.it

34. Giardino Storico della Reggia

Piazza Garibaldi, 21
43052 Colorno (PR)

La Reggia di Colorno was the summer palace of the rulers of Parma. Duke Francesco Farnese laid it out in the early 1700s as an Italian-style quincunx, but decorated with French-style broderies. Napoleon I's wife, Marie-Louise of Austria, replaced these with an English-style park – one of Italy's best.

The gardens have recently been remade to resemble the 18th-century style. The four parterres surround a circular pool with a fine fountain; there are no flowers, apart from a few irises. Hornbeam tunnels run along the sides, with windows cut in the leafy walls from which to admire the parterres. Lemon trees are put out for the summer in handsome terracotta pots that bear the arms of the Farnese, the Bourbons and Empress Marie-Louise. Outside in the park are overgrown woodlands and a lake with two small islands.

Town centre ☎ 0521 313 336 **Open** All year daily, dawn–dusk **Size** 6ha (15ac) **Owner** Provincia di Parma 🅿 🚻 ♿ 📷 ₩ www.comune.colorno.pr.it/ @ uff.turisticocolorno@libero.it

Giardino Storico della Reggia is a modern reinterpretation of a large baroque lay-out.

MARCHE

35. Villa Caprile

61100 Pesaro

The *giochi d'acqua* – water tricks – at Villa Caprile are among the best in Italy. If you see your guide poking a little stick into the ground, it means that you are about to be sprayed by jets of water coming from the paths, flower-beds, balustrading, steps and sculptures.

The house and garden were first made for the Mosca family in 1640. Queen Caroline of England lived here in 1817–18; French novelist Henri Stendhal and Casanova were among other famous visitors. Much of the structure of the garden is intact, though the planting is all 20th century. It is laid out on four levels cut from a steep hillside. The second terrace is the largest, with four box-edged compartments. Each has a tall trachycarpus palm at the centre and an identical quincunx, edged with santolina and filled with bright bedding plants. Many pots are put along the edge of this terrace, so that there is always much colour. The gates at the side lead along an avenue of clipped, 4-m high conical yews to a green theatre in hedged cypress. On the third terrace is a fine fountain of Triton, while the fourth has a fountain with a statue of Atlas. Further downhill a steep statue-lined avenue runs straight to the town of Pesaro. The plants are interesting, chosen to teach the students of the agricultural college.

NW of city centre on lower slopes of Monte San Bartolo. Approach from Via Adriatica ☎ Tel 072 121 440 **Open** Jun–Sep daily 3–7pm **Size** 3ha (7ac) **Owner** Istituto Agrario A. Cecchi 🅿 🄿 ♿ ⓦ http://scuole.provincia.ps.it/ita. cecchi/home_page.htm @ ita.cecchi@provincia.ps.it

36. Villa Imperiale

Via dei Cipressi
61100 Pesaro

Look at Villa Imperiale's garden with renaissance eyes, and you will understand why it

Villa Imperiale's hanging gardens were built for a renaissance scholar-prince.

was so highly regarded. But there is nothing to please the modern seeker of colourful plants, and the simple baroque broderies beneath the castle are a 1990s repro.

The gardens of the old castle behind the 17th-century villa, however, are unique. Alberti, Vasari and Castiglione all praised them. You enter by a long court-yard: its imposing brick walls (interrupted by Ionic pilasters) have niches for the display of classical pieces. Halfway up is a hanging garden with citrus trees and a long, low parterre. Right at the top, where the terrace covers the whole of the old castle's roof, is a modern parterre with a hexagonal design. Within the villa (designed in 1530 by Girolamo Gengi for Francesco Maria della Rovere) is a dramatic sequence of frescos – high quality, beautiful and complex. They occupy all the rooms on the *piano nobile* and are crammed with *trompe-l'œil* and idealised landscapes, offering an immediate insight into the late-renaissance aesthetic.

NW of city centre, near summit of Monte San Bartolo. Signed from Strada Panoramica Adriatica ☎ 072 169 341 **Size** 4ha (10ac) **Open** By appointment through tourist office **Owner** Conte Clemente Castelbarco Albani 🅿 ⓦ www.turismo.pesarourbino.it @ iat.pesaro@regione.marche.it

TOSCANA

37. Il Roseto di Cavriglia

Casalone
52022 Cavriglia (AR)

If you love roses, this is a garden you must see. It is the largest collection of roses ever assembled by an amateur – some 7500 different species and cultivars. The garden has been entirely made by Professor Gianfranco Fineschi since the 1960s among the vines and olive trees of his Chianti estate.

The layout of the garden grew organically to incorporate areas dedicated to different sections of the genus *Rosa*, including Gallicas, Moss Roses and Hybrid Perpetuals. Smaller areas celebrate lesser known byways of rose breeding, like the many hybrids of *Rosa banksiae* bred by Quinto Mansuino and his followers in Italy in the 1960s and 1970s. Modern roses are arranged according to breeder. Extensive areas are dedicated to the work of single families like the Meillands of France, the Kordes of Germany and the McGredys of Northern Ireland and New Zealand. Sections display the work of breeders from Argentina, Brazil, South Africa and minor European rose nations like Poland, Portugal and the Czech Republic. Vast numbers of Hybrid Teas and Floribundas are preserved here and nowhere else: Cavriglia's is the largest collection in the world. Around the outside of the garden is a breathtaking display of climbing roses and ramblers, fan-trained to display their flowers to advantage.

Il Roseto di Cavriglia is a garden of colour, scent and profusion – and a living dictionary of roses of the world.

2km from centre of Cavriglia on road to San Giovanni Valdarno
☎ 055 966 638 **Size** 4ha (10ac)
Open May–Jun daily dawn–dusk; other times by appointment
Owner Fondazione Roseto Botanico Carla Fineschi
P **WC** **♿** **⌂**
W www.rosetofineschi.org
@ info@rosetofineschi.org

It is hard to imagine that this perfect *Quattrocento* garden at Villa le Balze was made by an Englishman less than 100 years ago.

38. Villa le Balze
Via Vecchia Fiesolana, 26
50014 Fiesole (FI)

The garden of Villa le Balze is an early masterpiece of the English architect Cecil Pinsent, who also worked at I Tatti and La Foce. His clients were the American philosopher Dr Charles Augustus Strong and his wife Elizabeth Rockefeller.

The garden was made in 1914 on a very steep site; its main asset was its astounding view over the city of Florence. Pinsent left the aspect open in front of the house, where a narrow terrace is edged by plants in ornamental pots along the balustrade. To the sides are enclosed garden rooms. Best is the lemon garden next to the house, where four box-edged grass enclosures surround a circular pool with topiary and lemon trees in pots. The effect is so classically Tuscan that you might be visiting a 15th-century villa instead of one less than 100 years old. Elsewhere are a grotto, statues, rocaille work and a woodland of ilex.

On outskirts of Fiesole as you approach from Florence **☎** 055 59 208
Open By appointment
Size 1ha (2½ac)
Owner Georgetown University **WC**
W www.villalebalze.org

39. Villa della Petraia
Via della Petraia, 40
50141 Castello (FI)

Villa della Petraia was a much-loved country palace of the Medici Grand Dukes; it dominates the hillside north-west of Florence. Ferdinando I laid out the garden between 1568 and 1609; Justus Utens's paintings in the Museo Storico-Topografico 'Firenze Com'era' in Florence show this (and eleven other Medici gardens) as they were in 1599.

You approach from below and come first to the big parterre, originally a potager but now

Italy's greatest rose garden, Il Roseto di Cavriglia, has many arcades hung with colourful and scented rambler roses.

planted with ornamental plants of every kind. The terrace above has a broad tank along much of its length from which to water the numerous pots of flowering plants put out for the summer – large specimens of bignonias, campsis, plumbagos and hibiscus. At one end is a flower garden, recently restored and dedicated to ancient cultivars of tulips, narcissus and fritillarias. The retaining wall is planted to clipped orange trees.

A handsome staircase leads up the villa itself, where the gardens are designed in the 19th-century style, with shell-edged beds mounded up and planted with mosaïculture. A line of bougain-villeas in vast pots leads to the belvedere, with big views back to Florence. Behind the villa is Giambologna's statue of Venus combing her hair, and a fine 19th-century woodland park.

NW outskirts of Florence
☎ 055 452 691 **Open** All year daily 8.15am–5pm **Closes** 6pm Mar & Oct; 7pm Apr, May & September; 8pm Jun–Aug **Size** 4ha (10ac)
Owner The State 🅿 🚾 ♿
🆆 www.polomuseale.firenze.it/
   musei/petraia/default.asp

40. Giardini Boboli

Piazza Pitti, 1
50125 Firenze

The Boboli Gardens are by far the biggest and best in Florence – a statement of princely grandeur. They were begun in the 1540s, enlarged in the 1640s and constantly improved over the years. The quality of their features means that these gardens have become the most complete example of Tuscan garden art in all its manifestations over the centuries.

Standards of maintenance have deteriorated noticeably in recent years, but the gardens are still compulsory viewing for visitors to Italian gardens. Near the Pitti Palace is the Great Grotto begun by Giorgio Vasari in 1556, one of the earliest in Italy and subsequently much copied. You should climb through the great balustraded amphitheatre, up the steep hill, through a second, grassy amphitheatre to the statue of Abundance by Susini and thence to the Cavaliere garden (old roses and paeonies) at the highest point to be rewarded by extensive views of the city and its hinterland. On the way you pass the Kaffeehaus, the little Madama grotto, formal pools and fine fountains.

But the most striking feature lies down the long cypress avenue, which runs slowly to the south-west. Tunnels of trained, looped-over ilex trees lead off to the sides. The thick woodland hides a perfect 19th-century botanic garden: fine trees, a pool dedicated to water lilies and lotus, and a good collection of tender plants put out for the summer. At the end of the cypress avenue is a large baroque pool, with a balustraded island in the middle called the *isolotto*, guarded by statues of riders on sea horses rising from the water. Here, around a tall statue of Oceanus, is a collection of lemon trees in pots. Though furthest from the palace, the *isolotto* is the most famous of all the garden's features and, many would say, the most beautiful.

A rider rises from the pool surrounding the *Isolotto*, Giardini Boboli.

Near Ponte Vecchio, S of River Arno, behind Pitti Palace **C** 055 294 883
Open All year daily 8.15am–5pm
Closes 6pm Mar & Oct; 7pm Apr, May & Sep; 8pm Jun–Aug
Size 32ha (79ac) **Owner** The State
⊡ ⏢ ⛾ ♿ ⛩ ▦
W www.polomuseale.firenze.it/ musei/boboli/

41. Giardino dei Semplici (Orto Botanico)
Via Micheli, 3
50121 Firenze

Giardino dei Semplici is the name for the botanic garden in Florence. It was founded by Cosimo I for medical students in 1545, which makes it the third oldest in Italy (after Pisa and Padua). Unfortunately, its original layout was lost in the 18th century, and the present garden is a little formless. However, there are good collections of orchids, cycads, cacti, ferns and, of course, medicinal plants. Horti-cultural interest comes from azaleas in spring. Many plants are grown as specimens in pots. Good trees include large speci-mens of *Cupressus sempervirens*, *Ginkgo biloba* and a stunning 35-m high *Zelkova crenata*.

At Giardino dei Semplici, pots are put out for the summer.

Some of the potted lemons at Villa di Castello are among Italy's oldest and largest.

City centre near Piazza San Marco **C** 0552 757 402 **Open** All year Mon–Fri 9am–1pm **Closed** weekends **Size** 2.5ha (6ac) **Owner** Università degli Studi di Firenze
⛾ ♿
W www.unifi.it/unifi/msn/main_ita.htm
@ ortbot@unifi.it

42. Villa di Castello
Via di Castello, 47
50141 Castello (FI)

The Villa at Castello was the first and oldest of the Medici family's country houses: they acquired it in 1477. The magnificent garden – though much changed over the years – is still Florence's busiest and fills the hillside behind the broad palace. Grand Duke Cosimo I employed the sculptor Niccolò Tribolo to give the garden its first make-over in the 1530s. French writer Michel Eyquem de Montaigne praised its automata and *giochi d'acqua* in the 1580s.

The garden now appears as a series of square parterres, each containing a different pattern and planted with interesting shrubs and herbaceous plants, especially roses and herbs.

Ribbons of Florentine irises run up the centre. The box-edged alleys are lined with a very large number of citrus trees in pots. There are more than 500 of them, some (like 'Bizzarria') descended from the original plants cultivated by the Medici. Fruit trees and climbing roses are trained against the walls. At the top, a broad, flat terrace has another display of citrus fruits in pots of every size. Some of the pots are among the biggest ever cast. The large lemon house dates from the 18th century. Elsewhere are many statues (ancient, renaissance and modern) and the *grotta degli animali* (animal grotto), where marble figures of birds and animals saved from the Flood are surrounded by mosaics, rocaille and pieces of stalactite.

Western outskirts of Florence **C** 055 454 791 **Open** All year daily 8.15am–5pm **Closes** 6pm Mar & Oct; 7pm Apr, May & Sep; 8pm June–Aug **Size** 5ha (12ac) **Owner** The State
🅿 ⛾ ♿ ▦
W www.polomuseale.firenze.it/ musei/villacastello/

'Dorothy Perkins' roses drape over the balustrading at Villa la Pietra.

43. Villa la Pietra

Via Bolognese, 120
50139 Firenze

The garden at La Pietra was made between 1905 and 1930 by the American art dealer Arthur Acton. The house dates back to the 15th century, but the garden was not landscaped until the 19th century. Acton decided to remake it in the style of Florentine late-renaissance gardens. The result was an unqualified success: La Pietra was much visited, much admired and much copied. It has recently been extensively restored.

The approach is along a stately avenue of cypresses, no more than 100 years old, underplanted with ever-blooming China roses. The oldest part is the lemon garden, which dates back to at least the early 18th century: Acton embellished it with rocaille pilasters. All the other garden rooms are 20th-century: enclosed parterres, sunken pools, a green theatre, a shady pergola, an ilex tunnel, yew topiary and a large collection of antiquarian and architectural fragments acquired by Acton for imaginative re-use. Statues are everywhere – nearly 200 of them – including many by Antonio Bonazza and Orazio Marinali.

The flowers are few, apart from rambling roses and seasonal bedding; the garden's effects come from the play of light and shade, contrasts of form and textures, surprise views and sequences, and a charming American romanticism that pervades the whole and gives it *genius*.

About 1km NE of Piazza della Libertà ☎ 055 500 7201
Open By appointment and, in some seasons, Tue & Fri am. Telephone for details **Size** 23ha (57ac)
Owner New York University P WC
W www.nyu.edu/global/lapietra/
@ villa.lapietra@nyu.edu

44. Villa Pratolino (Parco Demidoff)

Via Fiorentina, 276
50036 Pratolino-Vaglia (FI)

The Medici villa at Pratolino once had a baroque garden of enormous importance and influence. Garden historians describe the most extensive and complex system of waterworks and automata that ever existed. The garden started to decline after the death of the last Medici, Grand Duke Gian Gastone in 1737. All disappeared in 1818 when the entire estate was remodelled in the German landscape style, with meadows and woodlands.

Giambologna's giant statue of the *Dio Appenino* at Villa Pratolino is grand and provocative.

The highlight of a visit today is the awe-inspiring *Dio Appennino* by Giambologna, an old giant who represents the spirit of the Apennine mountains. No photograph can convey the sheer size of this massive statue. The park is still of historic interest but in need of the substantial renovation that has now begun. So its interest for visitors will grow in years to come. Meanwhile, it is hard to imagine anywhere more remote from the city of Florence, some 15 minutes away.

10km N of Florence on the SS65
☎ 055 409 155 **Open** Apr–Sep Thur–Sat & pub hols 10am–8pm (8.30pm May–July); plus hols in Mar (10am–6pm) & Oct (10am–7pm)
Size 160ha (395ac)
Owner Provincia di Firenze
P WC
W www.provincia.fi.it/istrcult/Demidoff/Default.htm

45. Villa i Tatti

Via di Vincigliata, 26
50135 Settignano (FI)

The garden at I Tatti was made for the American art historian Bernard Berenson and his wife Mary after they bought the tumble-down farmhouse in 1905. They employed a young, untried English architect called Cecil Pinsent to extend the house and lay out the garden. Both were conscious exercises in Italianisation – the imposition of a style inspired by 16th-century Florence. The result is a charming and unique combination of ideas and inspirations taken from mannerist and baroque Tuscan gardens.

Berenson's reputation quickly turned I Tatti into a fashionable visitor attraction – and made Pinsent's name as a designer. The main feature is a series of small formal gardens (parterres and topiary) on either side of a long staircase down the hillside. Its levels are marked by intricate, pebble inlay work. At the bottom are formal tanks and a handsome double staircase. Elsewhere

Topiary terraces and pebble patterns at Bernard Berenson's Anglo-Italian garden, Villa i Tatti.

the visitor will find an ilex woodland, a long cypress avenue, a lemon house and (much loved by the Berensons) a meadow garden in the English style designed by the painter Aubrey Waterfield.

2km SE of Fiesole **C** 055 603 251
Open By appointment, usually Tue & Wed pm **Size** 30ha (74ac)
Owner Harvard University **P** **WC**
W www.itatti.it **@** info@itatti.it

46. Villa Gamberaia
Via del Rossellino, 72
50135 Settignano (FI)

Villa Gamberaia was the first of the Florentine villa-gardens to achieve cult status in the late 19th century. The house was built on a spur above the Arno valley in the early 1700s. It looks out over olive groves towards the city of Florence and beyond to the Chianti hills. Its original features still include a bowling green, a nymphaeum, a grotto garden, an ilex grove and formal parterres.

In the 1890s an artistic Romanian Princess called Joan Ghika converted the formal garden from box broderies to water parterres and planted a semi-circular apse of clipped cypresses beyond. A later owner added topiary (now rather too large and lumpy) and many of the garden's flowers, especially roses.

Even today, Villa Gamberaia makes a deep impression on visitors. The whole site is in perfect harmony with itself – hillside, house, garden and every component part. The American novelist Edith Wharton summed it up in 1903 – her analysis is still correct – when she wrote that Gamberaia '… combines in an astonishingly small space, yet without the least sense of overcrowding, almost every typical excellence of the old Italian garden: free circulation of sunlight and about the house; abundance of water; easy access to dense shade; sheltered walks with different points of view; variety of effect produced by the skilful use of different levels; and finally, breadth and simplicity of composition'.

Signed in Settignano, 5km NE of Florence **C** 055 697 205
Size 3ha (7ac)
Open Daily 9am–6pm
Owner Zalum family
P **WC** **&**
W www.villagamberaia.com
@ villagam@tin.it

47. Villa Torrigiani
Via del Gomberaio, 3
Loc: Camigliano
Capannori (LU)

Villa Torrigiani is a nice example of how Italian gardens were converted into English-style parks in the early 19th century. The house is fronted by a vast spread of very green grass, in lieu of the original baroque garden – one of the earliest in Italy to be inspired by André le Nôtre, whose only traces now are two shapely pools.

Torrigiani is approached along a broad, straight avenue, 1 km long and lined with grass verges and ancient cypresses. The house itself is a harmonious combination of architecture and ornament, perhaps the most exuberant and charming in all Tuscany. Around the lawns are some of the largest plane trees in Europe – vast and vigorous specimens of great beauty – as well as ancient camellias (always a speciality of Lucca) and hedges of bay. An arrangement of parterres

For over 100 years, Villa Gamberaia has been the perfect renaissance garden, though decorated with topiary and flowers.

The dramatic Theatre of Flora is only one feature of the outstanding garden at Villa Torrigiani.

and lemon trees at one side of the house leads to a dazzling 17th-century sunken formal garden called the Theatre of Flora. This rare and beautiful structure has a sequence of baroque staircases at one end and a nymphaeum at the other – its dome (watch out for squirting water) is capped by a statue of Flora. Here too are allegorical statues of the winds and some fine rocaille and pebble inlay work. Above the sunken garden is a long, rectangular pool, said to be a fish pond, but with balustrading and statues at its top end. Seldom do so many disparate features come so well together as at Villa Torrigiani.

10km NE of Lucca **C** 0583 928 041 **Open** Mar–first Sun in Nov, daily 10am–12 noon & 3–5pm **Closed** Tue **Size** 7ha (17ac) **Owner** Colonna family **P** **WC** **&** **@** villatorrigiani@villelucchesi.net

48. Villa Garzoni
Piazza della Vittoria, 1
Collodi (PT)

Your first sight of the garden at Villa Garzoni leaves no doubt about what you have come to see. You slip through the gate at the bottom and, suddenly, the whole dramatic confection rises in front of you: brilliant

bedding, intricate parterres, balustraded staircases and a long water-chain running down the hillside from a vast, white-painted statue of Fame blowing her trumpet. The impact is mind-blowing: no wonder that the villa is an icon of the Italian rococo.

Villa Garzoni was made over many generations, starting in 1632, though most of what we see now dates from the 1760s. The three double staircases are the centre of the composition: their rises run in parallel, creating a false perspective. Grottos fill the central sections of the staircases and terracotta

The grandest baroque staircase in Tuscany is at Villa Garzoni.

monkeys perch on the balustrades. Fountains, topiary and intricate broderies occupy the foreground. The view up the water-chain is framed by two large pediments, one fitted around a recumbent satyr and the other a satyress. Intricate pebble patterns carpet the ascent. Down by the entrance you notice the green theatre and pretty terracotta chairs. One of the terraces is planted with palm trees and ornamented with espaliered lemon trees in large terracotta pots. The standard of the floral displays is very high. Thick ilex woods fill the hillside on either side of the water-chain. Hidden within are terraced walks that have recently been reopened: the garden has undergone substantial repair and restoration and is now in better condition than for 50 years.

Collodi is 8km W of Pescia **C** 0572 429 590 **Open** All year daily 9am–12 noon & 2–5pm, but 9am–sunset in summer **Size** 5ha (12ac) **Owner** Villa e Giardino Garzoni srl **☐** **❚❚** **WC** **☐** **☐**

49. Palazzo Pfanner
Via degli Asili, 33
55100 Lucca

All the elements of the classic Italian baroque garden are here at Palazzo Pfanner, but concentrated within a small space. Its history is unknown: some attribute it to Filippo Juvarra, but others say that it was built earlier, by the Controni family in the 1680s.

You see the garden as soon as you enter the main portal of the palace: just beyond the spectacular stairs that lead to the *piano nobile* is a large octagonal pool with a fountain at its centre and a substantial collection of lemons in pots. Everywhere are statues – it is a very *busy* garden – including handsome renderings of the four seasons, the four elements, ancient gods and mythological heroes. All are surrounded by climbing roses and masses of bright seasonal bedding; the

Palazzo Pfanner is a perfect, small, enclosed garden within the walls of the city of Lucca.

7km N of Lucca
☎ 0583 406 265 **Open** Easter–Oct
daily 10am–1pm & 3–7pm
Closed Mon & Tue am
Size 9ha (22ac)
Owner Grabau family
🅿 🆆🅲 ♿
🆆 www.villagrabau.it
@ villagrabau@mclink.it

51. Villa Reale
Via Fraga Alta, 2
Marlia (LU)

Villa Reale is the grandest of the Lucca villas, and its gardens the most extensive and impressive. It takes its name from a sequence of royal owners – Elisa Baciocchi, Napoleon I's sister; the Dukes of Parma; the Austrian Grand Dukes of Tuscany; and King Vittorio Emanuele II.

The gardens' most important features date back to the 17th and 18th centuries: the large lemon garden has an enormous number of lemons in pots and four tall cones of clipped *Magnolia grandiflora*. It leads to a substantial balustraded water tank set with allegorical statues of the rivers Arno and Serchio and a nymphaeum that shelters a statue of Leda and the swan. Off to one side is the green theatre, Italy's oldest and most copied. It was first planted in 1624; the wings, stage lights and prompter's box are all of clipped yew.

garden is notable for its high standard of maintenance. In the best traditions of the baroque, it is theatrical, lively and entertaining.

Within old city walls, at NW corner
☎ 0583 991 667 **Open** Mar–Nov
daily 10am–6pm **Size** 1ha (2½ac)
Owner Pfanner family 🆆🅲 ♿ 🎑
@ dariopf@tin.it

50. Villa Grabau
Via di Matraia, 269
55010 San Pancrazio (LU)

Villa Grabau has one of the best 'English' parks in the Lucchese hills and a very fine lemon garden too. It is well maintained and well labelled, with lots of recent replanting – always a sign of a garden in good heart. The house faces south across the lawns. Two venerable bushes, now short trees, of *Osmanthus fragrans* occupy the terrace in front of the house.

You enter the garden at its southern edge, through a supremely beautiful gateway. The park is planted with a mix of deciduous and coniferous trees. As with all Lucchese gardens, the trees are not rare but include some very fine specimens, notably planes, ilexes and cedars. The positioning of the trees within the park is carefully planned to create a sense of beauty, space and enclosure; Edouard André may have had a hand in its design. Discreet laurel hedges conceal the estate farm buildings. Behind the house is the Italian garden, long since put to grass, with a remarkable fountain and tall, intricately curving hedges of ilex and laurustinus. The garden's faded outlines help to position over 70 lemon trees in large pots. The *limonaia* lies behind, a handsome building painted a deep pink and planted with climbing roses.

The parterres have gone at Villa Grabau, but the stairs, balustrading, fountain and lemon trees make a remarkably harmonious composition.

Villa Reale is the largest, grandest and most inventive garden in the rich hinterland of Lucca.

Elsewhere at Villa Reale are high hedges of ilex (some as much as 12 m tall); a large collection of old camellias; an impressive baroque water-theatre behind the house; an English-style park with good 19th-century conifers (especially cedars); a 1920s Islamic garden (rather out-of-place, but good of its type); and very good displays of seasonal bedding.

8km N of Lucca **C** 058 330 108 **Open** Mar–Nov Tue–Sun. Guided tours only: 10am, 11am, 12 noon, 3pm, 4pm, 5pm & 6pm **Size** 19ha (47ac) **Owner** Pecci-Blunt family
P WC ▦
@ villareale@cln.it

52. Villa Massei
Via della Chiesa, 53
55060 Massa Macinaia (LU)

Almost everything you see at Villa Massei has been made by the owners since they bought it in 1981. It is an American–Tuscan hybrid – romantic but restrained.

Leave your vehicle below the house and walk up slowly: you need a moment to prepare for the subtle, understated charms of this calm, unornamented, elegant garden. An extensive lawn in front of the house stretches into the distance, past a venerable cedar, to a long colonnade of round brick pillars festooned with 'Claire Jacquier' roses. Soft underplantings in cream and palest salmon lead to a pool enclosed within hedges. You return by one of the side aisles, planted with olive tree standards pruned to a leafy sphere.

Above are formal gardens, including a shrub-lined swimming pool, a masterpiece of landscaping with Mediterranean plants. Elsewhere are a rose garden; an avenue of cherries under-planted with native narcissi and wild orchids; and an English garden, its grass path curving through mixed borders, almost unreal in this super-Tuscan landscape. But the heart of the garden is an enclosed secret area behind the pillared loggia of the house. A wisteria-clad pergola leads to a cool grotto. To one side is a neat formal garden, perfectly proportioned, of simple box edgings filled with grass and pots of *Citrus mitis*. On the other side is an ancient

The new brick colonnade at Villa Massei is hung with 'Claire Jacquier' roses.

Villa Mansi's formal gardens have long disappeared, and the house now stands in a spacious 19th-century parkland setting.

camphor tree thought to be 200 years old – one of few in the Lucca area. The grotto itself, say the owners, is temporal perfection.

6km SE of Lucca
📠 0583 90 138 **Open** By appointment for groups **Size** 4ha (10ac) **Owner** Paul Gervais & Gil Cohen 🅿 🆆 www.agardeninlucca.com

53. Villa Mansi
Via delle Selvette, 242
Segromigno in Monte (LU)

Villa Mansi is one of the most handsome houses in the Lucca region. Its garden – now rather run-down – was equally impressive when first laid out by the fashionable Filippo Juvarra (1678–1736). Much was altered when the formal gardens were replaced by a landscape park, but the relics of the baroque layout are well worth a visit. A narrow water-chain runs over several small waterfalls to a small octagonal pool, under the eye of a stone soldier. At the lowest level lies a pretty fish pond, balustraded around with rustic rococo statues. A spacious 19th-century lawn makes a finer frame for the house than the baroque gardens it replaced. Around its edges, the grand old trees include hornbeam, tulip trees, cedars and planes.

📞 0583 920 234 **Open** Tue–Sun 10am–1pm & 3–6pm **Closes** 5pm Nov–Mar **Size** 5ha (12ac) **Owner** Claudia Salom 🅿 🆆 ♿ @ info@villamansi.it

54. Venzano
Mazzolla
56048 Volterra (PI)

Venzano is the most fragrant garden in this book and was designed by Australians Donald Leevers and Lindsay Megarrity. Almost every plant is intensely aromatic: the hedges are of bay, while rosemary and lavender cover the walls and bind the beds together.

The garden is a series of small terraces and enclosures with fine views over the Tuscan hills. Cistus, irises, paeonies, lilies, alliums, euphorbias, *Bupleurum fruticosum* – all the ingredients of the Mediterranean hillsides – have been brought together, often as improved forms, in ornamental mixes. Ixias, sparaxis, ipheions, narcissus and other bulbs give colour in springtime, while in autumn wild cyclamen line the lane running down to the property. A vine-covered pergola leads to a Roman well, its walls hung with maidenhair fern. A row of the dainty, constant-flowering *Nerium oleander* 'Petite Salmon' fills the courtyard garden. There are pots, too, of the *Crinum pedunculatum*, whose sweet-scented white flowers are set off by strong leaves that do not bend and break like other species do.

Nothing is irrigated: if you want to learn how to garden with plants in a Mediterranean climate, Venzano is the place to see. The small nursery is well known in Italy for its unusual plants.

Signed at entrance to Mazzolla, 8km SE of Volterra 📞 0588 39095 **Open** By appointment **Size** 1ha (2½ac) **Owner** Don Leevers 🅿 ♿ 🆆 www.venzanogardens.com @ info@venzanogardens.com

55. Orto Botanico di Pisa
Via Luca Ghini, 5
56126 Pisa

Pisa's botanic garden claims to be the oldest in the world, founded in 1544 as a

The Australian owners of Venzano have perfected the art of making English-style mixed borders in the unEnglish climate of Tuscany.

medical garden for the study
of useful plants. It was not,
however, moved to its present
site until 1591. None of its
original design remains, but it
is charmingly laid out and
full of interesting plants.

Close to the entrance are
two tall Chilean palms (*Jubaea
chilensis*) and a shaggy
Washingtonia filifera. The
systematic beds, off to the left,
are extensive and their 550 taxa
occupy one-quarter of the
garden. Nearby are a small
collection of medicinal plants
and some of the oldest trees in
the city: *Magnolia grandiflora*
and *Ginkgo biloba*, planted in
1787. The garden has four
glasshouses: a hothouse and
three dedicated to succulents
(250 taxa), palms and ferns.
The arboretum has many fine
trees and shrubs: the camellias
and rhododendrons are
especially good in spring.

City centre 🛈 050 560 045 **Open**
Mon–Sat 8am–5.30pm (5pm winter)
Closes 1pm Sat **Size** 3ha (7ac)
Owner Università di Pisa 🚾 ♿
🌐 http://www.dsb.unipi.it/hbp/
pagina.html
@ direzione@dsb.unipi.it

56. La Foce
Strada della Vittoria, 61
53042 Chianciano Terme (SI)

La Foce is the best inter-war
garden in Tuscany – an
Anglo-Italian hybrid made by the
English architect Cecil Pinsent
for the writer Iris Origo and her
husband Marchese Antonio.
All its structure is copied from
renaissance gardens – hedges,
parterres, lemon trees in pots –
but it also reveals an English
love of flowers.

It was made in stages on
a high, dry hillside with
extensive views across the

Val d'Orcia towards Mount
Amiata. The small enclosed
garden nearest the house is the
simplest: a fountain stands on
two stone dolphins, surrounded
by lawns and flower beds
edged in box. The lemon
garden is larger, with box
hedges around a slightly less
formal flower garden and
plinths for lemon trees in
summer. *Trachelospermum
jasminoides* covers the wall and
fills the garden with its intense
scent in high summer. The so-
called geometric garden has
triangular beds enclosed by
clipped box and planted with
Magnolia grandiflora, focusing
on a small pool, with a grotto
in the retaining wall. But the
most pleasing feature at La
Foce is a substantial pergola
of roses and wisteria, richly
underplanted with paeonies
and bulbs. It runs away from
the house for as much as 400
m, following the curves of the
hillside until it becomes a
broad path and passes through
an ornamental woodland
garden of Judas trees, flowering
quinces, pomegranates, shrub
roses, lavender and rosemary.

The views are breathtaking
and include a line of cypresses
(planted by the Origos) zig-
zagging its way up a hillside to
a farmhouse – a planting that
is now an icon of the Tuscan
landscape.

5km SW of Chianciano Terme
🛈 0578 69101 **Open** Guided tours
3pm & 4pm Wed, plus 5pm & 6pm
Apr–Sept **Size** 3ha (7ac) **Owner**
Marchesa Benedetta Origo 🅿 🚾
🌐 www.lafoce.com
@ info@lafoce.com

57. Giardino dei Tarocchi
Pescia Fiorentina
58100 Capalbio (GR)

Niki de Saint Phalle's
Tarot Garden is an
important essay in modernism.
It has nothing to interest the
horticulturist or botanist, but is
nevertheless extremely interesting
and enjoyable to visit. It is a
giant-sized sculpture garden,
cut from woodland and edged
by olive groves, within sight of

Iris Origo designed her garden at La Foce to take in the wider landscape,
including the volcanic peak of Monte Amiata.

Giardino dei Tarocchi is a garden of joy, fun and humour.

the sea. Saint Phalle worked on it from 1979 onwards – she took up residence in the sculpture called the Empress – and it has been open to the public since 1996.

Inspiration came from Gaudi's Parc Güell in Barcelona and Sacro Bosco at Bomarzo. Clever critics describe the Tarot Garden as an exploration of the human condition, where buildings and sculptures reflect the metaphysical qualities represented by the 22 main tarot cards and by the elements of life's experience, personality and self-knowledge. Saint Phalle said simply that her purpose was to make a garden of joy.

The sculptures are brightly coloured and covered with glittering ceramics, mosaics and mirrors. They have such names as the Sun, the Dragon, the Hermit and the Oracle. Most people take them at face value and enjoy the sheer fun of the site.

Via Aurelia (A12) exit Pescia Fiorentina **C** 0564 895 122
Open May–mid-Oct daily 2.30–7.30pm
Owner Niki de Saint Phalle
W www.nikidesaintphalle.com

58. Villa Chigi Cetinale
53018 Sovicille (SI)

Lord Lambton bought the Cetinale estate in 1977 and spent a fortune on restoring the historic house and garden. It is now a compulsory stop for anyone on a grand tour of gardens in Italy.

The villa was built in the 1680s for Cardinal Fabio Chigi and sits at the end of a long avenue. You pass through the gates and approach it across a formal garden of yew topiary and box parterres set with statues and lemon trees in pots: this classically Italian garden is a modern reconstruction, but very well done.

On the other side is a 19th-century avenue of cypresses that leads to an important baroque garden on the hillside some distance from the house. The lower flanks are called the *Tebaide*, a sacred wood studded with chapels, statues of saints and other aids to devotion. It helps to think of this as a Christian variation of the much more commonly encountered gardens devoted to the classical and profane. A long, straight flight of steps (some 200 of them) climbs through the ilex wood to a building known as the *Romitorio* at the top. It, too, was used for prayer, by monks who visited it by rota. Its views of the villa, the estate and the Sienese countryside are very extensive. Below the house is

a sequence of modern English-style gardens, planted with old-fashioned roses and thick herbaceous mixes in the Sissinghurst style – the best of their kind in Tuscany.

15km W of Siena **C** 0577 311 147
Open 9am–12 noon weekdays; by appointment **Size** 20ha (49ac)
Owner Lord Lambton **P** **&**

LAZIO

59. Giardini e Rovine di Ninfa
04010 Doganella di Ninfa (LT)

Ninfa is the most beautiful and romantic garden in the world. It is made among the ruins of a walled mediaeval city, which was abandoned in the 14th century and excavated about 100 years ago – a mediaeval Pompeii.

The princely Caetani family that owned it was more English than Italian and planted the garden in a completely English style. Every ruined house, church, workshop and fortification within the city seems to have climbing roses and other sweet-scented plants growing over it. The empty squares are busy with magnolias, cherries and Judas trees in spring. A river surges from a lake just above the garden and flows through the centre of the city. Wisteria drips from the bridges

Villa Chigi Cetinale's classic baroque garden was remade by the English Lord Lambton in the 1980s.

ABOVE: Giardini e Rovine di Ninfa: a garden within the ruins of a mediaeval town.
OPPOSITE: The wisteria-clad Roman bridge in Giardini e Rovine di Ninfa was once part of a highway from Rome to Naples.

that span it. Water from the lake and springs is diverted to run through the garden in innumerable streamlets and channels, so that almost every part is filled with the sight and sound of running water.

The plants came from English nurseries and revel in the cool freshness of the abundant water. Drifts of Japanese irises and arum lilies fill the streams and ditches. Roses like 'Mutabilis', 'Général Schablikine' and *Rosa roxburghii* (the double form) appear everywhere and, flowering for most of the year, provide a link throughout the garden. Ninfa is a garden without design; its structure comes from the mediaeval ruins.

There are no plant labels, statues or artefacts – nothing, in fact, to detract from its Elysian, dream-like quality. It is a garden quite unlike any other: a deserted mediaeval city now conquered by beautiful plants.

13km NNW of Latina
☎ 0773 633 935 **Open** Guided tours only. First Sat & Sun of month Apr–Oct, & third Sun Apr, May & Jun. By appointment for groups.
Size 8ha (20ac) **Owner** Fondazione Roffredo Caetani 🅿 🚻 ♿ 🏠 🌷

60. Villa Aldobrandini
Via Cardinal Massais, 18
00044 Frascati (ROMA)

Aldobrandini is the biggest and best of the many baroque villas in Frascati and clearly visible from Rome. It was built between 1598 and 1603 for Cardinal Aldobrandini, the nephew of Pope Clement VIII, and remained in the family until 1681, when it passed to the Pamphilj and later to the Borghese.

Pan plays his pipes at a corner of the enormous Water Theatre at Villa Aldobrandini.

The house was designed by Giacomo della Porta and Carlo Maderno to sit at the end of a 100-m driveway of clipped ilexes, with the main garden behind and to the sides. Orazio Olivieri laid out the gardens, including the Nymphaeum or *Teatro delle Acque* (the Water Theatre), which bristles with fountains and waterspouts; in the 17th century they made musical noises. The central statue of Atlas holding up the earth is flanked by Pan on one side and a centaur on the other. All are centrepieces for impressive fountains, fed from the stream that pours rapidly down the steep hillside behind. Here is the famous (and much-copied) pair of helter-skelter water spirals, known as the columns of Hercules, inlaid with patterned tesserae and encrusted with stalactites. Baroque castellations mark the ends of the terraces to the sides of the house. Ancient plane trees underplanted with hydrangeas lead to a formal garden in the conventional shape of a quincunx around a pool. This and a further parterre with star-shaped box hedges are rather threadbare now, though there are fine camellias along the side.

Villa Aldobrandini is badly maintained and in need of restoration, but still one of the greatest early baroque gardens of the world.

Town centre ☎ 069 420 331
Open Mon–Fri 9am–1pm & 3–5pm
Size 8ha (20ac) **Owner** Italian State
🅿 🚻 ♿ (most)

61. Orto Botanico di Roma
Largo Cristina di Svezia, 24
00165 Roma

Rome's botanic garden is not an ancient foundation: the Corsini family gave it to the Italian State in 1883, though its outstanding architectural feature is the Triton Fountain, designed by Fernandino Fuga in 1750.

You reach it along the Palm Avenue: look out for *Chamaerops humilis* var. *arborescens, Brahea dulcis,* a fine *Nannorrhops ritchieana,*

Orto Botanico di Roma has a good collection of palms and cycads.

the American *Rhapidophyllum hystrix*, and the unusual *Trachycarpus taki*. Further on, a woodland of umbrella pines (*Pinus pinea*) runs up the slopes of the Janiculum hill. Features here include a rather run-down rose garden, collection of bamboos, fern valley, rock garden and Japanese garden. At the bottom of the broad staircase known as *Il Scalone* is a vast plane tree thought to be 350 to 400 years old. Nearby are the *Giardino dei Semplici* (a medicinal herb garden), a 'perfumed' garden for the visually impaired, and three glasshouses – one for tropical plants, another for cacti, and the third for orchids. The garden has over 3500 taxa, including an 8-m high centennial *Yucca carnerosana* and good collections of nolinas and dasylirions, including *Dasylirion acrotrichum, D. glaucophyllum, D. serratifolium* and *D. longissimum.*

Trastevere area of central Rome
☎ 066 864 193
Open 9am–6.30pm (5.30pm winter)
Closed Tue & Aug **Size** 12ha (30ac)
Owner Università di Roma 'La Sapienza' ▣ 🚻 ♿
🔲 www.ips.it/musis/muort_f0.html

62. Villa Borghese
00197 Roma (ROMA)

Villa Borghese's gardens are among Rome's best – of immense historic, artistic and environmental importance. Cardinal Scipione Borghese, a nephew of Pope Paul V, laid out a large formal garden in the early years of the 17th century. It was turned over to the landscape style from about 1787 onwards, when Jacob More was commissioned to give the gardens a more 'natural' air. Nevertheless, they are still populated by innumerable buildings and statues from the original design – most notably by the eagles and dragons that represent the Borghese coat of arms.

The gardens of Villa Borghese have several entrances (the most famous being the Spanish Steps) and incorporate the Pincian, one of ancient Rome's seven hills. Their leading features – linked by a flowing structure of umbrella pines, Italian cypresses and holm oaks – include the lake, with Æsculapius' temple behind; the *Fontana dei Cavalli Marini* (sea horse fountain) in the style of Giovanni Bernini; and the *Tempietto di Diana* (little temple of Diana) built in 1789 with exquisite blue ceramic tiling.

Recent restoration has ensured that there is no more enjoyable a garden in Rome to visit and explore. The *giardini segreti* around Cardinal Scipione's Villa have recently been restored to their 17th-century glory and are open by prior appointment.

City centre ☎ 06 8530 4242
Open Daily dawn–dusk **Size** 80ha (198ac) **Owner** Comune di Roma
🅿 ▣ 🍴 🚻 ♿ 🖼
🔲 www.villaborghese.it

63. Villa Doria Pamphilj
00165 Roma

Villa Doria Pamphilj has the largest and finest historical park in Rome, but the worst maintained. Mussolini wrested it from the Doria Pamphilj princes in 1939. Their ownership dates back to the

Villa Borghese's extensive landscape is the grandest in Rome.

This little palace has a very pretty baroque garden, now separated from the vast park of the Pamphilj.

City centre on either side of Via Leone XIII [C] 0639 376 616
Open Daily 7am–dusk
Size 184ha (454ac)
Owner City of Rome
[P] [⊡] [WC] [&] (partly accessible)
[W] www.romabeniculturali.it/ villeparchi/

pontificate of Innocent X (1644–55), though the estate and its extensive woodlands of umbrella pines and ilex were frequently expanded by purchase until the late 19th century.

The original baroque garden (still owned by the Doria Pamphilj and visited only by appointment) is beautifully maintained, with a fine parterre around the central casino. Lemon trees are put out for the summer in their pots around a baroque pool, where a huge fruiting taxodium fills the bowl.

Beneath the villa – in the publicly owned part – are the ruins of further formal gardens, landscaped from the 1790s onwards. Here are empty fountains, vandalised grottos, broken pillars and statues with their heads knocked off. Their condition is shocking – but still worth seeing, as a place to ponder the glory that was counter-Reformation Rome.

64. Villa Adriana
Via di Villa Adriana, 21
00010 Tivoli (ROMA)

The Emperor Hadrian's Villa near Tivoli was built on an enormous scale over a ten-year period starting in AD 117. It is the most extensive ancient Roman complex known to us and contained a large number of gardens, as well as palaces and service buildings. It was built to impress and indeed has been very influential ever since it was first excavated in the 1490s.

The two features most relevant to garden historians are the *Teatro Marittimo* and the *Canopus*, which architects like Antonio da Sangallo and Giovanni da Údine tried to reconstruct in renaissance gardens. The *Canopus*, based on an Egyptian temple, is a long pool edged with a white marble colonnade and decked with statues. The *Teatro Marittimo* is an elegant folly contained within a watery moat.

The Canopus at Villa Adriana gives a good idea of how the Emperor Hadrian indulged himself at leisure.

The 100 fountains on this terrace at Villa d'Este were a symbol of the owner's power and wealth.

The site is, in any event, worth visiting for its 18th-century cypresses and the profusion of wild flowers, especially cyclamen, in spring and autumn.

Tivoli, about 20km E of Rome, SW of modern town ☎ 0639 967 900 **Open** Daily 9am–8pm **Size** 80ha (198ac) **Owner** Soprintendenza Archeologica del Lazio 🅿 🖼 🍴 🚾 ♿ 🏛
🕸 www.archeologia.beniculturali.it/ pages/atlante/S127.html

65. Villa d'Este

Piazza Trento, 1
00019 Tivoli (ROMA)

Villa d'Este was, from the start, recognised as the most impressive and complete mannerist garden in all Italy. It is still considered one of the wonders of the garden world, and is registered as a UNESCO World Heritage site. Its fame rests on its extent, and the complexity of its waterworks. It was begun in the 1560s by Pirro Ligorio for Lucrezia Borgia's son, Cardinal Ippolito II d'Este, but expanded by Cardinal Alessandro d'Este in the early 1600s. Cardinal Rinaldo d'Este then employed Giovanni Bernini in the 1660s to build the Bicchierone fountain.

The narrow terraces make it a hanging garden; visitors originally arrived at the bottom, where its splendour is immediately apparent. The modern entrance is through the palace at the top, but the number and size of the garden's features open out as you descend the terraces past ancient cypresses and extravagant fountains – including the *Rometta* (a tribute to Rome); the *Ovato* (backed by a nymphaeum); the Fountain of the Dragons; a many-breasted sculpture of Diana; the long walk called the Terrace of One Hundred Fountains; and the massive cascade below the Water Organ. The water-driven Owl Fountain is said to be so realistic that it impelled astonished songbirds to silence. But the garden is also peaceful and well maintained, and the central sequence of three broad fish ponds is a place of rare enchantment.

21km NE of Rome in town centre ☎ 0424 600 460 **Open** Tue–Sun 9am to 1hr before sunset **Size** 3ha (7ac) **Owner** Soprintendenza per i Beni Culturali
🖼 🍴 🚾 ♿ (prebooked) 🏛 🖼
🕸 www.villadestetivoli.info
@ villadestetivoli@telekottageplus.com

66. La Landriana

Via Campo di Carne, 51
00040 Tor San Lorenzo-Ardea
(ROMA)

Marchesa Lavinia Taverna made the garden at La Landriana on an open, empty site between 1967 and 1997. The Englishman Russell Page advised her in the early years but, with growing self-confidence, she dismissed him and became her own designer.

ABOVE: La Landriana's driveway is landscaped with repetition and scale.
OPPOSITE: The size and sophistication of Villa d'Este's waterworks were by far the most extensive in renaissance Italy.

Giardini del Vaticano's Eagle Fountain was made for the very rich Pope Paul V in about 1610.

67. Giardini del Vaticano
Viale Vaticano (VATICAN)

The Vatican Gardens are a series of pretty features rather loosely tied together by 19th-century landscaping. They reflect the changing tastes of the centuries, and the character of the individual popes across the ages: Leo XIII built the reproduction grotto at Lourdes and John-Paul II installed the Black Madonna of Czestochowa.

The earliest traces date back to the pontificate of Innocent VIII (1484-92), who built the Villa Belvedere. Bramante designed the Cortile del Belvedere for Julius II in 1504: in its day, this was the largest and most revolutionary garden in Europe. Pirro Ligorio, architect of Villa d'Este at Tivoli, built the exquisite mannerist Villa Pia for the Medici Pope Pius IV in 1560. Every part is dominated by the soaring presence of Bernini's massive dome.

Most of the fountains – there are 90 of them – date from the 17th century: best known is the Fountain of the Eagle, made by Jan van Santen for the Borghese Pope Paul V. Water for the fountains comes from Lake Bracciano, 50 km north, along an aqueduct built by the Emperor Trajan (AD 98–117).

The gardens were landscaped and restored in the 19th century: the formal Italian garden dates from this period, as do the groves of massive oaks (*Quercus ilex*), Italian stone pines (*Pinus pinea*) and cedars of Lebanon (*Cedrus libani*). Among the trees is an olive from the Garden of Gethsemane. And the gardens are alive with over 200 green parrots, descendants of a pair given to Paul VI by an Australian archbishop in about 1970.

The garden expanded to incorporate some 30 different compartments, by which time it was undoubtedly the best example anywhere in the Mediterranean region of a modern garden designed with plants. Some areas are dedicated to a single genus – the viburnum garden, magnolia garden, heather garden, and hydrangea garden – or to a distinct style, like the Italian garden and Spanish tank garden. Others are devoted to shade or to a single colour. The golden garden is especially effective, because it relies on leaf colour all through the year, while the grey garden is an entire woodland, where plants like cistus, santolina, helichrysum and artemisia gleam under a canopy of silvery olive trees. The white avenue is a long, narrow, rectangular garden enclosed within yew hedges. The planting is of uniformly white flowers with a long season, most especially the incomparable rose 'Schneewittchen' ('Iceberg'). The garden of the orange trees is an orchard of bitter oranges grown as standards and clipped into globes, underplanted with hundreds of *Myrsine africana*, also clipped into small spheres.

One of the most memorable features – quite unique – is a large area on a hillside, where grass paths wind among beds thickly planted with a single shrub, *Rosa* 'Mutabilis', which flowers continuously throughout the year.

25km S of Rome ⨀ 0601 014 140 **Open** Sat, Sun & pub hols Apr–Jun, Aug (Sun only) & Sept. Guided tours 10am, 11am, 12 noon, 3pm, 4pm, 5pm, 6pm. By appointment for groups **Size** 10ha (25ac) **Owner** Gallarati-Scotti family
🅿 🚾 ♿
Ⓦ www.giardinidellalandriana.it
@ info@landriana.com

⨀ 0669 884 676 **Open** Mar–Oct 8.45am–3.20pm (12.20pm Sat), except Sun & Holy Days. In winter 8.45am–12.20pm. Guided tours only; booking advisable (0669 885 100 for individuals; 0669 883 578 for groups) **Size** 23ha (57ac) **Owner** H.H. The Pope
🅿 🚾 ♿ 🍴 🎁
Ⓦ http://mv.vatican.va

68. Villa Lante
01031 Bagnaia (VT)

Water running down the hillside in endless different forms is the essence of Villa Lante's garden.

Villa Lante is one of Italy's greatest renaissance gardens – and very beautiful. It was the country palace of two Cardinal-bishops of Viterbo: Gianfrancesco Gambarra and Alessandro Montalto. The architects were Il Vignola and Pirro Ligorio, the specialist in waterworks who laid out Villa d'Este at Tivoli.

The villa has twin houses on either side of the garden's main axis, a most unusual and successful arrangement; the garden, too, is perfectly symmetrical. Your first sight is of the huge, balustraded water-parterre known as the Fountain of the Moors, where four blackamoors hold aloft the Montalto coat of arms. It is surrounded by extensive parterres in the mannerist style.

The rest of the garden is laid out on rising terraces, often overhung by vast plane trees, and said to be deeply imbued with mythological symbolism (Nature tamed by Man). First comes the semi-circular water organ, a hydraulic automaton designed in 1564 to accompany a group of instrumentalists. Further up are the *giochi d'acqua*, hidden water spouts to soak the unwary. The banqueting terrace has a long stone table with water running down the centre and jets that spurt right over the top to keep the diners cool but dry. Past the fountain of the river gods on the next terrace is Vignola's water-catenary – a long, gentle, channelled waterfall made of swirling stone in the shape of a crayfish.

The garden opens out towards the top, where a large, pyramidal fountain is supported by strange monsters, and two small temples are dedicated respectively to Pan and Diana. Right at the top is the ferny grotto from which spouts the water that is the source of all the garden's delights.

Villa Lante's water parterre is a superb example of the late-renaissance or mannerist style.

The words on the giant's lips at Sacro Bosco read, 'Abandon all thought …'

5km E of Viterbo ☎ 0761 288 008 **Open** Daily 9am–6.30pm (4pm winter) Guided tours **Size** 3ha (7ac) **Owner** Ministero per i Beni Culturali 🚻

69. Sacro Bosco
Bomarzo (VT)

Not everyone likes the Sacro Bosco di Bomarzo. It is not beautiful, orderly or colourful (though the cyclamen are pretty in autumn) and it fits within no historical category. It is simply a landscaped woodland filled with allegorical monsters, some mythological, others fantastic. They are not statues, but hewn from the rock. Even the church was carved from the living stone.

The surprise is to discover that the chief architect of the Sacro Bosco was the great Pirro Ligorio, who built Villa d'Este in Tivoli and took over the completion of St Peter's Basilica after the death of Michelangelo. His patron at Bomarzo was the soldier-scholar Pier Francesco Orsini,

heartbroken by the death of his first wife Giulia Farnese.

Work began in 1552, not on a garden of monsters (its modern nickname) but a valley of wonders: a marine monster with a sceptre on its head; an elephant carrying a tower on its back and munching a Roman legionary; a glorious dragon battling with a dog, lion and wolf; Hercules tearing Cacus apart with his bare hands; a crooked house, built at a tilt (disconcerting to walk inside); a giant tortoise with a woman on its back; and the famous child-eating giant, whose lips are an invitation to 'abandon all hope, you who enter herein'.

Bomarzo contradicts all the conventions of 16th-century art. Orsini's intention was to create a place of awe that would stun his guests and make them consider whether 'so many wonders are made for deception or for art'.

15km NE of Viterbo ☎ 0761 924 029 **Open** Daily 8.30am–dusk **Size** 3ha (7ac) **Owner** Bettini family 🅿️ 🖪 🚻 ♿ 🏛️

70. Villa Farnese
01039 Caprarola (VT)

The villa of the powerful Farnese family at Caprarola is a vast, pentagonal castle built by Antonio da Sangallo the Younger in about 1510. Cardinal Alessandro Farnese (a nephew of Pope Paul III) charged Vignola in 1559 with transforming the castle into an impressive palace, and laying out the gardens.

The 'lower' gardens are known as the Summer Garden and Winter Garden – both of them large and square – and are reached across a drawbridge over the castle moat. Each has four main quarters, subdivided into four further enclosures, planted with box, holly and cherry laurel – good examples of the late renaissance style.

Behind these gardens a path leads up through the wooded hillside, where springtime orchids and autumn-flowering crocuses grow naturally in the clearings. A long, broad avenue then runs to the exquisite Casino, to which the Farnese would escape for privacy. The way leads past pavilions with surprise fountains (*giochi d'acqua*), a long scalloped rill known as the *catena d'acqua*, statues, staircases, fountains, and a formal garden (built in 1620 by Girolamo Rainaldi) edged with herms and backed by tall Italian cypresses.

Eventually you reach the pebbled courtyard and shallow terraces that set off the Casino from the far side. It is a composition of supreme beauty that blends the elements of architecture, sculpture and garden design into a unique sequence of movement, elegance, harmony and drama.

Caprarola is 17km SE of Viterbo
☎ 0761 646 052 **Open** Daily all year by guided tours,10am (10.30am Sun & pub hols), 11am, 12 noon & 3pm. Other times by appointment for groups **Size** 20ha (49ac)
Owner The Italian State 🚾 🎫

Isola Bisentina's baroque garden is a successful modern re-creation.

71. Isola Bisentina
01023 Lago di Bolsena (VT)

Isola Bisentina exercises a powerful effect on the visitor's imagination. It is a volcanic island rising sheer from the waters of Bolsena, the largest volcanic lake in Italy. It belonged to the Farnese family for many years: Antonio da Sangallo was commissioned to build the palace, and Il Vignola the sumptuous baroque church Santi Giacomo e Cristoforo (now abandoned).

The formal garden is modern, made in the baroque style by the present owner's brother, Prince Giovanni Fieschi Raveschieri del Drago, a student of Frank Lloyd Wright. Its box hedges are surrounded by verbena, herbs, periwinkles, hydrangeas, palms and rose beds. He also restored the pretty cloisters, and planted the exquisite rose 'Purezza' against its columns.

The whole island has a melancholy air of neglect, both near the palace and in the parkland, woodland, abandoned kitchen garden and untended olive grove. Every visitor dreams of owning and restoring it. The ancient ilex trees are now a protected genotype.

Boat from Capodimonte
☎ 0761 799 820 or 0761 870 042
Open By appointment **Size** 17ha (42ac)
Owner Principessa del Drago 🚾

Water, fountains, statues and tricks abound at Villa Farnese.

Many consider Castello Ruspoli's parterres the finest in Italy; they are certainly among the oldest.

72. Castello Ruspoli
01039 Vignanello (VT)

Vignanello's castle has an historic topiary garden – one of Europe's best. It has belonged to the Ruspoli and their ancestors since 1531.

The feudal fortress was given a domestic make-over in 1610, when the formal garden was laid out by Ottavia Orsini, immediately across the moat at the back. There are 12 low-clipped parterres, each bordered by slightly taller hedging. The parterres have simple geometric designs but the long, rectangular layout is extensive – best seen from the *piano nobile* of the house, if this is permitted. At the centre is a small pond and modest fountain, all enclosed by semicircular stone balustrades.

The garden never had statues or paved paths and it is said that, originally, the parterres were laid out in rosemary and sage. Nevertheless, you can tell that the present design is old by the number of wild species like *Viburnum tinus* that, over the years, have seeded themselves into the box hedges.

Below the ramparts to one side is the not-too-secret *giardino segreto*, which was laid out early in the 20th century as a flower and fruit garden. Huge, clipped, evergreen oaks (*Quercus ilex*) offer delicious shade and coolness in the heat of the day.

15km E of Viterbo ☎ 0761 755 338 **Open** Sun 10am–2pm & by appointment for groups **Size** 2ha (5ac) **Owner** Donna Claudia Ruspoli 🚻

CAMPANIA

73. La Reggia di Caserta
Via Douhet, 2
81100 Caserta

King Ferdinand IV of Naples and Sicily (known as *Il Nasone* – 'Big Nose') built the enormous palace at Caserta and its spectacular gardens to rival his brother-in-law, King Louis XVI of France. Luigi Vanvitelli and his son Carlo were the architects, and the design occupied them from 1762 to 1779.

You notice the sheer scale of the formal water gardens as you pass through the arches of the palace and catch your first glimpse of the cascades. They stretch for 3 km up a broad, straight avenue lined with clipped ilex trees right to the top of a distant hillside.

Buses depart every half-hour to take you to the furthest end, where stupendous sculptures of Diana and her nymphs on one side are matched by Actaeon and his hounds on the other. The dramatic centrepiece is a huge fountain, whose waters arrive along a 20-km aqueduct from the central mountains of Italy. Ponder the vastness of the garden's conception, contrast it with the international

Diana and her handmaidens watch a group of Actaeon's hounds devour their master at La Reggia di Caserta.

insignificance of 18th-century Naples, and you have the measure of Ferdinand's delusions of grandeur. Then turn to the right and enter a totally different world – the first English landscape garden laid out in southern Italy: no lesser personalities than Sir William Hamilton and Sir Joseph Banks advised on its design and planting. All the elements of the English landscape park are here – sweeping lawns and classical follies – but tricked out with such un-English plantings as araucarias, palm trees and camphoras in place of beech and rhododendrons. A ruined portico leads down to the grotto, where you may catch the white marble figure of Venus bathing beside the pool.

This is one of the most imaginative, beautiful and romantic gardens ever made. Botanists will tell you that the huge, gnarled *Taxus baccata* at the edge of the pool dates back to the original plantings.

Town centre ☎ 0823 277 111
Open Daily 8.30am–6pm (but 5.30pm May & Sept; 5pm Apr; 4.30pm Oct; 4pm Mar; & 2.30 pm winter)
Size 400ha (988ac) **Owner** Ministero per i Beni Culturali
🅿 🚻 🚾 ♿ (partly accessible) 🖼
🌐 www.reggiadicaserta.org
@ reggiacaserta@tin.it

74. La Mortella

Via F. Calise, 39
80075 Forio
Isola d'Ischia (NA)

In 1949 the British composer Sir William Walton bought an abandoned quarry and a ruined granary, which he called La Mortella after the wild myrtles that grew there. In 1956 his wife Susana engaged the English landscape designer Russell Page to lay out a garden for them.

There are endless microhabitats in the Waltons' tightly designed, plant-led garden of La Mortella.

The quarry and its boulders gave it the appearance of a gorge: Russell Page turned this rocky valley into the central feature. Fountains, ponds, tanks and a Persian-style rill give a sense of watery abundance; sophisticated watering systems have created a luxuriant garden. The irrigation varies from mist to heavy spray, to satisfy the needs of all plants. The upper terraces are drier and rockier.

Within these many microhabitats grows a wide selection of plants. Susana Walton became an avid plantswoman, so that the garden now holds 3000 different taxa from all over the world. Sir William sent the tree fern *Dicksonia antarctica* back from a tour of Australia and it became the start of a large collection of subtropical ferns, interplanted with the beautiful creeping fern *Woodwardia radicans*, a rare native of Ischia. Lady Walton planted exotic trees like jacarandas, magnolias, bauhinias, chorisias, *Spathodea campanulata*, palms and flowering eucalyptus. Shrubs include metrosideros, and tropical bromeliads, and Araceae feature widely. The giant water lily *Victoria amazonica* and the jade vine *Strongylodon macrobotrys* flower in the tropical house. Elsewhere are spiky plants: cacti, succulents, aloes, cordylines, yuccas, puyas, phormiums and grasses.

The design is immensely satisfying, as is the contrast between light and shade, cool and hot. The standard of maintenance is exemplary.

On right as you approach Foro d'Ischia from port of Ischia
☎ 081 986 220
Open Apr–Oct Tue, Thur, Sat & Sun 9am–7pm
Size 2ha (5ac)
Owner Fondazione William Walton e La Mortella
🚻 🚾
🌐 www.ischia.it/mortella
@ mortella@pointel.it

Capodimonte tiled columns give structure to this convent garden of Chiostro di Santa Chiara.

75. Chiostro di Santa Chiara
Via S. Chiara, 49/c
80134 Napoli

This convent garden is worth a visit not for its horticultural interest (a few fruit trees and vegetables, and a tall umbrella pine) but for the double pergola that divides the cloister into four segments. Its supporting columns (octagonal in shape) and the benches beneath them are all completely encased in exquisite mid-18th-century Capodimonte tiles. Their shades of blue, green and yellow give a rustic simplicity to the painted subjects. Wreaths of flowers and fruit cover the columns, while the benches are backed by country scenes of shooting, fishing and similar secular activities.

The intention was to offer the younger nuns – many from good families but weak in their vocations – a sweet reminder of life outside the strictly enclosed order.

City centre 🄲 0811 957 5915 **Open** All year daily (except Wed) 8am–2pm
🆆🅲 ♿
🆆 www.santachiara.org
@ info@oltreilchiostro.org

76. Orto Botanico di Napoli
Via Foria 223
80139 Napoli

Thirty-five gardeners, 8000 species and a total of 25 000 plants of every kind, from tallest trees to smallest bulbs: these are the bare facts of Naples's beautiful and historic botanical garden. But it is also one of the most interesting and best maintained in Italy, with well-watered, grassy spaces and comfortable, broad paths.

The garden is high above Via Foria, from which one can admire a line of *Phoenix canariensis*, backed by vast oriental planes all along the promenade. The walls are topped by terracotta urns filled with *Fascicularia pitcairniifolia*. The arboretum has splendid specimens of many trees, including vast *Camellia japonica* seedlings 175 years old; notable examples of *Melaleuca decussata* and *Araucaria bidwillii*; and a large poison ivy tree (*Rhus toxicodendron*). Among the monocotyledons is a near-complete collection of Italian *Crocus* species. Cycads, palms and conifers are well represented, with *Pinus nigra* and *P. halepensis* both more

A line of Canary Island palms (*Phoenix canariensis*) runs behind the urns and balustrades of the approach to Orto Botanico di Napoli.

than 30 m tall. The fern garden covers a large area around a shady valley; structure comes from hundreds of *Dicksonia* and *Cyathea* tree ferns, and prominent in the understorey is the local speciality, *Woodwardia radicans*. The collection of citrus species and cultivars includes the rare Australian desert lime *Eremocitrus glauca* (syn. *Citrus glauca*), a xerophyte with tiny fruits. The attractive garden for cacti and succulents boasts fine specimens of *Machaerocereus eruca*, *Heliantocereus pasacana* and *Borzicactus ventimigliae*. The collection of 40 *Tillandsia* species (some 300 plants) includes a number of living holotypes – the original plants from which the species were first described and named. Medicinal plants are another interest. Elsewhere within the garden are habitat beds, where plants are grown that occur naturally together in deserts, sea-shores, rocky uplands and marshes.

City centre. Via Foria is the main road that leads out to the A2. Garden on left 🄲 081 449 759 **Open** Daily 9am–1pm, except pub hols **Owner** Università degli Studi di Napoli Federico II **Size** 12ha (30ac) 🆆🅲
🆆 www.ortobotanico.unina.it/

77. Giardini di Pompeii
80045 Napoli

No ancient Roman gardens have been so perfectly preserved as those of Pompeii and nearby Herculaneum; they remain as they were at the moment in AD 79 when Mount Vesuvius smothered them in volcanic ash.

The gardens tell us much about their inhabitants' way of life. Most were enclosed by a peristyle – these are town gardens – and formally planted with such evergreens as bay, myrtle, ivy, oleander, box and rosemary. Best known are the House of the Faun (with a sunken pool); the very large House of Julia Felix; the partly restored House of Octavius Quarto;

the House of Golden Cupids
(with lots of small statues);
and the House of the Vettii,
with fine frescos. Large houses
have as many as four such
peristyle gardens: smaller ones
have their walls decorated
with *trompe l'œil* country views
or garden plants to extend
their horizons into the
countryside. The base of the
garden wall of the House of
Ceius Secundus has painted
myrtles and ivies, while the
House of Lucretius Fronto
has frescos of fine decorative
fencing. Some gardens have
been reconstructed (like the
House of the Centenary),
while others were lost to
American bombing in
World War II.

Every visitor leaves
impressed by the level of
civilisation the comfortable
lifestyle suggests, and
strangely moved by the awful
fate of the city's inhabitants.

30km E of Naples, signed from
A3 Napoli–Salerno
C 081 850 7678
Open All year daily 8.30am–6pm
(earlier in winter)
Owner Ministero per i Beni Culturali
P ☕ ⊞ WC 盦 ⊞
W www.pompeiionline.net
@ info@pompeiionline.net

The sheer number and variety of
Pompeii's gardens give us an insight
into ancient Roman life.

The garden of Villa Cimbrone is eclectic and charming.

78. Villa Cimbrone
Via Santa Chiara, 26
84010 Ravello (SA)

Villa Cimbrone has quite
the most dramatic site
of any in this book, and the
garden is large, eccentric,
exciting, charming and
full of variety. It occupies
a promontory that was
bought by the English Lord
Grimthorpe in 1904: he spent
nearly 12 years laying out the
gardens with the help of a local
man (with no previous
experience of design) called
Niccolo Mansi. The result is
extravagant and capricious.

You enter though a vast
wooden door and immediately
encounter a long, broad walk
that runs far into the distance.
It draws you along, past
pergolas, pots and plinths
to an open Doric temple that
shelters a statue of Ceres.
The temple leads through to
a belvedere terrace, which is
lined with 18th-century busts
and perched 300 m above the
sea. The effect is breathtaking:
suddenly the whole Almalfi
coast lies below you.

The slopes and terraces of
the rest of the garden are also
full of interest. There are lawns
and shrubberies, statues and
topiary, a Byzantine pavilion,
a temple of Bacchus, a grotto
called Eve's (actually a
classical nymph), a rose
garden surrounded by
Gaudiesque ceramic tiles,
and much else besides. But
the decorative details and the
extensive plantings all pale into
insignificance beside the view,
the drama, the position and
the verve of that first long walk.

Fairly close to town centre; accessible only on foot **C** 089 857 459
Open Daily 9am–sunset **Owner**
Hotel Villa Cimbrone **Size** 8ha
(20ac) **⊞ WC &** (partly accessible) ⊞
W www.villacimbrone.com
@ info@villacimbrone.com

79. Villa Rufolo
84010 Ravello (SA)

The garden at Villa Rufolo
is famous for its historical
associations and splendid
position. Its design is simple –
the main feature is a Victorian

A Victorian, Italianate parterre, set with cycads, is the principal feature of this 'garden of Klingsor' at Villa Rufolo.

parterre – and its horticultural interest is limited to some cycads, cordylines, palms and a large *Brachychiton populneus*.

Villa Rufolo was restored in the 1850s by Francis Neville Reid, a British diplomat, whose restoration work left historical features intact from every important period in its history – Saracen, Norman and Gothic. The garden is surrounded by a colonnaded cloister on three sides and looks out towards the sea. In Reid's day it was festooned with climbing roses and an array of colourful plants. Richard Wagner visited it in May 1880 and found here the inspiration for Klingsor's magic garden music in *Parsifal*.

It is simply maintained, but still an enchanted place – above all for its wildly romantic position high above the rocky sea.

Town centre **[** 089 857 096 **Open** Daily 9am–8pm (6pm winter) **Size** 2ha (5ac) **Owner** Centro Universitario Europeo per i Beni Culturali **[WC] [ ]**

SICILIA

80. Orto Botanico di Catania
Via Antonino Longo, 19
95125 Catania

Catania's botanic garden was founded by the Benedictine Prior Francesco Tornabene in 1858, as an adjunct to the Faculty of Botany at the University. Its offices occupy a distinguished neoclassical building with a portico and white double colonnade.

Mount Etna is a constant presence: volcanic rock was used for the garden's layout and the soil is black volcanic grit. Three thousand square metres are dedicated to the *Hortus Siculus*, a garden for the island's own flora. Many of Sicily's endemics, like *Centaurea tauromenitana* and *Scilla sicula* grow here, mainly in systematic beds where some of the trees have grown to great heights. There are notable specimens of *Celtis aetnensis*, *Salix gussonei* and *Abies nebrodensis*. Catania also has one of the largest collections of cacti and succulents in Italy (some 2000 taxa), with a very strong hand

in Euphorbiaceae, Aizoaceae, Crassulaceae, Cactaceae and large, centennial examples of *Echinocactus grusonii* and arborescent euphorbias. Some of the palms (over 50 species) are of great height (*Washingtonia robusta* and *Syagrus romanzoffiana*) and others quite rare (*Trithrinax brasiliensis* and *Butia eriospatha*). Tall trees include *Toona sinensis*, the dragon tree (*Dracaena draco*) and *Phytolacca dioica*, which measures 13 m round the base. Other interesting plants include *Podocarpus neriifolius* with dark glossy leaves like an oleander's and a male specimen of the cycad *Encephalartos horridus*.

The garden is stylish and enjoyable to visit – and a haven from Catania's traffic.

City centre at top end of Via Etnea **[** 095 430 901 **Open** All year 9am–1pm, except Sun & hols **Size** 1.6ha (4ac) **Owner** L'Università di Catania **[WC] [ ]** **[W]** www.dipbot.unict.it/

81. Villa Imperiale del Casale
Loc. Casale
94015 Piazza Armerina (EN)

Villa Imperiale was the summer residence of co-Emperor Maximinius, who started building it shortly after his accession in AD 286. It is best known for its mosaics, which offer exciting insights into imperial life: the 'bikini girls' are now Sicilian mascots.

A reconstruction of the formal water garden at the heart of the Emperor's living quarters, Villa Imperiale del Casale.

But the huge palace, undis-covered until the 20th century, was constructed around a large, late-Roman garden. It is contained within a rectangular peristyle of the sort commonly seen at Pompeii, but very much larger. At its centre are three, low, conjoined pools, with marble sides and fish mosaics within. Their shape and structure do not resemble the neo-Roman pools that Leon Battista Alberti and other scholars emulated, based on the writings of the ancients.

Had Pompeii been discovered – or Villa Imperiale del Casale been excavated – in 1450, the history of renaissance gardens would have been rather different.

8km SW of Piazza Armerina
☎ 0935 680 036 **Open** All year daily 8am–7pm (or dusk, if earlier) **Size** 1ha (2½ac)
Owner Beni Culturali (Sicilia)
🅿 ▫ 🆆 ▫ ▫
🆆 www.regione.sicilia.it/beniculturali/

82. Taormina Gardens
98039 Taormina (ME)

Taormina has been a popular winter resort for wealthy aesthetes for more than 100 years. It has three good gardens to visit, though none is sufficiently distinctive to merit a journey on its own. All have dramatic views of Mount Etna and the sea.

The *Giardini Pubblici* (public gardens), some way down from the Greek theatre, are always open, meticulously maintained and full of interesting and colourful plants. Their greatest attraction is a series of eccentric towers made from architectural reclamation by the *émigrée* Englishwoman Florence Trevelyan in the 1900s.

Casa Cuseni on the road to Castelmola is an English Arts and Crafts garden, part-made by Frank Brangwyn in the 1910s and 1920s. One of its many ingenious enclosures is a plunge-pool, positioned to reflect Mount Etna's cone, so that you can dive into the volcano's moonlit image.

Florence Trevelyan built this garden tower at Taormina Gardens during the 1890s from architectural salvage.

Next door is *Madonna della Rocca*, made by the Austrian Daneu family, famous Palermitan dealers in antiquities. The garden displays an extensive collection of architectural fragments and some interesting plants and plantings.

The two private gardens:
☎ Tourist information office
094 223 243 **Open** Rarely and only by appointment

83. Villa Palagonia
90011 Bagheria (PA)

The reason for visiting Villa Palagonia is not the garden, but the walls that surround it, which are encrusted with more than 100 tufa statues of mythical beasts, anthropo-morphic animals, ladies (of every sort), knights, exotic birds, musicians and caricatures, all looking into the garden. They were created for Francesco Ferdinando Gravina e Alliata, who inherited the villa in 1749. Goethe visited it in 1787 and did not approve whatsoever: '… men with women's heads, women with men's heads, horses with dogs' legs and vultures' beaks, three-headed creatures in Paris fashions, bipeds with no feet, people with noses on their navels, soldiers, punchinellos, Turks, Spaniards … dwarfs, humpbacks, crouchbacks, cripples, nightmare faces all twisted and contorted …'.

It is perhaps inevitable that, although the garden comes straight from the fertile ground of the Sicilian rococo, modern commentators tend to see Gravina as a precursor of surrealism. Either way, Villa Palagonia is an extraordinary place to visit.

Bagheria is about 10km E of Palermo ☎ 091 932 088
Open All year daily 9am–1pm & 4–7pm (3.30–5.30pm from Nov–Mar) **Size** 2ha (5ac)
Owner Fondazione Villa Palagonia–Castronovo
🆆 ▫ ▫ ▫
🆆 www.villapalagonia.it
@ villapalagonia@villapalagonia.it

The walls and gates of Villa Palagonia are encrusted with bizarre but intriguing statues of strange creatures.

Francis II ordered this glasshouse from England in 1859 for Orto Botanico di Palermo, but it was unpaid for when the Bourbons fled from Sicily the next year.

84. Orto Botanico di Palermo

Via Lincoln, 2/A
90123 Palermo

Palermo's botanic garden is one of the most distinguished in the Mediterranean region. It moved to its present site next to the Villa Giulia (Europe's first public park) in 1786.

The layout is formal, with broad avenues crossing and criss-crossing each other. Architectural form comes from neoclassical statues, stately pools and very handsome glasshouses. A large area is given to systematic beds, some laid out according to the Linnaean system and others to conform to Silesian botanist Adolf Engler's classification. In recent years, areas have also been ordered in geographical and ecological groupings.

There is a total of 12 000 taxa in the garden. Palms are one speciality, with some 34 genera and 80 species represented. Both *Washingtonia* species flourish – the commonly seen *W. filifera* and rarer *W. robusta* – while the genus *Phoenix* is represented by *P. rupicola*, *P. reclinata*, *P. canariensis* and *P. theophrasti*. The collection of mature cycads is also good and includes *Cycas revoluta*, *C. circinalis*, *Ceratozamia mexicana* and *Zamia furfuracea*. Much of the collection of cacti and succulents is displayed in serried ranks of terracotta pots and is especially strong in *Aloe*, *Cereus*, *Crassula*, *Euphorbia* and *Opuntia*. But the most striking of all trees is a venerable *Ficus macrophylla*; its aerial roots have spread out over such a large area, smothering everything around it, that it now covers more than half a hectare. But throughout the garden there is much to interest the plant lover: indeed, many popular plants were introduced into garden cultivation from it.

City centre ☎ 0916 238 234 **Open** Weekdays 9am–5pm (6pm summer), but 8.30am–1.30pm weekends & pub hols **Size** 10ha (25ac) **Owner** Dipartimento di Scienze Botaniche, Università degli Studi di Palermo ♿ 🚻
W www.ortobotanico.palermo.it

85. Palazzina Cinese & Parco della Favorita

90143 Palermo

Ferdinand IV acquired several estates north of Palermo in 1798 to make a hunting ground that he called the Parco della Favorita. Then he employed Venanzio Marvuglia (1729–1814) to rebuild the palace, which is now known as Palazzo Cinese. The result is an exotic mixture of rococo, gothic, neoclassical, Turkish and oriental styles.

Favorita was laid out as a thickly planted, evergreen ornamental park, with straight avenues named after Diana, Hercules and Pomona. Some of the original features survive, somewhat vandalised, including the Hercules fountain with a copy of the Farnese Hercules at the centre. Traffic has recently been banned from Parco della Favorita, which has made it very popular with Palermitans, though it is best avoided at night.

The garden of Palazzina Cinese was made in the 18th-century French baroque style, with attractive parterres to which palm trees and roses were added later. It is open to the public by arrangement: contact the tourist office at info@palermotourism.com.

Northern outskirts of Palermo
Open All year daily dawn–dusk
Size 400ha (988ac) **Owner** Comune di Palermo 🅿 🚌 🍴 🚻 ♿ 🏛
W www.comune.palermo.it

Palm-trees and complicated rococo parterres are a fine complement for the fantastic Chinese-style palace of Palazzina Cinese.

86. Villa Malfitano

Via Dante, 167
90141 Palermo

Villa Malfitano is a High Victorian landscape garden, laid out in a very unEnglish climate. It was made from 1887 onwards by a rich English wine-merchant called Joseph Whitaker, and many of its plants came from the Orto Botanico di Palermo. Whitaker was interested in botany, and assembled a fine private collection of plants at Malfitano, though only the tougher trees and shrubs have survived the neglect of recent years.

The entrance drive is impressive, but it splits shortly after you enter; each branch leads to the house through an English-style park. There are cedars, pines, cypresses, dracaenas, jubaeas, washingtonias, livistonas and tree-yuccas. The rarest specimens include *Araucaria rulei* from New Caledonia and *Butia yatay* from Uruguay. All are set in grass: expansive lawns provide a green and English setting for their exotic forms.

In front of the house are traces of the original formal garden, but much more interesting is the huge *Ficus magnolioides* to one side. Most of the rest of the garden is crumbling. The glasshouses, pools and grotto cry out for restoration. But Malfitano is a wonderful place to see fine trees and to contemplate the greatness of England's commercial past.

City centre ☎ 0916 816 133
Open All year Mon–Sat 9am–1pm
Size 5ha (12ac)
Owner Fondazione Giuseppe Whitaker 🚻 ♿ ▦
🌐 http://web.tiscali.it/fon dazionewhitaker/

SARDEGNA

87. Orto Botanico di Cagliari

Viale S. Ignazio da Laconi, 11
09123 Cagliari

Cagliari's botanic garden is a place of great charm and interest. It was laid out in the 1860s on a site that dates back 2000 years: its ancient Roman features include a well and a cistern, whose water was essential to the garden's establishment.

The layout is classical: a long avenue leads straight from the entrance to a large, round pool at the centre of the garden. Around the pool are a collection of cacti and succulents (over 1000 taxa) and a section dedicated to the native Mediterranean flora, notably *Pinus halepensis*, *Rhamnus alaternus* and *Chamaerops humilis*. Smaller tanks are devoted to flowering lotuses (*Nelumbo nucifera*) and Egyptian papyrus plants (*Cyperus papyrus*).

The garden has areas dedicated to medicinal plants (many Italian universities have departments of pharmacology), cycads and palms (16 species). The best specimen trees include two large, shady *Ficus magnolioides*, the Osage orange (*Maclura pomifera*) and the flame tree (*Brachychiton acerifolius*).

W of old city next to Roman amphitheatre ☎ 0706 753 522
Open All year daily 8am–1.30pm, plus 3–6.30pm Apr–Sep
Size 5.5ha (14ac) **Owner** Università di Cagliari 🚻 ♿
🌐 www.cagliaridascoprire.it/ natura/ortobotanico.htm

Victorian hoops and arbours date back to the Villa Malfitano's first construction by Joseph Whitaker in 1887.

Gardens of Spain

Spain has made only a small contribution to the history of gardens, except for one very important and unique style – the Islamic gardens that existed in Andalusia up until the expulsion of the Moors in 1492. They were, moreover, different from other Islamic gardens in Persia or India, because they were characterised by small, introspective garden rooms, rather than expansive water gardens. Much has been written about them, but comparatively little remains: the best place to ponder their complexity is the archaeological site of Medina az-Zahra near Córdoba. The major part of what we see today, in the centres of Córdoba, Granada and Seville, though very beautiful, is a modern reconstruction.

The gardens of the Generalife at Granada and the Alcázares Reales at Seville are probably the most famous and most visited in all Spain. From about 1860 onwards, the Moorish gardens of Andalusia began to be copied, first tentatively and then enthusiastically all over the world so that, even today, Moorish ornament and decorative detail are popular in contemporary gardens throughout Spain itself.

Away from Andalusia, Spanish gardens vary considerably. This is partly a factor of climate: Galician gardens have a mossy luxuriance that comes from high rainfall and mild temperatures, whereas the box parterres and plane tree avenues of inland Spain are welded to the hot summers and cold winters. The elements common to all Spanish gardens, however, are trees and evergreens, shade and geometric form, and the presence of water.

The Italian renaissance style came to Spain during the 16th century, but was never widespread and did not give rise to exciting new art forms. Philip II made gardens at El Escorial and Aranjuez, but these survive in a modified form only. It was not until the accession of the Bourbon king Philip V that expansive gardens began to be made. Philip introduced the French baroque style and his two palaces at La Granja and Aranjuez have very fine gardens, made to impress. Thereafter, almost every king or queen of Spain seems to have created gardens and encouraged the establishment of botanic gardens. The English landscape style, however, made little impression on the Spanish countryside.

The history of Spain over the last 200 years is fraught with invasion, revolution and civil war. Historic gardens were neglected and almost all the famous ones had to be rescued and restored. This means that much of the original detail has been lost, though the structure and

OPPOSITE: Palm avenue, Jardines de Alfabia, Majorca

some of the larger plantings survive. Urban expansion has also seen the destruction of many aristocratic villa gardens.

Many of Spain's most interesting gardens are modern, dating from the 20th century. The middle classes often built or bought a large house and indulged a passion for botany or fantasy within the gardens. The jungly plant collection at La Concepción and the dramatic series of eccentric follies at Parc Samà are examples. Local authorities were conscious of the need to provide agreeable open spaces for growing cities. Some urban parks like El Buen Retiro in Madrid and Parc del Laberint in Barcelona are based on older structures, but others like Montjuïc are specifically modern and Parc Güell is a modernist classic. Almost every big city has fine public parks, including the Paseo del Parque at Malaga and the Jardín del Turia at València, both unfortunately beyond the scope of this book. Some of the youngest botanic gardens were founded by plant-loving foreigners, who wanted to display the riches of Spain's flora and the possibilities its climate offers for growing a wide range of exotic plants. Here belong Mar i Murtra, Pinya de Rosa and Viera y Clavijo. Others, including Botanicactus in Majorca and Jardín de la Marquesa on Grand Canary, have been developed specifically in response to modern tourism. In recent times, the inspirational Fernando Caruncho has become the best known of Spanish landscape designers, but unfortunately none of his gardens are yet accessible to the public.

ABOVE: Palms and a rocaille arch by Gaudí, Parc Güell, Barcelona
OPPOSITE: 19th-century Italian water garden, Jardines de los Reales Alcázares, Seville

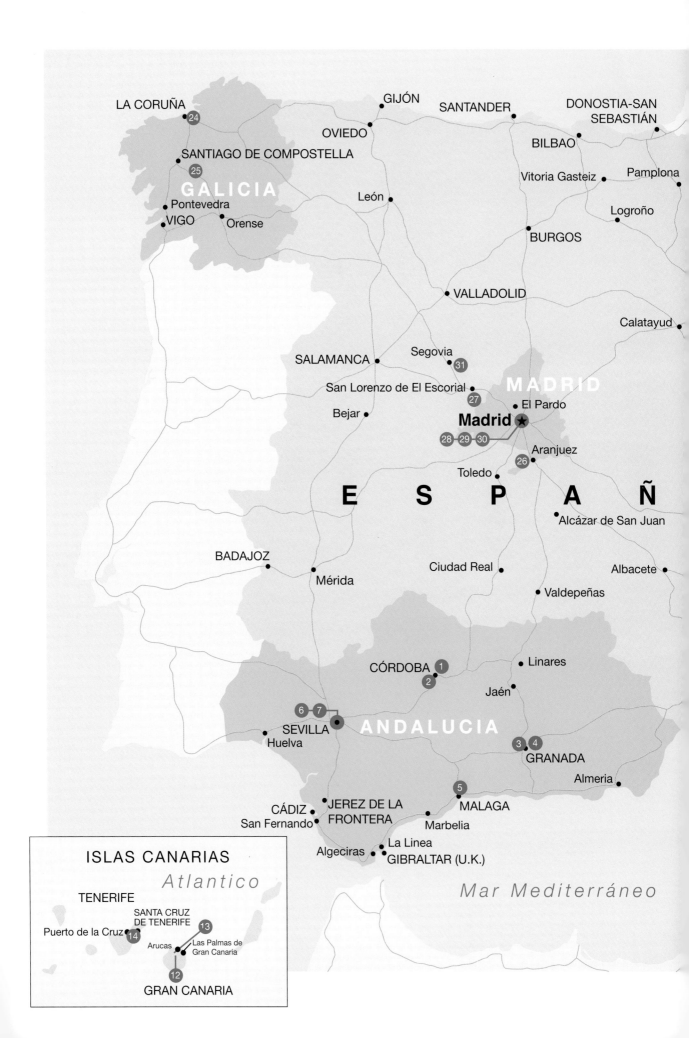

ISLAS CANARIAS

Atlantico

TENERIFE

SANTA CRUZ
DE TENERIFE

Puerto de la Cruz

Arucas

Las Palmas de
Gran Canaria

GRAN CANARIA

LA CORUÑA

GIJÓN

SANTANDER

DONOSTIA-SAN
SEBASTIÁN

OVIEDO

BILBAO

SANTIAGO DE COMPOSTELLA

Vitoria Gasteiz

Pamplona

GALICIA

León

Logroño

Pontevedra

VIGO

Orense

BURGOS

VALLADOLID

Calatayud

Segovia

SALAMANCA

MADRID

San Lorenzo de El Escorial

El Pardo

Bejar

Madrid

Aranjuez

Toledo

E S P A Ñ

Alcázar de San Juan

BADAJOZ

Ciudad Real

Albacete

Mérida

Valdepeñas

CÓRDOBA

Linares

ANDALUCIA

Jaén

SEVILLA

Huelva

GRANADA

Almeria

MALAGA

CÁDIZ

JEREZ DE LA
FRONTERA

Marbelia

San Fernando

La Linea

Algeciras

GIBRALTAR (U.K.)

Mar Mediterráneo

Gardens of Spain

1. Alcázar de los Reyes Cristianos
2. Jardín Botánico de Córdoba
3. Alhambra
4. Generalife
5. La Concepción
6. Jardins de los Reales Alcázares
7. Parque de María Luisa
8. Botanicactus
9. Jardí Botànic de Sóller
10. Jardines de Alfabia
11. Parc Casa March
12. Jardín Botánico 'Viera y Clavijo'
13. Jardín de la Marquesa
14. Jardín Botánico de Puerto de la Cruz
15. Jardí Botànic de Barcelona
16. Parc de Montjuïc
17. Parc de la Ciutadella
18. Parc del Laberint
19. Parc Güell
20. Jardi Botànic Mar i Murtra
21. Jardi Cap Roig
22. Jardí Botànic 'Pinya de Rosa'
23. Parc Samà
24. Pazo de Mariñán
25. Pazo de Oca
26. Jardines Reales
27. El Escorial
28. Parque del Buen Retiro
29. Real Jardín Botánico
30. Rosaleda 'Ramón Ortiz'
31. La Granja de San Ildefonso
32. El Huerto del Cura
33. Jardín Botánico de València

ZARAGOZA

CATALUÑA

Girona-Gerona

20 21 22 Lloret de Mar
Blanes

BARCELONA

15 16 17 18 19

23 Tarragona
Cambrils

Castellón
de la Plana

A

33 València

VALÈNCIA

ELCHE
32 ALICANTE

MURCIA

CARTAGENA

Puerto de Sóller

9
10 Sóller

11
Cala Ratjada

ISLAS

PALMA MALLORCA

BALEARES Ses Salines 8

GRAN CANARIA

IBIZA

FORMENTERA

N

SPAIN

★ National Capital

● Cities and Towns

— Major Roads

00 Spanish Garden

Adjacent Countries

Highlighted Spanish Region

0   50   100 Kilometres

0   50   100 Miles

ANDALUCIA

1. Alcázar de los Reyes Cristianos

Campo Santo de los Mártires
14071 Córdoba

Spain's oldest garden is the enclosed orange grove at the heart of the Alcázar de los Reyes Cristianos; it dates from the 9th century. The gardens outside the citadel are much more recent – and rather more interesting. The two large railed tanks near the entrance, although dating from the 19th century, were skilfully made to blend with the walls of the castle. The raised walk between them leads down some steep steps to a charming, shady formal garden with box hedges, citrus trees, ornamental shrubs and a fountain at the centre. This, too, dates from the 19th century. The main axis of the garden, however, lies away from the castle, and stretches out over a series of three spacious pools edged with clipped orange trees, roses and bedding plants. These date from the 1970s but capture the Moorish spirit of the Alcázar well – sweet scents, running water and handsome architecture. Elsewhere are cypress hedges, small enclosed gardens and statues of historic

19th-century water-tanks, Alcázar de los Reyes Cristianos, Córdoba

Parterre, Alameda del Obispo, Córdoba

Spanish persons, mainly kings and queens. They may not all be old, but the Alcázar gardens are among Spain's best.

Well signed in city centre
☎ 957 420 151 **Open** 15 Sep–30 Apr 10am–2pm & 4.30pm–6.30pm, Tue–Sat; May, June and 1–14 Sep 10am–2pm and 5.30pm–7.30pm, Tue–Sat; July–Aug 8.30am–2.30pm and 8pm–12 midnight, Tue–Sat; Sun & pub hols, all year 9.30 am–2.30 pm. **Closed** Mon **Size** 5.5ha (14ac) **Owner** Ayuntamiento de Córdoba
🅿 ♿ 🏠

2. Jardín Botánico de Córdoba

Avda de Linneo
14004 Córdoba

Córdoba's botanic garden is Spain's newest – opened in 1987 – and it is interesting to see what is considered important in the 21st century. The emphasis is upon conservation and visitor education. As well as traditional systematic collections, the garden has special collections of Spanish endemics and (in two glasshouses) tropical plants, cacti and succulents from the Canary Islands. Elsewhere the garden offers a small arboretum, a museum of palaeo-botany, a scruffy rose garden and an interesting collection of economic plants, including olive cultivars (Córdoba is a major centre for the olive industry). Also worth seeing are the historic gardens of the Alameda del Obispo, now part of the provincial agricultural college (Apdo 3092, 14080 Córdoba, cifa.cordoba.cap@juntadeanda lucia.es) about 1 km west of the botanic garden. Their main features are a sunken pool, a charming wisteria-clad tunnel and an unusual baroque maze of clipped orange-tree hedges.

Well signed. W of old city centre
☎ 957 200 077 **Open** All year daily 10am–6.30pm. **Closes** 3.30pm Sun. **Owner** Universidad de Córdoba
🅿 ♿ 🏠 ♿
🌐 www.uco.es/jardin-botanico/
@ jardinbotcord@telefonica.net

3. & 4. Alhambra & Generalife

Real de la Alhambra
18009 Granada

The historical significance of the Alhambra and Generalife lies in their influence upon garden architecture, design and decoration from about 1880 onwards: Granada's ornate Umayyad buildings were the most accessible example of the Moorish style in Europe – widely visited, painted, drawn and copied. They remain the most important and extensive source of Moorish garden style today, and essential visiting for anyone who loves beautiful and unusual ideas and details.

The plantings are fairly un-historical: *Magnolia grandiflora*, Hybrid Tea roses, wisterias and Banksian roses are some of the most commonly planted flowers (none was actually introduced into western gardens until centuries after the departure of the Moors). Sweet-scented flowers predominate, especially orange blossom. Elsewhere, native plants like laurustinus (*Viburnum tinus*) and bay trees (*Laurus nobilis*) have been allowed to proliferate. These are gardens for the senses: the sound of running water, the scent of flowers, and the sight of endless set-piece garden designs, each framed by Moorish windows, covered colonnades, rose-covered pergolas or arches cut from cypress trees.

The main parts of the Alhambra date from the mid-14th century, including the exquisite *Patio de los Leones* (lions). Like the *Patio de los Arrayanes* (myrtles), it is an enclosed courtyard with water, sculpture and plants that do not change from season to season. But its appeal rests on the extraordinarily rich decorative carving that surrounds it. The Daraxa garden, by contrast, is a perfect and (in Spain) rare example of a simple, enclosed renaissance garden, with cypresses, orange trees and box parterres. It dates from the 1530s; the fountain at the centre is later, from the 1620s. Outside, you come upon the *Torre de las Damas* (only the central arch is original) in front of an elegant pool and the *Jardines del Partal* which, like much of what we see today, is the result of creative restoration in the 1920s. The walk up through these gardens and along the lengthy path above the valley, looking towards the Generalife, is one of the most beautiful anywhere.

The Generalife itself has been so altered over the last 500 years that we do not really know what it looked like originally. The first gardens you pass through are all modern – mid-20th century – but sensitively designed to create a Moorish effect and laid out with cypress hedges, enclosed gardens, pergolas, roses and sweet-smelling plants. Eventually you climb up to the famous *Patio de la Acequia* (canal), where tiny jets (a modern addition) spurt water all along its length, with shady loggias at both ends and a colonnade along the side. The beds are usually filled with colourful seasonal bedding, while the views down to the Alhambra, with the Sierra Nevada behind, are breathtaking. Further steps lead up to the *Patio de los Cipressos*, so-called for the ancient cypress tree that grew there until recently, with pools, water jets and simple box hedges. Higher still is the house where the American writer Washington Irving lived in 1829; the sidewalls of the staircase have open channels at the top through which running water rushes down. The Generalife is not a garden for plants, but there are pleasant plantings of wisteria, oranges, oleanders and Banksian roses.

There are three things you need to know, however, before visiting the Alhambra and Generalife. First, you must buy your tickets in advance (see the website). Visits have a timed half-hour entry slot but, once inside, you may stay for as long as you wish. Second, the palaces and their gardens are very extensive, and you will need at least half a day to visit them. And, third, they are extremely popular so that, whatever the hour or season, you will never be alone to contemplate their extraordinary beauty.

Well signed. Best approached by bus no. 30 or taxi. **Open** Mar–Oct 8.30am–8pm daily & 10pm–11.30pm, Tue–Sat; Nov–Jan 8.30am–6pm daily & 8pm–9.30pm Fri–Sat. **Closed** 1 Jan & 25 Dec. **Owner** The State
P WC ♿ 🚻
W www.alhambradegranada.org

LEFT: *Torre de las Damas* and pool, Alhambra, Granada RIGHT: *Patio de la Acequia*, Generalife, Granada

LEFT: Thick underplantings, La Concepción, Malaga
RIGHT: Enclosed Moorish garden, Jardines de los Reales Alcázares, Seville

5. La Concepción

Ctra las Pedrizas, km 166
29014 Málaga

The garden at Finca La Concepción was planted by several generations of an Anglo-Spanish family called Livermore during the 19th century. Its botanical wealth and lushness are frankly astonishing, and merit a visit whatever the season or weather. It is a garden of many contrasts, but most interesting to garden lovers is the thickly planted collection of exotic evergreen trees around and below the house – vast palms (including towering specimens of *Jubaea spectabilis* and *Washingtonia filifera*), ancient cycads, *Ficus macrophylla*, large dragon trees (*Dracaena draco*) and the tallest Norfolk Island pine (*Araucaria heterophylla*) in Malaga province. Competition for light has turned this part of the garden into a jungle of evergreen leaves, with cool and shady walks weaving through the under-growth. Sweeping masses of clivias and agapanthus are used as underplantings. At the side of the house is a unique and spacious arbour. Under its intricate ironwork, covered with wisterias for scent in spring and shade in summer, the Livermores entertained in grand style.

Elsewhere stands a very fine curving avenue of plane trees, and a broad walk of palms leads up to the best of three gazebos, a classical rotunda on a point high above the Malaga road – a local landmark ever since it was built.

The estate was acquired by the city of Malaga in 1991, and the new owners have added several new, somewhat out-of-character attractions. Most are down near the entrance where the noise of passing traffic impinges on visitors, but the rest of the garden is a joy to explore.

Well signed. 7km N of Malaga on old road (N-321) ☎ 952 250 745 **Open** All year 10am–6.30pm Tue–Sun **Size** 3ha (7ac) **Owner** Ayuntamiento de Málaga

🅿 ❏ 🍴 🚾 ♿ 📷

6. Jardins de los Reales Alcázares

Plaza del Triunfo
41004 Sevilla

The gardens attached to the royal palace in Seville are, quite simply, the most beautiful in Spain. Prepare for a long visit and try to get there early, because the palace and gardens are both very popular with locals and tourists alike.

Every period of history is present in the designs and plantings. Alongside the sumptuous palace – half-Moorish and half-Renaissance – is a series of small, sunken, enclosed gardens, decorated with tiles, grilles, fountains, cypresses, oranges and sweet-smelling plants, starting with *Rosa* 'Fortuniana' in early spring. Tall walkways topped by ceramic urns (with R.A., for Reales Alcázares, and the royal crown in blue) give height to the design and protection for such tender plants as poinsettias. An elegant two-storey gallery runs right across the centre of the garden. The view on one side is of a long, 19th-century Italianate pool, edged by box hedges and orange trees. The other looks towards Charles V's pavilion, an astounding structure of great beauty, covered in distinctive tiles.

Throughout the garden, the plantings reflect the need for shade and sweet scents: palms, cypresses, myrtles, oranges and lemons give structure; roses and jasmine offer scent and colour.

City centre opposite cathedral ☎ 954 502 323 **Open** Daily (except Mon) 9.30am–5pm **Closes** 1.30pm Sun **Owner** The State 🚾 ♿ 📷

7. Parque de María Luisa

Avda de la Borbolla
41013 Sevilla

Seville's largest public park is also its most beautiful. Part of it dates back to 1893 when Princess María Luisa, the sister of Isabella II, gave 4 ha of her garden at San Telmo to the public. It was largely laid out, however, by the French architect J.C.N. Forestier in 1912 and remodelled by Aníbal Gonzalez for the Hispano-American exhibition in 1929.

Many of the exhibition's pavilions survive: most were built in the *neo-mudéjar* style and helped to establish an Andalusian vernacular norm for gardens. Grandest of all is the semi-circular *Plaza de España*, with an artificial lake at its centre and two brick mudéjar towers. In the *Plaza de América*, the Royal Pavilion (*Pabellón Real*) is now a museum of folk art and the Mudéjar Pavilion is the archaeological museum. Parque de Maria Luísa is jam-packed with pools and tanks, jets and fountains, pots, arbours, gazebos, pergolas, statues (several added since 1929), columns, and friezes, many of the latter covered in ceramic tiles from the Triana area of Seville. The trees have grown up – pines, poplars, planes, palms, magnolias and oranges – to provide shade and the beds are planted with bright bedding plants and roses. It is well maintained, a joy to visit any time, and free.

☎ 954 221 404
Open Daily 7am–11pm
Owner Ayuntamiento de Sevilla
🅿 ♿ 🍴 🚾 ♿
ⓦ www.parquesyjardines.sevilla.org

THE ISLANDS

8. Botanicactus

Ctra Ses Salines–Santanyí
Mallorca, Islas Baleares

Despite its name, Botanicactus is neither a botanic garden nor merely a collection of cacti. It is an ornamental garden, planted on a large scale like an upmarket public park, with three main sections. The first (2.5 ha) calls itself a Majorcan garden and has examples of the island's wild plants, as well as ornamental garden plants, including a river of cannas and a garden devoted to hibiscus. There is also a collection of 'millennial' olive trees and some ancient carob trees. The second section (4 ha) is a very large collection of cacti and succulents (notably aloes, agaves, opuntias, echinocactus, and saguaros, often underplanted with South African daisies, like drosanthemums and Hottentot figs), which builds up its impact through sheer scale and repetition.

Cacti and succulent collection, Botanicactus, Majorca

It has over 400 taxa and 10 000 plants. The third part (5 ha) is a vast water garden laid out around a lake. Elsewhere stand a collection of different palms and a hillside of cycads. There are no real rarities, though Botanicactus is very impressive to visit and fairly well maintained. The labelling, however, is almost non-existent.

Near south coast, 40km E of Palma
☎ 971 649 494 **Open** Daily 9am–5.30pm (7pm summer); Nov–Dec 10.30am–4.30pm
Size 5ha (12ac)
🅿 ♿ 🚾 ♿ ♿ ⚐
ⓦ www.botanicactus.com

Parque de María Luisa, Seville

9. Jardí Botànic de Sóller

Ctra Palma–Sóller, km 30.5
Apartat de Correus 44
07100 Sóller
Mallorca, Islas Baleares

Sóller's Botanic Garden was founded in 1985 and opened to the public in 1992. Its main object is to conserve endemic or rare plants of the Mediterranean islands and especially of the Balearics. It puts special emphasis upon educating school children and tourists (the website is very good), and is excellently laid out with a wealth of posters, notice-boards and pamphlets at every point of interest.

The design and plantings are intended to provide optimum growing conditions for the plants. There is a high central path from which one can see the different collections on either side. These include areas for all the different types of Majorcan flora: plants from stony river-beds, shady mountainsides and rocky shores; rare endemics; oak forest flora; mountain flora; plants of the maquis, scrub land and screes; and fresh-water flora. Other areas display the flora of the Canary Islands, Corsica, Sardinia, Sicily, Malta and Crete, and collections of plants used for medicinal, aromatic, culinary and ornamental purposes – from pharmacological herbs to indigenous fruit cultivars and ornamental cacti and succulents. All this is contained within a compass of little more than 1 ha – but it works. On the coast road, just past Deyá, is the Hapsburg palace of Son Marroig (*see* www.sonmarroig.com). Its garden is somewhat neglected, but it has a handsome Monopteros, positioned to enjoy spectacular views down to the rocky shore.

Right-hand side of main road from tunnel towards port ☎ 971 634 014
Open Daily 10am–6pm (2pm Sun)
Closed Mon **Size** 1ha (2½ac)
Owner Fundació Jardí Botànic de Sóller
🅿 🆆🅲 ♿
🎛 www.jardibotanicdesoller.org
@ fjbs@bitel.es

10. Jardines de Alfabia

Ctra de Palma–Sóller, km 17
07110 Jardines de Alfabia
Mallorca, Islas Baleares

Alfabia is by far the most interesting and enjoyable of the Majorcan gardens, both for its historic features and its mature trees. It is also extremely well maintained. The gardens are said to date back to the Moors, but nothing remains from that period.

There is a definite sequence to your visit. First, you go up a long, stepped walkway, restored in the mid-20th century and lined with palm trees. At the top, you turn right, down a gently descending pergola with views through the arches to formal gardens and orange trees on the right. A section of the pergola is tricked out with hidden water spouts to surprise the unwary. Its beams are laden with wisteria, jasmine, honeysuckle and other scented plants. In front of the house is a 19th- to 20th-century collection of ornamental trees and shrubs around a small lake – tall palms and bamboos. Almost the best feature is a large plane tree in the courtyard of the house as you exit through the front door. But the whole garden evokes a romantic reaction that makes you want to linger in contemplation of its beauty and timeless ambience.

On main road from Palma, just before Sóller tunnel ☎ 971 613 123
Open 9.30am–6pm (5pm winter)
Closes 1pm Sat & all Sun
Owner Zaforteza family
🅿 🖼 🆆🅲 🎛
@ www.jardinesdealfabia.com

Succulent collection, Jardí Botànic de Sóller, Majorca
OPPOSITE: Hidden water spouts, Jardines de Alfabia, Majorca

11. Parc Casa March
Cala Ratjada
Mallorca, Islas Baleares

These gardens may only be visited by prior arrangement with the tourist office in Cala Ratjada (Tel: 971 563 033). They are well worth the effort: the 60-ha estate occupies a spectacular headland and was laid out by the English designer Russell Page in the 1960s to hold Bartolomé March's collection of sculpture.

What the visitor therefore sees is a classy garden, an amazing array of modern sculpture and all in a stunning natural site. Design is paramount, and the gardens are completely subsidiary to the pieces of art. Page used the olive orchards and natural woodland of Aleppo pine as a background for some of the sculptures, notably the larger pieces by Henry Moore and Auguste Rodin. He also terraced the hillside and planted cypresses, standard *Magnolia grandiflora* and sweeps of agapanthus.

1km E of village centre
☏ 971 563 033 **Open** Strictly by appointment **Size** 60ha (148ac) **Owner** Fundación Bartolomé March

12. Jardín Botánico 'Viera y Clavijo'
Camino del Palmeral
Tafira Alta
35017 Las Palmas de Gran Canaria, Islas Canarias

The Botanical Garden in Grand Canary was founded in 1952 to conserve and study the flora of the Canary Islands, Madeira and the Azores. It was the brainchild of a Swedish botanist called Eric Ragnor Sventenius, who directed the garden until his untimely death in 1973, after which it was managed by the Englishman Dr David Bramwell. Jardín Botánico 'Viera y Clavijo' has been open since 1959 and, at 27 ha, is the largest botanic garden in Spain. All the many (and varied) habitats of the archipelago are represented, except the highest montane species. The 600 endemic taxa

Sculpture among the olive trees, Parc Casa March, Majorca

are displayed in an ornamental setting called the Jardín de las Islas. Micro-habitats have been made to grow important natural plant communities, including coastal plants; bog plants; the laurel forests (look out for the shrubby foxglove *Isoplexis chalcantha*); the pine forests (*Pinus canariensis*), with *Scilla latifolia* and *Isoplexis isabelliana* as two of the more attractive underplantings; palm forests (*Phoenix canariensis*); and more ornamental plantings like the dragon trees (*Dracaena draco*) and the popular giant house-leeks (*Aeonium* species). There is also a collection of cacti and succulents from around the world (300 taxa). Its scientific and conservation work has been of great international importance; as a garden, it is a pleasure to visit.

☏ 928 353 342 **Open** Daily 8am–12 noon & 1pm–6pm (but only 1pm–7pm on Sun and pub hols) **Size** 27ha (67ac)
🅿 🚾 ♿
🆆 www.step.es/jardcan/JARDCAN.html
@ jardincanario@grancanaria.com

13. Jardín de la Marquesa
Ctra Arucas–Bañaderos, km 1
Arucas
Gran Canaria, Islas Canarias

Arucas is the capital of the banana belt on Gran Canaria, and the Marquesa de Arucas's garden is surrounded

by plantations of bananas and strelitzias. It was laid out in the 1880s by a French architect – both house and garden are exotically over-ornamented – and expanded in the 1970s to add more interest for tourists.

The buildings include a watery grotto, Hindu summerhouses, bluestone fountains and a fantasy castle guarded by two castellated towers. The lake is exceptionally beautiful and surrounded by ancient palms (one of the best collections on the island) and an ancient 10-m dragon tree (*Dracaena draco*). Ornamental plants from tropical and subtropical regions are well represented, as are indigenous Canary Island plants – a total of 2500 species.

1km from centre on Bañaderos road
☏ 928 604 486 **Open** Mon–Sat 9am–12 noon & 2pm–6pm
Closes 12 noon Sat
Owner Marquesa de Arucas
🅿 🚻 🚾 ♿
🆆 www.jardindelamarquesa.com (but this is only a registered site name at present)

14. Jardín Botánico de Puerto de la Cruz
c/- Retama
Urb. la Paz
38400 Puerto de la Cruz
Tenerife, Islas Canarias

The botanic garden at Puerto de la Cruz was founded by Charles III in 1788 as an 'acclimatisation' garden. It is

Aloe arborescens, Jardín Botánico de Puerto de la Cruz, Tenerife

still referred to by some authorities as the Jardín de Aclimatación de la Orotava. The theory was that subtropical plants might be persuaded to adapt to the temperate conditions of Europe if they were first hardened off in a halfway climate. The first director was the Marqués de Villanueva del Prado who, through his own contacts, was able to introduce such novelties as the breadfruit tree.

The garden suffered some neglect during the 19th century, but its fortunes picked up after about 1950 and it is now well stocked, well run and a pleasure to visit. It is only about 2 ha, and its extensive list of plants (2500 taxa) barely squeezes into the handsome, railed rectangle it occupies on the hills above Puerto de la Cruz. The largest collections are palms, bromeliads, tropical araceae and exotic figs. Trees are always the great survivors of neglect: notable specimens here include the American mangosteen (*Mammea americana*); several araucarias; an ancient Canary Island pine (*Pinus canariensis*), forests of which grow on the slopes of Mount Teide south of the garden; more than 150 palm species; and a good collection of economic plants, including the camphor tree and rubber plant. Handsome specimens of *Ficus magnolioides* occupy large

spaces and there is an interesting collection of rootless, aerial plants like *Tillandsia dianthoides*. There are also plants of purely horticultural interest to please the visitors, such as cinerarias, which are popular greenhouse winter beauties in mainland Europe but actually native to the island.

Well signed. On edge of Puerto de la Cruz ▐ 922 383 572 **Open** Daily 9am–6pm (7pm Apr–Sep) **Size** 2ha (5ac) ▐P ▐WC ▐& ▐W www.icia.es

CATALUÑA

15. Jardí Botànic de Barcelona

Doctor Font i Quer, 2
Parc de Montjuïc
08038 Barcelona

Barcelona's Botanic Garden is brand new – opened in 1999 – and a real treat to visit. It has all the exhilarating modern design you would expect of Catalonia, plus a fascinating collection of plants laid out for visitors to study, enjoy and learn from. These are displayed geographically, and come from all the regions of the world with a Mediterranean climate. So there are distinct areas, each very extensive, devoted to Australia, South Africa, Chile, California, North Africa, the Canary Islands, the eastern Mediterranean and the Iberian Peninsular (plus the Balearic Islands). Each of these is broken down into further phytogeographic types so that, for example, the South African flora is represented by areas devoted to acid-soil bush, brushwood, coastal plants, fijnbos, Karoo, lowland plants, mountain woodland, savannah and the south-east woodland flora. This may sound dull, but the choice of plants is well made with ornamental horticulture in mind. The South African section, for example, has spectacular plantings of watsonias, pelargoniums and *Gazania* x *splendens*. The garden is also a joy for the non-gardener to walk around, and essential viewing for anyone making a garden in a Mediterranean climate.

Well signed in Parc de Montjuïc, northern side ▐ 934 264 935 **Open** Daily 10am–5pm. **Closes** 8pm Apr–Oct **Size** 14ha (35ac) **Owner** Ajuntament de Barcelona ▐P ▐WC ▐& ▐W www.jardibotanic.bcn.es

Good design and plantings, Jardí Botànic de Barcelona

16. Parc de Montjuïc
08038 Barcelona

Montjuïc – Montjuich in Castilian – is a fortified acropolis high above Barcelona Harbour. It has many of the city's recreational amenities, including two football stadiums, as well as the impressive ancient castle and the city's most upmarket cemetery. The whole hillside has been landscaped by the city council and there are several distinct gardens within the overall structure. The best way to visit them is to take a bus or taxi to the castle and amble down. The Jardins Mossèn Cinto Verdaguer, just below the castle, are a sequence of tanks, some filled with water lilies and other aquatics and others planted with hemerocallis, irises, nerines, amaryllis and agapanthus. The angular modern design is pleasing and creates a note of formality in the well-treed parkland setting. Elsewhere are large, abstract plantings of these and other plants in swirling beds. Here, and throughout Montjuïc (except for the botanic gardens), the standard of maintenance is only just acceptable – though the visit is still very worthwhile. The Jardins de Costa i Llobera have an extensive collection of palms, cacti and succulents on a very steep slope above the

Pools in Jardins Mossèn Cinto Verdaguer, Parc de Montjuïc, Barcelona

Giant fountain, Parc de la Ciutadella, Barcelona

port of Barcelona – and somewhat affected (as are the adjoining Jardins Miramar) by the noise of traffic below. There are patches of colour from underplantings of gazanias, drosanthemums, bauhinia, wigandias and grevilleas, but the garden relies for its effect upon the structure that comes from massed plantings of cacti, succulents and palms. The Jardins Miramar have a formal design with clipped hedges, bedding plants, white and yellow roses and lumpish modern statues. Its main attraction is the spectacular view of the city. A cable car runs down from Miramar to the port and makes an exciting end to your visit.

A rocky headland, SW of city centre **Open** All day, all year **Size** 100ha (247ac) **Owner** Ajuntament de Barcelona
🅿 ▯ 🍴 🚾 ♿
▥ www.bcn.es/parcsijardins/ pa_montjuic.htm

17. Parc de la Ciutadella
Barcelona

This public park – known in Castilian as the Parque de la Ciudadela – is large (17 ha) and popular, being right in the middle of the old city. Parts are in need of restoration but it is certainly worth a visit to see the magnificent fountain in

the north-east corner: statues of enormous griffons spew water from their mouths, and fountains, spouts and cascades run through eight different levels. At the top is a statue of Venus in her shell, backed by triumphal arches and a curved entablature, on top of which sits a vast bronze chariot pulled by four airborne horses. The young Antonio Gaudí helped to design it. Below is a lake with taxodiums in the water, palms on its islands and a life-sized model of a mammoth on its bank.

City centre **Open** Daily 10am–dusk **Size** 17ha (42ac) **Owner** Ajuntament de Barcelona
▯ 🚾 ♿
▥ www.bcn.es/parcsijardins/ pa_ciutadella.htm

18. Parc del Laberint
Carrer dels Germans Desvalls
08035 Horta-Guinardó
Barcelona

The Parc del Laberint is an unusual structure to find in Barcelona – a late 18th-century Italian baroque garden. It was made by the Marqués de Llúpia i d'Alfarràs in the 1790s and the main designer was an Italian called Domenico Bagutti. It was acquired by the City of Barcelona in the 1970s and completely restored in 1994; it is still the best kept garden in the city's

LEFT: Parterre and maze, Parc del Laberint, Barcelona RIGHT: Rocaille arches and spire, Parc Guëll, Barcelona

ownership. The heart of the garden is the magnificent clipped cypress-tree maze from which it takes its modern name. It is said to be the largest in Spain. The terrace above it has two splendid marble cupolas from which the outlines of the maze (and the cries of visitors lost in it) may be enjoyed in comfort. Steps lead up to a handsome neo-classical pavilion above a large, still tank; the views across the water and down to the maze are very satisfying. Off to the side and down to the lowest point lies a valley garden, known as the Romantic Garden, where a stream runs slowly through a sequence of large rectangular flower-beds, each devoted to a single taxon. Though the planting is somewhat unimaginative and municipal, it is a place of cool freshness and its reliance on plants for effect is a complete contrast to the formal parts of the garden. Elsewhere are parterres, classical statues, large terra-cotta pots, tanks, fountains and ancient trees. The whole garden is surrounded by wild woodland.

N of city next to velodrome
☎ 934 283934 **Open** Daily 10am–dusk **Size** 7ha (17ac)
Owner Ajuntament de Barcelona
P ⬛ WC ♿
W www.bcn.es/parcsijardins/pa_horta.htm

19. Parc Güell

Carrer Olt
08024 Barcelona

Parc Güell is Barcelona's top visitor attraction – jointly with the Church of the Sagrada Família – and always full of tourists. They come to see the architectural set pieces of Spain's greatest art nouveau architect – the entrance lodges, the hypostyle hall – and the eponymous Gaudí Museum.

But at Parc Güell you can also see how Gaudí applied his genius to the landscape. Apart from a few palm trees, he did not concern himself with planting the hillside: the background to the architectural features is mainly the natural woodland of evergreen oaks, pines and back-to-nature olive trees, with cistus and wild pistachios underneath. It is the decorative detail that is in evidence everywhere – zany rocaille columns, walls, seats, arches, arcading, vaults, vases and much else besides. It may not be obvious just how to obtain the same effects in your own garden, but there is much to look at and reflect upon.

Northern edge of Barcelona
☎ 934 243 809 **Open** Daily 10am–9pm (but 6pm Nov–Feb; 7pm Mar & Oct; 8pm Apr & Sep) **Size** 17ha (42ac)
Owner Ajuntament de Barcelona
⬛ 🍴 ♿ 🎁
W www.bcn.es/parcsijardins/pa_guell.htm

20. Jardí Botànic Mar i Murtra

Passeig Carles Faust 9
Apartat Correus 112
17300 Blanes–Girona
Barcelona

Mar i Murtra is a botanical garden laid out as a horticultural spectacle. It is seriously scientific, but wonderfully enjoyable to visit – the dramatic situation, the high standards of maintenance and the wealth of beautiful plants make it very popular (500 000 visitors p.a.). Its 16 ha were laid out by Karl Faust, a German businessmen living in Barcelona, between 1920 and 1952. Most of the headland is set out in the botanical fashion according to geographical habitat (e.g. deserts of southern Africa, Australian mallee and endemics of the Canary Islands) but done in such a way that it contributes considerably to the garden's aesthetic attractions. There are some 4000 species in all, and labelling is very good, so this is a garden that anyone who lives in a Mediterranean climate should visit. Purely horticultural features include a shaded cloister of climbing plants (*Aristolochia grandiflora* is the star performer) and – the highlight of the tour – a long staircase split into ten shorter flights of steps, leading down to an elegant monopteros known as the Temple of Linnaeus, high above rocky shores below. It is lined by cypresses, seasonal bedding and sweet-scented citrus trees: at the top is the Goethe plaza, where the lines of Goethe's poem 'Mignon' (*'Kennst du das Land ...'*) are inscribed on ceramic tiles in Catalan, Castillian and the original German.

1km from port, signed
☎ 972 330 826 **Open** Apr–Oct daily 9am–6pm; Nov–Mar 10am–5pm (but **closes** 2pm Sat, Sun and pub hols) **Size** 16ha (40ac)
Owner Fundació Karl Faust
🅿 ♿ ⊞
Ⓦ www.jbotanicmarimurtra.org
@ jbotanicmarimurtra@jbotanic marimurtra.org

21. Jardí Cap Roig
Paratge Cap Roig
Calella de Palafrugell
Gerona

Though sometimes billed as a botanic garden, Cap Roig is more of an early essay in conservation. It was bought by a Polish army officer Nicolas Woevodsky and his English wife Dorothy in 1926 – 40 ha of barren headland around a ruined castle. They planted pines to return the cape to its natural vegetation and create a nature reserve. Then they planted an English-style garden within the woodland, using colourful massed plantings. The Geranium Walk, for example, was 300 m long and planted with many different pelargoniums for its entire length. This is the style kept up today. There are still good plantings of arum lilies, agaves and seasonal plants like impatiens, while the design of the garden on its spacious terraces inspires the imagination of every garden-visitor. And the views are the best on the whole Costa Brava, Spain's most beautiful coastline.

C-66 to Palafrugell, then through Calella de Palafrugell to end of road
☎ 972 614 582 **Open** Apr–Sep daily 8am–8pm; Oct–Mar 9am–6pm
Size 40ha (99ac)
Owner Fundació Caixa de Girona
🅿 ♿ ⊞

22. Jardí Botànic 'Pinya de Rosa'
17300 Blanes
Gerona

Pinya de Rosa has the most complete collection of cacti and succulents in the world. It was started by a civil engineer called Dr Fernando Rivière de Caralt in 1945. There are over 7000 different taxa, including a near-complete collection of *Opuntia* species. They are arranged systematically, but also with a landscaper's eye for combinations of shape and colour: columnar, candelabra or globose forms are grouped together, some of them represented by hundreds of specimens. There are 32 beds devoted to agaves and 11 to aloes. Other succulents include goodly numbers of tall *Dracaena*, *Puya* and *Dasylirion* species and many examples of *Conophytum* and *Lithops*. The Mesembryanthemaceae are represented by 131 genera and 780 species in this family alone.

A high proportion of all the plants at Pinya de Rosa came from wild-collected seed of known provenance. There is always much to see, especially in winter when the aloes flower, but also in spring when the cacti come to their peak and the garden is knitted together with seedling California poppies. The garden has had problems recently; check the present position with the tourist office in Blanes (turisme@blanes.net).

Between Blanes and Lloret de Mar
☎ 972 355 290 **Open** Daily 9am–6pm
🅿 ♿ ⊞

23. Parc Samà
Ctra Vinyols
Cambrils
Tarragona

Parc Samà is one of the most glorious, extravagant and unusual gardens anywhere in Europe. As you approach across the flat, olive-growing plains of Baix-Camp, you see first a castellated, Disney-like

View from Goethe's plaza to Temple of Linnaeus, Jardí Botànic Mar i Murtra, Barcelona

LEFT: Rocaille bridges, pool and islands, Parc Samà, Tarragona
RIGHT: Sailors on stone boat in lower pond, Pazo de Oca, Pontevedra

tower perched high on a rocky pinnacle. Teetering above the road on a corner of the park wall, it is a good foretaste of the eccentricities inside.

You enter through the stableyard, and walk first towards the house, built in a romantic renaissance style by the young Marqués de Marianao in the 1880s. He was heir to a great colonial fortune – and spent it on his exotic park. The area around the house is thick with palm trees – it is one of the most extensive collections in Spain, not so much for its variety, as for the number of its plants. *Phoenix canariensis* and *Chamaerops humilis* are planted in quantity, as is *Trachycarpus excelsa*. As you walk into the woodland surrounds, you come across magnolias, cypresses, cedars, pines and avenues of plane trees. Then, from the fine fountain behind the house, you catch a glimpse of the garden's most exciting and unusual feature – a large lake (over 1 ha in area), fed by a canal and surounded by jagged, gothic rocaille. Three fantastic islands rise from the waters, like rocky outcrops in an oriental painting. Their summits are topped with palms; the largest has a viewpoint like a bandstand.

It reminds you of the castle turret you saw when you first arrived – but it is even more extraordinary.

On road from Cambrils to Montbrió; E15, exit 37 ☎ 977 826 514 **Open** Daily 10am–8.30pm (6pm winter) **Size** 14ha (35ac) 🅿 🚾 ♿

GALICIA

24. Pazo de Mariñán
Bergondo
Coruña

There are many country houses with gardens like Pazo de Mariñán throughout Galicia, but few are open to the public. Mariñán was given to the public in 1936 and has a good collection of plants that thrive in the mild, coastal climate of the Betanzos estuary. The garden is held together by granite stonework and intricate baroque parterres, dating from the early 1800s, from which several palm trees rise. It is sheltered by enormous camellias, also planted in the 19th century. The formal parts are decorated with granite statues, urns and fountains.

In the woodland are cypresses, *Abies nordmanniana*, and the oldest *Eucalyptus globulus* in Spain. The whole estate runs down to the water's edge and is surrounded by a granite wall.

E side of estuary, 3km N of Betanzos ☎ 981 777 001 **Open** 16 Sep–19 June Mon–Fri 11am–2pm & 4pm–7pm **Owner** La Diputación Provincial de A Coruña 🅿 🚾

25. Pazo de Oca
36685 A Estrada
Pontevedra

Pazo de Oca is the most famous garden in Galicia, a region renowned for high rainfall, ancient camellias, moss-laden trees and granite. The house and garden both date from the 1730s, which makes it one of the oldest Galician manor houses. It is also widely regarded as the most typical. The garden we see today was finished by 1743. It is particularly pleasant to visit in winter, when camellia petals fall on top of the last autumn leaves and the garden assumes a deep melancholy. Many of the camellias – some of them real trees – are over 100 years old, perhaps even twice that age. The old Reticulata hybrids are especially showy, but there are young plantings of Williamsiis too. You walk through the house to get to the gardens, past an elaborate *hórreo* (the traditional Galician granary) to the garden's outstanding (and unique) feature: two large tanks. Between them is a pathway (look out for the pretty ceramic vases) decorated with granite merlons and surrounded by ancient camellias and overgrown boxwood. At the centre of the lower pool is an almond-shaped island in the form of a ship, also of granite, with (granite) statues of 18th-century sailors in uniform at each end. The boat itself is laden with blue mophead hydrangeas. Elsewhere the garden is more open, with wild *Romulea bulbocodium* underfoot and a long avenue of limes.

30km SE of Santiago **Open** Daily 9am–dusk **Owner** Fundación Casa Ducal de Medinaceli 🅿 🆆🅲 ♿

MADRID

26. Jardines Reales
Plaza de Parejas
28300 Aranjuez

Aranjuez is famous for its whopping palace and extensive gardens, the latter little changed since the 18th century and much praised for their watery coolness. The river Tagus runs past the palace walls and the roar of its weir is a constant presence. There are three gardens. First comes the *Jardín del Parterre* (Garden of the Parterre), the formal garden in front of the palace as you arrive from Madrid. Its boxwood design, in the French style, dates back to

Casita del Príncipe, El Escorial, San Lorenzo de El Escorial

1746 but it has been much altered over the years; for example, by the addition of evergreen magnolias. Second –over a bridge – you come to the *Jardín de la Isla* (Garden of the Island) between the Tagus and its tributary the Jarama. It is the oldest part of the layout, with an extensive network of box-edged formal gardens, hornbeam hedges, statues, fountains and avenues of shade trees, mainly limes and plane trees. There are long walks along the river banks: its sheer size is impressive – as Philip V intended. Third, and further away, lies the *Jardín del Príncipe* (Garden of the Prince), a 150-ha landscape park in the English style, made by Charles

IV at the end of the 18th century and embellished with exotic trees, mainly from America. At its far end is the *Casa del Labrador* (Worker's Cottage), a mini-palace where the king could entertain more modestly and intimately than in Aranjuez itself.

Centre of town ☎ 918 911 344 **Open** Daily 10am–sunset **Size** 300ha (740ac) 🅿 🆆🅲 ♿ 🏛

27. El Escorial
San Lorenzo de El Escorial

Philip II started to build the Escorial in 1557 as a palace-monastery from which to rule his Most Catholic Empire. It is the largest renaissance building in Europe and its formal gardens, though insignificant in comparison, would be very impressive if attached to something smaller. They are on two levels, and filled with beautiful, simple, rather chunky parterres. Philip II had them planted with flowers, so that they resembled Turkish carpets.

The gardens of the nearby Casita del Príncipe are worth visiting in their own right. Laid out in 1772 for the future Charles IV, they are now dominated by 19th-century conifers, mainly sequoias, grown quite beyond their original purpose in the scheme of things. An extensive parterre

Boy with thorn sculpture, Jardines Reales, Aranjuez

leads up to a tank in the Portuguese style, and there are climbing roses on the walls. The wooded parkland has long, handsome avenues of plane trees and horse-chestnuts.

The Casita del Infante is also worth a visit: it is laid out in the baroque style, on descending terraces. Take into account, though, that the Escorial and its gardens are a large complex and you will need all day to do it justice.

50km NE of Madrid, signed from A6 **☎** 91 890 59 02 **Open** Daily 10am–6pm (7pm Fri–Sun). Sometimes **closed** lunch-time

P **WC** **♿** **🎁**

W www.patrimonionacional.es

28. Parque del Buen Retiro
28001 Madrid

Buen Retiro is a vast, well-maintained rectangular park right in the centre of Madrid. It was originally attached to a royal palace built by Philip IV in 1630, but has belonged to the city council since 1868 and is undoubtedly Madrid's favourite public park. It is also a popular refuge for cooing pigeons, twittering birds and stray cats.

The design is basically formal, with avenues of limes, horse-chestnuts, planes and celtis and straight paths, all running through a woodland mixture of pines, robinias and evergreen oaks. At the northern end is a large artificial lake (the *Estanque del Retiro*), with a vast equestrian memorial to King Alfonso XII (1922), framed by a semicircular colonnade. Further to the south, in the centre of the garden, is a very pretty crystal palace (the *Palácio de Cristal*) in front of a second smaller lake. Large, ancient trees of *Taxodium mucronatum* rise out of the water. At the southern end is a stunning French-style rose garden (its design based on Bagatelle's famous rose garden in Paris) made in 1915 and recently restored. It is bursting with colour, variety and scent. Elsewhere are an orchard of almond trees (very pretty in March) underplanted with lavender, a botanic trail (*itinerario botánico*) with notice boards drawing attention to some of the most interesting trees and shrubs, and many statues and fountains. Indeed, there is much to see in every part, and the best way to enjoy Buen Retiro is to wander around, relax, take a meal by the lake and watch your fellow-visitors.

Main entrance on Plaza de la Independencia; several other entrances. Retiro metro station exits directly into park **Open** Daily 6.30am–midnight (10pm winter) **Size** 119ha (294ac) **Owner** Ayuntamiento de Madrid

🅿 **🍴** **WC** **♿**

Glasshouses and bust of Linnaeus, Real Jardín Botánico, Madrid

29. Real Jardín Botánico
Plaza de Murillo, 2 28014 Madrid

Madrid's botanic garden is right next to the Prado Museum, so it is popular with tour organisers, as well as with schoolchildren on weekday mornings. It has occupied its present site since 1781, when its 8 ha were laid out on the three broad terraces, which still describe it today. The rise between levels is only a few steps, so the structure is not really noticeable, but there are broad walks that run the whole length of the garden and the lower level is held together by placing circular stone pools at every intersection.

This is Spain's premier botanic garden, and a joy to visit. Like many old gardens, it is dominated by large trees, some of which are native or naturalised, including celtis, elms, cercis and horse-chestnuts. Sometimes these ancient specimens make it difficult for the botanical collections underneath to flourish. The beds are a mixture of the scientific (systematically arranged for educational purposes) and the horticultural (for visitors to enjoy). Near the entrance are peonies, irises, rhododendrons and other collections of horticultural value, including a selection of Spanish-raised roses. Further along are

Rose garden, Parque del Buen Retiro, Madrid

collections of old garden roses (like *Rosa hemisphaerica*, 2 m tall and nearly twice as broad), a herb garden, a kitchen garden and collections of monocots, conifers and ferns. Up at the top, in a large pond, is the inevitable bust of Linnaeus, the father of modern botany, invariably with a pigeon on top. Among the champion trees are an ancient specimen of *Cupressus sempervirens* and a massive *Zelkova carpinifolia*. The collection is an interesting one and every visitor will find new plants or new surprises. Up near the pond, for example, is a copper beech (*Fagus sylvatica* Atropurpurea Group) close to a *Cornus capitata*, the former surely too temperate to survive a Spanish summer and the latter too tender to tolerate a Spanish winter. *How* is this possible? Like all good gardens, the Real Jardín Botánico raises these challenging questions though, alas, there are no books, guides or plant lists for sale that might provide visitors with answers.

City centre, next to Prado Museum ☎ 914 203 017 **Open** Daily 10am–9pm (6pm winter) **Size** 8ha (20ac) ♿ ♿ ♿ www.rjb.csic.es

Pergola, Rosaleda 'Ramón Ortiz', Parque Oeste, Madrid

30. Rosaleda 'Ramón Ortiz'
c/- Francisco y Jacinto Alcántara
Madrid

The Rosaleda 'Ramón Ortiz' in the 100-ha Parque Oeste is the best public collection of modern roses in Spain. It was formally laid out in the mid-1990s and planted with about 400 cultivars. A few, like 'Kalinka', 'Masquerade' and 'Fashion' are planted in large quantities, but most have one small section or bed to themselves, in which twenty to thirty plants are packed in. The overall effect is cheerful, bright and almost garish, but this is a splendid place to walk up and down to see what catches your eye, looking and learning about roses. A pergola of climbing roses fills the terrace that runs along the far side of the garden, and the ends are rounded off by curved arcades also packed with climbers. Labelling is good.

In Parque Oeste **Open** Daily 10am–9pm (or dusk, if sooner) **Size** 2ha (5ac) **Owner** Ayuntamiento de Madrid ♿ ♿

31. La Granja de San Ildefonso
San Ildefonso

French-born Philip V first conceived the palace and grounds of La Granja in 1721 as a Spanish Versailles. They are, however, quite distinct from the French prototype, depending more upon stupendous statuary, vast urns and the extensive use of water: there are 26 large fountains, each a monument in itself and most commemorating a mythological being. The approach from the village is spoiled by a

Cascada Nueva and palace, La Granja de San Ildefonso

planting of 19th-century conifers, but that makes you all the more appreciative of the gardens. The water staircase in front of the palace is called the *Cascada Nueva* and runs down from a large cupola; its sides are lined with monumental urns and statues. Parallel, and a little further up the hillside, is the sequence of Neptune pools, where vast copper statues of the sea-god and his attendants emerge from the waters. Recent restoration of these and all the other metal statues in the garden has returned them to their original glittering copper colour: the effect is rather startling.

The best way to see the garden is to wander freely along its avenues, which are all dead straight but offer endless options at every intersection. The avenues are mainly of limes and horse-chestnuts, and lined with hedges of beech or hornbeam. Do not miss the junction where the sculptures portray cherubs riding (rather perilously) on swans, and be sure to see the grandest of all the monuments, the tableau of Diana and her maidens. Philip V is said to have commented when it arrived from France: 'It has cost me two millions and amused me two minutes.' La Granja is fairly grim in winter, but a wonderful garden in which to enjoy shade and water in summer and, since it is 1200 m up, the season is always shorter than elsewhere.

11km SE of Segovia
☎ 921 470 019 **Open** Daily 10am–9pm (6pm winter). Fountains run 3pm–6pm Wed, Sat & Sun (summer only) **Size** 150ha (370ac)
🅿 🚻 ♿ 🔳 www.realsitio.com

VALÈNCIA

32. El Huerto del Cura
Porta de la Morera, 49
03023 Elche
Alicante

Huerto del Cura had an unusual beginning as a garden. It forms part of a huge grove of *Phoenix dactylifera* date palms at Elche

Palms and succulents, El Huerto del Cura, Alicante

near Alicante – some 200 000 trees, unique in Europe and now a World Heritage Site. About 100 years ago, one of these palms lost its 'heart', the tight ball of undeveloped leaves that forms the growth bud at the top of the tree. Instead of dying – the normal result – it sprouted seven distinct heads that continued to grow upwards, like a many-headed Hydra. This rare botanical phenomenon began to attract visitors and the grove was eventually acquired and preserved by a local priest (cura) from which it gets its name (El Huerto del Cura). Famous visitors like Alfonso XIII and Primo de Rivera have been honoured by commemorative plaques attached to other palm trees, but the original Palmera Imperial still flourishes, an extraordinary and impressive hulk, supported by guy-ropes and braces.

During the 1970s, the rest of the Huerto was turned into an ornamental garden and now has a loose, flowing design and a large number of exotic trees and shrubs, especially palms, cycads, strelitzias and bamboos, as well as sculptures, water features and some well-grown cacti. Almost all the plants are evergreen.

In high summer, when the temperatures may reach 40°C,

it is an oasis of coolness, shade and sweet scent. And the standard of maintenance is exemplary.

Well signed in Elche ☎ 965 451 936
Open Daily 9am–8.30pm (6pm winter)
Size 1.5ha (4ac)
🅿 🔳 🚻 ♿ 🔳 🌱
🆆 www.huertodelcura.com

33. Jardín Botánico de València
c/- de Quart, 80
E-46008 València

The University Botanic Garden in València moved to its present site in 1802, but fell into disrepair during the mid-20th century. It was substantially restored and replanted, however, in the 1980s. It is now well maintained, and designed to give instruction and enjoyment. You enter through a spanking new research building on the busy Calle Quart, and immediately travel back two centuries. The ground plan is unchanged since it was laid out in 1812. A long, broad drive runs straight ahead for the whole length of the garden, with box-edged systematic beds laid out on either side for almost its entire length. Off to the right is the palm collection – over 200 taxa, including some very tall washingtonias. Elsewhere are a rock garden for Spanish endemics, a collection of economic plants, another of medicinal plants, a plot devoted to timber trees, a horticultural collection of garden flowers, a cacti and succulents section (500 taxa, including the ones in a glasshouse), a latticed shade house and a most elegant, curving tropical house attached to a castellated tower.

City centre, 1km W of cathedral
☎ 963 156 800
Open Daily 10am–9pm (6pm from Nov–Feb, 7pm Mar & Oct, 8pm Apr & Sep) **Size** 4ha (10ac)
Owner Universitat de València
🚻 ♿
🆆 www.jardibotanic.org

Gardens of Portugal

Portuguese gardens are quite distinct: there is nothing like them anywhere else in Europe. The blue-and-white tiles known as *azulejos* are their most characteristic feature, closely followed by tanks of still water. Both were features taken from the Moors. Unlike Spanish tiles, Portuguese *azulejos* represent set-piece tableaux rather than patterns. And they are made to cover not just walls but every imaginable garden feature, including staircases, pools, fountains and pavilions.

The great gardens of Portugal are historical rather than horticultural. With few exceptions – Monserrate is one – botanic gardens are the only places to see a lot of interesting plants. The earliest Portuguese gardens show the influence of the Italian Renaissance. Statues, often with a distinct provincial charm, became a feature of Portuguese gardens when the baroque style became established early in the 18th century. The Lisbon earthquake of 1755 led to a rush of new garden building in the rococo style. The royal palace at Queluz is the best example. English-style landscape parks exist, especially in the north but also in the Sintra hills and at Buçaco. Modernism has not taken root, though Serralves Park in Oporto and the gardens of the Gulbenkian Museum in Lisbon are examples of what is possible in the Portuguese climate. The archaeological site at Conimbriga near Coimbra dates back to Roman times and its gardens attract a discerning minority.

Portuguese gardens are rich in their vegetation. Portugal has a super-temperate climate with rain in most parts of the country throughout the year. The average annual rainfall in Oporto exceeds 1150 mm, while Coimbra receives 940 mm a year. The result of this humidity, especially

ABOVE: Kitchen garden, Parque de Serralves, Oporto
OPPOSITE: Pool, tiles and staircase, Palácio dos Marquêses da Fronteira, Lisbon

in the north, is a remarkable luxuriance common to the natural vegetation of the countryside and the exotic plants grown in gardens. Portugal is the best place in Europe to see tree ferns.

Until very recently, there has been little restoration of historic parks and gardens. The Portuguese are a conservative people and sometimes lacking in initiative – as they are the first to admit. Almost every garden listed in this book has passed through long periods of neglect, when much of the interesting planting was lost. Trees are the great survivors, and almost all gardens have splendid collections of trees now in their prime.

Few gardens are open to the public, which is a pity because there are a large number of interesting private gardens in northern Portugal, especially in the Minho. As in neighbouring Galicia, many date from the 17th or 18th centuries, have a baroque structure and make a feature of camellias. From about 1700, camellias and other exotics began to be introduced from Portuguese colonies overseas. Many new camellia cultivars were later bred by Portuguese nurseries.

Horticultural skills are limited. Schools of ornamental and amenity horticulture do not exist. Standards of maintenance are often disappointing: Portuguese gardeners have a passion for tidiness and, in particular, for sweeping leaves off paths and raking the gravel underneath, but the disciplines of weeding, manuring and *cultivating* plants are rarely practised.

Water staircase, Palácio de Buçaco, Luso

Gardens of Portugal

1. Jardim Episcopal
2. Jardim Botânico da Universidade de Coimbra
3. Palácio de Buçaco
4. Jardim Botânico d'Ajuda
5. Jardim Botânico Universidade de Lisboa
6. Parque do Museu Calouste Gulbenkian
7. Palácio de Queluz
8. Palácio dos Marquêses da Fronteira
9. Parque de Monteiro-Mor
10. Parque Eduardo VII & Estufa Fria
11. Quinta do Palheiro Ferreiro
12. Jardim Botânico da Universidade do Porto
13. Parque de Serralves
14. Quinta do Meio
15. Quinta de Bacalhôa
16. Parque de Monserrate
17. Parque de Pena
18. Quinta da Regaleira

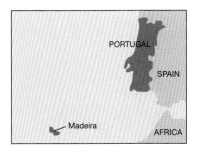

PORTUGAL

★ National Capital

• Cities and Towns

— Road

(00) Portuguese Garden

Adjacent Countries

Portugal

Staircase of kings, Jardim Episcopal, Castelo Branco

1. Jardim Episcopal

Largo Dr José Lopes Dias
6000-462 Castelo Branco

The bishop's garden at Castelo Branco is by far the most important in Beira Baixa. It is also a delicious example of the provincial rococo style. It was begun by Bishop João de Mendonça in 1725, continued by Bishop Caetano in the 1770s and is now a well-maintained national monument.

The design is formal and complex, but consists of a great number of enclosures on different levels, all tricked out in box, which has grown thick and high over the years. The box has been treated in a great many different ways, so that edgings may be low and straight, or high and battle-mented. Cubes, drums and chunky shapes fill some of the beds and line some of the walks. They help to create a sense of privacy and intimacy.

The walls, balustrades, steps, kerbs and tanks are all hewn from granite. So are the many allegorical and biblical statues that are displayed in the main garden rooms. They include four seasons, four points of the compass, the four cardinal virtues, the four evangelists, the twelve apostles, and the twelve signs of the zodiac (doubling up as months of the year). All

were locally carved in a slightly rustic style. Best known is the staircase lined with life-size statues of the kings of Portugal, each standing on a plinth inscribed with his name. Foreign conquerors (Portugal was once ruled by the kings of Spain) and those who submitted to alien invaders have been carved half-size, a nice example of garden-making as a political statement.

The central pool has an ornate cruciform shape, and elsewhere a large, traditional tank of water has its walls hung with tiles. The most remarkable pool is a low tank filled with narrow flower-beds arranged in ornate broderies around a central fountain. The curving, twisting, flowing shapes of the beds are carved in granite and filled with bedding plants, projecting just a little above the still water and seeming to float on the surface – beautiful, charming and uplifting all at once. The tank is an irregular tetrahedron – no two sides are the same length or parallel – but, seen from one end, it appears to be a completely regular rectangle.

Rococo architecture is full of *trompe-l'œil*, so it is nice to see an example in a rococo garden too. It typifies the charm of this garden – unique, entertaining and intimate.

Well signed, on NW edge of town
C 272 344 277 **Open** Daily
9am–7pm **Owner** Instituto
Português de Museus **P** **WC**
W www.cm-castelobranco.pt/jardim
_paco/jardim_paco.htm

2. Jardim Botânico da Universidade de Coimbra

Alameda Dr Júlio Henriques
3000-456 Coimbra

Coimbra's botanic garden is historical, beautiful and full of interesting plants. It was founded by the Marquês de Pombal in 1772 and designed by the British military architect William Elsden. Its central feature is a wide, circular parterre in the Italian style with a fountain at the centre, but there are also long, box-edged systematic beds to one side. The whole complex is most beautifully enclosed by high pillars and wrought-iron railings. The gardens are on different levels, and connected by broad walks, balustrades and staircases. Large specimens of *Cunninghamia lanceolata*, *Cryptomeria japonica* and *Erythrina crista-galli* date back to the 1790s, when the great Félix Brotero was the resident professor of botany. There are several glasshouses: *Victoria amazonica* is the star of the

Jardim Botânico, Coimbra

Estufa Pequena or 'small' greenhouse. On the slopes below the formal parts are a 10-ha arboretum (growing more than 50 *Eucalyptus* species and a splendid *Aesculus californica*) and many fine monocots, including a stunning avenue of 20-m high *Phyllostachys bambusoides*, a collection of watsonias, and drifts of *Doryanthes palmeri*.

City centre, just below university
C 239 822 897 **Open** Daily 9am–8pm (5.30pm winter)
Size 13.5ha (33ac) **Owner** Universidade de Coimbra **WC**
W www.uc.pt/botanica/jardim.htm

3. Palácio de Buçaco
3050-261 Luso

Buçaco is a palace garden in a forest: every part exudes history, architecture, botany, wilderness – and mystery. The palace, now an elegant hotel, was built in the neo-Manueline style by the Italian Luigi Manini for Carlos I, and finished in 1907, the year before the king's assassination. It is a glorious over-the-top confection, well worth a stay and not as expensive as you might suppose. Its formal gardens are not extensive,

but include a handsome box parterre and a pergola hung with wisterias (including the dark, double-flowered *Wisteria* x *formosa* 'Black Dragon'). Italianate stairs lead down to a woodland garden of lakes, surrounded by rhododendrons, azaleas, camellias and naturalised choisyas. Look closely and you will find a large number of interesting ornamental shrubs. The exotic plantings are enhanced by tall tree ferns and black swans. Elsewhere in the forest are 400-year-old *Cupressus lusitanica*, ginkgos, palms and a 19th-century collection of conifers. There are many paths to explore and enjoy: one of the best is the 3-km *Via Sacra*, lined with chapels, each with life-sized terracotta tableaux representing the stations of the cross.

25km from Coimbra, 3km from Luso **Open** Daily dawn–dusk **Size** 400ha (988ac) **Owner** The State
P **Tl** **WC**

4. Jardim Botânico d'Ajuda
1349-017 Lisboa

The handsome, spacious botanic garden next to the Ajuda palace was built to impress by Jose I in 1772 and is Lisbon's oldest. It was restored in the 1990s and is

LEFT: *Dicksonia* tree ferns, Palácio de Buçaco, Luso RIGHT: Snake fountain, Jardim Botânico d'Ajuda, Lisbon

now well maintained. The top terrace holds the systematic beds with some interesting, well-labelled plants. Look out for good trees, too, including *Ficus magnolioides*, *Grevillea robusta*, a large *Ocotea foetens* from Madeira, and a multibranched *Schotia afra*, trained over a vast frame (its crimson-pink flowers are stunning in mid-summer). A row of jacarandas runs the whole way along the top terrace and ancient glasshouses are stretched along the back wall. Look down on the classic 18th-century design of the terrace, with its distant views of the *Ponte 25 de Abril* and statue of Christ the King. The two large parterres are filled with ornamental bedding, arum lilies, dahlias and roses, and centre on a very fine fountain. Handsome trees pre-date the garden's restoration: a tall *Casuarina equisetifolia*, two *Ficus benjamina* and a circle of ancient and arborescent *Pittosporum tobira*.

Entrance in Calçada d'Ajuda
C 213 622 503 **Open** Daily 9am–8pm (6pm Oct–Mar)
Size 3.5ha (9ac) **Owner** Instituto Superior de Agronomia
P **WC** **W** www.isa.utl.pt/jardim

5. Jardim Botânico Universidade de Lisboa
Rua da Escola Politécnica, 58
1250-102 Lisboa

Lisbon's botanic garden is a wonderful, jungly, exotic place to see specimen trees planted in the late 19th century and now in their prime. They include many specimens that are the biggest and finest in Europe. In fact, they dominate the garden to such an extent that almost all the original underplantings have been crowded out.

The garden dates from the 1870s. Its design, on two levels around the university's old astronomic observatory, is formal at the top and fluid at the bottom, but everywhere obscured by the trees. There is a large, aerial-rooting *Ficus macrophylla* near the entrance, but most of the record breakers are down in the lower garden: vast *Chorisia crispifolia*, *C. insignis* and *C. speciosa*; a 25-m *Parrotia persica*; *Tipuana tipu*; the exquisite *Taxodium mucronatum*; a clump of ancient *Araucaria heterophylla*; large *Platanus* x *acerifolia*; and several *Metrosideros excelsus*, including a multi-trunked

specimen that covers a large area with subsidiary trunks formed from aerial roots. Here, too, are an avenue of 8-m tall *Phyllostachys bambusoides*, and excellent palms, including a circle of *Syagrus romanzoffiana*. Not all trees are labelled, but the garden is a haven from Lisbon's noisy traffic.

Main entrance on Rua da Escola Politécnica by Museu da Ciência. Subsidiary entrance (weekdays only) in Rua da Alegria **C** 213 921 802 **Open** Daily 9am–8pm (10am weekends & pub hols) **Closes** 6pm winter
Owner Universidade de Lisboa
WC **&** **W** www.jb.ul.pt
@ jb@fc.ul.pt

6. Parque do Museu Calouste Gulbenkian
Av. de Berna, 45A
1067-001 Lisboa

The gardens around the Gulbenkian Museum are a fine example of modern landscaping. At their centre is a lake, which pulls the buildings and landscape together and creates an introspective focus. The paths are all of concrete slabs, each laid at a slightly different level (not good for wheelchair users),

LEFT: Palms, Jardim Botânico, Lisbon RIGHT: Sculpture, Gulbenkian Museum, Lisbon

Baroque parterre, Palácio de Queluz

and their surfaces are scored first vertically, then horizontally to resemble wooden decking. Plants are not the gardens' strong point, though they include over 100 different taxa and a pleasant modern rose garden. The buildings themselves are covered in plants – yellow daylilies, blue agapanthus and pink, hanging pelargoniums on the administration buildings and Gulbenkian collection.

Main entrance on Av. de Berna; subsidiary entrances on Rua Marquês de Sá da Bandeira & Rua Dr Nicolau de Bettencourt **C** 217 823 000 **Open** Daily, except Mon 10am–5.45pm **Size** 3ha (7ac) **Owner** Fundação Calouste Gulbenkian
🖼 🍴 🚾 🏛 🅆 www.gulbenkian.pt

7. Palácio de Queluz
Lg. do Palácio Nacional
2745-191 Queluz

Queluz has the best rococo gardens in Portugal – perhaps even in Europe. The pink palace was built for Pedro III, while still a prince, and a French jeweller called Jean-Baptiste Robillon designed the gardens. You enter from the palace into the Garden of Malta, a sunken formal garden, once a tank of water, where box hedges and topiary surround a small pool. Alongside it lies the Hanging Garden (*Jardim Pênsil*) with more complex and exuberant shapes, set with Italian statues (in varying degrees of undress), English lead figures and ceramic urns, all enclosed by elegant balustrading. In older days, visitors approached it along a hedged avenue and passed between pillars (which commemorate Portuguese military and naval glories) to enter in front of a large basin with a statue of Neptune.

Down below the formal gardens is a long canal, covered in *azulejos* – panels with blue-and-white shipping scenes, linked by polychrome courtly scenes and still-life decorations, all as fresh as when first fired 250 years ago. Life-sized barges, cargoed by musicians, once plyed the water during royal festivities. There is little of horticultural interest, apart from lines of agapanthus, a

ragged row of *Magnolia grandiflora* and some tall trees in the park – limes, celtis and planes – but the baroque gardens and *azulejos* have the Wow Factor in abundance.

Well signed from IC 19 (Sintra–Lisboa) **C** 214 350 039 **Open** Daily, except Mon 10am–6pm **Owner** The State
🅿 🚾 ♿ 🏛

8. Palácio dos Marquêses da Fronteira
Largo de Sao Domingos de Benfica
11500 Lisboa

Fronteira has the best *azulejos* in Portugal: if you have time for only one garden in Lisbon, this is the one to see. The gardens are aligned on the side elevation of the house, and they beckon you away as you approach the front door of the palace. Pass round the corner and you discover a very large, square parterre with 16 elegant, box-edged segments – four squares, each with four beds. Each quarter has a pool at its centre, and there is an especially fine fountain at the centre of the whole garden.

Formal garden, Parque Eduardo VII, Lisbon

Yew topiary and statues mark the main points of the design. But the eye-catching highlight of the garden lies at the end – a dramatic, long, rectangular water-tank with broad baroque staircases at either end, leading up to pavilions at the top. The walls are tiled with 17th-century tableaux of the 12 Heroes of the Lusiads (Camoëns describes how they travelled to England to avenge the honour of 12 Portuguese ladies insulted and dishonoured by English knights) and surmounted by a balustraded terrace that runs between the two pavilions above the tank. The terrace's walls are inset with busts of Portuguese kings and queens in niches. Everything, including the walls around the great parterre, is covered in *azulejos* of the highest quality – mytholgical, satirical, martial, pictorial and decorative. There are further delights behind the house, including Venus's garden, with an exquisite rococo pool, a shell-grotto and statues of Apollo and Marsyas, but it is the memory of the amazing tank in the main garden that lasts longest.

On edge of Monsanto
[C] 217 782 023 **Open** Some week-day afternoons (telephone first)
Owner Fundação Fronteira [P] [WC]

9. Parque de Monteiro-Mor
Largo Júlio de Castilho
1600-483 Lisboa

The Parque de Monteiro-Mor surrounds two handsome old villas: one is now Portugal's museum of costume; the other a museum of the theatre. The formal garden between them is terraced around a pool: it was made by the third Marquês de Angeja, the Portuguese Prime Minister, in the 1750s. The magnificent trees on the terraces include a monumental copper beech, a spreading *Ficus macrophylla*, vast plane trees and camellias. Elsewhere are lines of hydrangeas, agapanthus and plumbago.

Most of the trees that are now the garden's glory date from the 1840s, after it was bought by the second Duque de Palmela, who imported rarities from English nurseries. He was advised by famous botanists of the day, including the Austrian Friedrich Welwitsch, who laid out the 5-ha woodland park as a botanical collection. Though now effectively abandoned and overrun by acanthus, vast strelitzias and seedling robinias, the old trees include several huge *Araucaria*

heterophylla, a rugged *Ginkgo biloba*, casuarinas, *Podocarpus elongatus*, *Pinus pinea*, *Phillyrea latifolia* and a very fine *Taxodium mucronatum*. The garden around the theatre museum has two large parterres filled with modern roses and maintained in the Portuguese fashion.

In Lumiar, a northern suburb of Lisboa [C] 217 590 318 **Open** Daily, except Mon 10am–6pm
Owner The State
[P] [II] [WC] [🏛]
[W] http://museudotraje-ipmuseus.pt

10. Parque Eduardo VII & Estufa Fria
1000-Lisboa

The Parque Eduardo VII is a large public park near the centre of Lisbon. It has an enormous, modern, formal garden, which stretches down the middle, and shady wooded areas on either side. The park also offers an avenue of jacarandas, large oleanders and a lake. In the north-west corner is the Estufa Fria, a 1-ha garden made in an old quarry covered by a slatted roof. This sheltered site was intensely landscaped, with pools and steps and viewing platforms for visitors to see over the whole body of the planting. Holes have been cut in the roof to accommodate some trees – mainly palms – which have grown too tall. Other plants include azaleas, monsteras, bananas, strelitzias, rubber plants, hydrangeas and ferns. The adjoining Estufa Quente has a glass roof and is noticeably warmer, with *Calathea zebrina* and bougainvilleas around its pool, plus seasonal bedding like primulas and cinerarias in winter. It leads to a small cactus house where the stars are knobbly *Peniocereus serpentinus*, pendulous *Euphorbia milii*, *Agave attenuata* and two very fine specimens of *Opuntia brasiliensis*.

Lisboa, NW of centre
☎ 213 882 878 **Open** Always
Owner The State 🅿 🖪 🍴 🆆🅲 ♿

11. Quinta do Palheiro Ferreiro
Rua da Estalagem, 23
São Gonçalo
9060-415 Funchal
Madeira

Quinta do Palheiro Ferreiro is the best example of a truly subtropical English garden in Europe. It was made by the Blandy family, which

has extensive interests in the wines and hotels of Madeira and bought the estate in 1885. The house was built in the Portuguese manor-house style, but was recently converted into a hotel to serve a new golf-course within the 320-ha estate. The 12-ha gardens are Victorian in design but well maintained and are full of interesting, mature plants. The thick surrounding woodland is mainly of *Pinus pinaster* and *P. canariensis*. The commonest underplantings are camellias, which seed themselves abundantly: there are over 10 000. Along one side of the drive leading down to the house is an overgrown camellia hedge up to 10 m high and nearly 1 km long, in every colour, shape and variation imaginable. Rare trees include *Leucadendron argenteum* from South Africa, and many proteas, magnolias, michelias, gardenias and bauhinias. South African bulbs are much used as underplantings: agapanthus, nerines, amaryllis, and naturalised freesias, sparaxis, ixias, lachenalias, and cyrtanthus. Native plants are represented by several *Aeonium* species and the incomparable

shrubby foxglove *Isoplexis sceptrum*. Rare plants from other north Atlantic islands include the waxy pink or white *Campanula vidalii* from the Azores and the endangered *Lotus berthelotii* from Tenerife. Other good gardens in Madeira include the Jardim Botânico da Madeira in Caminho do Meio and the Jardim Tropical Monte Palace (*see* www.montepalace.com).

6km NE of Funchal
☎ 291 793 044 **Open** Mon–Fri
9.30am–12.30pm
Owner Blandy family
🅿 🖪 🍴 🆆🅲
🆆 www.casa-velha.com

12. Jardim Botânico da Universidade do Porto
Rua do Campo Alegre, 1191
4150-181 Porto

Oporto's botanic garden started as a private estate known as Quinta do Campo Alegre. Its structure is in need of refurbishment, but the standard of maintenance is fairly good. The garden was largely planted by Henrique Andresen, a Portuguese-born German wine-exporter. It has belonged to the University of Oporto

LEFT: Lily pool, Quinta do Palheiro Ferreiro, Madeira RIGHT: Bougainvillea on terrace, Jardim Botânico, Oporto

LEFT: Giant trowel sculpture, Parque de Serralves, Oporto RIGHT: Rose garden, Jardim do Palácio Cristal, Oporto

since 1951. The entrance area is surrounded by rhododendrons, azaleas and kalmias, from which emerge some handsome trees of *Araucaria heterophylla*, a huge *Liquidambar styraciflua* and *Melaleuca armillaris*.

Three formal gardens have pride of place behind the imposing house: the central one, reached by a handsome staircase, is planted with modern roses, and the others, to the sides, with box-edged parterres. All three are enclosed by high camellia hedges composed mainly of 19th-century hybrids – including 'Mathotiana', 'Dom Pedro', 'Leeana Superba', 'Nicholsonii' and 'Mutabilis'. Off to one side – a modern addition – is a sequence of interlinked lily pools, surrounded by clivias and strelitzias. Go and explore the area below the formal gardens, starting with the very good collection of cacti and succulents, some in glasshouses, some in a large permanent planting outside. Still further down the hill is a woodland garden, rather spoiled by road noise. Here are some interesting rare trees, including a pair of *Bischofia javanica* and a grove of *Abies cilicica*.

W side of city **⌂** 226 002 153
Open Daily 9am–8pm (6pm Oct–Mar) **Size** 4ha (10ac)
Owner Universidade do Porto
WC **&** **W** www.fc.up.pt/bot
@ jardimvisitas@fc.up.pt

13. Parque de Serralves
Rua D. João de Castro, 210
4150-417 Porto

Parque de Serralves was laid out in the 1930s by the French landscape architect Jacques Gréber in a formal style that makes distinctly modernist use of materials. Parterres, pools, topiary and a water-staircase fill the broad terraces below the pink art deco house. The simple, unornamented surfaces are matched by monovarietal plantings – all extremely effective. Away from the house the mood changes. Here is a romantic woodland of native and exotic trees and shrubs – conifers, eucalyptus and oaks underplanted with camellias, rhododendrons and flowering shrubs. Highlights within the woodland garden include the largest rose garden in Portugal and a dark, rocky lake in the picturesque style. Avenues of horse-chestnuts and liquidambars ride out into

the countryside – the main axis runs straight from the house for 500 m. At the far end is a large kitchen garden, filled with scented plants and herbs, as well as fruit and vegetables. Allow lots of time to enjoy it all, including Oporto's stunning Museum of Modern Art near the entrance.

⌂ 226 156 546 **Open** Tue–Sun 10.00am–7.00pm **Closes** 8pm Sat, Sun & pub hols, Apr–Sep
Owner Fundação Serralves
P **⌂** **⫙** **WC** **&** **⊞**
W www.serralves.pt
@ serralves@serralves.pt

14. Quinta do Meio
Rua de Entre-Quintas, 219
4205-240 Porto

Quinta do Meio – now a numismatic museum called Casa Tait – was bought by William Tait in 1900. He and his daughter Muriel planted the garden in the English style, filling its box-edged parterres with rare plants. Almost all the plants have disappeared and been replaced by brambles, sycamores and acanthus, but the outlines of the formal garden and a few magnolias, fuchsias, roses and fruit trees survive. Near the house is a grove of ancient camellias and a vast hollow-trunked *Liriodendron tulipifera*. More liriodendrons and tall magnolias fill the upper terraces, now a back-to-nature woodland. The whole estate is pervaded by that spirit of melancholy all too common in old Portuguese gardens. The nearby Jardim do Palácio Cristal is also worth visiting – a spacious, pleasant public park with splendid views across the Douro. Near the entrance (flanked by a pair of large *Magnolia grandifolia*) are fine specimens of *Acacia melanoxylon*, araucarias, *Metrosideros excelsa*, an 18-m *Acer japonica* and *Brachychiton diversifolia*. Above the river is a sequence of handsome, modern rose gardens.

W side of city centre **C** 226 057 000 **Open** Tue–Fri 10am–12.30pm & 2pm–5.30pm; weekends 2pm–6pm **Closed** Mon **Owner** Câmara Municipal do Porto **P**

15. Quinta de Bacalhôa
Vila Fresca de Azeitão
Setúbal

Bacalhôa is an early baroque masterpiece, beautifully restored by its American owners some 50 years ago. The villa is earlier, in the Italian renaissance style, and was built mainly in the 1540s. The formal garden centres on a boxwood parterre around a fountain, best seen from the elegant, open Doric loggia behind. The parterres are punctuated by topiary yews. Beyond are the citrus orchards. A raised walkway leads you away, past beautiful green-and-white *azulejo* seats towards a large tank of water. Its longest side is filled by three elegant pavilions, linked by a roofed arcade. The tiled picture on the wall of *Susanna and the Elders* (1565) is the oldest *azulejo* in Portugal. From the parapets are views of Quinta da Bacalhôa's vines – it is a famous wine estate.

12km W of Setúbal, off N10 **C** 212 180 011 **Open** Tue–Sat 9am–5pm **P** **T** **WC** **&** **A** **W** www.azeitao.net/quintas/ bacalhoa.htm

16. Parque de Monserrate
2710-405 Sintra

Parque de Monserrate is an English garden: for over 150 years it belonged first to William Beckford and later to Sir Francis Cook and his grandson Sir Herbert. Beckford bought it in the 1790s and experimented with the gothic revival ideas he was later to incorporate into his fantasy at Fonthill Abbey in Wiltshire. He built a ruined chapel (gothic and castellated, but now engulfed by a vast *Ficus macrophylla*), a cromlech (like the folly at Fonthill) and a rocky cascade, where a stream bursts out over a great cataract and then races down a dark ravine, breaking and turning over boulders in a succession of different movements. Francis Cook, with help from Kew and botanical contacts, added rare trees and shrubs from all over the world: look for the tallest *Araucaria excelsa* in Europe, which is furnished with lower branches almost to ground level and the splendid *Cryptomeria japonica* 'Lobbii' on the lawn below the house. Elsewhere are such firs as *Abies nordmanniana* and *A. webbiana*, cedars, pines (including the Canary Island pine, *Pinus canariensis*), spruces, more *Araucaria* species, cypresses, Kauri pines, and swamp cypresses. Then in the 1920s, Herbert Cook gave the garden a horticultural overlay with new garden plants like hybrid rhododendrons, and spent his fortune on employing over 70 gardeners. The botanical and horticultural treasures are not well displayed – the garden is badly maintained by the local authority – but they are there for the knowledgeable visitor to discover and remain unparalleled in all Portugal. There are several other handsome quinta gardens on the way to Monserrate; the Palácio de Seteais is a five-star hotel.

Well signed from Sintra **C** 219 237 300 **Open** Daily 9am–7pm **Closes** 8pm summer & 6pm winter **Size** 143ha (353ac) **Owner** Fazenda Nacional **P** **WC** **W** www.parquesdesintra.pt/h/ frame_monserrate.htm **@** info@parquesdesintra.pt

Exotic architecture of Parque de Monserrate, Sintra

ABOVE LEFT: Duck house built as a castellated folly, Parque de Pena, Sintra RIGHT: Tree ferns and gothic follies, Quinta da Regaleira, Sintra OPPOSTIE: Exotic house sets off exotic garden, Quinta da Regaleira, Sintra

17. Parque de Pena

Largo Rainha Dona Amélia
2710-609 Sintra

Pena is an ultra-romantic royal fantasy on the highest peaks of the Sintra hills. King-Consort Fernando II built the remarkable Castle from 1840 onwards in a sort of German gothic style, with lots of Portuguese and Moorish decorative details. In the park he designed such follies as a gothic monk's grotto and a castellated duck-house, and he planted trees from all over the temperate world. But the best part today is the *Feteira da Rainha*, the spectacular woodland valley of ferns on the northern side. Here a glacial deposit of enormous boulders provides structure, while protection comes from a canopy of oaks (*Quercus robur*) underplanted by *Rhododendron ponticum*. The fully grown tree ferns – there are hundreds of them – are mainly dicksonias, with herbaceous davallias, woodwardias and blechnums underneath. The cumulative effect as you pass through them is awe-inspiring. Colour comes from camellias, azaleas, hydrangeas and large *Fuchsia magellanica*. In the lakes are black swans.

Signed from centre of Sintra
☎ 219 207 953 **Open** Tue–Sun 10am–6.30pm **Owner** The State
🅿 🖵 🍴 🚻 ♿
🕸 www.parquesdesintra.pt/h/frame_pena.htm
@ info@parquesdesintra.pt

18. Quinta da Regaleira

2710-567 Sintra

Both house and garden at Quinta da Regaleira are extraordinary – over-the-top, enormous and full of decorative symbolism that no-one really understands. They are also very enjoyable to visit.

The house was built and its grounds laid out by a Brazilian plutocrat called António Augusto de Carvalho Monteiro between 1904 and 1910. He hired the royal architect Luigi Manini to reproduce the effects that the Italian had already achieved for King Carlos I at Buçaco – a palatial neo-Manueline house and a sequence of garden follies in many different styles. Cynics say that Monteiro was a *nouveau riche* who thought that his garden would bring cultural credentials to ease his social climbing.

The thickly wooded garden is on a steep slope, crossed by a broad carriage drive and numerous narrow, steeper paths. The follies include romanesque towers, gothic turrets, Manueline decoration, picturesque grottos, dark chasms, secret passages, a labyrinth and caves.

The plants are very interesting: many vast plane trees, oaks and cypresses, with underplantings of hydrangeas, camellias, rhododendrons, muehlenbeckia, brunsfelsias and fuchsias, and a natural understorey of laurel, laurustinus, ruscus and bay. Elsewhere are *Fascicularia bicolor*, *Begonia* species and a fine planting of tree ferns at the top of the steep, sloping lawn in front of the house. Regaleira is a garden of style, exuberance, extravagance and sheer dottiness.

Well signed on road from Sintra to Colares ☎ 219 106 656 **Open** Daily 10am–7pm **Closes** 6.30pm Feb–Apr & Oct & 5.30pm Nov–Jan
🅿 🚻
🕸 www.maconaria.net/regaleira.shtml
@ regaleira@mail.telepac.pt

Gardens of France

It was in France that the civilisation of the Renaissance first received full expression outside Italy. After the accession of François I in 1515, French kings and courtiers built themselves magnificent houses and gardens in the image of the new learning – Fontainebleau and Chantilly are among the most splendid examples. Unfortunately, little remains from the 16th century, because the houses were altered and the gardens remade in later centuries. Nevertheless, the reproduction gardens at Chenonceau and Villandry give a good impression of these renaissance landscapes.

The Italianate gardens of the 16th century were the fertile soil that gave root to France's later architectural and landscaping greatness. During the first half of the 17th century, the classical French garden style was articulated, established and perfected – André Le Nôtre was its greatest exponent. It involved symmetrical parterres filled with broderies or turf, with *bosquets* on either side of a central avenue, extending as far as the countryside allowed, and enlivened by cross-axes. Le Nôtre worked at Sceaux, Chantilly and Vaux-le-Vîcomte, but the most complete expression of his genius is at Versailles, where he had an intelligent and enthusiastic patron in Louis XIV. From about 1660 onwards, France was the dominant and richest country in Europe, and its political might was reflected in the scale and confidence of French gardens over the next 100 years. Versailles is the most magnificent expression of royal power in Europe – perhaps in the world. Political power begets cultural influence: French baroque gardens were exported all over Europe during the following 100 years and Versailles was still being copied by the king of Bavaria in the 1870s.

Political dominance in Europe passed to England at the end of the Seven Years' War in 1763, and this coincided with the decline of the French baroque garden. The English landscape style was not immediately imported into France. Sir William Chambers's books on oriental gardening were, however, very influential and gave rise to the French belief that English gardening was really a reinterpretation of the Chinese style. The *anglo-chinois* style dominated the last 50 years of the 18th century: there are good examples of its preoccupation with the rustic and the rococo, with an oriental overlay, at Bagatelle and Chantilly.

Much was destroyed in the French Revolution, a disaster for both France and the rest of Europe. When the nobility returned in 1815, their gardens

OPPOSITE: Before the famous rose garden at Bagatelle was planted in the early 1900s, Empress Eugénie would sit under this Turkish pavilion and watch the young *Prince Impérial* take riding lessons.

Villandry's *potager* reaches a peak of colour and beauty in early autumn, when the vegetables are fully grown.

took on the true English landscape style practised by Brown and Repton, largely because they were cheaper to maintain. English-style parks were the preferred design throughout the 19th century, but increasingly supplemented by plantings of exotic trees; Ferrières and Trévarez are good examples. This interest in horti-culture is also seen in the quality and number of public gardens founded during this time, almost all with good collections of trees and other plants. The tradition of ornamental bedding was also developed: the French word is 'mosaïculture'. This used exotic plants and bright colours to create highly decorative garden displays. Municipal bedding in France is still the best in Europe: good design and a wide choice of plants are combined to make bold explosions of colour, complemented by very high standards of maintenance. Throughout France, from the Parc du Thabor in Rennes to the Parc de la Tête d'Or at Lyon, these displays of technical excellence are unmatched for horticultural interest and public amenity. Conspicuous spending on seasonal bedding is a matter of municipal self-respect.

From 1890 to 1940 a large number of historic French gardens were restored or newly made in the historic style by such architects as Edouard André, Henri and Achille Duchêne, and Jean-Claude Nicolas Forestier. These were the leading proponents of a return to classical French gardens, with made-to-measure baroque and rococo precedents to suit large country houses. Caradeuc in Brittany and Vaux-le-Vîcomte in Île-de-France are examples so fine that many visitors suppose these gardens to be ancient rather than modern. This desire to re-create the past continues on a lesser scale even today.

The real growth area in recent years, however, has been the result of cross-pollination with modern English gardens. It involves laying out gardens with the traditional shapes of the French Renaissance – squares, circles and, above all, quincunxes – then filling them with profuse expanses of colourful plants for maximum effect. These gardens may have less charm than the English, but they make more impact. They are more inventive, and their use of colour is much more tightly controlled than across the Channel. Some of the most rich and powerful of all modern gardens are to be found in France. There are good examples all over Touraine, Brittany and, especially, Normandy, where there is a high concentration of such gardens, including Plantbessin, Jardins du Pays d'Auge and Clos du Coudray.

French gardens differ enormously according to their regional location. History explains why the great Le Nôtre formal gardens are largely absent from the southern part of the hexagone: the French court was rooted in the north, at Versailles and Paris. Climate is important, too: there are four distinct types – Mediterranean, continental, temperate and alpine. Local traditions abound: every garden owner in the south of France must plant two cypress trees, one for peace and the other for prosperity. Normandy, especially Haute-Normandie, has a tradition of planting irises along the ridges of thatched roofs. Other local features are the palm-lined promenades of the Riviera and the cordylines of the Atlantic coast.

It is important to remember that French nurserymen and hybridizers played an important part in the development of gardens and garden plants. Without them we would have very few roses, lilacs, philadelphus, irises or water lilies. France's horticultural heritage is conserved through a system of national plant collections maintained by the *Conservatoire des Collections Végétales Specialisées*.

The garden-visiting market in France is growing rapidly, though it is still about one-third the size of the English market. This makes it all the more remarkable that France has so many excellent gardens open to the public. And the French love of formality remains – high-clipped hedges are a common feature, and beech, hornbeam, horse-chestnut or lime are cut into sharp rectangular shapes as high as 10 m. It is a taste that baffles and intrigues visitors from Germany and England, whose garden aesthetic is founded on natural forms. But it also gives French gardens a continuity of style that is one of their greatest charms.

The groves on either side of Versailles's main axis conceal a great number of ingenious and very beautiful features, like this fretwork pavilion in the *Bosquet de l'Encelade*.

FRANCE

★ National Capital

• Cities and Towns

— Major Roads

(00) French Garden

Adjacent Countries

Highlighted French Region

ÎLE DE FRANCE

Chantilly ⑲

0 — 25 Kilometres
0 — 25 Miles

⑨ Vernon

Saint-Germain

• Anet

VERSAILLES

㉑ ㉒ ㉓ ㉔ ㉕ ㉖ ㉗ ㉘

• Meaux

⑭⑨ ㊴ ★ Paris ㉙
㉞ ㊳ ㉟
㊱ ㊶ ㉜
㊸ ㊷
㊵ ㊳ ㉝ ÎLE DE FRANCE
㉟ Dreux
㉞ ㊳ ㉝

Chartres   Étampes   Fontainebleau

⑪ Vaux-le-Vîcomte

㉚

㉛

㉗

ANGLETERRE

Calais

BELGIQUE   ALLEMAGNE

Lille

LUXEMBOURG

La Manche

Cherbourg

⑮ Dieppe
⑰⑬
⑱   Amiens
⑭ ⑯

NORD-PAS-DE-CALAIS

PICARDIE

⑪ ⑩
Bayeux
⑥ ① CAEN
⑫ ④ ⑤ ② ⑦ ⑧ ROUEN
⑭
Coutances
㊴
Avranches
㊵ ③ NORMANDIE

Île de France
VERSAILLES ★ Paris
ÎLE DE FRANCE

CHALONS-
SUR-MARNE   METZ

LORRAINE

㊹ NANCY   ㊻

㊼

CHAMPAGNE-
ARDENNE   STRASBOURG

ALSACE

㊺

MULHOUSE

㊾ ㊽
BREST   ㊼
㊹ ㊺
BRETAGNE   ㊾
RENNES

LE MANS

⑦③

⑦⓪

ORLÉANS   Montargis

PAYS DE LA LOIRE   ⑦②   ⑦①
Nogent-sur-
Vernisson
⑦⑧   DIJON

ANGERS   ⑦④

Tours ⑥⑦   ⑦⑥ Besançon
⑤⑥   ⑥⑥ ⑥⑨
Langeais   ⑥⑤ CENTRE   BOURGOGNE
⑥⑧   FRANCHE-
NANTES ⑤⑤   COMTÉ
Cholet ⑤⑧   ⑤⑦   SUISSE
⑥⓪ ⑥①   ⑥②
⑤⑨ Luçon   ⑥③   ⑧⑤
POITIERS   ⑦⑨ ⑦⑤ ⑧④
F R A N C E   Nevers   GENÈVE
Villefranche-
LA ROCHELLE   Aubusson   Vichy   sur-Saone
Rochefort   ⑦⑦   • Saintes   LIMOGES   ⑧③ LYON
Golfe de
Gasgogne   POITOU-
CHARENTES   LIMOUSIN   ⑧⓪ CLERMONT-   Montbrisson   ⑨⑤
FERRAND   St Etienne   ⑧②
AUVERGNE   ⑧①   GRENOBLE
RHÔNE-ALPES   ⑨④
⑧⑥   Briançon
⑧⑦ BORDEAUX   ITAL

0 — 50   100 Kilometres
0 — 50   100 Miles

AQUITAINE

MIDI-PYRÉNÉES

LANGUEDOC-
ROUSSILLON   Alès   PROVENCE-
⑧⑨ ⑨⓪   ⑨⑤ ⑨⑦   ALPES-CÔTE D'AZUR
⑧⑧   MONTPELLIER ⑨① NÎMES   ⑨⑧ ⑨⑨ Mer.
TOULOUSE   Mazanet   ⑨②   Monaco
Bayonne   NICE
CANNES ⑨⑥

MARSEILLE

ESPAGNE   ⑨③ PERPIGNAN

Côte d'Azur

Mer Méditerranée

Gardens of France

1 Château de Brécy
2 Château de Canon
3 Château de Vendeuvre
4 Château d'Harcourt
5 Jardin des Plantes de Caen
6 Jardins de Plantbessin
7 Jardins du Pays d'Auge
8 Arboretum d'Harcourt
9 Musée Claude Monet
10 Château de Martinvast
11 Jardins du Château
   de Vauville
12 Jardin des Plantes de
   Coutances
13 Château de Miromesnil
14 Jardin Botanique de Rouen
15 Le Bois des Moutiers
16 Le Clos du Coudray
17 Parc Floral William Farcy
18 Château de Bosmelet
19 Château de Chantilly
20 Jardins de Valloires
21 Parc de Bagatelle
22 Jardin des Plantes de Paris
23 Jardin du Luxembourg
24 Jardins des Tuileries
25 Les Serres d'Auteuil
26 Parc des Buttes-Chaumont
27 Parc Floral de Paris
28 Parc Monceau
29 Château de Champs
30 Château de Fontainebleau
31 Château de Vaux-le-Vicomte
32 Château de Ferrières
33 Château de Breteuil

34 Château de Dampierre
35 Château de Groussay
36 Château de Versailles
37 Château de Courances
38 Domaine de
   Saint-Jean-de-Beauregard
39 Château de Malmaison
40 Musée Albert Kahn
41 Parc de Saint-Cloud
42 Parc de Sceaux
43 Roseraie du Val-de-Marne
44 Jardin Botanique du Montet
45 Jardin d'Altitude du
   Haut-Chitelet
46 Jardin Botanique du
   Col de Saverne
47 Parc de l'Orangerie
48 Château de la Roche Jagu
49 Kerdalo
50 Jardin Exotique de Roscoff
51 Parc de Trévarez
52 Château de Caradeuc
53 Parc du Thabor
54 Jardins d'Argences
55 Jardin des Plantes de Nantes
56 Château du Pin
57 Les Chemins de la Rose
58 Parc Oriental
59 Parc Floral de la Court d'Aron
60 Le Potager Extraordinaire
61 Jardin des Olfacties
62 Parc Floral d'Apremont
63 Prieuré Notre-Dame d'Orsan
64 Arboretum National de Chèvreloup
65 Château de Chenonceau

66 Château de Villandry
67 Jardin Botanique de Tours
68 Jardins de la Chatonnière
69 Château de Valmer
70 Arboretum des Grandes Bruyères
71 Arboretum National des Barres
72 Parc Floral de la Source
73 Roseraie de Pithiviers
74 Château de Bussy-Rabutin
75 Arboretum de Pézanin
76 Jardin Botanique de la
   Ville et de l'Université
77 Château de la Roche-Courbon
78 Arboretum de Balaine
79 Jardin-verger de Malicorne
80 Jardins de Cordès
81 Palais Idéal du Facteur Cheval
82 Château de Touvet
83 Parc de la Tête d'Or
84 Jardin Botanique 'La Jaÿsinia'
85 Labyrinthe-Jardin des Cinq Sens
86 Manoir d'Eyrignac
87 Jardin Botanique de Bordeaux
88 Château de Gaujacq
89 Bambouseraie de Prafrance
90 Jardins de la Fontaine
91 Jardin des Plantes de Montpellier
92 Jardin Méditerranéen de Roquebrun
93 Jardin Exotique de Ponteilla
94 Jardin Alpin du Lautaret
95 Les Colombières
96 Villa Ephrussi de Rothschild
97 Jardin Botanique de Menton
98 Jardin Exotique de Monte Carlo
99 Jardin Japonais

NORMANDIE

1. Château de Brécy
14480 Saint-Gabriel-Brécy

Stand at the back of the Château de Brécy and look at the formal gardens stretching up over five terraces. Nothing appears to have changed since it was built in the late 17th century. It is so old, indeed, that the design comes from renaissance Italy. The truth is, however, that only the walls remain from the 17th century and the pavilions from the 18th: the rest was remade by Jacques de Lacretelle in the 1960s and has been embellished by the present owners since 1992. Brécy is, nevertheless, one of the most beautiful and satisfying gardens in Normandy.

The spacious, gentle climb up the terraces takes you through a neat box-edged parterre, past a terrace devoted to *berceaux*, and another to ornamental water-tanks, to the pavilions on the top terrace. The steps and balustrading are topped by handsome stonework swags, urns and lions. Topiary shapes, Versailles cases and clipped box, yew and hornbeam add substance. Smaller gardens, full of interesting plants, lie off to one side, while the terraces themselves are intelligently planted in harmonious colour combinations: blue thistles and perovskias with white *Romneya coulteri*, for example, around the water-tanks. On the château itself is that most perpetual of climbing roses, 'Madame Alfred Carrière', and a curious climbing relation of the hydrangeas, *Decumaria sinensis*.

10km E of Bayeux
☎ 02 31 80 11 48 **Open** Easter–Oct Tue, Thu, Sun 2–6.30pm; also Sat in June **Size** 5ha (12ac)
Owner M. & Mme Didier Wirth
🅿 ⓌⒸ
@ babawirth@brecy.org

2. Château de Canon
14270 Mézidon-Canon

The garden at Canon was laid out at an interesting time, when the French formal style was giving way to the fashion for sinuous, natural 'English' parks. It was made between 1768 and 1786 by a free-thinking lawyer called Jean-Baptiste Elie de Beaumont, a friend of the English garden-writer Horace Walpole.

The château is small but very pretty. Statues and busts fill the lawn in front of it. The main formal garden lies behind and runs gently down to a formal lake, also set off by statues and herms. Woodland walks peppered with follies surround it: the main cross-axis cuts across the top of the lake, running between the *Temple de la Pleureuse* (Temple of Mourning) and a Chinese kiosk. But the best part of Canon is a unique series of thirteen small, high-walled gardens known as the *chartreuses*. These are said to date back to the time when Canon was a charterhouse and each monk tended his own walled plot but, in fact, Elie de Beaumont built them to ripen his fruit trees. Six are linked by archways along a straight path that runs from the entrance through to a small seated statue of Pomona. Each garden is planted with tall, late-summer plants that line the path along its length, including rudbeckias, heleniums, asters and dahlias. The view through the arches is one of the defining images of French gardening today.

20km SE of Caen ☎ 02 31 20 05 07
Open Easter–Jun 2–6pm weekends & pub hols; Jul–Sep daily (except Tue) 2–7pm **Size** 12ha (30ac)
Owner Mézerac family
🅿 ⓔ 🍴 ⓌⒸ ♿ 🏠
@ chateaudecanon@aol.com

The central walk through the *chartreuses* is a unique feature of the charming and historic garden of Château de Canon.

3. Château de Vendeuvre

14170 St-Pierre-sur-Dives

Vendeuvre is an extensive and fascinating garden to visit. Much has been made or restored to a high standard in recent years. The main gate frames a very pretty château (1750, made with pale stone) with a large, simple formal garden in front. Behind the house, small box parterres descend quickly to a sizable formal lake. On the far shore, you can see arches of clipped yew containing statues – except that, when you get round there, the statues turn out to be painted wood, the first of many surprises in this extra-ordinary modern garden. For, although there are traces of an older garden – notably a system of straight canals – most of the garden dates from the 1990s.

Off to one side, a fine old avenue of limes leads to a pyramid and thence to the *Jardin des Surprises* – a series of water jokes, inspired by renaissance Italy, which are set off by sensors as you move around the garden. They are, however, benign tricks, because the water is directed away from your path. A red-lacquered Chinese bridge squirts water from the beaks of pigeons and doves into the canal on either side as you pass over dry-shod. A tree bursts into a cloud of water jets. Elsewhere are a

Château d'Harcourt's modern multicoloured bedding recalls the *mille fleurs* plantings of classical French gardens.

grotto decorated with 200 000 ornamental shells, two small mazes, a 300-year-old plane tree and a lot of good colour planting. The standard of maintenance is exemplary.

30km SE of Caen ☎ 02 31 40 93 83 **Open** May–Sep daily 11am–6pm; Apr, Oct–Nov Sun & pub hols 2–6pm **Size** 12ha (30ac) **Owner** Comte Guy de Vendeuvre ⓟ ▢ ⑪ ⓦⓒ ♿ ⊞ ▦ Ⓦ www.vendeuvre.com ＠ chateau@vendeuvre.com

4. Château d'Harcourt

14220 Thury-Harcourt

The castle at Harcourt was destroyed by the Germans in World War II. Trees grow out of the rubble that was once its ground floor. But in the 1960s the late Duc d'Harcourt started to re-create the spirit of French renaissance gardens by planting a summer garden (*Jardin d'Eté*) with copious quantities of mixed summer bedding. You reach it by a long walk (look out for periwinkles in winter and cyclamen in autumn) from the castle. The narrow borders take the shape of a quincunx that fills a small valley. The corners are marked by standard hibiscus plants, but almost everything else is either a tender perennial or a tropical annual: dahlias, impatiens, cleomes, petunias, heliotrope, sweet-scented

stocks, zinnias, cosmos, ageratum, verbenas and much else – it varies from year to year. A pretty sight in full flower.

On edge of town, well signed ☎ 02 31 79 72 05 **Open** Apr–Sep daily 2.30–6.30pm **Closed** Sat in Apr **Size** 1ha (2½ac) **Owner** Duchesse d'Harcourt ⓦⓒ

5. Jardin des Plantes de Caen

5, Place Blot
14000 Caen

Caen's botanic garden (Jardin Botanique de la Ville et de l'Université de Caen) is well maintained and full of interest – a mixture of public amenity park and botanic garden. Most of the present design (like the best trees) dates back to the 1810s and 1820s, though the central glasshouse complex was built in the 1860s. The systematic beds include a section devoted to the flora of Lower Normandy, both wild species (953 of them) and those of horticultural origin. The magnificent glasshouses have a fine collection of exotics, including National Collections of *Peperomia*, *Rhipsalis* and *Cryptanthus* species. Palms and oleanders are put out for the summer.

The garden as a whole boasts over 5000 taxa; the extensive rock-garden alone has 1500

The water-squirts on top of Château de Vendeuvre's Chinese bridge point away from the passer-by.

Richly coloured bedding, including ornamental forms of maize, surrounds the systematic beds at Jardin des Plantes de Caen.

taxa and the pharmacological garden a fine collection of 600 medicinal plants. Even the geraniums in the summer bedding displays are each carefully labelled. The many good trees include *Ailanthus altissima*, *Toona sinensis* and *Albizia julibrissin*.

In town centre, NW end
📞 02 31 30 48 30 **Open** Times very variable, but open for most of day all year **Size** 3.5ha (9ac)
Owner City of Caen
🏠 🍴 🚻 ♿
W www.ville-caen.fr

6. Jardins de Plantbessin
14490 Castillon

Even within Normandy, so full of good modern gardens, Plantbessin stands out as exceptional for its tight design and splendid plantings. Though attached to a big house, the gardens are designed to be seen from the nursery behind, a self-contained display garden of plants for sale.

The gardens are laid out as two sequences of smaller gardens. The newer (*c.* 2000) is a series of formal gardens with a remarkable variety of hedges of different shapes and types, lots of topiary (all evergreen,

mainly box and yew), a very strong sense of design and direction, and many inspirational incidents. The style is Japanese at the top and almost baroque at the bottom. The older suite of gardens (started in 1986) is intensely planted in the modern English style, with a very wide variety of plant material used in interesting ways. The long, mixed border is a model of its kind. Many unusual shrubs are pruned into uncommon shapes, like variegated weigelas and philadelphus clipped into mounds. The plantings are thick, dense and luxuriant, but well controlled, and much is crammed into a small space without making it seem stuffed, just full of colour and shape. The standard of maintenance throughout is very high.

10km SW of Bayeux
📞 02 31 92 56 03 **Open** Mid-May–Oct Mon–Sat 2.15–5pm; also Sun July–Aug **Size** 1ha (2½ac) **Owner** Saint-Beuve family
P 🚻 ♿
@ sbch@waika9.com

7. Jardins du Pays d'Auge
Route des Trois Rois
14340 Cambremer

The Jardins du Pays d'Auge are a very pretty sequence of gardens in a gentle, fertile Normandy valley. All have been made since 1994, cut out of traditional farmland, and new areas are constantly taken into cultivation. Maturity comes from old hedgerow trees like *Acer campestre* and ashes, as well as the large number of Normandy farm buildings that have been brought from derelict farms and reconstructed here.

The names of the various gardens – the Green Room or the Garden of the Sun, for example – do not adequately convey the variety and ingenuity of the design and plantings. The main axis is a sequence of mixed borders backed by yew hedges, with bulk coming from clipped shapes of box and yew within the borders. Here, and throughout the gardens, the plantings are thick and the colour schemes impressive. The purple border is especially good. The rose garden, hornbeam arches and cloister garden are all unusually successful and imaginative.

Outside the long sequence of gardens are rather more relaxed areas, linked by close-cut lawns, which invite exploration up the slopes on either side. There are woodland areas, too, densely underplanted with ferns, hostas and Solomon's seal. Everywhere is a very wide choice of well-labelled plant material. These are one of the most impressive of the many excellent gardens made in Normandy in recent years.

The excellent modern gardens at Plantbessin combine firm structure with imaginative English-style plantings.

The Jardins du Pays d'Auge incorporate old Norman farm buildings into an inspirational modern design.

Well signed in village
☎ 02 31 63 01 81 **Open** Jul–Aug
daily 10am–6.30pm; May–Jun &
Sep–mid-Nov daily (except Sun)
9am–12 noon & 1.30–5.30pm
Closed Last 2 weeks Sep **Size** 3ha
(7ac) **Owner** Jacques Noppe
🅿 ▣ WC ♿ 🎁 🚾 🚾
Ⓦ www.cambremer.com
@ noppe@wanadoo.fr

8. Arboretum d'Harcourt
27800 Brionne

The 19th-century conifers are the most conspicuous feature at Harcourt and can be seen from afar. The arboretum was planted from 1833 onwards by the Société Royale d'Agriculture around the ruined walls of an astonishingly large mediaeval castle. The collection is not among the largest in France – there are about 500 different species and cultivars – but the stunning mediaeval architecture makes Harcourt a very worthwhile place to visit. The drive passes between two vast cedars of Lebanon (*Cedrus libani*) and along an avenue of mixed conifers of every sort, including pines, firs, spruces, sequoias and cryptomerias. The trees within the old walled garden include a very large and beautiful *Fagus sylvatica* 'Faux de Verzy', with tortuous,

zigzagging, pendulous branches. The castle keep, turned into a family house in the 18th century, is completely dwarfed by an enormous *Platanus × acerifolia*, thought to date from the 17th century.

8km SE of Brionne ☎ 02 32 46 29 70
Open Mar–mid-Nov daily (except
Tue) 2–6pm; mid-Jun–Sep 10.30am–
6.30pm **Size** 20ha (49ac) **Owner**
Département de l'Eure
🅿 ▣ WC ♿
@ harcourt@cg27.fr

Nineteenth-century conifers surround the mediaeval castle keep of Arboretum d'Harcourt.

9. Musée Claude Monet
84, Rue Claude Monet
27620 Giverny

Claude Monet's garden has been completely restored in recent years and looks better now than it did when the artist was alive. The most famous part is the Water Garden, reached by a subway under the road at the bottom of the original garden. But first you must pass through the astounding *Clos Normand*. This is made up of rectangular beds, fairly plainly designed. It is their planting that lifts them into the stratosphere of excellence: Monet liked his flowers bold, bright, exciting and profuse, with concentrated colours and interesting textures. And he expected every season to bring changing colours and new compositions. Much of the planting today is with annuals and bedding plants, ranged in long, overlapping rows. The effect is brilliant. Here, too, is the arcade of climbing roses edged with nasturtiums that spread across the broad, arcaded walk until they cover the surface and hide the gravel.

The Water Garden is fed by a willow-hung arm of the river Epte. Monet bought it in 1893, started work in 1895 and soon made the pond and the

Claude Monet's garden of water lilies is set off by a Japanese bridge and a large weeping willow.

Japanese Bridge. He planted wisterias, azaleas, iris, paeonies, bamboos, tamarisks and ferns; all have been faithfully restored in recent years. Here Monet came to muse, dream and paint the interplay of water, light and colour. From this spot he painted his first *Waterlilies* studies, which led to his marvellous *Décorations* series. Do visitors to Giverny enjoy fresh insights into his painting? Yes, most certainly. As the poet Gustave Kahn remarked in 1904, 'It helps you understand how such a gardener became a great painter.'

4km E of Vernon on D5
☎ 02 32 51 28 21 **Open** Apr–Oct daily (except Mon) 9.30am–6pm
Size 11ha (27ac) **Owner** Académie des Beaux-Arts 🅿 🚾 ♿ 🏛 🎫
🅦 www.fondation-monet.com/uk/ informations/index.html
@ contact@fondation-monet.com

10. Château de Martinvast
50690 Martinvast

Martinvast is a late 19th-century woodland garden in the English style. Many of the trees and older shrubs are now in their prime, especially ancient rhododendrons and tall conifers. It is a large and tranquil park for walking in – the owner recommends six discretely arrowed trails, so you should allow lots of time. You will see green woodpeckers in the woodland glades and black swans on the vast water-lily lake. The trachycarpus palms and banana plants show how mild the climate is.

The garden's recent history is a story of recovery from the destruction of the 1987 hurricane. The new plantings have much horticultural interest: young trees, modern rhododendrons and azaleas, and hydrangeas for late-summer interest. A young woodland of monkey puzzle trees (*Araucaria araucana*) is underplanted with camellias. Though a great pleasure to walk through at any time, it is undoubtedly best in May when the rhododendrons are in full flower (some of which are planted in the family's racing colours).

The substantial wooded park of Château de Martinvast is a place of tranquil beauty throughout the year.

5km SW of Cherbourg
☎ 02 33 87 20 80 **Open** Daily
8am–12 noon & 2–6pm **Closed**
Weekend mornings & Sat in winter
Size 60ha (148ac) **Owner** Comte
Christian de Pourtalès
🅿 ♿
@ de-pourtales@wanadoo.fr

11. Jardins du Château de Vauville
50440 Beaumont-Hague

The château at Vauville incorporates the remains of the original 12th-century donjon (or dungeon), but the subtropical gardens, started in 1947, are entirely modern. The intention has always been to see how many tender exotics, mostly from the southern hemisphere, can survive the exposed conditions on a rocky headland above the sea. Some 500 are now permanently established, and the list is growing. The structure and wind defences come from thickly planted barrages of cordylines, yuccas, bamboos, escallonias and *Cupressus macrocarpa*, all of them evergreen plants that filter the wind so that others can thrive in their lee. These include tree ferns, beschornerias, echiums, cacti, gunneras, amaryllis, senecios, aloes and dimorphothecas. A small stream has been dammed to provide damp conditions for crinums, osmundas and aquatics. Design is entirely second only to the climatic possibilities of individual plants. The results are fascinating.

15km W of Cherbourg
☎ 02 33 10 00 00 **Open** 2pm onwards. Guided tours only: weekends in Apr; daily Jul–Aug; Tue, Fri, Sat & Sun May–Jun, Sep–Oct **Size** 4ha (10ac) **Owner** Pellerin family
🅿 🖼 🍴 ♿ 🎁 ⛲
🆆 www.jardin-vauville.fr
@ jbotvauville@wanadoo.fr

12. Jardin des Plantes de Coutances
50200 Coutances

The Jardin des Plantes at Coutances was originally a private garden that was given to the municipality as a public park in 1852 and laid out in its present form shortly afterwards. It is an excellent example of the high standards that even small provincial towns set themselves in France.

A palm-lined staircase leads down from the town centre. Italianate terraces are set off by English-style lawns, with shrubby thickets, handsome trees, fountains and a maze. There is nothing rare, but there are nonetheless grand specimens of *Cedrus libani*, *Quercus ilex*, fern-leaved and copper beeches, and tulip trees. The whole garden is maintained to a high standard, and the bedding is both structured and lavish. It has the usual collection of sentimental statuary: best of

Jardin des Plantes de Coutances boasts hardy palms, bright bedding and high standards of maintenance.

all is a modern sculpture of Admiral Tourville, the 17th-century Maréchal de France, glaring down a long double alley of standard roses and bright bedding as if he were the *genius loci* of the garden.

In town centre, below cathedral square ☎ 02 33 76 55 55 **Open** Daily 9am–8pm **Closes** 5pm Oct–Mar **Size** 1.5ha (4ac) **Owner** Town of Coutances 🅿 ♿

13. Château de Miromesnil
76550 Tourville-sur-Arques

The 17th-century château at Miromesnil is very beautiful: simply proportioned Henri IV on one side and ornately Louis XIII on the other. The novelist Guy de Maupassant was born here in 1850. The *cour d'honneur* (the entrance courtyard) is flanked by panelled walls – bricks and stone have been used to create ornamental outlines on the surface. They are well covered by clematis, fruit trees and repeat-flowering climbing roses. Behind the house is a grass parterre enclosed by brick walls. Pillars frame a beech avenue that stretches away into the distance. But the chief

A barrage of tender exotic plants runs between the château of Vauville and the open sea.

Brilliant colours in the *potager* at Château de Miromesnil exemplify the modern French style of planting.

attraction at Miromesnil is the kitchen garden to the side of the house, first laid out in the 1970s by Comtesse Bertrand de Vogüé. It is thickly planted with vegetables, fruit and lots of roses, dahlias, colourful bulbs, annuals and perennials. There is colour at every season.

French commentators say that Château de Miromesnil is a very English garden, but it is actually the epitome of the modern French style of planting for colourful effect. Here, and in many other Normandy gardens, the French creative genius is supremely exemplified.

Off N27, 7km S of Dieppe
☎ 02 35 85 02 80 **Open** Apr–Oct daily 2–6pm; Jul–Aug 10am–1pm **Size** 10ha (25ac) **Owner** Société Civile D.B.M.
🅿 🚾 ♿ ⊞
🔲 www.chateaumiromesnil.com

14. Jardin Botanique de Rouen
Ave des Martyrs de la Résistance
76100 Rouen

Rouen's botanic garden is maintained to a very high standard as a public amenity. The bedding is among the best in France – the beds are lavishly planted with beautiful and spectacular colour effects. Palm trees and oranges are put out in *caisses* for the summer.

Among the many fine mature trees are a tall *Parrotia persica* near the glasshouses and a handsome male *Ginkgo biloba*. The glasshouses include a palmhouse (1880) and an orangery (1809). Elsewhere are a garden of scented plants, an extensive rose garden, a large iris garden, a rock-garden, an enormous collection of dahlias, a display of water plants and a collection of medicinal plants. There are some 5000 taxa in the open air and 3000 under glass. But ignore these statistics, if you wish, and just enjoy the garden for its colourful displays.

In southern part of city
☎ 02 32 18 21 30 **Open** Daily 8.30am–dusk **Size** 10ha (25ac) **Owner** City of Rouen
🔲 🚾 ♿

15. Le Bois des Moutiers
76119 Varengeville-sur-Mer

Le Bois des Moutiers is a chunk of late-Victorian England that has slipped its moorings and floated across to the coast of Normandy. The Arts and Crafts house and some of the garden's structure were designed by Edwin Lutyens for Guillaume Mallet in 1896: Gertrude Jekyll advised on the plantings. Jekyll's spirit hovers over the deep double borders that frame the short drive down to the front door. Their opulent beauty alone makes a visit worthwhile. Lutyens's genius is seen in the pergola that cuts across the entrance drive and is tricked out with ever-receding ornamental arches. Brick paths, yew hedges and topiary increase the sense of Englishness.

The park below the house runs down to a woodland garden, lushly planted with rhododendrons, azaleas, camellias, pieris, eucryphias and hydrangeas, with distant views of the sea. Though perhaps best in May, Le Bois

Dahlias and bananas are among thousands of colourful plants bedded out for the summer at Jardin Botanique de Rouen.

The clever perspectives of Edwin Lutyens's design at Le Bois des Moutiers are immediately apparent.

des Moutiers has colour and interest at every season. Corinne Mallet's nearby Shamrock garden (in Route du Manoir d'Ango) is also worth seeing in late summer; it has France's largest collection of hydrangeas, on which she is a world expert.

10km W of Dieppe
☎ 02 35 85 10 02 **Open** Mid-Mar–mid-Nov daily 10am–noon & 2–6pm **Size** 12ha (30ac) **Owner** SCI de la Haie des Moutiers 🅿 ▣ 🆆🅲 ♿ 🏛

16. Le Clos du Coudray
76850 Etaimpuis

Many consider Clos du Coudray the best new garden made in France during the last 20 years. It crams remarkable variety of designs and plants into a small area, yet never feels small-scale or crowded. The owner is a well-known horticultural journalist and the construction and planting of the garden have been avidly followed by his admiring readers.

It is a garden in constant expansion, and every addition brings new plaudits for its clever design, lavish planting and creative originality. Some of the highlights include: a very extensive rock-garden, a rose garden successfully underplanted with herbaceous

plants, a mixed border with hot colours, a hosta garden, a cool woodland area (look out for the National Collection of epimediums), many good water gardens, and borders for dahlias, hemerocallis and purple plants. The latest addition is a grass garden – surely the best in Europe – where the grasses are supplemented by a few flowering plants, like kniphofias, to give colour.

Clos de Coudray is in every way an exceptional garden, with more than 8000 different plants, all well cultivated and clearly labelled.

3km S of Saint-Victor-l'Abbaye
☎ 02 35 34 96 85 **Open** Apr–Oct daily 10am–7pm **Size** 1.5ha (4ac) **Owner** Jean le Bret
🅿 ▣ 🆆🅲 ♿ 🏛 👤
🆆 www.leclosducoudray.com
@ jardin@leclosducoudray.com

17. Parc Floral William Farcy
1, Rue Jehan Veron
76550 Offranville

This attractive and instructive garden was built on a flat pitch in the 1990s as part of a leisure complex on the edge of Offranville; William Farcy was the local man who turned the idea into a reality. The garden makes extraordinarily good use of a particularly long and thin site, and depends for its effectiveness upon clever design and well-chosen plants. Parts are formal (like the rose garden near the entrance, where richly planted box-edged compartments are framed by climbing roses on iron hoops), but most of the garden has a fluid design. Features include a herb garden, purple garden, lake and waterfall, hydrangea garden, grasses garden, walk planted

Le Clos du Coudray's pretty Norman cottage is surrounded by innumerable different gardens.

Parc Floral William Farcy is a modern garden of roses and companion plantings in box-edged beds.

with pastel shades, and a brilliant avenue of white-barked *Betula utilis*. The garden also displays a large number of narcissus, irises, paeonies, roses, hardy geraniums, willows, cornus and heathers: in short, there is always a lot to see. And it is full of good ideas for small gardens.

8km SW of Dieppe
☎ 02 35 85 40 42 **Open** April & 1–15 September daily (except Tue) 2–6pm (10am–6pm weekends & pub hols); May–Aug daily 10am–7pm; 15–30 Sep weekends only 10am–6pm **Closed** Tue May–Jun **Size** 2.5ha (6ac) **Owner** Mairie d'Offranville ⓟ ⓔ ⓦⓒ ♿
@ mairie.offranville.wanadoo.fr

18. Château de Bosmelet
76720 Auffay

Bosmelet is famous for its colour borders, though this is not obvious at first glance. The Louis XIII château has no formal garden, but is flanked by an exceptionally long (2.4-km) avenue of trees that stretches into the distance on both sides of the house. Everything is green and flowerless, a traditional expression of might.

All the action is in the beautiful, brick-walled garden off to one side, along a very handsome avenue of tall and ancient limes. Little remains

of the old plantings, except a huge bay tree, a clump of lilacs and a centennial *Magnolia* × *soulangeana*. But the opulence of the annual plantings is remarkable: colourful fruit, flowers, vegetables and herbs are grown ornamentally (and very effectively) on a large scale. This is an art at which the French surpass; at Bosmelet it is practised at the highest level. You enter along the short central axis, with mixed borders on either side and a pool at the centre. The really stunning effects are in the outer beds, where immaculate rows of flowers and vegetables maintain the colour throughout the season. The owners call it their 'rainbow *potager*'. The purple forms of cabbage, kale and

onions are especially beautiful. There is much to ponder and learn from at Bosmelet and even more to enjoy and admire.

Signed from Montreuil-en-Caux on D92 ☎ 02 35 32 81 07 **Open** June–Sep Fri–Sun & pub hols 1–7pm; Jul–Aug daily **Size** 60ha (148ac) **Owner** Baron Robert de Bosmelet ⓟ ⓦⓒ ♿ 🏛 ⓕ
ⓦ www.chateau-de-bosmelet.fr
@ bosmelet@laposte.net

PICARDIE

19. Château de Chantilly
60500 Chantilly

It is the sheer size of the flat and spacious garden at Chantilly that is most impressive: it was designed by Le Nôtre for the Prince de Condé in the 1660s and 1670s. The walk up from the entrance takes you to Constable Anne de Montmorency, an equestrian statue with the best overview of the design. Below lies a vast system of water parterres and fountains, fed by a grand central canal and tricked out with a few statues and urns, but otherwise wide open and unadorned. The system's source is the river Nonette, a tributary of the Oise.

The temptation is to view this watery expanse from the terrace and then turn back to

The art of colour grading is practised at the highest level in Château de Bosmelet's *potager*.

Château de Chantilly's extensive park and charming *hameau* are matched in beauty and importance by its spacious water gardens.

Eastern edge of town
☎ 03 44 62 62 60 **Open** Daily
10am–7pm (10.30am–5pm in
winter) **Size** 115ha (284ac)
Owner Institut de France
🅿 ⊡ 🍴 🚾 ♿ ⊞ ⊞
🅦 www.chateaudechantilly.com

20. Jardins de Valloires
80120 Argoules

The gardens at Valloires are large, well designed, well kept and full of horticultural interest. They have been developed by Gilles Clément since 1987 and now have the largest collection of shrubs in France (a remarkable achievement when you consider that the soil is chalk with a pH of 8.5 – hence, no rhododendrons, azaleas or camellias).

It is best to follow the suggested route, which takes you up from the entrance and round a small wood to a sudden viewpoint where the formal garden, stretching 200 m to the Château, opens out before you along the bottom of a broad, flat valley. Immediately below is a modern architectural garden, then comes a long expanse of mown grass, a colourful rose garden and the château itself, built from the ruins of a Cistercian abbey dissolved during the Revolution. Along one side is a lengthy avenue of Mount Fuji cherries (*Prunus serrulata* 'Shirotae') with a long, pale, pastel-coloured

visit the florid château (largely the work of the Duc d'Aumale in the 1870s), but this is a mistake. There are yet two huge gardens to discover beyond the water gardens: a 1770s so-called *anglo-chinois* garden to the right and an English-style park to the left. Both are excellent and worth exploring. The former has a hamlet of Normandy-style cottages in it; one of the buildings is a water-mill that doubles up as a restaurant (its speciality is *Crème Chantilly*). The 1820s English park is a delight, a wonderful place to idle away an afternoon and dream. Ancient plane trees are supplemented by tall, mature swamp cypresses (*Taxodium distichum*), planted in the 19th century and now the dominant trees in the landscape, with colonies of tuberous roots at their base. Eye-catchers include

a temple to Venus (modelled on the Temple of Vesta in Rome), a massive rock-garden, a series of fountains, a 'bridge of the worthies', and an *Île d'Amour* (Island of Love) presided over by a statue of Cupid.

The formal gardens at Jardins de Valloires stretch along the valley bottom towards the old abbey.

border below, cut into compartments by low hedges. Above the cherries, the ground rises steeply to a series of island beds planted to celebrate and display the diversity of the plant kingdom. The collections of lilacs, prunus, viburnums, spiraeas and deutzias (120 taxa) are especially good, but there are unusual species and cultivars of ornamental shrubs and trees everywhere. Some of the beds are colour-themed – blue or yellow, for example – and excellent use is made of groundcover: the massed plantings of *Geranium endressii* and *Aegopodium podagraria* 'Variegatum' are especially effective. The rose garden has a formal design and the roses are pale-coloured repeat flowerers, interspersed with colour-coded herbaceous plants, herbs, annuals and bulbs to ensure that the beds have a long season. Down at the lowest level is a very long, formal bog garden, with many forms of willow, poplar, alder, bamboos and much else.

The gardens are probably at their best in June when the roses flower for the first time.

12km S of Montreuil
☎ 03 22 23 53 55 **Open** Mid-Mar–mid-Nov daily 10am–6pm **Size** 8ha (20ac) **Owner** Le Syndicat Mixte pour l'Aménagement de la Côte Picarde 🅿 🄴 🍴 🆆🅲 ♿ 🎁 ⚲
🆆 www.jardinsdevalloires.com
@ contact@jardinsdevalloires.com

ÎLE DE FRANCE

21. Parc de Bagatelle
75016 Paris

Bagatelle is the best garden in Paris; some consider it the best in France. It is the garden with everything: a beautiful setting, a rich history and an amazing display of horticultural excellence.

The château was built in 1777 by the Comte d'Artois (later Charles X) as the result of a wager with his sister-in-law, Queen Marie-Antoinette, that he could finish it within 64 days. It has a pretty formal garden set with roses (edged with a fine collection of paeonies) and exquisite views across English-style parkland to majestic trees. Nearby is a stylised Chinese garden, made by the Scot Thomas Blaikie in the 1780s, with lakes, rock-faces, caverns, waterfalls, bridges, brooks and Chinese pavilions.

The formal garden was laid out in the 1840s by the English Marquess of Hertford, who also built the handsome orangery. This leads to the formal rose garden – a Jean-Claude Nicolas Forestier masterpiece – where 1200 different cultivars of every type are cultivated in a design of particular beauty. It is exceptionally lovely during its peak season at the end of May. Climbing roses are wound around huge, 5-m tall pillars; a series of pergolas and rope-swags accommodate further climbing roses; and many modern roses are grown as standards in box-edged beds, with a different, contrasting cultivar close beneath it. Every detail is an inspiration, and the standard of maintenance incomparable.

Nearby is a long suite of smaller gardens dedicated to irises, clematis, herbaceous plants and the art of bedding. Here, too, the horticultural interest and standards of cultivation are unmatched.

Bois de Boulogne, western Paris
☎ 01 40 71 74 60 **Open** Daily 8.30am–7pm **Size** 24ha (59ac)
Owner City of Paris
🅿 🄴 🍴 🆆🅲 ♿ 🎏
🆆 www.paris.fr

22. Jardin des Plantes de Paris
57, Rue Cuvier
75005 Paris

The Jardin des Plantes in Paris is France's premier botanic garden, founded in 1635. The view as you enter is immensely grand: a straight, flat avenue stretches 480 m, with a central alley laid out as a sequence of rectangles, stylishly planted with colourful bedding plants.

But this is a garden to learn about *all* plants. Four thousand taxa are displayed in the systematic beds known as *l'école de botanique* (the school of botany). Here, too, are ecological collections devoted to aquatics, woodlanders and littoral plants. The alpine garden is very impressive: 2000 taxa are cultivated in whatever conditions they require to flourish, from bogs to rocky crevices. Some are sheltered in winter to mimic the effect of snow cover in the wild. The iris garden is extremely pretty in May, when some 150 cultivars flower; it forms part of the collection of 600 herbaceous plants in a 'Dutch' garden. A small rose garden has a collection of species and tells

ABOVE: Parc de Bagatelle's collection of irises is popular with visitors in mid-May, just before the massive display of roses.
OPPOSITE: The wisteria avenue is one of many striking horticultural features at Parc de Bagatelle – the best garden in Paris.

There is an immense variety of horticultural interest in the historic Jardin du Luxembourg.

the history of rose breeding. There are good trees throughout, including several introduced here for the first time in Europe. Near the rose garden, a false acacia (*Robinia pseudoacacia*) from North America dates back to 1636; it is represented not by the original tree, but by suckers that came up from the roots once it had died.

The Mexican house, recently restored, has a landscaped collection of cacti and succulents from around the world. The Winter Garden is the name of the tropical house, with a dense collection of palms, ferns, jungle evergreens and economic plants. But throughout the garden and its glasshouses, you will find a wealth of plants to interest you and enjoy.

SE part of central Paris, near Gare d'Austerlitz 📞 01 40 79 56 01 **Open** Daily 8am–dusk **Size** 26ha (64ac) **Owner** Muséum National d'Histoire Naturelle
🅿 🚾 ♿ 🎁
Ⓦ www.mnhn.fr

Jardin des Plantes de Paris is France's premier botanic garden. It has a long history and a rich collection of plants for visitors to study and enjoy.

23. Jardin du Luxembourg
Bvd St-Michel
75006 Paris

The Jardin du Luxembourg is one of the liveliest public parks in Paris, but also full of historical interest, satisfying design features, good statues and welcome greenery. It is attached to the Palais du Luxembourg, built in the 1610s and now occupied by the Senate.

The present formal garden was spaciously laid out in the 1790s by Jean François Chalgrin, the architect of the *Arc de Triomphe*. Its box-edged parterres are filled with flowers in summer, and the large *bassin* at the centre is much loved by children with toy boats. Further away is a wooded English garden with winding walks, rolling lawns, a very large number of statues of literary heroes and some well-established fine trees, including ginkgos, tulip trees and paulownias. Within it lies the *verger*, where over 200 different apples and pears are grown and Paris's only inner-city apiary supports some 20 hives. The famous orangery was built in about 1840 and is used to overwinter orange trees, palms, oleanders and pomegranates.

Centre of Paris (left bank)
C 01 42 34 23 89 **Open** Daily 8am–dusk **Size** 23ha (57ac)
Owner French Senate
P ⊡ WC ⟐

24. Jardins des Tuileries
Place de la Concorde
75001 Paris

The Tuileries gardens were first laid out by Le Nôtre in the 17th century around the royal palace of the Louvre. They have been completely revamped since 1995 by two teams of modernist architects. The basic outlines remain, but the make-over includes flower gardens designed by Jacques Wirtz, a display of 18 pieces by Aristide Maillol (the usual nudes, but they fit in quite well) and the insertion of a modern sculpture garden with pieces by Max Ernst, Henry Moore and others. The main axis is aligned with the *Place de la Concorde* and the *Arc de Triomphe* beyond. Some say the overall effect is disrespectful of the past; others that it is insufficiently contemporary. But it is a very pleasant and lively space to promenade in the very heart of Paris.

Les Serres d'Auteuil's glasshouses, including the cacti house, are a pleasure to visit in winter.

Centre of Paris **C** 01 40 20 50 50
Open Daily 7.30am–dusk **Size** 30ha (74ac) **Owner** Musée du Louvre
WC ⏹ ⟐
W www.monum.fr

25. Les Serres d'Auteuil
3, Ave de la Porte d'Auteuil
75016 Paris

The glasshouses at Auteuil started life as the municipal nurseries for Paris, charged with producing bedding plants for public parks and gardens. Since the great palmhouse was restored for opening to the public in the 1990s, the complex has emerged as one of the most fascinating and rewarding gardens in Paris.

You enter between the two sober classical buildings that house the offices and encounter a spacious, elegant, sunken parterre. Its walls are decorated with ornamental pilasters and masks by Rodin. Beyond is the majestic palmhouse (a model of late 19th-century elegance), with two wings flanking a central dome where flourishes a tall *Phoenix canariensis*. Japanese carp occupy the pool; tropical birds inhabit a pretty *volière*. Here and in a further dozen glasshouses are some 6000 different taxa, many grown in quantity for ornamental effect. There are significant collections of orchids, begonias, bromeliads, ferns, azaleas, cacti, carnivorous plants, caladiums and palms. It is worth a visit at any season but comes into its own as a winter garden.

Outside are pretty themed gardens (Japanese, herb, English) and some good trees, including lagerstroemias and a massive *Pterocarya stenoptera*.

W of city centre, near Porte d'Auteuil **C** 01 40 71 74 00
Open Daily 10am–5pm (6pm in summer) **Size** 6.5ha (16ac)
Owner City of Paris **WC ⟐**
W www.paris.fr

26. Parc des Buttes-Chaumont
Rue Botzaris
75019 Paris

When Napoléon III laid out the Parc des Buttes Chaumont in 1862–67, it was still on the edge of an expanding city of Paris. Baron Haussmann

In the heart of Paris old trees, new borders and modern sculptures come together well in the Jardins des Tuileries.

The Temple of Sibyl at the top of a cliff-face is the focal point of Parc des Buttes-Chaumont's dramatic garden.

was one of the architects of this popular recreational park with panoramic views over the *Sacre Coeur*. He dynamited what remained of a limestone quarry and built a reproduction of the Temple of Sibyl at Tivoli on top of a 30-m cliff. You reach it over an iron suspension bridge, 63 m long. A waterfall cascades down the cliff-face into a lake. A cavern left over from quarrying was turned into a grotto with large stalactites.

The park is richly planted in the Victorian landscape style and many of the original trees are now in their prime, including a *Platanus orientalis*, *Zelkova carpinifolia* and an elegant weeping *Sophora japonica* 'Pendula'.

NE edge of city ⬛ 01 40 71 74 00
Open Daily 7am–8.15pm (later in summer) **Size** 25ha (62ac) **Owner** City of Paris 🄿 ⬛ ⬛ ⬛ ⬛
⬛ www.paris.fr

27. Parc Floral de Paris
16, Route de la Brasserie
Bois de Vincennes
75012 Paris

The Parc Floral was made to accommodate the 3rd Paris *Floralies Internationales* in 1969. It is now very much a family park, with children's play areas, a butterfly garden, puppet shows, mimes, concerts and open-air museum art exhibitions of contemporary artists.

Its horticultural interest, however, remains high. There are water gardens, an iris garden, a Mediterranean garden, a four-seasons garden, a bonsai garden, a pinewood underplanted with rhododen-drons and, best of all, the *Vallée des Fleurs*, where bulbs, annuals and bedding plants are displayed with great artistry in expansive, modernist swathes. Visitors of a retiring nature will find it quieter to visit on weekdays.

SE of city centre ⬛ 01 55 94 20 20
Open Daily 9.30am–dusk **Size** 28ha (69ac) **Owner** City of Paris
🄿 ⬛ ⬛ ⬛ ⬛ ⬛
⬛ www.parcfloraldeparis.com
@ cominfo@parcfloraldeparis.com

28. Parc Monceau
Bvd de Courcelles
75017 Paris

Philippe Egalité first laid out the Parc Monceau in the 1770s in the fashionable *anglo-chinois* style. The painter Louis de Carmontelle was the architect and he designed a riot of follies in every style from every epoch. The main survivor is the *Naumachie*, a lake such as was used for mock sea-battles in Roman times. Part of it is surrounded by a semicircular colonnade of Corinthian columns, some broken, some missing.

The Scottish landscaper Thomas Blaikie gave the park a make-over in the 1790s, making Monceau less formal, more relaxed and more English in style. Napoléon III converted it into a public park and his favourite architects Jean-Charles Alphand and Gabriel Davioud intensified its romantic feeling. During the 1860s they added a stylish bridge, a grotto and a cascade. Later, in the 20th century, came marble statues of such famous composers as Chopin and Gounod, and writers like Guy de Maupassant. The trees include a 30-m sycamore, a bulky *Platanus orientalis* nearly 200 years old, and fine purple beeches. The modern plantings are very colourful: there are masses of roses and some of the most extensive bedding in Paris.

The garden of Parc Floral de Paris was laid out for the *Floralies* in 1969, and its horticultural interest remains very high.

LEFT: The colonnade around the *Naumachie* is the highlight of the beautiful and historic Parc Monceau.
RIGHT: Château de Champs's rococo-style formal gardens were restored by the Duchênes in the 1890s.

NW of central Paris
☎ 01 40 71 74 00 **Open** Daily
7am–8pm (dusk in summer) **Size**
6ha (15ac) **Owner** City of Paris
🅿 🖼 🚾 ♿
📺 www.mairie8.paris.fr

29. Château de Champs
31, Rue de Paris
77420 Champs-sur-Marne

The original gardens at
Champs were laid out
by Claude Desgots in the
1710s, but destroyed in the
French Revolution. The
present ones were made in
a reproduction baroque style
by the Duchênes for Comte
Louis Cahen d'Anvers in
the 1890s.

The rococo-style broderies
are very elegant and extensive,
though dully planted with
groundcover roses for easy
maintance. They run down to
a pool and fountain called the
Bassin de Scylla and then
further down the hillside to
a massive statue of Apollo's
horses. Two green parterres –
mown grass in simple
quincunxes – lie to the sides
and are named after the statues
of Apollo and Diana at their
centres. Beyond is an English-
style park, maintained in a
relaxed manner for public
recreation. Here and there are
huge yew trees, said to be relics
of the original 18th-century
gardens. The whole complex
is a model of how to preserve
and show off a large historic
garden on a limited budget.

20km E of Paris ☎ 01 60 05 24 43
Open Daily (except Tue) 9.45am–
5.30pm (6.30pm in summer); mid-
Nov–Jan weekends only **Size** 85ha
(210ac) **Owner** The State
🅿 🚾 ♿ 🖼

30. Château de Fontainebleau
77300 Fontainebleau

The gardens around the royal
palace of Fontainebleau are
greatly reduced in splendour,
but still of great historical
interest and enjoyable to visit.
Le Nôtre's great parterre – the
largest *jardin à la française* he
designed – has recently been
partially reconstructed: its box-
edged beds filled with colourful
bedding give a fair impression
of its original splendour. The

Diana the huntress, attended by badly
controlled dogs, at Château de
Fontainebleau.

shady lime tree alleys that
surround it were added by
Napoléon I in the 1800s.

The large formal lake is the
oldest feature in the garden as
a whole – it is all that remains
of the Italian gardens laid out
by François I on his return
from the Italian wars in the
1530s. Its carp are said to be
even older, dating back to the
time of St Louis in the 13th
century. Beyond is the wooded
jardin anglais, made in 1812.
Diana's garden is named for
the spectacular fountain, made
in 1603, of the goddess of
hunting surrounded by four
urinating dogs. It owes its present
picturesque landscape to
Napoléon I and Louis-Philippe.

Town centre, 70km SE of Paris
☎ 01 60 71 50 70 **Open** Daily
9am–6pm (5pm in winter & 7pm
in summer) **Size** 200ha (494ac)
Owner The State (Ministry of
Culture) 🅿 🖼 🚾 ♿ 📷 🖼
📺 www.musee-chateau-
fontainebleau.fr
@ contact.chateau-de-
fontainebleau@culture.fr

31. Château de Vaux-le-Vîcomte
77950 Maincy

Louis XIV so admired the
château and gardens that
his finance minister Nicolas
Fouquet made at Vaux-le-
Vîcomte that he arraigned
him for embezzlement and
confiscated the property. They
are still the grandest privately

owned gardens in France. Le Nôtre was the architect, and Vaux-le-Vicomte was his first masterpiece.

The main gardens extend for 1.5 km, but such is the design that, wherever you stand, the château dominates the layout. It is a statement of power. Henri Duchêne remade the parterres in 1923 and they now have a pattern of complex broderies that exemplify the elegance of late baroque aesthetics. Clipped box hedges and trim yew cones are set in red gravel. Flowers are confined to the vast urns that lead down towards the formal lake and grottos at the far end. But Le Nôtre uses the perspective to suggest that these grottos are much closer than they really are; only when you approach the lake (whose function is to reflect a view of the château when you look back) do you realise that the grottos are, in fact, over 200 m away on the other side of a long, transverse canal, sunken so that you do not see it from the house.

The estate is enormous; it is well worth hiring an electric buggy to take you quickly round the garden to its furthest extremes. There is much, too, to admire in all the details – statues, masonry, urns, pools, flowers and woodland avenues.

5km E of Melun ◖ 01 64 14 41 90
Open Apr–mid-Nov daily 10am–6pm **Size** 33ha (81ac)
Owner de Vogüé family
🅿 ▣ 🍴 ♿ & 🏠 ▦
🆆 www.vaux-le-vicomte.com
@ chateau@vaux-le-vicomte.com

32. Château de Ferrières
77164 Ferrières-en-Brie

The park at Ferrières was once considered the most beautiful in France. Its glory has now faded, but it is still worth seeing. It was laid out in 1855 by Sir Joseph Paxton for Baron James de Rothschild. Paxton also designed the opulent square château in the Italian renaissance style. The short drive, some 200 m, is lined with formal gardens, giant urns, sunken pools and pretty seasonal planting. Make for the monumental staircase at the back of the house, guarded by *couchant* lions. Its handsome urns are planted with geraniums in summer. Below are massive butts of trim yew topiary and a meadowy lawn leading down to the lake and far into the distance.

Paxton laid out the park in the English style, creating vistas and landscapes with large clumps of blue Atlas cedars, wellingtonias, hornbeams and copper beeches. On the edge of the lake is an *Île d'Amour* (Island of Love), set among tufa grottos and planted with trees of weeping habit – ash, lime and sophora. Much has been lost over the years, but the giant redwood (*Sequoiadendron giganteum*), planted by Napoléon III on 16 December 1862, has survived even the hurricane of December 1999.

24km E of Paris ◖ 01 64 66 31 25
Open May–Sep daily 2–7pm; Oct–Apr Sun 2–5pm **Size** 125ha (309ac)
Owner Fondation Marie-Hélène et Guy de Rothschilde
🅿 🆆🅒 & 🏠
🆆 www.chateauferrieres.com
@ acceuil@chateauferrieres.com

33. Château de Breteuil
78460 Chevreuse

The spacious formal gardens at Breteuil were beautifully laid out by the Duchênes in the 1890s in the French baroque style. The central pool reflects the elegant Louis XIII façade of the house. Beyond the formal garden, a broad, grass ride lined with rhododendrons runs down to a small fountain and into the woods. A long walk takes you past some ancient chestnuts (*Castanea sativa*) with Solomon's Seal and helleborines underneath and meadowsweet around the lake. The less energetic will enjoy the old walled garden,

ABOVE: The plutocratic Rothschilds' love of style, opulence and scale are discernible still at Ferrières.
OPPOSITE: The extensive baroque gardens at Château de Vaux-le-Vicomte were one of the most successful 20th-century restoration projects.

LEFT: There are plans to restore more detail to the simple but historic layout of Château de Dampierre's gardens.
RIGHT: All of Château de Groussay's follies, including this Chinese pagoda, are no older than the 1950s.

which has recently been renamed the '*Jardin des Princes*' to commemorate Edward VII, who negotiated the *Entente Cordial* here while Prince of Wales. It has been charmingly converted into a designed combination of fruit, vegetables and flowers, with a central tunnel of climbing roses and other ornamentals. A box-hedged millennium maze made around a pretty little gazebo occupies the terrace below.

This strange little fountain lies beyond Château de Breteuil's formal garden, on the edge of the wood.

8km SW of Chevreuse
☎ 01 30 52 05 02 **Open** Daily 10am–sunset **Size** 70ha (174ac) **Owner** Marquis de Breteuil
🅿 🚻 🏧 ♿ 🏛 🖼
Ⓦ www.castle-france.com
@ contact@breteuil.fr

34. Château de Dampierre
78720 Dampierre-en-Yvelines

Le Nôtre laid out the gardens at Dampierre for the first Duc de Luynes. The formal gardens still cover a large area behind the château, but are now put to grass. The focal point is a semicircular pool fed by a spring, with a statue and ride up the hillside beyond. Off to one side are avenues of young horse-chestnuts around a large expanse of water, with a romantic dilapidated pavilion on an island at the end. Beyond the pavilion is the proper *Jardin Romantique*, an area of mown grass and serpentine paths set with rhododendrons, shrub roses and weeping willows, bordering a canal where yellow water lilies (*Nuphar lutea*) have taken over. The prevailing atmosphere is of delicious melancholy, but this, alas, will probably not survive the pending restoration.

4km W of Chevreuse on D91
☎ 01 30 52 53 24 **Open** Apr–mid-Oct daily 11am–6pm **Size** 60ha (148ac) **Owner** de Luynes family
🅿 🚻 🏧 ♿
@ contact@chateau-de-dampierre78.com

35. Château de Groussay
Rue de Versailles
78490 Montfort-l'Amaury

The garden, parkland and follies at Château de Groussay were all made by the Mexican mining millionaire Carlos de Béistegui. Most of them are in the style of the 18th century and compare well with genuine period pieces. Only a fortune founded on foreign investment could support such extravagances in depressed post-war France. Nevertheless, they bring to life the excitement, invention and fun of the rococo.

Béistegui started work on the grounds in 1950. The

prescribed route passes first through a new *potager* and then along a series of pretty horticultural enclosures in the modern English style. The first real eye-catcher is the Tartar tent, a large sheet-copper structure enamelled in blue and white stripes, with an interior covered in 10 000 blue Delft tiles. Down by the lake, you pass over a Palladian bridge, from which the outline of a pyramid on a rocky ledge is reflected. The Chinese pagoda occupies another part of the lake below the château while, at the end of an avenue in the woods, with spacious distant views, stands a tall observation column wound round by a spiral staircase. This is undoubtedly the most ambitious landscape park of modern times and the sequence of follies is a joy to discover.

On Route de Versailles, 2km from town centre ☎ 01 34 86 94 79 **Open** Apr–Sep Wed–Sun 10am–7pm **Size** 30ha (74ac) 🅿 ♿ 🏪 @ contact@groussay.com

36. Château de Versailles
78000 Versailles

Versailles is France's most visited tourist attraction. It is still the one historic landscape in France that no modern visitor should omit. The gardens and park, like the palace itself, were statements of royal power and wealth. They are still a symbol of French national grandeur. They were copied by kings and princes all over mainland Europe and, when you go there, it is easy to understand why.

Versailles is vast in concept and execution. You will need a long time to take it all in: hire an electric buggy to get round and buy a map. The first guide for visitors was written by King Louis XIV himself. The Sun King determined that the main axis should run from east to west, sunrise to sundown. The fountain of Apollo shows the sun god's chariot rising from the sea. Apollo's mother, Latona, dominates the central fountain.

Louis XIV's garden architect was André Le Nôtre. Throughout the 1660s he flattened hills, filled in marshes and planted thousands of trees. He brought the main axis down to the Neptune fountain and up to the Grand Canal, 3.5 km long. He made the fountains – 32 of them – that flow on Sunday afternoons in summer.

Versailles's gardens are also sublimely beautiful, full of architectural details of extraordinary originality. When you come across them for the first time, hidden gardens like *Bosquet du Dauphin* and the *Bosquet de la Girandole*, will make you gasp at their loveliness. The statues, urns, fountains and ornamental details are of the highest order, a treat for the eye. So is the architecture of the 13-m high orangery, where tender trees and shrubs in Versailles cases are protected in winter. The neat hedges of hornbeam, lime and field maple and the trellis work are further joys. Walk round the side of the palace

The scale of Château de Versailles's layout is a statement of royal and national power.

The statues, urns and vases at Versailles are chosen for their dramatic effect, both individually and *en masse*.

and admire the flower-filled parterres on either side. Ponder the bronze statues around the formal pools that represent the rivers of France. Then take off down into the *bosquets*, left and right of the main ride, and explore.

Louis XIV's shyer successors made additions to the park at Versailles on its north side: there is a separate entrance off Boulevard St Antoine.

The present gardens of the *Grand Trianon* were built mainly in the late 18th century – parterres, broderies, box hedges, yew cones and bright bedding – but there are plans to restore them to Le Nôtre's original layout.

Queen Marie-Antoinette built the *Petit Trianon* in 1774 and the model village called *Le Hameau* (the Hamlet) ten years later. Both have gardens laid out in the *anglo-chinois* style, with a romantic landscape of winding paths, lawns, lakes and tall trees. The rustic buildings are very charming in a slightly stagy way. Think of Marie-Antoinette milking the cows, while Dr Guillotin sets to inventing the guillotine.

25km SW of Paris **C** 01 30 83 78 00
Open Daily 7am–sunset **Size** 100ha (247ac) **Owner** The State
P E T WC ♿ ♨ ▥
W www.chateauversailles.fr

37. Château de Courances
91490 Milly-la-Fôret

Courances is one of the best examples of a renaissance water garden in France. The flat site on sandy soil is impressive for its spacious simplicity: it is a beautiful and thought-provoking landscape to visit. The approach is along a broad driveway, edged by a double canal and avenues of plane trees planted in 1782. The house was built in 1628 and given a face-lift in the late 19th century. It is contained within a formalised moat; stone dolphins spew water from the sides. It is perhaps most charming when the rambling roses trained around the edge are in flower. The Duchênes, father and son, made improvements between 1899 and 1914, and added the

box broderies behind the house. The view from the back of the château is iconic: long avenues, enclosed by high hedges of box, stretch out in the form of a *patte d'oie*. The broad central avenue holds a 250-m long formal lake, called *Le Grand Miroir*, in which the house is charmingly reflected. Elsewhere are other canals, formal lakes (one decagonal in shape) and a 'long water'.

For horticultural interest you need to visit the pretty Japanese garden, off to one side, made by the English designer Kitty Lloyd-Jones in the 1910s and replanted in the 1950s. Here are Japanese maples, pruned pine trees, weeping sophoras and thick underplantings of hellebores, hostas and much else – a complete contrast to the grand water garden.

The Anglo-Japanese garden in Château de Courances is an exotic contrast to the classical correctness of its park.

Geometric shapes, box hedges, good colour plantings and wacky-tacky sculpture at Domaine de Saint-Jean-de-Beauregard.

4km N of Milly 01 64 98 41 18 or 01 40 62 07 71 **Open** Apr–Nov Sat, Sun & pub hols 2–6pm **Size** 75ha (185ac) **Owner** Marquis Jean-Louis de Ganay

www.courances.net

info@courances.net

38. Domaine de Saint-Jean-de-Beauregard

91940 Les Ulis

There is only one thing to see at St-Jean-de-Beauregard – a large, walled garden, formally laid out in the 17th century and thickly planted in recent years with fruit and vegetables of every sort, with areas for colourful herbs, flowers and annuals. Four paths lined with trained pear trees lead to a pool at the centre. Along the walls are climbers like roses and beds with mixed plantings, though one is devoted to red-flowering currants. The garden is also full of home-made sculptures and bizarre scarecrows. The soil is light and sandy, and the standards of cultivation are good. The rest of the estate is rather run down, though there is a small parterre (not visitable) in front of the house, some nice young magnolias, a magnificent pigeon-house and avenues of horse-chestnuts. The estate is famous for its annual international *Fêtes des Plantes*.

28km SW of Paris 01 60 12 00 01 **Open** Mid-Mar–mid-Nov Sun & pub hols 2–6pm **Size** 20ha (49ac) **Owner** de Curel family

www.domsaintjeanbeauregard.com

info@domsaintjeanbeauregard.com

39. Château de Malmaison

Ave du Château

92500 Rueil-Malmaison

Only 5 ha remain of the 700-ha park that once surrounded Malmaison in the days of Empress Josephine. It is approached along a short drive but, if you duck through to the right-hand side, you enter a small rose garden – roses are the plants with which the Empress is most associated. The planting resembles the way roses were placed around the edge of formal lawns 200 years ago, but the roses are all modern. Josephine grew hers in pots under glass; unfortunately her fine conservatories have all disappeared.

Château de Malmaison: the Empress Josephine imagined her husband, Napoléon, as a new Apollo.

Beyond the house is an English-style park laid out before the then First Consul's wife bought the estate in 1799. The famous 'Marengo cedar' was planted to celebrate the news of Napoléon's first great victory over the Austrians in 1800. The garden is poorly maintained and largely of historic interest, but it is worth reflecting how many plants flowered here for the first time in France, including the tree paeony and the dahlia.

On western outskirts of Paris 01 41 29 05 57 **Open** Daily (except Tue) 10am–12.30pm & 1.30–5pm (6pm in summer) **Size** 5ha (12ac) **Owner** The State

www.chateau-malmaison.fr

40. Musée Albert Kahn

14, Rue du Port

92100 Boulogne-Billancourt

Albert Kahn (1860–1940) was an extraordinary figure – a banker, philanthropist, internationalist and Utopian. His gardens are an expression of his many interests.

There are about twenty gardens: Achille Duchêne designed the first one, a trellised *potager* and fruit garden, but later developments were Kahn's own work. Best known, and quite unique, is the blue garden, where blue cedars and spruces are underplanted with purple rhododendrons – especially cool and refreshing when they flower in May. Kahn's favourite was the Japanese garden, made by Japanese gardeners as

The Japanese garden at Musée Albert Khan reflects Khan's interest in oriental religion and his desire to promote world peace.

a tribute to his interest in Buddhism and Shintoism. But there is much more to see and ponder: a 'French' garden with climbing roses and hornbeam hedges, an 'English' garden, a Vosges forest garden, a rock-garden, and a bog garden are among the leading features. It was fairly common 100 years ago to create gardens of different styles within a large garden: the Villa Ephrussi de Rothschild is another good example. What distinguishes the Jardin Albert Kahn was Kahn's passionate belief that his garden could contribute to world understanding.

Western Paris, near Pont de Saint-Cloud ☎ 01 55 19 28 00 **Open** Daily (except Mon) 11am–6pm (7pm in summer) **Size** 4ha (10ac) **Owner** Département des Hauts-de-Seine 🅿 🍴 🚾 ♿ 🎁 🖼 🕸 http://membres.lycos.fr/cobalt03/bienvenu.html

41. Parc de Saint-Cloud
92210 Saint-Cloud

Le Nôtre laid out the magnificent gardens at Saint-Cloud in 1671 for the Duc d'Orléans, Louis XIV's only brother. The estate was later acquired by Queen Marie-Antoinette and became a favourite palace of the rulers of France until it was burnt down by the Prussians in 1870.

As always with the best French formal gardens, it is the scale of the design that is most pleasing to visitors. Above the site of the former palace, the Grand Perspective stretches in a straight line for over 2 km, across the orangery terraces, up the statue avenue, over the pool with 24 fountains and out along avenues of horse-chestnuts, square-cut at about 10 m. Across the valley are the earthwork outlines of earlier terraces, now abandoned, and a 19th-century English-style park.

Below the palace lies the Grand Cascade, a spectacular display of late 17th-century hydraulic expertise, powering a sequence of canals, fountains, water-staircases, statuary, jets, cascades and pools. Everywhere are good displays of bedding, with standard roses and urns, frothing with geraniums, in summer.

The whole park is presently undergoing restoration, which will make it even more enjoyable to visit. It is popular at weekends, but often almost empty of visitors on weekdays.

Avenues of clipped orange trees in Versailles cases are put out for the summer at Parc de Saint-Cloud.

Formality surrounds Parc de Sceaux's château; downhill are spectacular waterworks.

SW edge of city **C** 01 41 12 02 90
Open Daily 7.30am–dusk **Size**
460ha (1136ac) **Owner** The State
P ⊟ ⊪ WC ⅋ ▦
W www.domainedesaintcloud.fr

42. Parc de Sceaux
92330 Sceaux

Le Nôtre started to lay out the grand historical grounds at Sceaux for Jean-Baptiste Colbert, Louis XIV's finance minister, in 1670. The château is 19th century, built in the Louis XIII style to replace the original, destroyed during the French Revolution.

The approach to the château is along a double avenue of clipped limes, 10 m high. Recently restored formal gardens run down behind the house – neatly clipped yew cones, grass parterres, round *bassins*, seasonal bedding and hedges of yew and box, all very regular, simple and well done. Towards the bottom is a large, round pool on a terrace known as the *Terrasse des Pintades*, which forms part of the main transverse axis. Here you look down on the *Grande Canal*, the largest of the water-axes. Nearer the château is a secondary sequence of water gardens, remade in the cubist style in the 1930s, reusing some

bronze spouts designed by Rodin. The long, narrow cascade is called the *Allée des Cascades* and runs down to a large octagonal lake with a 10-m high fountain at its centre. Restoration continues: the impressive orangery has already reopened and work is now underway on the cascades.

Sceaux is a magnificent place for walking but, as with all Paris's old royal parks, the integrity of the landscape is compromised by tower blocks for social housing on its edges.

10km SW of Paris **C** 01 46 61 95 96
Open Daily 8am–dusk (7am in summer) **Size** 160ha (395ac)
Owner Département des Hauts-de-Seine
P ⊟ WC ⅋
W www.parc-de-sceaux.net

43. Roseraie du Val-de-Marne
Rue Albert Watel
94240 L'Haÿ-les-Roses

The rose garden at l'Haÿ – the prettiest in all Europe – was laid out in 1899 for Jules Gravereaux, a rich businessman who founded the Bon Marché chain of department stores. Edouard André, the designer, prescribed a tightly geometric layout, with a mix of stylish swags, pylons, archways, pillars, trellis work and tunnels draped with climbers and ramblers. It is a clever design – as well as stunningly beautiful – because it makes the garden seem much larger than it is.

The garden is entirely given to roses and nothing else – 16 000 bushes, representing over 200 species and 3000

Roseraie du Val-de-Marne is France's premier rose garden. Its central feature is a trellised semicircle swathed in 'Alexandre Girault' roses.

cultivars, most of them dating back to before 1950. Sections are devoted to collections of the different types of rose – Gallicas and Hybrid Perpetuals, for example – but most are planted for sheer effect, usually in neat box-edged beds. Others are grown as half-standards, or elegant, tall weepers. Many are tied onto rope swags, some running low to the ground. The famous trellis above the rose-theatre is hung with the Barbier rambler 'Alexandre Girault'. Everywhere are variety and ingenuity, colours and scents, charm and profusion. You cannot fail to be cheered and exhilarated by its panache, neatness and intense, romantic beauty.

5km S of Paris, off D126 or N20
☎ 01 43 99 82 80 **Open** Mid-May–mid-Sep daily 10am–8pm **Size** 1.7ha (4ac) **Owner** Département du Val-de-Marne 🅿 ▣ 🆆🅲 ♿
🆆 www.cg94.fr/nature/espaces_verts/parcs_departementaux/parcsf.htm

LORRAINE

44. Jardin Botanique du Montet
100, Rue du Jardin Botanique
54600 Villers-lès-Nancy

Nancy's botanic garden dates back to 1758, but moved to its present site in 1974. It sees its purpose – education and conservation – more clearly than many older establishments but is also laid out to attract and please visitors.

The design is fluid: only the rose garden has a formal outline. Large areas are given to plants of horticultural interest that were bred in Lorraine. There are fine collections of irises, paeonies and lilacs, a good dahlia garden and lots of rhododendrons, azaleas, camellias and acid-loving plants. Also worth seeing are the arboretum (mainly of northern hemisphere trees and shrubs), the collection of poisonous and medicinal

plants, and the alpine and systematic gardens. There is much to admire and learn about plants here.

The five modern glasshouses are good, too. They are interconnected, so you can walk through them as a sequence. The first is for aquatics and epiphytes, where *Victoria amazonica* has pride of place. Then come a tropical house (where economic plants like cacao are grown), a tropical rainforest house, a cacti and succulent house and one devoted to the conservation of threatened plants from tropical regions.

In new city, 1km E of Palais Ducal
☎ 03 83 41 47 47 **Open** Daily 9am–12 noon & 2–5pm **Closed** weekend mornings **Size** 20ha (49ac) **Owner** Conservatoire et Jardins Botaniques de Nancy 🅿 🆆🅲 ♿
🆆 www.cjbn.uhp-nancy.fr
@ pedagogiecjbn@grand-nancy.org

45. Jardin d'Altitude du Haut-Chitelet
88400 Xonrupt-Longemer

This handsome alpine garden has been developed since 1966 as an adjunct to

the Montet botanic garden in Nancy, but doubles up as a very attractive tourist destination. It lies at an altitude of 1226 m on the Route des Crêtes, the military road built by the Germans in 1914–18. It is charmingly laid out with large outcrops of rock, gravel areas, streams, pools, meadows and woodlands, so that it can accommodate the many different cultivation requirements of alpine plants. There are a complete display of the natural flora of the Vosges and large collections of plants from all over the world. Gentians, campanulas and ferns mix happily with lilies, orchids, dwarf willows and insectivorous plants – a total now approaching 3000 taxa. The high standard of maintenance adds to the pleasure of a visit.

On D430, near Col de Schlucht
☎ 03 29 63 31 46 **Open** Jun–Sep daily 10am–12 noon & 2–6pm (5.30pm in Sep); but 10am–6pm Jul–Aug **Size** 1.5ha (4ac) **Owner** Conservatoire et Jardins Botaniques de Nancy 🅿 ▣ 🆆🅲 ♿
🆆 www.cjbn.uhp-nancy.fr
@ pedagogiecjbn@grand-nancy.org

A *Colchicum* species: the range of plants at Jardin d'Altitude du Haut-Chitelet guarantees interest throughout the season.

Saverne's historic rose garden should be combined with a visit to its high-level botanic garden.

ALSACE

46. Jardin Botanique du Col de Saverne
67700 Saverne

Saverne's botanic garden was founded in 1931 to cultivate examples of the local flora. From the start, there was an emphasis upon medicinal plants and mountain plants from rocky habitats and high meadows. Local specialities include a hybrid between *Rosa villosa* and *R. alpina* that occurred in the uplands of Lorraine. The garden has a fine collection of alpines, peat-lovers and pharmacological plants and has recently added a display of aquatics. There is a small arboretum and a good number of ferns. Its lawns have no fewer than 20 species of self-sown wild orchids growing in them. The garden is probably at its most colourful in June, when the roses in Saverne's historic *Roseraie* are also at their peak.

On Col de Saverne, N4 towards Phalsbourg ☎ 03 88 91 21 00 **Open** May–mid-Sep weekends & pub hols 2–6.30pm; Jul–Aug weekdays 9am–6.30pm. Further details tourist office 03 88 91 80 47 **Size** 2.3ha (6ac) **Owner** l'Association des Amis du Jardin Botanique du Col de Saverne
🅿 🚻 ♿

47. Parc de l'Orangerie
Ave du Président Edwards
67000 Strasbourg

This is the best public park in eastern France. Its origins date back to Le Nôtre, who is said to have laid out some of the avenues, but the original Orangery was built in 1804 and the park substantially redesigned in 1835. It now has all the attributes of a public park – a zoo, a mini-farm, restaurants and rowing on the lake, as well as very fine displays of bedding, a good rose garden and ancient trees.

Strasbourg's botanic garden (28, Rue Goethe) is also worth seeing: its 3.5 ha boast 6000 taxa, including a good alpine garden, arboretum and glasshouses.

In old city, next to Palais de l'Europe ☎ 03 88 61 62 88 **Open** Always **Size** 26ha (64ac) **Owner** City of Strasbourg 🅿 🚗 🍴 🚻 ♿ (Strasbourg's botanic garden: ☎ 03 90 24 18 65 **Open**: summer daily 8am–7.30pm; spring & autumn 8am–6pm [10am weekends]; winter 8am–12noon & 2–4pm but **closed** Sun mornings)

BRETAGNE

48. Château de la Roche Jagu
22260 Ploëzal

La Roche Jagu is a large and solid mediaeval castle. Its gardens, set out in 1990, aim

Wicker-bound raised beds in the mediaeval-style garden of Château de la Roche Jagu.

to give an idea of how a mediaeval garden might have looked. Purists point out that it is wildly unhistorical, since many of its most effective plants (camellias, agapanthus, hemerocallis and penstemons) were not introduced until much later. Nevertheless it is fun to visit and very popular with tourists. The mediaeval designs take in a vineyard, a collection of medicinal herbs and raised beds encased in woven willow, surrounded by picket fences and hedges of bay, box and laurustinus. The plants include irises, pinks, roses, paeonies, lavenders, hops and honeysuckles. Outside the enclosures are long strips of useful crops, including linen and buckwheat. And the position is splendid, high on a steep hill opposite a bend on the estuary of the River Trieux.

20km N of Guingamp
☎ 02 96 95 62 35 **Open** Daily **Size** 30ha (74ac) **Owner** Conseil Général des Côtes-d'Armor
🅿 ▣ ⓦⓒ ♿ ▦ ▤
Ⓦ www.cotesdarmor.fr
@ chateaudelarochejagu@cg22.fr

49. Kerdalo
22220 Trédrazec

Peter Wolkonsky, a Russo-Polish prince, bought the farm at Kerdalo in 1965, attracted by the granite soil and mild climate of the Brittany coast. He gentrified the house and turned its valley into a botanical treasure house of captivating beauty.

Wolkonsky was an artist and applied his skills to the design and plantings. The layout is an eclectic mixture of styles – romantic, oriental, baroque, Italian, and jungly in a Rousseau-esque manner. Grottos, fountains and statues enliven the design. Pretty climbing plants cover the house – honeysuckles, roses, ceanothus, holboellia and clematis. The terrace looks down to an enclosed garden and a series of bog gardens, lakes and ponds made by damming the stream.

The hillside opposite Kerdalo's house was lavishly colour-planted on the grand scale.

Most of the plants, chosen for their form and colour, were obtained from English nurseries or arrived as gifts from English friends. Wolkonsky was not afraid to plant in masses: the hillside opposite the house has scores of yellow cypresses and the yellow-flowered evergreen *Cornus capitata*. Other notable specimens – all of them selected for their unusual shapes and forms – include the large-leaved *Magnolia delavayi*, the handkerchief tree (*Davidia involucrata*), monkey puzzles (*Araucaria araucana*), cork oaks (*Quercus suber*) and enormous specimens of *Pittosporum tenuifolium* 'Silver Queen'.

Kerdalo is now owned and gardened by Wolkonsky's daughter and English son-in-law, both of them even more knowledgeable horticulturists than the Prince. The future is bright.

2km N of Tréguier
☎ 02 96 92 35 94 **Open** Mid-Jul–end Aug daily, except Sun; Apr–June Sat & Mon 2–6pm **Size** 18ha (44ac) **Owner** Isabelle Wolkonsky-Vaughan
🅿 ▣ ⓦⓒ ♿

50. Jardin Exotique de Roscoff
B.P. 54
29682 Roscoff

Roscoff's Jardin Exotique is the best garden in northern France to see tender exotic plants, especially those from the southern hemisphere. These plants survive here due to the garden's unusually mild microclimate. There are few plants, for example, that would be hardy in Paris. It was created in 1987 as a tourist attraction and now houses over 3000 different plants.

Tender yuccas from Mexico, stately *Isoplexis* from Madeira and the Canary Islands are mixed with mimosas (*Acacia* spp.) from Australia, as well as banksias, eucalyptus (*Eucalyptus ficifolia* is brilliant in summer), leptospermums, grevilleas and callistemons. Echiums have naturalised,

Jardin Exotique de Roscoff: more tender exotic plants grow on this small, rocky outcrop than in any other garden in northern France.

especially *E. pininana*. The collections of *Protea*, *Kniphofia*, *Melianthus* and Restionaceae are certified by the *Conservatoire des Collections Végétales Spécialisées*. Throughout the garden are proteas, banksias, yuccas, palms and agaves, bulbs and ornamental flowering plants. There are innumerable mini-habitats, from barren rocks planted with cacti, aeoniums, agaves and aloes to shady valleys where streams keep tree ferns cool. Dense evergreen plantings protect the site from wind.

A granite outcrop, 18 m high, offers magnificent views of the many small islands in the bay of Morlaix and across Roscoff to the Île de Batz. Even the website is a model of excellence.

On N Britanny coast, SE of town centre **C** 02 98 61 29 19 **Open** Jun-Sep daily 10am–7pm; April–May & October 10.30am–12.30pm & 2–6pm; Mar & Nov 2–5pm **Closed** Dec–Feb **Size** 1.6ha (4ac) **Owner** Town of Roscoff
P ▣ WC & ▤
W www.jardinexotiqueroscoff.com
@ grapes@wanadoo.fr

51. Parc de Trévarez
Route de Laz
29520 Saint-Goazec

Trévarez is an opulent neo-gothic palace, built by the super-rich James de Kerjégu in 1894. His garden took 13 years to lay out: the scale is very impressive. Around the château are extensive parterres, avenues of beech, lime and hornbeam, and a fine Italianate *bassin* with comic animals in lead. The horticultural interest is in the park-like woodland garden, very much in the late 19th-century style, with extensive ornamental underplantings.

The figures tell it all: over 300 different camellias, 400 herbaceous plants and 1000 rhododendrons – a collection recognised by the *Conservatoire des Collections Végétales Spécialisées* and which makes a spectacular display in May. Summer brings the hydrangeas and fuchsias, which carry interest into early autumn. The garden is also good for spring bulbs, Japanese maples, magnolias and roses.

The Conseil Général has just finished a major upgrade of the whole estate. It includes four new gardens in a very contemporary style: the *Jardin des Agapanthes* (Agapanthus Garden) is straightforward, but the *Jardin des Miroirs* (Garden of Mirrors), the *Jardin de l'Entropie* (Garden of Chaos) and the *Jardin 'loup, où es tu'* (loosely translated as 'now you see me, now you don't') are rather more wacky.

5km S of Châteauneuf-du-Faou
C 02 98 26 82 79 **Open** Apr–Jun & Sep daily 1–6pm; Jul–Aug daily 11am–6.30pm; Oct–Mar Wed, weekends & pub hols 2–5.30pm
Size 85ha (210ac) **Owner** Conseil Général du Finisterre
P ▣ WC & ▤ ▤ ▤
W www.trevarez.com
@ administration@trevarez.com

52. Château de Caradeuc
35190 Bécherel

Caradeuc calls itself the Versailles of Brittany. Though this is a provincial boast, it nevertheless has an extensive garden of considerable

Edouard André was responsible for the scaled-down grandeur of Château de Caradeuc's formal garden.

Colour, opulence, plant interest and sheer style put Parc du Thabor among France's greatest public parks.

charm, beauty and interest that was redesigned by Edouard André in about 1900. The granite house appears at the end of a short avenue of lime trees. Between the drive and house is a large *jardin à la français*, thinly planted with floribunda roses in the 1960s style. A long, straight *allée* runs off to the side. Ignore it and make for the front of the house, where the spectacular main formal garden opens out to the left. It is no longer planted with bedding plants but the garden's superb structure is intact, with umbrella-shaped, variegated hollies and yews along the sides. It leads up to a commanding statue of Diana the huntress and beyond, past further garden buildings to a viewpoint overlooking the Rance valley. The views behind the house are also wide and distant. Mossy benches and lichen-encrusted statues remind us that Brittany is famous for its soft, mild climate.

30km NW of Rennes **Open** Easter–Sep 2–6pm weekends & pub hols; but Jul–Aug daily noon–6pm **Size** 40ha (99ac) **Owner** Marquis de Kernier **P WC & ⊞** @ caradeuc@free.fr

53. Parc du Thabor
35000 Rennes

Parc du Thabor is a typical French hybrid – part municipal park, part botanic garden – but wholly delightful to visit. Every part is maintained to a high standard. It dates back to the 18th century but has been expanded over the years. The fine mature trees, though few are labelled, include *Ginkgo biloba* and *Cedrus atlantica* 'Glauca'. There are also avenues of horse-chestnuts, oaks and limes, and a line of tall evergreen *Magnolia grandiflora*.

Spring brings extensive bulb displays (15 000–20 000 are planted every year) and fine rhododendrons, camellias and azaleas. A very good rose garden contains nearly 1000 different cultivars, mainly modern, including a large number of 'classic roses'. Climbing roses trained on swags surround the systematic beds of the botanic garden, themselves well maintained and full of interesting plants. Excellent and colourful bedding is extravagantly displayed in the so-called *Jardin Français* in front of the conservatory, some 60 000 plants every year. There are

good collections of dahlias and chrysanthemums and pleasant lakeside plantings. Parc du Thabor is a faultless example of a public amenity.

City centre **C** 02 99 28 55 55 **Open** Daily 7.30am–dusk **Size** 10ha (25ac) **Owner** City of Rennes **P ⊡ ¶ WC &** **W** www.rennes.fr @ jardins@ville-rennes.fr

54. Jardins d'Argences
50200 Saussey

The charming gardens at Argences have been entirely made since Philippe and Caroline Lecardonnel bought the 17th-century manor in 1989. They are the sort of gardens, now very fashionable in France, whose effects depend upon a combination of firm design in the French style and intimate English planting. The hedges are of yew, viburnum, euonymus and different forms of box. Clipped evergreens are also used in the borders to give structure – not just box, but also choisya, ligustrum and cloud-pruned junipers. Perhaps the most successful enclosure is the rose

LEFT: The charming formal rose garden at Jardins d'Argences is based on Edwardian models.
RIGHT: Famous author Jules Verne's centenary in 2005 was celebrated by special displays in his home town in the Jardin des Plantes de Nantes.

garden, made from an old tennis court. It is set about with box topiary, filled with David Austin roses and 'Iceberg', and underplanted with catmint, purple sage, alchemilla, lavender and geraniums. An armillary sundial fills the centre. The individual gardens at Argences are small, which makes the whole seem larger than it is. It continues to develop as the owners seek to improve it.

4km S of Coutances
☎ 02 33 07 92 04 **Open** Mid-May–mid-Oct daily 2–6pm **Size** 1.5ha (4ac) **Owner** Caroline Lecardonnel
🅿 🚾 🏛 🚻
🆆 www.jardins-argences.com
@ c.lecardonnel@wanadoo.fr

PAYS DE LA LOIRE

55. Jardin des Plantes de Nantes
15, Rue Gambetta
44000 Nantes

The Jardin des Plantes at Nantes dates back to 1807 and a *Magnolia grandiflora*
planted in that year still thrives. Other good specimens include a *Metasequoia glyptostroboides* (dating from 1955, one of the first planted in France), a fine *Torreya grandis* and a plant of × *Fatshedera lizei*, the strange intergeneric hybrid between a fatsia and an ivy that was bred by a Nantais nurseryman in 1910.

The garden's layout has the sinuous landscaped shapes of the 19th century. When the lakes and canals were excavated, the spoil was mounded to make a small hill. Another characteristic of the 19th century is the tradition of lavish bedding displays; the colour combinations are especially good. The collection of camellias, always popular in this part of France, includes some 200 ancient cultivars and over 400 modern hybrids from all over the world. The botanic parts of the garden display a good number of endemic plants of western France, and a collection of medicinal and poisonous plants. There are more treats in the glasshouses, most notably 4000 different cacti and succulents.

City centre, eastern edge
☎ 02 40 41 09 09 **Open** Daily 8.30am–6.30pm (but 5.30pm in winter & 8pm in summer) **Size** 7.5ha (19ac) **Owner** City of Nantes
🅿 🚾 ♿
🆆 www.jardins.nantes.fr
@ jardins@mairie.nantes.fr

56. Château du Pin
49123 Champtocé-sur-Loire

The 1920s Arts-and-Crafts garden around this handsome late-gothic château has been given new life over the last 20 years. Many interesting plants have been added without detracting from the highly structured design. Outside an elegant conservatory a large number of orange trees, bananas, daturas and oleanders are put out in pots for the summer. Down some steps is a lily pond (one of two), where some 60 topiary yews, clipped into many different shapes, march off into the garden. They are some of the best in France. Old yew hedges enclose a modern, double herbaceous border, carefully graded for colour effects. A so-called Persian garden has long pools

Rosa virginiana 'Alba' is among many rare and beautiful roses in Les Chemins de la Rose's fluid modern garden.

cut from turf with irises in narrow beds along the sides. Nearby is a garden planted entirely with yellow roses, against a background of lavender, acanthus and dark Italian cypresses. In the *potager* is a late-summer display of over 2000 dahlias; elsewhere are ancient trees, a collection of hydrangeas, sweeping lawns, naturalised cyclamen and a young arboretum. All is held together by the strength of the original design.

4km NW of Champtocé
☎ 06 11 68 61 81 **Open** Mid-Apr–mid-Oct weekends 2–6pm **Size** 5ha (12ac) **Owner** de la Celle family
Ⓟ ⑰ ♿
Ⓦ www.membres.lycos.fr/jardins/

57. Les Chemins de la Rose
Route de Cholet
49700 Doué-la-Fontaine

Les Chemins de la Rose is a modern rose garden, planned as a tourist attraction and opened in 1999. It also seeks to demonstrate the history of rose breeding in France, especially in the Anjou area. Its design is modern, with flowing island beds of roses of every kind, usually interplanted with clematis, shrubs and herbaceous plants, but often with other roses, too. Climbers are allowed to mound up into billowing clouds of colour or run up living props like pollarded willows. There are some 1300 different cultivars, and the number is growing every year. Some are very rare – including the white-flowered form of *Rosa virginiana*, and 'Cannabifolia' (the 'Cannabis Rose'). The collection of old roses is recognised by the *Conservatoire des Collections Végétales Spécialisées*. There is a sequence to the layout: rose types are grouped together so that you can make comparisons, but the easiest way to visit the garden – best in June – is to wander as the design takes you, through an ever-changing dream of colour, beauty and scent. The nearby municipal rose garden in the grounds of the old château in Doué-la-Fontaine is also well worth visiting.

2km SW of town centre
☎ 02 41 59 95 95 **Open** Mid-May–mid-Aug daily 9.30am–7pm; mid-Aug–mid-Sep daily 10.30am–12.30pm & 2–6pm **Size** 4ha (10ac) **Owner** Parc Zoologique de Doué-la-Fontaine Ⓟ ⬛ ⑰ ♿ ▦ ♿
Ⓦ www.cheminsdelarose.com
@ cheminsdelarose@unimedia.fr

58. Parc Oriental
49360 Maulévrier

Alexandre Marcel made the Parc Oriental around a lake between 1899 and 1913.

Parc Oriental's extensive Japanese-style garden is laid out around a large lake.

He was a celebrated Parisian architect with a passion for the orient, and had also worked for Léopold II at Laeken.

The château is now separately owned as an up-market restaurant, so the modern entrance to the gardens is some distance from the lake. It takes you along a pretty valley lined with a large number of very tall taxodiums. The park is full of symbols of Buddhism, Shintoism and Tao, but the overriding spirit is Japanese. Unlike most Japanese-style gardens of the day, the one at Maulévrier is very large. The oriental part, restored in 1987, consists of buildings in various East Asian styles and a large number of trees clipped in the Japanese cloud style – none of them Japanese in origin but all native to France (hornbeam, beech, hazel and lots of yews). There are rocky promontories, tea houses, open pavilions and a Cambodian temple with four guardian lions, brought in its entirety from the Paris Universal Exhibition of 1900.

The park is loveliest in spring when the cherries, magnolias, azaleas and wisterias flower and the Japanese maples are in young leaf. Piped oriental music and tinkling bells accompany you everywhere. Sometimes, in late summer, the whole garden is lit at night.

On southern edge of town, by river ☎ 02 41 55 50 14 **Open** Mar–Nov daily (except Mon) 2–6pm (but Jul–Aug daily 10.30am–7.30pm) **Size** 29ha (72ac) **Owner** Town of Maulévrier
🅿 ▣ 🆆 ♿ ▦
🎟 www.parc-oriental.com
@ contact@parc-oriental.com

59. Parc Floral de la Court d'Aron
85540 Saint-Cyr-en-Talmondais

Court d'Aron is a modern woodland garden, laid out around a series of shallow lakes. One of the lakes contains a large patch of the sacred Indian lotus (*Nelumbo nucifera*) – an impressive feat of horticulture at such a

Extensive and colourful carpet-bedding is a remarkable feature of Court d'Aron's garden of woods and lakes.

northerly latitude. Most of the other plantings rely on mass displays of colourful and exotic plants. The oak woodland is brilliantly lit up by swathes of bulbs in spring – crocus, narcissus and, especially, tulips. Among them are drifts of primulas, hardy geraniums, arum lilies and aquilegias. By summer, the main display comes from stretches of bright busy lizzies (*Impatiens*). Banana trees and lots of bamboos create a tropical effect. Elsewhere are

pseudo-Japanese gardens and an exhibition of bonsai. In the tropical house are orchids, bromeliads, *Tillandsia usneoides* and a small collection of carnivorous plants.

Well signed at 10km on D949 between Luçon & Les Sables d'Olonne ☎ 02 51 30 86 74 **Open** Easter–mid-Sep daily 10am–7pm **Size** 10ha (25ac) **Owner** Société Tropicalia
🅿 ▣ 🍴 🆆 ♿ ▦ 🚻
@ courtdaron85@aol.com

60. Le Potager Extraordinaire
Les Mares
85150 La Mothe Achard

Le Potager Extraordinaire is a low-budget, single-theme garden that grows as many ornamental forms of vegetable as possible. Fancy maize, variegated hops, yellow-leaved runner beans and giant sunflowers are among the subjects, and there are good collections of tomatoes (40 different varieties), courgettes and squashes. In one of the polytunnels, 30 different gourds of every conceivable size, colour and shape are grown on plants trained to the rafters; some of the longest gourds reach right down to ground level. Another polytunnel has less hardy, useful plants like manioc, loofahs, some 30 different hot

Le Potager Extraordinaire grows a large number of ornamental and edible gourds outside in late summer.

The smell of herbs in Jardin des Olfacties recalls the Mediterranean *maquis*.

CENTRE

62. Parc Floral d'Apremont
18150 Apremont-sur-Allier

Gilles de Cossé-Brissac started making the garden at Apremont in about 1970 and opened it to the public in 1976. It was an extraordinary undertaking, converting the valley below his ancestral turreted castle into an entirely new landscape and incorporating the hamlet that his grandfather had reconstructed in the mediaeval style in 1930. Brissac dammed the river Allier to make waterfalls, marshes and a series of lakes, and turned the meadows to mown grass.

Two styles dominate his creation. First, there is an English passion for horticulture – flowering trees, shrubs and herbaceous plants of every kind, many of them brought directly from across the Channel. Second, there is a series of very fine follies inspired by the 18th-century baroque, including a Turkish pavilion, a Chinese bridge (complete with pagoda) and a belvedere in the Russian neo-classical style. The White Garden, inspired by Sissinghurst in England, has white roses like 'Schneewittchen' ('Iceberg' or 'Fée des Neiges') interplanted with such white perennials as

pimentos, edible passionflowers, cotton, and the scented pea (*Phaseolus caracalla*). Elsewhere are a herb garden, some interesting soft fruit and a 'kitsch' garden brought to life by garden gnomes.

20km NW of Les Sables d'Olonne **C** 02 51 46 67 83 **Open** Jun–mid-Oct daily 10.30am–12.30pm & 2.30–6pm; but Jul–Aug 10.30am–7pm **Size** 2ha (5ac)
P ▢ WC & ⛨ ♿
W www.potagerextraordinaire.com
@ contact@potagerextraordinaire. com

61. Jardin des Olfacties
9, Rue Jean Mermoz
85220 Coëx

Coëx is a large village with little to attract the passing tourist – except this modern garden. The idea was to display plants chosen not for their flowers, form and colours, but for their scent. The best areas are below the entrance – a hillside is planted with rose beds and a well-designed herb garden with smells of lavender and curry plant (helichrysum). Look out for the olive tree – proof of the mild climate here. Below is a damp woodland, where the smells come from

underplantings of hostas, irises and azaleas. Beyond is a rather tacky Japanese-style garden (done on the cheap), a lake, a small cactus garden and lots of *Trachycarpus fortunei*. Everywhere you are tantalised by sweet smells, whose source you then seek to trace.

In village centre **C** 02 51 55 53 41 **Open** Mid-Apr–mid-Sep daily 2–7pm (but **opens** 10.30am mid-Jun–early Sep) **Size** 5ha (12ac) **Owner** Mairie de Coëx
P ▢ WC
W www.lejardindesolfacties.com
@ infos@lejardindesolfacties.com

Floral d'Apremont's modern garden combines lavish horticultural plantings (like this wisteria tunnel) with delightful rococo-style follies.

Many of the trees in the Arboretum National de Chèvreloup are still growing vigorously.

clematis, campanulas and geraniums. A 115-m-long pergola is smothered with white *Wisteria floribunda* and interplanted with pink robinias and clumps of blue *Iris sibirica* below. Trees with good autumn colour include *Pyrus calleryana*, *Malus transitoria*, *Malus toringoides* and *Nyssa sylvatica*. Other good trees are a large *Albizia julibrissin* and clumps of the Hungarian oak (*Quercus frainetto*). But the sheer profusion and variety of plants is remarkable – and the standard of maintenance very high.

15km SW of Nevers
☎ 02 48 77 55 00 **Open** Easter–Sep daily 10.30am–12.30pm & 2.30–6.30 pm **Size** 4ha (10ac) **Owner** Société Hôtelière d'Apremont
🅿 🚻 ⓦ 🚾 ♿ 🏛
ⓦ www.apremont-sur-allier.com
@ apremont-sur-allier@wanadoo.fr

63. Prieuré Notre-Dame d'Orsan
18170 Maisonnais

The gardens at the Prieuré Notre-Dame d'Orsan are a modern reinterpretation of a mediaeval garden, such as might have existed around this priory in the 15th century. They were begun in 1993 as a free interpretation of the gardens seen in miniatures and books of hours. Much emphasis is put upon using young growths of wood of various thicknesses to make raised beds, seats, fences, pergolas and frames. The features include a garden of 'simples' with medicinal plants in four raised beds, a hornbeam cloister with climbing roses (all modern), a tiny vineyard, some olives in pots, a *potager*, a fruit garden and a maze. The plantings are fairly unhistorical. Some visitors find the whole garden altogether too chichi and self-conscious. Others are moved by the mystical experience of walking in a calm, simple, spiritually charged place of quietness, where the certainties of pre-renaissance Christendom are deeply sensed.

25km W of Saint-Amand-Montrond
☎ 02 48 56 27 50 **Open** Apr–Oct daily 10am–7pm **Size** 1ha (2½ac)
Owner Patrice Taravella
🅿 🚻 🚾 ♿ 🏛
ⓦ www.prieuredorsan.com

64. Arboretum National de Chèvreloup
78150 Rocquencourt

The French national arboretum has had a mixed history. It sits next to the Trianon at Versailles and once formed part of the royal estate, but nothing remains of its historic plantings. What we see now was started in 1924, neglected between 1936 and 1960, vigorously restored after about 1965, and bashed by the hurricane of 1999. Less than half is open to visiting members of the public. This coincides largely with the collection of European trees, and excludes the very extensive groupings of Asiatic and American trees. Plantings are organised both botanically and geographically, and due weight is given to ornamental forms like horticultural selections and hybrids. Oaks, pines and sorbus are especially well represented and great thought has been given to their positioning. The arboretum as a whole is a remarkable collection; it is a pity that the entire site (and the magnificent glasshouse collections) are not open (even if only occasionally) to the public.

On N186 at NE edge of Château de Versailles ☎ 01 39 55 53 80
Open Apr–mid-Nov 10am–5pm Sat–Mon & pub hols **Size** 200ha (494ac)
Owner Muséum National d'Histoire Naturelle
🅿 🚻 🚾 ♿
ⓦ www.mnhn.fr

Swirling broderies and standard hibiscus in the modern Diane de Poitiers garden at Château de Chenonceau.

65. Château de Chenonceau

37150 Chenonceaux

Henri II gave Chenonceau to his mistress Diane de Poitiers in 1547. After his death in 1559, the king's long-suffering widow Catherine de Médicis confiscated the property and occupied it herself. This history is reflected in the two magnificent formal gardens first laid out after 1913, when the estate was bought by the Menier chocolate family and restored in the 1950s. The smaller garden, scrupulously designed around grass segments and a round pool in an early-renaissance style, is called the Garden of Catherine de Médicis. The much larger, showy garden on the opposite side of the castle, full of late-renaissance exuberance and colour, is known as the Diane de Poitiers Garden. Here the swirling santolina broderies are edged with bedding plants and *Hibiscus syriacus* cultivars are grown as standards. Both are good examples of the historical gardens that were popular in France in the first half of the 20th century.

Chenonceau is maintained to a very high standard and the estate raises some 130 000 bedding plants every year to ornament the gardens. Among the other classic tourist attractions of the Loire valley are the interesting gardens at Ussé, Amboise and Chaumont.

35km SE of Tours ☎ 02 47 23 90 07 **Open** All year 9am–7pm **Closes** earlier mid-Sep–mid-Mar **Size** 10ha (25ac) **Owner** Société Civile Chenonceau 🅿 ⬛ 🍴 🚻 ♿ 🎁 📷
🆆 www.chenonceau.com
@ chateau.de.chenonceau@ wanadoo.fr

66. Château de Villandry

37510 Villandry

Villandry is the apotheosis of the French renaissance garden – but a modern reconstruction dating from the early years of the 20th century, made by a Spanish doctor with his American wife's money. The château is genuine, dating back to the 1530s, and the main inspiration for the gardens were plans published in 1576 by the royal gardener, Androuet de Cerceau.

You enter the gardens through the largest section,

Château de Villandry is by far the finest example of a modern French renaissance garden.

the *potager*, where nine square designs tricked out in box, each with a different geometric pattern, are planted with vegetables chosen for their contrasting colours. It is an astonishing sight at any time of the year, but especially in summer and autumn when the vegetables are set off by narrow ribbons of bright annuals and bedding plants. The corners of the parterres are marked by neatly trained pear trees and arbours of trellis-work.

The *Jardin de l'Amour* (Love Garden), immediately below the château, is a parterre that depends upon its boxwood shapes for its effect. These represent allegories of love – hearts, *billets doux*, daggers, masks and fans. The colours of the bedding plants within the box compartments are charged with the sort of symbolism that the French relish (red for tragic love, yellow for jilted love).

Higher up are the music garden (more parterres), a simple water garden, alleys of boxed limes, a herb garden and a modern maze. The effects come from the size of the gardens, the variety and detail of their design, brilliant colours, the contrasts of height and level, and the exceptionally high standard of maintenance. There are over 50 km of hedges that have to be cut twice a year.

15km W of Tours ☎ 02 47 50 02 09 **Open** Daily 9am–sunset **Size** 5ha (12ac) **Owner** SCI du Château de Villandry

P ☕ 🍴 WC ♿ 🎁 ▦

W www.chateauvillandry.com

@ info@chateauvillandry.com

67. Jardin Botanique de Tours

33, Bld Tonnellé
37000 Tours

The botanic garden in Tours was founded in 1843 and the glasshouses were built in the 1890s. It is one of those wonderful French gardens that combine public amenity with botanical seriousness and very high standards of maintenance. History is represented by parterres, botany by systematic beds and a fine collection of plants, and popular tastes by magnificent displays of seasonal bedding. There is a herb garden, a heather garden, an arrangement of Mediterranean plants, a rock-garden, a display of lotuses and a spacious arboretum. Exceptional trees include a bulky, spreading *Ginkgo biloba*, planted in 1845; it is a male tree with a female branch grafted onto it. Near the glasshouses is a handsome avenue of evergreen magnolias, with bougainvilleas in Versailles cases between them. Inside the glasshouses (open afternoons only) are fine collections of cacti, succulents and bromeliads, as well as colourful exotics from all over the world.

Autumn bedding and a glimpse of the systematic beds in Tours's delightful municipal garden.

In western part of city centre ☎ 02 47 39 88 00 **Open** Daily 8am–4.30pm **Closes** 5.30pm spring & autumn; 8 pm Jun–Sep. Glasshouses open 2–5pm **Size** 5ha (12ac) **Owner** City of Tours

P ☕ 🍴 WC ♿

68. Jardins de la Chatonnière

37190 Azay-le-Rideau

La Chatonnière is a mediaeval castle that has been turned into a country house. Béatrice de Andia has been making the gardens since 1995. In fact, there are now some nine gardens around the château, and each has a fancy name like the 'Garden of Silence' or the 'Garden of Unreality'. However, they all share the same unity of style, energy and opulence: the

The stylistic effects in La Chatonnière's delightful gardens are created by large-scale planting and repetition.

This lavish and colourful bedding is only a prelude to Château de Valmer's prodigious *potager*.

whole valley is a feast of scent, colour and beauty, especially when the roses flower in early June. Vast quantities of dahlias, tulips, lilies, herbaceous plants and annuals appear throughout the garden, on the terraces, below the topiary, within the parterres, across the slopes, under the pergolas, around the white Carrara vases and into the surrounding woodland verges. Six hectares of meadows are filled with scarlet poppies in May and cornflowers in June. The *potager* – entitled the 'Garden of Prosperity' – is designed in the shape of a leaf, with paths along the veins, and planted with colourful fruit, vegetables and herbs at every season. Forget the symbolism and the clever-cleverness: these are gardens of supreme beauty. No-one could fail to be delighted and cheered by them.

3km NW of Azay-le-Rideau
☏ 02 47 45 44 40 **Open** Mid-Mar–mid-Nov daily 10am–7pm **Size** 70ha (173ac) **Owner** Béatrice de Andia
🅿 🚾 ♿ ♨
🆆 www.lachatonniere.com
@ deandia@aol.com

69. Château de Valmer
37210 Chançay

The impressive approach to such a small (but pretty) house as Valmer is explained by knowing that the original château was burnt down in 1948. You enter through a grand courtyard, past ancient weeping sophoras, over a dry moat and up past Florentine fountains and pretty brick-and-stone balustrading until you come to a large, rectangular yew enclosure, which represents the old chateau.

Here, and throughout the 16th-century upper terraces, the planting is simple and creates its effect by repetition – building up colour effects on a large scale. The rose garden is entirely planted with white roses – standards of 'Marie Pavié and little shrubs of 'Avon', plus a few white hibiscus. It is best appreciated from the gates and staircase high above. So, too, is the amazing *potager* below it – the largest and grandest in Touraine, with turrets at its corners – the annual miracle wrought by owner Comtesse Alix de Saint Venant and her head gardener, Sébastien Verdière. Its layout forms a giant quincunx, with a pool in the middle and parterres edged with box, nepeta and fruit trees trained low to within 50cm of the ground. Each quarter is itself a quincunx, richly planted and riotously colourful with more than 3000 different fruits, vegetables, salad plants and herbs. It is a sight to gladden the heart of any gastronome, but conservation and celebration of diversity is the message. Handsome Anduze pots, buttresses of yew, and lagerstroemias add structure, and all is presided over by a modern statue of St Fiacre, the patron saint of gardeners.

20km E of Tours ☏ 02 47 52 93 12
Open May–June 10am–12.30pm & 2–7pm weekends & pub hols; July–August daily (except Mon) 10am–7pm; Sep–early Oct daily (except Mon) 10am–12.30pm & 2–6pm
Size 6ha (15ac) **Owner** Comtesse Alix de Saint-Venant 🅿 ▣ 🚾 ♨
🆆 www.chateau-de-valmer.com
@ jardins@chateau-de-valmer.com

70. Arboretum des Grandes Bruyères
45450 Ingrannes

A flat site, sandy soil, lakes, pines, birches and, of course, heathers: Les Bruyères is an English woodland garden, a corner of Surrey snipped off and transported to the centre of France. It was started in 1973 and is now by far the best example of an English-style woodland garden outside Britain. It is a garden to walk around, along curving paths and through grassy glades, a landscape that changes with every footstep.

Five hectares are purely ornamental, loosely designed around an endless number of island beds. Plants are chosen for their contribution to the overall effect, and for their harmony with the natural woodland. The remaining 5 ha are a series of geographically laid-out arboreta that merge into the surrounding woodland.

There are four national collections recognised by the *Conservatoire des Collections Végétales Spécialisées*: 500 different heathers, 600 roses chosen solely for their scent, magnolias (300 plants) and flowering dogwoods from China and America (450). Other well-represented trees and shrubs are stuartias, oaks, hydrangeas, rhododendrons, cistus, junipers, pines, clethras and maples. And there is an emphasis upon trees threatened in the wild. So, it is a garden from which to learn, as well as an Elysian scene through which to stroll. All is organically managed.

On D434 about 1km S of Ingrannes ☎ 02 38 57 12 61 **Open** Mar–Oct daily 10am–6pm **Size** 10ha (25ac) **Owner** Association des Parcs et Jardins de France 🅿 🚾 ♿ 🆆 www.parcsdefrance.org @ parcsdefrance@wanadoo.fr

71. Arboretum National des Barres
45290 Nogent-sur-Vernisson

Les Barres is by far the most impressive arboretum in France; some 130 people work there. It was founded in 1821 by Philippe André de Vilmorin, a member of France's most distinguished family of nurserymen, whose main interest was improving the stock of forestry trees. Now it displays more than 2500 different trees from all over the world.

The arboretum is in three parts: the geographical collection, laid out in 1873, has the largest specimens, including a vast purple beech, a tall *Ginkgo biloba* and several sequoias over 50 m tall. The systematic collection (1894) has a large number of ornamental trees and shrubs – not just magnolias, rhodo-dendrons and wisterias but also handsome specimens of *Eucalyptus rodwayi, Carya cordiformis, Pinus coulteri* and the hardy rubber tree, *Eucommia ulmoides*. This was the era when Maurice de Vilmorin received many new introductions from French missionaries in China. The

arboretum has several living holotypes from these collections by Fathers David, Delavay and Fargès. Later additions came from the great English and American collectors like Joseph Rock and Kingdon Ward. The ornamental collection (started in 1941 when France was at war) is a splendid miscellany of horticultural variants, including weeping cedars and oak-leaved hornbeams.

2km S of Montargis ☎ 02 38 95 62 21 **Open** Mid-Mar–mid-Nov daily 10am–dusk **Size** 35ha (86ac) **Owner** The State 🅿 🚾 ♿ 🆆 🔲 www.arboretumdesbarres.com/index2.htm @ arboretum.des.barres@club-internet.fr

72. Parc Floral de la Source
45072 Orléans

The garden takes its name from the river Loiret, which has its source here. It surges out of a very large pool at a constant temperature of 12°C and is a substantial river from the start. Tree ferns line its edges. The château on the

LEFT: Arboretum des Grandes Bruyères is by far the best woodland garden in France.
RIGHT: Among the many horticultural spectacles at Parc Floral de la Source is this trial ground for new roses.

André Eve's mixed plantings at Roseraie de Pithiviers are a model example of how to combine garden roses with other plants.

hillside above the Loiret has very fine parterres on the valley slopes. Previous owners have included the English Lord Bolingbroke and Napoleon I's Marshall Davoust.

The garden has had several reincarnations, but has long been a showcase for the nursery trade around Orleans – France's most prestigious. The season begins with 100 000 bulbs flowering in the ancient oak woodlands. The very extensive iris garden (recognised by the *Conservatoire des Collections Végétales Spécialisées*) has over 1000 cultivars, best during the last two weeks of May. These are followed immediately by massive displays from the roses banked in a semicircle around the lake – 400 cultivars, mainly modern, of every colour. Late summer brings the *Potager Extraordinaire* to perfection. Its contemporary design (it starts with a living wall of osier willows) houses a very wide range of unusual and old-fashioned vegetables and herbs, all organically grown. Summer and early autumn also see the Dahlia Garden at its best, with over 150 cultivars of every type arrayed in large plantings.

Olivet, 8km S of Orléans
02 38 49 30 00 **Open** Daily 9am–6pm (2–5pm in winter) **Size** 35ha (86ac) **Owner** City of Orléans
W www.parcfloral-lasource.fr
@ parcfloraldelasource@wanadoo.fr

73. Roseraie de Pithiviers
Z.A. Morailles
45308 Pithiviers-le-Vieil

André Eve is a nurseryman and famous champion of old-fashioned roses. The display garden attached to his nursery was begun around 1990 and has examples of all the different roses in his catalogue, some 750 of them. They are grown as garden plants in association with other shrubs, clematis, herbaceous plants, grasses, bulbs and, above all, irises. All are chosen so that their peak bloom coincides with the flowering of the roses in May and June. The garden is informally designed and intensely planted in a cottage-garden style, apart from a very beautiful pergola of climbing and rambling roses all along one side. The

garden is small, yet seems enormous: you can spend hours and hours there soaking up the beauty, colour and scent.

2km S of Pithiviers 02 38 30 01 30
Open Weekdays 9am–12 noon & 1.30–5.30pm; but May–Jun daily
Size 1ha (2½ac) **Owner** Les Roses Anciennes d'André Eve
P ▢ WC ♿ ▢ ▢
W www.roses-anciennes-eve.com
@ info@roses-anciennes-eve.com

74. Château de Bussy-Rabutin
21140 Bussy-le-Grand

Bussy-Rabutin is an old castle converted to a country house in the 17th century. Its gardens are presently being restored to their 18th-century grandeur. The main feature is a charming and very extensive formal garden (wrongly attributed to le Nôtre) with box-lined edges, fountains and pools. The plantings include roses, paeonies and ancient pear trees, trained both as cordons and as very low hedges, no more than 50 cm high. The garden behind the house (set with ancient lime avenues) runs up to a remarkable statue of the abduction of Persephone.

10km SE of Montbard
03 80 96 00 03 **Open** Daily 9.15am–noon & 2–6pm (except Mon & some feast days) **Closes** 5pm mid-Sep–mid-May **Size** 8ha (20ac) **Owner** The State P WC ▢
W www.monum.fr
@ bussyrabutin@chateaux-france.com

Bussy-Rabutin's grand formal gardens, in a remote corner of France, have been restored to their former grandeur.

75. Arboretum de Pézanin
71520 Dompierre-les-Ormes

The Pézanin arboretum was begun by the nurseryman Philippe de Vilmorin in 1903, but abandoned in 1923 and not resumed again until 1970. Vilmorin was a collector of trees and planted over 1000 different taxa, of which no more than 200 survive, though extensive recent plantings have brought the total up to 600 again.

Three routes are signed around the collection: the best parts are dedicated to ornamentals and trees of botanical interest, old and new. The older trees include *Quercus × heterophylla* and several swamp cypresses with characteristic knobbly tubercles. The new plantings include a Burgundian forest of native species; a Canadian forest of North American species; a collection of maples (the sugar maples are part of the original plantings); 15 *Rhododendron* species; 27 different elms; 18 oaks; and all known cultivars of *Ginkgo biloba* (some 26). It is a National Collection recognised by the *Conservatoire des Collections Végétales Spécialisées*.

35km W of Macon
☎ 0385 502 386 **Open** Always
Size 26ha (64ac) **Owner** The State (L'Office National des Forêts)
🅿 🖪 🍴 🚾 ♿ 🏪 🚹
@ patrick.mazoyer@onf.fr

FRANCHE-COMTÉ

76. Jardin Botanique de la Ville et de l'Université
Place Maréchal-Leclerc
25000 Besançon

Besançon's botanic garden has been on its present site since 1956. It has by far the most interesting collection of plants in the Franche-Comté – over 4000 of them – and is therefore an excellent place to learn about horticulture in cold, continental climates. The many designed features include a peat garden, woodland garden, pharmacological collection, rock-garden and cliff garden, all created to display the great variety of wild plants. There is a fascinating collection of plants in the systematic beds and a good display of the native flora of Franche-Comté. In the glasshouses are collections of orchids, ferns, carnivorous plants, cacti and succulents, especially Aizoaceae, Crassulaceae and Cactaceae. There is, however, a dark cloud on the horizon: the university is reluctant to continue its present level of financial support.

In NW corner of city
☎ 03 81 61 57 78 **Open** Daily
7am–dusk **Size** 2ha (5ac) **Owner** Université du Franche-Comté
🅿 🚾 ♿
@ jardbotan@univ-fcomte.fr

POITOU-CHARENTES

77. Château de la Roche-Courbon
17250 Saint-Porchaire

The château from which La Roche-Courbon takes its name was built in 1465 and given a domestic facelift in the

The grand and extensive gardens of La Roche-Courbon date no further back than the 1930s.

Fruit, vegetables, herbs, roses and magnificent dahlias are all combined at Jardin-verger de Malicorne

17th century, but retains its warlike outline. It perches on a rocky promontory above the Charente marshes.

The gardens, however, are modern reconstructions, made in the 1930s and based upon 17th-century models. The entrance gate leads to a small formal garden, where low box-edged parterres are filled with colourful seasonal bedding. In front of the house is a large green parterre, edged with yew cones and clipped box shapes. Beyond is a *potager*, with apples and pears neatly trained in the French style. Urns, statues and vases provide focus points. Canals stretch away into the distance. But the glory of the garden is a great, formal *bassin* beyond the main parterre; it reflects the château from the hillside opposite and leads to a magnificent double water-staircase. The manipulation of water makes an impressive complement to the powerful castle. It comes as a surprise to learn that much of the garden floats on unseen islands of long wooden piles driven deep into the marsh.

20km NW of Saintes
☎ 05 46 95 60 10 **Open** Daily 10am–7pm (10am–12 noon & 2–5.30pm in winter) **Size** 5ha (12ac) **Owner** Chénereau family 🅿 🆆🅲 🆆 www.t3a.com/LaRocheCourbon/ @ LaRocheCourbon@t3a.com

AUVERGNE

78. Arboretum de Balaine
03460 Villeneuve-sur-Allier

Balaine is France's oldest and largest privately-owned arboretum, begun in 1812 by Aglaé Adanson and still owned by her descendants. Each generation has added to the collections and repaired the damage done from time to time by hard winters and freak winds. There is an English-style park, a *potager*, a rose garden, and a permanent display of sculptures. It is the trees, however, that visitors come to see – 650 different taxa, starting with 19 *Abies* species, 25 *Acer* and 13 *Alnus*. The rarities include *Abies alba* var. *nebrodensis*, *A. numidica* and *Betula humilis*, all vulnerable

or threatened in the wild. There is also a large number of outstanding specimen trees, including liquidambars, tulip trees, nyssas, pterocaryas, several wellingtonias, and a 35-m high swamp cypress (*Taxodium distichum*) on the edge of the lake behind the house.

The ornamental effects come from smaller trees and shrubs, and there is much to see at every season: wintersweet (*Chimonanthus*), *Garrya elliptica*, *Hamamelis* cultivars and mahonias in mid-winter give way to camellias, *Chaenomeles japonica* cultivars, corylopsis and many pieris in early spring, and clethras, *Oxydendron arboreum*, *Poliothyrsis sinensis* and tamarisks in August. The autumn colour is especially fine. The design of the arboretum, with its open glades, winding paths, streams and bridges, adds greatly to the enjoyment.

N of Moulins, off D27
☎ 0470 433 007 **Open** Mar–Nov daily 9am–12 noon & 2–7pm **Size** 20ha (49ac) **Owner** Couteix-Adanson family 🅿 🚻 🆆🅲 ♿ 🎪 👶 🆆 www.arboretum-balaine.com @ Arboretum.Balaine@wanadoo.fr

79. Jardin-verger de Malicorne

9, Route de Commentry
03600 Malicorne

Georges Delbard was an ambitious and successful nurseryman, who specialised in the breeding of fruit trees and roses. He began his *jardin-verger* (fruit garden) in 1950 in his home village of Malicorne. Delbard's idea was to make a collection of all the old fruit cultivars in France: there are now over 4500 different apples, pears, cherries, plums, peaches and apricots at Malicorne. The garden also demonstrates the many ways of training fruit trees, including cordons, palmettos and fans.

In 1994, Delbard started to convert the collection into a garden of beauty, by planting roses, bulbs and herbaceous plants among the fruit trees. He added two rose gardens (displaying his own hybrids), a dahlia garden, a *potager*, and collections of irises, hemerocallis, paeonies and annuals – all stylishly laid out and well maintained. The *jardin-verger* is thus a tourist attraction, a museum of old fruit and a demonstration garden, as well as an artistic creation of considerable beauty, where great emphasis is placed upon colours and scents.

Middle of Malicorne, 18km E of Monbard ☎ 04 70 64 33 34 **Open** Jun–Sep daily 10am–12 noon & 1–6pm **Closed** Sun mornings and Mon **Size** 1.6ha (4ac) **Owner** Delbard family 🅿 🚾 ♿ 🚻
🆆 www.jardinverger.com
@ jardinverger@delbardpro.com

80. Jardins de Cordès

63210 Rochefort-Montagne

The remarkable thing about the gardens at Cordès is that they should exist at all, perched on a rocky promontory 900 m high in the middle of the Auvergne. Yet they were designed by Le Nôtre in 1695 and have been recently very well revived and restored. The château is a real fortress, and the formal gardens occupy the only possible site, terraced up on either side of the sole access way. The approach gives way to large, straight-sided hedges of beech, 6 to 8 m tall. They are, in fact, double hedges, so that you can walk down the middle of them with only a strip of sky above you. These hedges enclose the two principal formal gardens – identical rectangular shapes cut into eight segments, with topiary at the corners and a round pool in the middle. The beds are put to grass, apart from a ribbon of seasonal bedding along their edges. The effect is both simple and majestic.

You have seen the best parts of the gardens by the time you arrive at the castle, but the courtyard has two small pools, edged with Irish yews, and fine views towards the Puy-de-Dôme.

20km WSW of Clermont-Ferrand ☎ 04 73 65 81 34 Open Easter–Oct daily 10am–12 noon & 2–6pm. By appointment in winter Size 4ha (10ac) **Owner** Pierre Péchaud 🅿 🚾

RHÔNE-ALPES

81. Palais Idéal du Facteur Cheval

26390 Hauterives

Ferdinand Cheval (1836–1924) was a country postman who dreamed of building a fantastic palace for himself. The garden itself does not merit a second glance, but what dominates it, and has made it famous throughout Europe, is the elaborately decorated confection called the *Palais Idéal*. This garden building is a monument of immense complexity, a masterpiece of rustic, naïve, primitive art, and a precursor of surrealism. It is a chaotic accretion of styles and details, some 26 m long, 14 m wide and 9 m high, and is highly over-ornamented. The whole building is tricked out with homespun proverbs and meaningful poems, and

Palais Idéal du Facteur Cheval is the eccentric but incredible realisation of a simple country postman's dreams.

decorated with stones, pebbles, tufa and fossils. One end is supported by three slender giants with lanky legs, some 8 m tall, and named as Vercingetorix, Archimedes and Caesar. The decoration includes writhing snakes, animals' heads, palm trees, cacti, snarling monsters and figures in niches.

The *Palais Idéal* incorporates a Swiss châlet, a mosque and a relief of the White House. The Egyptian Tomb and Hindu Temple have little resemblance to ancient Egyptian or classical Hindu architecture, but Cheval was less interested in realities than the spirit of things: in this he perhaps resembles many modern garden designers. The result must be the most extra-ordinary folly ever made: intense, exuberant and introspective all at once.

Well signed in village
☎ 04 75 68 81 19 **Open** Apr–Sep daily 9am–12.30pm & 1.30–6.30pm (7.30pm Jul–Aug); Oct–March 9.30am–12.30pm & 1.30–4.30pm (5.30pm Feb–Mar) **Size** 0.5ha (1ac) **Owner** Commune d'Hauterives 🅿 🚾 ♿ 🚻
🆆 www.aricie.fr/facteur-cheval
@ facteur-cheval@cg26.fr

82. Château de Touvet
38660 Le Touvet

The site of Touvet is stunning – halfway up a mountainside above the Isère valley with splendid views of the Alps to the east. This was still frontier territory when the renaissance fortress was converted into a turreted house and the formal gardens were laid out in the 1750s and 1760s.

The main feature is a water-staircase in the Italian style – Dauphiné was at that time more influenced by Italian fashions than French – which cascades down all the terraces, running over steps and reposing in *bassins*, until it reaches the pools at the lowest levels. On either side are complex, elegant box broderies in the rococo style, recently remade so that they give a good impression of what a late-baroque French garden looked like in its prime. Hornbeam hedges and yew fill the terraces. Statues, tufa niches and watery grottos furnish the enclosures. Modern roses grown as standards add form and colour in summer. An ancient *Magnolia × soulangeana* fills one of the lower gardens. Elsewhere are fruit gardens, a *potager* and a prairie garden. But the fountains, spouts and gushes of water accompany you everywhere.

The baroque water gardens at Château de Touvet have been restored to their 18th-century splendour.

Parc de la Tête d'Or's extensive modern rose garden is a popular place for bridal parties to be photographed.

30km from Grenoble & Chambéry
☎ 04 76 08 42 27 **Open** Easter–1 Nov 2–6pm Sun & pub hols; Jul–Aug daily **Size** 7ha (17ac) **Owner** Marquis de Quinsonas
🅿 🆆🅲
🆆 www.touvet.com
@ quinsonas@wanadoo.fr

83. Parc de la Tête d'Or
Place du Général Leclerc
69006 Lyon

This is one of the largest and most enjoyable public parks to visit in all Europe. It was laid out around an artificial 16-ha lake by Eugène and Denis Bühler in 1857–62. The structure comes from broad avenues, well-chosen trees and spacious areas of grass. The older trees include tulip trees, cedars, ginkgos and plane trees 40 m high. The seven entrances are all impressive, and the *Enfants du Rhône* gate has magnificent gilded ironwork. Throughout the park is a splendid selection of noble and sentimental statues; the most famous portrays a female centaur snogging a naked man, who lies sprawled across her back. The plantings, especially of seasonal bedding, are generous, colourful and maintained to a high standard.

The municipal botanic park, the largest in France, is an 8-ha enclave within the garden; its 6500 sq. m of glass include a most elegant palm house. The park is especially famous for its roses. The International Rosary covers 4 ha and has 30 000 roses (350 different sorts) in a fluid modern design. The collection of historic roses in the botanic garden reminds us that Lyon was once the world centre of rose breeding.

Elsewhere in the garden is an international trial ground for new roses, a zoo and a velodrome.

NE of city centre, near Palais de Congrès ☎ 04 72 69 47 60 **Open** Daily 6.30am–10.30pm **Closes** 8.30pm mid-Oct–mid-April **Size** 105ha (259ac) **Owner** City of Lyon
🅿 🖼 🍴 🆆🅲 ♿
🆆 www.lyon.fr

84. Jardin Botanique 'La Jaÿsinia'
74340 Samoëns

'La Jaÿsinia' is a garden devoted to alpine plants. It was laid out on a grand scale from 1906 onwards, in a way that seems quite surprising to us nowadays – the mountainside was dynamited to produce the required levels and the boulders bound into shape with steel rods. Hundreds of cartloads of good earth were transported from the valley to make the garden beds. Ernest and Marie-Louise Cognacq made the garden – they founded La Samaritaine department store in Paris – and Louis Jules Allemand was the designer. As well as 4500 different rock-plants from all over the world, the garden has areas of alpine meadow, woodlands, pools and streams.

At the top of the steep hillside are the ruins of a mediaeval fortress, a pretty baroque chapel, and stupendous views over the village, valley and peaks of Haut Savoie. The garden has close links with the Jardin des Plantes in Paris, which maintains a laboratory here.

In centre of Samoëns
☎ 04 50 34 40 28 **Open** Daily 8am–12noon & 1.30–8pm (3–6pm in winter) **Size** 3.5ha (9ac) **Owner** Commune de Samoëns
🅿 🚾

85. Labyrinthe-Jardin des Cinq Sens

Rue du Lac
74140 Yvoire

The Garden of the Five Senses was started in 1986 in a *potager* below the 14th-century castle. The intention was to re-create the atmosphere of a mediaeval garden through the use of symbolism and, in particular, by making a maze garden with the theme of the five senses. Hornbeam hedges and espaliered apples are used to make a cloister of four outdoor garden rooms for flowers that appeal to sight, touch, taste and smell. In the touch garden, for example, visitors are encouraged to feel the textures of different leaves. The fifth sense, sound, is represented by water and birdsong.

The garden is very highly praised by French visitors. They consider it poetic, a succession of little epicurean detours, a rediscovery of beauty, a timeless initiation, an awakening, a place to dream and meditate on courtly love, mythology and Paradise Lost. This is the sort of intellectual play that comes so easily to the French but may leave other nationalities slightly baffled. It doesn't matter. The green cloister is very pretty – and even foreigners say it has quite an atmosphere.

Village centre ☎ 04 50 72 88 80 **Open** Mid-April–mid-May daily 11am–6pm; mid-May–mid-Sep 10am–7pm; mid-Sep–mid-Oct 1–7pm **Size** 0.3ha (¾ac) **Owner** Bouvier d'Yvoire family
🅿 🚗 🍴 🚾 ♿ 🎁 ♻
🅆 www.jardin5sens.net
@ mail@jardin5sens.net

AQUITAINE

86. Manoir d'Eyrignac

24590 Salignac

The Manoir d'Eyrignac is old and has belonged to the owner's family for 500 years, but the garden is a modern re-creation of a 17th-century formal French garden. It dates from the 1960s, but was inspired – it is said – by traces of what existed at Eyrignac before the fashion for English-style parks swept away the original gardens. It is a good example of what can be achieved in a short period: solid hedges, ramparts and cones of box, yew and hornbeam set off by grassy paths and enclosures, all apparently much older than they really are.

The most striking feature is a long walk between drums of yew and scalloped hornbeam buttresses, rigorously cut to a regular template. The effect is very impressive. Elsewhere are a rondel of hornbeam with windows cut in its walls, a parterre (in front of the house), and a pool edged with clipped cones of potted box.

A new garden was added recently, formally designed

The solid, impressive and inventive formal gardens of Manoir d'Eyrignac are no more than 40 years old.

A charming collection of aquatic plants greets the visitor to the old botanic garden in Bordeaux's public gardens.

sasanquas to the many fine japonicas and reticulatas, all at their best from early February to April. The camellias are recognised as a National Collection by the *Conservatoire des Collections Végétales Spécialisées*. So is the collection of wisterias (45 different cultivars), many displayed on a 90-m pergola. Other specialities are clematis, pieris, daphnes, edgeworthias and over 250 different hydrangeas. Whatever the season, there is always much to see and admire, while the nursery offers over 3000 different plants for sale.

20km N of Orthez
☎ 05 58 89 24 22 **Open** All year 2.30–6.30pm **Closed** Wed **Size** 4ha (10ac) **Owner** Jean Thoby
P WC ♿ ♨
W www.thoby.com
@ pepibotanique@thoby.com

but planted with nothing but white roses like 'Iceberg'. The idea is to offer visitors a cool, scented, flowery alternative to the geometrical rigours of the older garden. The whole is maintained to a high standard.

14km NE of Sarlat
☎ 05 53 28 85 90 **Open** Oct–Mar daily 10.30am–12.30pm & 2.30pm–dusk; Apr–May 10am–12.30pm & 2–7pm; Jun–Sep 9.30am–7pm **Size** 3ha (7ac) **Owner** Patrick Sermadiras de Pouzols de Lile
P ♜ (summer only) WC ♿
W www.eyrignac.com/historique.htm

87. Jardin Botanique de Bordeaux

Place Bardineau
33000 Bordeaux

Bordeaux's public gardens date back to the 18th century, but were landscaped in their present form in the 19th century. Their lower levels are laid out along a lengthy, curving lake. There are good trees, especially taxodiums, and the usual collection of over-the-top 19th-century statues, but most is put to lawn. Summer brings a respectable quantity of bedding out, an art form at which the French excel.

The most interesting part is the rather ragged systematic beds in the old botanic garden, behind the fine neo-classical building that houses its offices. The collection of plants is in

the process of moving to a new site, further out of the city, but many well-established trees and shrubs will remain. These include an enormous *Magnolia acuminata* and a 15-m tall *Maclura tricuspidata*. The presence of large specimens of *Bauhinia grandiflora*, *Persea gratissima* and *Erythrina crista-galli* shows what is possible in the warm, maritime climate of Bordeaux.

In city centre, northern end
☎ 05 56 10 25 39 **Open** Daily 7am–sunset **Size** 10ha (25ac) **Owner** City of Bordeaux P WC ♿
W www.bordeaux.fr

88. Château de Gaujacq

125, Route du Bastennes
40330 Gaujacq

The Château at Gaujacq is built around a courtyard, like an Italian monastery. It gives the visitor a first taste of how unusual is the whole estate. One corner of the courtyard is filled by a very tall *Magnolia grandifolia*, but the modern garden lies outside. It is one of the best plantsman's gardens in France, with an exceptional nursery attached. The key to the design is a grass walk (edged with rounded *Lonicera nitida*) that leads off into numerous garden rooms.

Camellias are a major speciality: Gaujacq has 30 species and 600 cultivars, from the tall, scented

LANGUEDOC-ROUSSILLON

89. Bambouseraie de Prafrance

30140 Anduze-Générargues

'Bambouseraie' is the French word for a bamboo garden: it was invented to honour this garden at Prafrance – the biggest and best bamboosery in Europe – begun in 1855. The garden lies in a valley bottom, where flash floods are still a problem: the whole garden was 2 m under water in November 2002.

This is an enormous garden to visit, but the best parts are fairly accessible. The entrance drive runs along a 19th-century avenue of sequoias underplanted with 10-m tall bamboos. These gigantic specimens indicate the scale of the garden. To one side are clipped hedges of *Semiarundinaria makinoi*, a collection of bamboo taxa, dwarf Japanese maples in Anduze pots, a hedge of *Pleioblastus chino* f. *elegantissimus*, and a bamboo maze. Nearby is a forest of

The maze of clipped bamboos is one of Prafrance's many extraordinary features.

bananas – the garden has always grown other exotics, notably camellias in spring and Japanese maples for their leaf colour in autumn. Here, too, is the 'Laotian village', a hamlet where the houses and their furnishings are made from bamboo. Bananas (*Musa basjoo*), ginger plants, and pools with *Victoria cruziana* surround it. You may think that bamboos are unexciting; a visit to Prafrance will astonish and enthuse you.

2km from Anduze
☎ 04 66 61 70 47 Open Mar–Nov daily 9.30am–dusk **Size** 33ha (81ac)
Owner Muriel Nègre
🅿 🖼 🍴 🚾 ♿ 🏛 ♿
🌐 www.bambouseraie.fr
@ bambou@bambouseraie.fr

90. Jardins de la Fontaine
Quai de la Fontaine
30000 Nîmes

These gardens, now a public park, are some of the oldest and grandest historic gardens in the south of France. They lie at the end of the longest, widest avenue in Nîmes: you approach them over a canal and under an avenue of chestnuts, framed by urns and statues. They were laid out early in the 18th century around a surging spring – a sacred spot since Roman times. The water wells up in an arcaded *bassin* and connects

to a larger *bassin* with a balustraded parapet and magnificent statues, urns and oversized *putti* at the corners. The nymph on the island at the centre is Nemausa and represents the spirit of the place – the Roman city of Nîmes. Behind is a steep hillside, beautifully laid out as a wooded flower garden, with exquisite views of the fountains and old city.

City centre ☎ 04 66 76 70 01
Open Daily 7.30am–6.30pm
(9.30pm in summer) **Size** 3ha (7ac)
Owner City of Nîmes 🅿

Statues and urns abound in the gardens of La Fontaine, which were laid out around a surging spring.

91. Jardin des Plantes de Montpellier
163, Rue Auguste Broussonet
34090 Montpellier

This beautiful and historic botanic garden is the oldest in France. Henri IV founded it in 1593 as a 'living encyclopedia' of plants, with an emphasis on those of medicinal value. Its directors over the years have included Pierre Magnol, Pierre Marie Auguste Broussonet and Augustin-Pyramus de Candolle. It is still largely formally laid out.

The collections are not large for a botanic garden (4000 taxa) but include a ginkgo planted in 1794 next to the orangery (built in 1803) and a large pool filled with the lotus *Nelumbo nucifera*, brought back from the Egyptian campaigns in 1798 by the physician Alire Raffeneau-Delile. The rarest tree is *Cupressus dupreziana* (the Saharan cypress), which is nearly extinct in its native Algeria. There are handsome specimens, too, of *Liquidambar orientalis*, *Quercus castaneifolia*, *Carya illinoinensis* and *Zelkova serrata*. However, the large number of established specimens of *Quercus ilex* and *Celtis australis* – weed trees that have been allowed to grow up and overshadow the garden's structure – testify to an eventful history. It is not the best maintained of gardens but the sense of history and the beauty of its structure make it a delight to visit. Parts are likely to be closed at any time for much-needed restoration.

City centre, NW side
📞 04 67 63 43 22 **Open** All year Tue–Sun 12 noon–6pm (8pm in summer) **Size** 4.5ha (11ac) **Owner** Université de Montpellier 🚻 ♿
🆆 www.jardindesplantes. univ-montpl.fr
@ jdplantes@univ-montpl.fr

92. Jardin Méditerranéen de Roquebrun
Rue Chemin de Ronde
34460 Roquebrun

Roquebrun's exotic plantings merge into native Mediterranean *maquis* at the edges of its garden.

The breathtaking view of the Orb valley is enough to recommend this garden, which is made beneath the ruined castle on a very steep dolomitic rock-face. The south-facing aspect makes it possible to grow a surprisingly large number of plants; Roquebrun calls itself the 'Nice of the Hérault'. Some 4000 plants flourish here (over 400 taxa), including a wide selection of cacti and succulents – for example, aloes, yuccas, *Senecio serpens* and *Lampranthus emarginatus*. Many of them came from the Jardin Exotique at Monte Carlo.

They are supplemented by such flowering plants as bougainvillea, oranges, mimosas and masses of irises in spring.

A substantial area is given to native plants like *Aphyllanthes monspeliensis*, *Phlomis fruticosa*, *Bupleurum fruticosum* and *Cistus albidus*. Many are the traditional herbs of the Mediterranean – lavender, thyme and rue – but there are also economic staples like loquats, date palms, olives and pomegranates.

The Jardin Méditerranéen is not a garden for anyone with a poor head for heights – you begin the long, steep climb up to the garden from the river at the bottom of the village, but it is well worth the effort. And the smells of the *maquis* are delicious.

Just below castle; Roquebrun is 32km NW of Béziers
📞 04 67 89 55 29 **Open** Mid-Feb–mid-Nov daily 9am–12 noon & 1.30–5.30pm; but 9am–7pm Jul–Aug **Size** 2ha (5ac) **Owner** CADE (Collectif Agricole pour le Développement et l'Environnement) 🅿 🚻 🚽
🆆 www.jardin-mediterraneen.fr

93. Jardin Exotique de Ponteilla
Route de Nyls
66300 Ponteilla

This young garden is a remarkable 'find' in the middle of a flat, sandy plain. Though barely 20 years old, it is surrounded by evergreen trees as much as 20 m high,

The orangery and systematic beds are the best maintained at Jardin des Plantes de Montpellier.

Everything at Jardin Exotique de Ponteilla has been introduced to an empty site since 1986, including these palms, the pool and the waterfowl.

PROVENCE-ALPES-CÔTE D'AZUR

94. Jardin Alpin du Lautaret
05480 Villar d'Arène

making it completely secluded, a world apart from the open vineyards of the Roussillon. It is very much a horticulturist's collection, mainly of trees and shrubs, with seasonal plantings to give interest throughout the year. The layout is largely geographical, with broad paths named after such French botanists as Bougainville, but trees like eucalyptus run through the garden and, growing quickly, give much

of its structure. Areas are dedicated to specific plant types like palms, cacti and culinary herbs. The garden has a strong didactic purpose and is therefore of interest to people of all ages who want to learn about plants.

2km from Ponteilla, 8km SW of Perpignan **C** 04 68 53 22 44 **Open** Mid-Apr–mid-Oct daily 2–7pm **Size** 3ha (7ac) **Owner** Christian Allard **P WC &**

The site alone is reason enough to visit the garden at Lautaret. It straddles a spur above the Col du Lautaret, which is surrounded by peaks, glaciers and spacious alpine meadows. The garden has had a difficult history, and most of what we see today dates back no further than 1981. Nevertheless, it is France's best known alpine garden and a joy to visit during its short season of splendour. The figures tell it briefly: 2000 m above sea level and 2000 taxa from all over the world.

The design is excellent: it moves you along and enables you to inspect the plants at your own speed without other visitors (who may be many) getting in the way. And it supplies the individual plants

The Melje glacier provides an impressive background to Lautaret's famous alpine garden at 2000 m.

A trick of perspective elongates the progress of these steps at Les Colombières.

with whatever growing conditions they require – screes, meadows, bog, rocks, pinewoods and so on. There is a complete collection of local plants, including the endangered *Eryngium alpinum*. Plants are also arranged geographically and systematically, according to their botanical families. But quite apart from the beauty of the alpine plants themselves, the overall effect of the garden is intensely beautiful and the setting apocalyptic.

On N91, Col du Lautaret
☎ 04 38 78 43 66 **Open** Jun–Sep daily 9am–7pm **Size** 2.5ha (6ac) **Owner** Université Joseph Fourier de Grenoble P ☐ WC ♿ ⛶
W www.ujf-grenoble.fr/JAL/
@ station-alpine@ujf-grenoble.fr

95. Les Colombières
312, Route des Colombières
06500 Menton-Garavan

Ferdinand Bac laid out the garden at Les Colombières between 1918 and 1927 and lived there with his patrons, the Ladan-Bockairys, for many years. The garden is a circuit of features and follies high on the steep hillside above Menton. Each highlights a different theme, generally taken from classical mythology and charged with cultural imagery. It is the artist's masterpiece.

The circuit takes you from the Garden of Homer to the avenue of Nausicaä's fountain, the Rotunda, a bust of Nero surrounded by arches of cypress, Palladio's Casino (visually linked to the Rotunda), the

Roman temple, the *Allée des Jarres* (where ten enormous old oil jars line the route, its length stretched by tricks of perspective), Orpheus's rock and then down to the Spanish pool, with its sombre cypress avenue.

Bac preferred native trees – he admired the shape, shadow and tones of cypresses – though the garden also has the oldest carob tree in France. Space and light meant more to him than colour: Les Colombières is very self-controlled, almost austere, like a pilgrimage.

Off Bvd de Garavan, eastern Menton **Open** By prior appointment with the Patrimoine 04 92 10 97 10 **Size** 2.5ha (6ac) **Owner** Privately owned P

96. Villa Ephrussi de Rothschild
06230 St-Jean-Cap-Ferrat

This is by far the most opulent and impressive garden in the south of France. It was meant to be: Baronne Béatrice Ephrussi de Rothschild enjoyed displaying her wealth. She was an avid traveller and collector, so the garden she began around her Venetian-style villa in 1905 is made in many styles and displays a vast quantity of architectural and sculptural loot.

The house sits on top of the Cap Ferrat ridge, with magnificent views along the coast in both directions. In front of the house the Baronne placed a long, formal water garden leading up to a cascade and a copy of the Temple of Love in the *Petit Trianon* in Versailles. Tricks of perspective make the view seem much longer than it is. Below is a sequence of gardens in different styles, each made without regard for cost: a sultry, sunken Spanish garden, a Tuscan garden, a Japanese garden, an extensive cactus garden and a rose garden surrounded by the olive trees that grew here hundreds of years before the Riviera became fashionable as a winter resort. Throughout

The Venetian-style Villa Ephrussi de Rothschild and its gardens straddle the ridge of Cap Ferrat.

the garden are highly desirable artefacts – urns, ceramic vases, statues and swags. All the bric-a-brac that the Baronne could not find a space for elsewhere ended up in the stone garden: arches, fountains, sculpted capitals, gargoyles and statues are scattered among azaleas, hydrangeas, bergenias and fuchsias in the shade of camphor and Judas trees. And there are fine specimen trees throughout, including a massive *Ficus macrophylla* to one side of the formal garden.

Well-signed from entrance to Cap Ferrat 📞 04 93 01 33 09 **Open** Daily 10am–6pm (7pm Jul–Aug) **Closed** weekday mornings in winter **Size** 7ha (17ac) **Owner** Académie des Beaux-Arts (Institut de France) 🅿 🖥 🍽 🚾 ♿ 🏧 🎫 🔎 www.villa-ephrussi.com @ message@villa-ephrussi.com

Villa Ephrussi's garden offers a sequence of smaller gardens, each in a different style.

Jardin Botanique de Menton began as the private collection of an English plantsman.

97. Jardin Botanique de Menton

Ave St-Jacques
06500 Menton-Garavan

Jardin Botanique de Menton was an English plantsman's garden before it was acquired as an outstation for Paris's Jardin des Plantes in 1966. The authorities have developed the plantings considerably, so that it now displays over 1500 taxa, while also maintaining the charming, higgledy-piggledy structure of its former owner. The drive is lined with very tall palm trees (*Phoenix canariensis*); some still have marks where they were hit by shells during World War II.

In the gardens below the very attractive house are substantial specimens of *Jubaea spectabilis* and *Grevillea robusta* and an ancient *Cupressus goveniana*. The lotus and papyrus plants (*Nelumbo nucifera* and *Cyperus papyrus*) flourish in a pool. In the valley below the house is a good collection of citrus fruits: food plants are a particular interest here, as are economic plants and palms (over 80 species).

In the olive grove behind the house are many new plantings: a hedge of *Salvia greggii*, edgings of *Bulbine frutescens*, a very tall *Erythrina caffra*, and a pale yellow sport (that reverts a little) of *Russelia juncea*. The rarer plants include *Sophora toromiro*, now extinct in its native Easter Island.

Signed off coastal road, 1km E of town ☎ 04 93 35 86 72 **Open** Apr–Sep daily 10am–12.30pm & 3–6pm; Oct–Mar daily 10am–12.30pm & 2.30–5.30pm **Size** 1ha (2½ac) **Owner** Muséum National d'Histoire Naturelle 🅿 🚾 ♿
🆆 www.mnhn.fr
@ valrahmeh@mnhn.fr

98. Jardin Exotique de Monte Carlo

62, Bvd du Jardin Exotique
MC-98002
Monaco

Monte Carlo's Jardin Exotique claims to be 'the largest rock-garden in Europe', but it is devoted to cacti and succulents rather than alpine plants. It is both a tourist attraction (opened in 1933) and botanic collection, inspired by La Mortola just across the frontier in Italy. It is exceptionally well maintained.

The garden lies on a steep, south-facing cliffside high above Fontvielle, on the edge of the principality, with fine views over Monte Carlo's harbour and along the coast to Italy. A large *Chorisia speciosa* or kapok tree with a bulbous, prickly trunk stands by the entrance. A single path leads down – a long way down – through an ever-changing landscape of more than 6000 different cacti and succulent plants. Every tiny pocket is planted. Many plants are mature and of large size.

The view from the entrance to Jardin Exotique de Monte Carlo encompasses the whole coastline of Monaco.

They include the largest *Echinocactus grusonii* in Europe, thought to be about 120 years old, with half-a-dozen heads over a metre wide and many smaller shoots. Agaves include a very large clump of *A. stricta* (a species that divides after flowering, instead of dying), the rare *A. bracteosa* 'Mediopicta' and a large colony of the popular *A. attenuata*. Though there is a section for edible cacti like *Myrtillocactus geometrizans*, the displays are ornamental rather than taxonomic. Ornamental plants like *Aeonium arboreum* 'Atropurpureum', *Russelia juncea* and *Euphorbia milii* appear throughout the garden and bind the plantings together. It is especially fine in winter when the aloes and crassulas flower.

NW edge of Monaco, by frontier ☎ (377) 93 15 29 80 **Open** Daily 9am–6pm (or dusk if earlier) **Closes** 7pm mid-May–mid-Sep **Size** 1.2ha (3ac) **Owner** Mairie de Monaco
🅿 📷 🚾 ♿
@ jardin-exotique@monte-carlo.mc

99. Jardin Japonais
Ave Princesse-Grace
MC-98000
Monaco

The Japanese Garden in Monte Carlo was made by Ysuo Beppu and opened in 1994. It is convincingly designed, according to the canons of Japanese aesthetics, and superbly maintained. The central feature is a long lake, very irregular in shape and studded with stepping stones, lanterns, rocks, bridges and islands. It is fed by several small cascades. In the pool are more than 20 varieties of Koi carp. Other structures include a tea house and two sand gardens. The whole is enclosed by a Japanese tiled wall and bamboo fencing. The plantings, however, are rather westernised, with prominent lantanas, bulbinella, lotus, gardenias and cycads. Many European plants have been cloud-pruned: pines, tamarisks, lagerstroemia, olives, laurels and yews. It is therefore a hybrid creation, a Franco-Japanese garden, but very charming and peaceful. And it packs a lot into a small area.

On sea front, eastern edge of principality ☎ (377) 93 15 22 77 **Open** Daily 9am–7pm (6pm in winter) **Size** 0.7ha (2ac) **Owner** Mairie de Monaco 🚾 ♿

Jardin Japonais enjoys a charming combination of Japanese design and western plants and plantings.

Gardens of Germany

Germany has magnificent historic gardens, inspirational botanic gardens and imaginative modern ones. The rulers of Germany's many kingdoms, electorates, principalities, grand-duchies and duchies each wanted the most impressive palaces and gardens, the most fashionable styles and the best botanic collections. Berlin, Munich, Dresden, Hanover, Stuttgart, Cologne and Kassel have unusually rich and sumptuous historic gardens that compare favourably with capital cities anywhere in Europe. The scale and extravagance of lesser rulers is no less compelling: Dessau, Schwerin, Neustrelitz, Düsseldorf, Bayreuth, Würzburg and Weimar all have gardens and landscapes of major historic importance. Almost nothing survived the Thirty Years War (1618–48), but Germany's essential prosperity was restored by the end of the 17th century and presaged a flowering of parks and gardens that lasted through the 18th and 19th centuries until the country's collapse in 1918.

The first gardens were made in the Italian style – Wilhelmshöhe in Kassel and Herrenhausen in Hanover are good examples – but, by 1700, every German ruler was dazzled by Versailles and wanted to outshine the Sun King. The Wittelsbachs employed Dominique Girard, a Frenchman and a pupil of André Le Nôtre, to work at Schloß Augustusburg in the Rhineland, and Nymphenburg and Schleissheim in Bavaria. Traces of the French school of garden-making survive in every major German garden, even where subsequently overlaid by the English landscape style. The baroque was followed by the rococo: Germany has some of the best rococo palaces and gardens in Europe, from Berlin and Potsdam in Prussia to Würzburg and Veitshöchheim in Bavaria. Their wit, invention and sense of fun are captivating – light-hearted, exuberant gardens intended to amuse as much as to impress.

The English landscape movement spread quickly through Germany and, for the most part, co-existed with the baroque. The great gardens at Schwetzingen, Sanssouci and Wilhelmshöhe show how easily the old and new lie together. Some leading exponents were, however, fully committed to the freer forms of the landscape movement: Prince Franz of Anhalt-Dessau adopted the political and social thinking of the English enlightenment by landscaping his principality from end to end. His enormous landscape at Wörlitz, based on such precedents as Stowe and Stourhead, is only part of his

OPPOSITE: The formal, French-style parts of Schwetzingen's historic garden have all the charm of the late baroque.

Late-summer bedding in the 'Sicilian' garden – one of the many charming features in Sanssouci, Germany's most beautiful and enjoyable garden.

overall *Gartenreich*. Goethe at Weimar and King Karl Theodor in Munich were others who interpreted the landscape style as a political statement, as well as a source of beauty.

Once the Germans adopted the natural English style, they never reacted against it. Parks and gardens were continuously laid out as English landscapes until the middle of the 20th century. The landscape style developed new forms of compelling beauty in Germany long after the English had forgotten it. The dazzling genius of Peter Joseph Lenné moulded the entire landscape around Potsdam and western Berlin into one vast design of supreme beauty. Prince Hermann von Pückler, a student of Humphry Repton, advised at Babelsberg, while his own landscapes at Muskau and Branitz dominated mid- and late-19th-century thinking.

Germany's defeat in 1918 precipitated a political, social and cultural revolution. Almost all the palaces and estates of the former rulers of German states were confiscated – dynasties throughout Germany, not just the Hohenzollerns –

and transferred to the various *Länder* to maintain for public benefit. This explains why so many of Germany's heritage gardens are of historical interest rather than horticultural or botanical. All are freely visitable, from dawn to dusk. Properties of the nobility escaped a similar fate, at least until the communists dispossessed landowners in East Germany, but there is no tradition among Germany's aristocrats of opening their houses and gardens to the public. Good privately owned gardens are few.

Worse was to follow. The Allies' invasion and the German defeat of 1945 came at a heavy price. Almost all the gardens in this book were seriously damaged. Much of what we now see is the result of patient, tireless restoration in the post-war years or, in the case of eastern Germany, since the collapse of Soviet communist rule in 1990. A few historic gardens have been turned into tourist mega-attractions – Mainau and Ludwigsburg in particular – but most are faithfully maintained for public recreation and cherished as part of Germany's cultural patrimony. There are four UNESCO world heritage sites: Brühl, Potsdam, Gartenreich Dessau-Wörlitz, and Muskau.

The passing of aristocratic culture in 1918 led to the creation of urban parks, universally regarded as an important public amenity. The great civic gardens of Germany, including Grugapark in Essen and Dortmund's Westfalenpark, were often developed with federal money for garden shows: the biennial *Reichsgartenschau* or *Bundesgartenschau*, a local *Landesgartenschau* or the IGA (*Internationale Gartenbauausstellung*). The craft of gardening is exemplified here to a very high standard. Many have rose gardens, dahlia gardens, herb gardens, Japanese gardens, and *Bauerngärten* – cottage gardens, often laid out formally as a quincunx, and given more to vegetables, fruit and herbs than flowers. But these civic parks are also the leading exponents of Germany's New Planting. This style was first developed by the Potsdam nurseryman Karl Förster in the 1920s and 1930s,

then taken up in western Germany after 1945. It involves planting large quantities of herbaceous plants in an apparently random arrangement that allows the plants to grow, spread and seed as in nature. There are good examples at Westpark in Munich, Höhenpark Killesberg in Stuttgart, and Planten un Blomen in Hamburg, as well as Grugapark and Westfalenpark. The New Planting is also studied and exemplified at two experimental horticultural stations: Weihenstephan in Bavaria and Hermannshof in Baden.

Germany's botanic gardens are many and excellent. Their living collections, often laid out ornamentally, are places of pilgrimage for plant-lovers. The glasshouse collections are especially comprehensive. Even a small botanic garden will have an extensive collection of palms, cacti and orchids, and a *Victoriahaus* dedicated to flowering *Victoria amazonica*, grown every year from seed. The botanic gardens at Berlin, Munich and Bonn are among the world's most important.

The 'Bell' fountain at Herrenhausen (with 166 jets) was added in 1937 and restored after World War Two.

Gardens of Germany

1. Jensen Rosengarten
2. Botanischer Garten der Christian-Albrechts-Universität
3. Rosarium Uetersen
4. Rhododendronpark
5. Botanischer Garten der Universität Hamburg
6. Planten un Blomen
7. Schloßpark Lütetsburg
8. Herrenhausen
9. Berggarten
10. Botanischer Garten Göttingen
11. Botanischer Garten & Arboretum der Ernst-Moritz-Arndt-Universität Greifswald
12. Schloßgarten Schwerin
13. Schloßpark Ludwigslust
14. Schloßpark Neustrelitz
15. Botanischer Garten Münster
16. Botanischer Garten Bielefeld
17. Wasserschloß Nordkirchen
18. Westfalenpark
19. Botanischer Garten der Stadt Krefeld
20. Nordpark
21. Botanischer Garten der Universität Düsseldorf
22. Schloßpark Benrath
23. Grugapark Essen
24. Botanischer Garten Wuppertal
25. Botanischergarten der Stadt Köln
26. Schloß Augustusburg
27. Botanische Gärten der Rheinischen Friedrich-Wilhelms-Universität Bonn
28. Schloß Wilhelmstal
29. Schloßpark Wilhelmshöhe
30. Insel Siebenbergen
31. Palmengarten
32. Staatspark Hanau-Wilhelmsbad
33. Prinz-Georgs-Garten
34. Botanischer Garten der Technischen Universität Darmstadt
35. Europas Rosengarten
36. Schloßpark Charlottenburg
37. Tiergarten
38. Botanischer Garten und Botanisches Museum Berlin-Dahlem
39. Späth's Arboretum
40. Pfaueninsel
41. Schloß Klein-Glienicke
42. Freundschaftsinsel
43. Babelsberg
44. Neuer Garten
45. Schloßpark Sanssouci
46. Schloßpark Rheinsberg
47. Forstbotanischer Garten Eberswalde
48. Schloßpark Branitz
49. Muskauer Park
50. Schloß Georgium
51. Luisium
52. Schloß Mosigkau
53. Schloßpark Oranienbaum
54. Wörlitzer Park
55. Europa-Rosarium
56. Botanischer Garten der Martin-Luther-Universität Halle-Wittenberg
57. Rennsteiggarten
58. Schloßpark Gotha
59. Park an der Ilm
60. Schloß Belvedere
61. Schloß Tiefurt
62. Botanischergarten der Friedrich-Schiller-Universität
63. Botanischer Garten der Universität Leipzig
64. Clara-Zetkin-Park
65. Grosser Garten
66. Botanischergarten der Technischer Universität Dresden
67. Barockgarten Großsedlitz
68. Schloß Pillnitz
69. Hermannshof Schau- und Sichtungsgarten
70. Schloßpark Heidelberg
71. Schloßgarten Schwetzingen
72. Schloßgarten Weikersheim
73. Schloß Favorite
74. Alpengarten-Pforzheim
75. Schloßgarten Ludwigsburg
76. Höhenpark Killesberg
77. Park Wilhelma
78. Hohenheim Park & Botanischer Garten
79. Botanischergarten Tübingen
80. Botanischer Garten der Albert-Ludwigs-Universität
81. Insel Mainau
82. Park Schönbusch
83. Hofgarten Veitshöchheim
84. Hofgarten Würzburg
85. Botanischer Garten der Universität Würzburg
86. Schloß Rosenau
87. Schloßpark Seehof
88. Sanspareil
89. Schloßpark Eremitage
90. Botanischer Garten der Stadt Hof
91. Botanischer Garten der Universität Erlangen-Nürnberg
92. Hofgarten Ansbach
93. Botanischergarten der Stadt Augsburg
94. Weihenstephan Sichtungsgarten
95. Schloß Schleissheim & Schloß Lustheim
96. Westpark
97. Schloßpark Nymphenburg
98. Botanischer Garten München-Nymphenburg
99. Englischergarten
100. Schloß Linderhof
101. Schloß Herrenchiemsee

GERMANY

★ National Capital

• Cities and Towns

— Major Roads

⓪⓪ German Garden

Adjacent Countries

0   50   100 Kilometres

0   50   100 Miles

Jensen Rosengarten has roses of every kind displayed in a series of well-designed model gardens.

SCHLESWIG-HOLSTEIN

1. Jensen Rosengarten

Am Schloßpark 2b
24960 Glücksburg

Ingwer Jensen's rose garden – also known as Rosarium Glücksburg – is an immaculately maintained show garden for his nursery. Jensen is the leading apologist for old-fashioned roses in Germany and likes them to be grown in a garden setting alongside other plants. Clematis associate particularly well with roses in his yew-hedged model gardens: Jensen has 200 cultivars alongside some 500 different roses, including the largest selection of David Austin roses in Germany.

The garden, near Glückburg's historic castle, was designed in 1991 by Günther Schulze and is considered one of his best works. In front of the entrance pavilion is a lavender garden. A central walk leads past great banks of shrub roses in island beds and an arcade of climbing roses to a semicircle of 'Bonica' roses grown as standards around a seating area. A 20-m long bed of 'Maria Liesa' is reckoned to produce over one million flowers during the course of a summer.

Centre of Glücksburg
☎ 04631 60100 **Open** Mid-May–Sep daily 10am–6pm **Size** 1ha (2½ac)
Owner Rosen-Jensen GmbH
🅿 ⬛ ♿ 🎁 🌿
W www.rosen-jensen.de
@ info@rosen-jensen.de

2. Botanischer Garten der Christian-Albrechts-Universität

Am Botanischen Garten 1–9
24118 Kiel

Kiel's botanic garden was laid out to please and interest visitors – which it does. Although it is one of the oldest botanic foundations in Germany (1669), it moved to its present site in 1985. It has a youthful vigour that is most attractive.

An easy layout helps you on your way, as do placards that are informative but not intrusive. The entrance courtyard is brightly planted with modern roses and bedding plants and leads straight to the excellent systematic beds. The spacious rock-garden is designed for visitors to clamber around and look at the plants, which are geographically arranged. The stonework copies the structure of natural rock formations fairly convincingly. There are interesting areas

Kiel's botanic garden was designed not just for botanical display but also to delight visitors.

devoted to North American woodland plants, north European sand-dunes, alder swamps, a Mediterranean garden, a heather garden and a good display of Chinese shrubs. In the glasshouses are North American cacti, a fine array of South African succulents, orchids, tropical plants and economic plants like coffee, tea and cocoa.

3km NW of city centre, by A76 junction with ring road
☎ 0431 8804276 **Open** Daily 9am–6pm (3pm in winter) **Size** 8ha (20ac) **Owner** Universität Kiel
🅿 ♿ ♿
🆆 www.uni-kiel.de/Botanik/botgar
@ hortus@bot.uni-kiel.de

3. Rosarium Uetersen
Wassermühlenstr. 7
25436 Uetersen

The Rosarium occupies the entire public park at the centre of Uetersen. The garden is landscaped around two lakes, and roses are massed in beds cut out of the turf, each with as many as 200 roses of one variety. There are about 900 different sorts of roses (mostly modern) and 35 000 bushes. Climbers and ramblers are trained on tripod supports.

The area around Uetersen has long been known for its nurseries, and the Rosarium was founded in 1929 on the initiative of three international rose nurserymen – Kordes,

Rosarium Uetersen's handsome modern rose garden is laid out around two lakes.

Bremen's Rhododendronpark is Germany's best woodland garden.

Tantau and Krause. The latest roses from Kordes and Tantau are still the cornerstone of the display. From early summer to late autumn, it is a garden full of beauty, colour and scent. Roses are popular with Germans: the rose is their national flower.

Near town centre ☎ 04122 7140 **Open** Daily dawn–dusk **Size** 7ha (17ac) **Owner** City of Uetersen
🅿 ♿ 🍴 ♿ ♿
🆆 www.rosarium-uetersen.city-map.de

BREMEN

4. Rhododendronpark
Marcusallee 60
28359 Bremen

This magnificent woodland garden of oak and beech trees on the eastern edge of Bremen was founded by the German rhododendron society in 1936 as a permanent trial and display ground for rhododendrons – and a place of beauty to visit. It is well supported by the German nursery trade, whose heartland is the Bremen hinterland.

The plantings are landscaped in grassy glades and reflected in innumerable lakes, ponds and canals. Over 70% (some 700) of all rhododendron species grow here, and as many as 2000 different hybrids from around the world. It is the sort of botanical exercise at which German horticulturists excel. There is a complete historic collection of *Rhododendron*

indicum cultivars, with other areas devoted to German hybrids, Japanese azaleas and taxa suitable for the rock-garden.

An impressive range of glass-houses shelters tender species, including the large-leaved giants *R. giganteum* and *R. arboreum*, and epiphytic Vireyas.

Rhododendronpark doubles up as Bremen's botanic garden, with formal systematic beds displaying its living collections according to their place in the botanic order. Elsewhere are substantial collections of heathers and roses. A recent addition is *Botanika*, an educational experience within a new glasshouse complex, which uses jungle plants from the Himalaya and Borneo to teach visitors about ecology and diversity, as well as the sheer beauty of plants.

5km E of historic city centre
☎ 0421 36189779 **Open** Mar–Sep daily 7.30am–dusk **Size** 46ha (114ac) **Owner** City of Bremen
🅿 🍴 ♿ ♿ ♿ ♿
🆆 www.rhodo.org/park.php
@ info@botanika.net

HAMBURG

5. Botanischer Garten der Universität Hamburg
Hesten 10
22609 Hamburg

Hamburg's fine botanic garden moved to its new out-of-town site in 1979. It has a highly original modern design and two clear

Plants and culture at Hamburg University's botanic garden.

aims – to teach and give pleasure.

The educational part is a 3.5-ha systematic garden. Stand on the circular concrete islands in the lake and move across the wooden pontoons to the mainland. These are the starting points for a botanical family tree. Each bed represents a botanical order or section and is linked to its neighbours to illustrate the development of botanical divisions, classes, orders, and so on. It is beautiful, instructive and convincing. It is encircled by a geographical layout, where plants are displayed according to their natural distribution, including North America, East Asia and Europe.

The designed Japanese and Chinese gardens are extensive and eye-catching, especially when covered with spring flowers or autumn colours. Here, too, is a fine rock-garden concentrating on European alpines. And there are also display areas to interest garden owners: excellent collections of conifers and rhododendrons; dedicated gardens for daylilies, modern roses and irises; a very pretty north German cottage garden in front of a little thatched summer-house; plus a medicinal garden and collection of Bible plants. Thoroughly recommended.

At Flottbek, 9km W of city centre
☎ 040 42816476 **Open** Daily 9am–30 mins before dusk **Size** 10ha (25ac) **Owner** Universität Hamburg
🅿 🖻 🚾 ♿ ⚕
🔲 www.biologie.uni-hamburg.de/ bzf/garten/garten.htm
@ hortus@botanik.uni-hamburg.de

6. Planten un Blomen

c/o Regina Nierzwicki-Steinke
Klosterwall 8
20095 Hamburg

Planten un Blomen (dialect for 'Plants and Flowers') is part of a long string of public parks around the north and

Planten un Blomen has exemplary new-style herbaceous plantings.

west boundaries of inner-city Hamburg. It is wonderfully designed for leisure enjoyment, but also for horticultural interest.

The modernist design is perfect for German-style mass plantings, and large areas are given to seasonal bedding, steppe plantings and ground cover plants. The walled *Apotekergarten* (medicinal herb garden) has herbs planted according to the body parts they treat. The Japanese garden is the largest in Europe and was made in 1991 by a Japanese Professor from Osaka, Yoshikuni Araki. He also built the Japanese landscape garden in the grounds of the old botanic garden. Here, too, are the show houses of Hamburg's university botanic garden: they include a tropical house, cycad house, fern house, subtropical house and succulent house. And there is much else to see.

By City Exhibition Centre, in NW of old city ☎ 040 428544723 **Open** Daily 7am–11pm **Closes** 8pm Oct–Apr Glasshouses open weekdays: Mar–Oct 9am–4.45pm; Nov–Feb 9am–3.45pm & open weekends & hols Mar–Oct 10am–5.45pm; Nov–Feb 9am–3.45pm **Size** 47ha (116ac) **Owner** City & Universität Hamburg
🅿 🖻 🍴 🚾 ♿ 🏛 ⚕
🔲 www.plantenunblomen.hamburg.de
@ Regina.Nierzwicki-Steinke @hamburg-mitte.hamburg.de

NIEDER-SACHSEN

7. Schloßpark Lütetsburg

Landstr. 55
26524 Hage-Lütetsburg

Lütetsburg is a fine, moated castle in the flat, sandy heaths of north-west Friesland. It is one of the largest and most attractive privately owned gardens in Germany.

The structure dates back to 1790–1810, when Eduard Mauritz Graf zu Innhausen und Knyphausen laid out an

Schloßpark Lütetsburg's *cottage ornée* & rhododendrons.

5km E of Norden ☎ 04931 4254 **Open** May–Sep daily 8am–9pm; Oct–Apr 10am–5pm **Size** 20ha (49ac) **Owner** Graf Tido zu Innhausen und Knyphausen
🅿 🖥 🆆🅲 ♿ 🛗
W www.schloss-luetetsburg.de
@ tidozk@aol.com

8. Herrenhausen

Herrenhäuser Str. 4
30419 Hannover

Herrenhausen is the greatest early baroque garden in Germany. Its oldest structure is the Italian-style Great Cascade (1676), decorated with shells, stalactites and sculptures. It was the Electress Sophia (mother of George I of England), however, who made the present gardens from 1679 onwards and described them as her life's work.

The gardens are dominated by the Grand Parterre, approximately 200 sq. m: its beds have highly elaborate broderies and are richly planted with seasonal bedding. They are tricked out with decorative vases and sculptures of gods, seasons, virtues and continents, all painted white

extensive landscape garden in the Anglo-Chinese style. His picturesque lakes and romantic winding paths still give the garden its structure; he also built a number of very pretty garden buildings with thatched roofs in the *cottage ornée* style. These include the *Freundschaftstempel* (Temple of Friendship) and *Nordische Kapelle* (Nordic Chapel). The background to the landscaping is a fine woodland of native oaks: one has a low branch that has layered itself and formed a new tree. Good trees include *Quercus robur* 'Pendula' (dipping low into one of the lakes) and a handsome avenue of *Thuja plicata* 'Excelsa'.

The whole garden was given a horticultural makeover in the 1930s, when thousands of rhododendrons, azaleas and similar ericaceous plants were planted and it is for its spectacular spring flowering that Lütetsburg is best known today.

Hanover's palace was destroyed in World War II, but the gardens (known as Herrenhausen) have been handsomely restored.

to contrast starkly with the parterres. The large circular Bell Fountain at the centre has 166 jets and is especially beautiful when floodlit at night.

In 1699 the Electress Sophia doubled Herrenhausen's size by laying out the New Garden. It is divided into squares and triangles by formal *bosquets* and diagonal avenues. Each of its four quarters has an octagonal pool with a fountain at its middle. At the centre of the whole garden is the Great Fountain, capable of blowing a single jet of water 82 m into the sky at speeds of up to 140 kph.

Near the site of the former palace, destroyed in 1943 and never rebuilt, are the Fig Garden (where apricots and peaches are cultivated in forcing frames) and a parterre where oranges in pots are put out for the summer. The Hedge Theatre, laid out between 1689 and 1692, is Germany's oldest. Its narrow, deep stage has hornbeam hedges with numerous exits and entrances in the wings and is lined with strange Dutch figures of gilded lead. The maze (on the other side of the Grand Parterre) was added in 1937, one of many charming but unhistorical additions from that era – including the Bell Fountain itself.

NW outskirts of Hannover, 3km from centre **C** 0511 16847576 **Open** Garden: daily 9 am; **closes** 4.30pm Nov–Jan; 5.30pm Feb; 6pm Mar & Oct; 7pm Apr & Sep; 8pm May–Aug **Size** 50ha (123ac) **Owner** City of Hannover
P ⊡ ⑪ ⑾ ⑹ ⌂ ♿
W www.herrenhaeuser-gaerten.de
@ herrenhaeuser-gaerten@han-nover-stadt.de

9. Berggarten
Herrenhäuser Str. 4
30419 Hannover

The Berggarten was the private botanic garden of the Electors and Kings of Hanover, founded at the same time as Herrenhausen's palace gardens. Though badly damaged in World War II, it has a large collection of plants (11 000 taxa) and an air of

The Berggarten's *Paradiesgarten* in late spring.

horticultural excellence that makes it a delight to visit.

The display gardens include an iris garden; a rock-garden; the Desert and Steppe Gardens with drought-loving plants; a bog garden around a marshy lake; a new Prairie Garden made with North American perennials; and a pergola garden designed by Karl Förster that shelters Mediterranean plants.

The extensive herbaceous gardens are backed by an enormous specimen of the very rare *Fagus sylvatica* 'Suenteliensis', a prostrate form of common beech, trained over an iron arcade. Trees that survived the war include the oldest *Magnolia acuminata* in Germany and a splendid *Fagus sylvatica* 'Albovariegata'. The *Paradiesgarten*, a glade of

heathers edged with magnolias, rhododendrons and Kurume azaleas, is of miraculous beauty in late spring.

The glasshouses include an orchid house (one of the biggest collections in Europe), a tropical house, new rainforest house, Canary Island house and a good collection of cacti and succulents. It was here that African violets (*Saintpaulia ionantha*) first bloomed in Europe.

NW outskirts of Hannover, immediately behind Herrenhausen **C** 0511 16845780 **Open** *See* Herrenhausen **Size** 12ha (30ac) **Owner** City of Hannover
P ⊡ ⑪ ⑾ ⑹ ⌂ ♿
W www.herrenhaeuser-gaerten.de
@ herrenhaeuser-gaerten@han-nover-stadt.de

10. Botanischer Garten Göttingen
Untere Karspüle 2
37073 Göttingen

Göttingen's botanic garden comes in two parts – three, if you count the new arboretum. The old botanic garden has the more interesting designs and plants, but the new garden is worth seeing for its experimental plantings, especially of perennials. Both belong to the University of Göttingen.

The old botanic garden was laid out in 1736, in part of the city's defensive ditches, and displays more than 10 000 taxa. The systematic beds

Gaillardia aristata and other rock plants in the old garden of Göttingen's botanic garden.

(1200 taxa), pond, rock-garden and arboretum are especially fascinating, well planted and well maintained. Spring bulbs have naturalised throughout the woodland areas. A tunnel under the city's walls leads to the eight glasshouses: the collections of cycads, aroids, cacti and succulents, tropical water plants and ferns are especially good, and that of bromeliads (500 *Tillandsia* species) exceptional.

The New Botanic Garden, open night and day, is 3 km north of the city centre in Greisebachstraße and was founded in 1967 on a spacious 36-ha site. The rock-garden is one of the largest (5000 sq. m) and most richly planted in Europe, with innumerable different habitats. The collection of perennials is also extensive and there are inter-esting habitat plantings based on the woodland flora of North America, Europe and Asia.

The new arboretum across the road is the masterpiece of Germany's most distinguished dendrologist Andreas Bärtels, and a pleasure to explore.

Old city centre, on northern ramparts
☎ 0551 9964651 **Open** Daily 8am–6pm **Closes** 3pm weekends
Glasshouses: 9.30am–2.45pm
Size 4.5ha (11ac) **Owner** Universität Göttingen 🅿 📧 🚾
🇼 wwwuser.gwdg.de/~rcallau/botgart.htm

MECKLENBURG-VORPOMMERN

11. Botanischer Garten & Arboretum der Ernst-Moritz-Arndt-Universität Greifswald

Friedrich-Ludwig-Jahn-Str.
17498 Greifswald

Greifswald's botanic garden is in two parts. The arboretum is more inter-esting than the garden and glasshouses, because it suffered less from neglect during the communist years. It dates from 1934 and has some 1400 different trees and shrubs,

The arboretum at Ernst-Moritz-Arndt-Universität also has some attractive herbaceous plantings.

geographically arranged in the sort of plant combinations that occur in nature.

The flat, open site on sandy soil has been given bulk by planting lots of conifers that have thrived to protect other plantings. There are handsome specimens of *Juglans cinerea* and *Gleditsia caspica*, and a very attractive birchwood (lots of different species) underplanted by rhodo-dendron species.

Other features include a good heather garden, collection of dwarf conifers and sunken, sheltered fern garden. The botanic garden proper is in Münsterstraße and has a fine collection of plants in its elderly glasshouses. Best are the alpine garden, a collection of medicinal plants and large areas of naturalised aconites early in spring.

NE edge of town ☎ 03834 861130
Open Apr–Oct daily 9am–6pm
Closes 4.45pm Apr & Oct Garden and glasshouses at Münterstraße 2: open daily **Size** 8ha (20ac) **Owner** Universität Greifswald 🅿 🚾 ♿
🇼 www.uni-greifswald.de/~botgart

12. Schloßgarten Schwerin

Lennéstr. 1
19053 Schwerin

The Grand-ducal castle-palace at Schwerin occupies a small island between the Schweriner and the Burg lakes. Grand Duke Friedrich Franz II of Mecklenburg-Schwerin rebuilt it, rather extravagantly, in the 1840s and 1850s, using the French renaissance style with gilded pinnacles that glitter in the sun.

At the same time, Peter Joseph Lenné laid out a garden known as the *Burggarten* (castle garden): its dramatic staircases, arcades, grottos and shell-fountain are an architectural masterpiece. The palace is attached on the other side to a baroque formal garden 100 years older, laid out by a Frenchman called Jean Legeay. The parterres are simple grass now, edged by strips of flowers and enclosed by tall hornbeam tunnels. The central point is occupied by a splendid equestrian statue of Friedrich Franz II.

The parterres lead on to a very handsome formal lake,

The French-style palace at Schloßgarten Schwerin is set off by a baroque lake.

known as the *Kreuzkanal*, shaped like a double cross and unaltered by the later fashion for land-scaping. Along its sides are comic sandstone statues of gods, seasons and allegories – copies of the originals by Balthasar Permoser. At the end are the ruins of a formal waterfall and, off to the side, a Lenné landscape garden, which runs down to the lake. Good trees include cercidiphyllums and taxodiums.

Eastern edge of city ☎ 0385 5252920 **Open** Daily dawn–dusk **Size** 25ha (62ac) **Owner** Staatliches Museum Schwerin

🅿 📺 🆆🅲 ♿ 🚻 🏛
🆆 www.museum-schwerin.de
@ info@schloss-schwerin.de

13. Schloßpark Ludwigslust
19288 Ludswigslust

This is the largest park in Mecklenburg-Vorpommern. It lies on a flat site with avenues radiating out into a magnificent wooded landscape. In front of the palace is a series of broad cascades, all that remains of the 1730s baroque garden; the water is piped from 28 km away.

The palace was the chief residence of the Dukes and Grand Dukes of Mecklenburg-Schwerin from 1764 to 1837. Most of the garden buildings were added during that time: the *Steinerne Brücke* (stone bridge) in 1780; a grotto (1785); a monument to Duke Friedrich (1785); a palatial Swiss House (1789); a monument to the Duke's favourite horse (1790); the Mausoleum of Grand Duchess Helene Paulowna (1804–06); and, most remarkable of all for a Lutheran family, a brick-built Catholic church (1806–09) in the Hansa gothic style, the first in Mecklenburg.

The grounds around the Grand Duke's palace at Schloßpark Ludwigslust were landscaped by Peter Joseph Lenné in the 1850s.

But the joy of the garden today is the parkland, with its rhododendrons, beech woodland, a string of lakes, and ever-changing views as you walk. Peter Joseph Lenné was the architect of this final transformation in the 1850s. The rare trees include fine specimens of *Halesia monticola* (the snowdrop tree), taxodiums, sequoias and magnolias.

Town centre, at end of Schloßstraße ℂ 03874 28114 **Open** Daily dawn–dusk **Size** 120ha (296ac) **Owner** Staatliches Museum Schwerin 🅿 ▣ ⓦⓒ ♿ ▦ @ info@schloss-ludwigslust.de

14. Schloßpark Neustrelitz
17235 Neustrelitz

The palace at Neustrelitz was built on a bluff above its formal baroque gardens but was blown up by the communists in 1945. Though the palace and gardens were never rebuilt, it is still an enjoyable place to visit.

A line of white statues and urns runs through the middle of the lawns where once the gardens stood: a reproduction of the mythological twins Castor and Pollux, a 19th-century angel of victory, a heavily ornamented urn and, at the end, an elegant Ionic

Canova's *Hebe* in the formal garden at Schloßpark Neustrelitz.

temple to Apollo sheltering a copy of Canova's statue of Hebe and overlooking the Zierkersee. The view is flanked by lime trees (tapered to create the illusion of greater length), and a line of baroque sandstone statues of minor gods and seasons.

To one side is a magnificent orangery, designed by Karl Friedrich Schinkel in the 1840s, now converted to a restaurant. Elsewhere are a bust of Marshall Blücher and a memorial temple to Queen Luise of Prussia – both natives of Strelitz. The parkland around the temple was charmingly landscaped in the 19th century with exotic trees, now mature.

Edge of town ℂ 03981 253119 **Open** Daily dawn–dusk **Owner** Stadt Strelitz 🅿 ▣ 🍴 ⓦⓒ ♿ Ⓦ www.neustrelitz.de @ stadtinformation@neustrelitz.de

A rich diversity of plantings surrounds the landscaped lake in Münster's botanic garden.

NORDRHEIN-WESTFALEN

15. Botanischer Garten Münster
Schlossgarten 3
48149 Münster

Friedrich Wilhelm III of Prussia founded Münster's botanic garden in 1803 as an act of conquest. The king had seized the principality and established a university there; the site was taken from the Prince-Bishop's own garden to serve the new medical faculty as a physic garden.

There are 8000 taxa to admire and enjoy. The landscaped layout and gently curving walks make the garden appear much larger. Trees have grown up to such a size that the general effect is of light woodland, and this has been used to show underplantings to good effect – rhododendrons, ferns, candelabra primulas and the wild flora of beech- and birchwoods.

There is a splendid rock-garden above the lake (handsome gunnera and water lilies), a special site where Australian and New Zealand plants are displayed in summer, an area of wet meadows, a *Bauerngarten* (cottage garden), and six glasshouses open to the public. The excellent systematic beds were remade in a striking modern design in 2002 (you can walk on the woodchip beds), and a physic garden was added in 2005. Maintenance and labelling are of high standard.

In Schloßpark, city centre
C 0251 8323827 **Open** Daily 8am–5pm (4pm in winter)
Size 4.5ha (11ac)
Owner Universität Münster
P ⬜ WC ♿ ⊞
W www.uni-muenster.de/ BotanischerGarten
@ botanischer.garten@uni-muenster.de

16. Botanischer Garten Bielefeld

Am Kahlenberg 16
33617 Bielefeld

Bielefeld's botanic garden is not attached to any university, nor involved in any scientific research. It was laid out by the town council in 1912 as a place of beauty and learning – a horticultural cynosure rather than a botanic one.

The garden offers thousands of different plants, well maintained and immensely colourful. The town is especially proud of its trees, notably *Sequoiadendron giganteum* (planted 1912), *Nyssa sylvatica, Davidia involucrata* and *Paulownia tomentosa*. There is also a tall *Cunninghamia lanceolata* (rare in Germany) and an expansive Caucasian oak (*Quercus macranthera*).

The central feature is a pretty timber-framed building (*Fachwerkhaus*), dating to 1823

Achille Duchêne's parterres at Wasserschloß Nordkirchen.

and set off by extensive lawns and brilliant annual bedding. Behind it are ancient 'dwarf' Japanese maples and an extensive collection of azaleas and rhododendrons.

The other 'must-sees' are a well-labelled rock-garden, heather garden, beechwood garden with shade-loving plants, drifts of candelabra primulas, and a model vegetable garden.

SW of old city centre, 600m W of Sparrenburg **C** 0521 513178 **Open** Daily dawn–dusk **Size** 3.5ha (9ac)
Owner Town of Bielefeld
P ⬜ ⏹ WC ♿ ⊞ ⚑ ⊞
W www.bielefeld.de/de/un/boga
@ Botanischer.Garten@bielefeld.de

Bielefeld's botanic garden has splendid floral displays.

17. Wasserschloß Nordkirchen

Schloßstr.
59394 Nordkirchen

The 'Westphalian Versailles' is a magnificent palace on a square, moated island and is a masterpiece of early baroque architecture. It was built in 1703–33 for the Prince-Bishop of Münster, Friedrich Christian von Plettenberg, and was originally set about with formal gardens in the French and Dutch styles.

The present formal garden dates back to 1906–14, when the French garden architect Achille Duchêne made the parterres for the then Duke of Arenberg in a neo-baroque style. It was substantially restored again in 1991. The immensely grand central parterre, known as Venus Island, is an elaborate *parterre de broderie* in box filled with coloured gravel; plainer grass parterres enlivened by seasonal bedding surround it. Yew cones, urns, nymphs, goddesses, fauns, and busts of worthies set on plinths provide the decoration. Long avenues disappear off into the surrounding forest as they did 300 years ago.

30km SW of Münster **Open** Daily 9am–6pm; opens 2pm Sun
Size 170ha (420ac) **Owner** Fachhochschule für Finanzen, Nordrhein-Westfalen
P ⬜ ⏹ WC ♿ ⊞
W www.fm.nrw.de

18. Westfalenpark

An der Buschmühle 3
44139 Dortmund

Westfalenpark is one of Germany's great modern civic parks, with spectacular floral displays, wonderful public amenities and a particular speciality – roses. When the German national rose garden at Sangerhausen passed to East Germany after World War II, the West German Rose Society created a new display garden at Westfalenpark.

But there is much more to interest every gardener: fine trees, large displays of rhododendrons and azaleas, a lake with water lilies and bog plants, convincing steppe and moorland gardens, neat model gardens, collections of climbing plants, a vast wild garden, magnificent displays of bedding, and dedicated gardens for irises, delphiniums, hemerocallis, herbs and phlox. There are 50 000 roses in 3000 varieties.

The vast design encompasses the entire garden. Some areas have a theme, like the 'mediaeval rose garden' or the '*Jugendstil* (*art nouveau*) garden', but best of all is the '*Kaiserhain*', which ranks among the world's most beautiful modern rose gardens. Its design is spacious and fluid, enchanced by a sequence of changing angles and levels, lush underplanting and the subtlest imaginable grading of colours and shades.

Krefeld's botanic garden educates and delights visitors.

S of city centre, around TV tower
☎ 0231 5026100 **Open** Daily 9am–11pm Some gates **close** at 6pm or 9pm **Size** 70ha (173ac) **Owner** City of Dortmund
🅿 ☕ 🍴 🚾 ♿
🌐 www.westfalenpark.de
@ westfalenpark@dortmund.de

19. Botanischer Garten der Stadt Krefeld

Sandberg 2a
47809 Krefeld-Oppum

Krefeld's botanic garden began as a teaching garden in 1913, and in the 1980s underwent an extensive makeover. It is modern, attractive and inspirational. It is city-owned and attached to no university or research institute. Its purpose – admirably fulfilled – is to educate and delight the people of Krefeld. Its dead flat, sandy site near the River Rhine has a microclimate that enables plants like *Cunninghamia lanceolata* to flourish outside. There is also a fine young specimen of the monkey puzzle tree (*Araucaria araucana*).

The contemporary design makes possible the display of 5000 different taxa in a setting that is essentially horticultural. The features include an arboretum, bedding plants (instructive displays of annuals and herbaceous plants for home gardeners), a cottage garden, a display house (orchids, palms and tender plants are put out for the summer), a heather garden, rhododendron plantings, a rock-garden (good raised beds), a rose garden (mainly modern cultivars), a smell-and-taste garden, systematic beds, displays of water plants and marginals, spring bulbs, begonia trials, and a new Apothecaries' Garden with some 100 healing herbs, always of great interest in Germany.

5km E of Krefeld city centre
☎ 02151 540519 **Open** Apr–Oct daily 8am–6pm; Nov–Mar Mon–Thu 9am–3pm & Fri 9am–12 noon Glasshouses: all year Mon–Fri 9am–12 noon **Size** 3.6ha (9ac) **Owner** City of Krefeld
🅿 ☕ 🚾 ♿
🌐 www.wbboga.krefeld.schulen.net
@ postmaster@wbboga.krefeld.schulen.net

Westfalenpark is famous for its roses, but its natural plantings are also among Germany's best.

20. Nordpark
Kaiserswerther Str.
40474 Düsseldorf

Nordpark is – with Grugapark in Essen and Westfalenpark in Dortmund – one of the great modern civic parks for which the Rhineland is famous.

It was laid out in 1937 in a bold, geometric style, and large trees were transplanted for instant effect. Its spaciousness, strong design and extensive displays of colourful bedding make it a joy to wander around. The most impressive feature is the main formal garden, known as the Water Axis (*Wasserachse*); it is a long sheet of water with fountains along the edges and is surrounded by seats, modern urns and statues, like a traditional baroque garden but very much in the modern idiom. The fountains form great parabola of water, which is especially stunning when the afternoon light shines through it.

Elsewhere are excellent modern sculptures, a rose garden, lily pond, wisteria pergola, begonia garden, steppe garden plantings, fine rhododendrons and azaleas, and a good collection of young conifers. The Japanese garden, designed and made by Japanese gardeners in 1975, has clipped azaleas, thickets of Japanese maples, flowering cherries and tightly pruned bonsai pine trees – 10 m tall!

On River Rhine, 5km NW of city centre, adjoining Trade Fair Centre (*Messe*) ☎ 0211 8994839 **Open** Daily dawn–dusk **Size** 36ha (89ac) **Owner** City of Düsseldorf
🅿 🖼 🍴 🚻 ♿
🆆 www.stadt.duesseldorf.de
@ gruen@stadt.duesseldorf.de

21. Botanischer Garten der Universität Düsseldorf
Universitätsstr. 1
40225 Düsseldorf

Düsseldorf's botanic garden moved to its present site in 1974. There was a general movement at the time to relocate German universities outside their historic city centres: Düsseldorf opted for a concrete Valhalla surrounded by autobahns.

The garden is boldly laid out on a gently undulating site, and is designed to be seen from the main outer-circuit walk. This takes you through ornamental areas (medicinal plants, iris hybrids and heathers, for example) and geographical displays dedicated to interesting ornamental plants from North America, Japan, north-east Asia, the Caucasus and central Europe.

There is an extensive area of systematic beds; a fine alpine garden (complete with moraines, screes and volcanic tufa beds); ecological collections dedicated to the flora of heathlands, alpine moorlands, coastal sand-dunes

Düsseldorf's botanic garden is dominated by its geodesic dome.

and inland sand communities; and a collection of conifers bordering a lake. But the two outstanding features are a 3-ha wildflower meadow (especially colourful in May and June) and the geodesic glasshouse (of miraculous beauty) at the centre – a revolutionary structure of steel, aluminium and flexiglass. The plants are from Mediterranean-like climates – southern Europe, the Cape, California, Australia and the Canary Islands.

5km S of old city centre
☎ 0211 8112477 **Open** Apr–Sep daily 8am–7pm, but 1–7pm Sat & 10am–7pm Sun & hols; Mar & Oct 8am–6pm, but 1– 6pm Sat & 10am–6pm Sun & hols; Nov–Feb 8am–4pm (2.30pm Fri), but **closed** weekends **Size** 7ha (17ac) **Owner** Heinrich-Heine-Universität Düsseldorf
🅿 🚻 ♿ 🚻
🆆 www.botanischergarten. uni-duesseldorf.de
@ B.Garten@uni-duesseldorf.de

22. Schloßpark Benrath
Benrather Schloßallee 100–106
40597 Düsseldorf

This charming palace was one of several built as a hunting lodge for Karl Theodor, Elector of Pfalz (1724–99), by Nicolas de Pigage (1723–98). Part of the palace now houses the Museum for European Garden Art.

Nordpark has a spectacular Japanese garden.

Sculptures are an integral part of Schloß Benrath's baroque gardens and were often included to add grandeur to landscape gardens.

Nicolas de Pigage also laid out the park in the French style, and there is a very satisfying unity of design between the pink palace and its baroque gardens. On the terrace behind the palace, greenhouse plants in large containers are put out for the summer, as they were in the 18th century. On either side of the terrace are two small but delightful pleasure gardens. One, in the baroque style with a grass parterre and flower-border, is known either as the French Garden or the Electress's Garden; the other, more relaxed in style, is still called the Elector's Garden, though it was laid out in a fluid design by Peter Joseph Lenné in 1840.

The strongest part of the Schloßpark design is a long, straight canal (once flanked by avenues of lime), which stretches 470 m into the distance and is axially aligned on the palace. The canal also forms one side of a square woodland garden, which is geometrically laid out with eight avenues that intersect at the centre and has a circular walk within.

Elsewhere are an orangery, a rose garden, restored kitchen garden and fruit garden planted with old cultivars.

10km SE of Düsseldorf
☎ 0211 8993832 **Open** Daily dawn–dusk **Size** 63ha (156ac) **Owner** Stiftung Schloß und Park Benrath 🅿 🚻 ♿ 🍴 ⛲
🆆 www.schloss-benrath.de

23. Grugapark Essen
Virchowstr. 167a
45147 Essen

Grugapark first opened its gates for the Großen Ruhrländischen Gartenbauausstellung (garden show) in 1929 – 70 ha of public gardens, purpose-built to educate and entertain the people of Essen.

The scale and sheer variety of its contents are impressive, as is the consistently high standard of design, planting and maintenance. Horticulture, botany, ecology and public amenity combine to make a memorable visit. One way to get an excellent overview is to take a ride on its narrow-gauge railway, the *Grugabahn*.

The entrance opens onto a fountain whose five jets curve through the air in parallel lines with a flourish that sets the tone for the whole garden. The highlights include: two lakes (one dedicated to water lilies); lots of modern sculpture (surprisingly good); a camellia collection; a heather garden; a rose garden (all modern cultivars); a charming and extensive Japanese garden; a model kitchen garden; a herb garden; a cottage garden; a garden of the senses; a Mediterranean garden; an ecological garden; drifts of candelabra primulas; a terraced amphitheatre of dahlias; international seed trials; and the largest collection of dwarf conifers in Europe. The extensive rock-gardens include an alpine garden with a mountain stream and waterfall. Grugapark also has excellent (and massive) examples of a steppe garden and herbaceous plantings in the German natural style – these alone are worth the visit.

The beautiful, dense woodland garden is spectacular with rhododendrons in late spring. The glasshouses include one for tropical rainforest plants, a dry house for cacti and succulents, another for carnivorous plants, a bonsai collection and a show house filled with orchids in winter.

Grugapark Essen has very successful prairie plantings.

The botanic garden in Wuppertal was founded in 1890 as a school garden.

On SW edge of city, 4km from historic centre **C** 0201 8883106 **Open** Daily 9am–dusk **Size** 70ha (173ac) **Owner** City of Essen

P ⊘ ⑪ WC ♿
W www.grugapark.de
@ info@grugapark.essen.de

24. Botanischer Garten Wuppertal

Elisenhöhe 1
42107 Wuppertal

Wuppertal's botanic garden started life in 1890 as a school garden, and was taken over as a municipal botanic garden in 1929. It retains the happy air of a garden whose aim is to educate the young and give pleasure to all.

Its 4000 taxa occupy a south-facing slope, with the orangery, cactus house and water tower at the top. The layout follows the contours of the hill and is partly defined by the tree plantings. These include good specimens of *Quercus petraea, Davidia involucrata, Ailanthus altissima,* a tall *Liriodendron tulipifera,* an old purple beech and some pretty magnolias and flowering dogwoods. The main joys are a splendid rock-garden, a rhododendron walk, a steppe garden, a collection of herbs, and fine perennials. Best of all are the colourful seasonal displays and the wide range of tender ornamental plants put out for the summer on the sunny terraces.

At eastern end of Elberfeld area of Wuppertal **C** 0202 5634207 **Open** Apr–Sep daily 7.30am–7pm (9am weekends & hols) **Closes** 6pm Mar & Oct; 4.30pm Nov–Feb Cactus house: Mar–Oct Sun 3–5pm **Size** 2.5ha (6ac) **Owner** City of Wuppertal **P ⊘ WC ♿**
W www.stadt.wuppertal.de
@ botanischergarten
@stadt.wuppertal.de

25. Botanischergarten der Stadt Köln

Amsterdamer Str. 34
50735 Köln

This delightful garden is an amalgamation of a public park (laid out in 1862 by Peter Joseph Lenné) and the botanic garden, which moved here in 1914. Its centrepiece is the superb glasshouse known as

Cologne's botanic garden is spacious and full of interest at all seasons.

Flora, a soaring expression of civic pride that was intended to rival Sir Joseph Paxton's Crystal Palace in London. Almost everything was destroyed in 1945, but the gardens and their glasshouses have since been restored with increasing fidelity to the original design and plantings.

Cologne's botanic garden's prime function remains to educate and delight the one million visitors who come here every year. The living collections extend to over 10 000 taxa, with a particular emphasis upon plants of horticultural value – masses of irises, dwarf conifers, primulas, heathers, azaleas, lilies, magnolias, rhododendrons and plants suited for such microhabitats as woodland, sandy banks and bogs. The rock-garden, in particular, is outstanding, with 2000 different plants from the mountain ranges of the entire world. Some 5000 taxa grow in the superb glasshouses, where there are collections of economic plants (coffee, cocoa, pineapple, vanilla orchid, rice), lotuses and giant water lilies, cacti, and 150 camellias for winter colour. Even the summer flower displays – among the brightest and best in Germany – make a point of using unusual 'botanic' plants for ornamental effect.

What little remains of the pre-war plantings include massive specimens of the copper beech (*Fagus sylvatica* 'Atropurpurea') and the Caucasian wing nut (*Pterocarya fraxinifolia*).

1km N of old city, opposite zoo **C** 0221 560890 **Open** Daily 8am–dusk **Size** 5½ha (14ac) **Owner** City of Cologne **P ⊘ ⑪ WC ♿**
W www.stadt-koeln.
de/natur/parks/flora/

26. Schloß Augustusburg

Schloßstr. 6
50319 Brühl

The garden at Schloß Augustusburg, like its sumptuous palace, is a pure example of the early 18th-century

Schloß Augustusburg is a masterpiece of French baroque garden design.

baroque. It was made for the Elector of Cologne, Clemens August von Wittelsbach, between 1727 and 1729, by the Frenchman Dominique Girard, a pupil of Le Nôtre.

The outstanding feature is a matching pair of *parterres de broderie*, whose intricate pattern of swirling embroideries is elegantly worked in low-growing box, set off by gravel of different colours and seasonal bedding plants. The formal gardens are edged on three sides by double avenues of boxed limes. The main axis between the parterres leads down to a formal pool, fed by a shallow water staircase. It reflects the sky as you approach, and mirrors the grandeur of the palace when you look back.

Many tender plants are displayed along the terraces below the palace in summer, including large orange trees, palms and oleanders. The woodland park surrounding the formal garden was laid out in the English landscape style by Peter Joseph Lenné in the 1840s for King Friedrich Wilhelm IV of Prussia. In 1984 Schloß Augustusburg and its gardens were declared a UNESCO cultural world heritage site.

SE side of town, 15km S of Köln
☎ 02232 44000 **Open** Daily 7am–dusk **Size** 40ha (99ac)
🅿 📷 🆆🅲 ♿ 🚻 🎑
🅦 www.schlossbruehl.de
@ info@schlossbruehl.de

27. Botanische Gärten der Rheinischen Friedrich-Wilhelms-Universität Bonn
Meckenheimer Allee 171
53115 Bonn

Bonn's botanic garden is known throughout Germany for having recently produced the largest flower in the plant kingdom – the gigantic (and rather repellent) arum from Borneo called *Amorphophallus titanum*, whose flower reached 2.74 m high in 2003. Unfortunately, this record was beaten by a specimen in Park Wilhelma at Stuttgart, which achieved the incredible height of 2.91 m in 2005.

But there are many more reasons to visit Bonn, whose garden surrounds the historic, rococo Poppelsdorfer Schloß,

built by Prince-Bishop Clemens August in the 1740s. The castle was the most extravagant built by the Electors of Cologne, and only two ancient beech trees remain from its baroque garden; everything else was planted after the university took possession in 1818. The comparatively mild climate and inner-city site enable such tender trees as the monkey puzzle (*Araucaria araucana*) and lacebark pine (*Pinus bungeana*) to survive and flourish.

Conservation is a big part of the garden's remit. The glasshouses maintain reserve collections of threatened groups, like the epiphytic cacti of the tropical American forests, the endemic flora of the Cape Verde Islands, and the genus *Cyclamen*. Other

Bonn University's botanic garden is laid out around the palace of the Prince-Bishops of Cologne.

Hercules, 10 m high, dominates Schloßpark Wilhelmshöhe and the city far below.

glasshouses are dedicated to palms, ferns, mangrove swamp plants, *Victoria amazonica*, succulents and orchids. But everywhere, under glass and in the open, are good plants – well grown, well labelled and well displayed.

Southern part of historic city centre
C 0228 735523 **Open** Weekdays 9am–6pm (4pm Nov–Mar) Glasshouses: 10am–12 noon & 2–4pm **Size** 7.5ha (19ac) **Owner** Universität Bonn **P** ▣ **WC** ▣ ▦ ▧
W www.botgart.uni-bonn.de
@ botgart@uni-bonn.de

HESSEN

28. Schloß Wilhelmstal
34379 Calden

Landgrave Wilhelm VIII of Kassel built the splendid rococo palace of Wilhelmsthal between 1743 and 1761 as a summer residence. It was set off by an equally complex and exuberant garden, whose axes fanned out from the principal rooms. The ornate southern axis, originally built in 1756, has recently been restored and is a real eye-opener: a watery staircase and a long canal lead to an exquisite Chinese-style pavilion, decorated with gilded statues and fountains.

Most of the garden disappeared when the grounds were transformed into an English-style park in about 1800, but the landscaping was very well executed, leaving us with sweeping meadows and avenues that disappear into the woods, all overlooked by a neo-gothic watch-tower.

13km NW of Kassel **C** 05674 6898 **Open** Tue–Sun 10am–5pm (4pm in winter) **Size** 15ha (37ac) **Owner** Staatliche Schlößer und Gärten Hessen **P** ▣ **WC** ▣ ▦ ▦
W www.schloss-wilhelmsthal.de
@ info@schloesser-hessen

Gilded statues grace the Chinese pavilion at Schloß Wilhelmsthal.

29. Schloßpark Wilhelmshöhe
34131 Kassel

The magnificent 10-m statue of Hercules is the first thing you notice at Wilhelmshöhe. His muscular frame bestrides an octagonal pedestal at the top of a steep mountainside. The palace, visible from a great distance, is halfway up the mountain, and the old city centre of Kassel at its base is 6 km away.

The sheer size of the landscape is astonishing; Wilhelmshöhe claims to be the largest 'mountain park' in Europe. Landgrave Karl of Hesse built the dramatic cascade, pools, and rocky outcrops in 1699–1700 to echo the baroque gardens he had admired in Italy. Hercules is actually a bulked-up copy of the Farnese original.

The Elector Wilhelm I landscaped the mountainside 100 years later, adding the picturesque Ionic temple to Apollo near the palace and the *Teufelsbrücke* (Devil's Bridge) below the Octagon. Next came a vast (and very convincing) ruined Roman aqueduct and the neo-gothic, English-style ruined castle called *Schloß Löwenburg*. These are very substantial, theatrical and imposing buildings.

Wilhelm I was an admirer of the English landscape style; he planted trees, created meadows and made lakes and small waterfalls below the palace. His son, Wilhelm II, shared his horticultural interests and built the large (and very pretty) Great Glasshouse in 1822. Rhododendrons are a pleasing feature of the park in late spring and an important collection of old roses has recently been planted near the bottom of the park. But the most sublime experience at Wilhelmshöhe is the sight of the water cascading down its massive mountainside.

Above city of Kassel
☎ 0561 31680208 **Open** Park: daily dawn–dusk. Cascades run in summer Wed, Sun & hols, plus 1st Sat of month. They start 2.30pm at Octagon & reach Teufelsbrücke 3.10pm, aqueduct 3.20pm, Great Fountain 3.30pm. Löwenburg: Tue–Sun 10am–5pm (4pm in winter). Hercules and Octagon: daily mid-Mar–mid-Nov 10am–5pm. Great Glasshouse: daily 11am–4.30pm, but **closed** for a few weeks in winter **Size** 1000ha (2469ac) **Owner** Staatliche Schlößer und Gärten Hessen
🅿 ☕ 🍴 🆆🅲 ♿ ⛪ 👶 ♿
🆆 www.schloesser-hessen.de
@ info@schloesser-hessen.de

30. Insel Siebenbergen

Auedamm 18
34121 Kassel

Insel Siebenbergen is a horticultural island at the far end of the historic landscape belonging to Kassel's great summer palace of Karlsaue. It was made from spoil humped when the 'Swan Lake' was excavated in 1710. At first, it was planted with conifers, but it acquired its present design and a more general collection of plants from the 1830s onwards. It is a magnificent example of 19th-century landscaping for aesthetic effect with plants of every kind.

The plantings are thick and luxuriant, and the standard of maintenance quite unparalleled, even by German standards. Fine trees

There is exemplary planting and maintenance at Insel Siebenbergen.

include a vast three-trunked specimen of *Picea orientalis* and a handsome *Quercus robur* 'Concordia', but the structure comes from evergreen shrubs, azaleas, hydrangeas, fuchsias and rich herbaceous plantings in sweeps and drifts. They are complemented by dramatic summer bedding. Even the moat is thick with water lilies. 'Germany's most English garden' is a common verdict.

SW corner of Karslaue
☎ 0561 7392173 **Open** Easter–early Oct daily, except Mon 10am–7pm **Size** 1ha (2½ac) **Owner** Verwaltung der Staatlichen Schlößer und Gärten
🅿 ☕ 🍴 🆆🅲 ♿ ⛪ 👶 ♿
🆆 www.schloesser-hessen.de
@ info@schloesser-hessen.de

31. Palmengarten

Siesmayerstr. 61
60323 Frankfurt am Main

Frankfurt's Palmengarten is among the most interesting and best kept gardens in Europe, with an excellent layout and lots of plant appeal. It was established in 1868 as a private botanic garden – one of very few to have survived and flourished for so long.

You enter through a large glasshouse built in 1905, with carnivorous plants on the left and pineapples and tillandsias on the right. It is only the first of many fine glasshouses; Palmengarten has more than 1 ha under glass. The original palmhouse (1869) is one of Europe's largest, with displays of tropical plants and tree ferns, as well as subtropical palms. The *Tropicarium* is a huge, modern complex of 24 tropical glasshouses, divided and planted according to habitat, including semi-deserts,

Iris trials and one of the many glasshouses at Palmengarten.

The Crown Prince's pyramid on a small island is one of Wilhelmsbad's charming follies.

savannahs, mangrove swamps and monsoon regions. Other houses are dedicated to alpines and the woodland flora of sub-antarctic South America.

The grounds outside are bursting with colour and interest. Pergolas of modern climbing roses surround a formal rose garden and rococo pavilion. The steppe meadows are planted with dryland perennials from eastern Europe, central Asia and North America: maintenance comprises two mowings a year. The rock-garden has special areas of gravel, moraine, peat, acid soil, tufa and rock boulders to suit all tastes. Massed plantings of crocuses, tulips, narcissi, hyacinths, azaleas, rhodo-dendrons, hemerocallis, irises, peonies, lilies and dahlias are some of the other seasonal

highlights. At Palmengarten, the wow factor is abundant everywhere.

NW edge of city, bordering ring road
☎ 069 21233939 **Open** Daily 9am–6pm **Closes** Nov–Jan 4pm **Size** 20ha (49ac) **Owner** Gesellschaft Freunde des Palmengartens
P ⬛ 🍴 WC ♿ 🚼 ⛲
W www.palmengarten-frankfurt.de
@ info.palmengarten
@stadt-frankfurt.de

32. Staatspark Hanau-Wilhelmsbad
63454 Hanau-Wilhelmsbad

Wilhelmsbad is a ghostly relic of one of Germany's earliest landscaped gardens – romantic, evocative and full of nostalgia. It was laid out by Crown Prince Wilhelm of Hessen-Kassel between 1777

and 1785: the prince lived at Hanau and wanted to turn it into a profitable spa town. When his father died, the prince returned to Kassel, abandoning both Wilhelmsbad and its park.

Within a delightful, rather overgrown, romantic English park are some very charming follies, notably a pyramid, a deliberately ruined castle on an island in the lake, and a Chinese-style mound with a winding ascent, known as the *Schneckenberg* (Snail Hill). Most atmospheric of all is an ancient carousel, a contemporary cynosure when built in 1779; its horses and carriages seem not to have moved for 200 years.

3km NW of Hanau town centre
☎ 06181 83376 **Open** Daily dawn–dusk **Size** 29ha (72ac) **Owner** Staatliche Schlößer und Gärten Hessen P WC ⬛ ♿ 🖼
W www.schloesser-hessen.de
@ info@schloesser-hessen.de

33. Prinz-Georgs-Garten
Schloßgartenstr. 6b
64289 Darmstadt

Prinz-Georgs-Garten is a very pretty reconstruction of a small, enclosed baroque garden. It was made in 1748 by combining two existing gardens at right angles to each other – hence its 'L' shape – with a small palace at each end.

Prinz-Georgs-Garten: one of the sundials in the parterre.

The garden has a formal area, divided by central, cross- and diagonal axes, a small fountain in a central circular pool and some handsome sundials. The second parterre, in front of the *Prettlacksches Gartenhaus*, is lined with clipped yews, and decorated with a fountain, an Italian well-head and trained fruit trees. The bedding is unusually well done and a large number of orange trees are put out in white Versailles cases for the summer. Provincial Germany at its best.

Darmstadt city centre, adjoining Herrngarten **C** 06151 125632 **Open** Mar–Oct daily 7am–9pm; Nov–Feb 8am–5pm **Size** 1.8ha (4½ac) **Owner** Staatliche Schlößer und Gärten Hessen

P ◻ WC & ⊞ ▦

W www.schloesser-hessen.de
@ info@schloesser-hessen.de

34. Botanischer Garten der Technischen Universität Darmstadt
Schnittspahnstr. 5
64287 Darmstadt

Darmstadt's botanic garden has much to admire in its 4.5 ha: 9000 taxa, including an arboretum, a pinetum,

systematic beds, a rock-garden, beds of iris and hemerocallis, a heath garden, and a small lake edged with hefty taxodiums. The purple-flowering parasite *Lathraea clandestina* has naturalised upon the roots of poplars and willows.

The glasshouses have interesting collections, too: tropical water plants, economic plants, cycads, bromeliads and orchids. Many are put out for the summer in pots, including ferns, palms, banksias, eucalyptus and acacias.

But the real joy of the garden is its layout (it was designed in 1874 – the conifers are tremendous), with endless curving paths that make it appear much larger. And everywhere are well-labelled, interesting and unusual plants that you have not seen before and wish for your own garden.

Eastern edge of Darmstadt, 3km from historic centre **C** 06151 16 3502 **Open** Apr–Sep daily 7.30am– 7.30pm (12 noon Sun & hols); Oct– Mar 7.30am–4pm (12 noon Sun & hols) Glasshouses open weekdays: 9.30am–12.30pm & 1.30–3.30pm **Size** 4.5ha (11ac) **Owner** Technische Universität Darmstadt

P WC &

W www.tu-darmstadt.de/fb/bio/
   bot/BoGa.html

Beauty among the roses at Europas Rosengarten.

SAARLAND

35. Europas Rosengarten
Rudolf-Nebel-Weg 10
66482 Zweibrücken

Europe's Rose Garden is a very charming and successful civic park on the best German model. It was founded in 1914 but completely reworked in the 1960s and very well designed to give you lots of time to look at individual roses along the way, but keep the visitor traffic flowing. There are sculptures and memorials, a pretty trellised 'wedding pavilion' on a mound, a substantial lake, and good displays of annuals, bulbs and herbaceous plants.

But the roses steal the show: there are over 60 000 bushes in 2000 different varieties. Modern, repeat-flowering cultivars from all over the world predominate, and there are collections of older roses and shrubs. Labelling is good, which means that this is an excellent place to learn about roses and remember their names.

In city, NE of centre **C** 06332 871670 **Open** Daily Apr–Oct 9am–7pm **Closes** 8pm Jun–Aug **Size** 5ha (12ac) **Owner** Verein der Rosenfreunde Zweibrücken

P ◻ ⊪ WC & ⊞

W www.europas-rosengarten.de
@ info@europas-rosengarten.de

Darmstadt's botanic garden displays rare plants in a landscaped setting.

LEFT: Schloßpark Charlottenburg's central fountain is part of a large formal garden.
RIGHT: Tiergarten's immaculate and extensive bedding.

BERLIN

36. Schloßpark Charlottenburg

Spandauer Damm 20–24
14059 Berlin

Schloß Charlottenburg, Berlin's largest palace, was built in the closing years of the 17th century as a summer residence for the Electress Sophie Charlotte. The gardens were the first in Germany to be laid out in the French style; the architect was Siméon Godeau, a pupil of Le Nôtre.

The outlines remain today: the large formal garden running down to a formal lake has four parterres around a central fountain. The planting has been changed several times, though the latest revision (2001) is close to the baroque original, with its dramatic swirling broderies and colourful *mille fleurs* borders. Peter Joseph Lenné landscaped Charlottenburg between 1818 and 1835, turning the remoter parts of the palace gardens into a very beautiful English-style park.

Visitors should start on the palace terraces (where huge tender plants like palm trees are put out for the summer) and walk past the clipped yews, pleached limes and urns of the formal gardens to the statues above the lake, before turning along shady avenues and finally into the parkland – a very enjoyable sequence. At the far end of the lake an elegant iron bridge dating from 1799 (very early for cast-iron work) and a pretty rococo banqueting house called the Belvedere (1788). Karl Friedrich Schinkel's mausoleum of the Prussian kings lies to one side, constructed of red marble and surrounded by solemn yews and rhododendrons – a wonderful mood change from the exuberant formal gardens and the pastoral park.

Centre of W Berlin, a prominent landmark ☎ 0331 9694200 **Open** Daily 6am–8pm (9pm in summer) **Size** 53ha (131ac) **Owner** Stiftung Preußische Schlößer und Gärten Berlin-Brandenburg

🅿 🚗 🍴 🚾 ♿ 🏛 🎫
🅦 www.spsg.de
@ generalverwaltung@spsg.de

37. Tiergarten

Str. des 17 Juni
10785 Berlin-Tiergarten

Berlin's Tiergarten was completely destroyed in 1944 by war-stressed Berliners felling the trees for firewood but is once more the city's largest and best loved public park.

It was originally a hunting forest for the Electors of Brandenburg, but Peter Joseph Lenné was employed in the 1830s to lay it out in the English landscape style for public recreation. The thickly planted woodland is a pleasure to walk through, with underplantings of ornamental shrubs, most notably rhododendrons, interspersed with open spaces, lakes and self-contained gardens. The most enchanting is the Rose Garden, with a granite Italianate fountain at its centre and a handsome statue of Flora at one end. Roses of every kind are densely inter-planted with a rich mixture of herbaceous perennials and annuals chosen to create a sense of opulence. You could be 100 km from the city.

There are many sculptures and monuments throughout the Tiergarten – Goethe, Queen Luise, Friedrich Wilhelm III, Richard Wagner and Rosa Luxemburg are among the motley notables commemorated – but the magnificent gilded Angel of Victory column (*Siegessäule*) can be seen from every corner of the park.

Heart of Berlin, between Charlottenburg and Brandenburg Gate ☎ 0391 2961 **Open** Daily dawn–dusk **Size** 200ha (494ac) **Owner** City of Berlin

🅿 ▣ 🍴 🆆🅲 ♿

W www.stadtentwicklung.berlin.de

38. Botanischer Garten und Botanisches Museum Berlin-Dahlem

Königin-Luise-Str. 6–8
14191 Berlin

Berlin's botanic garden is Germany's biggest and best: the 22 000 taxa in its living collections guarantee its position among the world's top botanic gardens. Its history dates back to *c.* 1600, but it relocated to its current site in the early 1900s. The focal point of its design is an Italian garden, with rich displays of bedding plants fringed during summer with tender plants in large pots. It runs up to the huge tropical house (60 m long and 23 m high) at the centre of 16 interlinked glasshouses. Here are giant *Ficus* and bamboos, innumerable palms and Araceae, plus ancient specimens of cycads and *Welwitschia mirabilis* from Namibia. Other houses are devoted to begonias (over 100 species), orchids, bromeliads, African succulents, American cacti, South African plants, insectivorous plants, giant tropical water lilies (*Victoria amazonica* and *V. cruziana*), camellias, and a fine collection from Australia and New Zealand.

Elsewhere within the gardens are an extensive layout of systematic beds, a herb garden, medicinal garden and fragrance garden for public enjoyment. Thirteen hectares are devoted to geographical collections of the world's flora; a vast chain of rock-gardens runs through this area and displays the alpine flora of the great mountain ranges, including the Carpathians, Rockies and Atlas Mountains.

In the surrounding woodland are shade-loving plants, while herbaceous taxa and shrubs fill the glades between – all arranged geographically, so that each part is a perfect microcosm of an area's flora. The arboretum stretches to 14 ha; its 1800 trees are planted in taxonomic groups (Pinaceae, Fagaceae, for example), including fastigiate, pendulous or dwarf forms, many of them horticultural cultivars. The collection of conifers is especially impressive.

In S of city, near Dahlem U-bahn station ☎ 030 83850100 **Open** Daily 9am onwards **Closes** 4pm Nov–Jan; 5pm Feb; 6pm Mar & Oct; 7pm Sep; 8pm Apr & Aug; 9pm May–Jul **Size** 43ha (106ac) **Owner** Freie Universität Berlin

▣ 🍴 🆆🅲 ♿ 🏠 🚻

W www.bgbm.org

39. Späth's Arboretum

Späthstr. 80–81
12437 Berlin

Franz Späth laid out this arboretum in the 1870s. Späth came from a long line of successful nurserymen, and his nursery in Berlin became the most renowned in Germany. The arboretum is designed in the English style, with narrow paths winding through its arboricultural excitements

The formal gardens of Berlin's botanic garden run up to its enormous tropical house.

The famous nursery garden at Späth's Arboretum boasts fine mature trees.

to reveal idyllic open glades. It served as a private garden for the Späth family, as a trial ground and source of budwood for the nursery, and as a display garden for customers, among them the great chancellor Otto von Bismarck. Over some 1200 taxa represented by 5000 plants still grow here, and their dendrological interest is matched by their ornamental charm. There are fine specimens of *Quercus mongolica* var. *grosseserrata* and *Aesculus hippocastanum* 'Umbraculifera' and many Späth introductions, including *Prunus laurocerasus* 'Schipkaensis' and the type specimen *Juniperus* 'Pfitzeriana', the original parent plant of the millions now in cultivation.

SE Berlin ☎ 030 6366941 **Open** Apr–Oct Wed, Thu, Sat, Sun & hols 10am–6pm **Size** 5ha (12ac) **Owner** Humboldt Universität zu Berlin

🅿 ▣ 🍴 ⬚ ⬚ ⬚
ⓦ www.hu-berlin.de

40. Pfaueninsel

Pfaueninselchaussee
14109 Berlin-Zehlendorf

Pfaueninsel is a magic island, suspended in time. Though part of the overall landscaping that Peter Joseph Lenné designed for Potsdam and the Havel in the 1820s, it has an extraordinary air of

peace and enchantment that sets it apart from anywhere else in Germany. It can only be reached by ferry and, once you arrive, there is nothing to do but walk.

The Schloß is a strange, white, 'ruined' castle, with two towers joined by a suspension bridge. It was built for Friedrich Wilhelm II's mistress, Gräfin Lichtenau, in 1796 and connects across the lake with Schloß Glienicke and the Neuergarten. Near the Schloß are two very charming 1820s gardens, rare relics of a style now seldom seen. The Round Garden was designed around a pergola of robinia trunks hung with wisteria and colourfully

Pfaueninsel's eccentric Schloß is an integral part of Peter Joseph Lenné's landscape of Potsdam and the Havel.

planted with summer bedding. The Rose Garden, Germany's first, is planted with early varieties, grown in long, narrow beds, often as standards. But most visitors find that their curiosity is aroused by a distant gothic outline that leads them through an enchanted parkland of oaks and wild-flowers, past a Doric memorial to the much-loved Queen Luise, a house clad in bark, an aviary, the *Kavaliershaus* (a guesthouse designed by Schinkel) to the far end of the island. The gothic ruin is no more than some stables with a fanciful façade, and you realise that its only purpose was to make you explore the dreamlike beauty of this incomparable landscape from end to end.

Eastern side of Havel lake; ferry from Nikolskoer Weg ☎ 030 32091446 **Open** May–Aug daily 8am–8pm; Apr & Sep 8am–6pm; Mar & Oct 9am–5pm; Nov–Feb 10am–4pm **Size** 76ha (237ac) **Owner** Stiftung Preußische Schlößer und Gärten Berlin-Brandenburg

▣ ⬚ ⬚ ⬚ ⬚
ⓦ www.spsg.de
@ besucherzentrum@spsg.de

41. Schloß Klein-Glienicke

Königsstr. 36
14109 Berlin

Klein-Glienicke is an enchanting, compact, coherent, scaled-down landscape garden in a prominent position on the shores of the Havel. Karl Friedrich Schinkel built the neo-classical palace for Prince Karl of Prussia (the brother of Friedrich Wilhelm IV) in 1825–28. Schinkel also designed Klein-Glienicke's best known feature – the Lion Fountain beside the road: a pair of golden lions, high on two colonnaded plinths, spew jets of water into a pool below. Peter Joseph Lenné was the landscaper and created a perfect unity between the palace, flower gardens, pleasure grounds, park and wider landscape.

Prince Karl was an amateur

Schloß Klein-Glienicke is the perfect small, neo-classical estate.

archaeologist: some of the Greek and Roman inscriptions, wall paintings, reliefs and mosaïcs he brought back from his Grand Tour were incorporated into a classical temple. Nearby is a wonderfully romantic arrangement of fallen columns retrieved from Cape Sounion. At the tip of the garden is Schinkel's Casino, an exquisite neo-classical villa with neat colonnades on either side and delicious views across the Havel. Ludwig Persius later added an orangery, a Roman-style *Stibadium* (banqueting table) with a granite basin in front and, in the landscaped

park (open day and night), the *Gasthaus Moorlake*, a forester's lodge in the Swiss style.

By Glienicke Bridge on western edge of Berlin ☎ 030 8053041 **Open** Mid-Apr–mid-Oct weekends & hols 10am–5pm **Size** 81ha (200ac) **Owner** Stiftung Preußische Schlößer und Gärten Berlin-Brandenburg

🅿 🖼 🍴 🚾 🖼

🆆 www.spsg.de

@ besucherzentrum@spsg.de

BRANDEN-BURG

42. Freundschaftsinsel
Lange Brücke
14467 Potsdam

Freundschaftsinsel is the best known garden laid out by the German plant guru, Karl Förster (1874–1970). He first developed it as a show garden for perennials, shrubs, ferns and grasses between 1938 and 1940: his friend Hermann Mattern did the design. It fell into disrepair during the communist years but was comprehensively replanted in time for the *Potsdam Bundesgartenschau* (garden show) in 2001. Eighty thousand herbaceous plants were the core of the planting, and they included most of the

many delphiniums, phloxes and asters bred by Förster.

The backbone of the design is a long, curving pergola matched by curving beds, where rows of herbaceous perennials are prominently labelled. Elsewhere are ecological and steppe-style plantings, and magnificent mixed displays of annuals. Förster's private garden attached to his nursery at Am Raubfang 6, on the north-west edge of Potsdam, was also restored in 2001 and is open daily and freely throughout the year.

Centre of Potsdam **Open** Daily dawn–dusk **Size** 6ha (15ac) **Owner** City of Potsdam

🅿 🖼 🚾 ♿

🆆 www.foerster-stauden.de

@ info@foerster-stauden.de

43. Babelsberg
Park Babelsberg 11
14482 Potsdam

Schloß Babelsberg has a dreamy, romantic landscape garden on the shores of the Havel lake. The Schloß was designed by Karl Friedrich Schinkel for Prince Wilhelm of Prussia (later Emperor Wilhelm I of Germany) in imitation of George IV of England's neo-Norman Windsor Castle. The ubiquitous Peter Joseph Lenné laid out the park

Karl Förster's plantings at Freundschaftsinsel were restored in 2001 for the *Bundesgartenschau*.

Pückler-Muskau's Victorian garden at Babelsberg introduced colourful gardenesque flower-beds into the landscaped park.

(wooded on the eastern side and open and meadowy on the west) and linked it visually to Schloß Klein-Glienicke.

Prince Hermann von Pückler-Muskau took over as garden designer in 1843 and added the Victorian-style flower garden, still called the Pleasure Ground. It is a winding walk down a shallow valley beneath the castle, planted in the gardenesque style with flower beds and panniers, all enclosed by glazed palmetto tiles and richly planted with seasonal bedding. The formal rose garden is surrounded by a gilded gothic metalwork arcade.

The grounds are remarkable for the number of substantial and charming buildings. Some features have a utilitarian purpose like Persius's gothic *Maschinenhaus* (1843) with its electric generators and the *Flatowturm* (1856), a water reservoir disguised as a very tall tower. The *Siegessäule* (1868) or victory column was built to commemorate Bismarck's campaigns (an early example of German triumphalism) with a bust of the Iron Chancellor incorporated into its base.

Western side of Havel lake
☎ 0331 9694200 **Open** Tue–Sun 10am–5pm **Size** 135ha (333ac) **Owner** Stiftung Preußische Schlößer und Gärten Berlin-Brandenburg
🅿 ♿ & ▦
🆆 www.spsg.de
@ besucherzentrum@spsg.de

44. Neuer Garten
14469 Potsdam

The Neuer Garten (New Garden) was begun by Friedrich Wilhelm II in 1787 as a way of expressing his distaste for the baroque layout of Sanssouci. His mentor was Prinz Franz of Anhalt-Dessau, and he employed the Wörlitz designer Johann August Eyserbeck to lay out an extensive (and enchanting) park along the western side of Lake Heiliger.

The main palace within the landscape is the neo-classical *Marmorpalais* (Marble Palace), which is a key element in the mega-landscape of the Potsdam lakes. Friedrich Wilhelm surrounded the palace with delectable follies,

including a kitchen hidden in a ruined Roman temple, a gothic library, an Egyptian-style orangery and a pyramid that served as an ice house.

Peter Joseph Lenné worked on the landscape in 1816 and unified its various parts. Much later (in 1846), he also designed the pretty flower parterre on the garden side of the *Marmorpalais*. A second flower garden in front of the orangery followed in 1879 and boasts an excellent display of summer bedding and exotic plants – huge palms, oleanders, pomegranates and daturas.

At the far northern end of Neuer Garten you come to Schloß Cecilienhof, famous for being the venue of the Potsdam conference in 1945, but built by Crown Prince Wilhelm (son of the last Emperor, Wilhelm II) in a school-of-Lutyens, neo-Tudor style during the years 1913–17. English-style herbaceous borders and Arts-and-Crafts yew topiary surround it, while more parkland leads down to the shores of the Havel and the ruins of a shell grotto.

Northern edges of Potsdam
☎ 0331 9694244 **Open** All year, except Mon 9am–5pm (4pm Nov–Mar) **Size** 127ha (314ac) **Owner** Stiftung Preußische Schlößer und Gärten Berlin-Brandenburg
🅿 ♿ 🍴 ♿ & ▦
🆆 www.spsg.de
@ besucherzentrum@spsg.de

Edwardian-style topiary at Schloss Cecilienhof (at the northern end of Neuer Garten), where the Potsdam Conference met in 1945.

Schloßpark Sanssouci is Germany's most famous and beautiful garden. LEFT: The *Weinberg* terraces. RIGHT: A metal trellised pavilion on the top terrace by the palace.

45. Schloßpark Sanssouci

Maulbeerallee
14414 Potsdam

Sanssouci Park is by far the most beautiful, exciting and rewarding garden in Germany and, in my opinion, the world. It was started by Friedrich the Great between 1744 and 1770, expanded by Friedrich Wilhelm IV between 1826 and 1860 and finished by Emperor Wilhelm II between 1902 and 1913. It is a series of stupendous palaces and gardens joined together by Peter Joseph Lenné's brilliant, fluid land-scaping. You need all day just to see the principal sights.

Start at the bottom, along Am Grüben Gitter, pass between Ebenhech's sphinxes (1755), past the Great Fountain with its classical statues and excellent bedding, and up the *Weinberg* terraces, whose vines have long been famous. To the east is the *Bildergalerie*, which overlooks the Dutch garden (1764–66), the Neptune Grotto (1751–57)

and another pretty flower garden. The *Hauptallee* runs absolutely straight from here to the baroque *Neues Palais* 2 km away, a symbol of Prussian might to commemorate victory in the Seven Years War.

On the hillside to the west of Schloss Sanssouci are the ravishingly lovely Sicilian garden (arranged with subtropical exotics) and the cool, green Nordic garden, both made by Lenné for Friedrich Wilhelm IV in 1857. Next comes the Orangery (1851–60), an immensely impressive building inspired by Frederick Wilhelm's Italian travels. Tubs with palms, bay laurels and oranges are placed along the formal terrace in front. Below the orangery is the stately Jubilee terrace, built for Emperor Wilhelm II in 1913, above a copy of the famous equestrian statue of Friedrich the Great. West again of the orangery, a long lime avenue leads up towards a ruined rococo Belvedere (1770), the Dragon House (also 1770) in the style of a

Chinese pagoda, and a magnificent toy fort built for the many sons of Wilhelm II and fitted with miniature Krupp cannons.

Sanssouci's most famous building is the intriguing Chinese Teahouse (1754–57), a rococo fancy with life-size, gilded statues of oriental figures and gilded columns simulating palm trees. To the

Life-size, gilded figures surround Sanssouci's exquisite Chinese Teahouse.

south is *Charlottenhof* (1826–28), a pretty neo-classical Schinkel building; climbing roses festoon its walls. To the east is a charming flower garden, beautifully planted around a rustic central pergola with old roses and colourful bedding. The Roman baths on the edge of the nearby lake are built in the style of an Italian villa, and incorporate the Court Gardener's House, a Tea Pavilion and the Hall of Arcades. All have small but lavish flower gardens: tender plants intensify the Italian effect in summer. At the south-east of the grounds is the *Friedenskirche*, a Byzantine church designed for Friedrich Wilhelm IV by Ludwig Persius in the 1840s. The parkland to the west is known as the Marly Garden: it was landscaped by Lenné and sets off the architecture of the domed church elegantly.

It was Lenné's genius that welded the entire landscape of Potsdam together. Sanssouci is his masterpiece.

West side of Potsdam
☎ 0331 9694200 **Open** Daily dawn–dusk **Size** 190ha (444ac) **Owner** Stiftung Preußische Schlößer und Gärten Berlin-Brandenburg

🅿 ⬛ 🍴 🚾 ♿ 🏠 🖼
ⓦ www.spsg.de
@ besucherzentrum@spsg.de

46. Schloßpark Rheinsberg

Mühlenstr. 1
16830 Rheinsberg

Frederick the Great began Rheinsberg in 1734 while Crown Prince of Prussia. Its garden is large, important, harmonious and little visited and it is sometimes described as the precursor to Sanssouci.

The entrance from the town brings you over a moat, through a great archway and into the courtyard, which is open on the far side via an Ionic colonnade. This gives views over the lake and a formal garden in the foreground (with statues of Apollo and the four elements). Take the bridge leading to the orange parterre

Schloßpark Rheinsberg's orange parterre in summer.

(where citrus trees are put out in summer), then climb the Sphinx steps to a broad alley lined with limes and clipped spruces; this leads to an impressive gateway with pairs of tall Corinthian columns topped by statues of Flora and Pomona.

Friedrich gave the estate to his younger brother Prince Henry in 1744, who added a green theatre in 1758 – long and large, with many entrances for actors to enter or exit by the wings. Henry also built a pyramid, with a broken top, as his burial place. Thin hornbeam hedges enclose *bosquets* and the Salon, a very tall summer-house encircled by lime trees. A long walk past

two grottos leads to a dumpy obelisk known as the *Denkmal*, which Prince Henry erected in 1791 to commemorate another brother, Prince August-Wilhelm (1722–58), and the heroes of the Seven Years War.

Centre of Rheinsberg
☎ 033931 7260 **Open** Tue–Sun 10am–5pm (4pm in winter) **Size** 40ha (99ac) **Owner** Stiftung Preußische Schlößer und Gärten Berlin-Brandenburg

🅿 ⬛ 🚾 🏠 🖼
ⓦ www.spsg.de
@ besucherzentrum@spsg.de

47. Forstbotanischer Garten Eberswalde

Am Zainhammer 5
16225 Eberswalde

Eberswalde's arboretum is one of Germany's best places to see trees. It was founded as part of the Royal Prussian Forestry School in 1830. Parts are still dedicated to economic work – testing and selecting suitable timber trees – but there are some 1200 different trees arranged, for the most part, geographically.

The background is a fine woodland of native oaks, which flourishs on the thin, sandy soils of north Germany. Among the many handsome specimen trees are the American hazel (*Corylus americana*), *Tilia* 'Moltkei'

The Eberswalde arboretum also has a pretty rock-garden.

(with huge leaves), *Liquidambar styraciflua* (magnificent in autumn) and the rare Andalusian pine (*Abies pinsapo*). The underplantings of rhodo-dendrons and azaleas add charm in late spring, and the meadows are purple with wild *Geranium palustre* in summer.

Eberswalde is 57km NE of Berlin
C 03334 65562 **Open** Daily 9am–6pm (3.30pm Nov–Mar) **Size** 8ha (20ac) **Owner** Fachhochschule Eberswalde **P WC & ⊞**

48. Schloßpark Branitz
Kastanienallee 11
03042 Cottbus

The extravagant Prince Hermann von Pückler-Muskau retreated to Branitz in 1845 when debts forced him to sell his property at Bad Muskau. He set about landscaping it with zeal and energy.

The three main rides that open out in front of the Schloß were quickly put into place. Two lakes were excavated and the Pleasure Grounds finished by 1851: so were the blue garden, rose hill, kiosk and bust of the singer Henriette Sonntag in a gilded arcade. Only indigenous trees were allowed in the park. Excavating the lakes enabled Pückler to add gentle undulations. Streams, winding paths, follies and garden buildings bring movement and direction at every juncture.

The scale is vast – it is an unusually spacious landscape – and much was created almost instantly by the import of mature 100-year-old trees. Pückler's masterpiece, a vast mound of earth built in 1854–56 and unique in scale, was the Lake Pyramid. He was buried here (next to his wife) beneath a quotation from the Koran: '*Gräber sind die Bergspitzen einer fernen neuen Welt.*' ('Graves are the mountain peaks of a distant new world.') Its surface is covered by Virginia creeper, which turns brilliant scarlet in autumn.

Schloßpark Branitz's landscape is the embodiment of rural calm.

1km SE of Cottbus town centre
C 0355 7515221 **Open** Apr–Oct daily 10am–6pm; 11am–5pm in winter (**closed** Mon) Outer parts of park always open **Size** 100ha (247ac) **Owner** Stiftung Fürst-Pückler-Museum Park und Schloß Branitz
P ⊟ ⊞ WC & ⊞ ⊞
W www.pueckler-museum.de
@ info@pueckler-museum.de

49. Muskauer Park
02953 Bad Muskau

Muskauer Park is the masterpiece of Germany's great 19th-century landscaper, Prince Hermann von Pückler-Muskau (1785–1871). It is also the largest classical 19th-century landscape park ever made: 200 ha are in Germany and 350 ha across the river Neisse in Poland, connected once more by a bridge built in 2004.

Pückler was a roistering rogue of immense personal charm, who married for money and spent both his and his wife's fortune on laying out the grounds at Muskau. His travels to England after the Napoleonic Wars brought him into contact with Humphry Repton, whose ideas and influence can be seen at Muskau and at the many parks and gardens that Pückler himself designed later, not least for the Prussian royal family. At Muskau (his birthplace), the formal Pleasure Ground links the castle to the landscape – a Reptonian idea – but Pückler's ideas were unbounded in scale and extravagance. He diverted the

Muskau is the largest landscaped park in Europe.

river and planted on a grand scale, without regard for expense. He believed his landscaping was a work of art and would create a social utopia. It ruined him, and in 1846, Pückler sold Muskau to the wealthy Prince Friedrich of the Netherlands, who continued to work on the park with the constant help of Eduard Petzold.

Muskau is now a UNESCO World Heritage Site – and its magnificent mature parkland is a delight to explore. The lie of the trees and open spaces is as close to perfection as anyone ever achieved.

At Bad Muskau **C** 035771 51525 **Open** Daily dawn–dusk **Size** 550ha (1358ac) **Owner** Stiftung 'Fürst-Pückler-Park Bad Muskau'
P 🚇 🍴 WC ♿ 🎁 📮
@ stiftung@muskau.de
W www.muskauer-park.de

SACHSEN-ANHALT

50. Schloß Georgium
Puschkinallee 100
06846 Dessau

The landscape park around Georgium palace is so wooded and natural that you are surprised when you come across one of the many classical buildings and sculptures. It was made on the flood plains of the Elbe and parts are both jungly and swampy, though a causeway leads to the Elbe pavilion above the river. The park was laid out by Prince Johann-Georg of Anhalt-Dessau (Prince Franz's younger brother) from 1780 onwards and, as often in Germany, the oaks (*Quercus robur*) are especially fine.

The park is best in May when the trees are in new leaf and wildflowers speckle the undergrowth. The most striking folly is the *Ruinenbrücke* (ruined bridge), built in perfect imitation of an ancient Roman bridge. By the palace is the *Blumengartenhaus*, a small Ionic temple set off by an attractive display of bedding plants. More conspicuous, and now on an important road junction, are the Ionic columns of the *Sieben Säulen* (Seven Columns) of which, despite their name, there are actually eight.

In NW of town, 1km from centre
C 0340 613874 **Open** Daily dawn–dusk **Size** 60ha (148ac) **Owner** Förderverein 'Anhaltische Gemäldegalerie und Georgengarten' Dessau e.V.
P WC ♿ 📮
W www.georgium.de
@ info@georgium.de

51. Luisium
06846 Dessau

Luisium is an enchanting, self-contained, intimate landscape garden. It was begun in 1774 for Princess Luise von Anhalt-Dessau, wife of the great landscaper Prince Franz. Her *Landhaus* is small, tall, white and elegant. It looks over an immensely busy landscape, with beautiful rides in all directions inviting exploration.

On one side is a model landscape: a long, curving artificial lake; a white, wooden Chinese bridge; and a glade with, as its focal point outside the garden, the church tower at nearby Jönitz. On the other side is a *patte d'oie* of rides stretching out into the countryside.

The whole estate is protected by an embanked dyke, a rampart from which you can look out into the Elbe meadows and inwards to the constantly changing landscapes of Luisium itself. These fluid views in and out of the garden are one of its joys; features appear and reappear at different points. A stud farm,

The 'Roman' bridge at Schloß Georgium was built as a ruin in the 1780s.

Luisium's enchanting classical landscaping surrounds the Landhaus.

built with a gothic façade in the fields outside, is axially linked to an Eton-gothic summer-house inside the garden, known as the *Schlangenhaus*. There are many other fine features: a handsome orangery, picturesque castle ruins, gothic revival gatehouses, a small theatre, herms and urns.

The park itself is a beautiful classical composition of glades and groves, mainly of oak, lime, horse-chestnut and maple. Wild plants are encouraged: violets in spring and mushrooms in autumn. But what makes the greatest impression is the harmony between the whole park, its parts, and the world outside.

In Waldersee, 3km E of Dessau
☎ 0340 646150 **Open** Daily dawn–dusk **Size** 14ha (35ac)
Owner Kulturstiftung Dessau-Wörlitz
🅿 🚾 ♿ ▦
🆆 www.gartenreich.com
@ ksdw@ksdw.de

52. Schloß Mosigkau
Knobelsdorffallee 2/3
06847 Dessau-Mosigkau

Schloß Mosigkau has the only garden in Dessau imbued with the light-hearted spirit of the baroque. It was made by Princess Anna-Wilhelmine of Anhalt-Dessau (an aunt of Prince Franz) between 1752 and 1757. Pause on the main road at the bottom of the garden

(the modern entrance is at the back) and look down to the elegant ochre-yellow palace. This is how visitors arrived 200 years ago, along the short, straight driveway lined with seasonal bedding. It passes between two gate-lodges that, on closer examination, turn out to be large orangeries.

Tender plants in pots are a feature of the garden: the lawns are thickly strewn with oranges, daturas, Italian cypresses, oleanders, agaves and cordylines put out for the summer. Versailles cases hold bay trees clipped as umbrellas and tall pyramids of trachelospermum. On one side is a tall hornbeam maze with rather narrow paths and, at its centre, a venerable plane tree. Nearby is a charming summer-house in the Chinese rococo

style (1774). Its wooden pillars are made of tree trunks carved to resemble palm trees.

7km SW of Dessau ☎ 0340 521139
Open Daily dawn–dusk **Size** 2ha (5ac) **Owner** Kulturstiftung Dessau-Wörlitz
🅿 🖥 🚾 ♿ ▦
🆆 www.gartenreich.com
@ ksdw@ksdw.de

53. Schloßpark Oranienbaum
Schloßstr. 17
06785 Oranienbaum

Oranienbaum has the most extensive and exquisite Anglo-Chinese garden in Germany. Prince Franz von Anhalt-Dessau built it in 1795, influenced by the writings of the English architect William Chambers.

The main feature is a substantial tea house on the edge of a lake, whose waters are strewn with rocky islets and criss-crossed by Chinese bridges. Off to the side, on an artificial hill, is a five-storey Chinese pagoda that can be seen from a great distance. It is superficially similar to the one at Kew, but is brick-built with slate roofs and white Chinese woodwork for the balconies.

Oranienbaum – palace and town – were built as a unity in 1683 for Henriette-Catherina of Nassau-Oranien, the wife of Prince Johann-Georg of Anhalt-Dessau. The palace's extensive formal garden,

Bay trees in Versailles cases grace Schloß Mosigkau's entrance.

Oranges in tubs are put out for the
summer at Schloßpark Oranienbaum.

around a handsome central
fountain, is now put to grass.
Its edges are tricked out with
a large number of laurustinus
and Canary Island palms, and
bay trees, trachelospermums
and citrus in tubs.

The unusually long orangery
was built by Carlo Ignazio
Pozzi in 1812–18. It has
recently been well restored,
but too late to save the historic
collection of orange trees that
it once sheltered, all of which
were frozen by winter cold
during the long years of
socialist neglect.

13km ESE of Dessau
C 034905 20391 **Open** Daily
dawn–dark **Size** 15ha (37ac)
Owner Kulturstiftung Dessau-
Wörlitz
P WC & ▦
W www.oranienbaum.de
@ stadtinfo@oranienbaum.de

54. Wörlitzer Park
06786 Wörlitz

Wörlitz is the single most
important landscape
garden in Germany – breath-
takingly beautiful and blessed
with an apparently endless
number of delightful features.
It was laid out by Prince Franz
von Anhalt-Dessau (1740–
1817), a man of the European
Enlightenment, who travelled
widely in England and found
inspiration in such gardens as
Stourhead and Stowe.

The main circuit passes
over the Wolf Bridge, with a
wonderful glimpse down the
canal towards the Temple
of Venus (1794), best seen
when framed by *Rhododendron
ponticum* in early summer.
The Gothic House (1773)
is an imposing folly, whose
southern façade (based on
Shotover Park) was the first
gothic revival building in
continental Europe. Even
prettier is the northern façade,
inspired by Venice's finest
late-gothic church, Madonna
dell'Orto. Behind the Gothic
House, a short avenue frames
the Temple of Flora (1797–98)
– a copy of the original at
Stourhead.

Nearby is the elegant,
curving, wooden White Bridge,
which resembles Sir William
Chambers's Chinese bridge at
Kew. Elsewhere are copies of
the English Iron Bridge (1791)
and the Pantheon (1795–97).
But best of all is the Stein, an
imitation Vesuvius on top of a
huge boathouse made of vast
volcanic boulders and attached
to a pink-and-white villa called
Villa Hamilton in honour of
Sir William & Lady Hamilton's
house at Naples. The Stein
was ignited by a great fire that
spewed forth ashes, smoke
and flames. Red-tinted glass
portholes in the sides of
the 25-m cone were
illuminated from inside.
Water was pumped over the
lip of the cone to imitate
molten lava.

Prince Franz sought both to
beautify the landscape and
improve his estates. The park
was designed as a complex
system of spatial relationships,
with sight-lines (short and long)
and groups of trees planted
in the landscape style. The
aesthetics of architecture,
landscaping and painting
all contributed to the whole.
Seats, monuments and paths
have been positioned with a
deliberate effect in mind –
to offer the greatest variety
of mood and impressions
during a tour.

It goes without saying that
there are beautiful rhododendrons, pretty spring bulbs
and interesting individual trees
(*Quercus* × *heterophylla* dates back
to 1764 and is the first recognised hybrid oak), but all are
secondary to the park. You will
need all day and stout legs to
feel you have seen the best of it.

36km E of Dessau **C** 034905 20302
Open Daily dawn–dusk **Size** 120ha
(296ac) **Owner** Kulturstiftung
Dessau-Wörlitz **P ▢ ¶1 WC & ▦ ▦**
W www.gartenreich.com
@ ksdw@ksdw.de

55. Europa-Rosarium
Steinberger Weg 3
06526 Sangerhausen

Sangerhausen is a place of
pilgrimage for rose lovers
from across the world. It has
the largest collection of rose
cultivars ever assembled and is

ABOVE: The elegant, curving, Chinese-style White Bridge at Wörlitzer Park.
OPPOSITE: Wörlitzer Park's Temple of Venus, seen from Wolf Bridge.

Roses in ornamental mixed plantings, Europa-Rosarium.

different types, and make lists of possibilities for your own garden.

SE edge of town ☎ 03464 572522 **Open** Apr–Oct daily 8am–7pm (later in high season) **Size** 12.5ha (31ac) **Owner** VDR-Stiftung Europa-Rosarium Sangerhausen

🅿 🚪 🍴 🆆🅲 ♿ 🎪 ⚘
🆆 www.europa-rosarium.de
@ info@europa-rosarium.de

56. Botanischer Garten der Martin-Luther-Universität Halle-Wittenberg
Am Kirchtor 3
06108 Halle (Saale)

wonderfully designed for study and enjoyment. It was founded by the German Rose Society (*Verein Deutscher Rosenfreunde*) and opened to the public in 1903 with the aim of accumulating, testing and displaying every rose ever bred – a practice maintained year after year until the 1940s.

The garden's collection of early 20th-century roses represents an unparalleled horticultural heritage – if you want long-lost roses to restore a period garden, Sangerhausen is the place to find them. It currently has some 7500 different cultivars and 55 000 rose bushes laid out in a fluid design with light woodland at the edges and open lawns for

display. The roses are grouped according to their types, with extensive plantings of sections like Damask and Moss roses. The collections of Polyanthas, Hybrid Perpetuals, Noisette hybrids and ramblers of every kind are particularly extensive and the garden is unrivalled as a reference collection for Hybrid Teas of the first half of the 20th century.

Space is well used so that, though the garden is large and popular, it often seems intimate and private, with just enough around the corner to lead you on to new scenes of colour, beauty and scent. Sangerhausen is by far the best place in Europe to study the history of roses, reflect on the

Halle has a very attractive and visitable botanic garden that has recovered well from communist neglect. It has been on this site since 1698, which makes it one of Germany's oldest botanic gardens, and the present collections extend to a very respectable 12 000 taxa.

At its highest point is an octagonal observatory, designed in 1788 by Karl Gotthard Langhans, the architect of the Brandenburg Gate in Berlin. Nearby is the collection of 'ephemerals' – annual and biennial plants of great beauty in high summer. There are areas devoted to

Annuals by the observatory in Halle's botanic garden.

steppe plants from the eastern Mediterranean and central Asia; collections of herbaceous plants from America and eastern Asia; an excellent rock-garden that you can walk into; a collection of woodland plants like epimediums and *Hepatica transsilvanica*; a Mediterranean rock-plant garden; and a large area dedicated to systematic beds with many interesting and unusual plants. The arboretum is also systematically arranged and, despite the thin, sandy soil, has many fine ancient specimens, including *Sophora japonica, Acer campestre, Quercus cerris* and *Celtis occidentalis*. The unusual parasitic *Cuscuta reflexa* grows on an *Aesculus* species: its curling yellow stems resemble spaghetti.

The tropical house (1872) has a collection of economic plants like vanilla, banana, coffee and pepper, as well as orchids and ferns. The Victoria House (1902) has *Victoria cruziana* in the pool, surrounded by mangroves. Other glasshouses are devoted to cacti, flora of the Canary Islands, carnivorous plants and plants from the Mediterranean.

NW of Halle's old city centre, 200m beyond Moritzburg
☎ 0345 5526270 **Open** Apr–Oct 2–6pm weekdays & 10am–6pm weekends. By appointment for groups in winter **Size** 4.5ha (11ac) **Owner** Martin-Luther-Universität Halle-Wittenberg 🅿 ♿ 🚻 ♿ 🏠
🆆 www2.biologie.uni-halle.de/bot/garten.html
@ kustos@botanik.uni-halle.de

Gentiana lutea in flower in midsummer, Rennsteiggarten.

lilies, gentians and alpine thistles are the staples of the European collection, but the Caucasus, Rockies, Himalayas and Arctic tundra are also well represented.

Follow the 1 km circuit and dart off from side to side for a more detailed look at the different floras, and at the plants from calcareous, silicaceous or moorland soils. All are well labelled and well grown; the garden is neat, attractive and informative. June and July are probably the best months, but there is much to see in spring and autumn, too. The open site has wonderful views; on a sunny day it feels like the ante-room to Heaven.

33km S of Gotha ☎ 036842 22245 **Open** Mid-Apr–early Nov daily 9am–6pm (10am–5pm in Oct) **Size** 7ha (17ac) **Owner** Botanischer Garten für Gebirgsflora im Kulturbund e.V. 🅿 ☕ 🚻 🏠 ♿
🆆 www.rennsteiggartenoberhof.de
@ info@rennsteiggartenoberhof.de

58. Schloßpark Gotha
99867 Gotha

Gotha has one of the last baroque gardens made in Germany and one of the earliest landscape parks. The city is dominated by the vast 17th-century Schloß Friedenstein. It was the seat of one of the branches of the Saxon royal family: Queen Victoria's mother and husband were both members of its ruling house.

There are two distinct and stylish gardens in the surrounding Schloßpark. The oldest is the pretty and colourful orangery garden below the palace on the eastern side, laid out in the baroque style in 1747; at its peak, the large orangery housed some 3000 plants put out in tubs for the summer. The elegant English garden on the south side of the palace was first begun in 1766 (contemporary with Wörlitz) by Duke Ernst II of Sachsen-Gotha and Altenburg; the island in the lake has tombs of the ducal family. The amusing neo-gothic tea house dates from the 1780s, another early fashion import from England.

In city centre ☎ 03672 4470 **Open** Daily dawn–dusk **Size** 21ha (52ac) **Owner** Stiftung Thüringer Schlößer und Gärten
🅿 ☕ 🚻 ♿ 🏠 🖼
🆆 www.thueringerschloesser.de
@ stiftung@thueringerschloesser.de

THÜRINGEN

57. Rennsteiggarten
98557 Oberhof

This is a beautifully landscaped alpine garden at 850 m in the rocky, rolling hills of the Thuringian forest. It is ingeniously laid out both geographically and geologically in a series of rock-gardens that display over 4000 mountain plants from around the world. Auriculas, adonis, pinks, edelweiss, aquilegias, Turkscap

The palace of the Dukes of Sachsen-Gotha with restored formal gardens at Schloßpark Gotha.

59. Park an der Ilm
99423 Weimar

Johann Wolfgang von Goethe began to landscape the Park an der Ilm as an enchanting, Arcadian, English-style park in 1776. This was the year Duke Carl-August of Weimar gave him the *Gartenhaus*, a pretty 'garden house', as a summer residence. The house sits at the side of the Park and looks over a long river valley that stretches south from the centre of Weimar. Goethe laid it out as an English garden, with beds for vegetables, flowers, roses and a hollyhock walk. Its most famous monument is a sphere placed on a square base, whose significance is hotly debated by Goethe scholars.

The Park is a place of extraordinary beauty – classical, peaceful and fluent – but it is a beauty that reveals itself as you walk through it. The views in all directions change with every footstep, and are framed by handsome mature trees – oaks, ashes, limes and hornbeams. Goethe designed the beautiful *Römische Haus* (Roman House), high above the valley, in the 1790s as a summer residence for the Duke. There are many other monuments, including the *Künstliche Ruine* (Artistic Ruin) from 1784 and the snake stone (*Schlangenstein*) built in 1787 with the inscription *Genio huius loci* (the genius of this place).

Schloß Belvedere displays tender plants in pots during summer.

Southern edge of town
☎ 03643 545194 **Open** Daily dawn–dusk **Size** 48ha (119ac) **Owner** Stiftung Weimarer Klassik
P 🚻 ♿
W www.klassik-stiftung.de
@ info@klassik-stiftung.de

60. Schloß Belvedere
99425 Weimar-Belvedere

Romantic woodland walks, 19th-century formal gardens, good borders, rare plants and a stunning old orangery: the changing tastes of one of Germany's leading families can be traced in the gardens of Belvedere.

The exquisite baroque Schloß was built on a ridge by Duke Ernst-August I between 1728 and 1748. The Duke collected greenhouse plants and built a very large, horseshoe-shaped orangery east of the palace, which has recently been well restored. Goethe's friend and patron, Duke Carl-August (1757–1828), inherited his grandfather's love of exotica and made the orangery the focus of a vast, scientific collection of plants – the so-called *Hortus Belvedereanus*, with some 8000 taxa. Vast and ancient tender plants are still hoisted outside for summer display in cumbersome containers.

When Grand Duke Carl-Friedrich took over in 1811, his wife Maria Paulovna of Russia created the elegant English-style woodland park on the southern side of the Schloß. Here are broad walks sauntering down to a lake (and up the other side) and a series of agreeable monuments along the way, including the giant's grotto, a rock-garden, an obelisk and a shady stone bower. Best of all is the circular rose garden, built according to Humphry Repton's plans and drawings, and recently replanted with early 19th-century roses. Carl-Friedrich also created for his wife a series of charming, enclosed, formal flower gardens (1812) on the western side (still called the 'Russian' gardens) and a hornbeam 'green theatre' (1823). The flower displays in summer and autumn are unusually well done, even by German standards.

Magisterial landscaping at Park an der Ilm in front of Goethe's *Gartenhaus*.

2km S of Weimar **(** 03643 546962
Open Daily dawn–dusk **Size** 43ha
(106ac) **Owner** Stiftung Weimarer
Klassik

▣ ▣ ▥ ▥ ▥ ▥ ▥ ▥
▥ www.klassik-stiftung.de
@ info@klassik-stiftung.de

61. Schloß Tiefurt
Hauptstr. 14
99427 Weimar-Tiefurt

Two impressive periods of
German garden history are
represented in the sweeping
landscape park below Schloß
Tiefurt. Duchess Anna Amalia
littered the slopes and valley of
the Ilm with architectural
features and memorials in the
years after she adopted Tiefurt
as her summer residence in
1781. Best known is the 1799
statue in honour of Wolfgang
Amadeus Mozart, the first in
Germany. She wrote of Tiefurt:
'I want to put the gardens in
such a state as Fauns and
Nymphs would not be
ashamed to inhabit.'

Then, in the 1840s, Prince
Pückler-Muskau's pupil
Eduard Petzold reworked the
landscape with trees – defining
space, creating surprises and
providing a setting for the
monuments. Petzold gave
Tiefurt the generous shape

and form we see today, as well
as the paths that are such a
delight to explore. The flower-
beds around the palace and
the 1803 *Musentempel* (Temple
of the Muses) are planted
in the 18th-century style.
Duchess Anna Amalia
would be pleased.

2km NE of Weimar
(03643 545401 **Open** Daily
8am–dusk **Size** 21ha (52ac)
Owner Stiftung Weimarer Klassik
▣ ▣ ▥ ▥ ▥
▥ www.klassik-stiftung.de
@ info@klassik-stiftung.de

62. Botanischergarten der Friedrich-Schiller-Universität
Fürstengraben Nr 26
07743 Jena

Jena's delightful historic
botanic garden has over
12 000 different plants in its
collections, which is a lot by
any standard, and this includes
a famous alpine garden (2500
taxa), an arboretum (900
different trees and shrubs) and
the contents of five glasshouses.
Although it dates back to 1586,
the present garden owes its
existence to Goethe's lobbying
in 1794 to develop the present
site, part of the old ducal gardens.

Goethe is said to have planted
a *Ginkgo biloba* tree that still
thrives. There are fine specimens,
too, of the Hungarian oak
(*Quercus frainetto*), *Pinus
bungeana*, *Stewartia monadelpha*
and *Juglans mandschurica*.

In recent years the systematic
garden has been remade and
updated, and the habitat
collections for plants from
woodland, steppes, moors,
heaths and aquatics have been
renewed. The floral displays
are also good: spring bulbs
and irises, followed by rhododendrons, roses and dahlias.
The soviet glasshouses have
good displays of palms
(40 taxa), orchids, cacti, and
tropical and subtropical plants.
Victoria cruziana grows in one
of the pools, alongside tropical
epiphytes and denizens of
the mangrove swamps. The
Innenhof courtyard at the
centre of the glasshouse range
is a haven for exotic specimen
plants and succulents, most
effectively displayed in
summer.

In old city centre **(** 03641 949274
Open Daily 9am–5pm (6pm mid-
May–mid-Sep) **Size** 4.5ha (11ac)
Owner Friedrich-Schiller-Universität,
Jena ▣ ▣ ▥ ▥ ▥
▥ www2.uni-jena.de/biologie/
spezbot/botgar/

LEFT: The *Musentempel*, Schloß Tiefurt. RIGHT: Jena's botanic garden has a very fine collection of plants.

The new systematic beds at Leipzig Botanic Garden.

SACHSEN

63. Botanischer Garten der Universität Leipzig

Linnéstr. 1
04103 Leipzig

This is the oldest botanic garden in Germany, founded as a *Hortus Medicus* in 1580. It is full of interesting and unusual plants – a total of 8000 taxa are packed into the small, flat, leafy site. This means that visitors with horticultural interests will come across many plants that they do not know but wish to acquire. There are very good ornamental displays, too, notably of colourful annuals and half-hardy plants in summer and autumn.

The whole garden has been completely remade since the collapse of communism. The systematic beds are now laid out in a modern, fluid design, and the geographical and ecological collections will be reorganised shortly. The rock-garden is a delight, and comple-mented by an extensive area devoted to the steppe flowers of Europe and Asia. The spanking new glasshouse complex has separate areas for tropical and subtropical plants, while the historic 19th-century admin-istration buildings have been restored to their former elegance.

The many interesting trees include *Juglans nigra, Tetradium daniellii, Hovenia dulcis, Sinocaly-canthus chinensis* and a hollow-trunked *Parrotia persica* – proof that the old and the new coexist very happily in this most charming and historic of gardens.

1km SE of old city, in university area **C** 0341 9736850 **Open** Daily 9am–8pm **Closes** 4pm Nov–Feb; 6pm Mar, Apr & Oct Glasshouses: Tue–Sun1–6pm & 10am–6pm weekends; open only on request Oct–Mar **Size** 2ha (5ac) **Owner** Universität Leipzig **P WC &** **W** www.uni-leipzig.de/bota/ **@** botgasek@uni-leipzig.de

64. Clara-Zetkin-Park

Ferdinand Lassalle Str.
04229 Leipzig

Clara-Zetkin-Park is one of those German mega-parks that are best visited on a bicycle. It is a 1950s amalgamation of several public parks: one of them, the *Johannapark*, is important because it was laid out by Peter Joseph Lenné in the early 1860s. Rich flower plantings were an integral part of his scheme and are making their reappearance in this park now (based on Lenné's Marly Garden at Sanssouci).

There are good trees in the northern part, still known as the *Palmengarten*, but most of the park is made up of light woodland and grass, with lakes, avenues and bridges over the Elsterflutbett, which flows through the centre. The most ornamental area is the *Dahlienterrasse* (dahlia garden), richly embellished with noble and empowering East German sculpture.

1km SW of old city **C** 0341 1236099 **Open** Daily dawn–dusk **Size** 125ha (309ha) **Owner** City of Leipzig **P E TI WC &** **W** www.leipzig.de

65. Grosser Garten

Hauptallee 5
01219 Dresden

This garden is a place to let your imagination rip. It was once the greatest baroque garden in Germany – four times larger than Herrenhausen in Hanover. The outlines are still there, if you know how to look for them, but the garden lost out to invading armies in the 18th century (the Electors of Saxony were good at losing wars), wholesale landscaping in the 1810s, public access after 1919, ferocious bombing in 1945, and encroaching proletarian-isation under communist rule until 1990 – hence the modern-day boating lake, puppet theatre, miniature railway and children's play area.

But if you look out in any direction from the charming baroque Schloß at the centre, you will see long rides (the Hauptallee is over 2 km long),

The *Dahlienterrasse* in autumn – the most ornamental area in Clara-Zetkin-Park.

Grosser Garten's palace sits at the centre of the extensive formal garden.

interesting geometric outlines, and genuinely well-landscaped woodland glades in the distance. Near the Schloß are avenues of limes; a magnificent water basin with a tall, single jet playing in the middle; pretty, yellow-painted garden pavilions; and excellent summer bedding. One very charming leftover from DDR days is a dahlia trials garden, a real horticultural spectacle in late summer.

In SE corner of old city
☎ 0351 4456600 **Open** Daily dawn–dusk **Size** 150ha (370ac) **Owner** Staatliche Schlößer Burgen und Gärten Sachsen
🅿 🚗 🆆🅲 ♿ 🎁 📷
🅦 www.schloesser.dresden.de
@ info@grosser-garten-dresden.de

66. Botanischergarten der Technischer Universität Dresden
Stübelallee 2
01307 Dresden

Dresden's botanic garden was completely destroyed by Allied bombing in 1945. It now has 10 000 taxa of every type from every corner of the earth. The layout is basically geographical, but this is interrupted by feature gardens like the excellent alpine garden (mainly European species, but very comprehensive), a herb garden (medicinal and culinary) and

an impressive layout of systematic beds.

The extensive glasshouses include a *Sukkulentenhaus* for cacti and succulents (especially agaves, aloes and euphorbias) and a special collection from the Canary Islands. In the *Victoria-Haus* are economic plants like cocoa and pineapple, and epiphytic bromeliads like *Tillandsia usneoides*, as well as the giant water lily (*Victoria amazonica*). Plants in the *Große Tropenhaus* are mainly from tropical Asia and Africa, including coffee, bananas, peppers and cotton. Many are set out in their pots from May until autumn.

Part of Dresden Botanic Garden's cactus collection in summer.

In summer, they are joined by a colourful and unique display of annuals and vegetables grown from seed (some 800 taxa), chosen to help local people discover what will thrive in their own gardens.

On NE edge of Großer Garten
☎ 0351 4593185 **Open** Apr–Sep daily 8am–6pm; Oct–Mar 10am–3.30pm, 4pm or 5pm **Size** 3.3ha (8ac) **Owner** Technischer Universität Dresden 🅿 🆆🅲 ♿
🅦 www.tu-dresden.de

67. Barockgarten Großsedlitz
Parkstr. 85
01809 Heidenau

Großsedlitz is a huge baroque landscape, a series of formal compositions so spacious and elegant that they fill the visitor with admiration and amazement. It was begun by Count Wackerbart in 1719 and extended by King Augustus the Strong after 1723.

People who try to describe it mention axes and cross-axes, upper and lower, so that it becomes too complicated to understand. It is obvious when you are there, however, because almost the whole composition is immediately visible. There are, in fact, three set-piece views. One runs from the roof of the Lower Orangery

Only one wing of the palace at Barockgarten Großsedlitz remains, but the gardens flourish.

(actually a lawn), down across a splendid semi-circular parterre towards a grand double staircase at the far end, known as the *Stille Musik* because of its statues of musician cherubs. A parallel view runs from a second orangery across another parterre and over the Water Parterre to a wonderful baroque cascade (actually, never finished) tumbling down through woodland. The third cuts across the other views, links them up and ends with a distant prospect of the Sandstein Hills across the Elbe valley.

Everywhere are spacious monumental staircases, Italianate balustrades, vases, urns, fountains, a great number of 18th-century statues, and oranges and agapanthus put out in pots for the summer.

Heidenau is 20km SE of Dresden on S bank of River Elbe
☎ 03529 56390 **Open** Daily 8am–8pm **Closes** 6pm Oct & 4pm Nov–Mar **Size** 5ha (12ac) **Owner** Staatliche Schlößer Burgen und Gärten Sachsen ▯ ▯ ▯ ▯
▯ www.barockgarten-grosssedlitz.de
@ barockgarten@compuserve.de

68. Schloß Pillnitz
01326 Dresden-Pillnitz

Pillnitz is an exquisite rococo palace, matched by a fine baroque garden. The best way to arrive is by boat up the Elbe from Dresden, as did

King Augustus the Strong. It was Augustus, and Anna Constantia Gräfin von Cosel (one of his many mistresses), who started to lay out the garden in 1706. From this period we can date the hedge-gardens, recently replanted, known as the *Charmillen*.

But there is much else to see from every subsequent period here. Much of the garden was landscaped in the Anglo-Chinese style in the 1780s and worked over by Peter Joseph Lenné in the 1860s. Behind the *Bergpalais*, stately avenues of limes and horse-chestnuts run up towards a statue of Flora. To one side is Lenné's palm house; beyond lies the 'Chinese' lake (1791) and the Chinese pavilion.

Horticultural interest comes from the 1860s *Fliederhof* (Lilac

Garden) and an amazing *Camellia japonica*, brought from Kew in 1779 and kept alive only by encasing it every winter in a portable glasshouse. The tree is 9 m high and 11 m in diameter and reckoned (in a good year) to carry over 30 000 blooms between February and April. The azaleas make a very good display in May and the summer bedding is a delight. There is also a good collection of mature conifers – 200 cultivars were planted in the 1870s.

On N side of River Elbe, 13km SE of Dresden ☎ 0351 2613260 **Open** Daily 8am–dusk **Size** 20ha (49ac) **Owner** Staatliche Schlößer Burgen und Gärten Sachsen
▯ ▯ ▯ ▯ ▯ ▯ ▯ ▯ ▯
▯ www.schloesser-dresden.de
@ info-pillnitz@schloesser-dresden.de

Colourful bedding fills Schloß Pillnitz's palace courtyards and leads out into the park.

Experimental plantings in Hermannshof's show garden in June.

BADEN-WÜRTTEMBERG

69. Hermannshof Schau- und Sichtungsgarten

Babostr. 5
69469 Weinheim

Hermannshof's garden sets out to be both beautiful and instructive: it is the most important display garden for the 'modern German' style of gardening, where over 2500 perennials are trialled in a garden setting. It is also privately owned, so that its solutions are scaled down and directly relevant to private gardens.

The background is an established family garden with close-cropped lawns and a framework of old trees, including a stocky *Sequoiadendron giganteum* and a billowing *Magnolia × soulangeana*. What we see today, however, has come about since the modernist Urs Walser was appointed as the garden's director in 1979.

There are seven different but typical garden habitats: woodland, edge-of-woodland, steppe, rock-garden, water, water's edge and cultivated garden borders. Each is subject to three permanent trials. The first seeks to create plant combinations with pleasing harmonies and contrasts of colour or form. The second is a test of vigour, to discover which plants will co-exist without one variety dominating the others. The third is the finished product of the other two: balanced, low-maintenance, permanent plantings that offer interest and colour over a long period. The intention is to imitate nature. Plants are therefore arranged in drifts rather than clumps, and the same plant is repeated throughout a large grouping to give an impression of flourishing and self-seeding.

Town centre **(** 06201 13652 **Open** Daily 10am–7pm **Closes** 6pm Mar & Sep and 4pm (and weekends) in winter **Size** 2.2ha (5½ac) **Owner** Freudenberg family **P WC & ⚲**

70. Schloßpark Heidelberg

Schloßhof 1
69117 Heidelberg

Heidelberg Castle's garden has been an icon of garden historians since Salomon de Caux laid out the Elector Palatine Friedrich V's *Hortus Palatinus* here between 1616 and 1619. Little remains of the garden that was called, in its day, the eighth wonder of the world. Its hanging terraces,

Schloßpark Heidelberg's Father Rhein, in epoxy resin, offers a modern echo of the vanished *Hortus Palatinus*.

parterres, grottos, water organs and automata have disappeared. But such is its reputation that a copy of the original statue of Father Rhein now reclines lugubriously on a rocky bed surrounded by jets of water. It is enough to bring the Elector's gardens to life again. And the views of the red sandstone city of Heidelberg are worth the journey, however long.

By castle, city centre **(** 06221 538431 **Open** Daily 8am–5.30pm **Size** 4ha (10ac) **Owner** Staatliche Schlößer und Gärten Baden-Württemberg **⚲ ⏚ WC ⏏ ⊞**
W www.heidelberg-schloss.de
@ info@service-center-schloss-heidelberg.com

71. Schloßgarten Schwetzingen

68723 Schwetzingen

This is a garden of exceptional size and loveliness. Its design is completely original and spans both the highest expressions of the baroque and the inception of the landscape movement. It is crammed with beautiful incidents, yet retains a spellbinding harmony overall.

When the Elector Karl Theodor (1724–99) succeeded to the Palatinate throne in 1743, he employed Nicolas de Pigage to build long, curving extensions on either side of the castle. This semicircle was then mirrored by two curving pergolas of trellis-work, so that they enclosed a vast circle of formal gardens, lime avenues, low hedges and intricately planted flower borders – the perfect stage for courtly life.

The avenue beyond the great circle leads to the stag fountain, and thence to the lake, guarded by statues that represent the rivers Rhine and Danube. This area is dominated by the Temple of Apollo, on top of a rocky mound symbolising Mount Parnassus, where a statue of the sun-god stands beneath a cupola with a golden sun as its finial. It is a supreme expression of royal power – and superhuman beauty.

The mosque is the most extravagant of the many inventive features in Schwetzingen's delightful garden.

Schwetzingen's woodlands were originally *bosquets*, intersected by hornbeam *allées*. Karl Theodor employed Friedrich Ludwig von Sckell to convert the outer areas to the English landscape style in 1776. Some say this change represents a turning away from political absolutism towards the new Enlightenment. The lake, too geometric for liberal tastes, took on an irregular shape and the formal woodlands dissolved into handsome clumps and graceful meadows. Nicolas de Pigage then designed the temple of Mercury and the Elector's last fanciful folly, the extensive Turkish mosque, in 1785. It stands reflected in a large pool, flanked by two minarets.

But there is no end to Schwetzingen's marvels: the

Diana the Huntress at Schwetzingen symbolises Karl Theodor's love of the chase.

dramatic Fountain of the Birds, where visitors are sprayed with water from the beaks of birds on top of the encircling trellis-work; the wicked statue of Pan; the gold-painted statues of Atalanta; the long orangery; the exotic plants put out in summer in huge, white-painted tubs; the optical illusion known as the 'End of the World'; an arboretum planted by the head gardener after Karl Theodor's death in 1799; the 'Roman' aqueduct; the outdoor theatre surrounded by six sphinxes; the Temple of Minerva, where the Goddess of Wisdom is portrayed as the patron of horticulture; and the 'Rialto' bridge, which is a white-painted step-bridge in the *chinois* style. A spirit of optimism binds them all.

In town centre ☎ 06202 81484 **Open** Apr–Sep daily 8am–8pm; Mar & Oct 9am–6pm; Nov–Feb 9am–5pm **Size** 72ha (178ac) **Owner** Staatliche Schlößer und Gärten Baden-Württemberg
🅿 🚐 🍴 🚾 ♿ 🎁 🖼
🆆 www.schloesser-magazin.de
@ info@schloss-schwetzingen.de

72. Schloßgarten Weikersheim
97990 Weikersheim

The castle at Weikersheim has a delicious baroque garden that was first laid out between 1708 and 1730 by Graf Carl Ludwig von Hohenlohe. It is *provincial* baroque, full of charm, movement, humour and political messages.

The large parterres have a round pool at the centre, with a statue of Hercules killing the Hydra, a symbol of Carl Ludwig's supposedly wise political rule. The grass parterres are lined with pretty bedding and edged with a great number of mythological and allegorical statues – seasons, winds, elements, continents and divinities. They were intended to impress – and do. Between them are clipped oranges, pomegranates and flowering plants in Versailles cases: Graf Carl

Comic dwarf figures line the edge of Weikersheim's moat.

Ludwig greatly admired the French king's palace and park. Along the entrance wall are 16 dwarf statues, caricatures of domestic servants and tradespeople, including the jolly brewer, chambermaid, gardener and watchman. At the far end of the garden is a handsome sunken pool and a pair of curving orangeries, extravagantly trimmed with finials, balustrading, pilasters and statues. The good and great commemorated in stone include Caesar Augustus, Cyrus, Alexander the Great, Nimrod and, at the centre (magnificently arrayed with crown and orb), Graf Carl Ludwig himself.

Town centre; Weikersheim is 40km S of Würzburg ☎ 07934 992950 **Open** Apr–Oct daily 9am–6pm; Nov–Mar daily 10am–12 noon & 1.30–4.30pm **Size** 5ha (12ac) **Owner** Staatliche Schlösser und Gärten Baden-Württemberg
🅿 ⬛ ♿ 🚻 🎁 🖼
Ⓦ www.schloss-weikersheim.de
@ info@schloss-weikersheim.de

73. Schloß Favorite
76437 Rastatt-Förch

Schloß Favorite has a very pretty landscaped park around a large country palace built in the 1710s for the rich, pious and self-willed Sibylla Augusta, Margravine of Baden. It was laid out in the English

landscape style in 1791 with streams, meadows, trees and a lake with an island. Exotic trees (notably planes, limes and tulip trees) were added during the 19th century and have grown well. The park itself replaced the Margravine's original baroque garden, though it is not difficult to imagine the parterres that once filled the long rectangular lawn, framed by arched galleries in front of the palace. Exotic plants in pots are still put out in summer, including hibiscus, agapanthus and oleanders.

In Rastatt itself the formal *Schloßgarten* (restored in the 1980s) and baroque *Pagodenburg* garden are also worth seeing. *Pagodenburg* is an exact copy of the baroque

pavilion at Nymphenburg in Munich; its rose garden is very pretty in June.

5km SE of Rastatt ☎ 07222 41207 **Open** Daily dawn–dusk **Size** 30ha (74ac) **Owner** Staatliche Schlösser und Gärten Baden-Württemberg
🅿 ⬛ ♿ 🖼
Ⓦ www.schloss-rastatt.de
@ info@schloss-rastatt.de

74. Alpengarten-Pforzheim
Auf dem Berg 6
75181 Pforzheim-Würm

The show-garden at Alpengarten-Pforzheim is even more famous now than the excellent alpine nursery it was made to complement. It was begun in 1927, on a steep, wooded hillside on the northern edges of the Black Forest. There are over 3500 different taxa in the garden, but it is the size of the plants rather than their number that impresses. Japanese maples and dwarf conifers and low-growing rhododendrons planted 75 years ago have grown to considerable heights. The rock-garden is mainly of local sandstone with areas of imported limestone for plants that require more porous growing conditions. Troughs line the paths and there is a good shade-house. The collection of alpine primula species is very comprehensive, as are the saxifrages, gentians

A pretty landscaped park surrounds Schloß Favorite's baroque palace.

Alpine plants and small shrubs line the terraces at Alpengarten-Pforzheim.

and *Cypripedium* species. Flowering reaches a height in May and June; thereafter, the flowers are supplemented by summer bedding.

3km SE of Pforzheim **C** 07231 70590
Open Apr–Oct daily 8am–6pm (10am on Sun) **Size** 2ha (5ac)
Owner Carl family **P** ◻ **WC** ♿
W www.alpengarten-pforzheim.de
@ CAlpengarten@aol.com

75. Schloßgarten Ludwigsburg
Schloßstr. 30
71634 Ludwigsburg

Ludwigsburg is the largest palace in south-west Germany, with a most unconventional garden. Both were made by Duke Eberhard Ludwig between 1704 and 1733, but the historic garden has been much altered. It is now run as a public spectacle by a company called Blühendes Barock (Baroque in Bloom) and is extremely popular locally, though little known abroad. This is a pity, because Ludwigsburg is a real joy to visit.

The palace faces south, where the complicated, curling parterres in the enormous formal garden (remade in the 1950s) are extravagantly planted with a mixture of permanent and seasonal plantings – garish roses, thousands of bulbs, and brilliant bedding in summer and autumn.

Down beside the palace are two charming private gardens of the royal family, the *Friedrichsgarten* (named after one of the dukes) and the *Mathildengarten*, laid out as an English flower garden in the 19th century. Next comes the Upper East Garden, with more baroque gardens, handsome old trees, massed floral plantings, vast areas of spring bulbs, a Japanese garden (prettiest in late spring), a model fruit garden, a Mediterranean vine terrace and a neo-mediaeval castellated folly called the *Emichsburg* (which dates from 1798). In the Lower East Garden are a rhododendron garden (drifts of azaleas), a birdsong valley, expansive plantings of astilbes, a Japanese garden, a ruined Roman-style aqueduct, lakes, another modern rose garden, an area planted with thousands of lavender plants and the *Märchengarten* (fairytale garden) with entertainments like mazes, puppet shows and scenes from fairy tales.

Elsewhere – for this is a vast estate – are an ice house, more *parterres de broderies* and a fine garden around the adjoining Schloßpark Favorite. And everywhere are massed displays of flowers – Baroque in Bloom.

Schloßgarten Ludwigsburg has vast displays of 'Blühendes Barock' bedding in its enormous formal garden.

Annual meadow mixes are a speciality of Höhenpark Killesberg.

12km N of Stuttgart
☎ 07141 975650 **Open** Park:
Mid-Mar–early Nov daily
7.30am–8.30pm; *Märchengarten:*
9am–6pm **Size** 30ha (74ac)
Owner Staatliche Schlößer und
Gärten Baden-Württemberg
🅿 🚆 🍴 🚻 ♿ 🏛 ♿ 🎫
🅆 www.schloss-ludwigsburg.de &
www.blueba.de
@ info@schloss-ludwigsburg.de

76. Höhenpark Killesberg

Am Kochenhof
70192 Stuttgart

Killesberg is a popular public park, offering facilities for every imaginable family entertainment. But this is Germany, and so Killesberg's horticultural interest is also very high.

Much was planted for the International Garden Show in 1993, but Killesberg was originally designed by Hermann Mattern for the *Reichsgartenschau* (the predecessors of the international show) in 1939 and has a totalitarian scale and vision – powerful landscaping, spacious terraces and bold design complemented by lavish planting. Large sculptures, imposing fountains and expansive areas devoted to monoculture – closely planted with a single type of plant – reinforce the message.

The many excellent horticultural features include: a crocus lawn; a primula garden (60 different cultivars);

a valley of roses (almost all Hybrid Teas and Floribundas); a water lily lake; a dahlia garden (160 cultivars and 10 000 plants); a valley of astilbes; an arboretum of dwarf conifers; trials of bedding plants and annuals; beautiful seasonal bedding; and extensive wildflower meadows. Intimate it is not – but extremely impressive it is.

3km N of city centre
☎ 0711 2589225 **Open** Daily
dawn–dusk **Size** 50ha (123ac)
Owner City of Stuttgart
🅿 🚆 🍴 🚻 ♿
🅆 www.killesberg.de

77. Park Wilhelma

Neckartalstr.
70342 Stuttgart–Bad Cannstatt

King Wilhelm I of Württemberg built Park Wilhelma in the 1840s as a private garden in the Moorish style. The main entrance takes you through a sequence of five elegant glasshouses, individually dedicated to cacti, bromeliads, orchids (5000 plants) and many other tropical and subtropical plants.

The spacious colonnades around the pools and flowers of the enclosed Moorish garden are still the heart of the modern Park Wilhelma. At the centre is a vast circular pond (650 sq. m in area), which is heated to 30°C in summer. Tropical water lilies in bright, exotic colours grow alongside Indian lotuses, water hyacinths, *Victoria amazonica* and *V. cruziana*. Above the pool are south-facing subtropical terraces, where tender plants in pots are put out for the summer. Citrus trees, olives, figs, bananas and kiwis ripen here; daturas and hibiscus add colour and form; and the palm trees and cypresses are set so thickly that one can easily imagine oneself in the Mediterranean.

The conservatories are planted with succulents (huge pillar cacti and large prickly pears); useful tropical plants (papayas, cinnamon, sweet potatoes, cotton, cocoa, vanilla, coffee and pepper); tropical ferns; and temperate tree ferns. The new Amazon House is inhabited not just by kapok, mahogany, palms and banana-trees, but also by monkeys, birds and tropical fish.

Elsewhere are fine old trees (especially 19th-century conifers),

Tropical lotus and water lilies grow in Park Wilhelma's enclosed Moorish garden.

The systematic beds in Hohenheim's modern botanic garden provide a contrast to its landscaped follies and beautiful parkland.

the largest magnolia garden in Europe, and spectacular displays of bedding, from spring bulbs to roses, annuals and dahlias.

4km NE of city centre
C 0711 54020 **Open** Daily 8.15am onwards **Closes** 6pm May–Aug; 5.30pm Apr & Sep; 5pm Mar & Oct; 4pm Nov–Feb **Size** 27ha (67ac) **Owner** Staatliche Schlößer und Gärten Baden-Württemberg
P ⊡ ⓝ WC ⓰ ⓐ ⓑ ⓕ
W www.wilhelma.de
@ info@wilhelma.de

78. Hohenheim Park & Botanischer Garten
70599 Stuttgart

Hohenheim is a historic landscape park that has been occupied by an agricultural university since 1818 and now incorporates a modern botanic garden. The park was laid out by Karl II Eugen, Duke of Württemberg, between 1772 and 1793, and once had a large number of pretty follies and garden buildings. Three remain: a charming casino or *Spielhaus*, a Roman-style villa or *Wirthaus* and a classical ruin composed of three Corinthian columns and an architrave.

The duke's two special gardens were a complete collection of Württemberg plants and an American garden, where several tulip trees, planted in 1779, still survive. The conifers, added in the 19th century, are also very imposing. From the front of the palace, now occupied by students, an avenue of pollarded, 200-year-old Italian poplars leads down to the vineyard where the faculty of oenology trials over 100 different vines: the people of Stuttgart think highly of Württemberg wines.

In the modern botanic garden are about 7000 taxa, including some 5000 in the systematic beds and 1200 in the tropical and subtropical houses. *Begonia* species are a speciality – some 150 of them. There are also special collections of medicinal and economic plants, a garden dedicated to the writings of the remarkable local saint, Hildegard von Bingen (1098–1179), and a handsome Monopteros temple added in 1996.

14km S of Stuttgart
C 0711 4593080 **Open** Daily dawn–dusk **Size** 33ha (81ac) **Owner** Universität Hohenheim
P ⊡ WC ⓰
W www.uni-hohenheim.de
@ gartenbau@uni-hohenheim.de

79. Botanischergarten Tübingen
Hartmeyerstr. 123
72076 Tübingen

This is an exceptionally good botanic garden, purpose-built on the edge of the city in the 1960s and displaying some 12 000 taxa. It occupies an impressive site (a well-land-scaped, curving hillside) and its most famous feature, the glasshouse complex, is an imag-inative architectural statement. You see it across the valley as you enter at the top: the spacious polygonal *Tropicarium* (tropical house) is 12 m high and contains tall palms and bamboos; there are also houses for succulents, aquatics, alpines, and the flora of South Africa (excellent *Lithops*) and the Canary Islands.

The Fuchsia Pavilion commemorates Leonhart Fuchs, an early professor of botany at the university. The systematic beds fill the slopes below the glasshouses. The garden also has a splendid alpine garden geographically arranged with plants from eastern Europe, Switzerland, the Jura, the Himalaya and North America.

In the 5-ha arboretum is a vigorous collection of young trees and shrubs (more than

Autumn colour across the valley in Tübingen's botanic garden.

1000 taxa), including avenues of magnolias and ornamental maples, and many local cultivars of apple. Elsewhere are a pharmacological herb garden, collection of more than 100 grape cultivars, heath garden, and moorland garden. All are sensitively positioned, planted for effect and well maintained.

4km NW of old city centre
☎ 07071 2978822 **Open** Daily 8am–4.30pm; **closes** later on weekends **Size** 10ha (25ac) **Owner** Universität Tübingen 🅿 🚾 ♿
🆆 www.botgarden.uni-tuebingen.de

80. Botanischer Garten der Albert-Ludwigs-Universität
Schänzlestr. 1
79104 Freiburg im Breisgau

Freiburg's botanic garden was founded as a *Hortus Medicus* in 1620 and moved to its present site in 1912. It crams a lot into a small area – no less than 8000 different taxa. Many of these are in the glasshouses – a tropical house, subtropical water lily house, succulent house and fern house.

There is also much to see outside and the garden has been beautifully landscaped.

A church spire is used as a focal point for this border in Freiburg's botanic garden.

A spectacular waterfall of spring colour at Insel Mainau.

The university is especially proud of its old conifers (it refers to the Coniferetum, rather than a Pinetum) and has some mighty specimens of *Sequoiadendron giganteum* and *Cedrus atlantica*, as well as less-known trees like *Cephalotaxus* and *Calocedrus*. The gardens are laid out geographically – Asia, Japan, Australia, Pontic mountains, Mediterranean, and North America (good *Sassafras* and *Carya* species) – and according to ecotypes (alpine, coastal, heath, marsh and moorland). But there are also themed gardens like the Weinberg, where some 50 vine cultivars are trialled: Freiburg's wines are famous – at least in Baden.

NE of city centre, about 500m from cathedral ☎ 0761 2032872 **Open** Daily 8am–6pm Glasshouses open Tue, Thu & Sun 2–6pm **Size** 2ha (5ac) **Owner** Universität Freiburg 🅿 🖨 🚾 ♿
🆆 www.biologie.uni-freiburg.de
@ Botanischer.Garten@biologie.uni-freiburg.de

81. Insel Mainau
78465 Insel Mainau

Only superlatives can describe Mainau. This floral paradise is Europe's most visited garden and the best organised for visitors' enjoyment.

The 45-ha island belonged for many years to the Teutonic knights. The baroque palace was built in 1740 with splendid views across the lake, but the gardens were laid out by Grand Duke Friedrich I of Baden in 1853. Trees were his great interest: Mainau's excellent 19th-century conifers include a huge *Ginkgo biloba*, which the Grand Duke planted by the chapel in 1872; younger conifers include a 200-m long avenue of metasequoias.

Roses are a Mainau speciality: Friedrich I laid out the Italian-style rose garden in 1871. Three sides are enclosed by a pergola smothered in ancient climbing roses, though the bush roses are modern, brightly coloured and densely

planted to maximise their flower-power. Its beauty in early June is overwhelming; palms and cypresses surround it and increase its exotic allure. There are more roses in the lakeside garden – mainly shrub roses planted in 1969 – and now the dominant sight in early summer. Mainau has over 30 000 rose bushes.

Bedding is another Mainau speciality: some 400 000 bedding plants are raised every year for its displays, mainly pansies in spring and dahlias in autumn. They are planted by the lakeside in bright abstract swathes, best seen from the terraces above. Mainau boasts the largest display of dahlias in Germany: about 200 cultivars of every kind, and a total of 20 000 plants.

Spring bulbs are another of the garden's outstanding features: crocuses, narcissi and, above all, tulips extend through the cherry orchards in waves of different colour as far as the eye can see. You will never experience anything to match it.

On SW shores of Lake Constance
☎ 07531 3030 **Open** Daily 7am–8pm (or dusk, if sooner) **Size** 45ha (111ac) **Owner** Bernadotte family
🅿 🖪 🍴 🚾 ♿ 🏛 🚼 🖼
🆆 www.mainau.de
@ info@mainau.de

82. Park Schönbusch
Kleine Schönbuschallee 1
63741 Aschaffenburg

S chönbusch was the first and (many would say) the finest landscape park in southern Germany. It was laid out by the Portuguese Emanuel d'Herigoyen for the Archbishop and Elector of Mainz, Friedrich Karl von Erthal in 1775, but Friedrich Ludwig von Sckell took over in 1783 and completed it.

It was Sckell's first opportunity to apply the principles of landscape garden design he had learned in England. English parks have clumps of trees surrounded by meadows, but this is not always appropriate to the much more wooded landscape

ABOVE: Schönbusch's *Freundschaftstempel* is modelled on the Pantheon. OPPOSITE: Meadows planted with millions of tulips are an outstanding feature of Insel Mainau in spring.

of Germany. Sckell carved his park from the woodland, making glades, curving paths and rides – a delight to explore.

The pretty pink house is surrounded by grass and sits above a curving lake, with views over flowery meadows towards Aschaffenburg. Spoil from the excavations was used to form two long hummocks (the *Berg*), joined by a soaring arch called the Devil's Bridge (*Teufelsbrücke*). Other follies include: the extraordinary Light-house (*Aussichtsturm*); the Temple to Friendship (*Freundschaftstempel*); the classical Philosopher's House (*Philosophenhaus*); and the delicious banqueting house (*Speisesaal*), built in 1792 with a painted sky and murals of the surrounding park, so that guests have the illusion of dining outside.

2km S of Aschaffenburg
☎ 06021 625478 **Open** Daily dawn–dusk **Size** 168ha (415ac) **Owner** Staatliche Schlößer und Gärten Baden-Württemberg 🅿 🖪 🚾 ♿ 🖼
🆆 www.schloesser.bayern.de
@ sgvaschaffenburg@bsv.bayern.de

BAYERN

83. Hofgarten Veitshöchheim
Echterstrasse 10
97209 Veitshöchheim

V eitshöchheim is a triumph of the rococo – an exuberant, joyous, uplifting

garden. It was substantially built as a summer residence by Adam Friedrich von Seinsheim, Prince-Bishop of Würzburg, between 1763 and 1779. Some of the layout is a little earlier, and the lakes are 19th century, but the main features are all von Seinsheim's work.

The structure is, of course, formal, with seemingly endless hornbeam hedges and alleys of pleached limes. Within the *bosquets* are secret gardens planted with roses or fruit trees, hiding a fountain or protecting a latticed pavilion. Different views, cross-views and clever glimpses through trellis-work windows catch your eye with each step. Comic statues are everywhere: there are over 300 witty and

Trompe l'œil within the trellis-work at Hofgarten Veitshöchheim.

inventive sandstone *putti*, allegories, seasons and nymphs, bought between 1765 and 1768 from the workshops of Ferdinand Tietz, Germany's greatest rococo sculptor. Two unusually wacky *chinois* baldachins have curving cupola roofs supported by four sculpted palm trees and enormous pineapple finials. The green theatre and maze are worth seeking out and there is a charming *Schneckenhaus* (snail house) with mythological creatures made from shells and pebbles. The larger of two lakes has the Pegasus fountain at its centre, where statues of Apollo and the nine Muses on the heights of Mount Parnassus attend a huge winged horse as it rears to fly heavenwards. No garden offers such pure, hilarious *fun*.

Town centre, 11km N of Würzburg ☎ 0931 91582 **Open** Daily 7am– 8pm (or dusk, if earlier) Fountains operate 1–5pm every hour (on the hour) Apr–Oct **Size** 12ha (30ac) **Owner** Bayerische Verwaltung der staatlichen Schlößer, Gärten und Seen

🅿 🖭 🍴 🆆🅲 ♿ 🏛 🎏
🆆 www.schloesser.bayern.de
@ sgvwuerzburg@bsv.bayern.de

84. Hofgarten Würzburg
Residenzplatz
97070 Würzburg

The palace garden at Würzburg was one of the most opulent in Germany when Johann Prokop Mayer laid it out for the super-rich Prince-Bishop Adam von Seinsheim in the 1760s and 1770s. For many years, only the outlines remained, but recent restoration has brought back the splendour of this rococo masterpiece.

The gardens to the side of the palace are the only ones to retain traces of the original plantings – eight tall, conical yews around a central pool. The main gardens, behind the palace, have been very prettily replanted with arcades of clipped yew around a simple circular pool. The site then rises very steeply (it projects into a vast defensive bastion), over a series of three levels, rather like a theatre. Here are numerous charming enclosures looking down to the palace. Handsome staircases lead to arches and tunnels of laburnum and mulberry; arcades of thuya backed by

sweet-scented roses, lilacs and philadelphus; well-planted urns; and statues of dwarfs and *putti* on the balustrades.

But there are fine statues, urns and decorations throughout the garden, and a large number of tender plants put out for the summer. The summer bedding is particularly rich and exuberant, even by German standards.

City centre ☎ 0931 355170 **Open** Daily 7am–8pm (or dusk, if sooner) **Size** 9ha (22ac) **Owner** Bayerische Verwaltung der staat- lichen Schlößer, Gärten und Seen
🅿 🖭 🍴 🆆🅲 🏛 🎏
🆆 www.bsv.bayern.de
@ sgvwuerzburg@bsv.bayern.de

85. Botanischer Garten der Universität Würzburg
Julius-von-Sachs-Platz 4
97082 Würzburg

Würzburg's splendid botanic garden has been on its present site since 1960, but is an ancient foundation (1696) and one of its most distinguished alumni was Philip von Siebold (1796–1866),

These delightful conical yews date back to Hofgarten Würzburg's original baroque garden.

Naturalised campanulas thrive in Würzburg's botanic garden.

the founder of Japanese botanical studies. The present garden maintains a collection of some 150 taxa first described or collected by von Siebold, including such well-known garden plants as *Primula sieboldii* and *Hosta sieboldii*.

The garden has no fewer than 15 fascinating glasshouses, including an Alpine house and a Mediterranean house (with separate areas devoted to the flora of south-west Australia, California, Chile, South Africa and the Mediterranean region itself). The main range has tropical and subtropical houses, and one of the finest collections of cacti and succulents in Germany.

Some of the best outside features are a physic garden, a roof-garden (topped with gravel and designed with such plants as sedums, dianthus and thymes) and a *Bauerngarten* (literally Farm Garden) – a popular garden style in Germany that equates to an English cottage garden, where fruit, vegetables and herbs are more important than flowers.

The promising young arboretum is geographically laid out with trees and shrubs from all over the world, but also makes a speciality of central European flora.

SW edge of old city
☎ 0931 8886241 **Open** Apr–Sep daily 8am–6pm; Oct–Mar 8am–4pm **Size** 9ha (22ac) **Owner** Universität Würzburg 🅿 🚾 ♿
🆆 www.bgw.uni-wuerzburg.de
@ bgw@botanik.uni-wuerzburg.de

86. Schloß Rosenau
96472 Rödental-Coburg

Rosenau is the enchanted castle where Prince Albert was born. When Queen Victoria first saw it in 1843, she sighed: 'Were I not what I am, here would I have my true home.' The queen's enthusiasm is immediately understandable when you visit Rosenau today: it is the perfect romantic, intimate landscape garden.

The Schloß was reworked between 1806 and 1817 by Karl Friedrich Schinkel in the neo-gothic style for Prince Albert's father, Duke Ernst I of Sachsen-Coburg und Gotha. There is a very pretty formal garden by the entrance, but it is the parkland below that gives Rosenau its air of enchantment. No-one knows who designed it, but it is laid out in the English style, with grass expanses within ornamental woodland. The trees are all deciduous – beech, oak, ash and sycamore – while buttercups and *Geranium pratense* speckle the meadow. Its features include a lake, waterfall, grotto and orangery (which were added in 1826).

Rosenau is one of those great German landscapes whose intense beauty reveals itself only by walking through it.

5km NE of Coburg
☎ 09563 308410 **Open** Daily dawn–dusk **Size** 32ha (79ac) **Owner** Bayerische Verwaltung der staatlichen Schlößer, Gärten und Seen 🅿 🚗 🍴 🚾 🏛 🖼
🆆 www.sgvcoburg.de
@ rosenau@sgvcoburg.de

87. Schloßpark Seehof
96117 Memmelsdorf

The glory has departed from Seehof, once the greatest rococo garden in Germany, but the site remains immensely popular with visitors for its ability to conjure up its magnificent past.

The palace at its centre was built by Marquard von Stauffenberg, Prince-Bishop of Bamberg, between 1686 and 1693, but the garden owes more to Adam Friedrich von Seinsheim (bishop from 1757 to 1779), who also laid out the surviving masterpiece at Veitshöchheim.

Seehof was generally adjudged the bigger and better of the two: it had 400 sandstone statues from Ferdinand Dietz's studios, as opposed to Veitshöchheim's 300. Modern restoration has been slow but steady. The central cascade is working. A few statues have been

The colourful formal garden and Italian fountain at Schloß Rosenau look out over the parkland where Prince Albert played as a boy.

A restored fountain in front of Seehof's rococo palace.

recovered and returned. The main hedges and *allées* are in place again. And the scale is phenomenal. It reminds the people of Bamberg of the power and wealth of their prince-bishops, and explains the Bavarians' passion for the sophistication of the rococo.

7km NE of Bamberg
☎ 0951 409570 **Open** Apr–Oct Tue–Sun 9am–6pm Waterworks: every hour on the hour **Size** 21ha (52ac) **Owner** Bayerische Verwaltung der staatlichen Schlößer, Gärten und Seen 🅿 🔽 🆆 ♿ ⛲
🆆 www.schloss-seehof.de
@ sgvbayreuth@bsv.bayern.de

88. Sanspareil
96197 Wonsees

Sanspareil (meaning 'without equal') lives up to its name. There is nowhere like it anywhere – nor has there ever been. Imagine a wooded hill, studded with large outcrops of natural rock. Trace a trail through this untouched landscape of beech and ivy and give literary names to some of the more fanciful rock shapes. That is how Frederick the Great's sister, Wilhelmine, Margravine of Bayreuth, laid out the garden at Sanspareil in

the 1740s. Not that she built it herself, she explained: Nature was the real architect. All the Margravine did was to discover an allegory of the journeys of Telemachus and relate it to the position and shapes of the rocks. The path leads eventually to the grotto of Calypso, an extraordinary rock theatre encrusted with undressed stone like an Italian grotto, which the Margravine built as a ruin. It was a wild, aesthetic experiment that worked triumphantly.

Walking that hallowed path today is still a peerless experience. Nothing could be more different from the rococo gardens that were all the rage when Wilhelmine's sensibilities were first excited by the romantic potential of the site we still call Sanspareil.

25km W of Bayreuth ☎ 09274 330 **Open** Daily dawn–dusk **Size** 13ha (32ac) **Owner** Bayerische Verwaltung der staatlichen Schlößer, Gärten und Seen 🅿 🔽 🆆
🆆 www.schloesser.bayern.de

89. Schloßpark Eremitage
95448 Bayreuth

There are several good gardens in and around Bayreuth, but Schloßpark Eremitage is the most rewarding to visit. It started in 1664 as the Markgraf Christian Ernst's private zoo, but his son Markgraf Georg Wilhelm built a summer palace there in 1715, and a formal garden of *bosquets*, hornbeam tunnels and cascades. Georg Wilhelm also laid out the simple, flowery parterre in front of the old palace and the long, steep water-cascade that tumbles, rather crookedly, down the hillside to the river Main.

Georg Wilhelm's son, Markgrave Friedrich, gave the estate to his wife Wilhelmina in 1735. Markgravine Wilhelmina was a sister of Friedrich the Great of Prussia and just as keen on garden-making as her brother: one of the grottos she built in the surrounding woodland survives, as does a theatre built as a Roman ruin. Her finest addition was the orangery,

Calypso's grotto is the culmination of a visit to Sanspareil.

Modern bedding hints at the 18th-century splendour of Schloßpark Eremitage's baroque gardens.

now known as the *Neue Schloß*, which is a glittering, baroque octagon, encrusted with coloured glass chips, gold leaf, mirrors, crystals and pieces of tufa, crowned by a golden statue of Apollo and his horse-drawn chariot. The parkland is an English-style landscape: lush meadows, cool woodland, fine trees and rhododendrons.

4km E of Bayreuth
☎ 0921 7596937 **Open** Daily dawn–dusk **Size** 50ha (123ac) **Owner** Bayerische Verwaltung der staatlichen Schlößer, Gärten und Seen 🅿 💺 🍴 🚾 ♿ 🏛 🖼
🌐 www.schloesser.bayern.de
@ sgvbayreuth@bsv.bayern.de

90. Botanischer Garten der Stadt Hof
Stadtpark Theresienstein
95028 Hof

Hof's botanic garden was started in the 1930s in a corner of the town's beautiful Theresienstein park, which claims (wrongly) to be Germany's oldest. Its mission is to show the people of Hof what is possible in their own gardens – and to please visitors. The main features are a rose garden (mainly colourful modern cultivars), a herb garden that specialises in medicinal plants, a rock-garden, water lily lake, a shade garden, a golden garden and good mixed-colour plantings. Irises, heathers, lewisias and phloxes are other specialities. It is charming, popular and maintained to a high standard.

City centre, next to Theresienstein
☎ 0175 7528163 **Open** Apr–Oct daily 8am–8pm (or dusk, if sooner) **Size** 2ha (5ac) **Owner** City of Hof
🅿 💺 🚾 ♿
🌐 www.botanischer-garten-hof.de
@ info@botanischer-garten-hof.de

91. Botanischer Garten der Universität Erlangen-Nürnberg
Loschgestr. 3
91054 Erlangen

Though Erlangen's botanic garden is one of the smallest in Germany, it is one of the most accessible and enjoyable to visit. It is neatly laid out and well maintained, and its plants are displayed with an eye to horticultural beauty as well as scientific correctness. It has been on its present site since 1828 and supports some 4000 different plants. These are sometimes arranged according to habitats (steppe plants, moorland vegetation, bog plants, *garrigue*, coastal plants and a very pretty raised pool for water lilies) and sometimes geographically (including the excellent rock-garden, which also has some geological arrangements).

The fern garden, large physic garden, model kitchen garden (lots of old vegetable cultivars) and herb garden are also charming. The glasshouses include plants from the Canary Islands, an alpine house (plants from the Arctic Circle and Mediterranean mountains) and houses for cacti, succulents, subtropical water plants and economic plants from the tropics.

The adjoining Schloßgarten is also worth a quick visit.

Town centre, alongside Schloßgarten
☎ 09131 8522669 **Open** Daily 8am–4pm (5.30pm Jun–Aug) Glasshouses: Tue–Sun 9.30am–3.30pm **Size** 2ha (5ac) **Owner** Universität Erlangen
🅿 💺 🚾 ♿ 🚻
🌐 www.botanischer-garten.
   uni-erlangen.de
@ jakob.stiglmayr@rzmail.
   uni-erlangen.de

92. Hofgarten Ansbach
Schloßplatz
91522 Ansbach

It was in Ansbach's Hofgarten that agaves first flowered north of the Alps. That was in

Erlangen's botanic garden has an impressive collection of cacti.

Ansbach's orangery has a fine display of citrus trees in tubs.

1627, some 100 years before the garden assumed its present design and layout. It is baroque and formal, but restrained – *Protestant* baroque. The garden does not adjoin the Residence, so in 1731–43 the 'Wild' Margrave Karl Wilhelm Friedrich commissioned an orangery large enough to perform the design function of a palace, where he could entertain during the summer. It is a building of unusual length and beauty; orange trees in Versailles cases are put out for the summer in the formal garden in front – so are pomegranates, olives, pistachios, bay laurels and strawberry trees. The bedding is unusually well done.

Other features include the *Lindensalen*, a shady square of lime trees and fountains, a modern rose garden in box-edged parterres, a new 'seville' orange-house, and a historic avenue of 250-year-old lime trees.

Town centre ☎ 0981 9538390 **Open** Daily dawn–dusk **Size** 17ha (42ac) **Owner** Bayerische Verwaltung der staatlichen Schlößer, Gärten und Seen 🅿 ▣ 🍴 🚻 ♿ ▦ 🆆 www.bsv.bayern.de @ sgvansbach@bsv.bayern.de

93. Botanischergarten der Stadt Augsburg

Dr-Ziegenspeck-Weg 10
86161 Augsburg

Augsburg's modern botanic garden is run as a civic amenity by the city council – this is not uncommon in Germany when universities withdraw funding. It is, however, wonderfully maintained and full of inspirational designs and interesting, well-grown plants. Popular with visitors is the *Bauerngarten*, a formal kitchen garden planted in the cottage style. Tulips, annuals and bedding plants are planted in a sheltered, sunken garden, where pots are put out for the summer. The steppe garden displays plants from eastern Europe and the Mediterranean hills, while the rock-garden (red sandstone and limestone) sports a number of winter-hardy opuntias.

Other features worth looking at are a large Japanese garden, a modern rose garden, a fern garden, a medicinal herb garden and large herbaceous plantings. The glasshouses include a tropical house (rubber trees, tropical figs, epiphytes, orchids and lots of economic plants), a pool for *Victoria amazonica* and a new display house for plants from dry, hot climates – cacti, succulents, tropical euphorbias, and bulbs. The striking design incorporates a roof constructed of Teflon cushions.

SE of city, near zoo
☎ 0821 3246033 **Open** Daily 9am
Closes 5pm Nov–Feb; 6pm Mar, mid-Sep–Oct; 7pm Apr; 8pm mid-Aug–mid-Sep; 9pm May–mid-Aug **Size** 10ha (25ac) **Owner** City of Augsburg
🅿 ▣ 🚻 ♿
🆆 www2.augsburg.de
@ afgn.stadt@augsburg.de

The popular sunken garden at Augsburg's botanic garden.

Weihenstephan's experimental plantings in late spring.

94. Weihenstephan Sichtungsgarten
85350 Freising

The Display Garden (*Sichtungsgarten*) at Weihenstephan is a garden for *real* gardeners. It was founded by Munich's Technical University in 1947 as a test garden for horticultural plants of every kind. Ornamental trees, shrubs, herbaceous plants, annuals, fruit and vegetables are all here, for the most part grown in long beds separated by grass paths. But what makes Weihenstephan fascinating is the way that plants are grown in experimental combinations to demonstrate how they will look in any garden; it is the leading exponent of the 'German' style of garden planting.

The plant combinations may be of two plants that contrast vividly, or of several different plants that create a harmonious whole. The ecological combinations include a large alpine bed, a steppe planting, and areas for shade plants and heathlands. Roses are widely grown, as are paeonies, potentillas and grasses.

The university has several other gardens in Freising, seldom visited but well worth seeing. They include the *Lehrgarten* (Teaching Garden), *Kleingartenanlage* (Allotment Gardens) and the *Oberdieckgarten*, which has a pharmacological garden, rhododendron garden and scented garden. The *Schaugarten* (Show Garden) has fruit trees, window boxes and – a very German tradition – houseleeks (*Sempervivum* species) planted on a garden pavilion roof.

37km NW of München, on SE edge of Freising ☎ 08161 715110 **Open** Apr–Oct daily 8am–6pm (9am weekends) **Size** 7ha (17ac) **Owner** Staatliche Forschungsanstalt für Gartenbau Fachhochschule Weihenstephan 🅿 🚻 ♿ 👤 🚹 🎟 www.fh-weihenstephan.de @uschi.taetz@fh-weihenstephan.de

95. Schloß Schleissheim & Schloß Lustheim
Max-Emanuel-Platz 1
85764 Oberschleißheim

Schleißheim and Lustheim are two fine baroque palaces connected by formal gardens nearly 1 km long. Both were built by the Elector Max Emanuel of Bavaria: Lustheim in 1684 and Schleißheim in 1701. They face each other down a series of baroque parterres and water gardens: make time to walk the whole way between them and back. The long canal, designed by the Italian Enrico Zuccalli, was already in place by 1684; it ends by encircling Lustheim, which rises from the water like an enchanted dream. The connecting parterres and cascade were added by the Frenchman Dominique Girard, a pupil of Le Nôtre, between 1715 and 1724. The parterres

Extensive water gardens and baroque parterres run between the two palaces, Schleissheim and Lustheim; the colourful plantings reach their peak in late summer.

LEFT: Naturalised bulbs in habitat plantings of herbaceous and alpine plants, Westpark.
RIGHT: Long strips of bedding outline the extensive formal gardens of Schloßpark Nymphenburg.

are liberally planted with colourful bedding – wonderful in late summer. Avenues and *bosquets* fill the sides of the central axis, from which there are glimpses of further formal gardens and rides.

One of the excitements of the park is that it was never relandscaped in the English style. When the parterres at Schleissheim were enlarged by Karl Effner in the 1830s, he remained true to its period origins, which makes it one of the most important early baroque gardens in Germany.

17km N of München
☎ 089 3158720 **Open** Daily dawn–dusk **Size** 76ha (188ac) **Owner** Bayerische Verwaltung der staatlichen Schlößer, Gärten und Seen
P ☕ 🍴 WC ♿ 🎁 ▦
W www.schloesser.bayern.de
@ sgvschleissheim@bsv.bayern.de

96. Westpark

Westendstr.
81377 München

Westpark is a once-famous public park where modern German ideas on herbaceous planting are extensively displayed. It was landscaped by Rosemarie Weisse for the International Garden Show in 1983. The rose garden is planted with 20 000 roses and 500 cultivars (mostly from the 1970s) in island beds and has a curiously dated look now. However, the extensive habitat plantings of herbaceous and alpine plants have matured into real ecosystems and it is fascinating to see what has flourished over the intervening years: tulips, irises, geraniums, rudbeckias and Michaelmas daisies have flourished and radiate great swathes of seasonal colour.

Near a small lake are three oriental pavilions built for the Show – Chinese, Japanese and Nepalese – all slightly faded and partly hidden by mature display gardens. The effect is to increase their air of exotic mystery.

In SW of city, about 5km from centre. Best approached from Westendstraße ☎ 089 23392791 **Open** Daily dawn–dusk **Size** 72ha (178ac) **Owner** City of München
P ☕ WC ♿
W www.muenchen.de

97. Schloßpark Nymphenburg

80638 München

Visit the palace and park of Nymphenburg early in the morning, when the sun shines behind you as you approach. The palace is enclosed by a spacious *cour d'honneur*, whose curving walls are punctuated by pavilions – each a substantial house – and there are fountains and waterworks to admire here even before you pass beneath the porticos of the palace and into the Schloßpark proper.

Its scale and simplicity are what you notice first but, when these formal gardens were first laid out for the Elector Max Emanuel by Le Nôtre's pupil Dominique Girard in 1715, the parterres were put to complex broderies. Now they are filled with mown grass and lightly edged with bedding plants. The four sections (each enormous) have the circular Flora Fountain at the centre and then lead on towards the lake. Avenues and *bosquets* once radiated out from the parterre and lake, focusing on elegant rococo garden buildings, but their setting was altered by skilful landscaping by Friedrich Ludwig von Sckell in the 1790s. He retained the sections along the central axis – the basic structure of the parterre and the central canal with the cascade – but replaced the original geometric axis and avenue system with a more natural design. The

Pagodenburg (1716) is especially famous and much copied, but you should also see the *Badenburg* (1718) and the *Magdalenenklause* (1725). Later additions are the *Amalienburg* (1734, for Maria Amalia of Austria, the wife of the Elector Karl Albrecht) and the imposing urns and statues.

Sckell also left intact the long central formal canal; walk to the cascade at its end to appreciate the sheer size of the garden as it was originally laid out, and enjoy the distant reflections of the palace.

4km W of old city centre
☎ 089 179080 **Open** Jan–Feb, Nov daily 6.30am–6pm; Mar 6am–6.30pm; Apr & Sep 6am–8.30pm; May–Aug 6am–9.30pm; Oct 6.30am–7.00pm; Dec 6.30am–5.30pm **Size** 150ha (370ac) **Owner** Bayerische Verwaltung der staatlichen Schlößer, Gärten und Seen
🅿 ♿ 🍴 🚻 ♿ ▦ ▦
🆆 www.schloesser.bayern.de
@ sgvnymphenburg@bsv.bayern.de

98. Botanischer Garten München-Nymphenburg

Menzinger Str. 61–65
80638 München

When Munich's botanic garden moved to this site at Schloßpark Nymphenburg in 1914, the main consideration was that it should be better in every way than Berlin's. It is certainly more stylish, even today, and it has one of the largest collections of plants in the world – more than 14 000 taxa.

The design centres on the *Schmuckhof*, an ornamental sunken garden with colourful plantings throughout the year and large ceramic parakeets on its walls. To one side are the glasshouses, which lead off to a central show house. There are cacti houses, a 20-m high tropical house, an orchid house (2000 species) and many others – quite the equal of Berlin's. Maintenance, labelling, staging and display (inside and outside) are all exemplary.

The garden has every imaginable section (invariably of high horticultural merit): a spring garden, peony and iris beds, a systematically arranged arboretum, moor and heather gardens, a famous rock-garden, a rose garden, a rhododendron grove and fern gully, a collection of the protected plants of Germany (including *Cypripedium calceolus*), Bavarian plant communities, economic and medicinal plants, and systematic order beds. Keen horticulturists could spend a whole day in any one of them.

Western München, on N side of Nyphenburg Park; entrance in Menzinger Straße. Also accessible from Nymphenburg directly
☎ 089 17861310 **Open** Daily 9am–7pm (**closes** earlier Sep–Apr) Glasshouses: **closed** 11.45am–1pm **Size** 22ha (54ac) **Owner** Universität München ♿ 🍴 🚻 ♿ ▦
🆆 www.botmuc.de
@ botgart@botmuc.de

A ceramic parrot overlooks Munich's botanic garden, which has one of the largest plant collections in the world.

The Monopteros in Englischergarten was built on an artificial hill by Ludwig I in 1836.

99. Englischergarten
80538 München

Englischergarten is the German word for an English-style park in the style of Capability Brown. Munich's Englischergarten is Germany's best known and important as its earliest public park, quite apart from being a delight to visit.

It was laid out from 1789 onwards by Friedrich Ludwig von Sckell and the American-born Englishman Count Rumford and is now the largest city park in Germany. The landscape is beautifully moulded by clumps of beech extending the whole way up the wide valley. At the centre is the *Kleinhesselhoher See*, an artificial lake with three islands – boats may be hired. At the city centre end is a very elegant and conspicuous Monopteros, a white Ionic temple built by Ludwig I in 1836 on a small artificial hill. Nude sunbathing on its slopes increases its charms.

Even more popular with the people of Munich is the *Chinesischer Turm*, a squat pagoda based on Sir William Chambers's elegant precedent at Kew in England. It is surrounded by a beer garden with 7000 seats – Munich's second largest. Near the *Residenz* is a modern Japanese garden, a gift from Germany's old friend Emperor Hirohito in 1972.

City centre, extending for several km towards NE 0893 8666390 **Open** Daily dawn–dusk **Size** 370ha (914ac) **Owner** Bayerische Verwaltung der staatlichen Schlößer, Gärten und Seen

www.munich-info.de
gvenglischergarten@bsv.bayern.de

100. Schloß Linderhof
82488 Ettal

Charming, extravagant, theatrical and slightly louche: Linderhof is a rococo delight. 'Mad' King Ludwig II built it in the 1870s, high in the Alps and hard against the Austrian frontier, with snowy peaks for a backdrop. The whole ensemble – palace, gardens and park – resembles an operatic stage-set.

The Schloß is tiny, white and fizzing with architectural detail – a fantasy palace for a king

Schloß Linderhof ('Mad' King Ludwig's extravagant palace and gardens) resembles a rococo theatre-set.

The Latona fountain at Schloß Herrenchiemsee is a copy of the original at Versailles.

who lived in a fantasy world. Steps lead down to a rococo pool, where a gilded statue of Flora surrounded by *putti* conceals a fountain that shoots up to 30 m. Beyond the pool, the steps soar steeply, rising through terraces past a large bust of Queen Marie Antoinette to the temple of Venus at the top (Ludwig was not much interested in Venus: the court gardener, Carl von Effner, designed the garden). The flower beds and pots are crammed with bright colours, especially brilliant in late summer.

More extravagances fill the hillside behind the palace. A steep cascade runs down from an orangery. Formal gardens are contained within French trellis-work: look out for the large terracotta bust of Louis XIV. Here, too, is an English-style park, set among natural alpine meadows, a small white mosque with gilded domes (Ludwig II added an apse to hold his peacock throne) and Venus's grotto, where the king conjured up the first act of *Tannhäuser* by floating on a huge conch.

Halfway between Füssen and Oberammergau, 15km from Garmisch-Partenkirchen
☎ 08822 92030 **Open** Daily dawn–dusk **Size** 26ha (64ac) **Owner** Bayerische Verwaltung der staatlichen Schlößer, Gärten und Seen
Ⓟ ⬛ 🍴 🚻 🏛 🖼
Ⓦ www.linderhof.de
@ sgvlinderhof@bsv.bayern.de

101. Schloß Herrenchiemsee
83209 Herrenchiemsee

'Mad' King Ludwig II of Bavaria planned his extravagant palace and gardens on the island of Herrenchiemsee as a near-replica of Louis XIV's Versailles. He insisted that the formal gardens below the Hall of Mirrors be an accurate copy of the central axis laid out 200 years earlier by Le Nôtre in the 1670s. The fountains were especially important, so the water parterres have their bronze statues and fountains representing Fame and Fortune. Similarly, the main

fountain (the *Latonabrunnen*) is a perfect reproduction of the central fountain at Versailles. They all flow, rather better than the originals, for short periods twice an hour throughout the day.

The garden was begun in 1882, but no further work was done after the king's death in 1886; what we see today is only one-third of Ludwig's overall plans for the garden. The effect is grand and dramatic, and the baroque parterres are full of colourful plants in summer. Visitors who know the real Versailles will recognise every detail. The surrounding park occupies the whole 230-ha island and there is a 2-km walk from the landing stage.

By boat from Prien-Stock
☎ 08051 68870 **Open** Apr–mid-Oct daily 9am–6pm; mid-Oct–Mar daily 9.30am–4.15pm **Size** 42ha (104ac) **Owner** Bayerische Verwaltung der staatlichen Schlößer, Gärten und Seen
⬛ 🍴 🚻 ♿ 🏛 🖼
Ⓦ www.herrenchiemsee.de
@ sgvherrenchiemsee.de@bsv.bayern.de

Gardens of Great Britain & Ireland

Gardens and gardening are profoundly English activities. An interest in gardens pervades the national spirit as nowhere else in Europe. And until recently this was a specifically English activity, so that garden-making in Scotland, Wales and Ireland tended to be the preserve of English settlers or those who were influenced by English culture. There are, of course, records of ornamental gardening in every part of the British Isles before the Protestant reformation in the 16th century, but all the great gardens of Scotland, Wales and Ireland in this book were made by people who were culturally English. Regional variations are largely determined by soil and climate. Woodland gardens with conspicuous displays of rhododendrons are common in south England, west Scotland and much of Ireland and Wales. Rock-gardening is popular in Scotland and north England.

Modern English gardens are based on decorative horticulture. London is England's centre of gardening; it is in London that the Royal Horticultural Society (RHS) with 750 000 members runs its most important shows. Gardening is strongest as a national pursuit in the south-east of the country, where more than half the RHS's members live. But there are good gardens of every kind open to the public in every part of the British Isles. The industry is supported by some of the world's best nurseries and a constant flow of high-quality books and periodicals. The heroes of English gardening tend to be the makers of great gardens, especially those who write about them. And there is a tradition in England that owners should work in their own gardens; hands-on gardening shocks the continental well-to-do, who leave gardening to their gardeners. Great English gardeners

ABOVE: The Desert Wash at East Ruston Old Vicarage is an imitation Arizona desert.
OPPOSITE: The entrance to the 'rondel' garden conveys the spirit not only of Sissinghurst Castle but also of English mid-20th-century gardening.

The double borders at RHS Garden Wisley are the quintessence of the English horticultural tradition.

include the current Prince of Wales and his grandfather, King George VI.

The Protestant reformation cut Britain off from the civilisation of the Italian Renaissance. The English Civil War (1642–60) destroyed much of its cultural heritage. There are no important gardens older than the vast Dutch-style garden at Hampton Court, laid out by William III in the 1690s. The French baroque style was widely spread by the royal gardeners George London and Henry Wise between 1688 and 1714. But most formal gardens were swept away by the Landscape Movement, a uniquely English style promoted by Lancelot 'Capability' Brown and Humphry Repton, which spread very quickly from about 1745 onwards, first through England and then throughout Europe. A period of transition in the early 18th century was dominated by such designers as Charles Bridgeman, John Vanbrugh and William Kent. Also influential was William Chambers, whose fanciful books on Chinese gardens and executed plans for the Pagoda at Kew spawned a fashion for *anglo-chinois* gardens throughout Europe. The great landscape gardens like Stourhead, Blenheim and Stowe remain one of England's greatest contributions to European civilisation.

The Landscape Movement gave way in the 19th century to a fashion for Italianate gardens – Bowood and Shrubland are good examples – and to the rising importance of horticulture. Horticultural magazines exercised great influence, and writers like William Robinson promoted a wild, woodland style of gardening with plants. Gertrude Jekyll was probably the most important disciple of this movement, which developed into a study of how to use ornamental plants in a garden for artistic effect. Jekyll worked closely with the architect Edwin Lutyens and was conspicuous both as a writer and plantswoman: her style is still the English ideal that inspires most gardens today. Later practitioners include Norah Lindsay, Russell Page, Graham Stuart Thomas, Jim Russell, Lanning Roper and Peter Coats.

One legacy of Britain's imperial past is the large number of plants introduced from all over the world by plant hunters. Sir Joseph Banks (1743–1820) built up the great collections at Kew by corresponding with plant gatherers wherever the British had settled. The RHS sent David Douglas (1798–1834) to collect in North America. Sir Joseph Hooker (1817–1911) collected for Kew in New Zealand, the Himalayas and North Africa. British plant collectors dominated the first half of the 20th century: E.H. Wilson, George Forrest, Frank Kingdon Ward and amateurs like Reginald Farrer sent vast numbers of plants home to their sponsors and indirectly created many of Britain's great woodland gardens. There is a system of National Collections run by the National Council for the Conservation of Plants and Gardens (NCCPG), which has its offices at the RHS's garden at Wisley.

Unlike gardens in mainland Europe, the opening hours and dates of British and Irish gardens vary considerably from year to year. If a garden opens in 'mid-April', do not expect to find it open on 16 April – its first opening could be earlier or later, especially if Easter is early or late that year. It is essential to check before you plan your visit; fortunately most gardens have websites now. Remember that garden visiting is very popular in England. Major gardens, especially those belonging to the National Trust or RHS, are liable to be very busy. Members of these organisations are usually admitted free to their respective properties. The National Trust's portfolio of blue chip gardens is so comprehensive that no garden tour is complete without a visit to one or more of its properties. And membership of the RHS brings free access for its members to over 150 gardens throughout the United Kingdom and abroad.

The landscape movement began at Stowe Landscape Gardens when 'Capability' Brown was head gardener in the 1740s.

Gardens of Great Britain & Ireland

Ireland

1. Glenveagh Castle
2. Mount Stewart
3. Rowallane Garden
4. Annesley Gardens & Castlewellan National Arboretum
5. Talbot Botanic Gardens
6. National Botanic Gardens
7. Powerscourt Gardens
8. Mount Usher Gardens
9. Altamont Garden
10. Birr Castle Demesne
11. Derreen
12. Fota Arboretum & Garden
13. Mount Congreve
14. John F. Kennedy Arboretum

Great Britain

15. Castle of Mey
16. Inverewe
17. Dunrobin Castle
18. Cawdor Castle
19. Crathes Castle
20. Branklyn Garden
21. Arduaine Garden
22. Benmore Botanic Garden
23. Mount Stuart
24. Brodick Castle
25. Culzean Castle
26. Dawyck Botanic Garden
27. Royal Botanic Garden, Edinburgh
28. Logan Botanic Garden
29. Glenwhan Gardens
30. Castle Kennedy Gardens
31. Alnwick Garden
32. Wallington
33. Belsay Hall
34. Dalemain
35. Levens Hall
36. Newby Hall
37. Castle Howard
38. Bramham Park
39. Ness Botanic Gardens
40. Arley Hall
41. Tatton Park
42. Haddon Hall

43. Chatsworth
44. Renishaw Hall
45. Bodnant Gardens
46. Portmeirion
47. Powis Castle
48. National Botanic Garden of Wales
49. Dyffryn Botanic Garden
50. David Austin Roses
51. Biddulph Grange
52. Dorothy Clive Garden
53. Felley Priory
54. Packwood House
55. Cottesbrooke Hall
56. Hergest Croft Gardens
57. Abbey Dore Court
58. Spetchley Park
59. Hidcote Manor Garden
60. Kiftsgate Court
61. Westonbirt Arboretum
62. Blenheim Palace
63. Oxford Botanic Garden
64. Buscot Park
65. Stowe Landscape Gardens
66. Waddesdon Manor
67. Benington Lordship
68. Hatfield House
69. Sandringham House
70. East Ruston Old Vicarage
71. Anglesey Abbey
72. Cambridge University Botanic Garden
73. Shrubland Park
74. Helmingham Hall
75. Audley End
76. Glen Chantry
77. Beth Chatto Gardens
78. Tresco Abbey
79. Trengwainton
80. Trebah Garden Trust
81. Trelissick Garden
82. Caerhays Castle
83. Heligan Gardens
84. Lanhydrock
85. Cotehele
86. Antony

87. Mount Edgcumbe
88. Marwood Hill Gardens
89. RHS Garden Rosemoor
90. Knightshayes Garden
91. The Garden House
92. Bicton Park Gardens
93. Hestercombe Gardens
94. Tintinhull House
95. Abbotsbury Subtropical Gardens
96. Compton Acres Gardens
97. Iford Manor
98. Bowood House
99. Stourhead
100. Heale House Garden
101. Longstock Water Gardens
102. Mottisfont Abbey
103. Sir Harold Hillier Gardens
104. Exbury Gardens
105. Hinton Ampner
106. West Green House Garden
107. Osborne House
108. Savill Garden
109. Painshill Park
110. RHS Garden Wisley
111. Polesden Lacey
112. Capel Manor
113. Royal Botanic Gardens, Kew
114. Hampton Court Palace
115. Chelsea Physic Garden
116. West Dean Gardens
117. Denmans
118. Parham
119. Leonardslee Lakes & Gardens
120. Nymans
121. Wakehurst Place
122. Sheffield Park Garden
123. Pashley Manor
124. Great Dixter
125. Hever Castle
126. Penshurst Place
127. Great Comp
128. Bedgebury National Pinetum
129. Sissinghurst Castle Garden
130. Goodnestone Park

Kenmare
11

GARDENS OF GREAT BRITAIN & IRELAND

★ National Capital

• Cities and Towns

— Major Roads

00 Garden

Adjacent Countries

Great Britain/Ireland

| 0 | 50 | 100 Kilometres |
| 0 | 50 | 100 Miles |

N

Atlantic Ocean

North Sea

Irish Sea

Isle of Bute

Isle of Arran

Isles of Scilly

English Channel

SCOTLAND

NORTHERN IRELAND

NORTH ENGLAND

CENTRAL ENGLAND

EAST ENGLAND

WALES

SOUTH-WEST ENGLAND

SOUTH-EAST ENGLAND

ELAND

GREAT BRITAIN

FRANCE

Thurso
John o' Groats
15 Mey
Wick
17 Golspie
Poolewe 16
Nairn
Cawdor 18
Inverness
Aberdeen
19
Oban
21
Perth
20 Dundee
Lochgilphead
22 Dunoon
27 EDINBURGH
Rothesay GLASGOW
23
Ardrossan
Brodick Peebles
24 26 Stobo
Maybole 25 Alnwick 31
32
33
Ballycastle
Coleraine NEWCASTLE UPON TYNE
1 Londonderry
Letterkenny Ballymena Stranraer 30 29
Donegal NORTHERN IRELAND 28 Carlisle
Belfast ★ Newtownards Penrith
Saintfield 2 34
Sligo Ballynahinch 3 Kendal
Armagh 35 Ripon
Castlewellan 4 36 37
Dundalk York
Longford LEEDS 38
Drogheda
Athlone Malahide LIVERPOOL Sheffield
5 Llandudno 39 43 44
Dublin ★ 6 45 40 Chesterfield
Galway Enniskerry 7 Congleton 42
10 8 Stoke-on-Trent 53 King's Lynn 69
Birr Wicklow Porthmadog 51 Nottingham 70
Tullow 46 52 Norwich
Ballon 9 Bunclody Welshpool CENTRAL ENGLAND 71
Limerick Kilkenny 47 50 Wolverhampton Cambridge 72 74
13 14 Wexford 48 56 54 BIRMINGHAM 55 Northampton 73
Waterford Worcester 58 60 59 65 Stevenage Ipswich
k 12 Carmarthen Hereford Chipping 66 Welwyn Garden City 75 76 Colchester
48 57 Campden 62 62 Oxford 67 77
Abergavenny 64 63 Faringdon 68 112
CARDIFF 61 Tetbury 113 115 London
49 BRISTOL Chippenham Enfield
Barry Bath Reading 108 114 127 130
97 98 Woking 104 125 126 Canterbury
88 Taunton 93 94 99 100 101 Winchester 110 111 119 Crawley 122 123 124
Barnstaple Yeovil Salisbury 102 105 Horsham 116 118 128 129
Great Torrington 89 90 95 103 104 Chichester 117 120 121
Tiverton Southampton 107 Lewes
Exeter Bournemouth Newport
92 Poole 96 Isle of Wight
Bodmin 85 91 Weymouth
84 86
Truro 83 82 87 Plymouth
79 80 81 St Austell
78 Penzance Falmouth
Tresco St Mary's

IRELAND

1. Glenveagh Castle

Churchill
Letterkenny
Co. Donegal

American money and exquisite taste are responsible for the dramatic castle at Glenveagh and its beautiful gardens, which look down rocky slopes to Lough Veagh. Mrs John Adair was the rich American who built the granite castle and started to lay out the garden between 1870 and 1920. The gardens, however, were substantially remade between 1937 and 1975 by Henry McIlhenny, an artistic bachelor who was heir to the Tabasco Sauce fortune.

The gardens are a series of outdoor rooms, each with a different character. The 1-ha (2-ac) lawn in the Pleasure Grounds is fringed with rhododendron shrubberies, *Dicksonia* tree ferns and eucryphias, with massed underplantings of hostas, rodgersias and astilbes. Lanning Roper helped with the design, and Jim Russell advised on the planting: rare trees, tender shrubs, large-leaved rhododendrons and sweet-scented *R. maddenii*. A tree-like *Griselinia* dates back to Mrs Adair's days. The kitchen garden is bounded by herbaceous borders and planted with heritage vegetables, Irish apple cultivars and the rare, single-flowered *Dahlia* 'Matt Armour'. Pots, urns and topiary surround the elegant gothic orangery. The contrast between the luxuriant gardens and the barren landscape beyond is dramatic and one of the many pleasures found here.

14miles (22.5km) NW of Letterkenny **C** 074 9137090
Open Mid-Mar–early Nov daily 10am–6.30pm
Size 11ha (27ac)
Owner Heritage Service
P ⬛ ⬛ WC ⬛ ⬛
W www.heritageireland.ie

The grand formal gardens at Mount Stewart are Italianate in inspiration, but planted with tender trees and shrubs that have grown to a considerable height.

2. Mount Stewart

Grey Abbey
Newtownards BT22 2AD

Mount Stewart is by far the most important and exciting garden to visit in Northern Ireland. It was made by the super-wealthy Edith, Marchioness of Londonderry, between 1921 and 1959, taking full advantage of the mild climate on Strangford Lough and the rich, acid soil.

The Italian Garden in front of the house (not very Italian, but grand and formal) is laid out with vivid colours and quirky, inventive details like a line of carved monkeys on columns, representing politicians. Beyond the formal garden is a sunken Spanish garden around a pebbled pool – a stylish and convincing design. Off to one side is the Shamrock Garden, where Lady Londonderry planted an Irish harp (in yew topiary) in a bed that represents the Red Hand of Ulster.

The tender plants begin on the walls of the house itself: *Rosa gigantea* covers a large area and there are huge specimens of *Magnolia grandiflora*. Behind the house are the lake and woodland gardens: rhododendrons of every kind predominate, interplanted with tender cordylines, tree ferns, mimosas, clianthus, prostantheras, pittosporums and grevilleas, and underplanted in places with meconopsis and candelabra primulas. The edge of the lake is streaked with extended plantings of *Iris laevigata* and arum lilies. At one point, you catch a glimpse of a white stag in a glade.

For design, variety, plants and plantings, Mount Stewart is a place of miracles.

18miles (29km) E of Belfast
📞 028 4278 8387 **Open** Lakeside
gardens & walks: daily 10am–sunset.
Formal gardens: Apr–Oct daily
(& weekends in Mar) 10am–8pm
Closes 4pm March & 6pm Apr
& Oct **Size** 31ha (77ac)
Owner National Trust
P 🚻 **WC** ♿ 🚼 ▦
W www.nationaltrust.org.uk

3. Rowallane Garden
Saintfield
Ballynahinch BT24 7LH

Rowallane is a great plants-man's garden, famous for such plants as *Hypericum reptans* 'Rowallane' and *Viburnum plicatum* 'Rowallane'. It was largely made by Hugh Armytage Moore between 1903 and 1955, though some of the oldest trees date from the 19th century.

Plantsmanship dominates: even the walled garden is completely given to the display of plants, some grown against the walls because they are slightly tender, and others arranged rather more ornamentally. The National Collection of *Penstemon* species is here, alongside drifts of the Slieve Donard form of *Meconopsis* × *sheldonii* and *Primula* 'Rowallane Rose'. The plant of *Magnolia dawsoniana* was the first to flower in the British Isles.

Rowallane, now headquarters of the National Trust in Northern Ireland, has the largest collection of rhododendrons in Ireland.

Hugh Armytage Moore subscribed to the plant-collecting expeditions of E.H. Wilson, George Forrest and Frank Kingdon Ward and was always reluctant to discard surplus seedlings. He therefore started to plant up the fields outside the walled garden, which expanded rapidly as more farmland was converted to horticulture.

No garden can match Rowallane for rhododendrons on a sunny day in April or May, as you amble from a glade of *R. augustinii* to a line of *R. maccabeanum* or back through *R. yakushimanum* hybrids. It is a monument to its maker's love of plants.

1mile (1.6km) S of Saintfield
📞 028 9751 0131 **Open** Daily 10am–8pm (4pm mid-Sep–mid-Apr)
Size 21ha (52ac) **Owner** National Trust **P** 🚻 **WC** ♿
W www.nationaltrust.org.uk

4. Annesley Gardens & Castlewellan National Arboretum
Castlewellan
Co. Down BT31 9BU

There are two gardens at Castlewellan, though the distinction between them is slightly artificial. Annesley Gardens comprise a 5-ha (12-ac), 18th-century walled garden, which the then Earl of Annesley started to plant with ornamental trees and shrubs in the 1870s. The National Arboretum (of Northern Ireland) is the surrounding woodland, begun at the same time.

The walled garden remains the heart of the collection; it is where the plantings are most ornamental and standards of cultivation are highest. Magnolias, cherries and rhodo-dendrons grow here in grass. A path runs north to south down the centre, edged by herbaceous borders backed by yew hedges; an ornamental fountain punctuates its mid-point.

The woodland outside – the Arboretum – is a forest of exotic trees and huge rhododendrons. Twenty trees

The 18th-centuy walled garden at Annesley Gardens & Castlewellan Arboretum has an extensive collection of plants.

are the oldest existing specimens in the British Isles, 42 are the tallest or largest in the British Isles, and 50 in Ireland. The comprehensive collections of *Podocarpus* and *Eucryphia* and the fiery autumn colours extend the interest after the last rhododendrons have flowered.

The distant views of the Mountains of Mourne are a delight and the modern 'Peace Maze' in the nearby Forest Park is the longest hedge-maze in the world, presumably because it represents the journey to peace in Northern Ireland.

30miles (48km) S of Belfast,
4miles (6.5km) W of Newcastle
📞 028 4377 8664 **Open** Daily 9am–dusk **Size** 41ha (100ac)
Owner Department of Agriculture & Rural Development, Forest Service
P 🚻 **WC** ♿
W www.forestserviceni.gov.uk/ arboretum.htm

5. Talbot Botanic Gardens
Malahide Castle
Malahide
Co. Dublin

The Talbot Botanic Gardens at Malahide Castle were the lifetime achievement of Milo, Lord Talbot de Malahide,

There are no fewer than seven glasshouses within the walled garden at Talbot Botanic Gardens, each filled with a different collection of rare and tender plants.

10miles (16km) N of Dublin
☎ 01 8160014 **Open** May–Sep daily 2–5pm **Size** 9ha (22ac) **Owner** Fingal County Council
P ⊞ WC ⅃ ⅃
W www.fingalcoco.ie/ LeisureandTourism/

6. National Botanic Gardens

Glasnevin
Dublin 9

Ireland's premier botanic garden was founded on undulating ground on the south bank of the river Tolka in 1795 to promote a scientific approach to the practice of agriculture. Not until the 1830s did it take on a botanic mission.

The design of the garden is classically Victorian – fluid and inviting, with specimen trees and shrubs and dedicated gardens cut from the grass. Plants are generally grouped by genus (the collection of yew cultivars is especially interesting) and there is a large area devoted to systematic displays.

The glasshouses are historic, beautiful and of unusual design – the one known as the Curvilinear Range (1843) has a good collection of cycads and orchids. The great Palm House (1882) is very strong on tropical plants from Central America. The cactus and fern houses (surrounded by borders

between 1942 and 1973. Talbot was a British diplomat with a passionate interest in botany, who travelled all over the world to extend his collections. As his knowledge developed, his greatest interest became the flora of Tasmania and Chile. The gardens still have over 5000 different taxa, which is a remarkable achievement on a dry, limey soil.

The castle is an ancient fortification, dating back to the first English invasions of Ireland in the 12th century. Its handsome parkland has been proletarianised since it was sold to the government in 1973, but once you enter the 1.5-ha (4-ac) walled garden,

you are truly in the realm of Flora, a series of secret gardens each with its own character and range of uncommon and tender plants. There are seven glasshouses for the real rarities, including a collection of *Primula auricula* cultivars and a Victorian house dedicated to Australasian plants. Here and in the 7 ha (18 ac) of woodland gardens outside are extensive collections of *Escallonia*, *Syringa*, *Philadelphus*, *Nothofagus* and *Pittosporum*, as well as the English National Collection of *Olearia*. You may wonder why an English National Collection should be grown by an Irish parks department, but Ireland is like that.

Mature trees line the banks of the river Tolka at the National Botanic Gardens, Dublin.

of arum lilies and white watsonias) each have extensive collections, including a 400-year-old tree fern presented by the Melbourne Botanic Garden in the 1890s.

The gardens have always been a focal point for horticulture and the dissemination of plants in Ireland. They also act as a public park (entry is free) and you will see Dubliners enjoying the lawns around the long pond. But you can wander off to look at the tree collections, the dedicated beds for annuals, the paeony border or the rose garden, and find yourself alone. The many fine trees include a magnificent *Zelkova carpinifolia* near the new herbarium and the tallest *Platanus × hispanica* 'Suttneri' (21 m) in the British Isles.

3miles (5km) N of Dublin city centre
☎ 01 804 0300 **Open** Daily 9am–6pm (10am–4.30pm in winter & 10am Sun) **Size** 20ha (50ac) **Owner** Office of Public Works
🅿 🍴 🚾 ♿
🌐 www.botanicgardens.ie
@ botanicgardens@opw.ie

7. Powerscourt Gardens
Powerscourt Estate
Enniskerry
Co. Wicklow

Powerscourt is a monumental house with vast formal gardens filling the hillside below, but both are more than matched by the splendid prospect of the Great Sugarloaf Mountain as an off-centre focal point.

Start with the glorious Palladian house, built in 1730, and walk slowly down the amphitheatre of terraces, dating from the mid-19th century when the 7th Viscount Powerscourt sought to improve his estate. Vast urns line the staircase on either side (look out for the sulky cherubs) until you arrive at statues of two winged horses, made in Berlin in 1869, and the large round pool with the Triton fountain at its centre.

The 7th Viscount was also a noted tree collector; his

Powerscourt has the grandest Italianate formal gardens in Ireland, but is dominated by the distant view of Great Sugarloaf Mountain.

arboretum, towards the bottom of the slope, is one of Ireland's finest. Halfway down lies a Japanese garden, made in 1908 for the 8th Viscount Powerscourt, with lots of twists and hummocks, a red lacquered bridge to catch the eye, and several tall trachycarpus palms. The herbaceous borders in the walled gardens are magnificent.

The only downside to your visit is that Powerscourt is an extremely popular destination and sometimes it feels as if half the population of Dublin is there with you.

12miles (19km) S of Dublin
☎ 01 204 6000 **Open** Daily 9.30am–5.30pm (dusk in winter) **Size** 19ha (47ac) **Owner** Powerscourt Estate
🚾 🅿 📷 ♿ 🍴 🚉
🌐 www.powerscourt.ie

8. Mount Usher Gardens
Ashford
Co. Wicklow

'Robinsonian' is the word that most people find to describe the garden at Mount Usher: the cantankerous Irishman William Robinson started

to preach a more natural, wilder form of gardening just at the time that Mount Usher was bought by the Walpole family in 1868.

The Walpoles were plantsmen, and they filled the fields with trees and shrubs on either side of the river Vartry that runs through the middle of the garden. The river now has four bridges and they provide some of the best views of Mount Usher, so wild and Elysian indeed that the gardens sometimes seem to have no structure at all. And yet, as you wander along its paths and through its glades, you realise that it is the plants that really matter here – over 5000 different taxa. Many have grown prolifically or to great heights: *Pinus montezumae* has naturalised over a large area; the *Cornus capitata* is the tallest in the British Isles at 18 m; and the *Nothofagus dombeyi* is the largest in Ireland. Eucalypts, magnolias, eucryphias (including *Eucryphia × nymansensis* 'Mount Usher') and Japanese maples are especially well represented. The Palm Walk and Azalea Ride are substantial design features. Crocuses are a bonus in late winter, bluebells in late spring and cardiocrinums in high summer.

The river Vartry is the central design feature of the remarkable collection of plants at Mount Usher Gardens.

30miles (48km) S of Dublin
☎ 0404 40205 **Open** Mid-Mar–Oct daily 10.30am–6pm **Size** 8ha (20ac) **Owner** Mrs Madelaine Jay
🅿 ⬛ ⓦⓒ ♿ 🏛
🅦 www.mount-usher-gardens.com
@ mount_usher.gardens@indigo.ie

9. Altamont Garden
Tullow
Co. Carlow

Altamont is one of those charming, beautiful woodland gardens that could only have been made in Ireland. It was laid out between 1923 and 1999 by Corona North – a knowledgeable, energetic and slightly scatty plantswoman – and her father Feilding Lecky Watson.

There is a hint of formality around the elegant 18th-century house and a new and extensive double border in the walled garden, but the rest of the garden is beautifully and informally planted with rare trees and elegant flowering shrubs. A 10-m tall *Rhododendron augustinii*, grows by the house – Lecky

Watson subscribed to several Himalayan expeditions – but paths lead away towards a large lake, a woodland garden, a bog garden and a shady glen that runs down to the river Slaney. The banks of the lake are planted to offer an everchanging sequence of beautiful compositions. Magnolias, azaleas, hydrangeas, cherries, davidias, tulip trees and taxodiums are underplanted with hostas, candelabra primulas, astilbes and blue meconopsis. The magnificent orange *Rhododendron cinnabarinum* was planted in 1917. The drier areas have carpets of bluebells and wild daffodils in the spring, followed by paeonies, naturalised lilies, colchicums and cyclamens.

Near Ballon, between Tullow & Bunclody ☎ 059 91 59444 **Open** All year Mon–Fri 9am–5pm (3.30pm Fri); 10am–6pm weekends in summer **Size** 16ha (40ac) **Owner** Office of Public Works
🅿 ⓦⓒ ♿ 🏛
🅦 www.heritageireland.ie
@ altamontgardens@opw.ie

10. Birr Castle Demesne
Birr
Co. Offaly

Gardening has been a passion for the owners of Birr for at least 100 years. The result is a huge collection of trees and shrubs assembled from all over the world – old camellia hybrids from Portugal, home-bred magnolias and a very large number of plants grown from seed collected in China and the Himalayas. The older features include an elegant river walk, a large park with wild flowers, a good woodland garden, the tallest box hedges in the world and the largest grey poplar (*Populus × canescens*) in the British Isles.

The plant collections are impressive, some from the great 20th-century plant hunters (Frank Kingdon Ward, Roy Lancaster and Yu) and are supplemented by gifts from such famous gardens as Nymans in Sussex, where Lord Rosse's mother, Anne, lived. The finest feature is the formal garden designed by Anne Rosse in 1935 within the old walled garden. Here are a cloister of arched hornbeams, a lilac avenue, crinums, peonies and two rose gardens.

25miles (40km) S of Athlone
☎ 0509 20336 **Open** Daily 9am–6pm (or dusk, if earlier) **Size** 53ha (130ac) **Owner** Earl of Rosse
🅿 ⬛ ⓦⓒ ♿ 🏛 🚹
🅦 www.birrcastle.com

11. Derreen
Lauragh
Killarney
Co. Kerry

If ever a garden deserved to be called 'a jungle', it is Derreen. Not an impenetrable jungle, of course, but one where the luxuriance of the mossy, lichen-encrusted vegetation suggests that the garden has been hacked out of a primaeval forest. Nothing could be further from the truth: Derreen was a bare and barren peninsular in the gale-swept Atlantic Ocean until about 1870. That was when

GARDENS OF GREAT BRITAIN & IRELAND 221

Lord Lansdowne, later Viceroy of India, began to clothe the rocky wasteland with thuyas, tsugas, griselinias, pittosporums and olearias. Then he set to planting a wide spectrum of plants within the shelter of these pioneer species, and they flourished in the mild, wet climate.

The garden is, in fact, carefully designed in the Robinsonian tradition as a wild or woodland garden. Southern hemisphere plants are well represented – including drimys, leptospermums and eucalyptus – but the woodland is also rich in camellias and conifers from eastern Asia and North America. The rhododendrons are amazing, especially the large specimens of *R. falconeri*, *R. sinogrande* and *R.* 'Loderi King George'. Best of all are the tree ferns, filling a valley to become a wood within a wood, and seeding in their thousands.

15miles (24km) from Kenmare on the Castletown Rd **C** 064 83588 **Open** Apr–Oct daily 10am–6pm **Closed** Mon–Wed in Aug. **Size** 24ha (60ac) **Owner** Charlie Bigham
P ◻ **WC** ♿

12. Fota Arboretum & Garden

Carrigtwohill
Co. Cork

Fota is an island in Cóbh harbour, linked to the mainland by a causeway, with a romantic sense of remoteness. It is famous for its trees, most of which were planted by the Smith-Barry family during the 19th century. The trees flourish in the mild, frost-free air and include such record-breakers as *Eucalyptus muellerana* (36 m), *E. globulus* ssp. *bicostata* (28 m), and *Chamaecyparis lawsoniana* 'Columnaris' (30 m), as well as an amazing *Pittosporum tenuifolium* (normally a shrub) at 20 m. Southern hemisphere plants include exceptional mimosas, lomatias, melaleucas, pseudopanax and the very rare *Dacrycarpus dacrydioides* and *Phyllocladus trichomanoides*.

The grounds are laid out as a landscaped park (though a golf course intrudes into part of it), and one of the pleasures of a visit is the scale of its design, quite apart from the trees. Victorian conifers (huge redwoods and wellingtonias) dominate the plantings, but there are handsome groups of *Dicksonia* tree ferns, phormiums (a National Collection), bananas, *Cornus controversa* and cordylines, and a spectacular specimen of *Phoenix canariensis*, more than 100 years old.

There are also four walled gardens to explore (one recently restored as a rose garden with a large selection of climbers on the walls), a handsome conservatory and a collection of Irish-bred daffodils for spring display. The autumn *Cyclamen* are a bonus.

14miles (22.5km) E of Cork **C** 021 4812728 **Open** Arboretum: daily 9am–6pm (5pm Nov–Mar). Walled gardens: Apr–Oct Mon–Fri 9am–6pm **Size** 11ha (27ac) **Owner** Office of Public Works
P **WC** ♿
W www.heritageireland.ie

13. Mount Congreve

Kilmeaden
Co. Waterford

There is nowhere like Mount Congreve, the largest horticultural garden in Europe and, as yet, little known. It is the lifetime work of Ambrose Congreve, who was born in 1907 and started gardening around his Georgian ancestral home when he was 11 years old. The facts are: 9000 different rare trees and shrubs, 3500 cultivars of rhododendrons, 650 named camellias, 350 cultivars of Japanese maples, 25 gardeners and 16 miles (26 km) of paths, including half a mile (almost 1 km) of hostas.

But even more impressive is Congreve's style of planting in large quantities – 6, 10, 25 or 50 of each variety 'to make the proper statement when the garden matures'. A whole hillside is planted with scarlet embothriums and a walk

down to the river Suir is lined on one side with 100 *Magnolia campbellii* at 10-m intervals and on the other with 100 *Magnolia sargentiana* var. *robusta*. One of the walled gardens has four double herbaceous borders arranged month by month, one each for May, June, July and August. The vast glasshouses have huge collections of orchids, bromeliads, fuchsias, cyclamens, begonias and house-plants. In the oak woodlands are near-complete collections of prunus, acers, azaras, eucryphias, michelias, pittosporums, pieris, berberis, viburnums, cornus and ericas.

All will be willed to the Irish State and be more regularly open to the public in future.

5miles (8km) from Waterford on Cork Rd (N35) **C** 051 384115 **Open** Strictly by appointment. Apr–Oct Thu only 9am–5pm **Size** 44ha (110ac) **Owner** Ambrose Congreve
P **WC**
@ congreve@eircom.ie

14. John F. Kennedy Arboretum

New Ross
Co. Wexford

This excellent young arboretum was founded in 1968 as a memorial to the late president, with financial help from Irish-American citizens. The Kennedy homestead at Dunganstown is 4 miles (6.5 km) away. The site is a fine one and rises from 36 m to the summit of Slieve Coillte at 271 m – it is worth climbing to see the magnificent views (you can also drive there).

The great pleasure of a visit to this arboretum is seeing such a wide variety of different trees growing vigorously as they enter their prime. The 4500 different taxa (shrubs as well as trees) are arranged taxonomically in lines and groups, often with considerable artistry, for example around the lake. In another part, a duplicate collection is arranged geographically in some

200 plots – equally fascinating, because it gives you the chance to see whole ecosystems. Special features include an 'ericaceous garden' with 500 different rhododendrons and many varieties of azaleas and heathers. There is also a slow-growing conifer collection, hedge collection, display of groundcover plants, and selection of climbing plants on a series of stone and timber shelters. In summer you can do your sightseeing the lazy way and chug around on a miniature railway.

8miles (13km) S of New Ross
☎ 051 388171 **Open** May–Aug 10am–8pm; Apr & Sep 10am–6.30pm; Oct–Mar 10am–5pm
Size 252ha (623ac)
Owner Office of Public Works
P ⬛ WC ♿ ▦
@ jfkarboretum@opw.ie

SCOTLAND

15. Castle of Mey
Thurso
Caithness KW14 8XH

The wonder about the garden at the Castle of Mey is that it exists at all. The castle is built close to the rocky shore of Britain's most northern coastline, a barren outpost of wind, rain, salt and persistent cold. But visit it on a sunny day in July or August and you could scarcely imagine a more charming garden. It was designed for the annual visit of the mother of Queen Elizabeth II and entirely planted for late summer display. The walled kitchen garden is divided by internal hedges that protect a series of small compartments. Vegetables, fruit and herbs are grown on a royal scale, and areas are given to sweet peas, dahlias, roses and *Primula florindae*, last to flower of all the Asiatic primulas and also the most sweetly scented. In the charming glasshouses are colourful, well-grown pot plants to be enjoyed here and displayed in the castle.

The tender plants in the Castle of Mey's conservatory reach their high point in August, when Prince Charles is in residence.

Between Thurso & John o' Groats
☎ 01808 851473 **Open** Mid-May–Jul & mid-Aug–Sep Sat–Thur 10.30am–4pm **Size** 1.6ha (4ac)
Owner Queen Elizabeth Castle of Mey Trust P WC ▦ ♿ ▦
W www.castleofmey.org.uk
@ castleofmey@totalise.co.uk

16. Inverewe
Poolewe
Ross and Cromarty IV22 2LG

Inverewe is known worldwide as an extraordinary garden, well worth the long journey to visit, but preferably on a sunny, dry day in May. It was one of the first subtropical gardens to be made in western Scotland by establishing shelter belts against the Atlantic gales and planting exotics in their lee. This was the achievement of its owner Osgood Mackenzie between 1862 and 1922. Spectacular large-leaved Himalayan rhododendrons (Mackenzie's greatest interest), magnolias, eucalypts, tree ferns, palms and nothofagus are underplanted with drifts of erythroniums, blue meconopsis and candelabra primulas, including the brilliant red *P*. 'Inverewe'. Among the surprises is *Isoplexis sceptrum* from Madeira, while drimys and hoherias are so much at home that they self-seed. The paths are often narrow and sometimes steep, but they heighten your sense of exploration, and the way to visit Inverewe is to wander wherever something catches your eye. Down in the semicircular walled garden, just above the rocky shores, expanses of crocosmias, watsonias, dieramas, agapanthus, gazanias and galtonias make a brilliant summer display.

6miles (10km) NE of Gairloch
☎ 01445 781200 **Open** Daily 9.30am–9pm **Closes** 4pm Nov–Mar
Size 20ha (50ac) **Owner** National Trust for Scotland P ▦ WC ♿ ▦ ♿
W www.nts.org.uk
@ inverewe@nts.org.uk

Inverewe's woodland gardens provide shelter to a large number of exotic plants that are too tender to grow in most of Britain.

This grand 19th-century parterre at Dunrobin Castle has recently been restored and improved by the addition of trellised pyramids.

17. Dunrobin Castle

Golspie
Sutherland KW10 6SF

Dunrobin Castle is the largest house in northern Scotland, built in the 1850s for its largest landowner the Duke of Sutherland. The designer for both house and garden was Sir Charles Barry, architect of the Houses of Parliament in London. The garden's formality, striding down to the Dornoch Forth, complements the French château style of the house. Three immensely grand parterres surround the fountains, two traditionally bedded out (but brilliantly and colourfully done) and one planted with hardy geraniums and *Ceratostigma willmottianum*, underplanted with tulips and lilies. One of the parterres has recently been re-made, and thereby much improved: some 20 fretwork pyramids have been planted with clematis and climbing roses in a modern reinterpretation of 19th-century grandeur.

Elsewhere are lots of interesting plants: *Akebia quinata*; huge clumps of gunneras; tall fuchsias (including *F. 'Dunrobin Bedder'*); *Ceanothus thyrsiflorus* with eccremocarpus threading through it; huge maples, limes and horse-chestnuts (much taller than one might expect so far north); a long herbaceous border where plants grow unusually tall; and extensive rhododendron woodlands. But the parterres are the best feature, whether seen from the castle above or looking up at the castle from their colourful midst.

1mile (1.6km) N of Golspie
☎ 01408 633177 **Open** Apr–mid-Oct daily 10.30am–5.30pm (4.30pm Apr–May & Oct) **Size** 2ha (5ac) **Owner** Sutherland Trust
🅿 ☐ 🆆🅲 🏠 🎁 📷
🆆 www.gardens-scotland.co.uk/dunrobin.html
@ info@dunrobincastle.com

18. Cawdor Castle

Nairn IV12 5RD

Cawdor is a proper castle, with baronial turrets and a romantic history as the 14th-century home of the Thanes of Cawdor. It has several gardens: best is the very enjoyable flower garden, laid out in 1710, whose clipped yew hedges are covered in *Tropaeolum speciosum*. Here are large herbaceous borders, areas devoted to lilies and galtonias, spring-flowering trees and shrubs, an arch of rambling roses and a Victorian lavender-edged garden with shrub roses. The oldest garden, dating back to 1620, is known simply as the Walled Garden and was once the castle's kitchen garden. It was given a let's-have-fun make-over in the 1980s and now sports a holly maze, a laburnum walk, and coloured planting schemes.

The turrets of Cawdor Castle rise up between two clipped cones of strangely leaning yews.

Also worth seeing, especially in spring, is the Wild Garden below the castle, where ancient trees (huge limes and fine Victorian conifers) were underplanted in the 1960s with azaleas, rhododendrons and spring bulbs.

6miles (10km) SW of Nairn
☎ 01667 404401 **Open** May–Sep daily 10am–5.30pm **Size** 1.4ha (3½ac) **Owner** Dowager Countess Cawdor 🆆🅲 🍴 ♿ 🏠 🎁 📷
🆆 www.cawdorcastle.com
@ info@cawdorcastle.com

19. Crathes Castle

Banchory AB31 5QJ

Crathes is a turreted castle in a cold, forbidding area of eastern Scotland. All the

The rich colour-plantings at Crathes Castle make this an outstanding Scottish example of mid-20th-century gardening.

Branklyn Garden is one of Britain's outstanding small gardens and has a remarkable series of rock-gardens with many different habitats.

more remarkable, therefore, is the lavishness of its walled flower garden. It started as a kitchen garden and much of its charm depends upon ancient yew hedges and curious topiary dating back to the early 18th century. But the garden itself is 20th-century and was developed before World War I and later in the 1920s and 1930s by Lady Burnett, a friend of Lawrence Johnston of Hidcote – Crathes is the best example of the Hidcote style in Scotland. The picturesque Golden Garden was added by the National Trust for Scotland in the 1970s.

The whole is divided into eight distinct gardens, each with its own character. These include a white border (older than Sissinghurst's), a misty blue garden, and a dreamy, high summer double border with pastel shades for long Highland evenings. The garden is intensively planted to give colour all year round but is probably best in late summer when the reds, oranges, yellows and purples of the Upper Garden are at their most clamorous.

15miles (24km) W of Aberdeen
☎ 01330 844525 **Open** Daily 9am–sunset **Size** 1.5ha (3¾ac) **Owner** National Trust for Scotland
WC P ⫪ ⛓ ⛭ ⛆ ⛫
W www.nts.org.uk
@ crathes@nts.org.uk

20. Branklyn Garden
116 Dundee Rd
Perth PH2 7BB

Branklyn is the leading exponent of the Scottish tradition of rock-gardening. It was made between 1922 and 1967 by John & Dorothy Renton. They used local granite in its design, and added a small area of limestone for such plants as pulsatillas and gentians that are native to the Dolomites and other European mountain ranges. Most of their plants came from the Himalayas, and they subscribed to the leading plant collections of the day by Reginald Farrer and George Forrest.

Plants hold sway. They are planted where the conditions best suit them and most resemble their natural habitats. Highlights include trilliums, primulas, erythroniums, dwarf rhododendrons, lilies like *L. nepalense* and notholirions, the National Collection of *Cassiope* cultivars, woodland areas of sorbus and birches, a fine collection of Japanese maples, and the famous 'Branklyn' group of *Meconopsis*. Plants are placed to show off their individual beauty to maximum effect, whether on an artificial rock-face or in conjunction with others. Large specimen plants provide focal points. And the design ensures that you walk round slowly, looking at all the plants and pondering their beauty.

On eastern edge of Perth
☎ 01738 625535 **Open** Apr–Oct daily 10am–5pm **Size** 0.8ha (2ac) **Owner** National Trust for Scotland
P WC ⛓ ⛭ ⛫
W www.branklyngarden.org.uk

21. Arduaine Garden
by Oban PA34 4XQ

Arduaine is one of Scotland's famous West Coast rhododendron gardens, where tender exotica flourish in the mild, damp climate. It also has a unique collection of modern hybrids, planted by two retired rhododendron nurserymen in the 1970s and

Lush plantings and tender exotics flourish in the sheltered glades of Arduaine, one of Scotland's famous rhododendron gardens.

Tender rhododendrons are a speciality of Benmore Botanic Garden, and its setting is incomparable.

1980s. But the garden dates back to 1897, when the rocky shoreline was first tamed by a retired tea-planter called James Campbell. He planted the specimens of *Rhododendron arboreum* subsp. *zeylanicum* (now the tallest in the British Isles) and the vast, multi-stemmed *R. barbatum*. South American plants also flourish, including eucryphias, *Puya chilensis, Gevuina avellana* and *Philesia magellanica*. The underplantings boast expanding colonies of *Primula denticulata* and *P. helodoxa, Narcissus cyclamineus, Cardiocrinum giganteum, Meconopsis betonicifolia* and *Myosotidium hortensia*. The whole garden is protected by a barrage of conifers and 12-m griselinias.

On A816 between Oban & Lochgilphead ☎ 01852 200366 **Open** Daily 9.30am–sunset **Size** 8ha (20ac) **Owner** National Trust for Scotland
W www.nts.org.uk

22. Benmore Botanic Garden
Dunoon PA23 8QU

Benmore Botanic Garden was acquired by the Royal Botanic Garden, Edinburgh, in 1929 as a place to accommodate the many species introduced by plant

collectors like George Forrest. The magnificent redwood avenue, now in its prime, is much older, having been planted by a former owner, Piers Patrick, in 1863: there is no finer entrance to a garden in Britain. Patrick also planted the collection of conifers, one of the best in Scotland. Subsequent owners, especially the Younger family, planted ornamental trees and shrubs of every kind.

Benmore is a living textbook of the genus *Rhododendron*: over 400 species and subspecies and hundreds of hybrids and cultivars grow here. The Royal Botanic Garden realised that the mild, wet climate would also make possible the cultivation of tender plants from lower altitudes in Bhutan, Tasmania and Chile. The Bhutanese glade has fine *Betula utilis, Sorbus thibetica, Abies densa*, juniper scrub and herbaceous underplantings. The Tasmanian Ridge is planted with *Athrotaxis laxifolia, A. selaginoides* and *Nothofagus cunninghamii*. The Chilean Rainforest Glade has a background of *Araucaria araucana, Austrocedrus, Fitzroya, Podocarpus* and *Nothofagus*, underplanted with *Chusquea* bamboos and *Desfontainea spinosa*, all grown from wild-collected seed.

The whole garden is spacious, educational and beautifully maintained.

7miles (11km) N of Dunoon
☎ 01369 706261 **Open** Mar–Oct daily 10am–6pm **Closes** 5pm Mar & Oct **Size** 61ha (150ac) **Owner** Royal Botanic Garden, Edinburgh
P ☒ WC ☒ ☒ ☒ ☒
W www.rbge.org.uk
@ benmore@rbge.org.uk

23. Mount Stuart
Isle of Bute PA20 9LR

There is much to see at Mount Stuart, and all on a plutocratic scale. The house is gothic, palatial, pink, and quite extraordinary; do not fail to visit it. The gardens go back to the early 18th century – you can still see a lime avenue nearly 300 years old, but most of them date from the late 19th-century and later.

By the entrance is a mature Victorian pinetum with magnificent firs, larches and Douglas firs. In front of the house lies a 1-ha (2-ac) rock-garden, designed around two streams and a pond by Thomas Mawson in the 1890s and thickly planted with rare plants. The planting has been reworked several times since then and includes small trees, like the rare *Reevesia pubescens* and tender *Michelia doltsopa*.

The kitchen garden was redesigned by the late Lord Bute with help from Rosemary Verey in 1990. It has a geometrical, box-edged layout, with two stylish fruit cages, two herb gardens (culinary and medicinal), a large glass pavilion planted with tender plants and an extensive area of herbaceous plantings in the German style (a later addition). Mount Stuart also has a tropical greenhouse, acres of bluebells and established rhododendrons, and a 'wee' garden of 2 ha (5 ac) planted with tender exotics from Australia and New Zealand.

5miles (8km) S of Rothesay
☎ 01700 503877 **Open** May–Sep daily 10am–6pm **Size** 122ha (300ac) **Owner** Mount Stuart Trust
P ☒ ☒ WC ☒ ☒ ☒ ☒
W www.mountstuart.com
@ contactus@mountstuart.com

24. Brodick Castle

Isle of Arran KA27 8HY

Brodick is famous for its rhododendrons, but even without them would be a place of pilgrimage for horticulturists. Take its record-breaking trees, for example: Brodick has Britain's tallest *Nothofagus nervosa* (32 m), *Drimys winteri* (22 m), *Embothrium coccineum* (21 m) and *Leptospermum scoparium* (12 m). The garden was substantially planted between 1923 and 1957 by Molly, Duchess of Montrose, one of those hands-on aristocratic gardeners so characteristic of the British gardening scene. The Duchess also supported the leading plant collectors of her day, including George Forrest, Joseph Rock, Frank Ludlow and Frank Kingdon Ward.

The older conifers, however, date back to the mid-19th century, as does the walled garden (recently restored as it was in the 1890s), but it is the woodland garden that offers most to the visitor. The hillsides are riven with streams and the spectacular large-leaved rhododendrons like *R. sinogrande, R. maccabeanum* and *R. falconeri* revel in the sheltered, damp, frost-free conditions. They also include such difficult species as *R. protistum*. Magnolias, camellias, crinodendrons and eucalyptus are underplanted with drifts of candelabra primulas, hydrangeas, ferns and even the American pitcher plant (*Darlingtonia californica*). Bluebells and daffodils add their seasonal colour; there is not a more perfect woodland garden on a sunny day in early May.

Ferry from Ardrossan to Brodick ☎ 01770 302202 **Open** Park: daily 9.30am–sunset. Walled garden: Apr–Oct daily 10am–4.30pm **Size** 32ha (80ac) **Owner** National Trust for Scotland
🅿 🚻 🅦🅒 ♿ 🏛 🛈 🖼
W www.nts.org.uk
@ brodickcastle@nts.org.uk

25. Culzean Castle

Maybole
Ayrshire KA19 8LE

Culzean Castle sits on a rocky headland high above the Northern Straits. Its gardens date back to the 17th century – the deer park is older still – and are stylishly maintained by the National Trust for Scotland.

On the terraces behind the castle are richly planted mixed borders with some unusual plants – *Mutisia decurrens* and *Acca sellowiana*, for example, flourish in the maritime climate. Kniphofias, galtonias and *Salvia guaranitica* are also much in evidence. The centrepiece is a handsome fountain, while tender plants in pots fill the conservatory.

Walk your way down towards the walled gardens, past the very handsome Camellia House (1818) in the gothic style, now filled with oranges and lemons. The great range of glasshouses includes a vinery (1890s) planted with Victorian table grapes. The central paths in the second walled garden are planted with some of the best herbaceous borders in Britain. The landscaping of the estate is also worth exploring, especially the walk down through the woods to the Swan Lake with a gothic cottage and, higher up, the Pagoda, dating from 1814. Good trees are everywhere, including the tallest Irish yew (*Taxus baccata* 'Fastigiata') in Britain at 20 m.

2miles (3km) W of Maybole
☎ 01655 884455 **Open** Walled garden: Good Friday–Oct daily 10.30am–5pm Park: daily 9.30am–sunset **Size** 51ha (125ac) **Owner** National Trust for Scotland
🅿 🚻 🅦🅒 ♿ 🏛 🛈 🖼
W www.culzeancastle.net
@ culzean@nts.org.uk

26. Dawyck Botanic Garden

Stobo EH45 9JU

Dawyck is a regional outlier of the Royal Botanic Garden in Edinburgh. It is essentially a woodland garden

Dawyck Botanic Garden lies in a cold, upland valley but is famous for its trees and rhododendrons.

with a very fine collection of trees, including the fastigiate beech (*Fagus sylvatica* 'Dawyck'), which was first found here in about 1850. Dawyck is in a very cold part of Scotland, high in the hills and north-facing, so that the climate is more continental than temperate. The garden is laid out on grassy terraces above the house and around a peaty stream called Scrape Burn.

The trees for which the garden is famous were first planted in the 1830s: the Naesmyths who owned Dawyck at that time subscribed to the great plant-hunting expeditions of the day, including those of David Douglas. This explains the many fine North American conifers in the valley around the stream. In the early 20th century, the owners received plants from the early Chinese collections of E.H. Wilson.

The garden is also famous for its rhododendrons (the scented azalea terrace is especially good in late May when the meconopsis flower, too), berberis and cotoneasters. Millions of snowdrops and daffodils flower in spring, and the autumn colours are excellent.

The cantilevered roof of the main glasshouse in Edinburgh's Royal Botanic Garden creates uninterrupted space inside.

8miles (13km) SW of Peebles
☎ 01721 760254 **Open** Feb–Nov
daily 10am–6pm **Closes** 4pm Feb
& Nov; 5pm Mar & Oct **Size** 24ha
(60ac) **Owner** Royal Botanic
Garden, Edinburgh
🅿 ◩ WC 🏠 🛈
🆆 www.rbge.org.uk
@ dawyck@rbge.org.uk

27. Royal Botanic Garden, Edinburgh

20A Inverleith Row
Edinburgh EH3 5LR

The 'Botanics', as Edinburgh people call it, is one of the friendliest and most interesting gardens in Britain. It is inter-nationally renowned for its collection of plants from temperate and tropical regions around the world. So far as possible, these have been displayed in a naturalistic setting that hints at their native habitats. The rock-garden is about 1 ha (over 2 ac) in extent and composed of many different microhabitats, most of them helped by the naturally light sandy soil and low rainfall. More than 5000 species (from areas as diverse as high mountains, the Arctic regions and the Mediterranean) flourish in the mounds and gullies of sandstone and conglomerate alongside the stream and in the screes.

The arboretum has nearly 2000 different trees, many seldom seen in cultivation.

There are also extensive areas dedicated to rhododendrons, azaleas, heathers, Chinese mountain plants and systematic demonstration gardens. The landscaping in the glasshouses is particularly attractive and recreates a series of different environments from arid deserts to humid tropics. These include a Tropical Aquatic House; Fern House; Orchid and Cycad House (some of the cycads are 200 years old); South American Aquatic House (bromeliads as well as water plants); Arid Lands House (an excellent collection of the flora of Arabia); Peat House (the world's largest collection of *Vireya* rhododendrons); and Tropical Rock House (gesneriads and members of the ginger family). The newly restored Temperate Palm House, built in 1852, is the tallest in Britain at 23 m high. Labelling and maintenance are excellent.

1mile (1.6km) N of city centre
☎ 01315 527171 **Open** Daily
10am–7pm **Closes** 6pm Mar & Oct;
4pm Nov–Feb **Size** 29ha (72ac)
Owner Board of Trustees
🅿 ◩ WC ♿ 🏠 🛈
🆆 www.rbge.org.uk
@ info@rbge.org.uk

28. Logan Botanic Garden

Port Logan
Stranraer DG9 9ND

Logan is a subtropical outlier of the Royal Botanic Garden in Edinburgh. 'Subtropical' is not the word

Cordylines and tree ferns are among the many subtropical plants that flourish in Logan Botanic Garden, where the climate is mild and damp.

for Scotland's climate, but the absence of frost on parts of its west coast makes possible the cultivation of plants from the world's subtropics.

The garden was begun in the 1870s and acquired by Edinburgh in 1969. The tree ferns (*Dicksonia antarctica*) in the walled garden – almost a forest of them – date back to its beginnings and are underplanted with the smaller fern *Blechnum chilense* to create an impression of lush fertility. The formal lily pond is partly framed by a diagonal avenue of 10-m high centennial cabbage palms (*Cordyline australis*), supplemented by echiums from the Canary Islands and Madeira. The summer display of tender plants – salvias, dieramas, osteospermums, diascias, argyranthemums, verbenas and gazanias – is the most brilliant in Scotland. Here, too, is a pretty peat garden planted with meconopsis, primulas, trilliums, gaultherias and dwarf rhododendrons. The woodland garden, beyond the walls and past an avenue of *Trachycarpus fortunei*, has 40 species of *Eucalyptus*, with an understorey of tree ferns, olearias, lepto-spermums, callistemons, fuchsias, crinodendrons, drimys, embothriums, desfontainias and eucryphias. Their miraculous profusion at Logan is one of Scotland's jolliest sights.

14miles (22.5km) S of Stranraer
☎ 01776 860231 **Open** Mar–Oct daily 10am–6pm **Closes** 5pm Mar & Oct **Size** 12ha (30ac)
Owner Royal Botanic Garden, Edinburgh
🅿 🖫 🆆🅲 ♿ 🏚 ⚘
🅦 www.rbge.org.uk
@ logan@rbge.org.uk

29. Glenwhan Gardens
Dunragit
by Stranraer DG9 8PH

Many fine gardens on the west coast of Scotland and Ireland have been won from rocky moorland, bog and scrub. Glenwhan is especially interesting as a recent example

Vast drifts of candelabra primulas flourish in Glenwhan – an excellent modern plantsman's garden.

where the process is ongoing, because this plantsman's garden has been entirely created by its present owners since 1979. Their first action was to dig out two small lakes and plant shelter belts of native trees – Scots pines, oaks, rowans and willows. A series of roped terraces – planted with heathers, azaleas, small conifers, golden elders, hardy fuchsias and massed Rugosa roses – rises above the lakes towards a small folly at the peak.

The wonderful views of Luce Bay and the Mull of Galloway help to explain why Glenwhan has thrived – the mild air and plentiful rainfall make for many horticultural oppor-tunities. Plantings are now sufficiently established to create microhabitats for plants with special requirements, like large-leaved *Rhododendron fictolacteum*. Among the new plantings are many interesting southern hemisphere plants, including eucalyptus and olearias around the summerhouse, embothriums, eucryphias, callistemons and dicksonias. Scottish standbys abound: meconopsis, candelabra primulas, erythroniums and trilliums flourish. The range of plants is immense, and their cultural needs take precedence over design. But the gardens are an education and inspiration to all who have the patience to take a long-term view of their gardening.

Signed from Dunragit
☎ 01581 400222 **Open** Apr–Oct daily 10am–5pm **Size** 5ha (12½ac)
Owner Tessa & William Knott
🅿 🍴 🆆🅲 ♿ 🏚 ⚘
🅦 www.glenwhangardens.co.uk
@ tess@glenwhan.freeserve.co.uk

30. Castle Kennedy Gardens
Rephad
Stranraer DG9 8BX

Castle Kennedy is a ruined keep, destroyed by fire in 1716. Lochinch Castle (where *Buddleja* 'Lochinch' originated) is its 1860s replacement, ¾ mile (1 km) to the north. The garden between them lies on an isthmus, with the dark Black Loch to the east and the sparkling White Loch to the west. The landscaping dates to the 2nd Earl of Stair (1720–50), who had been ambassador to France and admired the splendour of Versailles. Grand grassed mounds and terraces, rides, ridges and earthworks give the garden its highly original structure.

The horticultural interest comes from Castle Kennedy's walled garden, a riot of herbaceous colour in the summer, with *Callistemon* species among the interesting tender shrubs against its walls. Elsewhere are plants from Sir Joseph Hooker's Himalayan expeditions (magnificent *Rhododendron arboreum*), an avenue of monkey puzzle trees

Alnwick Garden is the grandest new garden in Britain and is full of good design and plants.

(*Araucaria araucana*) raised from the original seed sent from Chile and a semicircle of crimson *Embothrium coccineum* interplanted with flower-decked *Eucryphia × nymansensis*. There are more conventional flower borders in the area beside Lochinch Castle.

5miles (8km) E of Stranraer
☎ 01776 702024 **Open** Apr–Sep daily 10am–5pm **Size** 30ha (75ac)
Owner Lochinch Heritage Estate
🅿 ◲ 🚻 ♿ ⛱
🆆 www.castlekennedygardens.co.uk
@ info@castlekennedygardens.co.uk

NORTHERN ENGLAND

31. Alnwick Garden
Denwick Lane
Alnwick NE66 1YU

The Alnwick Garden is new, enormous, and very well made. There is an immense amount to see and admire – good design, interesting ideas, striking plantings and unusual plants. It is the brainchild of the Duchess of Northumberland and the masterpiece of the Belgian designer Jacques Wirtz. The central feature is a grand water cascade in the baroque style, with curving edges and hornbeam arcades reminiscent of the château of Belœil in Flanders. It leads to the Ornamental Garden in the old kitchen garden of the Duke of Northumberland. Its criss-cross design creates about 20 different box-edged areas, put to fruit, vegetables, herbs and especially flowers – whole beds are dedicated to a single genus, like roses, hellebores, irises, Japanese anemones and delphiniums, with much to see in every season.

Other features include an enormous Tree House; a David Austin rose garden (tightly and beautifully designed with pergolas, climbers, shrub roses and mixed plantings); the poison garden (ivy, yew, cannabis and amanitas are among the plants); a bamboo labyrinth; and a 'serpent garden', which displays the many ways that water can be made to move. But Alnwick is a sumptuous, inspirational and fascinating garden, remarkable for its high standards of construction and exemplary maintenance.

Centre of Alnwick ☎ 01665 511350
Open Daily 10am–7pm (4pm in winter) **Size** 16ha (40ac)
Owner Alnwick Garden Trust
🅿 ◲ 🚻 🆆 ♿ ⛱
🆆 www.alnwickgarden.com
@ info@alnwickgarden.com

32. Wallington
Cambo
Morpeth NE61 4AR

The garden at Wallington is one of many made for the National Trust by Graham Stuart Thomas. There are other features of interest, including a massive display of daffodils around the classical house and

Graham Stuart Thomas designed and planted the modern garden at Wallington, a flagship property of the National Trust in north-east England.

a park that 'Capability' Brown may (or may not) have helped to design – he was born in nearby Kirkharle. But the joy of a visit is to stumble for quite a distance through a dark woodland, until suddenly you arrive at the old walled garden. It lies on a steep, south-east-facing slope (essential in this cold, inland part of Northumberland) and is most irregularly shaped. Mixed borders, sweeping lawns and a trickling stream lead to the conservatory at the top, where an ancient, tree-like specimen of *Fuchsia* 'Rose of Castile Improved' is the star turn. Beyond, in front of further glasshouses, is a late-summer border of dahlias, cannas and foliage plants in purple, red and orange. Below is a miraculous early-autumn border in blue and yellow – Thomas at his most perceptive. The National Collection of *Sambucus* species and cultivars grows in the old orchard.

Shrub roses – this is *Rosa hugonis* – flower early in the protection of Dalemain's walled garden.

6miles (10km) NW of Belsay
☏ 01670 773600 **Open** Daily 10am–7pm **Closes** 6pm October & 4pm Nov–Mar **Size** 41ha (100ac) **Owner** National Trust
🅿 🚻 🆆🅲 ♿ 🎁 👶 ♨ 🖼
W www.nationaltrust.org.uk

33. Belsay Hall
Belsay
Newcastle upon Tyne NE20 0DX

The gardens at Belsay have one outstanding and unique feature: a wildly picturesque quarry garden. When Sir Charles Monck built the Greek Revival house in the early 19th century, he cut the stone from the rock-face behind the house. His descendants transformed this wilderness into garden – a sequence of gloomy chasms, corridors and pinnacles 4.5 ha (11 ac) in extent that shelters all manner of exotic and tender plants. Rhododendron species flourish in the protective shade, climbers scramble 10 m up the cliffs and spring bulbs carpet the base. The ravines create a microclimate that allows such

plants as *Trachycarpus fortunei* and eucryphias to flourish in this cold upland site. Elsewhere are good bedding, herbaceous plantings, a magnolia terrace, some of the oldest Douglas firs in England and 0.8 ha (2 ac) of hardy hybrid rhododendrons – alas, not visitable, but a magnificent sight from the terrace of the house.

10miles (16km) NW of Newcastle
☏ 01661 881636 **Open** Apr–Oct daily 10am–6pm (4pm Oct); Nov–Mar Thu–Mon 10am–4pm **Size** 16ha (40ac) **Owner** English Heritage
🅿 🍴 🆆🅲 ♿ 🎁 👶
W www.english-heritage.org.uk

34. Dalemain
Penrith CA11 0HB

Dalemain is a garden of great charm in a fine position on the edge of the Lake District. It has an intimacy seldom found among good gardens open to the public. The entrance to the garden is a 16th-century terrace, very few of which remain in the British Isles. Then comes a kitchen garden with fruit trees planted 250 years ago, though the overall 'feel' of Dalemain is Edwardian.

Most of the plantings are modern, including the formal knot garden (tulips, herbs, white *Viola cornuta* and agapanthus) and the long and richly planted herbaceous

border that overlooks the park and the Lakeland Fells. The mixed borders and roses are dreamily English, particularly the Rose Walk, which boasts more than 100 old-fashioned roses and leads to a gazebo hung with *Clematis tangutica*. Nearby is the wild garden with drifts of meconopsis and martagon lilies in late spring. The fine trees include a tulip tree (*Liriodendron tulipifera*) and the largest *Abies cephalonica* in the British Isles.

4miles (6.5km) SW of Penrith
☏ 01768 486450 **Open** Apr–Oct Sun–Thu 10.30am–5pm; Nov–Dec & Feb–Mar Sun–Thu 11am–4pm **Closed** Jan **Size** 2ha (5ac) **Owner** Robert Hasell-McCosh
🅿 🍴 🆆🅲 ♿ 🎁 👶 ♨ 🖼
W www.dalemain.com

35. Levens Hall
Kendal LA8 0PD

Levens is famous for its topiary – huge, overgrown, comical chunks of box and yew. Some is said to be left over from a simple formal parterre laid out in 1694 and supplemented by fashionable golden yews in the 19th century. Some is more recent: successive generations have been good about replacing plants and restoring the garden when necessary. Peacocks, arches, umbrellas, top hats, corkscrews and chess pieces are to be found, but many defy naming. The arbours and high

Levens Hall is the most famous topiary garden in Britain; most of the plantings are at least 150 years old.

yew hedges, some of them crenellated, are spangled with scarlet *Tropaeolum speciosum* and the parterres planted annually with 15 000 plants, so that there is always lots of colour to highlight the topiary. The standard of maintenance is unusually high and the ha-ha (also built in 1694), which divides the garden from the park, is said to be the oldest in England.

5miles (8km) S of Kendal
☎ 01539 560321 **Open** Mid-Apr–mid-Oct Sun–Thu 10am–5pm
Size 4ha (10ac) **Owner** C.H. Bagot
🅿 🍴 🆆🅲 ♿ 🏠 ♿
🆆 www.levenshall.co.uk
@ housekeeping@levenshall.co.uk

36. Newby Hall
Ripon HG4 5AE

Newby is known as 'the Hidcote of the North' – a plantsman's garden in the Arts-and-Crafts style, of the sort more commonly seen in southern England. It manages to combine firm but inventive design, a great number of

Newby Hall is the finest example in northern England of a garden in the 'Hidcote' style.

different features, and considerable artistry. Its axis is a bold, wide and very long grass walk, lined by yew-backed, double herbaceous borders stretching gently down from the elegant 17th-century house to the river Ure. Few visitors ever arrive at the river – instead, they are diverted to one side or the other to explore some of the many ornamental paths and gardens that lead off it. That was the intention of the garden's creator, Major Edward Compton, who inherited Newby and laid it out between 1921 and 1977. He designed the long walk as a corridor, from which to enter garden rooms filled with different plants at their best throughout the seasons. These formal enclosures – there are many more of them than at Hidcote – are strongly designed, thickly planted and set among informal areas of woodland garden.

But for many visitors it is the plants that they remember – so many new and interesting ones. They include the National Collection of *Cornus* and a comprehensive collection of shrubby salvias, many of them collected in Central and South America by the owner's brother, Dr James Compton.

3miles (5km) SE of Ripon
☎ 01423 322583 **Open** Apr–Sep Tue–Sun & bank hol Mon 11am–5.30pm; also Mon Jul–Aug **Size** 10ha (25ac) **Owner** Richard Compton
🅿 🍴 🆆🅲 ♿ 🏠 ♿ 🖼
🆆 www.newbyhall.co.uk

37. Castle Howard
York YO6 7DA

Castle Howard is typical of many of England's great gardens – an important historic landscape with a major horticultural spectacle grafted onto it. The house is palatial, the largest in Yorkshire, designed by John Vanbrugh in 1699 for the 3rd Earl of Carlisle. Vanbrugh also laid out the park on a heroic

The rose garden is a charming modern feature among the splendours of 18th-century landscaping at Castle Howard.

scale, furnishing the five axes with important buildings and natural features: the lake, terraces, statues and waterfalls down to the new river are all his. Vanbrugh's masterpiece (built in 1724–26) is the Temple of the Four Winds. The Mausoleum was designed by Nicholas Hawksmoor in 1728.

In front of the house are the relics of a vast 19th-century parterre, whose centre point is the Atlas fountain built by William Andrews Nesfield in the 1850s. Within a walled garden is a series of grand 1980s rose gardens designed by Jim Russell to display every type of rose from ancient to modern. Russell also laid out an arboretum and a historic collection of rhododendrons and other ericaceous plants in a part of the estate called Ray Wood. The collections of Forrest, Rock, Kingdon Ward, Ludlow and Sheriff are represented, as are more recent plant hunters. The aim is to create one of the most comprehensive collections of hardy woody plants in Europe – 6500 taxa so far.

15miles (24km) NE of York
01653 648333 **Open** Daily 10am–6pm (or dusk, if earlier) **Size** 405ha (1000ac) **Owner** Castle Howard Estates Ltd
www.castlehoward.co.uk

38. Bramham Park

Wetherby LS23 6ND

Bramham is the finest French formal garden in Britain. It was made by the first Lord Bingley in the 1700s and 1710s and ornamented with garden buildings by his daughter in the 1730s and 1740s. And it survived the landscaping fashions of 'Capability' Brown. Bingley was his own designer, which explains why Bramham is less regular than real French gardens of the period.

The approach is memorable: a long driveway winds through the woods, turns a corner, and suddenly reveals the magnificent Palladian house, framed by spacious avenues. The garden is made up of long, straight rides carved through dense woodland and edged with tall beech hedges, neatly cut. The way to visit it is to start walking, and keep walking, as the vistas take you. Loggias, statues, temples, and obelisks draw you along. The parkland turf is speckled with cowslips and harebells. There are features of breathtaking beauty, like the recently restored *patte-d'oie* and a sequence of formal cascades running down to a square, lake-sized pond. You cannot fail to be cheered and delighted by the superlative grandeur of Bramham. And you may be the only visitor.

5miles (8km) S of Wetherby
01937 846000 **Open** Apr–Sep daily 11.30am–4.30pm **Size** 28ha (68ac) **Owner** George Lane Fox
www.bramhampark.co.uk
judy.fisk@bramhampark.co.uk

39. Ness Botanic Gardens

Neston CH64 4AY

Ness was laid out in 1898 by Arthur Bulley, a rich cotton merchant in Liverpool with a passionate interest in plants and plant hunting.

The French formal style is clearly seen in the view of clipped avenues at Bramham Park.

Arley Hall can fairly claim to have the oldest herbaceous borders in England, first planted in 1846.

He sponsored such plant collectors as George Forrest and Frank Kingdon Ward and even set up his own seed company to distribute the seeds they imported from China and the Himalayas. *Primula bulleyana*, *Gentiana sino-ornata* and *Pieris formosa* var. *forrestii* are among his introductions.

Ness is just above the mild, windy estuary of the river Dee and still retains the 'feel' of a private garden – beautifully laid out, but horticulturally rather than botanically. The large rock-garden is outstanding, with an enormous range of different environments (south-facing and north-facing, limestone and sandstone, sunny, shaded and damp) – alpine and rock plants of every kind grow here, alongside some overgrown dwarf conifers. There are notable collections of *Betula* and *Sorbus*, *Salix* and *Cotoneaster*, rare plants of the British Isles, rhododendrons, hollies, lilies, camellias and heathers. Add the fine herbaceous borders, water plants and good glasshouse collections and you will probably find that Ness is one of those gardens where you remain longer than you intended.

2miles (3km) SE of Neston
☎ 01513 530123 **Open** Daily 9.30am–4pm (5pm Mar–Oct)
Size 26ha (65ac) **Owner** University of Liverpool 🅿 ⬛ 🆆🅲 ♿ 🏛 ♿
🆆 www.nessgardens.org.uk/

40. Arley Hall
Great Budworth
Northwich CW9 6NA

The gardens at Arley Hall are famous for their double herbaceous borders, laid out by the present owner's forebears in 1846. They are probably the oldest devoted solely to herbaceous plants and are still extremely beautiful, though they have been constantly changed and updated over the years. The yew hedge behind them, yew buttresses and the dumbwaiter yew topiaries at either end add much to their beauty. To one side is a short avenue of evergreen oak (*Quercus ilex*) clipped as 10-m high cylinders. Elsewhere are pleached limes (near the entrance), a parterre laid out by W.A. Nesfield, fine

18th-century parkland by William Emes, a Victorian 'Rootree' (old tree stumps, rocks and a secret grotto), lots of shrub roses, two walled gardens, and Lord Ashbrook's arboretum, underplanted with rhododendrons, azaleas and flowering shrubs.

5miles (8km) W of Knutsford
☎ 01565 777353 **Open** Apr–Sep Tue–Sun & bank hols 11am–5pm; also weekends in Oct **Size** 5ha (12½ac) **Owner** Viscount Ashbrook
🅿 🍴 🆆🅲 ♿ 🏛 ♿ 🖼
🆆 www.arleyhallandgardens.com
@ enquiries@arleyhallandgardens.com

41. Tatton Park
Knutsford WA16 6QN

Tatton is a most inviting garden to explore – full of history, interest, beauty and variety. Humphry Repton probably laid out the parkland, but there are also two very early formal gardens – a beech maze dating from around 1795, and the gardenesque Charlotte's Garden, full of trellis-work and flower beds shaped as petals, designed by Lewis Wyatt in 1814. Wyatt also accounted for the adjacent conservatory in 1818, now crammed with colourful tender plants.

The great Sir Joseph Paxton designed the formal Italian garden with complicated and richly planted parterres that set off the house so well, while his

Sir Joseph Paxton designed this formal garden – one of many outstanding features throughout Tatton Park.

son-in-law George Stokes built the palatial palm house, now a fernery. Later came a Japanese garden (1910–13), the largest in Britain and the only one in northern England. It combines a tea garden with a representation of Mount Fuji and an island with a Shinto shrine. Other good things to see include the sunken Edwardian rose garden, some excellent topiary, fine mixed borders, the African hut, and the massed plantings of rhododendrons and azaleas around a pool.

3miles (5km) NW of Knutsford
☎ 01625 534400 **Open** All year Tue–Sun 10am–6pm (11am–4pm in winter) & bank hol Mon **Size** 20ha (50ac) **Owner** National Trust
P **Ⅱ** **WC** **&** **🏛** **♿** **🚻**
W www.tattonpark.org.uk

42. Haddon Hall
Bakewell DE45 1LA

No other garden in England so lacking in horticultural interest is as charming and delightful to visit as Haddon. It is hard to say why visitors find it all so beguiling – but they do, and so will you. The mediaeval castle with a Jacobean make-over contributes to the magic, as does the setting above a beautiful, unspoiled valley.

The garden was laid out by the 9th Duchess of Rutland in

Roses, delphiniums and clematis contribute to the dreamy beauty of Haddon Hall's garden.

the 1910s and 1920s along six much older terraces, connected by handsome stone staircases, above the river Wye. One terrace has a square pool with a fountain at its centre; others give picturesque views of an ancient stone bridge across the river. The Duchess planted formal features like yew trees to add to the structure, but her great passion was for roses, and it is for these most beautiful of flowers that the garden is now known. Bright Hybrid Teas and Floribundas predominate, but shrub roses and wild rose species are also well represented. Climbing roses flourish against the walls,

alongside ceanothus and clematis. Bulbs give colour in spring and autumn. Sixty different cultivars of delphinium in the herbaceous borders are supplemented by tender perennials and annuals, hardy and half-hardy. But go in rose time, when there is no more beautiful and romantic garden in England.

1½miles (2.5km) S of Bakewell
☎ 01629 812855 **Open** May–Sep daily 12noon–4.30pm; Apr & Oct Sat–Mon **Size** 2ha (5ac) **Owner** Lord Edward Manners
P **📷** **Ⅱ** **WC** **🚻**
W www.haddonhall.co.uk

43. Chatsworth
Bakewell DE45 1PP

Chatsworth's garden and grounds have been open to the public for nearly 200 years, and the estate has the happy knack of making everyone feel a welcome guest. It is by far the grandest garden in the north Midlands – a huge and beautiful park (the work of 'Capability' Brown) into which successive Dukes and Duchesses of Devonshire have inserted formal designs, flower gardens, magnificent garden buildings and major horticultural interest. Some of its best features antedate Brown's landscaping, including the unique Great Cascade, built in about 1700, and the

The Grand Cascade at Chatsworth is the oldest and most impressive in Britain.

Canal, dug at the same time as a sheet of water to reflect the southern façade of the house.

The glory days of Chatsworth's garden were the 1830s and 1840s when Sir Joseph Paxton and the 'bachelor Duke' built the Emperor fountain, the rock-garden (huge boulders surrounded by conifers), the arboretum, the pinetum and the 'conservative wall', whose function was to hold the heat to ripen fruit trees early. The horticultural interest embraces a tulip tree avenue, the bamboo walk, Victorian yews of different hues, a rose garden, cottage garden, kitchen garden, borders in orange and blue and white and, rather surprisingly in this cold climate, record trees like the tallest *Pinus strobus* (42 m) in the British Isles.

8miles (13km) N of Matlock
☎ 01246 582204 **Open** Mid-Mar–mid-Dec daily 11am–6pm (10.30am Jun–Aug) **Size** 43ha (105ac) **Owner** Chatsworth House Trust
🅿 🚻 ᵂᶜ ♿ 🏠 👶 🍴
Ⓦ www.chatsworth.org

44. Renishaw Hall
Sheffield S21 3WB

Renishaw is a stylish and enjoyable garden to visit. It was laid out around 1900 by Sir George Sitwell, an amateur designer who wrote about Italian gardens and applied Italian renaissance principles to the garden he made at Renishaw. Symmetry, proportion, scale and shadow still govern what we see today: yew hedges, pools, fountains, grass and statues – a garden that would not be out of place in Tuscany or the Veneto.

What has changed, however, are the plantings. Sitwell decreed that nothing should interfere with the correctness of his design, but his descendants have fleshed it out with old-fashioned roses and soft-coloured herbaceous plantings. The results are unusually charming: it is the sort of Anglo-Italian hybrid that many English garden

Sir George Sitwell designed the stylish gardens at Renishaw Hall in the Italian style.

owners make in Italy. The house has some surprisingly tender plants on its walls, including *Acacia dealbata* and *Cytisus battandieri*, and the bluebell wood is planted with rhododendrons, camellias and magnolias.

7miles (11km) NE of Chesterfield
☎ 01246 432310 **Open** Apr–Sep Thu–Sun & bank hol Mon 10.30am–4.30pm **Size** 3ha (7ac) formal gardens, plus woodlands **Owner** Sir Reresby Sitwell 🅿 🍴 ᵂᶜ ♿ 👶
Ⓦ www.sitwell.co.uk

WALES

45. Bodnant Gardens
Tal-y-Cafn
Colwyn Bay LL28 5RE

Bodnant is the largest, the best and the most influential garden in Wales. The house is grand and ugly, built by Henry Pochin in the 1870s, but its setting is magnificent, with views across the valley of the river Conwy to the Carneddau mountains. Pochin and his descendants, now in their fifth generation, have all been passionate horticulturists, and Bodnant has one of the finest collections of plants in Britain.

The splendid, broad terraces below the house are full of interest – a deep herbaceous

border, tender climbers against the retaining walls, two enormous cedars, a formal lily pond, a rose pergola, and many specimens of *Magnolia grandiflora*. The lowest terrace is dominated by an elegant 18th-century gazebo known as the Pin Mill, which looks across a pool towards a grassy green theatre, edged with cut cubes of yew topiary. Plantings of pencil-thin cypresses help to create an intensely Mediterranean feel on clear summer days.

The wild and woodland areas are known as the Dell and run down to an old mill and a fast-flowing stream, whose banks are planted with hostas, astilbes, bergenias and meconopsis. Tall specimen trees (some of the redwoods are massive, including the tallest in the British Isles at 47 m) give structure to an amazing collection of ornamental shrubs and small trees, notably magnolias, hydrangeas, rhododendrons, camellias and embothriums, all arranged for horticultural effect – colour gardening on the grand scale. The famous 55-m long laburnum arch curves back to the top terrace and presents an unforgettable spectacle in early June.

8miles (13km) S of Llandudno
☎ 01492 650460 Open Mid-Mar–early Nov daily 10am–5pm **Size** 32ha (80ac) **Owner** National Trust & McLaren family 🅿 🍴 ♿ 👶
Ⓦ www.bodnantgarden.co.uk

46. Portmeirion
Penrhyndeudraeth LL48 6ET

Portmeirion is a little village where the architect Sir Clough Williams-Ellis worked out his Italianate fantasies. He once said that, to make a successful garden, a man must start when he is absurdly young and live to be absurdly old. He was over 40 when he bought Portmeirion from his uncle in 1925, but he lived to be 95 and established the subtropical gardens we see today.

The gardens in Portmeirion are mainly formal, with a

The Italianate village of Portmeirion on the west coast of Wales is surrounded by subtropical gardens and extensive woodland gardens.

mixture of Mediterranean plants, exotic palms and architectural bric-a-brac of every period. Other attractions include tree ferns, gunneras, phormiums, ginkgos and holm oaks. Williams-Ellis bought up further estates in later years, by which he acquired one of the chief attractions of the gardens at Portmeirion today – the collection of rhododendrons and azaleas known as the Gwyllt Gardens. *Rhododendron arboreum* has grown to enormous size and in some parts still forms impenetrable thickets. The peak display comes in May, though the mainstay of late summer and autumn is thousands of hydrangeas throughout the Portmeirion estate. One garden, almost at the furthest end of the estate and planted with a background of eucalypts, is known as the 'ghost garden' because of the way the wind whistles in the leaves.

3miles (5km) E of Porthmadog
☎ 01766 770000 **Open** Daily 9.30am–5.30pm **Size** 28ha (70ac)
Owner Portmeirion Ltd
🅿 🚻 ♿ 🍴 👶 ♿ 🏠
🆆 www.portmeirion-village.com

47. Powis Castle
Welshpool SY21 8RF

The gardens at Powis Castle are famous for their hanging terraces draped with bulky, overgrown yews and flamboyant summer bedding. The yews are relics of the original formal garden, laid out in the Italian style in the 1690s, and are now so large that they bulge over the walls of the steep terraces below the castle. These walls protect all manner of rare and tender plants, including Banksian roses, hoherias, scented rhododendrons and a large *Acca sellowiana*. Colourful plantings have for long been a speciality of the terraces, supplemented in summer and autumn by annuals and tender exotics. The balustrades, urns and 17th-century lead statues from John Van Nost's foundry add to the drama, enhanced by views of the rhododendrons and azaleas on the ridge opposite. These are in an area known as the Wilderness, first planted as a landscape garden in the 18th century, but now deliciously overrun by ornamental trees and shrubs: Powis has National Collections of *Aralia* and *Laburnum*.

In the dry moat are further gardens, with rich colour plantings, a collection of old fruit trees and an Edwardian garden of roses, delphiniums, campanulas and hollyhocks. And look out for the silver-leaved *Artemisia* 'Powis Castle', a gift to gardeners everywhere.

1mile (1.6km) S of Welshpool
☎ 01938 551920 **Open** Early Apr–late Oct Thu–Mon 11am–6pm
Size 9.7ha (24 acres)
Owner National Trust
🅿 ♿ 🍴 🚻 👶 ♿ 🏠
🆆 www.nationaltrust.org.uk

48. National Botanic Garden of Wales
Middleton Hall
Llanarthne
Carmarthen SA32 8HG

When the new Welsh botanic garden opened its gates in 2000, it was a symbol of the principality's new-found self-confidence and the first national botanic garden to be made in the United Kingdom since the 18th century. It is very well designed, in a modernist

The Great Glasshouse at the National Botanic Garden of Wales, designed by Sir Norman Foster, is the largest single-span greenhouse in the world.

idiom, and is especially suitable for educational visits, which means that there is much to see and learn from.

The garden occupies the site of an old estate called Middleton Hall, which has a fine double-walled garden. It has its fair share of Welsh themes, including an ethnobotanical display of native pharmacological plants and a collection of endangered native plants, which includes the microspecies *Sorbus leyana*. You enter the garden along the Broadwalk, 220 m long and planted with herbaceous plants. The double-walled garden comes next, with an Auricula Theatre and an exposition of systematic beds, based not on traditional taxonomy but genetic studies of evolution.

The garden's most impressive feature – alone worth the journey – is the Great Glasshouse, the largest single-span glasshouse in the world. Sir Norman Foster designed it, and the American Kathryn Gustafson landscaped the interior. It concentrates upon the Mediterranean floras of the world, which are cheaper to maintain than tropical plants. For the problem with this garden is that it does not receive the visitor numbers necessary for its maintenance and further development. This is a pity (because there is so much to admire and enjoy), but it is not untypical of the Welsh attitude to gardens and gardening.

7miles (11km) E of Carmarthen
☎ 01558 668768 **Open** Daily 10am–6pm (4.30pm in winter) **Size** 41ha (100ac) **Owner** Trustees of the National Botanic Garden of Wales 🅿 💻 🍴 🆆🅲 ♿ 🏠 🚻
🆆 www.gardenofwales.org.uk
@ info@gardenofwales.org.uk

49. Dyffryn Botanic Garden

St Nicholas
Cardiff CF5 6SU

Dyffryn is the most sumptuous garden in south Wales. The house was

Dyffryn Botanic Garden has a great number of different garden designs and features, as well as an impressive collection of plants.

built in the 1890s for a coal magnate called John Cory, who commissioned the landscaper Thomas Mawson to lay out the garden. After Cory's death in 1910, the estate passed to his son Reginald, one of Britain's most distinguished horticulturists.

Dyffryn has a large number of different designs and enclosures. There are about 30 of them, including a fernery, a limestone rock-garden, an outdoor theatre (originally used to display Reginald Cory's collection of bonsai), a yew-enclosed rose garden, pools, courtyards, statues and the remarkable Pompeian Garden, based on gardens seen by Reginald Cory and Thomas Mawson on a tour of Italy. The whole complex is currently undergoing restoration – for example, the 100-m double herbaceous borders in the old walled garden have recently been replanted – but it is a great joy to explore garden after garden, and wonder at the combination of good design and wonderful plants.

The woodlands that surround the enormous lawns contain many rare trees (some of them record-breakers) and magnificent underplantings of rhodo-dendrons and azaleas. In the Bathing Pool Garden is an *Acer griseum* grown from the first seeds collected in China by E.H. Wilson in 1901.

4miles (6.5km) N of Barry
☎ 02920 593328 **Open** Daily 10am–6pm **Closes** 5pm Oct & 4pm winter **Size** 22ha (55ac) **Owner** Vale of Glamorgan Council 🅿 💻 🆆🅲 ♿ 🚻
🆆 www.dyffryngardens.org.uk

CENTRAL ENGLAND

50. David Austin Roses

Bowling Green Lane
Albrighton
Wolverthampton WV7 3HB

David Austin is Britain's leading rose breeder, renowned for his new strain of 'English' roses. These combine the shape and scent of old-fashioned roses with the colours, health and florifer-ousness of modern types.

The formal, enclosed display gardens adjoining Austin's nursery are impressive: five different sections, each extensive and thickly planted with old-fashioned roses and his own hybrids (over 700 different cultivars of old roses, shrub roses, climbers, ramblers and species, plus a few classic Hybrid Teas and Floribundas). The Long Garden is the largest, with an impressive display of old roses and a forest of brick pergolas for climbing roses and ramblers. Roses are grown as garden plants in mixed beds in the Lion Garden and there

The nursery's display garden at David Austin Roses is crammed with densely planted 'English' roses, ramblers and old-fashioned roses.

is a good range of wild roses in the Species Garden. But the best displays come from Austin's own roses, densely planted and maintained to an extremely high standard. They dominate the Victorian Garden and the beautiful Renaissance Garden, designed around a long rectangular pool and an elegant Tuscan loggia. The garden is embellished with sculptures by David Austin's wife. Groups are sometimes allowed to see the breeding houses and trial grounds.

Signed in Albrighton
☎ 01902 376376 **Open** Daily (except Christmas–New Year) 9am–5pm **Size** 0.8ha (2ac) **Owner** David Austin P ▣ ⑪ ⑩ ⑥ ⑨
W www.davidaustinroses.com

51. Biddulph Grange
Biddulph
Stoke-on-Trent ST8 7SD

The garden at Biddulph is quirky, original and delightful. It was made between 1842 and 1872 by James Bateman, an important amateur garden designer, plantsman and writer, and provides the earliest example of a garden being divided into a series of smaller rooms, each designed and planted to a different theme. Some are so inventive that they still seem rather wacky – the Dragon Parterre, for example, which is dominated by a golden cow (or, possibly, buffalo) or the

stumpery, where carefully excavated and inverted tree stumps form a framework for trailing ivies and other plants. One of the more eccentric novelties is the 'upside-down tree' replanted with its roots in the air between the Rhododendron Ground and the Lime Avenue. Others are the Egyptian courtyard with its sphinxes and pyramid, a bowling green and quoits ground, the Chinese Garden (surprisingly large and beautiful, with a joss house, temple and section of the Great Wall) and the ferny Scottish glen. There are also areas devoted to collections of plants – a *Wellingtonia* avenue, a fine pinetum and the Dahlia Walk – but it is the sheer creativity of the garden rooms that visitors remember.

3½miles (5.5km) SE of Congleton
☎ 01782 517999 **Open** late Mar–Oct Wed–Sun & bank hol Mon 11.30am—5.30pm **Size** 6ha (15ac) **Owner** National Trust P ▣ ⑩ 🏠 ⑨
W www.nationaltrust.org.uk
@ biddulphgrange@nationaltrust.org.uk

52. Dorothy Clive Garden
Willoughbridge
Market Drayton TF9 4EU

Dorothy Clive's is a plantsman's garden, but one that satisfies the eye even without flowers. Its name commemorates the invalided wife of a local industrialist,

The golden cow, sheltered by an oriental temple, is one of many original features at Biddulph Grange, an extraordinary 19th-century garden.

Though best known for its rhododendrons, Dorothy Clive Garden also has first-rate conifers and mixed borders.

who started the garden in 1940 so that she should have a place of recreation. It lies on a high, windy hillside, with an old quarry towards the top, but the shelter provided by native oaks and beech means that it can be quite still at the centre, while a gale rages in the tree-tops.

The quarry holds a magnificent collection of rhododendrons, many of them the horticultural hybrids that are so underestimated by grand rhododendron garden owners. At the centre of the quarry is a spectacular, long, stepped waterfall – obviously artificial, but so well made that you do not mind. Other features include a fine bog garden, an extensive alpine scree (one of the best in England), a gravel garden, an impressive collection of ornamental trees and eye-catching flower borders.

7miles (11km) NE of Market Drayton **☎** 01630 647237 **Open** Mid-Mar–Oct daily 10am–5.30pm **Size** 5ha (12ac) **Owner** Willoughbridge Garden Trust **P ◻ WC &** **W** www.dorothyclivegarden.co.uk **@** info@dorothyclivegarden.co.uk

53. Felley Priory
Underwood
Nottingham NG16 5FJ

Felley has one of the finest modern gardens in Britain, though the beautiful priory dates back to 1150. The design is formal but the plantings are informal – and the combination is astonishing.

Handsome yew hedges fill the garden with their bulk: some have been turned into objects of topiary, with curvy tops and bobbles, peacocks, swans and turrets. Elsewhere are mediaeval-style wooden palings.

Plants determine the plantings, with a very large number of interesting ones in flower at every season. Bulbs are used in great numbers: snowdrops, cyclamens and massive displays of daffodils in spring. The herbaceous borders do not make a show until midsummer. Shrubs are a major interest, and Felley has good collections of magnolias, cornus, hydrangeas, *Paeonia suffruticosa* and viburnums. The rose garden has some 90 different old-fashioned roses, beautifully grown, trained to maximise flowering, and interplanted with clematis, paeonies and agapanthus. Plantsmanship is in evidence everywhere– all the plants seem to be the best forms – and there is a cheerful confidence, almost a swagger, about the whole garden, which makes it a joy to visit.

10miles (16km) NW of Nottingham, near M1 Jct 27, on A608 **☎** 01773 810230 **Open** All year Tue, Wed & Fri 9am–12.30pm; also 9am–4pm 2nd & 4th Wed of Mar–Oct & 11am–4pm every 3rd Sun of Mar–Oct **Size** 1ha (2½ac) **Owner** The Hon. Mrs Chaworth-Musters **P ◻ WC & ✿**

Felley Priory is an exemplary modern garden that combines firm design, rare plants, good colour-sense and immense charm.

Packwood House is famous for its herbaceous borders and superlative topiary.

54. Packwood House

Lapworth
Solihull B94 6AT

Packwood is famous for its astounding topiary. Vast clipped yew trees are said to represent the Sermon on the Mount. The tallest, on a mound, is Christ, surrounded by the twelve apostles, the four evangelists and a multitude of smaller yews. The size of the yew trees (as much as 15 m high) is very impressive, but so are their individual characters (no two are the same), their close planting and the way they grow out of mown grass. And yet, they probably date no further back than the mid-19th century.

The walled garden below the topiary is exceptionally lovely. A sunken garden has a small rectangular pool, surrounded by yew hedging and excellent double borders. Around the brick walls are blocks of bright roses, grown in compartments defined by yew hedges that slope up like buttresses – a very effective foil for the mono-planting. And above the gardens, running between two charming gazebos, are some of the best herbaceous borders in England. The whole garden is imbued with a sense of magic.

2miles (3km) E of Hockley Heath
☎ 01564 783294 **Open** Mar–Oct Wed–Sun & bank hol Mon 11am–5.30pm **Closes** 4.30pm Mar, Apr & Oct **Size** 2.8ha (7ac)
Owner National Trust
🅿 🚻 ♿ 🎁 🍴 🖼
🆆 www.nationaltrust.org.uk

55. Cottesbrooke Hall

Northampton NN6 8PF

Cottesbrooke is one of the loveliest Queen Anne houses in England: some say that it was the model for Jane Austen's *Mansfield Park*. The formal garden in front of the house was laid out by Sir Geoffrey Jellicoe in 1938: cones of yew and thick parterres provide the structure, with classical statues at the centre – Venus, Diana, Hermes and Eros. The urns and pots, here and throughout the garden, are filled with exotic annuals, agapanthus and conservatory plants in summer.

Around the house is a series of beautiful flower gardens, walled or hedged, including the long double herbaceous border known as the Terrace Garden (a magnificent example of colour planting) and Sylvia Crowe's Pool Garden with water lilies and climbing roses. Roses are a constant theme throughout the garden.

Cottesbrooke is wonderfully rich in statues, including four of the worthies made by Peter Scheemakers for the Temple of Ancient Virtue at Stowe. And across the beautiful parkland lies a bluebell wood, where rhododendrons prosper and the banks of a stream are richly planted with water irises, candelabra primulas, rheums and gunnera.

10miles (16km) N of Northampton
☎ 01604 505808 **Open** May–Jun Wed, Thu 2–5.30pm; Jul–Sep Thu only **Size** 20ha (50ac) **Owner** Mr & Mrs A.R. Macdonald-Buchanan
🅿 🍴 🚻 ♿ 🎁
🆆 www.cottesbrookehall.co.uk

56. Hergest Croft Gardens

Kington HR5 3EG

Hergest Croft is an extremely important woodland garden and arboretum that has been developed by three generations of Banks plantsmen since 1896. It demonstrates considerable artistry in the display of large-scale plant associations, and good design in a series of recent improvements. The azalea garden is especially successful: the extensive plantings of azaleas blend and run their colours over a very large area. Even here, however, it is the trees that catch the eye – an *Abies grandis* at 45 m and the tallest *Davidia involucrata* var. *vilmoriniana* in Britain. The nearby Maple Garden was begun in the 1980s to accommodate the flood of new plants coming out of China with British collectors:

Cottesbrooke Hall is an outstanding garden in the Arts-and-Crafts style, set in a majestic parkland.

magnolias, sorbus and birches are much in evidence, as well as maples.

Park Wood is a separate area, across the park and over a stream. Here is a very fine collection of rhododendrons, both species and hybrids, and many more record-breaking trees. The kitchen garden is noted for its magnificent double herbaceous borders, but the collection of unusual fruit and vegetable cultivars is also interesting. Gentians line the entrance and exit: *G. acaulis* in spring and *G. sino-ornata* in autumn. But it is the trees that give Hergest Croft its distinction: the finest collection in private hands in Britain.

Signed from A44 ☎ 01544 230160 **Open** Apr–Oct daily 12.30–5.30pm (noon–6pm May–Jun) **Size** 23ha (56ac) **Owner** W.L. Banks
🅿 ▣ ♿ ⬚ ▦ ⚐
🆆 www.hergest.co.uk

57. Abbey Dore Court
Abbey Dore
Hereford HR2 0AD

Abbey Dore is one of those very English gardens that combine good design and good plants with a shrewd eye for colour and form. It has been made entirely by the present owner since 1967, on both banks of the fast-running river Dore. The design is a mixture of semi-formal terraces and woodland wilderness – ferns, pulmonarias and hellebores line the river walk, which leads over a bridge to a meadow garden with enough ornamental trees and shrubs to be called an arboretum, as well as naturalised bulbs, a pond and rock-garden.

But the high point of visiting Abbey Dore is the walled garden and two long borders, thickly planted for year-round interest in purple, gold, blue-green and silver. The herbaceous plantings are particularly good. Like all plantsman's gardens, the emphasis changes as plants flourish or fail, but the momentum is kept up by

Spetchley Park is a well-designed plantsman's garden; unusual plants have been collected by the Berkeley family for over 100 years.

constant replanting and reorganisation. It is the joy of seeing good plants and thinking of how best to display them that gives Abbey Dore its distinctive character.

Midway between Hereford & Abergavenny ☎ 01981 240419 **Open** Apr–Sep Tue, Thu, weekends & bank hols 11am–5.30pm **Size** 2.5ha (6ac) **Owner** Mrs Charis Ward
🅿 🍴 ♿ ⬚ ⚐
🆆 www.abbeydorecourt.co.uk

58. Spetchley Park
Worcester WR5 1RS

Spetchley is a splendid large-scale plantsman's garden, surrounded by a classic English landscaped park. The Berkeley family have been amassing this fascinating collection of unusual plants for over 100 years – an unusually long period. One result is that certain plants have naturalised over a large area – *Lilium martagon* and *Tulipa sprengeri*, for example. Another is that venerable specimens of ancient rarities are grown alongside modern excitements: the laciniate walnut (*Juglans nigra* 'Laciniata') has been growing quietly against one of the walls of the walled garden since the early 20th century. And it is in the walled garden that there is most to see. It is split into several ornamental areas, each with a distinct design and

planting; paeonies, columbines and masses of bulbs run everywhere.

Roses are a constant theme, and bushes of every type appear throughout, from 19th-century climbers to the latest and brightest Floribundas. The main rose garden is outside the walled garden, next to the fountain garden and not far from the conservatory, which is crammed with unusual plants. There is much to see, too, in the park and in the woods behind the walled garden: a root house, for example, a magnificent *Quercus × hispanica* 'Lucombeana' and the tallest × *Cupressocyparis leylandii* 'Silver Dust' in Britain.

3miles (5km) E of Worcester ☎ 01453 810303 **Open** Apr–Sep Wed–Sun & bank hol Mon 11am–6pm; also 11am–4pm Oct weekends **Size** 12ha (30ac) **Owner** R.J. Berkeley
🅿 ▣ ♿ ⬚
🆆 www.spetchleygardens.co.uk

59. Hidcote Manor Garden
Hidcote Bartrim
Chipping Campden GL55 6LR

Hidcote was one of the most influential gardens of the 20th century. It is an Arts and Crafts masterpiece created by the American plantsman and plant collector Major Lawrence Johnston after

Lawrence Johnston named this enclosed courtyard at Hidcote Manor 'Mrs Winthrop's garden' after his mother.

his mother bought the estate for him in 1907. It was designed as a series of outdoor rooms, each with a different character and separated by walls and hedges of many different species.

Hidcote has a firm architectural structure (many of Lawrence Johnston's ideas came from France and Italy), combined with a wide range of plants. The planting is exuberant and a model example, much copied, of how to place plants to create contrasts and harmonies. Some of the rooms are very small (like Mrs Winthrop's garden – no more than a courtyard with a potted cordyline at the centre) and others like the Long Walk and the Great Lawn give a wonderful sense of space.

Among the most famous features are: the mixed borders, richly planted with old roses and companion plants; the red borders, which were among the first hot borders in the country when planted in 1913; the sunken 'bathing pool' garden, where a huge circular swimming pool fills a hedged compartment; and the woodland area or wilderness, sometimes known as Westonbirt, where Johnston planted long vistas that run from end to end, but disappear and reappear as you follow the paths back and forth. Hidcote remains an inspirational

garden to visit, with much to admire and learn from.

4miles (6.5km) NW of Chipping Campden ☎ 01386 438333 **Open** Apr–Oct Sat–Wed 10.30am–6pm (5pm in Oct) **Size** 4.2ha (10.5ac) **Owner** National Trust
🅿 🚻 🍴 🆆🅲 ♿ 🎁 🎁 🎁
🆆 www.nationaltrust.org.uk

60. Kiftsgate Court
Chipping Campden GL55 6LN

It helps to think of Kiftsgate as the twin of Hidcote: their founders, Heather Muir and Lawrence Johnston were friends and gardened in the same way, with tight design, a wide choice of plants, and a

thoughtful use of colour. They differ, however, in that Hidcote has ossified since the National Trust took over in 1948, whereas Kiftsgate has changed and improved immeasurably under the guardianship of Mrs Muir's daughter, Diany Binny, and granddaughter, Anne Chambers.

Some of the plantings are textbook examples of how to do things: there is no better colour garden than the yellow border, where gold and orange are set off by occasional blues and purples. It makes you blink at its perfection. The Four Squares garden is tricked out in pink, lilac and purple, and the high-summer Wide Border in crimson, mauve,

Kiftsgate Court, a neighbour and friendly rival of Hidcote Manor, is still developing under the guidance of the third generation of passionate gardener owners.

purple and grey. Each repays detailed study. The double borders of *Rosa gallica* 'Versicolor' were among the first 'old' rose borders to be planted before Graham Stuart Thomas revived interest in them in the 1950s; Thomas also named the eponymous *Rosa filipes* 'Kiftsgate', now some 30 m high. The garden as a whole is remarkable for its tender plants – abutilons, echiums, azaras, and natural-ised *Geranium palmatum*. Modern additions include a striking contemporary water garden. And the bluebells are stunning in late May.

4miles (6.5km) NW of Chipping Campden, opposite Hidcote Manor
☎ 01386 438777 **Open** May–Jul Sat–Wed 12noon–6pm & Apr, Aug–Sep Sun, Mon, Wed 2–6pm
Size 1.5ha (4ac) **Owner** Mr & Mrs J. Chambers
🅿 ▣ 🚾 ♿
Ⓦ www.kiftsgate.co.uk
@ info@kiftsgate.co.uk

61. Westonbirt Arboretum
Tetbury GL8 8QS

Westonbirt is the finest old arboretum in the British Isles, with one of the most important collections of mature trees and shrubs in the world. There are over 18 500

Westonbirt Arboretum attracts most of its visitors when the maples display their autumn colours in October.

of them (representing 3700 species and cultivars) planted in open farmland from 1829 to the present day, beautifully landscaped and spaciously planted.

The estate belonged to the Holford family – all passionate dendrologists – until taken into public ownership in 1956. Now it calls itself the 'National Arboretum'. The Holfords were careful to plant for decorative effect, to create a 'picturesque' landscape on a grand scale – hence the grand rides framed by carefully chosen ornamental

trees. Further features were created within the resultant woodland: there are fine spring displays of rhododendrons, azaleas and magnolias, and oceans of bluebells in the part called Silk Wood. The collections of most British plant hunters from David Douglas in the 1830s onward are well represented, including those of E.H. Wilson, who was born at nearby Chipping Campden. The maple glade is famous, especially when it colours up in October. Silk Wood has a National Collection of hundreds of Japanese maple cultivars.

3miles (5km) SW of Tetbury
☎ 01666 880220 **Open** Daily 10am–8pm (or dusk, if earlier)
Size 243ha (600ac) **Owner** Forestry Commission 🅿 ▣ 🍴 🚾 ♿ 🏠 ♿
Ⓦ www.forestry.gov.uk/westonbirt

62. Blenheim Palace
Woodstock
Oxford OX20 1PX

Blenheim was built by Queen Anne after 1705, as a reward for the first Duke of Marlborough's soldiering, and named to commemorate his victory over the French at the battle of Blenheim in 1704.

Vanbrugh, Bridgeman, Hawksmoor and Wise worked

The Frenchman Achille Duchêne laid out the formal gardens at Blenheim Palace less than 100 years ago.

here: the Grand Bridge, the triumphal arch and the Column of Victory date from the 1720s. The huge 810-ha (2000-ac) park was landscaped in the 1760s by 'Capability' Brown, who also built the Grand Cascade. The formal gardens around the palace were made (with American money) in the early 20th century by the Frenchman Achille Duchêne and are a perfect complement to the monumental architecture of the palace. The Water Terraces centre on a Bernini fountain and took five years to build. The Italian garden focuses on the neo-classical Mermaid Fountain and is decked with orange trees and 'Mme Caroline Testout' roses in summer. There is a pretty Victorian rose garden and, in the old walled Pleasure Gardens, a modern maze and lavender garden. The arboretum has some interesting trees, including four fine, upright incense cedars (*Calocedrus decurrens*), and a mass of bluebells in May. In 1908, Winston Churchill proposed to his future wife, Clementine, in the Temple of Diana.

8miles (13km) N of Oxford
01993 811091 **Open** mid-Feb–Oct daily 10.30am–5.30pm (dusk, if earlier) Park: open daily
Size 41ha (100ac) **Owner** Duke of Marlborough
www.blenheimpalace.com

63. Oxford Botanic Garden
Rose Lane
Oxford OX1 4AZ

Oxford has the oldest botanic garden in England, first laid out in 1621: the handsome gateways were added ten years later and an ancient yew dates from 1645. The garden has kept its original rectangular design and many of its statues and ornaments. Long, narrow systematic beds occupy almost every part of the walled garden, though the university

Oxford Botanic Garden is England's oldest botanic garden and also one of the most visitor-friendly.

does try to make them look attractive as well as interesting to plant lovers. There are good and representative collections of almost every type of plant, including a grass garden, ferns, carnivorous plants and the National Collection of hardy *Euphorbia* species. The tree of *Sorbus domestica* f. *pomifera*, planted in 1791, is probably the largest in Britain.

The area outside the walls was annexed in 1947 and designed to be of horticultural interest: here you will find a new water garden, rock-garden, herbaceous border, bog garden, spring walk and autumn border. The Harcourt Arboretum at Nuneham Courtenay is an outlier of the garden, planted since 1950 in an oak woodland, and well worth a visit – especially in May, when filled with vast oceans of bluebells.

In city centre 01865 286690
Open Daily 9am–5pm (4.30pm Nov–Feb; 6pm May–Aug) **Size** 1.8ha (4½ac) **Owner** University of Oxford
www.botanic-garden.ox.ac.uk
postmaster@botanic-garden.ox.ac.uk

64. Buscot Park
Faringdon SN7 8BU

Buscot has a magnificent water garden designed by Harold Peto in the early 1900s – a masterpiece even by the likes of this most masterly of garden architects. It stretches straight from the handsome house over hundreds of metres down a sequence of gentle steps and then along a narrow, straight canal with a stout Italianate bridge as a focal point. Finally it breaks out into a lake at the bottom with a temple as the viewcatcher on the other side. The design of the water garden has a strength and dynamic that make it entirely self-contained.

But there is much more at Buscot, including a *patte d'oie*, focused on the Theatre Arch, and innumerable pleasure gardens hidden between the three avenues. The modern

A grass walk leads down to Buscot Park's magnificent water garden designed by Harold Peto.

The Palladian bridge, though not the earliest in England, is one of Stowe's most celebrated features.

gardens laid out by Lord Faringdon from about 1980 in and around the old walled kitchen garden are also excellent. Here are a sumptuous double herbaceous border (whose use of yellow and purple foliage creates a sense of brightness even in dull weather), a garden planted with quadrants, each designed to represent a season, neatly trained fruit trees and a tunnel of Judas trees (*Cercis siliquastrum*).

3miles (5km) W of Faringdon
☎ 01367 240786 **Open** Apr–Sep Mon–Fri 2–6pm & alternate Sat & Sun **Size** 20ha (50ac) **Owner** National Trust & Lord Faringdon
🅿 💺 🚾 👶 🖼
🆆 www.buscotpark.com

65. Stowe Landscape Gardens
Buckingham MK18 5EH

Stowe is enormous – and extremely important to the history of gardens. John Vanbrugh, Charles Bridgeman and William Kent all worked here. Even more important, it was while 'Capability' Brown was head gardener at Stowe in the 1740s that he developed his skill in simplifying formal gardens and creating the distinctive curves and contours that we now recognise as the English landscape garden.

Stowe is an extraordinary place to visit, and not always easy, because part is occupied by a golf course and another

by a school. But the main structures belong to the National Trust, and a discursive amble around them is both a delight and an education. The number, size and quality of its garden buildings are all exceptional, and these features are joined by delicious landscaping.

The vistas, valleys, trees and lakes more-or-less prescribe your circuit, starting by the mighty Temple of Concord above 'Capability' Brown's superb Grecian valley (1740s). It was Brown's first major essay in landscaping, and created an idyll that has never ended. It leads into the Elysian Fields (1731), the paradise for ancient heroes. Kent's Temple of Ancient Virtue (1735) honours Socrates, Homer, Lycurgus and Epaminondas. The Temple of British Worthies (1737) has statues of Alfred the Great, the Black Prince, Queen Elizabeth I, John Milton and twelve further historic persons – Stowe was a highly fashionable garden with a strong political message.

Further down is the Palladian Bridge (1738), which leads to the main garden below the palatial house. Other features include Vanbrugh's Rotondo, Charles Bridgeman's ha-ha (the longest ever built), the Temple of Venus, the Hermitage, Dido's Cave, the elegant Doric Arch, a gothic temple and much else besides. Just keep walking: Stowe is the key to the 18th-century English enlightenment.

3miles (5km) NW of Buckingham
☎ 01280 822850 **Open** Mar–Oct Wed–Sun 10.30am–5.30pm plus bank hols & weekends in winter
Size 304ha (750ac) **Owner** National Trust 🅿 💺 🚾 👶 🏠 🖼
🆆 www.nationaltrust.org.uk

66. Waddesdon Manor
Aylesbury HP18 0JH

Sometimes the National Trust works harmoniously with a descendant of the family that originally donated a property to the charity. Waddesdon is a good example, for the great garden, first laid out in the 1870s and 1880s for the French Baron Ferdinand de Rothschild, is now admin-istered by the English 4th Lord Rothschild.

The house is a renaissance-style château. The Baron's garden designer was the French landscaper Elie Lainé, who levelled the crown of a hill and planted it with mature trees, as well as creating the drives, banks and formal gardens that were essential to the design. The result is one of the finest Victorian gardens in Britain, which has been meticulously restored since 1990 by Lord Rothschild. Garden features are excavated, repaired and reopened every year. The results include a grand park, a delicate aviary built of cast-iron trellis-work in the German rococo style, a new rose garden planted with a large number of 'Miss Alice' roses (named for Baron Ferdinand's sister, Alice

Summer bedding is still practised with all the opulence of the 19th century at Waddesdon Manor; blue and yellow are the Rothschilds' heraldic colours.

de Rothschild), and splendid formal gardens extravagantly filled with bedding plants.

Formal bedding in the parterres was always a Waddesdon speciality, but now the designs change every season to reflect the themes of current exhibitions in the house. In the woodlands are naturalised snowdrops, scillas, daffodils, bluebells, lilies-of-the-valley and autumn crocuses.

6miles (10km) NW of Aylesbury
C 01296 653226 **Open** late Mar–mid-Dec Wed–Sun & bank hol Mon 10am–5pm; weekends only for rest of year **Size** 67ha (165ac) **Owner** National Trust **P** **🅿** **🍴** **WC** **♿** **📷** **♨** **🏪**
W www.waddesdon.org.uk
@ waddesdonmanor@nationaltrust. org.uk

67. Benington Lordship
Benington
Stevenage SG2 7BS

Benington Lordship has *charm* and a profusion of good plants. The eclectic architecture sets the scene: a Georgian house with an Edwardian add-on, a neo-Norman gateway in Pulhamite, and the ruins of a real Norman castle, complete with a dry moat flooded by snowdrops in late winter. The garden is both ancient and modern; the best features have all been developed since Sarah Bott and

her husband moved here in 1971. The rose garden, in front of the house, has modern roses underplanted with lavender, irises and bergenias. The Edwardian rock-garden is thick with bulbs and small specimen trees. Drifts of *Scilla bithynica* cover every part of the garden, making a sea of blue in early spring – no other English garden has such a spectacle. Best of all are the breath-taking double herbaceous borders (planted in gentle pastel

shades), which tumble down a slope by the entrance to the kitchen garden. Many consider them the best in Britain.

4miles (6.5km) E of Stevenage
C 01438 869668 **Open** All year by appointment **Size** 3ha (7ac)
Owner R.R.A. Bott **P** **WC**
W www.beningtonlordship.co.uk

68. Hatfield House
Hatfield AL9 5NQ

Hatfield is a Jacobean house of great historic importance. Its gardens are mainly modern, but very appropriate, instructive and enjoyable to visit. An 1890s parterre called the East Gardens is the outstanding feature: in 1977 Lady Salisbury enclosed it on either side with avenues of 'topiarised' evergreen oaks and replanted the formal beds. She also made the Knot Garden, in front of the Old Palace, basing her designs on traditional English patterns. Four central beds surround a small pool: the corners of the beds are marked by pyramids of box. Three are knots; the fourth is a gravel maze, to remind

In the 1970s, Lady Salisbury created Elizabethan-style knot gardens at Hatfield House to complement the Old Palace.

us that Hatfield already had a maze when Queen Elizabeth I visited it in the 16th century.

The Elizabethan fruit garden is represented by pomegranates that are put out in summer, another link to the earliest gardens at Hatfield. The planting is true to the period, too: every plant is one that would have been introduced to England before 1620. They include clove carnations, ancient roses and a collection of historical tulips given by the *Hortus Bulborum* in Holland. The kitchen garden is also worth seeing – lots of rare vegetables; like the rest of the garden, it is organically maintained.

3miles (5km) S of Welwyn Garden City ☎ 01707 287010 **Open** Mid-Apr–Sep daily 11am–5.30pm East Gardens: open Thu only (**closed** Aug) **Size** 17ha (42ac) **Owner** Marquess of Salisbury

🅿 ♿ 🍴 🚻 ♿ 🏛 ⚘ 🎏
🆆 www.hatfield-house.co.uk

EAST ENGLAND

69. Sandringham House
King's Lynn PE35 6EN

Sandringham is a rambling, ugly, homely, neo-Jacobean monster, built in the 1860s as a country house for the future King Edward VII. Its grounds were laid out in the late-Victorian landscape style; the best feature is two splendid lakes, with their Pulhamite banks, cascades, boat-house, rock-garden and feeder streams, richly planted with dwarf conifers, ferns and water plants. Among the many fine specimen trees are oaks planted by Queen Victoria and Queen Mary.

King George VI employed Sir Geoffrey Jellicoe in the late 1940s to redesign the gardens around the house to offer greater privacy; Jellicoe responded with a fine series of formal gardens, enclosed by yew hedges and romantically

Queen Elizabeth II remodelled the woodlands around the royal residence at Sandringham House as ornamental gardens.

planted with high-summer colour when the royal family was in residence. But the 1940s were times of great financial stringency, and most of the gardens built for Edward VII were allowed to fall into ruins, including the 3-ha (7-acre) walled kitchen garden.

Queen Elizabeth II employed Eric Savill in the 1960s to renew and replant the shrubberies and woodland walks in the style exemplified by Savill Garden in Surrey. Savill also planted the splendid herbaceous borders. The garden is now in good heart again, which just shows that even a garden can be a measure of its owners' changing lifestyles.

7miles (11km) NE of King's Lynn ☎ 01553 612908 **Open** Mid-Apr–Oct (except when Queen in residence) daily 10.30am–5pm (4pm in Oct) **Size** 24ha (60ac) **Owner** H.M. The Queen

🅿 ♿ 🍴 🚻 ♿ 🏛 ⚘
🆆 www.sandringhamestate.co.uk
@ visits@sandringhamestate.co.uk

70. East Ruston Old Vicarage
East Ruston
Norwich NR12 9HN

This is by far the most interesting and ambitious garden to have been made in England during the last 20 years: in 1988, it was an empty field. It combines superb architectural design with exceptional plantsmanship, and has been conceived and executed on a grand scale.

Quick-growing shelter belts and a position close to the sea enable many tender exotics to grow happily outside. The garden has been designed as a series of 'rooms', getting larger the further you move from the house. These include superb long borders abundantly and richly planted; a box parterre annually bedded out with unusual and original plant combinations; a gravelled forecourt with large groups of *Aeonium* 'Zwartkop' and various echeverias; and a large exotic garden with unusually bold plantings of palms and bananas. The Mediterranean Garden ('Mediterranean' in the broad sense) has clouds of yellow Australian mimosa, a very dark blue rosemary from Spain and *Beschorneria yuccoides* from Mexico. The Desert Wash, covering 0.5 ha (1 ac), is an imitation Arizona desert, where the only rainfall is one of tumultuous thunderstorms every year. Plantings include *Trithrinax campestris* palms from Argentina and the Mexican blue palm (*Brahea armata*), plus dasylirions, agaves, aloes and other succulents.

East Ruston also has a pretty no-nonsense vegetable garden, a cutting garden, woodland

East Ruston Old Vicarage is the most ambitious and exciting new garden in Britain, begun in 1988 and full of original design features.

walks, wildflower meadows, a walled garden and a spectacular corn field, brimming with field poppies, cornflowers and corn marigold. See it and marvel.

4miles (6.5km) E of North Walsham
☎ 01692 650432 **Open** Late Mar–Oct Wed, Fri, weekends & bank hols 2–5.30pm **Size** 13ha (32ac) **Owner** Graham Robeson & Alan Gray
🅿 🍽 🚾 ♿ ⚘
ⓦ www.e-ruston-
    oldvicaragegardens.co.uk
@ erovoffice@btinternet.com

71. Anglesey Abbey

Lode
Cambridge CB5 9EJ

The gardens at Anglesey Abbey are the grandest, the most ambitious and the most impressive to come out of 20th-century England, and were made (with American money) by the first Lord Fairhaven between 1927 and 1966. He also collected classical and renaissance statues, urns and busts, and designed his garden to display these symbols of wealth and taste.

The house is a neat, neo-Jacobean mansion, surrounded by vast expanses of fine flat lawns. Fairhaven created movement by planting long avenues of majestic trees, now in their prime, of ilex, lime and hornbeam. Finest is the 800-m Coronation Avenue of horse-chestnuts, planted in 1937 for the coronation of King George VI, and especially beautiful in May. Yew hedges enclose single-theme gardens like the Rose Garden and the Dahlia Garden (the best in a National Trust property), which doubles up in spring as the Hyacinth Garden. The Temple Lawn encloses a circle of white marble columns. Twelve busts of Caesars are lined in the Emperors' Walk. And the National Trust has added a winter garden with large plantings of different snowdrops, bright-stemmed trees and shrubs and glistening evergreens – quite out of character with the rest of the garden, but good enough of its kind. The bulbs are stunning at every season.

5miles (8km) NW of Cambridge
☎ 01223 810080 **Open** Mid-Mar–Oct Wed–Sun & bank hol Mon 10.30am–5.30pm Winter Garden: Nov–mid-Mar Wed–Sun
Size 40ha (98ac)
Owner National Trust
🅿 🍽 🚾 ♿ 🎁 ⚘ 🖼
ⓦ www.angleseyabbey.org

72. Cambridge University Botanic Garden

Bateman Street
Cambridge CB2 1JF

Oxford may be older, but most people would agree that Cambridge is better. This is one of the most beautiful botanic gardens in the world, fluently laid out on a level site and so filled with good and interesting features that you

Classical columns and statuary are set off by clipped yew hedges and fine trees at Anglesey Abbey.

Syringa persica flowers in the best of Britain's university gardens – Cambridge University Botanic Garden.

are effortlessly drawn along as if in a happy dream.

The garden has been here since 1831, and some of the older trees date from shortly thereafter: the *Sequoiadendron giganteum* is the oldest in Britain and the vast Caucasian wingnut (*Pterocarya fraxinifolia*) dates from the 1840s. At the heart of the garden are the beautifully designed systematic beds, almost 1 ha (2 ac) of mainly herbaceous plants with some 1600 species. The leading ornamental feature is the limestone rock-garden, whose plantings (best in spring and summer) are arranged geographically. It overlooks a small water lily lake. The nearby woodland garden has excellent specimens of *Dipteronia sinensis*, *Tetracentron sinense* and the hardy paw-paw (*Asimina triloba*); the fine dawn redwood (*Metasequoia glyptostroboides*) was grown from the original introduction of seed into the UK in 1948 and, at over 22 m, is one of the largest specimens in the British Isles.

Other good features include the Winter Garden (mainly coloured stems and bark), collections of endangered Fenland plants, a complete hand of native *Sorbus* species, limes, philadelphus and no less than nine National Collections – *Alchemilla*, *Bergenia*, European *Fritillaria*, *Geranium*, shrubby *Lonicera*, *Ribes*, *Ruscus*, European *Saxifraga* and *Tulipa*. The

Glasshouse Range holds about 3000 species of plants in some ten houses that open out from a long corridor, including a Temperate House, Alpine House, Wet Tropical House, Palm House, Succulent and Carnivorous Plant House and a display conservatory. And do not miss the Cambridge oak (*Quercus* 'Warburgii'), arguably the most beautiful tree in England.

1mile (1.6km) S of city centre
☎ 01223 336265 **Open** Daily 10am–4pm in winter (5pm in spring & autumn; 6pm in summer) **Size** 16ha (40ac) **Owner** University of Cambridge
🅿 🖼 🚾 ♿
🌐 www.botanic.cam.ac.uk/

73. Shrubland Park

Coddenham
Ipswich IP6 9QQ

Shrubland Park is famous for the grand Italianate garden designed by Sir Charles Barry in the 1850s. The house is built on the edge of a plateau, with fine views south across the Gipping valley towards Ipswich. Barry's 'grand descent' is a wide formal staircase, edged with vases and urns, which runs from the terrace of the house to the fountain garden and renaissance-style loggia below. It is surrounded by box hedging, clipped yews, laurels, firs, cedars, and holm oaks, all of which increase its Italianate character. The 'green

terrace' runs from the fountain garden for some 400 m towards a Swiss châlet, passing several 19th-century gardens on the way – the French Garden (laurel hedges and busts), heated walls for fruit-growing and a low box-edged maze. Behind the loggia, around a wooden summer-house, is the 1850s wild garden; William Robinson was asked to simplify and replant it in the 1870s. In the park (Humphry Repton advised on its landscaping in 1789) are vast, ancient Spanish chestnuts, billowing rhodo-dendrons, a bamboo walk and the estate's ice-house. But the splendour of the 'grand descent' is every visitor's abiding memory.

2miles (3km) N of Claydon
☎ 01473 830221 **Open** Mid-Apr–Aug Sun & bank hol Mon 2–5pm; plus Wed Jul–Aug **Size** 16ha (40ac) **Owner** Lord de Saumarez
🅿 🚻 🚾
🌐 www.shrublandpark.co.uk

74. Helmingham Hall

Stowmarket IP14 6EF

The garden at Helmingham is wonderfully harmonious – it complements the moated 15th-century manor-house perfectly – and has all been made by Lady Tollemache since 1975.

The garden is set in the spacious 160-ha (400-acre) deer-park, loosely studded with vast centennial oaks grown to their full spread. The formal garden, 100 m long, is planted with billowing Hybrid Musk roses, underplanted with soft-coloured herbaceous perennials and edged with *Lavandula angustifolia* 'Hidcote'. Roses are the main theme of the walled kitchen garden, too, built of brick in 1745. The central grassy path, 120m long, is lined with climbing roses underplanted with pale-coloured herbaceous plants to blend with the roses.

Nearer the house is a new series of knot gardens and old-fashioned rose gardens planted in 1982, which look as if they

Double herbaceous borders, backed by rambling roses, frame a grass walk leading to the mediaeval house at Helmingham Hall.

have been here for hundreds of years. This is gardening on a large scale and makes its impact through simplicity and repetition. One reason the garden is so successful is that the roses and their companion plantings all fall within a narrow colour range: it is a discipline from which every garden owner can learn. So admired are the results that Lady Tollemache is now a professional garden designer.

9miles (14.5km) N of Ipswich
☎ 01473 890799 **Open** May–mid-Sep Wed & Sun 2–6pm **Size** 4ha (10ac) **Owner** Lord Tollemache
🅿 🚇 🆆🅲 ♿ ⛺ ♨
🆆 www.helmingham.com
@ events@helmingham.com

75. Audley End
Saffron Walden CB11 4JF

Audley End is a historic landscape that has taken on a new lease of life as an organic showpiece. 'Capability' Brown landscaped the park in 1763, but the most interesting historical feature is the parterre garden behind the house towards Robert Adam's Temple of Concord. This dates from the 1830s and has 170 geometric flower beds crisply cut from the turf and planted

with original varieties of perennials, bedding plants and annuals for spring and summer. There is nothing to match it as an example of the post-landscape formal gardens that were considered smart for a few years before the fashion for Italianate gardens took root.

Nearby are the Elysian Garden, designed in the 1780s by Placido Columbani (one of very few Italians working in England at the time), and the Victorian pond garden in the 'picturesque' style. The kitchen garden is now run jointly with Garden Organic, the UK's national organic pressure

group, as a working organic garden. It looks much as it would have done in late Victorian times with vegetables, fruit, herbs and flowers to supply the household. The vinehouse is one of the earliest and largest in the country, with vines over 200 years old.

1mile (1.6km) W of Saffron Walden
☎ 01799 522842 **Open** Apr–Sep Wed–Sun & bank hols; also weekends Mar & Oct 10am–6pm **Size** 41ha (100ac), including parkland **Owner** English Heritage
🅿 🍴 🆆🅲 ♿ ⛺ ♨ 🎁
🆆 www.english-heritage.org.uk

The parterre behind the house at Audley End is designed and planted as it originally looked in the 1830s.

Innumerable different habitats have enabled the owners of Glen Chantry to create an exceptional plantsman's garden.

76. Glen Chantry

Ishams Chase
Wickham Bishops
Witham CM8 3LG

The English make very fine plantsman's gardens: Glen Chantry is an exceptional example. It displays a very large number of plants in quite a small space, and all are cultivated in optimum conditions to suit their particular needs. The owners have created it from a bare hillside since 1976, with endless microhabitats: scree beds, peat beds, raised beds and an artificial stream are part of the story, but so is a winding pattern of ebbing and flowing island beds. Along the centre of these beds are trees and shrubs that screen the two faces from each other and make it possible to plant both sides of a path with the same colour. The owners also practise 'vertical planting', which means that season after season different plants are seen to perform within the same patch: in one small area, for example, the spring-flowering fritillaries, erythroniums and corydalis are covered in summer by hostas, grasses and rushes.

Glen Chantry is a model of what devoted plantsmanship can achieve: educational, functional and beautiful all at once. And the standards of maintenance are outstanding.

Halfway between Wickham Bishops and Witham ☎ 01621 891342 **Open** Apr–Aug Fri–Sat 10am–4pm **Size** 1ha (2½ac) **Owner** Sue & Wol Staines ᴾ ▣ ᴡᴄ ♿ ✿
ᵂ www.glenchantry.demon.co.uk

77. Beth Chatto Gardens

Elmstead Market
Colchester CO7 7DB

The renown that surrounds Beth Chatto is founded partly on her herbaceous plant nursery and her writings, but rises most particularly from her wonderful, varied, beautiful and instructive gardens. Chatto started to make them in 1960, on land unfit for farming but with three distinct ecologies: hungry sand and gravel, a spring-fed hollow, and dry shade beneath ancient oaks. When she began planting, she followed the principle of finding the right plant for the right place, and thus turned problem areas into flowery solutions, though her plants are chosen as much for their foliage and form as for their flowers.

On the thin, dry soils are plants from Mediterranean climates: broom, salvias, potentillas, verbascums, and the tree-like *Genista aetnensis*. Chatto dammed the ditch to make a water garden of remarkable luxuriance around a series of ponds: the lush plantings include gunneras, astilbes, lysichitons, hostas,

phormiums, water-irises and the ostrich fern (*Matteuccia struthiopteris*). Bulbs, aconites, cyclamens, erythroniums, dicentras and natural woodlanders carpet the oak woodland.

But the gardens are most famous now for the gravel garden, begun in 1992 on the site of an old car park, where drought-resistant sun-lovers have been planted in a fluid sequence of island beds. It is a horticultural experiment to discover which plants will survive an English drought – cistus, lavender, ornamental thistles, euphorbias and many more. All are arranged with supreme artistry, perhaps Chatto's greatest gift to fellow gardeners.

7 miles (11km) E of Colchester ☎ 01206 822007 **Open** Mar–Oct Mon–Sat 9am–5pm; Nov–Feb Mon–Fri 9am–4pm **Size** 2ha (5ac) **Owner** Beth Chatto ᴾ ▣ ᴡᴄ ♿ ✿
ᵂ www.bethchatto.co.uk
@ info@bethchatto.fsnet.co.uk

SOUTH-WEST ENGLAND

78. Tresco Abbey

Isles of Scilly TR24 0PU

There is nowhere like the island gardens of Tresco: these were the first subtropical gardens in northern Europe,

Beth Chatto is one of England's most influential garden writers; the Gravel Garden is a recent development in her gardens.

The gothic ruins of the mediaeval Tresco Abbey are surrounded by cacti, succulents and palm trees in this great subtropical plantsman's garden.

and inspired such famous gardens as the Giardini Hanbury in Italy. They were first designed and planted by Augustus Smith in 1834: his successors have been equally passionate in their search for tender plants that will grow outside on Tresco's south-facing terraces as nowhere else in Britain – cacti, date-palms, erythrinas, heliconias, echiums, furcraeas, strelitzias and naturalised pelargoniums. The collection is especially strong in plants from South Africa, Australia and New Zealand but, even though any account of Tresco reads like a list of plants, it is still very much an ornamental garden that strives for horticultural effect.

The terraces, steps and artefacts, and the placing of plants, all contrive to create a strong and satisfying garden. The oldest specimens include Canary Island palms, a large number of aeoniums from both the Canary Islands and Madeira, agaves from America and puyas from Chile. The hotter, drier terraces at the top suit South African and Australian plants; those at the

bottom provide the humidity that favours the flora of New Zealand and South America. No matter what time of the year, there is always a lot of colour and much of interest: proteas and acacias in winter (there are more than 300 plants in flower even at the winter equinox); the shrubby foxglove (*Isoplexis sceptrum*); mesembryanthemums and agapanthus in summer. There is also a shady area where tree ferns and *Musschia wollastonii* flourish. The standards of maintenance are exemplary.

Direct helicopter flight from Penzance, or boat from St Mary's
☎ 01720 424105 **Open** Daily 10am–4pm **Size** 7ha (17ac) **Owner** Robert Dorrien Smith
🖼 🚾 ♿ 🏠 ♿
Ⓦ www.tresco.co.uk

79. Trengwainton
Madron
Penzance TR20 8RZ

Trengwainton has one of the best collections of tender plants on the Cornish mainland, thanks to the

Bolitho family, who started planting seriously only in 1925. Much came as seed from such collectors as Frank Kingdon Ward: some rhododendrons flowered here for the first time in the British Isles, among them *R. maccabeanum*, *R. elliottii* and *R. taggianum*.

The walled gardens were built in 1820 to the supposed dimensions of Noah's Ark, using brick, rather than the local granite, which is slow to warm up. There are five compartments and the dividing walls between them have steeply banked-up soil on their western sides for forcing early vegetables. Now these compartments are dominated by large flowering trees, especially magnolias. There is also an especially fine specimen of *Magnolia sargentiana* var. *robusta* near the house. The woodland valley, sheltered by beech and oak, has splendid collections of rhododendrons, camellias and hydrangeas, and a stream lined with astilbes, primulas, tree ferns and bamboos. Bluebells grow wild here, but you will also see watsonias, galtonias, acacias, *Myosotidium hortensia* and the tallest *Xanthoceras sorbifolium* (7 m) in the British Isles.

Tree ferns surround this contemplative pool in Trengwainton's woodland garden.

2miles (3km) NW of Penzance
☎ 01736 363148 **Open** Mid-Feb–
Oct Sun–Thu 10am–5pm (5.30pm
Apr–Sep) **Size** 41ha (100ac)
Owner National Trust
P ⬚ WC ⅏ ⬚ ⬚
W www.nationaltrust.org.uk
@ trengwainton@nationaltrust.
org.uk

80. Trebah Garden Trust

Mawnan Smith
Falmouth TR11 5JZ

Trebah is a beautiful
Cornish garden on either
side of a hidden, wooded
valley that runs right down to
the sea. The house sits at the
top, with magical views at all
seasons: no visitor could resist
the urge to explore.

Trebah belonged originally
to the Fox family, leading
Cornish Quakers, who
established the garden in the
period 1850–1900. The many
specimens of record-breaking
plants include the tallest
Chusan palm (*Trachycarpus
fortunei*) in the British Isles
at over 15 m. Vast, tree-like
rhododendrons and evergreen
shrubs give the lightly wooded
valley an unusually exotic and
romantic outline. A stream
trickles down the middle,
disappearing into thickets and

**Trebah Garden Trust's wooded valley
is lined with giant rhododendrons,
record-breaking trees and rare plants.**

Rhododendrons mix with rare plants in Trelissick Garden's great subtropical
collection.

re-emerging in an enormous
boggy patch of *Gunnera
manicata* before passing
through 0.8 ha (2 ac) of blue
and white hydrangeas and
running safe to the sea.

The plants are many and
varied. Cacti, agaves, aloes,
bromeliads and puyas flourish
at the top, but it is the size and
age of the ornamental trees
and shrubs down the valley
that most amazes.
Rhododendron 'Trebah Gem',
Cornus capitata and *Podocarpus
totara* are among the most
spectacular, and bluebells,
candelabra primulas, watsonias
and daffodils are also
abundant in due season.
Trebah is a place of wonder.

4miles (6.5km) SW of Falmouth
☎ 01326 252200 **Open** Daily
10.30am–5pm **Size** 10ha (25ac)
Owner Trebah Garden Trust
P ⬚ WC ⅏ ⬚ ⬚
W www.trebah-garden.co.uk
@ mail@trebah-garden.co.uk

81. Trelissick Garden

Feock
Truro TR3 6QL

Trelissick has a stunning
position on the estuary of
the river Fal. Its beautiful neo-
classical mansion looks across
south-facing parkland to the
sea. It is still occupied by the
Copeland family, who planted

much of the garden in the
1950s.

The garden's position means
that it has a wonderful
collection of tender plants:
bananas, phormiums,
Prostanthera rotundifolia,
naturalised echiums, tree ferns
and old *Photinia* species and
cultivars, some as much as
6 m high. *Erythrina crista-galli*,
cannas and hedychiums are
also among the many good
things that overwinter outside.

The terrain is very varied,
with shady north-facing
woodland for rhododendrons,
grassy dells, south-facing walls
and steep slopes with some
good young plantings like
Quercus rhysophylla. A young
orchard is planted with old
Cornish apple cultivars, of
which there is a surprisingly
large number. Summer
holiday-makers have a large
collection of over 100 cultivars
of hydrangeas to admire,
some in a special walk. But
venerable conifers, daffodil
drifts, camellias and a fig
garden also add to the
garden's magic.

5miles (8km) S of Truro
☎ 01872 862090 **Open** Daily
10.30am–5.30pm (4pm in winter)
Size 10ha (25ac)
Owner National Trust
P ⬚ WC ⅏ ⬚ ⬚
W www.nationaltrust.org.uk
@ trelissick@nationaltrust.org.uk

82. Caerhays Castle

Gorran
St Austell PL26 6LY

Caerhays is the largest and finest woodland garden in south-west England. Its collections of rare plants are astounding: if trees and shrubs are your interest, Caerhays should be compulsory viewing. Its special collections of camellias, magnolias and rhododendrons mean that it is essentially a spring garden; there is much to see from the first day it opens its garden gates.

The castle is impressive, built by John Nash in the early 1800s, but the garden dates from the first years of the 20th century, when J.C. Williams began to sponsor E.H. Wilson's collections and, later, George Forrest's in China. Williams is best known for his hybridising: *Camellia × williamsii* was named for him and some of the original plants still flourish at Caerhays, including 'J.C. Williams', 'Mary Christian' and 'Saint Ewe'. Magnolias were a special interest (think of *M.* 'Caerhays Surprise' and 'Caerhays Belle') and there are currently over 40 species, 170 named cultivars and some 250 (as yet) unnamed seedlings in the Caerhays collection.

There are rare trees throughout the garden. Plants have

Heligan Gardens have been restored as they were in Edwardian times and are now a major tourist attraction.

invariably been placed according to their cultural requirements, which take precedence over the niceties of garden design. Caerhays has the tallest specimen of *Emmenopterys henryi* (18 m) in the British Isles and 37 other record-breaking trees, including eight *Acer* species. Just keep walking: you will stumble upon many magnificent flowering trees and vast sweeps of camellias and rhododendrons in this glorious garden.

Between Mevagissey & Portloe
☎ 01872 501310 **Open** Mid-Feb–May daily 10am–5pm
Size 24ha (60ac) **Owner**
F.J. Williams
🅿 🚗 ⓦⓒ 🏛 ⚇ 🖼
🎟 www.caerhays.co.uk
@ estateoffice@caerhays.co.uk

83. Heligan Gardens

Pentewan
St Austell PL26 6EN

Heligan is a working garden that has been restored as it was 100 years ago. It claims to be the largest garden restoration project in Europe – it is certainly the most interesting in Britain. Its productive kitchen gardens (there are five walled gardens) are of particular interest: they boast over 300 cultivars of fruits, herbs and vegetables,

some of them no longer commercially available (there is a strong emphasis on heritage varieties).

Many of the garden buildings are once again fulfilling their original functions: fruit stores; tool and potting sheds; pineapple pits; a dark house; peach, vine and melon houses; manure-heated frames; and bothies for bachelor gardeners. One of the glasshouses is devoted to Victorian cut flowers and ornamental plants. In the 8-ha (20-ac) pleasure grounds are an Italian Garden, a Sundial Garden, a New Zealand Garden, the Crystal Grotto, the Alpine Ravine, summerhouses, pools, superb herbaceous borders and a magnificent collection of rhododendrons, dating from Sir Joseph Hooker's expedition to the Himalayas in 1849–50. The 9-ha (22-ac) Jungle Garden is a luxuriant valley where a stream runs through four ponds, past ancient conifers, bamboo tunnels, palm-lined avenues, bananas, gunneras and the largest collection of tree ferns in Europe.

5miles (8km) S of St Austell
☎ 01726 845100 **Open** Daily
10am–6pm (5pm in winter)
Size 81ha (200ac) **Owner** Heligan
Gardens Ltd
🅿 🚗 🍴 ⓦⓒ ♿ 🏛 ⚇
🎟 www.heligan.com

Caerhays Castle is the birthplace of many camellias and magnolias. This is *Magnolia* 'Caerhays Belle'.

Lanhydrock has a very extensive display of tulip cultivars, as well as a huge collection of magnolias.

84. Lanhydrock
Bodmin PL30 5AD

Lanhydrock is a castellated mansion, mainly 19th-century, in a grand setting. The formal garden in front of the house is still there in outline – immaculately trimmed Irish yews and simple box-edged beds of modern roses in grass – but there is plenty of horticultural interest behind. The Victorian-style parterres to the side of the house are used for seasonal bedding, including a grand display of over 100 different tulip cultivars in spring – the best collection in south-west England.

Behind the family church, a woodland garden is planted with splendid magnolias – two vast trees of *M.* × *veitchii* 'Peter Veitch' and a large *M.* 'Yellow Fever' are among the real stunners in April – but the collection as a whole is enormous (140 different species and cultivars) and spills over into the woodland behind. Here, too, is a colourful under-planting of large rhododendrons in spring. Hardy plants are not forgotten, though: there are large herbaceous borders and a formal garden known as the herbaceous circle. Crocosmias feature in large numbers; Lanhydrock has over 60 taxa in its National Collection.

2½miles (4km) SE of Bodmin
☎ 01208 265950 **Open** Daily 10am–6pm (dusk, if sooner) **Size** 12.5ha (31ac) **Owner** National Trust
🅿 🍴 🚾 ♿ 👶 🖼
🕸 www.nationaltrust.org.uk
@ lanhydrock@nationaltrust.org.uk

85. Cotehele
St Dominick
Saltash PL12 6TA

Cotehele is an ancient manor house, scarcely altered since it was built in the 15th century. The garden, by contrast, has been largely made by the National Trust since it was acquired in 1947; Graham Stuart Thomas was its begetter. All that gave structure were some ancient trees (*Liriodendron tulipifera* and *Cercis siliquastrum*) and some Victorian terraces that look down a sheltered, wooded valley to the Tamar estuary. Today the terraces are simply planted with roses, primulas and wallflowers.

In the woodland are camellias, rhododendrons and shade-loving plants, kept damp by a small stream; mimulus and candelabra primulas line its sides, and *Gunnera manicata* thrives around a pool at the bottom. A 16th-century dovecote, still inhabited by white doves, is surrounded by azaleas, cherries and *Rhododendron arboreum*

Cotehele's thickly planted garden is laid out on a series of steep terraces.

hybrids. *Jasminum mesnyi* and *Rosa bracteata* are among the tender plants that clamber up the granite walls. Above the house are yew hedges, cork oaks, splendid magnolias and the yellow-stemmed ash (*Fraxinus excelsior* 'Jaspidea').

9miles (14.4km) N of Saltash
☎ 01579 351346 **Open** Daily 10.30am–dusk **Size** 5.5ha (14ac)
Owner National Trust
🅿 🍴 🚾 ♿ 👶 🖼
🕸 www.nationaltrust.org.uk
@ cotehele@nationaltrust.org.uk

86. Antony
Torpoint PL11 2QA

Antony is a historic garden in a stunning position with an amazing collection of plants, notably rhododendrons, magnolias and camellias. It is also a garden of great beauty and surprising contrasts.

The area around the house belongs to the National Trust. Here are the yew walk (ending in a colossal Burmese temple bell, flanked by stone lanterns dumped here in the 1890s); a fine modern summer garden (Hybrid Musk roses, lilies, irises, phlox and paeonies); a collection of over 600 early *Hemerocallis* hybrids from the USA; and several record-breaking trees – best of all is a vast and shaggy cork oak (*Quercus suber*), dating from the 19th century.

The house looks down over extensive lawns and along three straight avenues (Humphry Repton may have designed them) to the Tamar estuary; the views alone justify the visit. The Woodland Garden above the river still belongs to the Carew-Pole family, who gave the rest to the National Trust. It has a huge collection of magnolias, rhododendron species and hybrids; four linked ponds; a 19th-century conifer dell with giant redwoods (*Sequoiadendron giganteum*), *Cryptomeria japonica* and *Taxus baccata* 'Dovastoniana'; and a vast collection of camellias (which includes the National Collection of *Camellia japonica* cultivars).

A Burmese temple bell is one of many unusual features in the great woodland garden at Antony.

5miles (8km) W of Plymouth, 2miles (3km) NW of Torpoint
☎ 01752 812191 **Open** Apr–Oct Tue–Thu & bank hol Mon 1.30–5.30pm; also Sun Jun–Aug **Size** 14ha (35ac) **Owner** National Trust & Carew-Pole Trust 🅿 ⬛ 🆆 ♿ ♿ 🖼
🆆 www.nationaltrust.org.uk
@ antony@nationaltrust.org.uk

87. Mount Edgcumbe
Cremyll
Torpoint PL10 1HZ

Mount Edgcumbe dominates the sea approaches to Plymouth Sound. A long, stately grass drive climbs from the shore, through ancient oak woods interplanted with large ornamental trees, to the mid-16th century castellated house at the top of the hillside.

The extensive formal gardens are down on the waterside, protected by a clipped ilex hedge 10 m high. They include an Italian garden (dating, rather unusually, from the 1790s); a French garden (made when England was at war with France); the 18th-century Thomson's Seat; a 1760s orangery; a balustraded terrace with statues of Venus, Apollo and Bacchus; and a fern dell with ivies and tree ferns. Recent additions include an American plantation and a New Zealand garden, complete with geyser.

Behind the house is the 18th-century Earl's Garden, where the fine old trees include an even older lime tree, a large *Quercus × hispanica*, and a *Pinus montezumae*. Here, too, are classical garden houses, an exotic shell seat, splendid Victorian herbaceous borders planted in red and blue, elderly rhododendrons, and echiums 4 m high. Mount Edgcumbe also boasts the British Isles's tallest cork oak (*Quercus suber* at 26 m) and a National Collection of camellias with over 1000 cultivars.

Best visited by ferry from Plymouth
☎ 01752 822236 **Open** Formal gardens & park: All year dawn–dusk Earl's Garden: Apr–Sep Sun–Thu 11am–4.30pm **Size** 4ha (10ac) plus 324-ha (800-ac) park **Owner** Cornwall County Council & Plymouth City Council
🅿 ⬛ 🍴 🆆 ♿ 🖼 🖼 🖼
🆆 www.mountedgcumbe.gov.uk

88. Marwood Hill Gardens
Marwood
Barnstaple EX31 4EB

Marwood Hill is the purest example of a plantsman's garden in England. There are no fashion statements and no concessions to other people's trendy tastes: it is a collection of plants, and little more – but what a collection!

The gardens were made by Dr James Smart between 1949 and 2002: his bronze statue now surveys the valley below his house with a questioning eye. He dammed the valley to create ponds, pools, a scree garden and bog garden – more habitats for plants – and grew tender plants on the south-facing slopes and woodlanders on the northern. Every conceivable type of plant is here, but especially trees and shrubs. Birches and eucalypts were among Smart's favourites, but there are also many magnolia species and hybrids from all over the world, including the home-grown *M. sprengeri* 'Marwood Spring'. A camellia wood mainly of Sasanquas and Japonicas is matched by a large glasshouse filled with Reticulata hybrids. A pergola has 12 different wisterias on it – its colour extended by interplanting clematis and climbing roses. Primulas and astilbes dominate the bog garden. Hundreds of different hydrangeas flower from

Mount Edgcumbe displays a great variety of formal and informal gardens in a magnificent seaside setting.

The pools and ponds at Marwood Hill Gardens were created to increase the microhabitats and opportunities for planting.

midsummer to late autumn. Rhododendrons were another Smart passion. But the sheer scale and variety of the plantings is amazing: there is no better place in the south-west to learn about plants of every kind.

5miles (8km) NW of Barnstaple **C** 01271 342528 **Open** Daily 9.30am–5pm **Size** 8ha (20ac) **Owner** Dr J.A. Snowdon

P ▣ ▣ WC ♿

W www.marwoodhillgarden.co.uk
@ marwoodhillgardens@netbreeze.co.uk

89. RHS Garden Rosemoor
Great Torrington EX38 8PH

Rosemoor is the best of the Royal Horticultural Society's regional gardens. It was first planted by Lady Anne Palmer in the 1960s, and many of the most interesting plants date from that period – wonderful magnolias, rhododendrons and ornamental trees. After Lady Anne gave it to the RHS in 1988, the Society set about developing an adjoining site in as many ways as possible to interest, educate and enthuse its visitors. It has been remarkably successful: Rosemoor has a great variety of designs, styles, plants and plantings in both its formal 'rooms' and in the more natural parts. Whatever your

interests or whatever the season, you cannot fail to find ideas and inspiration here.

Some of the gardens are themed by plants: the Queen Mother's rose garden for modern roses, and its companion shrub rose garden containing over 200 cultivars, are major features in summer and autumn. Others demon-strate how to garden well in particular circumstances or seasons: the Winter Garden, Stream-and-bog Garden and Shade Garden are good examples. Yet others are intended to inspire creativity: the Spiral Garden has cool, soft, pastel colours, while the Square Garden contains hot plantings. The cottage and herb gardens are more informal and separated by a *potager* with decorative

vegetable planting. Rosemoor is deservedly one of the major tourist attractions in the south-west.

1mile (1.6km) S of Geat Torrington **C** 01805 624067 **Open** Daily 10am–6pm (but 5pm Oct–Mar) **Size** 26ha (65ac) **Owner** Royal Horticultural Society

P ▣ ▮ WC ♿ ▣ ♿

W www.rhs.org.uk/rosemoor
@ rosemooradmin@rhs.org.uk

90. Knightshayes Garden
Tiverton EX16 7RG

Knightshayes is uniquely beautiful. It calls itself 'a garden in a wood', and that was the aim of Sir John and Lady Amory when they started to make it in 1945. The choice of styles was forced on them by the position of the house, halfway up a windy hillside surrounded by ancient oakwoods. They took their inspiration from the Savill Garden and were helped in the early years by Sir Eric Savill himself.

The original canopy is now supplemented by magnolias, birches, *Nothofagus* and *Sorbus*. The garden reveals itself as a series of walks and glades, with beautiful rhododendrons, camellias and rare shrubs underplanted by hellebores, erythroniums, foxgloves, cyclamens and bluebells. Closer to the house are the stately formal gardens,

Eucalyptus, conifers and other evergreen trees and shrubs now occupy the site of an old tennis court at RHS Garden Rosemoor.

This circular pool at Knightshayes Garden, surrounded by yew hedging, is set off by a single specimen of *Pyrus salicifolia* 'Pendula'.

enclosed by immaculately clipped and castellated yew hedges. Alpine treasures and small bulbs grow here in raised beds. The old bowling lawn is filled by a vast circular pool and a single weeping pear, (*Pyrus salicifolia* 'Pendula'), which is pruned to thin out its canopy of branches – an iconic planting that no visitor ever forgets.

2miles (3km) N of Tiverton
☎ 01884 254665 **Open** Mar–Oct daily 11am–5pm **Size** 20ha (50ac) **Owner** National Trust
🅿 🍴 🚾 ♿ 🏠 ♿ 🖼
🆆 www.nationaltrust.org.uk
@ knightshayes@nationaltrust org.uk

91. The Garden House
Buckland Monachorum
Yelverton PL20 7LQ

The Garden House is one of the few but fortunate private gardens that have enjoyed a succession of good garden-makers to improve and expand them over the years. It was first developed by a great plantsman, Lionel Fortescue, between 1945 and 1981. He insisted upon choosing only the best cultivars and growing them well; almost all Fortescue's plantings still flourish.

The setting is spectacular: a ruined ecclesiastical site on the edge of Dartmoor, with stupendous views. Fortescue's work survives above all in the terraced walled garden behind the house, where plants of every kind are dominated now by magnolias, eucryphias, rhododendrons and hoherias.

After 1981, The Garden House was improved in quite a different way by the new curator, Keith Wiley. He developed 2.5 ha (6 ac) of inter-connected gardens, each dedicated to a single theme. The South African garden replicates the spring flowering of the Veldt – best in July and August. Nearby is the Quarry Garden, where natural outcrops are covered by such plants as rock roses and creeping thymes around a series of ponds fed by a waterfall. The Cottage Garden is a wildflower meadow, where the native campions and ox-eye daisies are joined by such plants as *Alchemilla mollis* and astrantias. Other areas include a maple glade, lime avenue, spring garden, herbaceous beds, wisteria bridge and bulb meadow.

2miles (3km) W of Yelverton
☎ 01822 854769 **Open** Mar–Oct daily 10.30am–5pm **Size** 4ha (10ac) **Owner** Fortescue Garden Trust
🅿 🚾 🌱
🆆 www.thegardenhouse.org.uk
@ office@thegardenhouse.org.uk

92. Bicton Park Gardens
East Budleigh
Budleigh Salterton EX9 7BJ

Bicton was laid out by the rich and eccentric Lord Rolle between 1800 and 1842 and was a vehicle for his passionate interest in plants. He has bequeathed us one of the most varied, interesting and beautiful gardens in England.

At the heart of Bicton is the Italian Garden; it dates back to 1735 but was given its formal beds 100 years later. Above it lies England's finest pre-Paxton palm house, built in the 1820s from 18 000 tiny panes of glass – a building of

Modern habitat plantings at The Garden House fill the foreground of this view down to the village church.

The 1820s palm house at Bicton Park Gardens is a period masterpiece, glazed with thousands of tiny panes of glass.

unsurpassed elegance. Few privately owned gardens have such a profusion of further glasshouses today – Bicton has the Tropical House, where the Bicton orchid (*Lemboglossum bictoniense*) first bloomed in 1836; the landscaped Arid House for cacti and succulents; and the Temperate House for horticultural displays. Other fine monuments include the flint Shell House (with rare seashells) and the rustic Hermitage built in 1839 overlooking a water garden.

The trees in the world-famous Pinetum and Arboretum are impressive and include the tallest *Abies cephalonica* (41 m) ever recorded in the British Isles. But do not miss the rare American Garden, the early 19th-century rose garden, the Mediterranean Garden, the Stream Garden, the tree ferns in the Fern Glade and the rugged *Wisteria sinensis*, thought to be Britain's oldest at over 180 years.

4miles (6.5km) N of Budleigh Salterton ☎ 01395 568465 **Open** Daily 10am–6pm (5pm in winter) **Size** 25ha (63ac) **Owner** Simon & Valerie Lister P 🍴 WC ♿ 🎁 🚻
W www.bictongardens.co.uk

93. Hestercombe Gardens

Cheddon Fitzpaine
Taunton TA2 8LG

Sir Edwin Lutyens laid out the formal garden at Hestercombe in 1904 and Gertrude Jekyll planted it in 1906. It was probably their most successful collaboration: meticulous restoration has made it the best example of an Edwardian garden in Britain. There is a handsome conservatory and a fine Dutch Garden, but the centrepiece is the Great Plat, a sunken formal garden, surrounded by raised terraces, pergolas and all the Lutyens hallmarks: iris-choked rills, seats, relieved staircases and pools, where reflections twinkle on recessed apses.

Gertrude Jekyll's planting is bold and simple – good plants, well-used, with bergenias to the fore. The combination of Lutyens's design and Jekyll's planting is extremely photogenic: Hestercombe is a rewarding garden in which to learn about symmetry, balance and proportion. Beyond it, half-veiled by the pergola, lies the undulating Vale of Taunton, quintessentially English. And, as Lutyens intended, the whole design distracts the eye from the hideous house.

Behind the house lies an earlier garden, elegantly landscaped by Coplestone Warre Bampfylde in the latter half of the 18th century: 16 ha (40 ac) of lakes, temples, combes and woodlands. It is the perfect complement to the intense design and plantings of Lutyens and Jekyll. And the gardens are extremely well run for visitors' enjoyment.

4miles (6.5km) N of Taunton
☎ 01823 413923 **Open** Daily 10am–5pm **Size** 20ha (50ac)
Owner Hestercombe Gardens Trust
P ☕ WC 🎁 🚻
W www.hestercombegardens.com
@ info@hestercombegardens.com

94. Tintinhull House

Tintinhull
Yeovil BA22 8PZ

Tintinhull is a small masterpiece, famous for its tight design and use of colours. The house is a very pretty,

Lutyens's design and Jekyll's plantings at Hestercombe Gardens frame a view of the Vale of Taunton.

Tintinhull House has one of the smallest, but most influential, Arts-and-Crafts gardens in England.

small late-17th-century manor, built sideways on to the road.

The strongly geometrical garden was made in the mid-20th century by Phyllis Reiss, who diverted attention from the road by creating a strong parallel axis centred on the main façade. Internal walls and hedges define a number of smaller compartments, while paths, steps and clipped box mounds give substance and direction at all seasons. A wide range of plants is displayed most ornamentally.

The most famous garden within the garden has a long rectangular pool at the centre, a roughly classical summer-house at one end, and lawns edged with borders on either side. One is composed of the bright bold colours of scarlet, yellow, orange and white, while the other is dominated by pastel pinks, mauves, blues and pale yellows. Yet they are also mirror images of each other because each uses grey-leaved plants and striking leaf shapes as well as colour.

The health of such a garden as Tintinhull depends on the calibre of its carer, and the National Trust was fortunate in the 1980s to have Penelope Hobhouse as its tenant. Under her tutelage the garden was intensified in the spirit of Mrs Reiss's original precepts. Some of the high standards have been lost since then, but Tintinhull is still an incomparable lesson in the sculpting of space and the use of plants as elements of design.

5miles (8km) NW of Yeovil
☎ 01935 823289 **Open** late Mar–Oct Wed–Sun & bank hol Mon 11am–5pm **Size** 0.8ha (2ac)
Owner National Trust
🅿 🆆🅲 🔼
🆆 www.nationaltrust.org.uk

95. Abbotsbury Subtropical Gardens
Abbotsbury
Weymouth DT3 4LA

Abbotsbury is a sheltered, subtropical woodland garden in a lush valley: the soil is so rich that it has the tallest native English oak (*Quercus robur*) at 40 m in the British Isles. It was begun by a botanist Earl of Ilchester in the early 19th century and is beautifully maintained by his descendants, with an emphasis on rare and tender plants, which are still being added. Camellias, hydrangeas, rhododendrons, azaleas and magnolias fill the valley with colour (there is a new Magnolia Walk) and blue-bells and naturalised candelabra primulas flourish underneath.

But the real thrills come from the collections of the exotic and the unknown: palms, eucalypts, tree ferns, cannas, bananas, cordylines, phormiums, watsonias and probably the largest clump of *Gunnera manicata* in England. Tender specialities include *Photinia nussia*, *Leucadendron argenteum* and *Pittosporum crassifolium*, but there are hundreds more. All seem to revel in the informal, jungly layout of woodland paths, glades, ponds and pools, and the romantically overgrown walled garden. The Mediter-ranean garden, Himalayan glade and New Zealand garden are exceptional, and the sub-tropical displays of summer bedding outstanding. It is a place of wonder.

Halfway between Weymouth & Bridport ☎ 01305 871387
Open Daily 10am–6pm (dusk in winter) **Size** 8ha (20ac)
Owner Ilchester Estates
🅿 🍴 🆆🅲 ♿ 🎁 ♨
🆆 www.abbotsbury-tourism.co.uk/gardens.html

The colonial style of Abbotsbury's visitor centre matches the exotic splendours of its gardens.

The Italian garden at Compton Acres Gardens is the most spacious of several distinctly styled enclosures at this popular 1920s masterpiece.

96. Compton Acres Gardens

Canford Cliffs Rd
Poole BH13 7ES

Compton Acres is a 1920s masterpiece – a series of totally unconnected but highly entertaining gardens, all in different styles joined by tarmac paths. They include an Egyptian Court Garden, a Spanish Water Garden, the Roman Gardens and the Canadian Woodland Walk.

There was a fashion in the early 20th century for this sort of living guide to garden style and Compton Acres is by far the most comprehensive example still in existence. It is also extremely well maintained. The Italian Garden is one highlight, though it bears only a light resemblance to Italian renaissance gardens: a long rectangular pool runs between a little temple at one end and a pair of bronze wrestlers at the other, with yellow cypresses, pink clematis and copious quantities of bedding along the sides. The Japanese Garden is, however, a real treat, quite the best in England, and properly laid out by Japanese craftsmen with paths, stepping stones, bridges, herons, stone lamps, bronze cranes, a sturdy waterfall and a scarlet tea house, all disposed around an irregular pool and edged with azaleas, cherries, maples and bamboos. Doubtless it is very anglicised,

but it is also very beautiful and makes a thrilling end to the circuit.

Well signed in Canford Cliffs
☎ 01202 700778 **Open** Daily 9am–6pm (or sunset, if earlier) **Size** 4ha (10ac) **Owner** Red Sky Leisure Ltd
🅿 🖼 🍴 🚾 ♿ 🎁 ⚘
🆆 www.comptonacres.co.uk

97. Iford Manor

Bradford-on-Avon BA15 2BA

Iford is a beautiful and romantic garden, where an Italianate design is complemented by luxuriant English-style plantings. It was Harold Peto's own garden – a site for the wealthy Edwardian designer to house his collections of statues and architectural marbles.

For students of garden design, it is the key to Peto's ideas and skills, because Iford shows not just what he was capable of doing but what he liked enough to do for himself. That said, the design was dictated by the unusually steep site, to which Peto responded with characteristic energy. Formal terraces run along the contours, connected by handsome Italianate staircases. The top terrace is of exceptional beauty, running from a classical, semicircular stone seat, past an Ionic colonnade, statues, sarcophagi, urns, pillars and an octagonal gazebo to a Romanesque cloister.

Elsewhere are sheltered courtyards, a Japanese garden, a wisteria-clad pool and endless architectural caprices. Italian cypresses, phillyreas, acanthus and other Mediterranean species provide the background to later plantings – Lanning Roper added shrub roses and companion plants in the 1960s. Horticultural interest comes from these and from a meadow of naturalised anemones and martagon lilies.

7miles (11km) SE of Bath
☎ 01225 863146 **Open** May–Sep Tue–Thu, Sat–Sun 2–5pm; also Sun Apr & Oct **Size** 5ha (12ac) **Owner** Mrs E. Cartwright-Hignett
🅿 🚾
🆆 www.ifordmanor.co.uk

The architect Harold Peto designed his own garden at Iford Manor to hold his magnificent collection of classical pieces.

The formal garden in front of Bowood House was designed in the Italian style in 1818.

98. Bowood House

Calne SN11 0LZ

Bowood is well organised – it makes you feel welcome – and there is much to see. The 18th-century house sits at the top of a splendid 'Capability' Brown landscape, sweeping gently down to a long lake, with a classical temple and rustic cottage on the far side. The dam at the neck of the lake was landscaped by Charles Hamilton of Painshill to create a long cascade running between large rocks, an impressive and picturesque feature surrounded by woodland.

The house is set off by two formal terraces. The upper one was designed by Smirke in 1818 (very early for Italianate architecture) and the lower by Kennedy in 1851; both are well planted with colour throughout the season. Behind the house is a 19th-century pinetum, laid out geographically, with oceans of grass to separate the continents. The conifers are joined by deciduous trees and there are glimpses of the lake below as you wander among the splendid specimens.

In the oak woods above the house is the Robert Adam mausoleum, based on the Pantheon, surrounded by 24 ha (60 ac) of rhododendron drives with names like Lady Shelburne's Walk. Large rhododendrons have been planted here continuously for over 150 years. Their peak flowering in May is complemented by vast expanses of bluebells. Maintenance everywhere is excellent.

Between Calne & Chippenham
☎ 01249 812102 **Open** Apr–Oct daily 11am–6pm Rhododendron walks: late-Apr–early Jun **Size** 81ha (200ac) of grounds **Owner** Marquis of Lansdowne
🅿 🚗 🍴 🚻 ♿ 🎪 🖼
W www.bowood.org

99. Stourhead

Stourton BA12 6QD

Stourhead was so famous in the 18th century that its owner Henry Hoare had to build an inn to accommodate the visitors who came to admire it. It still has a powerful effect today.

Hoare started laying out the garden in the 1740s, as a sequence of pictorial views and experiences – uplifting, melancholy, sublime and Arcadian. He dammed the river Stour to make the lake and started building: the Temple of Flora, the Pantheon and Pope's Grotto were all finished between 1745 and 1755. A new phase of building began in the 1760s, with the Corinthian Temple of Apollo, the stone bridge and the incorporation of a gothic cross from Bristol. After 1780, his grandson Colt Hoare added such features as the gothic cottage and hermitage.

Beech, oak and larch were the original trees planted, supplemented by conifers in the 19th century. Then between 1900 and 1950 Sir Henry Hoare embellished the landscape with exotic plantings of rhododendrons, azaleas and such ornamental trees as davidias and copper beeches. The prescribed route (apparently inspired by Virgil)

The view of Stourhead's Temple of Concord across the lake is one of the defining images of the English landscape style.

is anti-clockwise and reveals an ever-changing series of picturesque views across the lake – majestic, harmonious, noble and provocative. The later plantings may indeed quarrel (as the National Trust maintains) with the 18th-century aesthetic, but there is no more ravishing place to explore on a fresh May morning, when the air is sweet with the scent of azaleas.

3miles (5km) NW of Mere
☎ 01747 841152 **Open** Daily 9am–7pm (or dusk, if earlier) **Size** 41ha (100ac) **Owner** National Trust
🅿 🍴 🚻 ♿ 🏛 ♿ 🏠
🆆 www.nationaltrust.org.uk

100. Heale House Garden

Middle Woodford
Salisbury SP4 6NT

Many consider Heale to be the prettiest house in southern England – and its garden complements it. The house dates back to the 17th century but was sympathetically extended in the 1890s. Then, in the early 1900s, Harold Peto laid out the garden at the bottom of a timeless, broad, chalk valley, with the river Avon and its leats flowing through. You can see Peto's craftsmanship in the Italianate garden architecture: the balustrade above the river launch, the formal pools and the terraced walk up an avenue of mop-headed robinias (a recent replacement for the original laburnums) to the west of the house.

On an island among the leats is a scarlet-lacquered Japanese bridge leading to a Japanese garden, complete with a tea house that straddles the water. The bridge looks as new as it did when built 100 years ago, but it also seems completely at home here among overgrown Japanese maples and other plants of Japanese origin. The old kitchen garden is exceptionally beautiful, with cob walls, clipped evergreens, tunnels of trained apples and pears, and excellent mixed borders.

Heale's walled kitchen garden has been planted with shrub roses alongside the old fruit trees.

Everywhere are Hybrid Musks, climbing roses and skilful colour combinations, not to mention drifts of cyclamens in autumn, and woodlands full of snowdrops and aconites in late winter.

4miles (6.5km) N of Salisbury
☎ 01722 782504 **Open** Daily 10am–5pm **Closed** Mon, except bank hols **Size** 3.2ha (8ac) **Owner** Mr & Mrs Guy Rasch
🅿 🍴 🚻 ♿ 🏛 ♿

SOUTH-EAST ENGLAND

101. Longstock Water Gardens

Longstock
Stockbridge SO20 6EH

The water gardens at Longstock are unique: dozens of small islands and all-but-islands linked by small bridges and intensely planted with water-loving plants. Water is not just a feature of the garden, but the dominant theme. The drifts of ligularias, astilbes, lysichitons, primulas, kingcups, hemerocallis, musks, water irises and lilies are often reflected in the pools that form between the islands. The ground is so soft that the islands seem to float, and a remarkable accumulation of peat has allowed such calcifuge plants as *Meconopsis*

betonicifolia to flourish in this chalky valley. Around the perimeter are swamp cypresses, liquidambars and the cut-leaved alder (*Alnus glutinosa* 'Laciniata'); further away are oaks and Scots pines.

On the other side of the road lies a splendid arboretum, with a vast collection of well-spaced specimen trees now approaching the prime of their life. At the top, by the nursery, is a beautiful, long pergola of fruit, rambling roses and clematis, and the National Collection of *Buddleja*. Standards of maintenance are excellent.

Longstock Water Gardens have beautiful, expansive groupings of ornamental aquatics and marginals.

Graham Stuart Thomas designed and planted the walled rose gardens at Mottisfont Abbey to hold his own historic collection of old roses.

1½miles (2.5km) NE of Longstock village ☎ 01264 810894 **Open** Apr–Sep 1st & 3rd Sun in month 2–5pm **Size** 4ha (10ac) of water garden; 26ha (65ac) of arboretum **Owner** John Lewis Partnership
🅿 🆆🅲 ♿ ⚲
🆆 www.longstockpark.co.uk

102. Mottisfont Abbey

Romsey SO51 0LP

Mottisfont Abbey is a pretty, late 17th-century manor-house, embedded in later enlargements and extensions. It sits in a beautiful chalk valley, where a broad spring surges out and runs down to feed the river Test. One of the London planes (*Platanus × hispanica*) near the river is the largest in England at 42 m.

Three significant designers worked here in the mid-20th century – Russell Page, Sir Geoffrey Jellicoe and Norah Lindsay – but the pride of the garden is its National Collection of old and historic roses in the walled garden. At its core is the very large number of old roses discovered, assembled and preserved by Graham Stuart Thomas, and made popular through his writings. Thomas himself designed the layout and worked on the herbaceous interplantings that complement the roses in high summer. Companion planting was one of his greatest skills, and Mottisfont its supreme

exposition. The Gallicas, Damasks, Albas and Centifolia roses, along with the Portlands, Bourbons and Hybrid Perpetuals, combine exceptionally well with softly coloured foxgloves, pinks, hardy geraniums and forms of *Linaria purpurea*. The climbers on the weathered brick walls are trained to maximise their flowering. Many would say that in mid-June this is the most English garden in the world.

4½miles (7km) NW of Romsey ☎ 01794 340757 **Open** Mar–Oct Sat–Wed 11am–5pm, but daily in Jun 11am–8.30pm for roses **Size** 11ha (28ac) **Owner** National Trust
🅿 🍽 🆆🅲 ♿ 🎁 ⚲ ▦
🆆 www.nationaltrust.org.uk

103. Sir Harold Hillier Gardens

Jermyns Lane
Ampfield
Romsey SO51 0QA

Ignore the word 'Gardens': this is the most important modern arboretum in the UK, spaciously laid out on an undulating site from 1953 onwards. It has the greatest collection of wild and cultivated woody plants in the world: over 12 500 taxa, totalling 44 000 plants.

The arboretum was established by the late Sir Harold Hillier: Hillier's Nursery aimed at the time to offer for sale every cultivar of every tree or shrub that was hardy in the British Isles. It has so many unique features that you will need all day to see more than a fraction of its riches. These include the collection of poplars called the Populetum, the magnolia avenue, a maple valley, the largest winter garden of its kind in Europe and National Collections of *Carpinus, Cornus, Corylus, Cotoneaster, Hamamelis, Ligustrum, Lithocarpus, Photinia, Pinus* and *Quercus*.

The planting and landscaping have been done with more ornamental effect than usual among arboreta, but it is the sheer number and variety of trees and shrubs here that makes the most lasting impression: each time you visit, wherever you walk, and

Sir Harold Hillier Gardens is the greatest modern arboretum in the British Isles, but also has ornamental features like this double border, 200 m long.

whatever the season or weather, you will find interesting plants that you have never seen before. And every part of the arboretum is an education and a pleasure.

2½miles (4km) NE of Romsey
☎ 01794 368787 **Open** Daily 10am–6pm (dusk, if earlier)
Size 73ha (180ac) **Owner** Hampshire County Council
🅿 🚻 🆆🅲 ♿ 🏠 ⚘
🆆 www.hilliergardens.org.uk/

104. Exbury Gardens

Exbury
Southampton SO45 1AZ

Exbury is England's best known rhododendron garden, laid out on an expansive level site running down to the Solent. It has more than *one million* rhododendrons and countless magnolias and camellias, too. Lionel de Rothschild, who started to plant it in 1919, sought to acquire every tree or shrub that would grow there.

The house is Palladian, and very beautiful. Before it stretches a long grassed glade, framed by vast 18th-century cedars and tree-like rhododendrons, including 'Loderi King George'. But the garden is mainly designed as woodland paths, glades and ponds, planted with rare trees and rhododendrons. The best known feature is the Azalea Bowl, where Kurume azaleas in bright, contrasting colours surround a small lake; their blazing reds, shocking pinks, fuchsias, mauves and whites are reflected in the still water. Tradescantias, gunneras, hostas, iris and, especially, candelabra primulas, flourish in the water garden and along every boggy ditch.

Other things to see include the famous de Rothschild nerines, a new hydrangea walk, a new garden of herbaceous perennials and grasses, and the 0.8-ha (2-ac) rock-garden (but even that is planted mainly with alpine rhododendron species from the Himalayas). A small train will help you round in summer, but

Kurume azaleas in light oak woodland run down to one of the lakes at Exbury Gardens.

remember – you need a lot of time to look at one million rhododendrons.

3miles (5km) S of Beaulieu
☎ 02380 891203 **Open** Mar–Oct daily 10am–5.30pm (or dusk, if earlier) **Size** 81ha (200ac)
Owner Edmund de Rothschild
🅿 🅿 🚻 🆆🅲 ♿ 🏠 ⚘
🆆 www.exbury.co.uk

105. Hinton Ampner

Bramdean
Alresford SO24 0LA

For quality, ingenuity, design and taste, Hinton Ampner ranks among England's greatest 20th-century gardens,

alongside Sissinghurst and Hidcote. Its gardens were laid out by Ralph Dutton, 8th and last Lord Sherborne, between 1935 and 1985. Dutton was an educated and scholarly man, who sought to create a unity between the house, garden, park and wider landscape. His eye for line was matched by a fine sense of historical propriety. Dutton placed his statues, buildings, axes and views with exquisite judgement to lead you subtly along the exact route that he intended. The terraces he built below the house extend far beyond its baseline, but always end in features like a statue, an avenue or some gates. Dutton was careful to choose soft-coloured plants that do well on chalk and then planted lots of them, always using the best forms: among them are buddlejas, lilacs, philadelphus, cotoneasters, weigelas and shrub roses. The lowest terrace has yews clipped into the shapes of staddlestones, interplanted with pink tulips in spring and pink dahlias in autumn – an astonishing *tour de force*.

There is much else to enjoy here, including the dell garden in an old chalk pit and the landscaping of the village church.

1mile (1.6km) W of Bramdean
☎ 01962 771305 **Open** Mid-Mar–mid-Oct Sat–Wed 11am–5pm
Size 5ha (12½ac) **Owner** National Trust 🅿 🅿 🆆🅲 ♿ ⚘ 🏛
🆆 www.nationaltrust.org.uk

The distant views in the splendid 'Hidcote-style' garden at Hinton Ampner House are always framed and focused.

106. West Green House Garden

Hartley Wintney
Basingstoke RG27 8JB

West Green is an Australian's garden in England. Marylyn Abbott's other garden in Mittagong, New South Wales, is much visited; West Green is utterly English and no less visitable. The house is early Georgian, with classical busts along its garden façade, which looks onto a 'theatre lawn'. The centrepiece is, however, the old walled garden off to one side, where box-edged beds overflow with plants in clever colour combinations that are changed from year to year. Lavish bedding and large plantings create wonderful effects throughout the garden. The fruit cages are elegantly designed in trellis-work and even the fruit and vegetables are grown in decorative ways.

Elsewhere are a grand water-staircase; a charming, small topiary garden, where water lilies flourish in small water tanks sunk into the ground; a dramatic new Persian water garden; a lake, and much else to admire. Drama, colour, innovation and humour are everywhere. This is a garden to inspire, amuse and delight.

2 miles (3km) W of Hook
☎ 01252 844611 **Open** Apr–Sep
Wed–Sun & bank hol Mon 11am–
4.30pm **Size** 3ha (8ac) **Owner**
Marylyn Abbott **P** **ⅱ** **WC** **&** **♿**
W www.westgreenhouse.co.uk

Queen Victoria's husband, Prince Albert, designed the grand Italianate terraces at Osborne House.

107. Osborne House

East Cowes PO32 6JY

Osborne was Queen Victoria's private house: Prince Albert laid out the spectacular Italianate terraces between the elegant Italianate palace and parkland below in 1847. The house conveys a very good impression of the queen's family life and the garden is undoubtedly the finest early Victorian garden in England. Grass shapes are cut from gravel and planted, at their centres, with exotic cordylines, phormiums and agaves. Statues, urns, magnificent fountains, pools and balustrades serve to ornament and define the garden. The seasonal displays of massed bedding remain impressive, and modern topiary (a stag of *Lonicera nitida*) rubs along with ancient umbrellas of clipped holly. It is all immensely Italianate and a delight to explore.

In the park are many fine trees, including stately cedars, trachycarpus palms, and cork- and holm-oaks. The walled kitchen garden was redesigned and replanted in the 1990s; there are magnificent displays of tender plants in the conservatory, colourful lines of annuals and perennials for cutting, and pots with the royal cipher 'V&A'. Further away is Swiss Cottage, where the royal children each had a plot of their own to cultivate; heritage vegetables and fruit are grown organically. Everything about Osborne is enchanting and offers insights into the past.

On N coast of Isle of Wight
☎ 01983 200022 **Open** Apr–Oct
daily 10am–5pm (4pm in Oct) **Size**
20ha (50ac) **Owner** English Heritage
P **ⅰ** **ⅱ** **WC** **&** **♿** **♿** **♿** **♿**
W www.english-heritage.org.uk

108. Savill Garden

Wick Lane
Englefield Green
Windsor TW20 0UU

King George V and his wife Queen Mary commissioned Sir Eric Savill to lay out this garden in 1932. It is, quite simply, the finest woodland garden in England, developed on an undulating site framed by magnificent oaks and pines. King George VI so admired it that he insisted the garden should bear Sir Eric's name.

The woodlands contain unrivalled plantings of camellias, rhododendrons, azaleas, maples, hydrangeas and flowering dogwoods, underplanted with subtle drifts of bulbs, ferns and herbaceous plants. The bog garden is especially effective, with large groupings of meconopsis, primulas, astilbes, hostas and wild narcissi, especially

The gardens at West Green House are ingeniously designed and full of subtle colour sequences.

The Savill Garden, and the adjoining Valley Garden in Windsor Great Park, are the best examples of large-scale woodland gardening in England.

Narcissus bulbocodium in March. The gravel garden is one of England's oldest and largest, planted with a fine display of drought-tolerant plants (many of them rare) and plants that benefit from the mulching effect of the gravel. In high summer, the rose garden and set-piece double herbaceous borders are worth a long trip to see. Extensive and intelligent use is made of a wide range of summer perennials in the borders. The raised beds, the cool greenhouse and the monocot border are each full of interest in due season.

The neighbouring Valley Garden is larger and a little wilder, with more shrubs and fewer herbaceous plants, but the principle is the same: huge trees of oak, beech, sweet chestnut and Scots pine are underplanted with camellias, rhododendrons, azaleas and hydrangeas. The Punch Bowl is a natural combe filled with terrace upon terrace of brightly coloured Japanese Kurume azaleas. And the plant interest is extremely high: the two gardens share no less than seven National Collections: *Ilex, Magnolia, Mahonia, Pernettya, Rhododendron* (species & Glenn Dale azaleas), ferns, and dwarf, slow-growing conifers.

3miles (5km) W of Egham
☎ 01753 847518 **Open** Daily 10am–6pm (4pm Nov–Feb)
Size 14ha (35ac) & 41ha (100ac)
Owner Crown Estate
🅿 🖻 🍴 ⓦⓒ ♿ 🏛 ♦
Ⓦ www.savillgarden.co.uk

109. Painshill Park
Portsmouth Rd
Cobham KT11 1JE

Painshill is a remarkable landscape garden – one of the most famous in its day – and was laid out between 1738 and 1773. Its maker, Charles Hamilton, was a plantsman, painter, designer and creature of the Enlightenment – influential, but not wealthy. His money-making schemes, all incorporated into the landscape, included a tile factory and vineyard, yet none was successful and he went bankrupt.

Hamilton's lasting achievement was to transform a barren heathland into ornamental pleasure grounds and parkland of dramatic beauty.

A long, narrow 5.5-ha (14-ac) lake is at the centre of the design: with sweeps of mown grass, it offers a setting for the garden's most famous features, the white gothic temple and the crystal-lined grotto, which are connected across a Chinese-style bridge. Hamilton sought to provoke the greatest variety of moods: other features include a ruined abbey, a Turkish tent, a gothic tower, a cascade and a hermitage.

Though a pioneer of the naturalistic landscape style, Hamilton was also a great plantsman and imported many new species from North America for his shrubberies. The garden still appeals to visitors on many levels, but your first visit is always an exciting and satisfying exploration.

On western edge of Cobham
☎ 01932 868113 **Open** Mar–Oct daily 10.30am–6pm; Nov–Feb daily 11am–4pm **Size** 64ha (158ac)
Owner Painshill Park Trust
🅿 🖻 ⓦⓒ ♿ 🏛
Ⓦ www.painshill.co.uk
@ info@painshill.co.uk

110. RHS Garden Wisley
Woking GU23 6QB

Wisley is the headquarters of the Royal Horticultural Society, and therefore the most important horticultural

Charles Hamilton built this white gothic ruin to draw visitors around the lake as they toured his picturesque landscape garden at Painshill Park.

Wisley, the headquarters of the Royal Horticultural Society, is the largest horticultural display garden in the world.

demonstration garden in Europe. It has many incidents of great intrinsic value – the vast Pulhamite rock-garden that fills an entire hillside, for example – but its true worth lies in its comprehensiveness: everything that a gardener could possibly want to see and learn from is here to delight, instruct and inspire.

Sir Thomas Hanbury of La Mortola gave the garden to the Society in 1903 for 'the encouragement and improvement of the science and practice of horticulture in all its branches'. It is still a trials garden, where the Society practises the perfect cultivation of every type of plant that can be grown in the British Isles, from alpines to hothouse orchids, whether in the open ground or in artificial conditions. This is supported by an important system of trials that grow, test, examine and make awards to flowers, fruit and vegetables.

The many features include an alpine meadow carpeted with *Narcissus bulbocodium* in spring and *Crocus sativus* in autumn; the finest Pulhamite rock-garden in Britain; woodland areas, where magnolias and tall rhododendrons give shelter to meconopsis, hellebores and snowdrops; huge patches of candelabra primulas; a Mediterranean garden; a fine

collection of roses; a double herbaceous border (130 m long); a pinetum; the best collection of heathers in England; more than 670 apple cultivars; model fruit, vegetable and ornamental gardens; and formal gardens designed by Sir Geoffrey Jellicoe and Lanning Roper. The only problem is the sheer size of it all: allow a whole day for a visit.

3miles (5km) E of Woking
☎ 01483 224234 **Open** Daily 10am–6pm (but 9am on weekends) **Closes** 4.30pm Nov–Feb **Size** 97ha (240ac) **Owner** Royal Horticultural Society
P 🅿 🍴 WC ♿ 🎁 🚻
W www.rhs.org.uk/gardens/wisley

111. Polesden Lacey

Great Bookham
Dorking RH5 6BD

'Edwardian opulence' is a cliché – but at Polesden Lacey it is a reality. This was the home between 1906 and 1942 of Mrs Ronald Greville, a political hostess with a vast fortune to spend on the elegant house and extensive gardens. It is placed on the edge of a valley with beautiful views to the south. A historical anomaly is the 425-m long terraced walk, laid out by the playwright Richard Sheridan when he lived here in the 1790s; the return is through Mrs Greville's extensive rose

Rose pergolas, dripping with rambler roses, are just one of many bold horticultural features in the grand 20th-century garden of Polesden Lacey.

garden, which has some 2000 plants of 20th-century Hybrid Teas and walls and pergolas dripping with popular Edwardian rambling roses, including 'American Beauty', 'Dorothy Perkins' and 'Excelsa'. The old walled garden boasts another large rose garden, iris beds, and a lavender garden. An excellent herbaceous border runs for 140 m along one of the outside walls. Elsewhere are a rock-garden, a croquet lawn, elegant grass terraces, fine views over the park and snowdrops.

3miles (5km) SW of Leatherhead **C** 01372 452048 **Open** Daily 11am–5pm **Closes** 4pm Nov–Feb **Size** 12ha (30ac), plus landscaped park **Owner** National Trust
P ⬛ WC ♿ ⬛ ⬛ ⬛
W www.nationaltrust.org.uk/ polesdenlacey

112. Capel Manor
Bullsmoor Lane
Enfield EN1 4RQ

Capel Manor is a horticultural college: its extensive and wide-ranging gardens are laid out for teaching and for public enjoyment – which amounts to the same thing. In the National Gardening Centre, dozens of small model gardens are designed and planted by

The art of bedding is one of the numerous displays at the great teaching garden, Capel Manor.

trade sponsors to give state-of-the-art ideas to students and visitors for their own gardens. An influential gardening magazine, *Gardening Which?*, sponsors twelve such gardens and carries out trials and experiments (long-term and seasonal) in another part of the grounds.

There is also a series of themed gardens laid out for all to learn from: a walled garden, a herb garden, a knot garden, a disabled person's garden, a shade garden, an Italianate holly maze, a magnolia border, a pergola, a Japanese garden, alpine beds and some

historical re-creations. Other themes include Mediterranean, modern, cottage, rustic, family and minimalist gardens. What brings it together is the extraordinary user-friendliness of it all: there is so much variety that you cannot fail to learn something, even if some of the gardens are not quite to your taste.

1½miles (2.5km) SW of Waltham Cross **C** 08456 122122 **Open** Mar–Oct daily 10am–6pm; Nov–Feb weekdays only **Size** 12ha (30ac) **Owner** Capel Manor Corporation
P ⬛ WC ♿ ⬛ ⬛
W www.capel.ac.uk

113. Royal Botanic Gardens, Kew
Richmond TW9 3AB

Everyone knows that Kew can fairly claim to be the world's leading botanic garden, but sometimes they forget to tell you that Kew is also one of the most enjoyable to visit. It is laid out in a flat, park-like setting on the banks of the river Thames. It was begun by Augusta, Princess of Wales, in the 1750s: William Chambers designed the orangery, the Temple of Arethusa and Bellona, the incredible ruined arch and the iconic pagoda (1762). 'Capability' Brown landscaped it, Sir Joseph Banks

The great palm house at Royal Botanic Gardens, Kew, is set off by colourful displays of summer bedding.

Sir William Chambers's pagoda at Kew inspired dozens of copies throughout Europe.

helped with the plantings, and in due course the garden was revived by Sir William Hooker in the 1840s.

Kew's botanic garden has an incomparable collection of plants and is therefore of great interest to plant lovers. And there are many horticulturally themed gardens, including the azalea garden, the bamboo garden, the unique berberis dell, the comprehensive grass garden (550 species), the holly walk (600 of them – some specimens are as high as 30 m), the juniper collection (Europe's largest), the lilac garden, the rhododendron dell (700 plants), the pinetum (lots of record-breakers) and the rock-garden (over 2500 different plants, geographically arranged).

The glasshouses likewise contain a vast collection of plants. Decimus Burton built the Palm House (1844–48) and the Temperate House, twice its size, in 1859. The modern Princess of Wales Conservatory has ten distinct climatic zones, ranging from arid to moist tropical: among its most striking plants are a 160-year-old *Protea cynaroides* from South Africa and a *Jubaea spectabilis*, so tall that it is the world's largest indoor plant. Other glasshouses to visit include the hot and humid water lily house, the alpine house, the bonsai house and the unique filmy fern house. And all the buildings, not just

the eye-catchers, are beautifully integrated into the superb landscape.

W London ☎ 02083 325655 **Open** Daily (except 24–25 Dec) 9.30am– 6.30pm (7.30pm weekends) **Closes** 5.30pm mid-Feb–last Sat Mar; 6pm early Sep–end Oct; 4.15pm Nov–Dec **Size** 122ha (302ac) **Owner** Trustees of the Royal Botanic Gardens
🚾 🅿 🍴 (three) ♿ 🎁 📖
Ⓦ www.kew.org
@ info@kew.org

114. Hampton Court Palace

Hampton KT8 9AU

Hampton Court is by far the largest example of a formal garden in England to have survived the landscaping movement. It is also the most important royal garden: William III was responsible for the main features we see today. His vast Privy Garden (private garden) has recently been restored as it was in 1702. Every detail is accurate: note, for example, how widely the roses and other plants are spaced in their slightly raised beds – an exact copy of the horticultural practices of the time.

Walk along the raised embankment above the East Garden and imagine the king conversing with his courtiers and supplicants below. William III laid this part out, too, with 12 marble fountains and the Long Water, which cuts right through the deer park for nearly 1 mile (1.5 km). Queen Anne added the semicircular canals in 1710. On the other side of the Privy Garden is the Pond Garden, a sunken formal garden in the Elizabethan style, dating from the early 1900s, with magnificent displays of spring bulbs and bedding. Nearby is the Great Vine (actually 'Black Hamburgh') planted in 1768 on the advice of 'Capability' Brown: it produces, on average, 300 kg of grapes every year. On the other side of the palace are the extensive wilderness gardens, a mass of naturalised daffodils in spring, and the Maze (famous in England, but actually quite easy to navigate). Other areas in the Wilderness have considerable horticultural interest, including the rose garden, herbaceous garden, and walls covered with climbing plants.

Spring bedding is practised at a high level in the Pond Garden at Hampton Court; the tunnel behind belongs to the Privy Garden.

S of London, in Hampton
☎ 08707 527777 **Open** Daily
10am–6pm (4.30pm Nov–Mar)
Size 24ha (60ac) of formal gardens
& 243ha (600ac) of deer park
Owner Historic Royal Palaces
P ▣ ⅰⅰ WC & ⬚ ▦
W www.hrp.org.uk

115. Chelsea Physic Garden

66 Royal Hospital Rd
London SW3 4HS

The Chelsea Physic Garden is the second oldest botanic garden in England and a world away from London's busy traffic. It was founded in 1673 as an Apothecaries' Garden and still maintains 5000 taxa within its small compass. The pond rock-garden, dating from 1773, is the oldest in England and includes among its rocks some Icelandic lava brought to the garden by Sir Joseph Banks. The central London microclimate allows the largest olive tree in Britain to flourish and a grapefruit tree (*Citrus × paradisi*) to crop regularly. The Chilean wine palm (*Jubaea chilensis*) grows well, and *Cordyline australis* reaches full size. Australian banksias flourish against the office wall, alongside *Clematis cirrhosa* var. *balearica*.

The heart of the garden is still its extensive botanical order beds, displaying a vast number of rare and interesting plants, including the form of *Rosa chinensis* known as 'Crimson Bengal', which flowers throughout mild winters. A historical walk draws attention to the great number of plants first introduced to Britain by the garden and its curators, including *Hibiscus rosa-sinensis* and the tea-plant (*Camellia sinensis*). The garden remains the perfect London refuge and is of intense interest and charm.

Between Royal Hospital Rd and
Chelsea Embankment
☎ 02073 525646 **Open** Apr–Oct Wed
12noon–5pm & Sun 12noon–6pm
Size 1.5ha (4ac) **Owner** Chelsea
Physic Garden Co. WC ▣ & ⬚
W www.chelseaphysicgarden.co.uk
@ enquiries@chelseaphysicgarden.
co.uk

A statue of Sir Hans Sloane commemorates one of Chelsea Physic Garden's benefactors.

116. West Dean Gardens

West Dean
Chichester PO18 0QZ

West Dean is a beautiful Edwardian mansion with a sweeping view of the South Downs. Gertrude Jekyll and Harold Peto both worked here. Jekyll's Wild Garden has just been restored: irregular paths, open glades, shady patches, streams, ponds and lots of interesting plants. Peto's magnificent 100-m pergola is draped with rambler roses, wisteria, clematis and honeysuckle, while the borders along its sides are thickly planted with hostas,

Harold Peto designed the pergola for the sumptuous Edwardian garden at West Dean.

pelargoniums, ferns, iris, dicentras and spring bulbs. Also worth seeing is the arboretum, with National Collections of *Aesculus* and *Liriodendron*, and the tallest *Cupressus goveniana* and *Ailanthus vilmoriniana* in Britain.

But West Dean's chief glory is its kitchen garden, an outstanding example of Edwardian self-confidence, where fruit and vegetables are still grown in quantity and variety to a standard unseen for 100 years. Its 16 glasshouses and frames are dedicated to orchids, house plants, strawberries, vines, cucumbers, aubergines, peppers, nectarines and peaches. Outside are orderly rows of cabbages, carrots, lettuces and beetroot, many of them grown from heritage seed. The walls, about 1 mile (1.5 km) in extent, are covered in trained fruit-trees – over 200 different apples, pears and plums, with an emphasis upon the conservation of older cultivars. Fruit-trees are also grown as cordons, goblets, domes and chalices; the pear arch is especially handsome. The hot border is planted with rich red, orange and yellow herbaceous plants, which reach their high point when the fruit and vegetables are also at their peak.

6miles (19km) N of Chichester on
A286 **☎** 01243 818210 **Open** Mar–
Oct daily 11am–5pm (10.30am
May–Sep); Nov–Feb Wed–Sun
11am–4.30pm **Size** 36ha (90ac)
Owner Edward James Foundation
P ⅰⅰ WC & ⬚ ▮
W www.westdean.org.uk
@ gardens@westdean.org.uk

117. Denmans

Fontwell
Arundel BN18 0SU

Denmans is the show garden of England's leading garden designer. It is designed to give you lots of ideas for your own garden, which it does superbly.

John Brookes's tenets include a commitment to form and texture as well as colour, a passion for easy care, and a

There are many useful lessons to learn in Denmans display gardens, attached to a leading designer's house.

style that is more fluid and informal than many. Denmans makes especially good use of gravel as a mulch to walk upon and get closer to the plants. Sometimes it suggests movement; on other occasions it creates a casual, jungly effect. The flint Walled Garden has several sections, including a dry gravel stream bed with informal plantings. Impressions are created by cutting the grass to different heights. There are damp-loving plants beside the stream, and a brilliant, hot herbaceous corner. The mild climate allows such plants as mimosa and callistemon to flourish outside.

Plants are an integral part of the design: Brookes knows his plants well and how to display them. Time and again, you are taken aback by the stunning contrasts and harmonies of his plantings.

Halfway between Chichester & Arundel ☎ 01243 542808 **Open** Daily 9am–5pm (dusk in winter) **Size** 1.6ha (4ac) **Owner** John Brookes & Michael Neve
🅿 ▣ ♨ ♿ 🏛 👤
🆆 www.denmans-garden.co.uk
@ denmans@denmans-garden.co.uk

118. Parham
Storrington
Pulborough RH20 4HS

Parham – Elizabethan house and 20th-century garden – is a quintessence of charm. Both are supremely beautiful,

the very image of an English idyll. Their setting is an ethereal deer park, with a landscaped lake, a cricket ground, fallow deer and bulky ancient oaks.

The garden was begun by the Hon. Clive Pearson and his wife in the 1920s and has been frequently replanted and embellished by their descendants. Most of it is held within the old brick-walled garden: 4 ac (1.6 ha) of firm design and crisp outlines contrasting with rich and exuberant plantings. Here are magnificent gates, lush borders, colour plantings in yellow, blue and mauve, old and new fruit trees, lots of roses, a herb garden, cutting borders, fine statuary, box-edged vegetable borders and endless smaller gardens to explore – all maintained to the highest standard.

Lanning Roper and Peter Coats are among the designers who worked here: their aim was to achieve, '… Edwardian opulence … without being too purist'. The garden is now spreading to areas outside, with fine borders against its outer edges and the recent addition of a brick-and-turf maze.

Midway between Pulborough & Storrington ☎ 01903 742021 **Open** Easter–Sep Wed, Thu, Sun & bank hol Mon 12noon–6pm **Size** 4.5ha (11ac) **Owner** Parham Park Trust
🅿 ▣ ♨ ♿ 🏛 👤 ▦
🆆 www.parhaminsussex.co.uk
@ enquiries@parhaminsussex.co.uk

119. Leonardslee Lakes & Gardens
Lower Beeding
Horsham RH13 6PP

Leonardslee is best known as a rhododendron garden, planted on an enormous scale by Sir Edmund Loder in 1889. The rhododendrons spill through the oak woods and across the greensand valleys. One combe is filled from top to bottom with a cataract of sweet-scented yellow azaleas (*Rhododendron luteum*), underplanted with native bluebells and all reflected in one of Leonardslee's seven lakes. It was here that Sir Edmund made his *Rhododendron × loderi* crosses, and some of the original plants, more like trees now, can still be seen.

Parham has dreamy colour planting schemes – an art form at which the English excel.

The Pulhamite rock-garden contrasts with the valleys of rhododendrons and azaleas at Leonardslee.

Rhododendrons and azaleas are everywhere, but so, too, are camellias and magnolias. And there are very fine collections of other ornamental trees and shrubs: maples, oaks, liquidambars, hickories and nyssas ensure that beauty in spring is followed by fine autumn colour. The banks of the lakes and streams are densely planted with candelabra primulas, lysichitons and gunneras. Other features include a magnificent Pulhamite rockgarden about 100 years old, which sports a striking clump of *Trachycarpus fortunei* palms, and a strange blend of dwarf conifers and very bright Kurume azaleas.

And if you should bump into a wallaby, it may help to know that Sir Edmund introduced them nearly 100 years ago and they have thrived and multiplied.

4miles (6.5km) SW of Handcross
☎ 01403 891212 **Open** Apr–Oct daily 9.30am–6pm **Size** 100ha (250ac) **Owner** Loder family
🅿 🍴 🚻 🎁 ♿
🆆 www.leonardslee.com
@ gardens@leonardslee.com

120. Nymans
Handcross
Haywards Heath RH17 6EB

Nymans is one of many great plantsman's gardens that were made about 100 years ago in the wooded hills of Sussex. It differs from most, however, in enjoying a strong overall design and mustering its plants with a fair degree of artistry. It was made by Leonard Messel, a London banker, who sent his head gardener's son, Harold Comber, to collect plants in South America. Messel planted first a pinetum, then an arboretum, a rock-garden, a heather garden (the first of its kind in England), a Japanese garden, and a rhododendron woodland. All are major features still today.

A lengthy pergola is planted with forms of *Wisteria floribunda* from end to end with lines of *Iris sibirica* along the outside; in a good year they flower together in mid-May. The walled garden has four elaborate and matching pieces of topiary (drums, globes and crowns) at its central point and opulent yellow-and-blue herbaceous borders, as well as a pioneering collection of old roses and a vast assembly of magnolias and camellias. It was here that *Magnolia × loebneri* 'Leonard Messel' and *Eucryphia × nymansensis* 'Nymansay' originated.

4miles (6.5km) S of Horsham
☎ 01444 400321 **Open** Mid-Feb–Oct Wed–Sun & bank hol Mon; also 11 am–4 pm weekends in winter **Size** 12ha (30ac) **Owner** National Trust 🅿 🍴 🚻 ♿ 🎁 ♿
🆆 www.nationaltrust.org.uk/nymans

A rose-covered dovecote stands close to the ruined mansion at Nymans.

121. Wakehurst Place
Ardingly
Haywards Heath RH17 6TN

Wakehurst Place has been a country outlier of the Royal Botanic Gardens at Kew since 1965 but has a long horticultural history and a lot to show for it.

Most of the planting began after Gerald Loder bought the estate in 1903 and began to introduce exotic trees and shrubs into the undulating, wooded site. Near the house are two walled gardens, rather cottagey, one planted in pastel shades and the other full of good topiary. A monocotyledon border runs along the outside of the walls, with superb displays of lilies, grasses, kniphofias and hedychiums. The waterlily-filled pond leads to an Asian heath garden, where dwarf rhododendrons, cotoneasters, potentillas, gaultherias and junipers from the Himalayas, China and Japan jostle for attention – note the wonderful masses of *Rhododendron yakushimanum*.

Below is the Iris Dell, planted with Japanese cultivars of water iris (*Iris ensata*) against a brilliant background of Kurume azaleas (Wakehurst has significant connections with Japan). The water garden is surrounded by sheets of blue meconopsis and the giant Himalayan *Cardiocrinum giganteum*. Other good features include a bright spring border, magnificent magnolias and rhododendrons, Japanese maples, a wildflower meadow, a Himalayan glade, a bog garden and two pinetums.

Wakehurst's many rare trees include the King William pine (*Athrotaxis selaginoides*), *Torreya nucifera* (17 m high) and two cultivars of *Chamaecyparis lawsoniana* ('President Roosevelt' at 15 m and 'Winston Churchill' slightly shorter at 13 m). The National Collections include *Betula* and *Nothofagus*, as well as *Hypericum* and *Skimmia*. And, for the botanically minded, there is even a nature reserve dedicated to Cryptogams – mosses, liverworts, lichens and filmy ferns.

The country outlier Wakehurst Place offers a greater range of microhabitats than Kew Gardens itself.

5miles (8km) SE of Crawley
☎ 01444 894066 **Open** Daily 10am–6pm (4.30pm in winter) **Size** 127ha (314ac) **Owner** Royal Botanic Gardens, Kew
🅿 🚗 🍴 🚻 ♿ 🏠 ♿
🌐 www.kew.org

122. Sheffield Park Garden

Uckfield TN22 3QX

Sheffield Park is a famous landscape garden – both 'Capability' Brown and Humphry Repton worked here – drowned by a deluge of 20th-century ornamental plantings. The structure is intact and three of the five lakes are relatively uncluttered, but the reason to visit the garden nowadays is the great number of exotic trees and shrubs. The finest trees actually date back to the 19th century: wellingtonias and redwoods, cedars and *Pinus pinaster*. Within the collection is a large number of British 'record' trees and some mass plantings of historical importance – the groves of *Nyssa sylvatica*, for example, are unique in Britain.

The underplantings are nicely balanced between the spring flowerers (rhodo-dendrons and azaleas, with daffodils and bluebells) and the autumn colourers (amelanchiers, maples, fothergillas, nyssas, sorbus and taxodiums). Some of the plantings offer interesting contrasts of colour and shape, while the colourful displays are doubled by their reflections in the lakes. And in autumn there is an incomparable display of *Gentiana sino-ornata*.

10miles (16km) N of Lewes
☎ 01825 790231 **Open** Mid-Feb–mid-Dec Tue–Sun, bank hols 10.30am–6pm; also Mon May & Oct **Size** 49ha (120 ac) **Owner** National Trust 🅿 🚻 ♿ 🏠 ♿
🌐 www.nationaltrust.org.uk/sheffieldpark

The lakes designed by 'Capability' Brown at Sheffield Park were surrounded with exotic trees and shrubs during the 20th century.

123. Pashley Manor

Ticehurst TN5 7HE

Pashley Manor is a Victorian garden that has been given a modern facelift over the last 20 years. It opened to the public in 1992 and was good enough by 1999 to receive the accolade of Garden of the Year. The house is two-faced with a fine half-timbered Elizabethan structure as you approach down the drive and a Georgian façade on the garden side.

The Victorian garden – nothing very special – contributed a framework of fine old trees, fountains, springs and large ponds or small lakes. The new garden was designed by Anthony du Gard Pasley, a leading landscape architect with a particular empathy for the lush Edwardian style of planting. His designs have pulled the old garden together and added a sumptuous series of new enclosed gardens, where colour gardening is practised to brilliant effect. Pashley Manor is also one of the best English gardens to study the art of bedding; over 12 000 tulips (60 different varieties) are planted every year.

1½miles (2.5km) SE of Ticehurst
☎ 01580 200888 **Open** Apr–Sep Tue–Thu, Sat & bank hol Mon 11am–5pm **Size** 5ha (12½ac) **Owner** James & Angela Sellick
🅿 🍴 🚻 ♿ ♿
🌐 www.pashleymanorgardens.com
@ info@pashleymanorgardens.com

124. Great Dixter

Dixter Rd
Northiam TN31 6PH

Great Dixter is an influential garden: its owner between 1953 and 2006 was the popular horticultural journalist, Christopher Lloyd. Sir Edward Lutyens designed the garden's layout for Lloyd's father, an expert on topiary: the backbone is still an Edwardian structure of brickwork, yew hedges, steps, walls, doorways and Arts and Crafts details. Christopher Lloyd respected this structure,

Christopher Lloyd's ever-changing Long Border was the trial ground for his experiments in plant combinations at Great Dixter.

but was more interested in plants – how to grow and use them. He had a remarkable eye for combining plants in harmonious groupings throughout the year.

The garden's most admired feature is the Long Border, about 65 m long and 4.5 m deep, which has always been a showcase and trial ground for experiments in planting. Shrubs, herbaceous plants, bulbs and bedding are used here and exhibit a wide variety of weaving colours, heights and textures, and are unified as much by good foliage as by flowers.

Lloyd adored change and sought to refine and improve his garden all the time. He was one of the first English garden owners to use lots of annuals and tender perennials to extend the season of colour into autumn. His Tropical Garden is a jungle of bold exotic leaves, shapes and colour. He was also a pioneer of meadow gardening, which he perfected on either side of the entrance path and, more particularly, below the house: crocuses, daffodils, fritillaries, snowflakes and colchicums are naturalised in their thousands alongside such flowering plants as primroses and *Geranium pratense*.

13miles (21km) N of Hastings
☎ 01797 252878 **Open** Apr–Oct Tue–Sun & bank hol Mon 2–5pm
Size 2ha (5ac) **Owner** Lloyd Trusts
🅿 🚾 📷 ♿
🌐 www.greatdixter.co.uk
@ office@greatdixter.co.uk

125. Hever Castle
Edenbridge TN8 7NG

Hever Castle was the childhood home of Queen Anne Boleyn, but the formal garden was entirely made in the early 1900s by its new owner, William Waldorf Astor. It was one of the most opulent and delightful gardens made during that extravagant decade, when the display of wealth reached its apogee. Near the house are an immaculately trimmed yew maze (its four quarters are symmetrical, which makes it easy to get to the centre) and some good yew topiary, including free-standing specimens and rows that represent the pieces on a chess board. In the woods above is Anne Boleyn's walk, a peaceful

At the end of Hever Castle's extensive Italian garden, a classical portico frames a view of the artificial lake.

place to saunter through superb rhododendrons and bluebells at their peak in May.

But the outstanding feature is the 2-ha (5-ac) Italian garden, built to house Astor's collection of statuary and architectural loot from Italy. A pergola runs its whole length on one side, edged with a series of cool, dripping, mossy fountains. Opposite is the Pompeian wall, where sculpture, urns, sarcophagi and all manner of up-market bric-a-brac are displayed with ostentatious style, often surrounded by tender flowering shrubs, in a series of exquisite Italianate gardens. At the end, you burst out onto a theatrical terrace, known as the Piazza, and a 14-ha (35-ac) lake, hand-dug by 800 workmen in less than two years – quite breathtaking.

3miles (5km) SE of Edenbridge
☎ 01732 865224 **Open** Mar–Nov daily 11am–5pm (4pm in winter)
Size 16ha (40ac) **Owner** Broadland Properties Ltd 🅿 🍴 🚾 ♿ 📷 ♿ 🖼
🌐 www.hevercastle.co.uk

126. Penshurst Place
Tonbridge TN11 8DG

Penshurst is a historic garden of great importance. It has substantial remains from the 16th century, which escaped the fashion for landscaping in the 18th century. Its present structure dates to the 1850s, when the then Lord De L'Isle called in the architect George Devey (a precursor of the Arts & Crafts movement) to lay out an idealised Elizabethan garden, divided into small, self-contained garden rooms, each with its own style and character. These were reworked 100 years later by the fashionable designers Lanning Roper and John Codrington, who are responsible for the beautiful colour combinations in all the plantings. A vast Italianate parterre dominates the immediate pleasure garden in front of the castellated house. Another parterre is planted as the Union Jack –

Yew topiary and yew hedges give structure to this view of the castle at Penshurst Place.

once a fashionable and patriotic feature that is seldom seen today.

The real pleasure of this garden is to wander in and out of its enclosures, each so different but bound together by good design – there is over 1 mile (1.5 km) of yew hedging. The magnolia garden, nut orchard and 100-m bed of herbaceous paeonies are exceptional.

5miles (8km) W of Tonbridge
☎ 01892 870307 **Open** Mid-Mar–Oct daily 10.30am–6pm **Size** 4.5ha (11ac) **Owner** Viscount De L'Isle
P ⧉ ⊞ WC ⧗ ⧇ ⌗
🆆 www.penshurstplace.com
@ enquiries@penshurstplace.com

127. Great Comp

St Mary's Platt
Borough Green
Sevenoaks TN15 8QS

Eric Cameron bought Great Comp, a 17th-century manor-house, in 1957 and created the modern garden out of rough woodland and paddock. It is a model of how to garden successfully on a large scale. The key is close planting – using the widest possible choice of herbaceous plants and small shrubs as groundcover, in order to minimise maintenance. But Great Comp also has a large collection of plants, over 3000 different taxa, from conifers to heathers; magnolias and rhododendrons are especially well represented, plus a large number of different salvias in the formal Italian garden.

One curiosity is the large number of 'ruins' in the garden – modern follies made to resemble relics of lost cottages or farm buildings. They are fun to explore, add character, and sometimes afford good viewpoints.

2miles (3km) E of Borough Green
☎ 01732 886154 **Open** Apr–Oct daily 11am–5.30pm **Size** 2.8ha (7ac) **Owner** Great Comp Charitable Trust P ⧉ WC ⧗ ⧇ ⌗
🆆 www.greatcomp.co.uk
@ greatcompgarden@aol.com

128. Bedgebury National Pinetum

Park Lane
Goudhurst
Cranbrook TN17 2SL

Bedgebury Pinetum is the national conifer collection: it claims to be the biggest and best in the world. It was founded as a joint venture between the Forestry Commission and the Royal Botanic Gardens at Kew: the first plants for the pinetum were raised at Kew in 1921 and planted out at Bedgebury four years later. The collection has over 10 000 trees, made up of 330 different species and more than 2000 cultivars. The rare, historically important and endangered trees include some 56 vulnerable or critically endangered species and five NCCPG National Collections: *Chamaecyparis lawsoniana* cultivars, *Juniperus*, *Taxus*, *Thuja*, and × *Cupressocyparis*. There are 18 record tree species, including two broad-leaved, and some of the oldest and largest examples of conifers in Britain.

But Bedgebury is also very enjoyable to visit – the pinetum occupies gently hilly ground and areas are land-scaped around a series of lakes and streams. Every part has been laid out so that the form, colour and texture of mature conifers can readily be seen. There are also fine oaks and maples and colourful azaleas and rhododendrons. Planting continues, and maintenance is good.

4miles (6.5km) S of Goudhurst
☎ 01580 211044 **Open** Daily 10am–6pm (4pm in winter) **Size** 130ha (320ac) **Owner** Forestry Commission
P ⧉ ⊪ WC ⧗ ⧇ ⌗
🆆 www.bedgeburypinetum.org.uk
@ bedgebury@forestry.gov.uk

The garden at Great Comp excels in its use of colourful heathers and combinations of conifers.

Vita Sackville-West's White Garden at Sissinghurst, where all the plants are green, grey and white, has been much copied by other English garden owners.

129. Sissinghurst Castle Garden

Sissinghurst
Cranbrook TN17 2AB

The name of Sissinghurst is known wherever gardens are made in the modern English style: many consider it the most important and influential garden of the 20th century. It was begun in 1930 by Sir Harold Nicolson and his wife Vita Sackville-West, in and around the moat, walls, cottages and outbuildings that surround a 15th-century tower. Nicolson was responsible for the structure – the paths, hedges, axes and focal points – while Sackville-West undertook the planting in her characteristically romantic and exuberant style. It was the combination of these two complementary talents that made Sissinghurst a source of wonder and inspiration to this day.

The famous set-pieces are even better when you walk through them than they are in books and photographs: the white garden, cottage garden, 'rondel', old-fashioned rose garden, nut-plat and lime walk are still a revelation, an education and an inspiration. There are two reasons for this. First, the design is so good that your progression from room to room is invariably a sequence of anticipation and delight. Second, the garden is always developing, as new plants are added and worked into the borders. Such was the Nicolsons' intention, for they insisted that the National Trust should continue to keep the garden up to date. The design is therefore unaltered and unalterable, but the plantings continue to be governed by the Gertrude Jekyll principles of which Sissinghurst is the supreme exemplar.

6miles (10km) E of Goudhurst
☎ 01580 710700 **Open** Mar–Oct Fri–Tue 11am–6.30pm (10am Sat, Sun and bank hols) **Size** 2.2ha (5½ac) **Owner** National Trust
🅿 ▢ 🍴 📶 ♿ 🏪 ♿ 🖼
W www.nationaltrust.org.uk/ sissinghurst

130. Goodnestone Park

Wingham
Canterbury CT3 1PL

There is so much to see at Goodnestone: a handsome Palladian house, a fine chestnut avenue, 18th-century parkland, formal 19th-century terraces, and a 1920s woodland garden, best in spring when the rhododendrons and camellias are in flower. But the outstanding feature is the walled garden, with three enclosures each about half a hectare, enclosed by beautiful, old weathered bricks and festooned with clematis, jasmine, honeysuckles, climbing roses and an enormous wisteria. A long, broad, grass walk runs down the middle towards the flint tower of the parish church, a focal point just beyond the furthest wall. Drifts of shrub roses, peonies, penstemons, clematis and herbaceous plants fill the borders, stuffed with interesting plants and arranged to create pretty colour combinations – even the kitchen garden has flowers. Other features include the alpine garden (raised beds and sinks planted with gentians and other tiny treasures) and the stylish conservatory greenhouse filled with tender exotics.

2miles (3km) NW of Aylsham
☎ 01304 840107
Open Apr–Sep Wed–Fri, bank hols & some Sun 11am–5pm
Size 5.5ha (14ac)
Owner Lady FitzWalter
🅿 ▢ 📶 ♿ ♿
W www.goodnestoneparkgardens. co.uk
@ enquires@goodnestonepark gardens.co.uk

Despite a dry climate and thin soil, Goodnestone Park's walled garden is lushly planted and always full of colour.

Gardens of the Netherlands & Belgium

Few traces remain of gardens in the Low Countries prior to the mid-17th century. By then the Dutch preoccupation with horticulture was already established: tulipomania is its best known manifestation. But Dutch nurserymen and horticulturists were also avid collectors and breeders of roses, irises, hyacinths and narcissus, as can readily be seen from 17th-century flower paintings. At the same time, the maritime empire of the Dutch East India Company brought not only herbs and spices back to the Low Countries, but also exotic ornamental plants from the Cape of Good Hope and India.

A new style of garden design began to develop during the 17th century as the Dutch Republic established itself and sought a distinct cultural identity. The emergence of the typical Dutch garden can be explained in part by climate and terrain, but it also embodied the Calvinist virtues of modesty, domesticity and a horror of display. Horticulture and the cultivation of fruit and vegetables were a spiritual duty. A rectilinear system of straight drainage canals was fundamental to the layout of Dutch gardens; so, too, was the planting of trees along the boundaries. The flatness of the terrain precluded terraces, fountains, or cascades, but the constant presence of water means that many gardens are bathed in reflected light and the sky seems to fill them twice over.

The earliest gardens that have survived date from the 1670s and 1680s, and were influenced by the emerging styles of the French baroque, but always adapted to Dutch tastes and conditions. Thus, gardens tended to be introspective and not to stretch their vistas over the surrounding countryside. Het Loo is undoubtedly the most important and influential garden to emerge at this time, and a model for Hampton Court in England.

The landscape movement spread quickly from England to the Netherlands. Examples of its earliest manifestations on the mainland of Europe are the gardens of Beeckestijn and Twickel. It was considerably developed in the 19th century by such designers as Jan David Zocher junior (1791–1890), whose romantic vision of an Arcadian landscape filled with exotic plants was immensely popular and produced gardens like Rosendael and De Keukenhof. The German Eduard Petzold, a pupil of Prince Hermann von Pückler-Muskau, was also active in the Netherlands in the latter half of the 19th century. But the revival of the formal garden was as strong

OPPOSITE: Dutch garden owners are skilful creators of shapes and users of colour, as seen at Botanische Vijvertuinen Ada Hofman.

towards the end of the 19th century in the Netherlands as in any other country, and the chief architect was the ubiquitous Frenchman Edouard André, assisted by Hugo Poortman, at such gardens as Warmelo and Weldam in Gelderland. As in England, this romantic reinterpretation of renaissance gardens was accompanied by a greater emphasis upon horticulture and, initially, this meant gardens were planted according to the principles articulated by Gertrude Jekyll. But the ideas of the German Karl Förster also took root, so that the gardens of such designers as Mien Ruys show a trend away from the romantic English style towards a looser style that was more in tune with the surrounding countryside. Piet Oudolf is probably the leading exponent of this style in modern times.

When modern-day Belgium formed part of the Spanish Netherlands, it took its culture from France and the United Provinces rather than Spain. The influence of the Netherlands has always been strong in Flemish-speaking parts and, as a general rule, it is here that horticulture has been strongest and the gardens more frequently modest and introspective. Catholicism, however, kept all Belgians-to-be in touch with the culture of renaissance Rome, so that their earlier gardens often owed as much to Italy as to the Netherlands. Nor were they noted for innovation or quick to follow fashion: the Parc de Bruxelles in 1776 was the last large formal garden laid out in north-west Europe. The bishops of Liège, princes of the Church with vast estates, tended to follow French fashions, as did such families as the Princes de Ligne, who had large landholdings in Hainault. The upshot is that, even before Belgium was cobbled together in 1830, there were two very distinct communities with differing cultural roots – the Flemings and the Walloons. By then there was only one acceptable style of garden design – the rather romantic development of the English landscape garden that used exotic plants, especially conifers and rhododendrons, in a fluid, rolling mixture of grass and woodlands. Old gardens were remade in its likeness, and the landscape style was universally adopted for public parks.

The 19th-century fashion for rock-gardens and winter gardens encouraged the further expansion of horticulture. Belgium produced some of the greatest nurserymen of the day. New technologies enabled Alphonse Balat to build beautiful glasshouses for the Belgian king and nobility. Plants influenced design well into the 20th century. Not until the 1950s did René Pechère emerge as a designer and restorer of formal gardens.

There are no significant gardens in Luxembourg, but horticulture remains strong in both Belgium and the Netherlands. Ghent is the seat of the international garden show, held once every ten years, known as the *Floralies*. The Dutch nursery trade is still the most significant in Europe. Horticultural diversity is guaranteed by national organisations dedicated to the conservation of old cultivars: the *Stichting Nationale Plantencollectie* in the Netherlands and *Vereniging van Botanische Tuinen en Arboreta* (*Association des Jardins Botaniques et Arboreta de Belgique*) in Belgium both maintain National Collections of plants. And the horticultural tradition in these two countries has also bequeathed us an unusually large number of arboreta and plantsman's gardens, like Trompenburg and Kalmthout, many of which grew directly from the activities of an individual nursery.

Spring and early summer are the best seasons for garden visiting: April for bulbs, May for rhododendrons and June for roses.

Gardens of the Netherlands & Belgium

The Netherlands

1 Menkemaborg
2 Hortus Haren
3 Fraeylemaborg
4 Mien Ruys Tuinen
5 Priona Tuinen
6 Botanische Vijvertuinen Ada Hofman
7 Hortus Bulborum
8 Beeckestijn
9 Hortus Botanicus Amsterdam
10 De Keukenhof
11 Hortus Botanicus Leiden
12 Westbroekpark
13 Cultuurtuin Botanische Tuin Delft
14 Arboretum Trompenburg
15 Kasteel de Haar
16 Kasteel-Museum Sypesteyn
17 Botanische Tuinen Utrecht
18 Von Gimborn Arboretum
19 Botanische Tuin Belmonte & Botanische Tuin De Dreijen
20 Paleis Het Loo Nationaal Museum
21 Kasteel Rosendael
22 Kwekerij Piet Oudolf
23 Het Warmelo
24 Kasteel Weldam
25 Kasteel Twickel
26 Jan Boomkamp Tuinen
27 De Tuinen van Appeltern
28 Kasteeltuinen Arcen

Belgium

29 Arboretum Kalmthout
30 Plantentuin Universiteit Gent
31 Nationale Plantentuin van Belgie Domein van Bouchout
32 Serres Royales
33 Parc de Bruxelles & Jardin Botanique de Bruxelles
34 Domein Bokrijk
35 Kasteel Hex
36 Château Beloeil
37 Château d'Enghien
38 Kasteelpark Coloma
39 Mariemont Park
40 Château de Seneffe
41 Château d'Annevoie
42 Les Jardins de Freÿr

THE NETHERLANDS & BELGIUM

★ National Capital
• Cities and Towns
— Major Roads
⓪⓪ Garden

Adjacent Countries

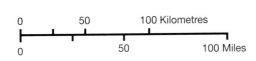

0   50   100 Kilometres

0   50   100 Miles

The gardens at Menkemaborg surround the illustrious moated castle.

THE NETHERLANDS

1. Menkemaborg

Menkemaweg 2
9981 CV Uithuizen

Menkemaborg is a lordly, brick-built water-castle, with black-and-white shutters and a sequence of gardens that have been freely restored as they were in 1705.

The castle is surrounded by a broad, rectangular moat and approached by a single bridge. The edges of the moat are planted with bird cherries (*Prunus padus*) grown as tight-clipped standards; one side has a thick yew hedge with scalloped edges. Rectangular box-edged compartments give an impression of space and order. They are sparingly planted, in the early 18th-century fashion, with garden plants that were widely grown at the time, including roses, irises, paeonies and columbines. The pleasure garden has a trellised pavilion, arbours and arches. A tunnel of pear trees and an orchard of ancient apple cultivars give structure to the kitchen garden, where heritage vegetables and herbs are grown. Modern statues in the 18th-century style are placed throughout the gardens. There is also a maze with an ancient plane tree at its centre.

The whole garden is wonderfully harmonious and restrained – the perfect complement to the castle.

22km NE of Groningen
☎ 0595 431970 **Open** May–Sep daily 10am–5pm; Mar, Apr, Oct–Dec daily (except Mon) 10am–12 noon & 1–4pm
Closed Jan–Feb **Size** 4ha (10ac)
Owner Museum Menkemaborg
🅿 🚻 ♿ 🎁 🖼
🔲 www.menkemaborg.nl
@ menkemaborg@castel.nl

2. Hortus Haren

Kerklaan 34
9751 NN Haren

Hortus Haren is the largest botanic garden in the Netherlands, with an amazing Chinese garden grafted on, but it resembles most closely the great civic gardens of western Germany.

The original garden was laid out in the 1930s to display wild flowers in a natural setting: a meadow, a heath, a swamp, a peatbog, an alpine meadow, several woodland mixes, ditches, damp valleys

ABOVE: One of many entrances to the beautiful and complex Chinese garden at Hortus Haren.
OPPOSITE: Hortus Haren's spectacular Chinese garden is the most extensive in Europe.

and dry slopes. The garden took a more horticultural turn when the glasshouses were built in 1966. They are divided into several climate zones, including tropical mountains (tea-plants, cinnamon and brunfelsias), monsoon areas (rubber trees and tamarinds) and desert lands (the *Yucca aloifolia* dates to 1891). They also include a tropical water lily house for *Victoria cruziana*, an orangery and a house for economic crops, including cassava, peanuts and cotton.

The very fine rock-garden has an impressive number of different habitats. The stone had to be imported: red sandstone from Hanover, hard blue limestone from the Ardennes, red rock from Oland in Sweden, slate from the Eiffel, and soft limestone from Münster. There is also a rather dull Celtic garden and an English garden (not very convincing), subdivided into four rooms – a summer-flowering cottage garden, an old-rose garden, a topiary garden and a herb garden. But, the Chinese Garden (1995), said to be an authentic copy of a Feng Shui garden from the Ming Dynasty, is stunning. It is very large and filled with every component in the vocabulary of Chinese gardening: a long, zig-zagging, covered walk, meandering pathways, tea houses, small pavilions, bonsai, rock-gardens and beautiful flowering plants that rather overwhelm the structure.

You need a long time to find your way around and see every part from every intended angle, but it is worth the effort; there is nothing so extensive, complex and beautiful outside China itself.

4km SE of Groningen
☎ 0505 370053 **Open** Daily
9.30am–5pm **Size** 20ha (50ac)
Owner Stichting Behoud
Groene Hortus
🅿 💬 🚾 ♿
🔲 www.hortusharen.nl
@ info@hortusharen.nl

3. Fraeylemaborg

Hoofdweg 30
9621 AL Slochteren

The garden at Fraeylemaborg is a wonderful example of how formal gardens were adapted and lost in response to the English landscape movement. Fraeylemaborg itself is a handsome water-castle – mainly stone-built, moated, and more ornamental than military – but almost nothing remains of its French-style baroque garden laid out by Henric Piccardt, a friend of William III, in the 1690s.

The garden was landscaped in the 1820s by Lucas Pieters Roodbaard, then a fashionable architect in Friesland, who gave the formal pools a natural, irregular outline and replaced the *allées* by curving paths and a series of glades that run down the long, thin site for 1.5 km. But the eye is still drawn down the central axis, and from time to time you encounter a statue or a small pond in the shape of a clover leaf that escaped the moderniser's hand in the 19th century. The walk from glade to glade, past rustic bridges and fine trees, is a simple delight at every season. Some slightly surprising modern sculptures will accompany you on the way, and there is a vast, spreading walnut tree (*Juglans nigra*), leaning at a perilous angle just beyond the moat.

19km E of Groningen
☎ 0598 421568 **Open** Daily
dawn–dusk **Size** 26ha (65ac)
Owner Gerrit van Houten
Stichting
🅿 🍴 🚾 ♿ 🎁 🖼
🔲 www.fraeylemaborg.nl
@ info@fraeylemaborg.nl

Fraeylemabourg's gardens were landscaped in the 19th century; some arresting installations have recently been added.

The older compartments at Mien Ruys's gardens were very influential and have now been declared National Monuments.

Border, for example), others to specific types of plants like the Mixed Border and Herb Garden, and others still to special effects, like the Yellow Garden. But the result is one of the most stimulating and varied gardens in western Europe.

30km NE of Zwolle **C** 0523 614774
Open Apr–Oct daily (except Mon) 10am–5pm (opens 1pm Sun)
Size 2ha (5ac) **Owner** Stichting Tuinen Mien Ruys
🅿 🖪 WC ♿ 🚻
W www.mienruys.nl
@ tuinen@mienruys.nl

4. Mien Ruys Tuinen
Moerheimstraat 78
7701 CG Dedemsvaart

Mien Ruys (1903–99) dominates the story of 20th-century gardens and gardening in the Netherlands. Her father was a famous nurseryman (he raised *Helenium* 'Moerheim Beauty') who encouraged her to study in Berlin and southern England. Ruys returned with a sound understanding of how Gertrude Jekyll and Karl Förster used plants in the garden. Herbaceous plants became her main interest, and she was a major influence on such designers as James van Sweden, who brought new landscaping styles into the US.

Ruys began experimenting in her parents' garden in 1924: the lavishly planted Wild Garden was followed in 1927 by the Old Experimental Garden, based on English borders. The garden now contains some 25 different areas, each with a distinct character, but many have been added since her death. Some are dedicated to habitats (the Water Garden and the Sun

5. Priona Tuinen
Schuineslootweg 13
7777 RE Schuinesloot

Priona Tuinen is one of the leading 'natural' gardens in the Netherlands. If you have old-fashioned views about what constitutes a weed, then this is not the place for you. Henk Gerritsen and Anton Schlepers were inspired initially (in 1978) by the gardens of Mien Ruys and Piet Oudolf, but went on to develop a series of gardens that challenges our preconceptions about what plants to grow, and *how*.

Priona Tuinen: anarchic topiary is one of many original and charming features in this important garden.

Ada Hofman's inventive combinations of shape, colour and water is typical of her Botanische Vijvertuinen.

Weeds or wildflowers? Priona Tuinen's flower meadow is mown to enable such weeds as rose-bay willowherb and sorrel to establish themselves among the species that were actually planted – *Symphytum caucasicum*, *Geranium pratense* and *Campanula rapunculus*. Old-fashioned flowers in the Cottage Garden are combined with weedy wild flowers, while the Long Border (35 m) appears for much of the year to have been planted for minimum maintenance: however, it comes into flower late in the season when the weeds and grass are hidden by well-chosen flowering plants. The vegetables in the Vegetable Garden have gone to seed – parsnips, salsify, leeks, carrots and cabbages are all encouraged to flower. And the garden bulges with surreal ornaments and cheeky topiary, perilously close to kitsch.

Henk Gerritsen (Anton Schlepers died of Aids in 1993) is, however, a control freak. He is quite clear about his driving principle: the wilder the planting, the greater the need for strong design if the result is still to be considered a garden. His hedges are crisp and structural, the paths are immaculately mown and swept, and every feature is a model of ecological integrity.

2km N of Slagharen **C** 0523 681734 **Open** May–Sep Thu–Sat 10am–5pm; Sun 2–6pm **Size** 1.5ha (4ac) **Owner** Stichting Priona Tuinen

P **⊡** **WC** **&** **♿**

W www.prionatuinen.com

6. Botanische Vijvertuinen Ada Hofman
Westeindigerdijk 3
7778 HG Loozen Gramsbergen

Ada Hofman has built up the largest, most complex series of water gardens in the Netherlands: 30 gardens, 50 ponds and 3000 different taxa. All have been made, with enormous vigour and creativity, since 1987. The ponds are of differing sizes, aspects and depth; at their heart are three larger pools. Plantings are often reflected in the water – so is the sky – which makes the gardens appear spacious, colourful and bathed in light. Fountains and sculptures, even a topiary dolphin leaping through a hoop, provide focal points.

Between the pools are many other inventive features: glittering rock-gardens made from blocks of glass, a Japanese garden, and a Chinese garden (complete with pond) on the roof of Ada Hofman's own house. There is an unusually varied choice of materials – this is an immensely colourful and *busy* garden – and many trees and shrubs have been cut or trained into unusual shapes.

This life-sized sculpture portrays her husband helping Ada Hofman from the lake after a planting session at her Botanische Vijvertuinen.

All is organically managed – the water is usually beautifully clear – and there is therefore lots of wildlife: fish, frogs, newts and salamanders, as well as insects and birds. This is surely the most ingenious and instructive modern garden in the Netherlands.

4km E of Hardenberg
☎ 0524 562448 **Open** Apr–Oct daily (except Mon) 10am–5pm **Size** 2.5ha (6ac) **Owner** Ada Hofman
🅿 ☐ 🆆🅲 ♿ ☂
🆆 www.adahofman.nl
@ vijvertuin@adahofman.nl

7. Hortus Bulborum
Zuidkerkenlaan 23A
1906 AC Limmen

The Hortus Bulborum was founded in 1928 for the conservation of historic bulbs: it now harbours more than 3500 cultivars of hyacinths, crocuses, irises, fritillarias and, especially, daffodils and tulips. The oldest date back to the 16th century, and several can be identified from 17th-century paintings, but perhaps the most flamboyant and fascinating are the mid-20th century tulips, which show an immense variety in their colours and shapes.

All the bulbs are grown in small, square blocks on the flat, sandy site, and tend to be dead-headed, in the Dutch manner, just as they seem to be reaching the peak of their splendour. It is fascinating, even if you know nothing about bulbs, to walk up and down between the blocks and study the ones that catch your eye. You leave mesmerised by their beauty and diversity, and with long lists of cultivars you would like to grow yourself, if only you could find them commercially. The garden does sell a few surplus bulbs every year, but gives priority to those who are restoring period gardens.

9km S of Alkmaar ☎ 0251 231286 **Open** 6Apr–16May daily 10am–5pm (opens 12pm Sun) **Size** 1.5ha (4ac) **Owner** Stichting Hortus Bulborum 🅿 ☐ 🆆🅲 ♿ ☂
🆆 www.hortus-bulborum.nl
@ info@hortus-bulborum.nl

8. Beeckestijn
Rijksweg 136
1981 LD Velsen-Zuid

Beeckestijn is an important historic garden, lightly restored in the 1960s and again in the 1990s. The house is baroque and fairly sober, with a few rococo frills, and is surrounded by excellent formal gardens dating from about 1720.

Formal box-edged beds line the turning circle in front and are filled with colourful bedding. The main gardens, however, are on either side, with a variety of geometric layouts, including serpentine walls for fruit growing, a herb garden, an orchard and pots of tender plants put out for the summer. The main axis leads away behind the house between double lime avenues punctuated by white statues on plinths, until you come to a formal *bassin*, fountain and a cross-avenue.

The serpentine walks in the woodland are part of the landscape garden, designed by Johann Georg Michael in the early 1770s and one of the first in the Netherlands. Here, too,

Hortus Bulborum is a living museum of the history of bulbs, especially Dutch tulips.

The modern gardens at Beeckestijn have been designed and planted in the baroque style.

are the ice house, a gothic ruin and a hermitage. It is all very calm, spacious and stylish.

4km N of Haarlem 0255 567200 **Open** Daily dawn–dusk **Size** 18ha (44acres) **Owner** Museum Beeckestijn Gesloten
www.beeckestijn.nl
museum@beeckestijn.nl

9. Hortus Botanicus Amsterdam

Plantage Middenlaan 2a
1018 DD Amsterdam

Amsterdam's botanic garden is one of the smallest, oldest and neatest in the world; it is also very enjoyable to visit. It was founded as a medicinal herb garden in 1638 and now crams over 6000 plants into its tiny compass. It still has a good herb garden, with a fine fig tree (*Ficus carica*) in the centre, but the emphasis now is more upon conservation and education.

The habitat plantings include a bed devoted to plants from the sandy dunes of northern Holland. There is a magnificent *Quercus* × *turneri* near the entrance; elsewhere are good specimens of *Platanus* × *hispanica* and *Ginkgo biloba*. The systematic beds are laid out in a semicircle, installed in 1863, but now arranged according to molecular systematics. *Firmiana simplex* and *Eriobotrya japonica* flourish against the wall of the laboratory.

There is a fine range of glasshouses, which shelter (among many other good plants) an important collection of South African cycads. These include *Encephalartos woodii* (grown from offsets from the only plant of this species ever found – a male form) and a specimen of *E. altensteinii*, brought from the Eastern Cape some 300 years ago (which puts it among the oldest pot plants in the world). This is also the first garden in the Netherlands to acquire the Australian living fossil tree, *Wollemia nobilis*.

Carnivorous *Sarracenia* species grow outside and flower at Hortus Botanicus Amsterdam.

In old city centre, SE side 020 6259021 **Open** Daily 9am–5pm (10am weekends) **Closes** 4pm Dec–Jan & 9pm Jul–Aug **Size** 1.2ha (3ac) **Owner** Universiteit van Amsterdam
www.hortus-botanicus.nl
info@dehortus.nl

10. De Keukenhof

Stationsweg 166a
2161 AM Lisse

Keukenhof is probably the best known garden in the Netherlands: it is undoubtedly the most visited during its short season of opening. Even though some 700 000 visitors pass through its gates in spring, the magnificence of the floral displays distracts you completely, and it is not difficult, for example, to take photographs without people invading the frame.

Keukenhof is a show-garden for the Dutch bulb industry

No garden is so colourful or intensely visited during its spring season as De Keukenhof.

and has been on this site since 1949. The park was landscaped in 1840 by Jan David Zocher junior, whose woodlands, glades and lake set off the bulbs so well. The way to visit it is to wander wherever the fancy leads you, letting yourself be drawn by the vast, free-style sweeps of colour. There are set-pieces like the river of blue *Muscari*, but most of the garden is large scale, abstract and brilliantly coloured. The standard of maintenance is exceptional, even by Dutch standards, and you cannot fail to find your visit an uplifting and enjoyable experience.

20km S of Haarlem **C** 0252 465 555 **Open** Usually last week in Mar–mid-May (*see* website) **Size** 32ha (79ac) **Owner** Koninklijke Algemeene Vereeniging voor Bloembollencultuur
P **⊞** **❚❙** **WC** **⛎** **⛉** **⚑**
W www.keukenhof.nl
@ info@keukenhof.nl

11. Hortus Botanicus Leiden

Rapenburg 73
2300 RA Leiden

Leiden has the oldest university in the Netherlands (1575) and the oldest botanic garden laid out by Carolus Clusius in 1593. The *Laburnum anagyroides* that Clusius planted in 1600 still survives. Later on, Philipp von Siebold and the great Linnaeus himself also worked here. Much of the garden has been restored in recent years to celebrate these historic antecedents.

The entrance garden, with a tulip tree (*Liriodendron tulipifera*) planted in 1682, is based on a map of 1739. The Clusius Garden has the four simple beds of its original 16th-century design, subdivided into further rectangles. The von Siebold memorial garden is Japanese in style and combines a structure of stones and gravel with western-style plantings of Japanese plants. Plants come first, and the long, thin garden manages to display more than 15 000 taxa. The collection of *Paeonia* species is extensive, and the fern garden is shaded by a dozen ancient arboresent honeysuckles (*Lonicera maackii*). Fine trees include *Pinus nigra, Pterocarya fraxinifolia, Diospyros lotus*, two large *Zelkova serrata* and a line of ancient oaks along the canal that runs from end to end of the garden. In the Winter Garden are cycads and lithops from southern Africa and insectivorous plants from the Dutch East Indies. *Victoria amazonica* has a house to itself: its cast-iron arches copy the rib pattern of the plant's leaves,

Primula pulverulenta and *Iris pseudacorus* flourish in a boggy patch at Hortus Botanicus Leiden.

Westbroekpark is known for its impressive plantings of rhododendrons and roses.

and the roof sports a gold-plated crown. The French architect Daniel Marot built the orangery in the 1740s. Some 250 plants are put out in pots for the summer, including olives, lemons, oleanders, brugmansias, plumbago and callistemons.

In old city centre, SW corner **C** 071 527 7249 **Open** Apr–Oct daily 10am–6pm; Nov–Mar daily 10am–4pm (except Sat) **Size** 2.6ha (6ac) **Owner** Universiteit Leiden
P ▪ ⊓ WC ⅃ ⊞
W www.hortus.leidenuniv.nl
@ hortus@hortus.leidenuniv.nl

12. Westbroekpark
Kapelweg
2587 BK Scheveningen

Westbroekpark was named after the garden director Pieter Westbroek, who first laid it out in the 1920s. Ignore the mini-golf course and the boating on the lake: the park has a fluid English landscape style, planted with fine shrub borders, handsome ornamental trees, superb rhododendrons and good bedding.

At the garden's heart is the best public rose garden in the Netherlands, first planted in 1960 and now the seat of the Dutch international rose trials. Here are some 20 000 roses,

planted for the main part in the 1960s style, with 50 or 100 plants of one rose cultivar massed in oblong or triangular beds cut out of the turf. It is an impressive sight when the roses' first flowering is at its height in early July.

The horticultural content has recently been doubled by making Westbroekpark the national hardy-plant garden, which means that a vast array of herbaceous plants now surrounds the display of roses.

East end of Scheveningen, towards Den Haag **C** 070 350 28 63 **Open** Daily dawn–dusk **Size** 18ha (45ac) **Owner** City of Den Haag
WC ▪ ⊓ ⅃
W www.denhaag.nl/westbroekpark/

13. Cultuurtuin Botanische Tuin
Julianalaan 67
2628 BC Delft

Delft's botanic garden is not historic – it was founded in 1917 – but it is full of interest to plant lovers. It has 7000 different taxa, of which 2000 grow in the glasshouses. The garden also has ten National Collections: Cannaceae, Cercidiphyllaceae, Eucommiaceae, Hamamelidaceae, *Lavandula*, Marantaceae, Musaceae, Platanaceae, Theaceae and Zingiberaceae. For non-botanists this means that the garden has some very interesting and beautiful

Plants are put out for the summer against a glasshouse wall at Cultuurtuin Botanische Tuin, Delft.

Arboretum Trompenburg has extensive collections of plants of all kinds and is immaculately maintained.

ornamental plants, including lavender, cannas, bananas, ginger plants and witch hazels.

The arboretum has a fine *Pinus wallichiana*, a very tall *Acer campestre* and a *Crataegus monogyna*, which (grown as a tree) reaches 20 m. The glasshouses specialise in plants from the Dutch East Indies but also have collections of cacti and orchids. One of the houses has a pool for *Victoria cruziana*. Field horsetail (*Equisetum arvense*) and Japanese knotweed (*Fallopia japonica*) are problem plants in parts of the garden.

On SE edge of old city centre
☎ 015 2782356 **Open** Mon–Fri 8.30am–5pm; Sat 10am–3pm; & Sun 12–4pm (Jun–Aug only) **Size** 2.5ha (6ac) **Owner** Technische Universiteit Delft
🚻 ♿
🕸 www.tnw.tudelft.nl
@ botanischetuin@tnw.tudelft.nl

14. Arboretum Trompenburg
Honingerdijk 86
3062 NX Rotterdam

Arboretum Trompenburg started life in 1857 on the edge of Rotterdam as the country retreat of the Smith family. Jan David Zocher junior helped with the lay out.

Some fine ashes, a *Thuja plicata* and *Taxodium distichum* date from these early days, followed shortly thereafter by *Gymnocladus dioica, Pterocarya fraxinifolia* and *Fraxinus xanthoxyloides* var. *dumosa*.

Trompenburg grew to its present size and importance after James van Hoey Smith took over in the 1920s; enthusiasm and a passionate interest in trees continues to this day under the guidance of his son, Dick van Hoey Smith.

Trompenburg is not a large arboretum, but takes its place among the world's best for the extraordinary richness of its collections: its five National Collections are *Fagus, Hosta, Quercus, Rodgersia* and *Rhododendron*, which include some 100 *Fagus*, 750 *Hosta* and 300 different *Quercus*. *Fagus sylvatica* 'Aurea Pendula' and *Acer palmatum* 'Asahi-zuru' are outstanding in late spring and *Yucca filamentosa* is grown as groundcover underneath *Cedrus atlantica*. The plantings are so colourful and varied that Trompenburg does not appear as being principally an arboretum – just a garden of exceptional beauty with a fascinating collection of very rare plants.

The layout, too, is charming, with a large number of white-painted bridges over the

canals. *Acer palmatum* 'Trompenburg' is well known, but Dick van Hoey Smith has also been responsible for introducing 12 new cultivars of beech and 10 of oak. And Trompenburg also boasts a good pinetum (150 *Chamaecyparis*), a rose garden, a heather garden, hundreds of rhododendrons, a patch of *Aesculus parviflora* 40 m long, massed displays of bulbs and an extensive collection of cacti and succulents under glass. Maintenance is of the highest standard.

2km E of old city centre
☎ 010 2330166 **Open** Mon–Fri 9am–5pm; weekends 10am–4pm (but **closed** Sun Nov–Mar) **Size** 6ha (15ac) **Owner** Stichting Arboretum Trompenburg
🚻 💼 ♿
🕸 www.trompenburg.nl
@ arboretum@trompenburg.nl

15. Kasteel de Haar
Kasteellaan 1
3455 RR Haarzuilens

De Haar is a stunning late-mediaeval castle. It was completely revamped in the neo-gothic style between 1892 and 1912 by Baron Etienne van Zuylen, who had the good fortune to marry a Rothschild heiress. It was her money that paid for the opulent (and very beautiful) castle and for the new gardens. Their landscape architect was the fashionable Henri Copijn, who began by removing the entire village of Haarzuilens and re-siting it 1.5 km to the west. Then he laid out the fine formal gardens in the baroque style: box-edged broderies, a rose garden, a 'Roman' canal and a very grand canal garden. He also built a vast kitchen garden. Clipped yews lead out into the park, which Copijn remodelled in the 19th-century idiom – gently curving paths, groves and glades, pools and lakes, picturesque bridges, aviaries and a deer park. True to the Rothschild tradition, he imported 7000 40-year-old trees from all over the province of Utrecht to give instant maturity to the plantings.

12km W of Utrecht ☏ 030 6778515
Open Daily (except Mon) 10am–5pm
Size 100ha (247ac) **Owner** Van Zuylen family
🅿 🖪 🆆 ♿ 🚻 🖼
🆆 www.kasteeldehaar.nl
@ informatie@kasteeldehaar.nl

16. Kasteel-Museum Sypesteyn

Nieuw Loosdrechtsedijk 150
1231 LC Loosdrecht

Sypesteyn was the fantastic creation of Jonkheer C.H.C.A. van Sypesteyn (1857–1937) and probably the last castle to be built in the Netherlands. Van Sypesteyn was convinced that his family had once owned a castle here, and he set to re-creating it from about 1910 onwards. He had already written a book about old Dutch gardens, in which he insisted that gardens should be simple and noble (based on a historic symbiosis of house and garden) and devoid of picturesque landscape effects. So he laid out his grounds as they might have been in about 1600, with a formal garden on the same island as the castle – a simple pattern of box parterres enclosed by hornbeam hedges and pleached limes.

The formal garden at Kasteel-Museum Sypesteyn is a fine example of early 20th-century historical reconstruction.

Over the moat are a number of anachronistic trees (including *Davidia involucrata*, which was not introduced from China until the 20th century), a small topiary garden and plantings of astilbes and hostas. A slender *patte-d'oie* leads out into the woods, where the purple rhododendrons are pretty in late spring.

22km NW of Utrecht
☏ 035 5823208 **Open** May–Sep daily (except Mon & Fri) 10am–5pm & weekends only Apr & Oct (opens 12 noon weekends)
Size 5ha (12½ac) **Owner** Stichting Kasteel-Museum Sypesteyn
🅿 🖪 🆆 ♿ 🚻 🖼
🆆 www.sypesteyn.nl
@ info@sypesteyn.nl

17. Botanische Tuinen Utrecht

Harvardlaan 2
3584 CV Utrecht

Utrecht's botanic garden is on the post-war, out-of-town campus of the university, but occupies an extraordinary military bastion known as Fort Hoofddijk, part of a complex system of military defences last renewed in the 1880s. The garden dates to 1963, and the stony ruins were quickly transformed into a vast rock-garden. It is one of the best in the world and alone worth the journey to see.

The garden's numerous habitats include peat gardens, extensive woodland areas, a swamp speckled with cotton

Botanische Tuinen Utrecht's enormous rock-garden, with its vast collection of plants, was made from the ruins of Utrecht's ancient fortifications.

Handsome conifers and the extensive collection of rhododendrons are typical of the plantings at Von Gimborn Arboretum.

grass, and a series of rock-faces thickly covered by ramondas and haberleas. The other collections were moved here from the old site in central Utrecht, including the systematic beds (though the trendy hexagonal 1960s design looks rather tired now) and a collection of native plants. The most recent addition has been the Theme Gardens, a 1990s miscellany of the hip and the charming. They include a meadow garden, a Japanese garden, a fine display of annuals, a garden of religion and a vampire garden.

The glasshouses make a speciality of South American plants, especially Bromeliaceae, Orchidaceae, Costaceae, Annonaceae and the flora of Suriname. The 6500 taxa include National Collections of Crassulaceae, *Arisaema*, *Arisarum*, *Trillium* and *Penstemon*.

4km NE of city centre
C 030 2535455 **Open** Mar–Dec daily 10am–4pm **Closes** 5pm May–Sep **Size** 8ha (20ac) **Owner** Universiteit Utrecht **P 🍴 WC ♿ 🏛**
W www.bio.uu.nl/bottuinen
@ botgard@bio.uu.nl

18. Von Gimborn Arboretum

Velpereng
3940 Doorn

Max von Gimborn was a rich ink-manufacturer with a passion for trees.

He started planting the eponymous arboretum in 1924 and the University of Utrecht took over two years after his death in 1964. Conifers were von Gimborn's main interest, and the holotype plants of *Pinus pumila* 'Globe' and *Chamaecyparis lawsoniana* 'Gimbornii' are among the trees still growing here.

The arboretum was landscaped by a Dutchman called Gerard Bleeker and the plantings, though basically systematic, are graded for decorative effect. The conifers, in particular, are sensitively used to create both mass and attractive combinations. Autumn colour, especially from the maples, is excellent,

and the *Hamamelis* give a good display in winter.

The arboretum has seven National Collections: *Euonymus*, *Fraxinus*, *Laburnum*, *Magnolia*, *Rhododendron*, *Syringa* and *Tsuga*. The *Tsuga* Collection is uniquely fascinating, because of the large number of selected cultivars and the sheer size and beauty of the mature specimens. It is worth walking right to the end of the arboretum to see them, especially in late spring when the main rhododendron collection is in flower nearby.

23km E of Utrecht, between Driebergen & Doorn **C** 0343 412144
Open All year Mon–Fri 8.30am–4pm; weekends 10am–4pm (5pm May–Sep) **Size** 27ha (67ac)
Owner Universiteit Utrecht
P 🔲 WC ♿
W www.bio.uu.nl/bottuinen
@ botgard@bio.uu.nl

19. Botanische Tuin Belmonte & Botanische Tuin De Dreijen

Generaal Foulkesweg
6703 DS Wageningen

These two gardens belong to the University of Wageningen and both are on Generaal Foulkesweg – Belmonte at 94 and De Dreijen at 37.

Wageningen is the centre of excellence for Dutch

Palms and cycads are put out in summer in Botanische Tuin Belmonte and Botanische Tuin De Dreijen – two great gardens of trees, shrubs and hardy plants.

The baroque gardens at the royal palace of Het Loo are the grandest in the Netherlands.

horticultural education, and both gardens have outstanding plant collections. They have no less than 19 National Collections between them, including *Aesculus*, Caprifoliaceae, *Catalpa, Cornus, Deutzia, Hosta, Hydrangea, Philadelphus, Rhododendron* and Rosaceae.

Belmonte surrounds a hill, from which there are fine views of the Rhine and the garden itself. It has belonged to the university since 1951. Its two outstanding ornamental collections are of maples (dazzling in autumn) and the Rosaceae. The latter includes many rare cultivars of Japanese cherry and a great number of *Malus* species and cultivars. But the magnolias and the rhododendron and azalea walks are also first-rate, and there is some adventurous underplanting with wildflower meadow mixes.

De Dreijen is older and has belonged to the university, then the National Horticultural School, since 1896. Its systematic beds have an unusually comprehensive and interesting display of shrubs and herbaceous plants, including lilacs, weigelas, hostas, wisterias, hydrangeas and asters. The rose garden displays over 600 cultivars of every kind, and the fine mature trees include a handsome specimen of the seldom-seen *Juglans ailanthifolia* var. *cordiformis*.

On SE edge of Wageningen
☎ 0317 483182 **Open** Daily dawn–dusk **Size** 17ha (42ac) and 6.5ha (16ac) **Owner** Wageningen Universiteit 🅿 🚾 ♿
🆆 www2.wur.nl/botanische_tuinen
@ Henk.deLeeuw@wur.nl

20. Paleis Het Loo Nationaal Museum
Koninklijk Park 1
7315 JA Apeldoorn

Het Loo is the grandest historic garden in the Netherlands. Prince William III of Orange bought the site in 1684 and started building in the following year. He expanded it considerably in the 1690s, after he became king of England and had access to English money.

Het Loo then passed to his successors as Stadtholders and kings of Holland, until Queen Wilhelmina bequeathed it to the nation in 1962. It had by then been entirely converted to the English landscape style, but the decision was taken in 1970 to restore much of the garden to its original 1690s format.

Het Loo is *not* the Dutch Versailles. No attempt was made to extend its lines into the distant countryside: it was intended as an expression of princely self-respect, not of regal power. Nevertheless, the architect was the Frenchman Daniel Marot and the layout is in some ways French-inspired – symmetry, strong axes, elaborate parterres, hornbeam tunnels, fountains, *bassins* and statues. But it is surrounded, like Hampton Court, by raised walks in the renaissance manner, and hidden from public view.

The sunken Great Garden centres on a splendid fountain of Venus, surrounded by eight parterres with extremely elaborate patterns. Only their edges are planted (rather sparsely) in the 17th-century manner with such period plants as fritillaries, tulips, paeonies and *Rosa gallica* 'Versicolor'. Fountains fill the main cross-axis: the two modern globe fountains are especially striking (one of the world; the other of the skies) and lead to massive Italian-style cascades at the edge, where water spills down from the surrounding walks. Statues, urns and balustrading supply the ornament.

The rest of the garden has been more lightly restored but it is worth climbing the semicircular colonnade at the furthest end to look down on the King's Fountain with huge pots of billbergias around its edge. Versailles cases with tender plants (not just orange trees) add interest here and in the two gardens at the sides of the palace, known respectively as the King's Garden and the Queen's Garden.

What cannot be conveyed by words, but is clear from photographs, is the perfect union between the sober house and the orderly garden – and the thrill you get from walking in it.

4km NW of Apeldoorn
☎ 055 5772400 **Open** Daily (except Mon) **Size** 30ha (74ac)
Owner The State
🅿 🚗 🍴 🚾 ♿ 🏛 🎫
Ⓦ www.paleishetloo.nl
@ info@paleishetloo.nl

21. Kasteel Rosendael

Rosendael 1
6891 DA Rozendaal

The gardens at Kasteel Rosendaeal were begun in the 1660s and improved by Baron Lubbert Torck in the 1720s: baroque at first, but with some rococo added on. The royal architect Daniel Marot advised on the changes and helped to install the shell gallery, shell grotto, gazebo, trick fountains, cascade and formal star-shaped wood. The formal gardens disappeared when the landscape movement took hold and Jan David Zocher junior designed the splendid English-style park in 1836.

The rococo architectural features were, however, never removed so that, when the castle passed to the *Stichting Het Geldersch Landschap* on the death of the last Torck in 1978, there was every possibility of restoring them. In fact, the shell gallery had already been repaired in 1972, the park followed in the 1980s, and the orangery, grotto and trick fountains in the 1990s. The shell gallery is the real sensation: a semicircular wall with niches, fountains, benches and a pavilion, all intricately and exuberantly patterned with shells, stones and coloured glass. Bright ribbons of bedding plants curve through the grass that

runs down to the lake, but the rose garden and the rhododendrons are also stunning. All is maintained to a very high standard: visitor satisfaction is guaranteed.

5km NE of Arnhem ☎ 026 3644645
Open Mid-Apr–Oct daily (except Mon) 11am–5pm **Size** 45ha (111ac)
Owner Stichting Het Geldersch Landschap 🅿 🚗 🍴 🚾 ♿ 🏛
Ⓦ www.mooigelderland.nl

22. Kwekerij Piet Oudolf

Broekstratt 17
6999 DE Hummelo

Piet Oudolf claims to be the founder of New Wave planting, an extension of the German school of planting developed by Karl Förster in Potsdam. His designs have won great acclaim in western Europe and the US for his use of perennials in a natural way. 'Natural' is an important word to describe his work: his plantings take their inspiration from nature, and the plants must therefore look spontaneous, though assembled with artistic skill.

The private garden attached to his nursery exemplifies his approach. The design is firmly structured, with clean paths of brick and stone, and beds edged with the same materials. Hedges give mass and create enclosure, but there is a stunning group of short hedges cut at an angle and others cut into billowing, cloud-like shapes. All the borders, each so differently planted, have hedges as a background.

Structural considerations apply also to plants: shape and texture are more important than the transient flowers. Oudolf likes plants to grow into each other in imitation of nature. Ornamental grasses are much in evidence. The garden is *extremely* well designed but planted within a rather narrow definition, and you may come away thinking it a pity that he doesn't use shrubs, roses and climbers, too. There is an austerity here that some visitors may not sympathise with.

The house, rose garden, lake, baroque garden, shell grotto and landscaped park are all visible in this picture of Kasteel Rosendael.

Piet Oudolf's mastery of contrasting textures is well displayed in his own garden, where abstract plantings are contained within firm but unusual geometric frames.

9km NW of Doetinchem
☎ 0314 381120 **Open** Jun & Aug
(closed Jul) daily (except Mon)
10am–4 pm **Size** 1ha (2½ac)
Owner Piet & Anja Oudolf
🅿 🚾 ♿ 👶
W www.oudolf.com

23. Het Warmelo

Stedeke 11
7478 RV Diepenheim

Het Warmelo is a pretty manor house with a wonderful series of gardens from different periods. It is popular with visitors, partly because its owner in the 1950s and 1960s was Prince Bernhard of the Netherlands.

The oldest part is the English-style landscaped park from which there are ravishing views of the house across a lake, canal and moat. Next came the 19th-century pinetum, replanted 100 years later for ornamental effect by Prince Bernhard's mother. But the best feature is the formal gardens (clipped topiary and an elegant pool – all very rococo), designed for Baroness Creutz in the 1920s by Hugo Poortman; it was the Baroness who really made Het Warmelo what we see today.

Elsewhere are splendid plantings of rhododendrons and azaleas, a baroque rose garden, a 'well' garden with two rills, and a garden room, hedged in yew, with a large fuchsia collection (350 cultivars, 3000 plants).

7km SW of Goor ☎ 0547 351280
Open May–mid-Oct Tue &
Thu 1.30–5pm; & (May only)
Sun 10am–5pm **Size** 7ha (17ac)
Owner Avenarius family 🅿 🚗 🚾 ♿
W www.kasteelwarmelo.nl
@ warmelo@worldonline.nl

24. Kasteel Weldam

Diepenheimseweg 114
7475 MN Markelo

The garden at Weldam is a fine example of late 19th-century historical restoration – a romantic re-interpretation of a classical 17th-century Dutch design. It was laid out in the 1880s after a plan by the Frenchman Edouard André, who gave the job to his young pupil, Hugo Poortman; the moated house was revamped at about the same time.

Most of the garden was put to formal shapes: yew and box, cut as elaborate parterres, with cones and bobbles to give vertical emphasis. The intricate *parterres de broderie* are especially fine. Orange trees (a powerful symbol of Dutch identity) are put out for the summer in *caisses de Versailles*. Other features include a maze (replanted in 1999) and a 145-m long beech tunnel. André's make-over worked around some of the larger trees that had been planted either when the garden was landscaped or when the craze for conifers hit the Netherlands in the 1840s. So there are also fine specimens of such trees as *Pinus cembra* and *Taxodium distichum* to enjoy. And the 1890s saw the addition of a rose garden and lots of rhododendrons, which brighten up the garden for much of the year.

The baroque pool and topiary at Het Warmelo date to the 1880s.

2km W of Goor ☏ 0547 361533
Open All year, Mon–Sat 9am–
4.30pm **Size** 4.5ha (11ac) **Owner**
zu Solms-Sonnenwalde family
🅿 🚻 ♿ 🏛 ▦
🆆 www.weldam.nl

25. Kasteel Twickel

Twickelerlaan 7
7495 VG Ambt Delden

The gardens at Twickel have much in common with Weldam – they belonged until recently to the same family, though the brick-built castle, surrounded by a rectangular moat, is much larger. The formal gardens fill an area between the moat and a handsome orangery (1833), with parterres designed by Hugo Poortman in the early 1900s surrounding a simple round pool. Ancient orange trees and many other tender plants are put out here for the summer. To the sides are further formal gardens with box-edged enclosures planted with bulbs and seasonal bedding, and some very fine topiary.

Even more enjoyable is the landscaped park beyond, one of the oldest in the Netherlands. It was begun in the 1790s, re-made by Jan David Zocher junior in the 1830s and improved by the German Eduard Petzold in the 1880s. Many of the established trees date to the 19th century.

But what makes Twickel outstanding is the input of Countess Marie van Heeckeren van Aldenburg Bentinck (1879–1975) from 1922 onwards. She was a plantswoman in the English manner and planted ornamental trees and shrubs throughout the park. Rhododendrons now frame the views of the castle across the lake and there are fine mixed borders within the light oak woodland. *Iris sibirica* has naturalised in the meadows.

2km N of Delden ☏ 0743 761020
Open May–Oct Tue–Sat
Owner Stichting Twickel
🅿 🚻 ♿ 🏛 ▦
🆆 www.twickel.nl
📧 info@twickel.nl

This lake is only one of more than fifty model gardens at Jan Boomkamp Tuinen.

26. Jan Boomkamp Tuinen

Hesselerweg 9
7623 AC Borne

There are over 50 model gardens at Boomkamp's garden centre, which has one of the largest displays of plants for sale in Europe. Every imaginable style is offered, ancient or modern, European or exotic, and the standards of workmanship and maintenance are enviable.

The English garden has herbaceous plantings in the Jekyll style; the French garden is quiet and formal, with splendid yew topiary. There are water gardens, a butterfly garden, a rose garden, a shade garden, a roof garden, conservatories, a Japanese garden, and an ever-changing exhibition of garden sculpture. In short, there is something for everyone, though you will inevitably see gardens that are not to your taste.

2km SE of Borne ☏ 074 2664181
Open Daily 10am–5pm **Size** 6ha
(15ac) 🅿 🍴 🚻 ♿ 🏛 ♿
🆆 www.boomkamp.com
📧 gardens@boomkamp.com

27. De Tuinen van Appeltern

Walstraat 2a
6629 AD Appeltern

This is the biggest and best assembly of show gardens in Europe – some 180 of them.

Nothing is for sale (though there are cafés and restaurants along the way) and there are no grand vistas or dominant themes. What makes the garden exceptional is the way that designers, nurseries and suppliers of materials all contribute their skills and products. Everything is labelled, and the name of the contributor noted.

The gardens aim to inspire, but also to inform and empower visitors to make or develop their own garden. Every style is represented but every design is self-contained and can be studied in detail. The exhibits vary in size from a tiny balcony garden to large water gardens – as always in the Netherlands, water is everywhere, but in many different forms.

The only way to visit the gardens is to wander round, looking at everything and noting what you like – it may be a combination of plants, a new material for surfacing paths, a detail of a Japanese garden or the layout of a vegetable garden. It is hard to imagine a more varied and inspirational place for garden lovers to visit (although you may not like everything you see). And the standard of maintenance is excellent. There is only one grudge – a long walk from the car park to the entrance.

This dolomitic rock-garden is one of 180 show gardens at De Tuinen van Appeltern.

24km W of Nijmegen
☎ 0487 541732 **Open** daily
10am–6pm (5pm Mar, Oct–Nov)
Size 8ha (20ac) **Owner**
Ben van Ooijen
🅿 🚻 🚾 ♿ ✚
W www.appeltern.nl
@ info@appeltern.nl

28. Kasteeltuinen Arcen

Lingsforterweg 26
5944 BE Arcen

Seldom has a historic garden been so overwhelmed by trendy modern accretions as Kasteeltuinen Arcen. The castle is large and handsome, a good example of the Dutch late renaissance style, surrounded by its moat. The gardens have all been made since 1988, however, and are designed to absorb large numbers of visitors. It is very popular with German tourists. Some of the designs are conventional, others imaginative, even madcap.

The main water garden has a stylish series of neo-baroque terraces. The rose garden, dispersed around ten smaller gardens, displays over 500 cultivars and 20 000 plants. A pseudo-Italian garden, where slender cypresses and palms are put out in the summer, is pretty enough, but a world away from the new water-and-sculpture garden, where water lilies are required to interact with grasses and sculptures. The glasshouses are stylishly designed and full of interest, as are the model gardens in various styles – European and oriental, practical and beautiful.

Elsewhere are a garden of rhododendrons, an 'Aceretum' for Japanese maple cultivars, a hosta garden, an iris garden, a rock-garden, a 'twilight kingdom' of water and perennials, and an 'avant garden' with an aluminium floor. Will you enjoy it? Yes, very much.

13km N of Venlo ☎ 077 4736020
Open Apr–Oct daily 10am–5pm
(6pm May–Sep) **Size** 32ha (80ac)
🅿 🚻 🚾 ♿ ✚
W www.kasteeltuinen.nl
@ info@kasteeltuinen.nl

BELGIUM

29. Arboretum Kalmthout

Heuvel 2
2920 Kalmthout

The oldest trees at Kalmthout go back to the 1850s, when it was a nursery run by Charles Van Geert. The arboretum owes its fame and remarkable collection of trees (and other plants), however, to the de Belder family, who acquired it in 1952.

One of Kalmthout's greatest strengths is the way the rare trees, shrubs and herbaceous plants are displayed in harmonious plantings, with some beds devoted to a single colour scheme. Another is the way that the de Belders, who collected wild seed all over the world, selected improved forms of almost every plant they grew.

The site is flat and must once have been quite featureless; now it is so absorbing and introspective that it comes as a surprise, from time to time, to hear an express train whizzing

The lake is a fine feature of the horticultural paradise at Arboretum Kalmthout.

along the eastern boundary. The older trees include a remarkable *Pseudolarix amabilis* and some of the *Hamamelis* hybrids for which the arboretum is especially famous.

The design consists of island beds and glades between them that draw you on; the effect is quite Elysian. Long views do exist – the avenue of large conifers is one – but the design evolved by making beds around groups of specimen trees. The landscape also benefits from a spacious lawn in front of the house and a very pretty lake at the end of the garden; both features open up the design to the sky.

Among the plants especially well represented in the collection are rhododendrons (600 taxa), roses, *Malus*, Japanese maples, hydrangeas and magnolias, as well as hostas, astilbes and much more besides. But the sheer beauty of Kalmthout alone would justify a long journey to see it at any season.

24km N of Antwerpen
☎ 03 666 6741 **Open** Mid-Mar–Nov daily 10am–5pm **Size** 12ha (30ac) **Owner** Province of Antwerp
P ☐ ⓘ WC ☐ ☐ ☐
W www.arboretumkalmthout.be
@ info@arboretumkalmthout.be

30. Plantentuin Universiteit Gent

K.L. Ledeganckstraat 35
9000 Gent

Ghent's botanic garden has been on this site since 1903; it is well laid out and full of interesting plants, with more than 10 000 taxa and 4000 sq. m. of greenhouses.

Near the entrance are a large pond, a vast weeping beech, some handsome conifers – including the Mediterranean umbrella pine (*Pinus pinea*), fine rhododendrons, and a rock-garden originally created in the 1950s with Marshall Aid. The systematic garden has recently been reorganised to reflect phylogenetic relationships. There are good collections of hardy plants here and throughout the

Rhododendrons and mature conifers surround the lake at Plantentuin Universiteit Gent.

garden. The arboretum is arranged geographically, in three regions: Europe, Asia and America. Of special interest to young visitors are the exotic vegetables in the kitchen garden and the collection of carnivorous plants. The three glasshouses date mainly from the 1970s: a palm house, a subtropical house and a Victoria house. The collections of Araceae, *Begonia*, Bromeliaceae, Cyperaceae, *Hoya*, Orchidaceae and *Pelargonium* are especially good. The cactus house is also visitable, but only on Sunday mornings between 11am and noon.

S edge of old city centre, by Citadel Park ☎ 09 2645073 **Open** All year Mon–Fri 9am–4.30pm; weekends & pub hols 9am–12 noon **Size** 2.75ha (7ac) **Owner** Universiteit Gent
P WC ☐
W www.plantentuin.ugent.be
@ Chantal.Dugardin@UGent.be

31. Nationale Plantentuin van Belgie Domein van Bouchout

Nieuwelaan 38
1860 Meise

Belgium's national botanic garden moved here in 1939 – not a good year for peaceful change in Europe. The estate had belonged to Leopold II's loopy sister Charlotte, Empress of Mexico, and the handsome castle projecting into the lake is still the centre of the garden's spacious layout.

The garden has all the facilities and displays that you would expect of a national centre of botanic excellence. The glasshouse complex, for example, is known as the Plant Palace and covers 1 ha with 13 large greenhouses and 22 small collection houses. They have recently undergone restoration and renewal, which means that the plant collections look young and vigorous, not tired and overcrowded. The range of habitats includes tropical, subtropical, arid and evolution houses, but one of the most enjoyable is the Spring House, where rhododendrons and camellias flower two months ahead of their relations outside. By far the most beautiful is a stand-alone house originally designed in 1854 by Alphonse Balat, the royal architect, to grow *Victoria amazonica*; it has a uniquely elegant gothic design, complete with a royal crown on top, and is surrounded by a semicircle of taxonomic beds.

The outdoor collections are extensive, but it is worth singling out the magnificent avenues of old beeches; exceptional numbers of

The Balat glasshouse at Nationale Plantentuin van Belgie was designed in 1854 to grow the largest of all water lilies, *Victoria amazonica*.

rhododendrons, magnolias and hydrangeas; the pinetum (here called the Coniferetum); a chichi garden of medicinal herbs; a collection of North American deciduous trees; and the Mediterranean terraces, where plants like *Chamaerops humilis* survive the Belgian winter. Exceptional trees include huge liriodendrons and taxodiums near the castle, a towering *Sequoiadendron giganteum* at 45 m and an *Ulmus glabra* 'Cornuta' at 35 m. Corydalis and polygonatum grow wild in the woods, the songbirds are full-throated, and Canada geese are constant companions.

12km N of Bruxelles city centre
☎ 02 2600970 **Open** Daily 9.30am–6.30pm **Closes** earlier in winter **Size** 92ha (227ac) **Owner** Belgian State
🅿 🖱 🆆🅲 ♿ ⊞
🆆 www.br.fgov.be
@ office@br.fgov.be

32. Serres Royales
Avenue du Parc Royal
1020 Laeken

Leopold II – king of the Belgians between 1865 and 1909 – built this extraordinary series of glasshouses to indulge his passion for botany and plant collecting. It is probably the most beautiful glass complex ever built and immensely popular with visitors. Even on a weekday you will find yourself accompanied by vast crowds, but so impressive is the architecture and so extensive are the botanic collections, that this will not impair your enjoyment.

The architect was Alphonse Balat, who constructed a castle entirely of metal and glass: monumental pavilions, glass cupolas and wide corridors that cross the site like vast shopping arcades. The first part to be built, between 1874 and

The spectacular glass dome of the Winter Garden at Serres Royales gives height to palms.

1876, was the Winter Garden, but the building continued for 30 years, boosted by Leopold's profits from the Congo.

The plants are important historically and botanically – most of the very tall palms date back to Leopold's days – but they are displayed in the 19th-century manner for horticultural effect. The camellias, azaleas, hydrangeas, begonias, orchids and fuchsias are especially fine – comprehensive collections, superbly grown.

Northern outskirts of Bruxelles
☎ 02 5512020 **Open** Times vary (*see* website): usually mid-Apr–mid-May **Size** 2.5ha (6ac) **Owner** H.M. The King of the Belgians
🅿 🖱 🆆🅲 ♿ ⊞
🆆 www.monarchie.be

33. Parc de Bruxelles & Jardin Botanique de Bruxelles
1030 Bruxelles

There are two fine parks in the historic centre of Brussels. The Parc de Bruxelles was laid out between 1774 and 1787 as a public park on the site of the old royal palace, destroyed by the French in 1745. It occupies a rectangle between the present royal palace and the Belgian parliament building. Its 14.5 ha are formally and symmetrically designed with a *patte d'oie*, a large pool (plus modern fountain), avenues of lime, oak and elm, and some 30 mythological and classical 18th-century statues. Parterres, seasonal bedding and roses add decoration.

The 3.75 ha Jardin Botanique is a fraction of what survived after the national botanic garden was moved to Meise in 1939. It is dominated by its fine orangery and fronted by formal gardens and green copper statues, mainly of classical themes.

René Pechère, an able modern landscaper, redesigned the formal gardens as a sequence of hexagons in the 1950s. Annuals and bedding make for colour in summer,

The old orangery at Jardin Botanique de Bruxelles is set off by modern formal gardens.

when bananas and albizias are also put out. Here, too, are a young avenue of *Magnolia grandiflora* 'Galissonnière', a very large *Acer palmatum* and perhaps the most northerly olive tree in Europe. Across a road lies an English-style park where tall trees blot out the surrounding skyscrapers.

City centre **Open** Parc de Bruxelles: daily dawn–dusk; Jardin Botanique: daily 8am–9pm (6pm in winter) **Owner** Région de Bruxelles-Capitale

34. Domein Bokrijk
Bokrijklaan 1
3600 Genk

Bokrijk's arboretum is only a small part of a much larger park devoted to the countryside; its adventure playground is the largest in Europe. The arboretum is quite a distance from the other attractions and was established in 1965 among scrubby birchwoods on poor, acid, sandy soil, sometimes not very well drained. Though initially laid out systematically, it was landscaped in the 1980s and underplanted with shrubs and herbaceous plants.

The collections are very interesting and enjoyable to visit. Conifers are one speciality, but the arboretum also has the National Collection of bamboos and the largest assembly of hollies (*Ilex* species and cultivars) in Europe. *Malus, Camellia, Acer* and *Hibiscus* are also very well represented and, since these all perform at different seasons, there is always much to see. By the mock-renaissance castle in the old kitchen garden is a good collection of roses. Elsewhere are a herb garden, fern garden, Mediterranean garden, wetlands garden and young woodland garden.

10km NE of Hasselt (follow signs to Kasteel, not Museum) ☎ 011 265361 **Open** Apr–Sep daily 10am–6pm **Size** 18ha (44ac) **Owner** Province of Limburg

☑ www.bokrijk.be
@ bokrijk@limburg.be

35. Kasteel Hex
3870 Heers

The gardens at Hex are among the most renowned in Belgium. The substantial house was built by Count Charles-François de Velbrück, Prince-Bishop of Liège, between 1770 and 1784. His (very beautiful) landscaped park, one of the earliest in Belgium, remains as he intended, but the formal gardens were restored in the 1910s, then simplified in the 1990s by Jacques Wirtz.

Wirtz's Prince's Garden has three terraces filled with box-edged compartments planted with old and aromatic garden flowers. The Chinese Garden has also been remade around a remarkable late 18th-century polychrome Buddha.

But Hex is best known today for its old roses and its *potager*. The roses were planted by Countess Michel d'Ursel between 1970 and 1997 and constitute one of the largest collections in Belgium – and

The formal Prince's Gardens at Kasteel Hex are simple but extensive.

Stone sea-horses guard the huge lake that dominates the important garden at Château Beloeil.

certainly the most beautifully planted. The box-edged *potager* is formally laid out and traditionally cultivated with a very large range of unusual vegetables and fruit.

The whole estate is imbued with an unmatched charm and sense of style. If only the gardens were open more frequently …

28km NW of Liège **☎** 012 747341
Open By appointment (*see* website)
Size Gardens: 12.5ha (31ac)
Park: 150ha (370ac)
Owner d'Ursel family
P **WC** **♿**
W www.hex.be
@ gardens@hex.be

36. Château Beloeil
Rue du Château 11
7970 Beloeil

Beloeil is by far the most famous and important historic garden in Belgium. Its scale is staggering, and the beauty and invention of its features were once unparalleled. The features are now rather simplified and standards of maintenance are not as good as they used to be, but Beloeil is still a grand and splendid place to visit.

The house is a copy of the original, burnt down in 1900.

The gardens are dominated by a vast stretch of water, 450 m long and 130 m wide, which frames the castle in a grand reflection. The present layout dates to the late 1750s and is very much in the French style, with a long *allée* that extends out through woodland and into the open countryside beyond. But the great joy of a visit is the series of formal gardens, lesser canals and pools that run parallel to the formal water on either side. Best of all is a circle of great hooped arches of hornbeam like the tracery of a Romanesque church.

20km NW of Mons **☎** 069 689426
Open Mid-May–mid-Nov daily
1–6pm; also weekends in Apr
Size 25ha (63ac) **Owner** Prince
de Ligne **P** **☐** **WC** **♿** **▦** **▨**
W www.beloeil.net
@ fondation.ligne@skynet.be

37. Château d'Enghien
7850 Enghien

Enghien is a grand and important historic landscape, which the town has been restoring since 1986. The very unusual 17th-century sunken garden was laid out by Count Antoine d'Arenberg

The baroque parterres at Château d'Enghien were one of the first features to be restored in the 1980s.

(better known as Père Charles) as a quincunx with a shell-lined pool at the centre. Period plants fill the parterres, which are surrounded by balustrades and guarded by pavilions. At the end of a long double avenue of beech is the Garden of the Seven Stars, a heptagonal marble pavilion at the top of a hill where seven long *allées* meet; the design is thought to represent the seven planets known at that time. A further garden has been planted with a huge collection of dahlias (540 cultivars at the last count) and yet another of roses.

Elsewhere are fine statues, a Temple of Hercules, splendid purple beeches (by the château), back-to-nature woodlands and a water-tower with a collection of automatons.

In Enghien, 37km SW of Brussels
📞 02 3971020 **Open** Apr–Oct daily 10am–6pm; Nov–Mar weekends only 10am–5pm **Size** 182ha (449ac) **Owner** City of Enghien
🅿 🚾 ♿
🕸 www.enghien-edingen.be
@ tourisme.enghien@skynet.be

38. Kasteelpark Coloma
J. Depauwstraat 25
1600 Sint-Pieters-Leeuw

Coloma is a beautiful moated castle in the Flemish style, built of brick in the early 1500s, and now surrounded by a landscaped park. But it also boasts the largest rose garden in Belgium: 3000 different roses and 60 000 rose plants. The design is imaginative and the collections are excellent.

There are three principal areas. First comes a complete collection of Belgian-raised roses; few are ever seen abroad, but many are excellent. Next is a collection of historical roses of every sort, systematically and stylishly displayed. The third and largest collection is of roses from all over the world – a representative selection arranged country by country and breeder by breeder. German and British roses are especially comprehensive, but minor countries like Israel, Hungary and Switzerland each have

their place. There are also collections from Canada and Australia – two rose-growing nations whose roses are seldom seen in west Europe.

Near village centre; Sint-Pieters-Leeuw is 18km SW of Brussels
📞 02 3764436 **Open** Mid-May–Oct daily (except Mon) 10am–8pm **Size** 15ha (37ac) **Owner** Province of Vlaams-Brabant 🅿 🖵 🚾 ♿ 🎫
@ toerisme@sint-pieters-leeuw.be

39. Mariemont Park
100 Chaussée de Mariemont
7140 Morlanwelz

Mariemont takes its name from Charles V's sister, Mary of Hungary, who built a hunting lodge here in the 16th century, though her garden (along with every subsequent make-over) was destroyed during the French Revolution.

Everything we see today is due to the coal magnate Nicolas Warocqué, who bought the estate in 1830, and his land-scaper, Charles-Henri Petersen. It was Warocqué's grandson,

The woodland park at Mariemont has splendid underplantings of Belgian azaleas.

Raoul, who bequeathed the château and its gardens to the community in 1917.

Petersen enclosed the entire estate with a brick wall and laid out its grounds in the English landscape style, with curving drives that lead you through old woods of beech and oak. The Warocqué family then planted it with exotic trees and shrubs: cedars, sequoias, araucarias, ginkgos and many other conifers (all now in their prime), alongside purple cut-leaved and weeping beeches. The approach runs along a double avenue of ordinary beeches, 1 km long. Bluebells, magnolias, tulip trees, azaleas, rhododendrons and magnificent specimens of *Acer pseudoplatanus* f. *variegata* add colour in spring, followed by roses of every sort – there is a wonderful sunken garden surrounded by loops of 'Paul's Scarlet Climber'. The garden also has a very important collection of sculpture, including Rodin's *Burghers of Calais*.

A school of horticulture occupies the old stables; students are responsible for the high standards of maintenance, the magnificent potagers and fruit gardens, and the splendid bedding schemes. Seven hundred thousand visitors a year in a region dominated by industry are testimony to Mariemont's excellence.

On SE edge of La Louvière, 30km W of Charleroi ☎ 064 212193 **Open** Daily 9am–6pm but 10am–5pm Oct–Feb **Size** 45ha (111ac) **Owner** Ministère de la Communauté française

🅿 ▦ 🍴 🚻 ♿ 🏛 ▥ ▦
Ⓦ www.musee-mariemont.be
@ info@musee-mariemont.be

40. Château de Seneffe
9 Rue Lucien Plasman
7180 Seneffe

The château at Seneffe was built in the 1760s, but has long lost its original gardens and, indeed, a series of new gardens laid out in the 1910s. What we see now is modern, designed in the 1990s by Belgium's veteran landscape architect, René Pechère.

All that remains from the more distant past are a fine early 19th-century landscape garden, a small theatre built as a folly in 1780, and a large orangery. The approach to the château is framed by beautiful classical colonnades and statues, and the main garden runs down from one side. It is laid out on three shallow terraces, strictly geometric and formal, but modern rather than baroque – a stylish and successful reinterpretation of the classical French garden.

Simple parterres and pools occupy the central axis, but low, box-edged gardens run along the sides, with ranks of box and yew cut into cubes, and empty chambers of clipped hornbeam enclose the sides. The garden in front of the very pretty orangery has also been remade, as has the main *bassin* behind the château with its 15-m fountain.

In Seneffe, 10km NE of La Louvière ☎ 064 556913 **Open** Daily 8am–6pm (4pm in winter) **Size** 22ha (55ac) **Owner** Ministère de la Communauté française

🅿 ▦ 🚻 ♿ 🏛 ▦
Ⓦ www.chateaudeseneffe.be
@ chateaudeseneffe@hotmail.com

Château de Seneffe's parterre was redesigned in a minimalist style in the 1990s.

Château d'Annevoie has the best water gardens in Belgium, set on a hillside and fed by natural springs.

41. Château d'Annevoie

Rue des Jardins
5181 Annevoie

Annevoie's spectacular water gardens were laid out between 1758 and 1778 by Charles-Alexis de Montpellier. The owners like to call them 'European-style' gardens because, though basically inspired by great French gardens, they incorporate certain elements taken from the Italian Renaissance and the English landscape movement. Nevertheless, it is the omnipresence of water that gives them their defining character; Annevoie has more than 20 pools, canals, grottoes and *bassins*, and 50 fountains, jets and cascades.

Uniquely among Belgian gardens, the entire system of waterworks relies on gravity alone. The large reflecting pool fed by bronze dolphins emphasises the elegant architecture of the château. A flight of fountains descends to a twin-level waterfall. This races into an octagonal pool with a powerful central jet at its centre, then runs into a fan fountain and yet another waterfall. There are hornbeam tunnels, an avenue of copper beeches, and a parterre filled with flowers, but these are irrelevant beside the magnificence of the water displays.

Halfway between Namur and Dinant 082 611555 **Open** Apr–Oct daily 9.30am–6.30pm **Size** 28ha (70ac) **Owner** de Montpellier family

P 🚻 WC ♿ 🏠 📷
W www.jardins.dannevoie.be
@ info@jardins.dannevoie.be

42. Les Jardins de Freÿr

5540 Hastière

This handsome castle above the river Meuse has belonged to the Beaufort family since the 15th century. The present building dates from the late 16th century, and the gardens, more recent, to the 1760s, though they were almost lost to neglect in the middle of the 20th century and restored in the 1970s.

The gardens are laid out on terraces on one side of the castle. The entrance is on the lowest level, and passes between twin gate-lodges, which turn out to be orangeries, the oldest in the Low Countries. These lead to a quincunx of limes and then past slender formal pools, where orange trees are lined up in white cases for the summer. Some are reckoned to be 350 years old – the oldest in Belgium. The limes mark a transverse access that seems to run from the edge of the Meuse (though actually the road runs between the garden and the river) up to a very handsome rococo banqueting house known as *Frédéric Salle* in honour of Frédéric, Duc de Beaufort-Spontin, the heir to the castle when it was built. This is framed on either side by extensive *bosquets* with tall hedges of hornbeam – there are said to be 6 km of hedges here.

The whole ensemble is immensely satisfying and beautiful and a fair match for the natural grandeur of the river valley.

6km SE of Dinant 082 222200 **Open** Guided tours Jul & Aug daily (except Mon) 11am, 2.30pm & 4pm & weekends Apr–Jun & Sep **Size** 3ha (7ac) **Owner** Beaufort family

P 🚻 WC ♿ 🏠 📷
W www.freyr.be
@ info@freyr.be

The handsome rococo banqueting house on the top terrace at Les Jardins de Freÿr is known as *Frédéric Salle*.

Gardens of Scandinavia

Denmark and Sweden have both played leading roles upon the European stage. The cultural legacy of their political eminence includes a wealth of royal and aristocratic houses and gardens, many of them restored and well maintained to this day.

Great Danish gardens begin with King Frederik IV, who started to build grand baroque gardens at Frederiksberg on his accession in 1699, and at Fredensborg and Frederiksborg in the 1720s. All have splendid gardens still, though Frederiksberg (now a public park) is presently an unrestored English-style landscape. The English landscape movement was quickly embraced by the Danes, whose temperate climate and gentle rolling countryside were well suited to its adoption. Gardening in modern times has become a popular interest with a horticultural trade (based in Funen), specialist societies and publications to support it. The cultivation of churchyards as public gardens is an unusual Danish tradition.

During the 17th century, Sweden was the greatest power in northern Europe. The statues in the royal gardens at Drottningholm came to Stockholm as spoils of war. Queen Christina (who reigned 1640–54) employed the French-man André Mollet as royal gardener, and the Tessins worked in Sweden until 1728 (both father and son worked on Drottningholm). The English landscape movement was introduced at Hagapark and Drottningholm by Fredrik Magnus Piper in the 1780s, and provided the preferred model for gardens that has lasted ever since. The Arts-and-Crafts ideas of Rudolf Abelin at Norrviken created a minor ripple early in the 20th century and Swedish landscape architects led a modernist fashion for clean lines and gardens empty of ornament, but both these approaches to gardens and gardening are at variance with popular Swedish horticulture, which is founded (as throughout northern Europe) upon the pleasure of growing plants.

There is little to see in the way of historic gardens in Norway and Finland, which both lacked a royal or aristocratic culture. Each has, however, good botanic gardens and a respectable tradition of horticultural seriousness of purpose. All four Nordic countries have been at the forefront of public amenity design in recent years, and visitors will see many stylish and innovative treatments of public parks and land surrounding public buildings. It should also be recorded that a love of nature and of growing things runs deep in all four countries.

OPPOSITE: The recently restored baroque gardens at Denmark's Frederiksborg are one of the greatest assertions of monarchical power in Scandinavia.

Gardens of Scandinavia

Norway

1. Arboretet og Botanisk Hage
2. Vigeland Park
3. De Naturhistoriske Museer og Botanisk Hage

Sweden

4. Botaniska Trädgården Uppsala Universitet
5. Hagapark
6. Bergianska Botaniska Trädgården
7. Drottningholms Slottsparken
8. Göteborgs Botaniska Trädgård
9. Trädgårdsföreningen
10. Norrvikens Trädgårdar
11. Fredriksdal

Finland

12. Kasvitieteellinen puutarha Turku
13. Helsingin yliopisto Kasvitieteellinen puutarha
14. Mustilan Kotikunnassäätiö

Denmark

15. Fredensborg Slotspark
16. Frederiksborgs Barokhave
17. Gerlev Rosenpark
18. Frederiksberg Have
19. KVLs Have
20. Botanisk Have Københavns Universitet
21. Rosenborg Slotshave
22. Egeskov Slot
23. Liselund Park

SCANDINAVIA

★ National Capital

• Cities and Towns

— Major Roads

⊙ Gardens

Adjacent Countries

0	100		300 Kilometres
0	100		200 Miles

NORWAY

1. Arboretet og Botanisk Hage

Universitet i Bergen
Mildeveien 240
5259 Hjellestad

Bergen's arboretum and botanical garden were founded in 1971 on a rocky peninsular above the sea. Their scientific function is to evaluate the suitability of plants for Norwegian parks and gardens.

This is also a most beautiful and interesting place to visit, especially when the rhododendrons flower from May to June and the roses in July. The rhododendrons are planted in large groups to increase their impact; there are some 4000 plants, composed of 200 species and 400 cultivars. There is also a spectacular heather garden, interplanted with dwarf conifers, at its best in late August. Other ericaeous genera are well represented, including *Cassiope*, *Andromeda*, *Vaccinium* and *Gaultheria*. The extensive rock-garden relies mainly on natural rock for its structure and there is a remarkable Moss Garden, where hummocks of different mosses cover the soil, the rocks and the trunks of trees. The expansive design of the garden is a great asset.

23km S of Bergen ◖ 55 98 72 50
Open Daily dawn–dusk **Size** 50ha (123ac) **Owner** Universitet i Bergen
🅿 ▣ 🆆 ♿
W www.uib.no/arboretet
@ post@sah.uib.no

2. Vigeland Park

Kirkeveien
0116 Oslo

Vigeland is Oslo's leading tourist attraction: a powerful and moving sculpture park dedicated to the work of Gustav Vigeland (1869–1943).

Vigeland himself designed the main axis along a double avenue of limes, laid out the grounds and modelled the

The many depictions of the human form at Oslo's Vigeland Park have a profoundly moving effect upon most visitors.

sturdy life-sized sculptures. There are over 200 of them, in granite or bronze, naked humans of all ages – parents, children, siblings and lovers. They occupy an 850-m progress, which leads first to the 100-m-long bridge, where the best known sculpture is a bronze of an angry small boy.

The ground rises towards the Fountain, the largest piece in the garden, where the giants at the centre hold up the basin, surrounded by 20 groups that represent the cycle of man's life from birth to death and from death to birth again.

Towards the top of the garden is the Monolith, a single piece of carved granite, 17.3 m high, which tells of Man's longing for the spiritual life. The final

piece, right at the top, is the Wheel of Life, carved as a garland of men, women and children, and intended as a symbol of eternity.

W side of Oslo ◖ 23 49 37 00
Open Daily dawn–dusk **Size** 32ha (80ac) **Owner** City of Oslo
🅿 ▣ 🆆 ♿ 🚻 🍴
W www.vigeland.museum.no

3. De Naturhistoriske Museer og Botanisk Hage

PO Box 1172
Blindern
0318 Oslo

Oslo's botanic garden was founded in 1814 by the new University of Norway. Several trees, including an *Ulmus glabra* and *Aesculus hippocastanum*, are older and date back to when the estate was privately owned and known as Tøyen – the old manor-house is integrated within the design. A splendid avenue of fastigiate oaks (*Quercus robur* f. *fastigiata*) marches up from the furthest corner. As with most north European gardens, spring comes late: the *Hamamelis* are the first to flower in March, while the magnolias are at their best in mid-May.

The garden has two focal points. One is the old house, which has a neo-baroque garden in front, with box hedging and lime arches around a fountain. The other

The rock-garden at Oslo's botanic garden is outstanding; note the fine clump of *Veratrum nigrum* on the left.

is the old glasshouses, which also have a semi-formal setting and look pretty reflected in the formal ponds. The Palm House (1868) has three sections – cacti, tall palms and plants from Mediterranean regions. As well as tropical water lilies, the Victoria House (1876) has good collections of orchids, ferns, aristolochias and tropical staples like sugar (*Saccharum officinarum*) and ginger (*Zingiber officinale*).

Perhaps the best features are the circular systematic beds, with many interesting plants, and the beautifully landscaped rock-garden, whose 1500 species are roughly arranged geographically in American, Asiatic and European sections (though this is modified by the individual plants' requirements for specific conditions). The collections of *Trillium*, *Dicentra*, *Primula*, *Asarum*, *Lilium* and *Daphne* are especially strong.

In Toyen, just below Munchmuseet (Munch Museum) ☎ 22 85 16 30 **Open** Daily 7am–5pm (8pm Apr–Sep); but opens 10am at weekends. Greenhouses: daily (except Mon) 11am–4pm **Size** 15ha (37ac) **Owner** Universitetet i Oslo
▪ ▨ ▪ ▪
▨ www.toyen.uio.no/botanisk

SWEDEN

4. Botaniska Trädgården Uppsala Universitet
Villavägen 8
752 36 Uppsala

Uppsala University's botanic garden has a long and distinguished history. It dates back to 1655 but its most famous incumbent was Carl Linnaeus, who began teaching botany here in 1741. It moved to its present site in 1789, at the instigation of Carl Peter Thunberg.

The garden's main buildings are axially aligned on Uppsala's castle, for which the large, modern, formal 'baroque' garden serves as a visual grounding. One of its strangest features are lines of

Carl Linnaeus is honoured in Uppsala's historic botanic garden below the town's renaissance castle.

topiary spruces, clipped into pyramids. Pollarded limes surround the pool, and hedges enclose good collections of paeonies and old roses. The garden now has 11 000 species and cultivars displayed in different sections: economic beds, rock-gardens, peat beds and annual beds, plus areas for research and education. Plants are chosen for their ornamental and horticultural value, as well as their botanical interest: the alpine and herbaceous plants are especially comprehensive and attractive.

Everything has been recently renewed and replanted to celebrate the tercentenary

of Linnaeus's birth in 1707. This includes the glasshouses – the cool orangery and the Tropical Greenhouse, which houses some 4000 species from warmer climate zones.

Linnaeus's garden (entrance in Svartbäcksgatan 27) is now called the Linnaeus Garden. The formal garden with a geometric layout has been restored according to a plan from the 1750s. The entrance passes between two ancient limes to reveal Linnaeus's long, low, rich-yellow laboratory at the far end, approached along an ornamental double border. It was here that Linnaeus first expounded the binomial system of nomenclature, which is now applied to all living creatures. Pause to consider the enormity of that inno-vation: scientific history was made here and you walk on hallowed ground. To the sides are systematic beds where plants are labelled with pieces of white-painted slate. In the orangery are four 250-year-old laurels dating back to Linnaeus.

City centre, near castle
☎ 018 4712838 **Open** Daily 7am–8.30pm (7pm Oct–Apr) Glasshouses: Mon–Thu 9am–3.30pm; 9am–2.30pm Fri. Linnaeus Garden: May–Sep daily 9am–9pm (7pm in Sep) **Size** 13.5ha (33ac) **Owner** Uppsala Universitet
▪ ▪ ▨ ▪
▨ www.botan.uu.se
@ botanical.garden@botan.uu.se

Linnaeus's own garden at Uppsala has been well restored to its original 18th-century format.

Sweden's finest landscape garden at Hagapark has three gold-and-blue painted Turkish tents dating from 1790.

5. Hagapark

Haga Norra
115 59 Stockholm

Hagapark is the finest landscaped park in Sweden, laid out by Gustavus III in the 1770s and 1780s on the edge of Lake Brunnsviken, just north of Stockholm. The architect was Fredrik Magnus Piper, who had travelled widely in England studying the landscape style.

Hagapark has large, open expanses of undulating grass, woodland areas where lily-of-the-valley grows, winding paths and lots of mature trees, especially oaks and limes. There is no better place in Sweden for a good exploratory walk.

Within the landscape are several delicious monuments, built as small banqueting houses for the king. These include a brightly coloured Chinese pavilion, a Moorish house and the Temple of Echo, an open, arcaded, circular building, rather like a bandstand. Even more impressive are three Turkish pavilions in swirling blue and gold, designed by Louis Jean Desprez in 1790. One is now a museum, and another operates as a café-restaurant.

N edge of city ☎ 08 4026130
Open Daily dawn–dusk **Size** 120ha (296ac) **Owner** H.M. The King of Sweden
P ⬛ WC ♿ ▦
W www.hagatradgard.se

6. Bergianska Botaniska Trädgården

Frescati
104 05 Stockholm

Stockholm's botanic garden occupies a charming site on the shores of Lake Brunnsviken, more or less opposite Hagapark. It is stylishly laid out with a design that is both modern and elegant, and the standard of maintenance is very high.

Stockholm's botanic garden, known as the Bergianska, is stylishly laid out and full of interesting plants.

Drottningholm is Sweden's greatest royal palace; its gardens are a statement of national might.

The garden was founded in 1791 but moved here in 1885 and is jointly administered by the Academy of Sciences and Stockholm University. The Academy runs the Mediterranean part of the remarkable conservatory and the orangery (1926), and the university is responsible for the outdoor areas, the *Victoria* greenhouse (very pretty, built in 1900, something between a hexagon and a dome in shape) and the tropical areas in the conservatory.

The garden as a whole has some 9000 taxa, which makes it a very interesting place for plant lovers to visit. The highlights include a good systematic garden near the entrance, a Japanese garden (1991), a rhododendron valley, several wildflower areas, a good rock-garden, large areas of naturalised bulbs, a very good collection of *Syringa* species and cultivars, a herb garden, a kitchen garden and a collection of some 45 Swedish apple cultivars. Look out for the European mistletoe (*Viscum album*) growing all over a North American maple (*Acer saccharinum* f. *laciniatum*).

4km N of Stockholm city centre
☎ 08 54591717 **Open** Daily dawn–dusk Glasshouses: 11am–5pm
Owner Stockholm Universitet
🅿 🚉 🚻 ♿
🆆 www.bergianska.se

7. Drottningholms Slottsparken
178 02 Drottningholm

Drottningholm is the most impressive of Stockholm's palaces, built at a time when Sweden was the dominant power in northern Europe. It is also where the royal family actually lives.

The extensive baroque garden was laid out in the 1680s and 1690s for Queen Hedvig Eleonora by the Tessins (father and son), who based their work on plans by Le Nôtre. King Gustaf VI Adolf restored it, rather simply, in the 1960s.

The design is not typical of grand baroque gardens: two large grass parterres below the palace lead to a pool with a fountain of Hercules at the centre, but this is followed by a series of small water gardens, in the form of quincunxes,

with lots of fountains and round pools, fed by a wall of cascades. All the bronze statues, including Hercules, came to Sweden as booty from the Thirty Years War. Further away are hedges of hornbeam, lime and fir that hide a series of *bosquets*, one of which contains a green theatre. Double avenues of limes enclose the entire formal garden on each side.

The Chinese Pavilion at Drottningholm is surrounded by other oriental features, such as this birdcage.

Beyond lies Gustavus III's English-style park, designed by Fredrik Magnus Piper in the 1780s, with ponds, canals, bridges, winding walks, expanses of grass and clumps of trees. The follies include a gothic tower, a Turkish tent, and copies of antique statues that the king brought back from Italy in 1784. Best of all are the Chinese Pavilion and its outbuildings (1753), a pink-and-green rococo extravaganza high in the woods above the formal garden. The whole complex – palace, gardens and park – is a UNESCO-listed World Heritage site.

W of city centre on Lovön Island
☎ 08 4026200 **Open** Daily dawn–dusk **Size** 150ha (370ac) **Owner** H.M. The King of Sweden
🅿 🔲 🚾 ♿ 🏛 🎫
🔲 www.royalcourt.se

8. Göteborgs Botaniska Trädgård

Carl Skottsbergs Gata 22 A
413 19 Göteborg

Gothenburg's botanical garden is Sweden's biggest and best. It is regularly voted the country's most popular garden and, if you visit, you will understand why: it combines botanical breadth with horticultural enthusiasm and sets out to please and delight its visitors. It has never been an academic garden, yet it has over 16 000 taxa, and its enormous rock-garden has received three stars in the *Guide Michelin*. It is a *natural* rock-garden that merges into the indigenous scrubland at the top, with many different habitats (including areas for woodland- and peat-loving plants) and a sequence of cascades, ponds and streams. Plants are arranged geo-graphically (Europe, Asia and America) and include everything from Swiss Edelweiss to hardy cacti from Canada. The sheer number and beauty of well-grown plants is inspirational.

The Japanese Glade is a large garden around a lake designed in the Japanese style, though the plants (all Japanese, too) are allowed to grow freely: the magnolias, azaleas, cherries and cercidiphyllums are especially colourful. The extensive Rhododendron Woodland valley, best from mid-May to early June, is also outstanding – one of the largest collections in Scandinavia, with more than 200 species and at least twice as many cultivars. Spare some time to wander round the arboretum and, if you visit in late April or early May, through the Wood Anemone Valley, where the native *Anemone nemorosa* covers the slopes like snow.

Gothenburg's glasshouses are extensive: they contain 4000 different plants, including some 1600 orchids, spread between four houses. The Tropical House has economic plants like coffee and cardamom. The begonias share their house with tillandsias and the epiphytic staghorn fern. Other houses include the Cactus House, the Australian/South African house (splendid xanthorrhoeas and proteas), two Tropical Mountain houses and a house for sarracenias.

S of city centre ☎ 031 7411106 **Open** Daily 9am–sunset **Size** 40ha (100ac) **Owner** Västra Götalandsregionen 🅿 🔲 🍴 🚾 ♿ 🏛
🔲 www.gotbot.se
@ botaniska.tradgarden@gotbot.se

Gothenburg's botanic garden displays an exceptional level of horticultural interest.

The Trädgårdsföreningen in central Gothenburg has Scandinavia's largest collection of roses.

9. Trädgårdsföreningen

Slussgatan 1
401 23 Göteborg

Trädgårdsföreningen – the horticultural society's garden – was founded in 1842 to promote horticulture. It was laid out as an English-style landscape park and its older trees include a handsome pair of fastigiate elms (*Ulmus glabra* 'Exoniensis'). The magnificent Palm House was added in 1878 and based on London's Crystal Palace. It is owned by Gothenburg's Botanic Garden and, in addition to the tropical palm house, has areas dedicated to camellias, Mediterranean plants, tropical water lilies and epiphytes.

The entire north-east end of the garden, however (accounting for one-third of its total area), is occupied by Sweden's largest rose garden or *Rosarium*. This is a comparatively recent venture: the first plantings were made in 1986 and now total some 5000 rose plants and 2600 different cultivars. Roses of every kind are grown, some displayed in groups (e.g. collections of old-fashioned shrub roses), and others in mixed borders – a tremendous spectacle in July. Other areas are devoted to dahlias, cacti and perennials.

In city, slightly E of centre
☎ 031 365 58 58 **Open** Daily 7am–9pm (**closes** earlier autumn & winter); open 9am at weekends Palm House: daily 10am–5pm (4pm in winter). **Size** 15ha (37ac)
Owner City of Gothenburg
🅿 ⬚ 🍴 🚾 ♿
🆆 www.parkochnatur.goteborg.se
@ tradgardsforeningen@ponf. goteborg.se

10. Norrvikens Trädgårdar

269 91 Båstad

Norrviken was a ground-breaking garden when its owner Rudolf Abelin started to lay it out between 1906 and 1942. It introduced a new style into Sweden, influenced both by Italian formality and English plantsmanship, but based on the principles of the Arts-and-Crafts movement.

Abelin was a wealthy amateur who had travelled widely and developed a particular interest in fruit-growing. It was Italian gardens that he took as the foundation for his design – a single main axis leads from the distant entrance, along colour-controlled borders, across the baroque garden, through the house and as far as the Mirror Pool and the sea beyond (a constant presence). Features

Norrvikens Trädgårdar is an Arts-and-Crafts garden with an inspirational design and bold, adventurous plantings.

The kitchen garden at Fredriksdal has been laid out in the 18th-century style with many heritage strains of fruit and vegetables.

along the way include an archway of mulberries, a cherry orchard, an antique glasshouse, a Japanese garden, an English woodland garden (good rhododendrons), and very fine water gardens. The plantings are large-scale and usually in soft pastel colours. The baroque garden in front of the house is intended to contrast with the natural plantings that surround it. The trees include the oldest *Chamaecyparis lawsoniana* in Sweden.

The paths are raked daily so that yours will be the first footprints on the surface if you arrive when the garden opens, which is recommended because you will then have the sun directly behind you as you approach, and the garden soon gets crowded.

In recent years, Norrviken has acquired a new purpose as a place for innovative sculptures, installations and events. Opinions are divided on whether the new and the old sit well together. But tender plants are cleverly used in unusual ways, and standards are everywhere top-notch. Norrviken remains a garden of outstanding invention, beauty and interest.

3km NW of Båstad █ 0431 369040 **Open** Mid-Apr–Sep daily 10am–5pm **Owner** Tage Andersen
🄿 ▣ 🍴 🆆🅲 ♿ 📷
🅆 www.norrvikenstradgardar.net
@ norrviken@swipnet.se

11. Fredriksdal
Gisela Trapps väg 1
S-254 37 Helsingborg

Fredriksdal is a fine example of a manor-house garden, with lots of different things to admire and enjoy. The main entrance, along a drive lined with bulky hawthorn hedges, leads straight to the extensive rose garden, planted with well-grown old and shrub-type roses. Around the manor-house are high hornbeam hedges and tunnels, a relic of the original late 18th-century layout.

Off to one side is a splendid sequence of productive gardens in the 18th-century style, some enclosed by low wattle fences. These include a formal herb garden, a fruit garden with many old cultivars of rhubarb, an orchard with some 50 Swedish apples, and a kitchen garden where heritage vegetables are grown. The original kitchen garden is now laid out as a sequence of botanic systematic beds, though a few old trees have been kept, including three unusual cultivars of beech (*Fagus sylvatica*), labelled as 'Aspleniifolia', 'Buxifolia' and 'Laciniata'. There are further venerable beeches in the 19th-century English-style parkland, where a pretty gothic summerhouse provides a good focus.

NE edge of Helsingborg
█ 042 10 45 00 **Open** Apr–Sep daily 10am–6pm; Oct–Mar 11am–4pm
Closes 7.30pm Jun–Aug **Size** 56ha (138ac) **Owner** City of Helsingborg
🄿 ▣ 🆆🅲 ♿ 🚻
🅆 www.museum.helsingborg.se
@ fredriksdal@helsingborg.se

FINLAND

12. Kasvitieteellinen puutarha Turku
Ruissalon puistotie 215
20100 Turku

The Botanical Garden of the University of Turku moved to its present site in 1956 and supports 6000 taxa. Some 7 ha around the glasshouses are put to the collections – edible plants, roses, meadow flowers, rock-plants, and a good collection of water lilies in a chain of small lakes. The ornamental landscaping and the inclusion of horticultural cultivars make this a most enjoyable garden to visit.

The surrounding woodland is planted as an arboretum, roughly divided into three geo-graphical areas – Europe, Asia and North America – for trees and shrubs. Look out for the rare endemic hybrid rowan, *Sorbus* × *meinichii*. The collection of *Betula* species and selections is unusually comprehensive. The six glasshouses have a wide range of tropical and subtropical plants – the display of cacti is especially good.

5km SW of Turku on Ruissalo peninsular █ 02 2761900
Open Regularly, all year **Size** 21ha (53ac) **Owner** University of Turku
🄿 ▣ 🆆🅲 ♿
🅆 www.sci.utu.fi/biologia/puutarha/
@ puutarharuissalo@utu.fi

13. Helsingin yli-opisto Kasvitieteellinen puutarha
Unioninkatu 44 *or*
Kaisaniemenranta 2
00014 Helsinki

Helsinki University's botanic garden has been on its inner-city site since

Helsinki's botanic garden, seen here in autumn, is dominated by its beautiful palm house.

Kumpula Campus and is also worth seeing (but only by prior appointment).

Central Helsinki, on W side of Unioninkatu Street ☎ 09 19150033 **Open** Daily 7am–8pm (9am weekends) **Closes** 5pm Oct–Mar **Owner** University of Helsinki

🅿 ☕ 🚻 ♿ 🎁
Ⓦ www.fmnh.helsinki.fi
@ hortus-botanicus@helsinki.fi

14. Mustilan Kotikunnassäätiö
Mustilantie 55
47200 Elimäki

Mustila is Finland's largest arboretum, founded in 1902 as a trial ground for exotic conifer species. The biggest test is always winter-hardiness, for this is an area where temperatures may plummet to -40°C; severe winters wipe out the less hardy plants roughly once every ten years. Nevertheless, the arboretum contains some 1000 taxa, of which only about 100 are conifers now. They are often grown in dedicated stands, where they can best be evaluated for forestry – Finland is a major exporter of timber. The big blocks of trees like *Picea engelmannii* (1921), *Larix sibirica* (1928) and *Abies lasiocarpa* (1939) are very impressive. The Douglas firs (*Pseudotsuga*

1829. It has a very attractive layout, with its systematic beds neatly displayed in front of the splendid principal glasshouse. Among the mature trees is a very fine specimen of *Quercus macrocarpa*.

Ornamentals are also grown, and the garden has an exceptional collection of *Lonicera*, *Prunus* and *Ribes*. There are some 3000 taxa in the outdoor collections and 1000 in the glasshouses. The Palm House dates back to 1889 but was destroyed by bombing during World War II. Only two plants survived: a single *Cupressus sempervirens* and some seeds of *Victoria cruziana* at the bottom of the frozen pool.

A new botanic garden operates at the University's

Large areas of rhododendrons turn the arboretum at Mustila into a colourful woodland garden during summertime.

menziesii) grow to 35 m high and quickly outperform the native conifers, while *Picea omorika* and *Larix kaempferi* both reach 30 m and more.

Mustila's horticultural highpoint arrives in June, when 8000 rhododendrons flower in the Rhododendron Valley, and 4000 on the Azalea Slope, many of them products of an azalea-breeding program at Helsinki University. This coincides with peak visiting time, but the arboretum is large enough, even at weekends, for visitors to feel alone in this exotic Nordic forest.

115km E of Helsinki **C** 05 3776678 **Open** Daily dawn–dusk **Size** 120ha (296ac) **Owner** Arboretum Mustila Foundation

P ⌷ WC ♿ ⚐

W www.mustila.com

@ arboretum@mustila.com

DENMARK

15. Fredensborg Slotspark

Slottet 9
3480 Fredensborg

Fredensborg is the Danish royal family's favourite palace, on the eastern shore of Lake Esrum, and the historic gardens are among Denmark's largest. Frederik IV (reigning

1699–1730) based them on gardens he had seen in Italy, with straight avenues fanning out from the palace, but Frederik V employed a Frenchman (appropriately named Nicolas-Henri Jardin) in the 1760s to lay out the central Broad Avenue and fill the *bosquets* with pleasure gardens.

The grounds are peppered with memorials to deceased heroes and commemorations of military success. The Norwegian Valley (*Nordmandsdalen*) is of special interest: a grassy arena arrayed with some 68 sandstone sculptures of simple Norwegian and Faroese people of all ages, completed by the sculptor Johann Gottfried Grund between 1764 and 1784. The Queen's Private Garden has all the horticultural interest (a wonderful modern orangery, kitchen gardens, herbaceous borders and a viewing mount with a spiral of box-hedging that leads to the top) but is generally open only in July. Also worth seeking out are the oldest Norway spruces (*Picea abies*) in Denmark.

15km SW of Helsingør **C** 033 403187 **Open** Daily 9am–5pm **Size** 120ha (296ac) **Owner** H.M. The Queen of Denmark

P ⌷ ⌷ WC ♿ ⚐ ▦

W www.kongehuset.dk

@ nce@ses.dk

16. Frederiksborgs Barokhave

3400 Hillerød

The spectacular baroque garden at Frederiksborg Castle is a near-exact modern re-creation of the original laid out by Johan Cornelius Krieger for Frederik IV in the 1720s. The castle was built by Christian IV between 1600 and 1620, and partially rebuilt in the 1860s after a fire. It lies on an island in a lake, and the gardens are across the water on the mainland, axially aligned on the castle.

The 1990s make-over retained a sequence of pools at the furthest point, but reinstated the historic avenues and *bosquets* below. Nearest to the castle are four box parterres with yew obelisks and complicated broderies set in gravel that spell out the monograms of four Danish monarchs, including the present Queen Margrethe II. They are edged with flowers similar to those known in the 18th century. The entire confection is enclosed by steep, mown-grass banks and down the centre runs a broad cascade. The whole composition is immensely impressive, as indeed it was intended to be. The first sequence of *bosquets* (further up towards the pools) has pools and

The 18th-century statues in the Norwegian Valley at Fredensborg make a powerful impression.

The beds at Frederiksborg are planted with period plants and contained within very neat topiary.

fountains, hornbeam hedges, pleached limes and sweet-scented shrubs – lilac, *Philadelphus* and roses; the second terrace is filled with fruit trees rather than flowers.

Off to the north and west is a large landscaped park, dating to the 1850s, with magnificent trees, rhododendrons and flowering trees.

Centre of Hillerød, 24km SW of Helsingør ☎ 033 926585 **Open** Daily 10am–9pm (7pm Mar–Apr, Sep–Oct & 4pm Nov–Feb) **Size** 90ha (222ac) **Owner** H.M. The Queen of Denmark
🅿 ♿ 🍴 🚾 ♿ 🛝 🎫
🎦 www.ses.dk

17. Gerlev Rosenpark
Tørslevvej 10B, Gerlev
3630 Jægerspris

Gerlev was, until recently, best known for its arboretum of native Danish trees and shrubs. Part of the arboretum has, however, been turned over to a collection of old roses, which are now the principal attraction for visitors.

Historically, there are actually two collections: Valdemar Petersen's assortment of some 800 cultivars and a complete inventory of roses bred by the Poulsen family.

Petersen was the nurseryman who revived the Danes' enthusiasm for old roses. He had a particular interest in wild rose species and primary hybrids, and these fill a double border, nearly 200 m long, at the centre of the garden. The Poulsen roses are displayed in a series of free-form beds, planted according to the year in which the roses were introduced, starting in 1912. The whole history of Denmark's most famous rose breeders is displayed here, including the Floribunda roses (which the Poulsens 'invented' in the 1920s).

There are some 5500 plants in all at Gerlev, but it is the sheer variety of roses that is of most interest.

4km SW of Frederikssund (over bridge) ☎ 038 113205 **Open** Daily dawn–dusk **Size** 10ha (25ac) **Owner** Velux Foundation 🅿 🚾 ♿

18. Frederiksberg Have
Frederiksberg Runddel
2000 Frederiksberg

Frederiksberg is a popular public park in Copenhagen, but it began life in the early 1700s as a royal palace with a fine baroque garden made for

Gerlev Rosenpark has an extensive collection of Danish roses; some are accompanied by complimentary ornamental plantings.

The elegant Chinese bridge at Frederiksberg leads to a dramatic rococo Chinese *Lusthus*.

Frederik IV. At the end of the 18th century it was converted into an English-style park, and so it remains today, apart from the ancient double avenues of lime trees on either side of the grass terraces below the ochre-yellow palace, now the Danish Royal Military Academy.

The grounds run down to a sinuous waterway, a sort of cross between a canal and a lake, which encircles several islands. The landscape is mainly wooded, with a large open area at the centre – it has a broad, spacious feel that is very attractive to explore. It also holds a series of ornamental buildings of immense beauty and import-ance. These include the Swiss Cottage (1801) and the neo-classical Apis Temple (1802), but by far the most attractive is the rococo Chinese *Lusthus* (1799), on one of the islands, reached by a fine bridge. Alas, it is open only on Sunday after-noons from May to September.

The park is well maintained, with pretty spring bulbs, a rose garden and good bedding in summer. Though firmly in the suburbs of Copenhagen, it also harbours a heronry.

In SW of København **Open** Daily dawn–dusk. Chinese *Lusthus*: May–Sep Sun 2–4pm **Size** 32ha (80ac) **Owner** The Municipality

🅿 ♿ 🍴 🚾 ♿ 🎦

19. KVLs Have
Bülowsvej 17
1870 Frederiksberg

The garden of the Royal Veterinary and Agricultural University was first laid out in 1858. The oldest trees include a magnificent *Ginkgo biloba* (above the rock-garden and pool at the centre of the garden) and a splendid line of three *Rhus* species – *R. potaninii*, *R. chinensis* and *R. verniciflua*.

Magnolias and azaleas are prominent in spring, but this is also an excellent place to see well-cultivated plants (6000 different taxa) at all times of the year. There are good displays of perennials, daffodils, martagon lilies and colchicums, but the best areas are the rose garden and display beds. You reach the long rose garden by a pergola of climbing roses; a selection of the best modern cultivars occupies the centre and billowing masses of shrubs and climbers line the edges. All are beautifully colour-graded: white, pink, red, orange, yellow and back to white again.

The trials and displays of bedding plants are a major feature in summer and autumn, immensely colourful

The trial grounds for summer bedding plants at Denmark's Royal Veterinary and Agricultural University are a delight.

The Palm House is the focal point of Copenhagen's magnificent botanic gardens.

and full of interest. The bedding schemes within the garden itself show a sophisticated use of colour.

Western København **☎** 35282828 **Open** Daily dawn–dusk **Size** 8ha (20ac) **Owner** Den Kgl. Veterinær-og Landbohøjskole
P **WC** **♿**
W www.lbh.kvl.dk
@ halj@kvl.dk

20. Botanisk Have Københavns Universitet

Gothersgade 140
1353 København

Copenhagen's botanic garden has the second largest collection of plants and the only gene bank for wild species in Scandinavia. It is a wonderful place to look at plants. It was founded in 1600, but moved to its present site in 1872; the splendid rock-garden is actually on a section of the old ramparts, while the lake once formed part of the city moat.

The garden has 13 000 taxa, including a collection of 1000 annuals grown according to their taxonomic groupings. It also has some 1000 native plants of Denmark, arranged both taxonomically and in such ecological areas as dunes and wet meadows. There is

a good compact section of leguminous trees and shrubs and a fine pinetum dominated by *Pinus nigra* subsp. *nigra*.

Microhabitats are exploited, for example, to grow *Rhododendron rex* in the shade of the conifers, and *Cistus* species not far away in the extensive rock-garden, where the Greek mountains, the Alps, the Caucasus and Greenland are especially well represented. Greenland plants are also a feature of the moraine scree, which supports some 1400 species.

The order beds are extensive: perennials account for about 1000 different plants, and there is a notable collection of irises. A large area is devoted to smaller rhododendrons and similar ericaceous plants like kalmias, and the collection of roses, old and new, is also comprehensive. If you come in June, you will see parasitic orobanches growing on the roots of the *Berberis* collection.

The regal Palm House complex dates back to 1872 and is divided into five climatically different sections: tropical water plants (including *Victoria cruziana*); plants of economic importance (from date palms to tree tomatoes); tropical rain-forest plants (everything from bananas to

a historic collection of old cycads); a savannah house; and a Mediterranean house. Other houses open to visitors have good collections of bromeliads, epiphytic cacti, orchids, epiphytic *Begonia* species, and representatives of the flora of Madagascar. Tender plants like *Zantedeschia aethiopica* 'Green Goddess' and *Opuntia phaeacantha* grow against the walls.

Just N of old city centre
☎ 035 322240 **Open** Daily 8.30am–6pm **Closes** 4pm & all Mon Oct–Apr. Most glasshouses: daily 10am–3pm (but some less frequently & for shorter periods) **Size** 10ha (25ac) **Owner** Københavns Universitet **P** **☐** **WC** **♿** **♨** **🏛**
W www.botanic-garden.ku.dk
@ bothave@snm.ku.dk

21. Rosenborg Slotshave

Øster Voldgade 4 B
1350 København

Rosenborg is a magnificent renaissance castle, built by Christian IV in the early 1600s. The surrounding park and garden (also known as *Kongens Have* or King's Garden) is currently the subject of a major exercise in prestige restoration and improvement.

The network of 18th-century lime avenues still supplies much of the structure and follows the lines of the original 17th-century layout. The copper lions (with rather goofy expressions) date back to Christian IV's time and the Hercules Pavilion (1773) is another outstanding feature.

The pretty new rose garden behind the castle uses only old cultivars of roses (e.g. *R. gallica* 'Versicolor' and *R. hemisphaerica*), so it has only a fleeting season. It is, however, beautifully laid out, with chunks of box, lavender and *Santolina* as evergreen fillings and a rather terrifying copper statue of Queen Caroline Amalie (1796–1881) at the end.

Early spring sees a magnificent, if equally ephemeral, carpet of crocuses in a very striking formal pattern, though the 250-m-long double herbaceous borders offer colour all through the seasons. Good

scented garden and grey garden. None of them is worth a second glance, but worthy old trees include specimens of *Populus tremula* 'Erecta' and *P. wilsonii*.

30km S of Odense ☎ 062 271016 **Open** May–Sep daily 10am–5pm **Closes** 6pm Jun & Aug; 8pm Jul **Size** 20ha (50ac) **Owner** Count Michael Ahlefeldt-Laurvig-Bille
🅿 ▣ 🍴 🚻 ♿ ♿ 🏛 🖼
🆆 www.egeskov.dk
@ info@egeskov.dk

23. Liselund Park
Langebjergvej
4791 Borre

Liselund has for long been famous as the finest example of a 'romantic English' landscape in Denmark, a subtle and charming composition of grass, woodlands, lakes, islands, waterfalls and bridges. It was laid out by Anders Kirkerup for Antoine Calmette, the governor of Møn, in 1793.

The garden is on chalk downland and, in 1905, a landslide dropped two-thirds of it into the sea, but what remains is exquisitely laid out and populated by charming follies. These include a tiny Chinese tea house; a Norwegian hut (painted inside to resemble Pompeii); and a Swiss hut that was originally a gardener's cottage (with a good overview of the garden), where Hans Christian Andersen wrote *Fyrtøjet* (*The Tinder-Box*). Calmette also built a small thatched manor-house (more like a doll's house) called *Liselund Slot*, which was designed for short visits and simply furnished. It is now a museum. The 'new' castle, built in 1887, is an upmarket hotel.

NE end of island of Møn ☎ 055 812178 (museum) **Open** Daily dawn–dusk **Size** 6ha (15ac) **Owner** Danish Ministry of Culture
🅿 ▣ 🍴 🚻 ♿ 🖼

The stylish new rose garden behind Rosenborg Castle uses only old cultivars.

trees include a very broad, dark-leaved purple beech and a multi-stemmed pterocarya.

Central København: entrances in Øster Voldgade, Gothersgade, Kronprinsessegade and Sølvgade ☎ 33 13 47 65 **Open** Daily 7am–sunset **Size** 12ha (30ac) **Owner** Slots- og Ejendomsstyrelsen
▣ 🍴 🚻 ♿ 🏛 🖼
🆆 www.ses.dk
@ sesmail@ses.dk

22. Egeskov Slot
Egeskov Gade 18
5772 Kværndrup

Egeskov is a stately home with lots of family entertainment to attract visitors. The moated castle dates back to 1554 but was tarted up in the 1890s. The same has happened, more recently, to the gardens.

The Renaissance Garden was laid out in 1962 by Ferdinand Duprat, who also designed the formal garden at La Roche-Courbon. Its main features are animal topiaries and a parterre of French fleurs-de-lys on a ground of red gravel. The organic kitchen garden is good – well displayed and neatly kept – and there is a charming *Fuchsia* garden with over 100 cultivars.

The English-style park, too, is worth seeing, classically laid out around a lake. But the best feature is a beech maze, thought to be 300 years old and closed to visitors, but replicated in bamboo for visitors to explore. Of the two further mazes, the willow maze (1990) has an observation tower at the centre that anxious parents can access from outside. The modern gardens include a herb garden,

Gardens of North-east & Eastern Europe

The gardens of Poland and the ex-Soviet Union are a mixed bunch: visiting them is a slightly hit-and-miss affair. Almost all the old botanic gardens and many of the parks attached to palaces and large country houses suffered serious damage during World War II. Present-day lack of funding means that many of the gardens that were well maintained in Soviet or communist days have fallen apart. Some botanic gardens (Tbilisi is an example) have been pillaged by citizens in search of firewood and others by nurserymen in search of interesting stock. Hothouse collections have been wiped out by shortages of water, electricity or fuel. But it is worth remembering that similar ups and downs have often affected gardens in western Europe. Despite these troubles, most botanic gardens in this chapter have managed to maintain good plant collections and most historic gardens have begun to see significant programs of restoration. It should also be said that gardens and plant collections are often maintained only by amateur enthusiasts, working without support, desirous of recognition and desperate for foreign contact.

Communism has a lot to answer for. It was an inherently inefficient system that delivered bad management. Nor was Communism conducive to the preservation of bourgeois culture; had Poland, for example, remained in the western orbit between 1945 and 1990 it would still have as many good gardens to visit as Germany or France. English-style parks, specimen trees and collections of elderly conifers are often the only relics of the once great gardens of eastern Europe.

Russia and Poland took their garden culture from the west. Peter the Great

ABOVE: Emperor Paul I brought the Neptune fountain to Peterhof from Nuremburg in 1799.
OPPOSITE: The leaning tower and ruined arch give an Italianate air to the landscape at Arkadia in Poland.

The Komarov Botanical Garden was founded by Peter the Great; parts of it were prettily landscaped in the early 19th century.

modelled his botanic garden at St Petersburg on Amsterdam's, and the Summer Gardens on Dutch canal gardens. Warsaw's baroque came from France and the landscape movement spread quickly from England at the behest of Catherine the Great. Nevertheless, nothing can prepare the visitor for the sheer size of imperial gardens in Russia: Peterhof and Tsarskoe Selo are among the largest, grandest and most extravagant gardens ever made. These symbols of power and achievement were readily adopted by the Communists, who quickly repaired the extensive war damage wrought by Germany during World War II. But Communism also ensured that throughout eastern Europe there is now a complete absence of gardens made by landowners or the middle class – and, hence, no Arts-and-Craft movement and no ornamental plantings on the English or German model. The gardens that have survived are either of national and historic importance, or attached to botanical institutes.

Poland was carved up during the latter half of the 18th century between Europe's three most predatory and expansionist powers: Russia, Austria and Prussia. Nevertheless, Polish culture and learning survived under foreign rule, and there is nothing except climate to distinguish the gardens of the different parts of Poland. The real upheaval came in 1945, when the political boundaries were moved significantly to the west to incorporate the German province of Silesia and eastern Pomerania, which had been Prussian for many centuries. The Communists then extinguished middle-class culture, and all the more vigorously for it being German. What remains for us to visit today are the palaces and landscapes of such national importance that they were spared obliteration and are now being restored as and when funds are available: the royal palaces of Warsaw are splendidly maintained and the country estates of the great families like the Potocki, Radziwiłł and Czartoryski will follow suit. Some have been repossessed by their original owners, or sold to new buyers and restored in some degree. But few are open to the public and their potential for popular tourism has yet to be realised. The botanic gardens are also well-managed and full of interest. There is much to discover and enjoy in Poland, including the many collections of roses and lilacs that are grown, largely for their exceptional hardiness, throughout eastern Europe.

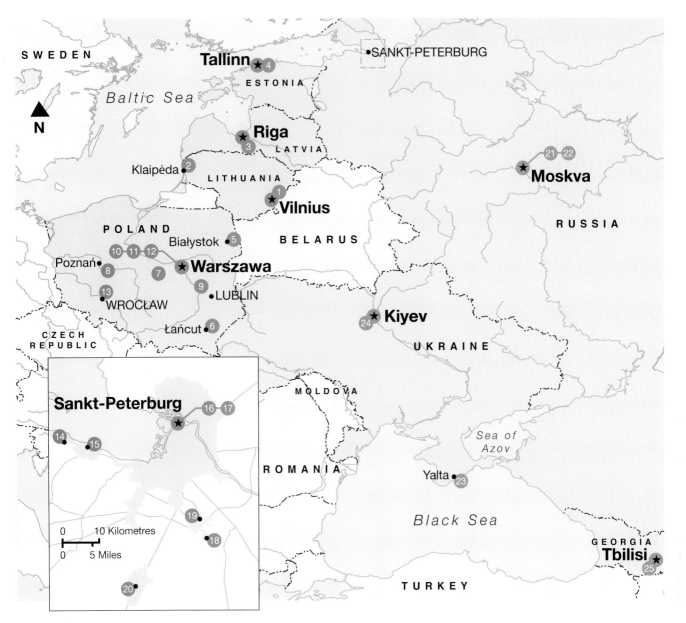

Gardens of North-east & Eastern Europe

Lithuania
1. Botanikos Sodas, Vilnius
2. Palangos Botanikos Parkas

Latvia
3. Latvijas Nacionālais Botāniskais Dārzs

Estonia
4. Tallinna Botaanikaaed

Poland
5. Pałac Branickich
6. Łańcut Park Zamkowy
7. Nieborów & Arkadia
8. Kórnickie Arboretum
9. Czartoryski Park
10. Park Łazienkowski
11. Ogród Botaniczny Uniwersytetu Warszawskiego
12. Wilanów Pałac

13. Ogród Botaniczny Uniwersytetu Wrocławskiego

Russia
14. Oranienbaum Palace Gardens
15. Peterhof
16. Komarov Botanical Garden
17. Summer Gardens
18. Pavlovsk
19. Tsarskoe Selo
20. Gatchina Palace
21. Moscow University Apothecaries' Garden
22. Main Botanic Garden

Ukraine
23. Nikitsky Botanical Garden
24. Central Botanical Garden, Kiev

Georgia
25. Tbilisi Botanic Garden

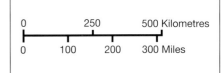

NORTH-EAST & EASTERN EUROPE

★ National Capital

• Cities and Towns

— Major Roads

(00) Garden

Adjacent Countries

0	250	500 Kilometres

0	100	200	300 Miles

LITHUANIA

1. Botanikos Sodas, Vilnius

Kairėnų Dvaro Parkas
Kairėnų 43,
10239 Vilnius-40

Relics of the Frenchman Edouard André's work have survived in the delightful botanic park at the Baltic resort of Palanga.

The Botanic Garden of Vilnius University was founded in 1781 and moved to its present location on an old estate called Kairenai in 1974. The systematic beds are still in the centre of Vilnius at Vingis Park, where the trees include an especially fine *Phellodendron amurense*. The new garden suffered considerably from underfunding in the 1990s but has since been salvaged by good management; it now has lots to offer visitors, much of it new.

The house at the centre of the estate has disappeared, but there remains a fine old water-mill, plus some newly restored stables and a number of follies around the park. There is a total of nearly 10 000 taxa in its various departments, but the interest to visitors lies in the garden's commitment to the conservation of old, locally bred horticultural cultivars. Bulbs are one speciality, but so are dahlias, paeonies, lilacs and soft fruit. These collections are extensive, still growing and well displayed – a joy to visit.

5km NE of city centre **C** 5231 7933
Open May–Oct daily dawn–dusk
Size 200ha (494ac), not all fully developed **Owner** Vilnius University
P ☐ WC &
W www.botanikos-sodas.vu.lt
@ hbu@gf.vu.lt

2. Palangos Botanikos Parkas

Vytauto g. 15,
Palanga

The botanical park in the cheerful, popular resort of Palanga is attached to the Tiškevičius Palace, now the home of the National Amber Museum. The park was built by the Tyszkiewicz family, who owned the town from 1824 until expropriated in 1940. It was laid out on a flat site by the Frenchman Edouard André over a period of three summers during the 1890s. The park combines formal 'French' designs with a flowing English-style land-scape and a collection of exotic trees and shrubs, now reaching maturity.

The palace was designed by the German Franz Schwechten and completed in 1897. From its balustraded terrace, a double staircase curves down to the brightly planted parterres and a statue of Christ with His arms outstretched in blessing by the Danish neo-classicist Berthel Thorwaldsen. Beyond is the English parkland, with pretty white bridges over the streams and a fine collection of firs, cypresses, larches, ashes, limes, maples and horse-chestnuts, plus banks of rhododendrons and azaleas. Behind the palace is a semi-circular rose garden.

Palanga has one of the mildest climates in Lithuania, so this is one of the few gardens where *Magnolia kobus* manages to bloom without losing its flowers to frost. Elsewhere in the park are some fairly hideous modern sculptures. But this is one of the best maintained parks in the Baltic states and a civilised contrast to the razzmatazz of Palanga itself.

Vilnius's botanic garden has assembled a fine collection of azaleas and rhododendrons that are hardy down to -40°C.

In town centre **C** 8460 49270
Open Daily dawn–dusk **Size** 86ha
(212ac) **Owner** Town of Palanga
P ▣ WC ♿ ▦
W www.pgm.lt
@ botanikosparkas@takas.lt

LATVIA

3. Latvijas Nacionālais Botāniskais Dārzs

Miera iela 1
2169 Salaspils

The National Botanic Garden of Latvia claims to be the largest in the Baltic states, with more than 15 000 taxa, including 5000 trees and shrubs and about 1400 hot-house plants. It was founded in 1956 on the site of a much older nursery; its remit includes the introduction of new plants, research into ornamental gardening and popularising the results.

The garden is laid out in a natural style, with woods, open areas, ponds and a stream. An avenue of *Thuja* greets you at the entrance, with an attractive collection of juniper cultivars, heaths, heathers and potentillas; their evergreen nature gives structure and colour to the garden, even in deep winter. The cheerful rosarium contains some 1000 cultivars and boasts a number of very interesting, super-hardy, Latvian-raised Rugosa hybrids. The collections of lilacs and clematis include many cultivars bred in Latvia, and hardy shrubs like *Philadelphus*, *Forsythia*, *Spiraea* and *Weigela* are also well represented. There are over 760 different *Tulipa* cultivars, 700 *Allium* and 170 Juno irises, and good collections of such herbaceous plants as paeonies, daylilies, astilbes, phlox and clematis. Large areas are given to annuals, which build up to a spectacular crescendo of colour in August and September: the mass plantation of kochias (*Bassia scoparia*) in many different shades is breathtaking.

The glasshouses have a respectable number of cacti

Latvia's main botanic garden at Riga is full of horticultural colour as well as botanic interest.

and succulents, orchids and bromeliads, plus two unusual and colourful collections of gerberas (150 taxa, including 32 varieties bred here) and chrysanthemums (300 taxa).

18km SE of Riga **C** 9445440
Open Daily 8am–8pm (but 9am–4.30pm Oct–Mar). Orangery: Mon–Fri 9am–noon & 1–4pm
Size 126ha (311ac) **Owner** Latvian Academy of Sciences
P WC ♿ ⚥
W www.nbd.gov.lv

ESTONIA

4. Tallinna Botaanikaaed

Kloostrimetsa tee 52
11913 Tallinn

Tallinn Botanic Garden was founded in 1961 and still has a youthful vigour about it. Plantings are spacious, and much of the structure has yet to reach its full size. One of its main purposes is to show visitors what can be grown in Estonian gardens and it therefore has a wide range of horticultural cultivars.

Among the 1600 perennials, for example, are 58 astilbes, 178 irises and 335 paeonies. The collection of bulbs is also impressive: some 272 tulips, 180 narcissus and more than 100 each of crocuses and alliums. The rose garden is especially interesting and

includes a chronological display of historical roses, a modern assortment of bedding roses, climbers, shrub roses and 74 species roses. There is also a good arboretum, a colourful display of rhododendrons, a lilac garden, a charming collection of heathers at the highest point of the garden, and well-planted boggy areas around the nine small ponds. The six glasshouses (which display some 2400 taxa) include a palm house, an orchid house, a succulents house and two tropical houses.

E of city centre **C** 6062 679
Open May–Sep daily 11am–7pm. Glasshouses **close** 4pm **Size** 123ha (304ac) **Owner** City of Tallinn
P WC ♿
W www.tba.ee
@ aed@tba.ee

POLAND

5. Pałac Branickich

Kilińskiego 1
15-089 Białystok

The Branicki palace is a beautiful baroque building right in the middle of the ugly industrial town of Białystok. It was built by Count Jan Klemens Branicki in 1726, destroyed in World War II, and rebuilt almost immediately thereafter.

Today the palace is a medical university, but the formal

ABOVE: The boxwood formal gardens at Nieborów are enclosed by magnificent hedges.
OPPOSITE: The ruined Roman aqueduct at Arkadia is one of Europe's most impressive landscape statements.

gardens and park are freely accessible. The crisp parterres, guarded by sphinxes, are among Poland's best, and intended to be viewed from the platform behind the palace. The central *allée* runs on into the English-style park and ends at a pretty garden pavilion. The other buildings in the park, in various states of repair, include an orangery and two pavilions, one Italian and the other specifically Tuscan.

City centre 📞 085 652 30 05 (tourist office) **Open** Daily dawn–dusk **Size** 10ha (25ac) **Owner** City of Białystok

🅿 🚻 ♿ 🏛 🚻

6. Łańcut Park Zamkowy

ul. Zamkowa 1
37-100 Łańcut

The palace at Łańcut was built as a fortress for Prince Stanislaw Lubomirski in the 1630s, converted to its present form by the wealthy Polish nationalist Princess Izabela Czartoryska in the 1790s and restyled in the French neo-baroque style by her descendants 100 years later.

Łańcut's garden and park went through similar remodel-ling. Czartoryska used the old five-pointed bastions as a ha-ha and built two magnificent

structures on the inside – an Italianate conservatory with an Ionic portico (1799) and an elegant semicircle of columns (with composite capitals) that once surrounded a statue of Venus. The park beyond was then laid out in the English style, with winding paths and clumps of trees; the follies include a picturesque castle (1808) and a menagerie (1828). The park was reworked, enlarged and enclosed between 1890 and 1905.

Fine trees are the principal legacy of this last make-over (restoration has only just begun) and include Poland's oldest ginkgo, huge plane trees, poplars, pterocaryas, beeches and oaks. But you should also see the Italian garden, rose garden and mixed borders, all dating back to 1900.

Czartoryska's reputation as a moderniser saved Łańcut from complete destruction (but not from proletarianisation) in the communist years; it will be interesting to see how quickly it returns to its turn-of-the-century glory.

Town centre 📞 017 225 20 08 **Open** Daily 8am–dusk (park always open) **Size** 36ha (90ac) **Owner** Muzeum-Zamek w Łańcucie

🅿 📷 🚻 ♿ 🏛 🚻
🆆 www.zamek-lancut.pl
@ muzeum@zamek-lancut.pl

7. Nieborów & Arkadia
99-416 Nieborów

Nieborów is a magnificent palace of the Radziwiłł family, originally built in the 1690s but converted into a neo-classical beauty by Prince Michał Radziwiłł in the 1780s. The remoter parts are landscaped in the English style, especially around two lakes, though two of the canals nearer the house are still formal in shape.

The gardens around the house are formal and geometrical, enclosed by hedges of hornbeam or lime, as much as 10 m high. Two enclosures have bronze eagles perched on tall columns, now surrounded by red and yellow Floribunda roses, and there are two orangeries with wooden shingles on their roofs. A pair of vast and ancient plane trees dominates the parterre behind the house. Nieborów is well maintained and enjoyable to visit, but would benefit from further restoration.

The real excitement is the landscape park laid out by Michał Radziwiłł's wife, Helena, some 5 km away, along a lime avenue. Arkadia was her name for it, intended to conjure up Rousseau-esque ideas of happiness, love, death and beauty.

Behind Arkadia's Temple of Diana at the top of the lake is an extraordinary assemblage of classical follies.

The centrepiece of the design is a placid lake with an island where a copy of the philosopher's tomb is inscribed *Et in Arcadia Ego*. A cluster of grand and thought-provoking monuments occupies the further end of the lake. Here is the Temple of Diana (1783), guarded by sphinxes on the lakeside but extended into the park behind as a semicircular rotunda; its interior is furnished with classical pieces, and its pediment inscribed *Dove pace trovai d'ogni mia guerra* ('Here I found peace after all my struggles'). Nearby lies the Sanctuary of the High Priest, an extraordinary evocation of a classical villa, with the most complicated and beautiful use of old brick, chunks of ironstone and fragments of classical architecture, all moulded into a unique and harmonious whole. At the head of the lake is a hefty Roman-style aqueduct, brick-built to resemble a ruin in the *Campagna*. Other buildings include a Greek Arch, a Gothic House and the House of the Margrave, each as different from each as imaginable, yet blending to create the illusion of a lost Arcadia in a sylvan landscape.

In early summer, the air is sweet with the scent of elderflower, the bees buzz in the lime trees and damselflies skim the water's surface. Go early in the day and you may be the only visitor in this enchanted landscape.

80km W of Warszawa
046 838 56 35 **Open** Daily (except Mon) 10am–dusk **Size** Nieborów: 25ha (62ac) & Arkadia: 15ha (37ac) **Owner** Oddzial Muzeum Narodowego w Warszawie
www.nieborow.art.pl

8. Kórnickie Arboretum

ul. Parkowa 5
62-035 Kórnik

Kórnik was once a handsome country estate with the finest arboretum in Poland. The arboretum and (slightly dotty) 1850s castle designed by Karl Friedrich Schinkel are still here, but recovering from bad management and poor funding. That said, Kórnik is a stunning park to visit at almost any time of the year.

The sheets of snowflakes (*Leucojum vernum*) and scillas in early spring are almost unbelievable, and the park is especially colourful when the magnolias, azaleas and rhododendrons flower a little later. Kórnik has also been involved recently in breeding new Preston lilac hybrids.

The arboretum dates to the 1840s, when Count Tytus Dzialynski started collecting trees and shrubs and adapted the exisiting landscape park to hold his collections. Dzialynski's son, Jan, a passionate dendrologist, then built up an exceptional holding of conifers. Kórnik has about 3500 different trees and shrubs. There is beauty and interest at every step. Older than the arboretum itself are a 300-year-old lime (*Tilia cordata*) and a 30-m beech (*Fagus sylvatica*), 200 years old. Many trees are Poland's largest specimens, including specimens of *Liriodendron tulipifera*, *Magnolia acuminata* and the hardy rubber tree (*Eucommia ulmoides*).

20km SE of Poznań
061 817 00 33 **Open** Daily dawn–dusk **Size** 30ha (74ac) **Owner** Instytut Dendrologii PAN
www.idpan.poznan.pl
idkornik@man.poznan.pl

9. Czartoryski Park

ul. Czartoryskich 8
24-100 Puławy

It was Princess Izabela Czartoryska in the 1790s who rebuilt the family palace at Puławy and laid out its English-style park. She and her husband were children of the Enlightenment and conspicuous Polish patriots, with an immense fortune matched by instinctive good taste. Her landscape architect was an Englishman called James Savage.

A double avenue of lime trees frames the drive to the pink palace, now the seat of the Institute of Soil Science and Plant Cultivation, but it is the garden buildings that are the main attraction. These include a conservatory with a Doric portico (1790), the Marynka Palace (1794), a small Chinese pavilion and a marble sarcophagus (1801) in the Roman style. But the most impressive is the splendid Corinthian Temple of Sybil (1802), modelled on the Temple of Vesta at Tivoli, which is regarded as the first Polish museum because it housed the Princess's collection of nationalist items. When this was full, she built the Gothic House (1809) and used it to house a second collection.

The park and its buildings were seriously neglected and damaged by pollution in communist years. Some of the follies are still boarded up, but plans for their restoration are afoot. The good trees include a multi-stemmed *Tilia tomentosa* and an immense *Populus nigra*.

50km NW of Lublin ☎ 081 886 34 21 **Open** Daily dawn–dusk **Size** 25ha (63ac) **Owner** Instytut Uprawy Nawozenia i Gleboznawstwa 🅿 🚾 ♿ ▦
🅦 www.iung.pulawy.pl
@ iung@iung.pulawy.pl

Puławy's magnificent Temple of Sybil was built to house a collection of Polish national memorabilia.

10. Park Łazienkowski
Agrykola 1
00-460 Warszawa

Łazienki is Poland's last royal palace, a Palladian monument to the ill-fated King Stanisław August Poniatowski, who ruled from 1764 to 1795. The palace is at the centre of the whole design, an exquisite confection in a delightful, watery setting – on an island in a lake – where Ionic colonnades connect it to the parkland, and gondolas ply their trade on the elegant lake.

The beautiful parkland is a mixture of formal avenues and informal English-style park, with lakes and grassy glades within the woodland. There are several further palaces and houses within it, including the Belvedere, the Ujazdowski Palace, the White Cottage,

The Greek theatre at Łazienki is on an island in the lake, where gondolas ply their trade.

and the Myślewicki Palace. The parkland binds them together and provides a setting for some exquisite classical follies. One of the most impressive is the full-size Greek theatre (on an island), which is still used for outdoor performances. The large Orangery looks onto a fine formal garden, tricked out with classical-style statues and busts. The Hermitage, the Egyptian Temple, the Temple of Diana and the New Orangery (now an upmarket restaurant) are also worth discovering.

S of city centre ☎ 022 621 62 41 **Open** Daily 7.30am–dusk **Size** 78ha (193ac) **Owner** The State
▣ 📶 📶 ♿ 🏛 🖼
W www.lazienki-krolewskie.com
@ info@lazienki-krolewskie.com

11. Ogród Botaniczny Uniwersytetu Warsawskiego

al. Ujazdowskie 4
00-478 Warszawa

Warsaw University Botanic Garden is still on the site between Łazienki and the Belvedere Palace that the Russian Emperor Alexander I gave to the university in 1818. It has had a chequered history, including near-complete destruction during the Warsaw Uprising (1944). The few trees that survive from the 19th century include a two-trunked *Sophora japonica*, a mighty *Acer campestre* and, largest of all, a majestic *Carya cordiformis*.

The garden has a good systematic display, with lots of interesting plants to look at; a collection of Polish native plants; habitat plantations; areas devoted to medicinal and other useful plants; a rock-garden (the *Alpinarium*); an iris garden; a handsome rose garden set in a 19th-century geometrical design; a splendid collection of paeonies; and an extensive planting of lilacs, at their best in May.

The whole garden is well maintained, with much of horticultural interest; plants grow well in the light, sandy soil.

The Polish Academy of Sciences also has a visitable

Warsaw's botanic garden has a fine collection of roses laid out in a 19th-century geometrical design.

botanic garden, founded in 1974 some 20 km south of central Warsaw at Powsin. It has some 7000 taxa and offers special open days for popular genera like magnolias and roses (*see* www.ogrod-powsin.pl for details).

S of city centre, close to Łazienki Park ☎ 022 628 75 14 **Open** May–Oct daily 9am–8pm (10am weekends) **Size** 5ha (12ac) **Owner** Uniwersytetu Warsawskiego
▣ 📶 📶 ♿ 🏛 🖼
W www.ogrod.uw.edu.pl/
@ ogrod@biol.uw.edu.pl

12. Wilanów Pałac

ul. St.K.Potockiego 10/16
02-058 Warszawa

Wilanów is an exquisite ochre-yellow baroque palace built in the 1680s by King Jan III Sobieski. The main formal garden is on two terraces, and attractively planted with summer bedding. On one side are high-clipped hornbeam *bosquets* and, on the other, a box-edged parterre planted with colourful modern roses.

There are more excitements in the wooded park, with its winding waterways, columns and memorials in the German landscape style. The Chinese temple is a stunning piece of imaginative fancy, apparently based on the Englishman Sir William Chambers's designs. The brick-built pumphouse that feeds the fountains is disguised as a castle, its design also based on English precedents. Both these, and the English-style park, were laid out by the Potocki family in about 1800. Palms and other tender exotics are put out for the summer in front of the fine conservatory. Statues, urns, vases, sarcophaguses, columns and obelisks are everywhere.

Wilanów is noted for its profusion of exuberant baroque statuary, much of it the result of extensive recent restoration.

The jolly exuberance of the palace and its formal gardens makes an abiding impression.

SE of city **C** 022 842 81 01
Open Daily (except Thu)
10am–dusk **Size** 43ha (106ac)
Owner The State

P ⬛ ⏹ WC & ⬛ ⬛

W www.wilanow-palac.art.pl

13. Ogród Botaniczny Uniwersytetu Wrocławskiego

ul. Henryka Sienkiewicza 23
50-335 Wrocław

Wrocław University Botanic Garden was founded by King Friedrich Wilhelm III of Prussia in 1811; Wrocław was then (and up until 1945), the German city of Breslau.

The garden is attractively spread around a long, curving lake, spanned by two elegant bridges; at its heart is the large section devoted to systematic beds, laid out according to the Engler taxonomic system around a bust of Linnaeus. All types of plants are here, and you will make the acquaintance of many that are new to you.

The garden has only a small arboretum, because trees are dispersed throughout; large, old specimens include *Carya ovata* and *Pterocarya fraxinifolia*. There is also a good but rather oddly designed rock-garden, which incorporates a geological cross-section of a local hard coal deposit, complete with petrified fossil plants.

Decorative plants of horti-cultural value are prominently displayed, including *Acer platanoides* 'Globosum' and *Sophora japonica* 'Pendula'. The collections of paeonies

The parterres in front of the baroque palace of Wilanów are now filled with modern roses.

ABOVE: Catherine the Great laid out the grounds around her Chinese palace at Oranienbaum in the landscape style.
OPPOSITE: The fountain-lined canal at Peterhof leads from the Baltic sea to the great fountain that depicts Samson ripping apart the jaws of a lion.

1750s and then to Catherine the Great's jolly rococo house (1768), known as the Chinese palace. It is more *anglo-chinois* than Chinese, and looks over a pretty lake, landscaped with venerable oaks. Other features are lost in the woods, but there are dank walks, most of them straight, among limes, alders, Norway maples and spruces, and the natural flora of geraniums and astilbes is attractive.

Oranienbaum – so-called because Menshikov displayed large numbers of orange trees – is not the most important or best maintained of properties around St Petersburg, but some restoration is underway and it makes a splendid contrast to the busy popularity of nearby Peterhof.

On coast, 40km W of Sankt-Peterburg 812 422 80 16 **Open** Daily 7am–7pm **Size** 300ha (741ac) **Owner** The State

RUSSIA

14. Oranienbaum Palace Gardens
Dvortsovy pr., 48
189510 Lomonosov

The baroque palace at the centre of the Oranienbaum estate was built for Peter the Great's counsellor, Prince Alexander Menshikov, in the 1710s. It sits high above a rather tatty parterre, connected to it by a gorgeous baroque staircase. To the sides are *bosquets*, some of them planted with fruit trees and hedges of lime and *Aronia*.

The view on the other side of the palace is quite different – a lake laid out much later, with relics of a landscaped park beyond. Woodland walks lead first to the dilapidated villa built for Peter III in the

(120 cultivars), lilies, daylilies, dahlias, chrysanthemums and irises (250 cultivars) are also good. In the four public glasshouses, the tropical and subtropical collections include Bromeliaceae, Araceae, Orchidaceae, cacti and succulents (1300 taxa) and an exceptional number of glasshouse aquatics (300 taxa).

The garden as a whole has some 11 500 taxa. It also owns the 150-ha Wojsławice estate near Niemcza, whose arboretum is famous for its conifers, rhododendrons and azaleas.

NE of city, within old walls 071 322 59 57 **Open** Apr–Oct daily 8am–6pm. Glasshouses: daily 10am–5pm **Size** 7.5ha (19ac) **Owner** Uniwersytetu Wrocławskiego
www.biol.uni.wroc.pl/obuwr/
obuwr@biol.uni.wroc.pl

15. Peterhof
Razvodnaya ul., 2
191041 Sankt-Peterburg

Peter the Great built the palace and laid out the gardens at Peterhof after his defeat of the Swedes at the battle of Pultava in 1709. It was a statement of imperial victory, symbolised by the fountain-statue, at the centre of the lower garden, of Samson ripping apart the jaws of a lion. Peter modelled it on Versailles and employed the French architect Jean-Baptiste Le Blond to build the palace and lay out the formal gardens. The fountains are the most comprehensive in Europe.

If you come by road, the glittering domes of the palace draw you down through the stately upper garden. A sequence of grand pools and fountains is flanked by parterres, arcades, avenues, formal gardens and *bosquets*. The Neptune fountain came from Nuremburg, where it had lain unused since the 1660s.

The landward approach to Peterhof leads through a spacious sequence of pools and avenues towards the gilded roofs of the palace.

The lower park, below the palace, is a very extensive network of straight avenues punctuated by cascades, fountains and monuments of every imaginable design. It is best approached from the sea, early on a summer morning when the sun lights up the 64 fountains and 225 gilded statues of the main cascade. Their number and excellence, all glistening and spurting with water-jets, are quite outstanding. The view down the cascade, over the Samson fountain, past lion statues and along the central canal (itself a wooded avenue lined with fountains) out into the Baltic Sea is by far the most emblematic in Russia.

But there is much to see and admire throughout, including the Chessboard Hill cascade (a black-and-white surface); the Triton fountain; the Adam and Eve fountains (with attractive pavilions); the Marly lake right at the western end (the name comes from Louis XIV's hunting lodge at Marly, now lost); a vast semicircular orangery; and a landscaped garden around the 19th-century Cottage Palace at the extreme eastern end.

Peterhof is Russia's grandest palace-garden and should on no account be missed.

On coast, 30km W of Sankt-Peterburg. Best visited by hydrofoil from central Sankt-Peterburg
☎ 812 427 5287 **Open** Daily (except Mon) 9am–8pm. Fountains run: mid–May–mid-Oct 11am–5pm **Size** 200ha (494ac) **Owner** The State
🅿 🖥 🍴 🚻 ♿ 📷 🖼
W www.peterhof.ru
@ admin@peterhof.ru

16. Komarov Botanical Garden
Professora Popova ul., 2
197376 Sankt-Peterburg

Peter the Great founded St Petersburg's botanic garden in 1714 for the cultivation of medicinal herbs. During the 19th century it became the repository for Russian botanical exploration, as collectors brought plants here from all over the world. The garden still has an excellent rock-garden and interesting sections devoted to the regional flora of the Caucasus, Central Asia and North America.

The layout is informal, remade in the English land-scape style in the 19th century. The total number of taxa is uncertain; some Russian sources say 6700, others 12 000. The elegant glasshouses, currently undergoing resto-ration, have a large collection of tropical and subtropical plants, especially cycads, palms, rhododendrons and orchids. The outdoor collections are good on ferns, Chinese and Japanese plants, bamboos, conifers, tulips and lilacs.

Northern part of old city centre
☎ 812 234 1237 **Open** Daily (except Fri) 11am–4pm **Size** 20ha (50ac) **Owner** Russian Academy of Sciences 🅿 🚻 ♿
W www.spbrc.nw.ru
@ binadmin@OK3277.spb.edu

17. Summer Gardens
191186 Sankt-Peterburg

The Summer Gardens are historically important and popular with members of the public. They were laid out in the French style in 1703 for Peter the Great, but damaged by serious flooding in 1777.

What we see today is essentially the gardens as redesigned shortly thereafter by Catherine the Great. They still have their formal shapes, with long parallel avenues going north-south from the river and west-east towards the Summer Palace but, in place

Victoria amazonica has a house of its own at Komarov Botanical Garden in St Petersburg.

St Petersburg's Summer Gardens are thickly populated with fine anatomical specimens barely disguised as allegories, nymphs, virtues and minor deities.

of parterres and fountains, the gardens are shaded by tall trees, mainly limes and Norway maples. Long, straight canals enclose the garden on either side. Scattered plantings of lilacs and *Philadelphus* add scent in early summer, when the paeonies and hostas are also in flower. Some 80 statues adorn the northern end by the river: endless representations of nymphs, virtues, seasons, muses and allegorical figures.

The neighbouring Michailowskiy Park has recently been restored as it was when first laid out by Alexander I's court architect, Carlo Rossi, in 1803.

On river, opposite Summer Palace **C** 812 314 0374 **Open** Daily (except Tue) 10am–10pm **Size** 11ha (28ac) **Owner** St Petersburg City Council **P** **WC** **&** **▦**

18. Pavlovsk

Revolyutsii ul., 20
189623 Pavlovsk

Pavlovsk is the ochre-coloured palace outside St Petersburg that Empress Catherine II ('The Great') built for her son and heir, Paul I. The architect was the Scotsman Charles Cameron, an admirer of the renaissance architect Palladio, who began work in 1779.

The remarkable park we see today was developed, year by year, throughout the next 20 years. Paul's wife, the Empress Maria Feodorovna, soon took sole charge; she was a princess of Württemberg and much influenced by Rousseau-esque ideas about the landscape.

Pavlovsk sits above a great landscaped valley of the Slavyanka River and is best

The Temple to Friendship is one of many beautiful and imposing monuments in Pavlovsk's park.

No Russian landscape has such a display of artistry, power and wealth as Tsarskoe Selo; this is the Hermitage that faces the palace at the end of the formal gardens.

seen by crossing one of the fine bridges and exploring the far bank, where Cameron's classical Cold Baths and the Apollo Colonnade lie. These, and all the monuments throughout the English landscape park, are of supreme beauty.

Return by the tall, handsome, circular Doric Temple to Friendship and explore the area immediately behind the palace, where a series of even more exquisite buildings leads from garden to garden – rather more formal than the flowing landscape style of the surrounding park. Here are the graceful Ionic Three Graces Pavilion, the classical Aviary, and a rustic Dairy on the French model (now a run-down restaurant) – all linked by lime avenues and formal gardens.

Beyond are the restored Rose Pavilion, the Monument to Parents, and a charming area decorated with statues of the Muses and Allegories called the Star, where 12 avenues radiate out into the park. If you wander yet further afield, you will encounter numerous bridges, cascades, gateways and statues, plus very fine meadows, woods and parkland.

But be sure to visit the palace itself, too; it is stuffed with good things from all over Europe and some excellent pieces designed by Maria Feodorovna herself.

30km S of Sankt-Peterburg
☎ 812 470 2155 **Open** Daily 10am–6pm (5pm in winter) **Size** 607ha (1499ac) **Owner** The State
🅿 ➤ 🍴 🚻 ♿ 🏛 🎏
🅆 www.pavlovsk.org
@ admin@pavlovsk.org

19. Tsarskoe Selo
Sadavaya ul., 7
Pushkin
Sankt-Peterburg

Tsarskoe Selo is large, important and uniquely beautiful. You will need all day to do it justice – and a lot of walking.

Start in front of the Catherine Palace. The formal gardens, dating back to Empress Elizabeth I in the 1740s, run gently down to the Hermitage pavilion. Immediately outside the palace are complex broderies worked out in coloured mineral surfaces – crushed brick, charcoal and pale gravel, as well as grass. Note the tall trees that follow: Empress Catherine the Great gave the order in 1762 that the trees and hedges in the formal gardens should no longer be pruned, but allowed to grow naturally. The tall limes are, therefore, historically correct, even though they interfere with views to and from this most important façade of the blue-and-white rococo palace.

The Empress turned her attention throughout the 1770s and 1780s to creating the stunning landscape park, aided by a team of English and German gardeners, who took their inspiration from contemporary English designs. Its centrepiece is the lake, surrounded by the grandest imaginable pavilions and ornaments. The so-called grotto is a mini-palace of the most intricate design, while the Palladian bridge is a copy of Stowe's. Elsewhere are a victory column on an island in the lake, a pyramid, a gothic church, a mosque and a semicircular colonnade, planted with climbing plants and guarded by two large lions. Best of all is the Chinese village, composed of ten substantial villas in the oriental style, with their roofs turned up at the corners and painted pale yellow, orange and green. It is approached by any number of Chinese bridges, including an ingenious one at the intersection of two canals, served by four staircases, one rising from each of the four quadrants.

The adjoining Alexander Park has canals, lakes, avenues, an English landscape garden, an artificial hill called Mount Parnassus, and a landscaped lake. Here and throughout Tsarskoe Selo the architectural and decorative detail is infinitely varied and fascinating.

25km S of Sankt-Peterburg
812 465 5308 **Open** Daily 9am–8pm (or dusk) **Size** 566ha (1398ac) **Owner** The State
W www.tzar.ru
& www.pushkin-town.net
@ tzar@spb.cityline.ru

20. Gatchina Palace

Krasnoarmeisky pr., 1
188350 Gatchina

Gatchina is both the saddest and the most exciting of the imperial palaces and parks around St Petersburg. The palace is smart and full of gob-smacking decoration,

but the park has barely begun to recover from 70 years of communist neglect; visit it now, while it is still deep in beautiful melancholy.

Catherine the Great's German gardener, Johann Busch, laid out the park in the 1770s for her favourite Count Grigory Orlov in the English style. To Busch we owe the lakes and woodlands that give Gatchina its brilliance and charm when the sun is shining. Her architect, Antonio Rinaldi, bequeathed us such monuments as the Eagle Pavilion and the Eagle Column (the eagle was Orlov's heraldic device).

In 1783 the Empress bought back Gatchina and gave it to her son, Paul, who preferred formal gardens, but made several additions to the park. One was the Temple of Venus (based on the original at Chantilly), but by far the most interesting was the Birch House, made for Emperor Paul by his wife, the Empress Maria Feodorovna. It resembles no more than a pile of birch logs, until you notice a key hole or a drainpipe and realise that the simulated wood disguises a pavilion with a rich and exquisite interior. It, too, awaits restoration.

Meanwhile, enjoy the neglect and decay, safe in the expectation that improvements will soon arrive.

45km S of Sankt-Peterburg
271 134 492 **Open** Daily dawn–dusk **Size** 700ha (1728ac) **Owner** The State
W www.gatchina.ru

21. Moscow University Apothecaries' Garden

Prospect Mira, 26
129090 Moskva

This is the oldest botanic garden in Russia; it is also the best maintained and most interesting to visit. Peter the Great founded it in 1706 and planted a Siberian larch (*Larix sibirica*) that still survives. Still older is a white willow (*Salix alba*) near the lake, which predates the garden itself. It was at first a garden of medicinal plants but has belonged to Moscow University since 1805.

Avenues of limes date from the 18th century, though the garden was landscaped in the 19th century. Now its main functions are education, conservation and public amenity. Colourful borders and a long tank dominate the entrance, but the most interesting parts are off to one side – a woodland garden with interesting trees (a good stand of *Phellodendron amurense*) and a growing collection of ferns.

One of the many fine bridges that tack together the watery landscape at Gatchina.

Autumn colour on *Betula procurva* in the well-managed Moscow University Apothecaries' Garden.

The glasshouses, and much of their collections, were brought from Germany in 1945 as war reparations. Some specimens are ancient, including an *Encephalartos altensteinii*, thought to be 300 years old. Among the garden's 18 000 taxa are the largest collections of gesneriads, begonias and orchids in Russia. All are in the process of being transferred to a new range, whose tropical house is 33 m high; its four sections are each 1600 sq. m.

Unfortunately, funding for the garden remains a problem, and the areas devoted to the native flora of the former Soviet republics have now been abandoned.

9km due N of city centre
☎ 095 977 9044 **Open** Daily dawn–dusk **Size** 340ha (840ac) **Owner** Russian Academy of Sciences ▣ WC ♿
W www.gbsad.ru
@ infor@bgsad.run

UKRAINE

23. Nikitsky Botanical Garden
National Research Centre
98648 Nikita
Yalta

Yalta's botanic gardens are remarkable for two reasons. First, they are one of the few botanic gardens of the old Soviet Union that are still

---

Skilful management and fund-raising have enabled the garden to rebuild its historic glasshouses (built in 1891, though the *Cycas circinalis* is over 200 years old) and lay out new areas for education and facilities.

NE of city centre ☎ 095 280 5880 **Open** Daily 10am–6pm (8pm May–Sep) **Size** 6.5ha (16ac) **Owner** Moscow University
P ▣ WC ♿
W www.hortus.ru
@ artyomparshin@mtu-net.ru

22. Main Botanic Garden
Botanicheskaya, 4
127276 Moskva

This enormous garden was founded in 1945 as a showpiece for pan-Soviet botany. At its centre are thick natural woodlands of oak (*Quercus robur*), birch and Norway maple (*Acer platanoides*). Within this are large stands of exotic and native trees and shrubs, including good collections of plants like lilacs, which survive the cold winters. Indeed, it is a good garden to discover just what will survive in such a zone.

Moscow's Main Botanic Garden has suffered from underfunding since this photograph of doronicums and birches was taken in communist times.

thriving and well maintained. Second, they are a Mediterranean paradise for plants, with beautiful views of the Crimean coast.

The gardens were founded in 1812, originally as a silkworm farm, but soon developed as a repository for other useful plants. Exotic plants seldom seen in Ukraine include myrtles, *Feijoa, Chamaerops* and an olive grove, 160 years old. Stone pines (*Pinus pinea*) from Italy grow alongside wellingtonias from California. There are extensive thickets of Chinese bamboos, palm trees, pistachios, *Arbutus* and such economic species as figs and persimmons.

Horticultural research and the breeding of new plants has always been a priority, and the garden has important collections of roses (2000 cultivars), *Clematis*, chrysanthemums and fruit and nut trees. There are also two nature reserves: one for the native flora of *Quercus pubescens* and junipers and the other for a mixture of natives and exotics, including *Pinus halepensis* var. *stankewiczii* and metasequoias.

5km E of Yalta **⬛** 065 433 5530 **Open** By appointment **Size** 1000ha (2469ac) **Owner** Ukraine Academy of Agrarian Sciences **P** **WC** **⬛**
W www.nbg.crimea.ua
@ nbg@yalta.crimea.ua

24. Central Botanical Garden, Kiev

Tymiriazivs'ka 1
252014 Kiyev

Kiev's main botanic garden is also the prettiest. It was founded in 1936 and contains over 13 000 taxa. The collections of tropical and subtropical plants in the glasshouses (more than 3000 species) are probably its single greatest asset, especially its orchids. It is, however, best known locally for its enormous lilac garden, running down to the Vydubitsky Monastery. Native plants are well represented, especially the flora of the Crimea, but there

are sections, too, for the Caucasus, Carpathians and Russian Far East.

Also worth finding are the pinetum, a fine rose garden (lots of historic cultivars, unknown in western Europe), and the displays of paeonies and magnolias. The collections of useful plants are unusually comprehensive, notably Ukrainian cultivars of medicinal, edible and economic plants, especially fruit trees.

West bank of Dnieper (southern end), near Vydubitsky Monastery **⬛** 044 295 4105 **Open** Daily 10am–8pm (5pm in winter) **Size** 130ha (321ac) **Owner** Ukraine Academy of Sciences **P** **⬛** **WC** **&**

GEORGIA

25. Tbilisi Botanic Garden

St Botanikuri N 1
380005, Tbilisi

Tiflis's botanic garden is the oldest in the Caucasus, with a thriving collection of endemic plants of the region. It once formed part of the palace gardens of King George XII (who reigned 1756–95) and is still by far the best place

to see one of the world's richest floras, all brought together in a charming and fascinating garden high above Tiflis.

At least, that is how it was until the early 1990s. Since then, the garden has suffered from civil war, pillage, uncertain water supplies, power cuts and lack of funds to such an extent that it seemed fated to close forever. A cry went out in 2003 to the citizens of Tbilisi to aid the garden in its plight, and hundreds of citizens gave their time, labour and money to restore it.

The garden's collections are threefold: Georgian endemics, endangered plants of the Caucasus, and an arboretum. Some 70 ha are untouched native vegetation, where *Acer monspessulanum* var. *ibericum* and *Celtis caucasica* are among the tree-cover species. The garden itself is the place to see such rarities as *Populus salicifolia, Iris elegantissima, Lilium georgicum* and *Ophrys oestrifera* subsp. *oestrifera*.

City centre, above Rustaveli Ave **⬛** 032 723 409 **Open** By appointment **Size** 128ha (316ac) **Owner** Georgian Academy of Sciences **P** **WC**
W www.acnet.ge/botang.htm
@ manel@geo.net.ge

The collection of Georgian endemic plants at Tbilisi Botanic Garden displays the richness of the Caucasian flora.

Gardens of Central Europe

Imperial Austria dominated and determined the development of garden design throughout Central Europe. Almost no gardens survive from the years before the siege of Vienna in 1688, but the century that followed was characterised in Austria by a powerful surge of self-confident building. Fischer von Erlach and Lukas von Hildebrandt interpreted the French style for the emperors and leading nobles, clerical and lay. Consequently, Austria has magnificent baroque gardens in and around its imperial capital: Schönbrunn and the Belvedere must be counted among Europe's top ten. Many were later reworked in the English landscape style, and some have recently been restored to their 18th-century glory. But Vienna has a concentration of baroque splendour unmatched in Europe.

The Czechs have been quick since 1990 to reclaim their glorious history of architecture and the arts. Restoration projects have put their great 18th- and 19th-century gardens back on the tourist map, and provided an appropriate setting for their many historic houses. Here, and in Slovakia and Hungary, large-scale landscape gardens and arboreta were made until the outbreak of World War I in 1914.

Slovakia has been slower to come to terms with its heritage. Gardens were not part of the indigenous Slovak culture. Many of its historic landscapes were associated with the Hungarian ascendancy, and those where restoration has begun, like the arboretum at Mlyňany, are represented as Slovak achievements with no reference to their oppressors.

Hungary itself always took its culture from abroad – Austria, France, Italy and England were the sources for Hungarian

ABOVE: The park at Lednice in the Czech Republic is one of the most extensive and complex in Europe.
OPPOSITE: Swiss alpine gardens like 'La Thomasia' are often set among breathtaking scenery.

The rococo Privy Garden (imperial private garden) at Schönbrunn in Austria has recently been handsomely restored.

ideas on houses, gardens and the decorative arts. Despite the strong movement for independence from Austria in the 18th-century and the nationalist movement of the 19th, nothing sprang from indigenous Hungarian forms. Not for nothing did Austrian statesman Prince von Metternich declare that Asia begins at the eastern edge of Vienna ('*Asien beginnt an der Landstraße*'). In Hungary, as in Slovakia and the Czech Republic, much was lost in the years of Communism. The post-communist laws of land restitution have also impeded progress: garden restoration is a low priority for returning owners, while many historic estates are still occupied by special schools, institutes and lunatic asylums with no funding and precarious security of tenure.

Switzerland is a small republic of mountain cantons populated by religious dissidents, who never adopted the aristocratic culture that gave other countries their enduring historical gardens. Nevertheless, both Italy and France influenced the design of middle-class gardens in the 17th and 18th centuries, and a fashion for English landscapes followed in the 19th. Few private gardens are regularly open to the public; the visitable Swiss gardens today (all superbly run) are public parks, botanic gardens, and high-mountain alpine gardens.

Prague's botanic garden has excellent naturalistic plantings of short herbaceous plants and alpines.

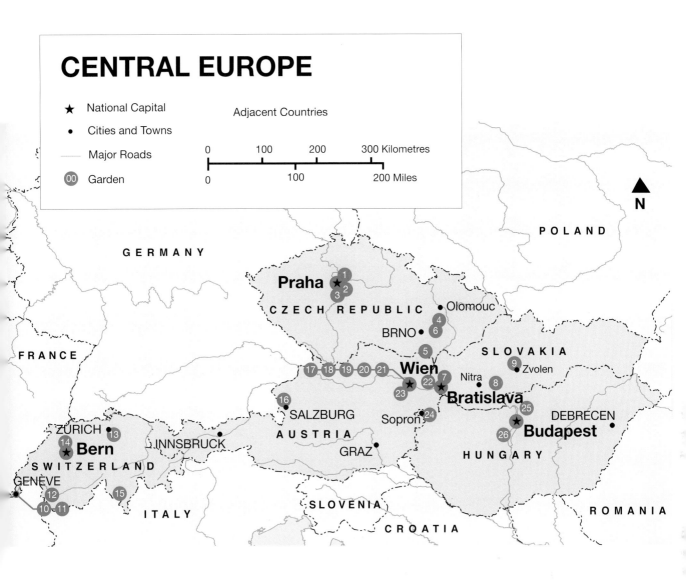

Gardens of Central Europe

Czech Republic
1. Pražská Botanická Zahrada
2. Průhonice Park
3. Konopište
4. Arcibiskubsky Samek a Zahrady Kroměříž
5. Zámecký Park Lednice
6. Státní Hrad Buchlov

Slovakia
7. Botanicka Zahrada UK Bratislava
8. Arborétum Mlyňany
9. Arborétum Borová Hora

Switzerland
10. Conservatoire et Jardin Botanique de la Ville de Genève

11. Parc de la Grange
12. Jardin Alpin de Pont de Nant 'La Thomasia'
13. Botanischer Garten der Universität Zürich
14. Botanischer Garten der Universität Bern
15. Isole di Brissago Giardino Botanico

Austria
16. Mirabellgarten
17. Schloßpark Schönbrunn
18. Volksgarten, Burggarten & Stadtpark

19. Schloßpark Belvedere
20. Alpinum Wien
21. Botanische Garten der Universität Wien
22. Schloß Hof
23. Rosarium Baden bei Wien

Hungary
24. Nagycenk
25. Vácrátóti Botanikuskert
26. Martonvásári Kastélypark

Prague Botanic Garden: alpine gardens flourished even under Communism.

Venezuela). Each is ornamentally landscaped. The plants are exceptionally well displayed and chosen not so much for their botanic importance as for their educational interest and beauty.

The baroque gardens of the nearby castle of Troja have recently been restored and are also well worth a visit.

N of city centre, near Zoo
■ 234 148 111 **Open** Daily 9am–7pm (6pm in Apr; 5pm in Oct & 4pm in winter). *Fata Morgana* **closed** Mon **Size** 18ha (44ac)
Owner City of Prague
P ■ WC ♿ ♦ ▣
W www.botanicka.cz
@ info@botanicka.cz

CZECH REPUBLIC

1. Pražská Botanická Zahrada

Nádvorní 134
171 00 Praha 7-Troja

Prague's botanic garden is a place to see well-grown plants and contemplate the Czechs' love of horticulture. When it was founded in 1969, the intention was to extend it to 130 ha, but little was done to plan or plant it until 1992, when the city of Prague took over and pegged it to 18 ha (still large by modern standards). It already has 20 000 different taxa, and the number is growing.

The rock-garden is exceptional, with many different habitats and some larger areas given to prairie-style plantings. The enormous Japanese garden (1.5 ha) is not very convincing but a pleasant winding landscape with a few oriental features, including an area of water and rocks, and another of cherry trees, rhododendrons, azaleas, *Iris kaempferi* hybrids and Japanese maples. Elsewhere are an excellent display of rare bulbs, an alpine house, a heath-and-heather garden, a Mediterranean collection and a vineyard.

Fata Morgana is the pretty name for a stylish, south-facing glasshouse, 400 m up the hillside. Its slinky, 'S'-shaped structure is tucked into the hillside, so that one side is sheer rock for its entire length. It is divided into three sections: dry climates, tropical (complete with frogs and fish in the pools) and the mountain flora of Asia and the Andes (notably the rare vegetation of the Roraima-Tepui formation in

2. Průhonice Park

252 43 Průhonice

Průhonice is an important arboretum with a good horticultural collection of other plants. The way to see it is to start walking and keep walking, until you are exhausted: there are 40 km of winding paths. Count Ernst Emanuel Silva-Tarouca

The rhododendron collection at Průhonice is the best in the Czech Republic and its arboretum the largest in Central Europe.

acquired the estate (by marriage) in 1885 and remodelled the house, unfortunately not visitable, in what is politely called the Czech neo-renaissance style.

Tarouca was a passionate plantsman and, although his main legacy was trees, he also had a painterly eye for ornamental effects. Walk to the end of the first lake when the rhododendrons and azaleas are flowering in early June, and look back at the castle, reflected in the water and framed by colour; it is the perfect postcard view. Průhonice has a large collection of 8000 rhododendrons (but only 100 cultivars) and good collections, too, of roses, hemerocallis, paeonies and water lilies. The assembly of *Iris* species is said to be the world's largest. The arboretum accounts for about 1500 taxa: 1200 are broad-leaved trees and 300 are coniferous (these have thrived especially well). Look out for the type plant of *Pinus heldreichii* 'Smidtii' in the woods.

The whole estate is laid out not in the English landscape style but in imitation of the woods and meadows of Bohemia. It is tacked together by wooden bridges, natural rock-gardens, 10 ha of lakes, and wonderful views across open, flowery clearings.

20km SE of Prague 🄲 271 015 290 **Open** Apr–Oct daily 7am–7pm (but 8am–5pm in winter) **Size** 244ha (603ac) **Owner** Institute of Botany, Academy of Sciences of the Czech Republic 🄿 🄲 🆆🄲 🄶
🆆 www.ibot.cas.cz

3. Konopište
Mendelova 131
256 01 Benešov

When the German commander-in-chief Admiral Tirpitz visited Konopište to stay with Grand Duke Franz-Ferdinand of Austria in 1913, it was widely assumed that they were planning a joint military venture. In fact, they were both

The opulent and extensive rose garden at Konopište is the highlight of a visit to Grand Duke Franz-Ferdinand's vast and impressive domain.

passionate about roses, and the Admiral had come to see the Grand Duke's collection.

Franz-Ferdinand – the Austrian emperor's heir – bought the Konopište estate in 1887, and laid it out in the grand manner. The castle (well worth visiting) is an 1890s gothic extravagance and the park is a wooded landscape with some rather more formal areas to display the Grand Duke's Italian sculptures, urns and fountains. Franz-Ferdinand's arboretum has grown to maturity and has a fine collection of conifers and ornamental forms of beech and oak; look out for the tall *Quercus robur* 'Concordia' on the edge of the rose garden.

The extensive rose garden is still the most exciting feature, designed in 1910 in an Italianate style, with Venus on top of a tall column at the centre, surrounded by four obelisks perched on stone spheres. It has recently been well restored (but not so well replanted) and is both impressive and attractive, with its beds cut out of the grass, red roses, urns, statues and firm geometry. Above it is a cast-iron conservatory in the classical style. On the terrace below are a pretty water garden and small lake, designed and planted by an Englishman called Marcham in 1913.

45km SE of Prague 🄲 317 721 366 **Open** Apr–Sep daily 9am–6pm **Size** 340ha (840ac) **Owner** The State 🄿 🄲 🄗 🆆🄲 🄶 🄵
🆆 www.zamek-konopiste.cz
🄰 info@zamek-konopiste.cz

4. Arcibiskubsky Samek a Zahrady Kroměříž
Snemovní nám. 1
767 01 Kroměříž
Zlín

Kroměříž has the best preserved early baroque garden in central Europe – so important and beautiful that it is now a UNESCO World Heritage site. It was laid out beyond the city's walls by Italian designers for the Archbishop of Olomouc in the 1660s around an octagonal rotunda, from which paths stretch straight in eight directions. The paths are lined with hedges of lime and hornbeam at least 5 m high; sometimes they arch over to make a tunnel. The areas in between are put to formal gardens of many different designs – box broderies, mazes and simple grass plats.

Only half the 11-ha garden has been restored; in the parts still to be recovered are two mounds: perfect vantage points from which to admire the rest of the garden. And all along one side is a most elegant white colonnade,

Zámecký Park's grand tropical glasshouse contrasts with its English-gothic palace; its formal gardens are magnificent.

244 m long, set with statues and busts of classical gods and mythical heroes. The whole design seems to have leapt from a renaissance book of garden patterns and impresses the visitor by its sheer size, quite apart from its beauty.

The glasshouses (including a grand, old-fashioned 18th-century palm house) near the entrance have a fine collection of tropical plants; citrus and agapanthus are put out for the summer in pots.

Kroměříž has a second garden, around the Archbishop's palace, a 19th-century landscaped park, with lakes drawn from the river Morava. The handsome garden buildings here include a Pompeian Colonnade, some elegant bridges, a Temple of Friendship, and a Chinese pavilion. The rare trees and rhododendrons are said to be the best collection in Moravia.

45km S of Olomouc; 60km E of Brno 🄲 573 502 011 **Open** Park: daily dawn–dusk Garden: Apr–Oct daily 10am–6pm **Size** 65ha (161ac) **Owner** The State
🅿 🖻 🍴 🆆🅲 ♿ 🛗 🎴
🅦 www.azz.cz
@ zamek@azz.cz

5. Zámecký Park Lednice
691 44 Lednice

The Lednice estate is a UNESCO world heritage site, and rightly so. It is a vast complex of sumptuous palace buildings, gardens, parks, lakes and semi-wild countryside, entirely developed by the super-rich Liechtenstein princes between 1249 and 1945. One of its popular names is 'The Garden of Europe'.

The palace received its last make-over in the mid-19th century: it was given its theatrical English-gothic appearance between 1846 and 1858, when the enormous tropical glasshouse, designed by an Englishman, was somewhat incongruously attached to the house.

The gardens around the palace are formal, extensive, and undergoing restoration. They were given a Victorian-English format in the 1850s, with clipped cones of yew replacing the older baroque parterres. Most lie to the side of the house in a series of slightly disconnected designs, enclosed by hedges of box or yew, but the colourful seasonal bedding is palatial in scale.

The garden buildings lavished around the English-style park are many and of the highest quality. The most conspicuous are the 1790s Turkish minaret, visible from a large area, and the *Janův Hrad* (John's Castle) built as a mediaeval ruin in 1807. Elsewhere are temples (the Three Graces, Diana, Apollo and others), a Roman aqueduct, an Egyptian obelisk and a classical colonnade. Allow plenty of time to explore

A baroque rotunda dominates the formal gardens at Kroměříž, seen here from one of the glasshouses attached to the Archbishop's palace.

and discover them. The many good trees include the tallest *Torreya californica* in the country.

65km S of Brno, off motorway to Bratislava 519 340 128 **Open** Daily dawn–dusk **Size** 270ha (667ac) **Owner** The State
www.lednice.cz
szlednice@iol.cz

6. Státní Hrad Buchlov
687 08 Buchlovice

The house at Buchlovice is a baroque gem, elegantly enclosed by two curving wings. It dates from the early 1700s, and probably had an Italian architect. The baroque garden that surrounds it is perfectly in keeping: a whisper of low box hedges around a fountain, wrought-iron gates and steps leading up to the courtyard, itself lightly decorated with baroque hedging and plants in pots. A broad terrace stretches out behind the house and leads down to another formal garden around a fountain, but this is simpler, with grass squares surrounded by box hedges and all enclosed by hornbeam tunnels.

Many of the owners of Buchlovice were enthusiastic tree planters, and the main reason to visit the estate now is to see splendid collections dating from the 1790s and the 1850s. Some trees were planted rather close to the

Bratislava's botanic garden has an especially interesting sequence of rock-gardens.

house, like a vast *Sophora japonica* (which blocks off one of the terraces), but the fine specimens are numerous – huge limes, many weeping beeches, elegant conifers, large examples of *Magnolia acuminata*, and a multi-stemmed *Pterocarya fraxinifolia* behind the house. A stream runs through part of the park, where lilacs, rhododendrons and azaleas add colour in spring. White peacocks add an exotic dimension.

50km E of Brno 572 434 240 **Open** May–Sep daily (except Mon) 9am–5pm (but 6pm Jul–Aug); Apr & Oct weekends & pub hols only, 9am–4pm **Size** 19ha (47ac) **Owner** The State
www.zamek-buchlovice.cz
zamek@zamek-buchlovice.cz

SLOVAKIA

7. Botanicka Zahrada UK Bratislava
Botanicka 3
841 04 Bratislava

The Comenius University Botanic Garden doubles up as a focal point for botanic research in Slovakia and a pleasant destination for visitors. It was founded in 1942 and has a collection of about 5000 different plants. The large rose garden is the ornamental centrepiece, planted for colour with some 125 cultivars. The rock-gardens are probably the most interesting exhibits and have extensive collections of the endemic Slovak flora, as well as attractive displays of plants from mountain ranges around the world.

Also worth seeing are the Japanese garden, rhododendrons and azaleas, and *Poncirus trifoliata*, flourishing outside without winter protection. The glasshouses have sections devoted to tropical and subtropical plants, Australian species, palms, orchids, cacti and tropical aquatics (for example, *Victoria cruziana*).

Just N of Danube & W of E62 265 421 311 **Open** Apr–Oct daily 9am–6pm **Size** 5ha (12½ac) **Owner** Univerzita Komenského
www.uniba.sk
jaroslav.bella@rec.uniba.sk

The formal garden at Státní Hrad Buchlov is hemmed in by magnificent mature trees: *Sophora japonica* (on right) hides a wing of the house.

Arborétum Mlyňany was badly managed in communist times, but has a respectable collection of young conifers.

chinensis and several forms of *Q. mongolica*. Maintenance is fairly low-key, and labelling is poor, but knowledgeable tree lovers will be amazed by the size and number of the trees.

30km E of Nitra ☎ 376 334 571 **Open** Daily 7am–6pm (9am weekends & pub hols) **Size** 67ha (165ac) **Owner** Slovak Academy of Sciences P ⬛ WC ♿ 👥 🎁 W www.arboretum.sav.sk @ arboretum_mlynany@nextra.sk

8. Arborétum Mlyňany
Vieska nad Zitavou, no. 178
951 52 Slepčany

Count István Ambrozy-Migazzi began to make the arboretum on a hillside at Mlyňany, with distant views of the Tribeč mountains, when he came to live here in 1892. He wanted to grow as many 'foreign' plants as possible, to discover what would survive in this corner of what was then Hungary. He imported thousands of trees and shrubs, especially from nurseries in Germany, France and England, and inserted them into the native woodland.

However, political changes forced him to leave Mlyňany in 1914 and he never returned. Eventually the estate was taken over by the Slovak Academy of Sciences which, from the mid-1950s, began to enlarge the collections.

The original sense of spacious parkland and exotically planted woodland has been lost as the older trees have grown together over the years. Younger plantings have, however, benefited from the protection of established oaks and hornbeams. Exotic oaks are one of the arboretum's specialities: look out for fine old specimens of *Quercus* × *hispanica* 'Ambrozyana' (named from Mlyňany; another introduction was *Thuja occidentalis* 'Malonyana'), *Q.* × *libanerris* and *Q. robur* 'Cucullata'. The newer plantings include a shapely *Populus simonii, Fraxinus*

9. Arborétum Borová Hora
Borovianska cesta 2171/66
960 53 Zvolen

The arboretum at Zvolen dates to 1964 and exists mainly as a resource for the research station attached to the technical university. One of its purposes is to identify and propagate geographic variability within native tree species: Zvolen has almost 1100 tree species and what makes it fascinating to visit are the *forms*, because they are being trialled for release in our gardens. There are only 12 species of *Picea* here, but 89 forms and cultivars – a unique collection. Likewise, there are 49 cultivars of *Pinus*, 39 *Sorbus*, 36 *Acer*, 25 *Salix* and 28 *Fagus* (the latter derived from a single species, *F. sylvatica*).

Even more interesting is the collection of 700 beautiful roses, assembled to test winter-

Blue *Salvia nemorosa* speckles the meadows in Arborétum Borová Hora at Zvolen.

hardiness and conserve historic cultivars. These include some 116 cultivars bred by Jan Böhm in Bohemia in the 1920s and 1930s and by Rudolf Geschwind in what is now Slovakia between 1867 and 1910. These represent an inestimable gene bank for future breeding, though many of the plants are over-pruned and under-fed. The policy of continuous planting means that there are also lots of youngish trees and shrubs to see.

The arboretum is on a steep hillside and spread over a large area, so be prepared for lots of walking.

On northern edge of Zvolen, 2km from centre **C** 455 320 814 **Open** All year Mon–Fri 7am–3.30pm **Size** 48ha (119ac) **Owner** Technická univerzita Zvolen **P ⬛ WC ♿** **W** www.alpha.tuzvo.sk

SWITZERLAND

10. Conservatoire et Jardin Botanique de la Ville de Genève

1, ch. de l'Impératrice
1292 Chambésy/Genève

Geneva's botanic garden was begun by the great Swiss botanist Augustin-Pyramus de Candolle in 1817 and moved to its present position in 1904. Its 10 000 taxa include some fine old trees (especially oaks, such as *Quercus robur*) that date back to its days as a private garden; the five bulky plane trees (*Platanus × hispanica*) that march up towards the glasshouses are thought to be nearly 300 years old.

The design is fluid, like an English-style park, with good displays of bedding, roses, tulips, dahlias and irises to please all visitors. The high standard of maintenance also adds considerably to one's enjoyment. The domed conservatory (built as recently as 1987, just above the lakeside main road, with a viewing gallery 8 m up) has an ornamental display of palm

The design of the elegant new conservatory in Geneva's botanic garden is based on classical forms.

trees at the centre, as well as good collections from tropical regions and a dry area for cacti and succulents. The Winter Garden and other houses (including one for *Victoria cruziana*) are also worth visiting.

The extensive rock-garden offers many different habitats, including walls of tufa rock. It is mainly laid out geographically, with a surprisingly large collection of Mediterranean plants and a mission to conserve the flora of the canton of Geneva, which is supported by an alpine outstation in the mountains at Bourg-St-Pierre (Valais).

Other newish features are the prairie garden (not very successful), a garden that illustrates the history of the rose, and a garden for medicinal plants.

N of old city centre, by Palais des Nations **C** 022 418 51 00 **Open** Apr–Sep daily 8am–7.30pm. Glasshouses: daily (except Fri) 9.30–11am & 2– 4.30pm **Size** 18ha (44ac) **Owner** City of Geneva **P ⬛ ⑪ WC ♿ ⬛ ⬛** **W** www.ville-ge.ch/cjb/

11. Parc de la Grange

Ave William Favre
1205 Genève

Parc de la Grange is the best of the many public parks in Geneva – beautifully laid out, well maintained and welcoming. Structure comes

Parc de la Grange's delightful rose garden is just above Lake Geneva.

from the older trees that were part of an English-style park laid out in the 19th century by the philanthropist William Favre, who gave the estate to the city in 1918. Ancient oaks and cedars date back to his tenure, as do the tall *Acer monspeliensis* along the eastern edge.

The main attraction nowadays is the rose garden, started in 1944 and now Switzerland's largest at 1.2 ha, with 200 different varieties and 12 000 bushes. It is formally laid out around an Italianate pavilion just above the shore of Lake Geneva. Pools and terraces add variety to the layout, where roses are generally grown in single-cultivar blocks. It makes no claim to be a comprehensive collection, but sets out to delight the visitor: the colour and scent at midsummer are astonishing.

E end of city, 1.5km from Pont du Mont-Blanc ☎ 022 418 50 00 **Open** Daily 7am–6pm (or sunset) **Size** 21ha (52ac) **Owner** City of Genève ▢ ▢ ▢ ▢ ▢ ▢ www.ville-ge.ch

12. Jardin Alpin de Pont de Nant 'La Thomasia'

Pont de Nant
1888 Bex/Plans-sur-Bex

High rock-gardens are a feature of Switzerland, and 'La Thomasia' is one of the best. It lies at an altitude of 1260 m in an alpine meadow at the top of a mossy, wooded valley.

The garden was first laid out in 1891 by a local family of amateur botanists called Thomas. It has no formal design, just a series of 70 humpy rockeries laid out geographically, but each designed to suit the growing conditions required by a group of plants – sun or shade, rock or moraine, calcareous or calcifuge. In satisfying these requirements, each is technically as perfect as possible. 'La Thomasia' also has a stream, several pools, a bog and a marshy area.

'La Thomasia' is typical of Switzerland's excellent high-alpine rock-gardens, geographically arranged and richly planted.

Some 3000 taxa grow here from mountains around the world, but for foreign visitors the Swiss collections are probably the most interesting: the majority are collected in the Vaud itself. Europe, Asia and North America are the main divisions, though there are three small beds for South America and New Zealand at the centre.

The only way to visit 'La Thomasia' is to wander round each bed, peering to make sure you miss nothing. It is a superb gallery of the high-mountain flora of the world, and all in a breathtaking setting of mountains and glaciers.

Up valley from Bex ☎ 024 498 13 32 **Open** May–Jun & Sep daily (except Tue) 11am–6pm; Jul–Aug daily 11am–7pm; Oct daily (except Tue) 1–5pm **Size** 1ha (2½ac) **Owner** Canton of Vaud ▢ ▢ ▢ www.botanique.vd.ch

13. Botanischer Garten der Universität Zürich

Zollikerstr. 107
8008 Zürich

Zürich University's botanic garden moved here in 1977; the old site in the city centre is still worth a visit, too. The new one has 9000 different plants. Its most striking feature are three glasshouses, each hemispherical in shape, with a ribbed structure that looks almost futuristic. They are dedicated respectively to tropical, subtropical and savannah plants, though the total area under glass is actually quite modest.

Next in interest is the rock-garden – always good in Swiss botanic gardens – whose core collection of alpine species is surrounded by plants from other European mountains and around the world. The ground orchids are especially attractive in late spring.

The water garden has a large number of well-designed tanks, most of them raised above ground level for better display – this works especially well for the water lilies. Elsewhere are a trendy bee-garden (bee-friendly plants), a garden of bright herbaceous plants, and a spring garden. The garden also plays host to a number of sculptural pieces (some better than others).

2km SE of city centre
☎ 044 634 84 61 **Open** Mar–Sep daily 7am–7pm (but 8am–6pm weekends); Oct–Feb daily 8am–6pm (but 8am–5pm weekends). Glasshouses: open later & shut earlier **Owner** Universität Zürich
🅿 ▣ 🆆 ♿ ⌗
🅆 www.bguz.unizh.ch
@ enz@systbot.unizh.ch

14. Botanischer Garten der Universität Bern

Altenbergrain 21
3013 Bern

Berne University's botanic garden occupies a small triangle of land on the northern side of the river Aare and has been here since 1859. If you enter from the bridge called *Lorrainebrücke*, you have a bird's-eye view of much of the garden, including the systematic beds.

The focal point of the garden's original design was the handsome administration building, but this is now rivalled by three splendid modern glasshouses, which seem to hang on the hillside – especially conspicuous (and visitable) in winter. They are dedicated respectively to tropical plants (mainly economic, like palms), ferns (including cycads) and cacti.

The handsome rock-garden has 1500 taxa and is divided into no less than 13 geographical or habitat sections. Perhaps the most interesting are the areas devoted to Swiss flora at the centre and the subalpine meadow flora of the Valais. The rock-garden department works closely

Berne's botanic garden is made on a steep river bank; its systematic beds can be seen from the bridge above.

with the mountain garden (*Alpengarten Schynige Platte*) near Wilderswil. Also worth seeking out are the woodland garden and little herb garden.

Space is at a premium, so many of the traditional areas of a botanic garden are necessarily small but Bern is, nevertheless, a very enjoyable garden to visit. It manages to cram 6000 taxa into its small compass and is maintained to a high standard.

City centre (northern part) across river from Kunstmuseum
☎ 031 631 49 45 **Open** Daily 8am–5pm (but 5.30pm Mar–Sep) **Size** 2.5ha (6ac) **Owner** Universität Bern 🅿 ▣ 🆆 ♿ ⌗
🅆 www.boga.unibe.ch/
@ info@botanischergarten.ch

15. Isole di Brissago Giardino Botanico

6614 Brissago e isole

The garden at Brissago occupies the largest of a group of little islands – indeed, Brissago is the only one that the ferry runs to. It is impossible to imagine a more un-Swiss site, almost frost-free and much closer in every way to such gardens as Villa Taranto in Italy than to anything in Switzerland.

The garden was laid out between 1885 and 1927 by an Irish adventurer, who called himself Baron St Leger, and his mysterious wife. Their accomplishment was to turn a barren mudflat into a sub-tropical paradise for plants. The garden has no real design; the baroness was a pupil of William Robinson, and for her the pleasure of making a garden was to grow as many beautiful and exotic plants as possible. But it is easy to find your way round and there is no end to the stunning views and satisfying compositions.

The outstanding features of the garden at Isole di Brissago today are its conifers and palms; a line of the comparatively hardy Chusan palm (*Trachycarpus fortunei*) curves along the edge of the embankment on the eastern side.

Baron St Leger had a characteristic Victorian interest in economic plants: there are two species of banana at

The *Trachycarpus fortunei* palms originally planted along the shore at Brissago have begun to seed themselves around the island.

Brissago (*Musa basjoo* and *M. textilis*) and specimens of the papyrus sedge (*Cyperus papyrus*) and the Japanese paper bush (*Edgeworthia chrysantha*). Today, the Swiss authorities maintain the island to a very high standard, and fill it with colourful bedding and bulbs.

Towards northern end of Lake Maggiore. Ferry runs from western side. **C** 091 791 43 61 **Open** Late Mar–late Oct daily 9am–6pm **Size** 2½ha (6ac) **Owner** Canton of Ticino

P ⊡ **⫪** **WC** **占** **⊞**

W www.isolebrissago.ch

@ decs-isole.brissago@ti.ch

AUSTRIA

16. Mirabellgarten

Mirabellplatz 4
5020 Salzburg

The Mirabelle Garden epitomizes the easygoing charm of Austria. It was first laid out in the 1690s as a setting for the bishop's new palace (now the city's offices). Fischer von Erlach was the architect of the palace, but there is barely an echo of his work in the gardens now. Everything has been reworked so frequently, pastiche upon pastiche, that little or nothing has survived.

Nevertheless, the rococo-style garden is a delight to visit. Meticulous standards of floriculture and maintenance are one reason, as are the changes of scale offered by later additions to the gardens, such as the hornbeam theatre, the rose garden, the Dwarf Garden (with 18th-century statues of vertically-challenged persons) and the aviary. One genuine survival is four Italian statues of mythological set-pieces like Pluto's abduction of Prosperina (apparently they also represent the four elements of fire, air, water and earth); these statues once stood in the centre of the baroque parterre. Nowadays, the parterres are grassed over, but the grass is the background for extravagantly planted

Salzburg's Mirabellgarten is a charming pastiche around the relics of the original rococo garden.

broderies of bright bedding plants in colourful pseudo-rococo swirls that gladden the heart and lift the spirits.

N of river Salzach, at NW corner of Marktplatz **C** 0662 80 72 **Open** Daily dawn–dusk **Size** 5ha (12½ac) **Owner** City of Salzburg

P ⊡ **WC** **占** **⊞** **⊞**

W www.stadt-salzburg.at

17. Schloßpark Schönbrunn

1030 Wien

Schönbrunn Palace is massive, grand and beautiful. It was intended to outshine Versailles – as an imperial palace, not a mere royal one. The gardens, too, are enormous, dating back to 1690, after the siege of Vienna, when they were laid out by Jean Trehet, a French pupil of Le Nôtre. The baroque outlines remain to this day – a long central axis flanked by diagonal *allées* with *bosquets* in between and *millefleurs* plantings.

The entire garden was much improved by the Empress Maria Theresa in the mid-18th century, so that most of its features date from 1740 to 1780. The main parterre was reworked, new walks and vistas opened up, and the garden extended in all directions. The Empress added the Neptune fountain at the centre, the picturesque Roman ruin, the obelisk fountain, the *Schöne Brunnen* well-house (the springs after which the palace is named) and the Gloriette (worth climbing up to for the view of Vienna). All were symbols of imperial power, wisdom, justice and stability. The palm house was added in the 1880s and the sundial house in the early 1900s, to accommodate Emperor Franz Joseph's ever-growing collection of plants.

Of special interest today is the newly restored Privy Garden, surrounded by fretwork arcades of Virginia creeper. The sunken part by the palace is filled with large citrus trees and standard lantanas in summer,

Citrus trees and lantanas are put out in summer to adorn the Privy Garden (imperial private garden) at Schönbrunn.

Schönbrunn and its gardens were built as symbols of imperial splendour.

while the parterres above are meticulously maintained.

What is remarkable about Schönbrunn's gardens is their scale, their beauty and the harmony between the various features and the palace itself. They are imperial in a way that Versailles can never be, and much less brash. Naturally, their importance is recognised by their listing as a UNESCO World Heritage Site.

5km SW of old city centre
☎ 01 877 50 87 **Open** Park: opens 6am in summer & 6.30am in winter; **closes** some time between 5.30pm & 8.30pm according to season. Privy Garden: Apr–Oct daily 9am–5pm (6pm Jul–Aug) **Size** 160ha (395ac) **Owner** The State
P ➤ ⛨ WC ♿ ⛺ ▦
W www.schoenbrunn.at

18. Volksgarten, Burggarten & Stadtpark
1030 Wien

The centre of old Vienna has no open spaces, but the city has a necklace of splendid public parks around its ring-road. Three of the best are the Volksgarten, Burggarten and Stadtpark.

The Volksgarten is the oldest, close to the Hofburg (Vienna's imperial palace) in the west of the city. It was laid out in the English landscape style in 1819 and made popular by concerts conducted by Johann Strauß the Elder. It has a very fine display of roses, plus seasonal floral displays, lakes and statues of the famous, including the Empress Elisabeth, but the most imposing structure is a copy of the Parthenon, called the *Theseustempel*.

Also part of the Hofburg complex, and originally the emperor's private garden, is the Burggarten, also landscaped in the English style in 1819 and best known for its statues of famous artists, including Mozart (rather kitsch – vulgarity is everywhere just below the surface in Vienna) and Goethe.

The Stadtpark is a 65-ha English-style park, on the south-east edge of the ring-road, first opened in 1862. The famous gilded statue of Johann Strauß the Younger

is here, but so are Brückner, Schubert and Lehár. The trees include a fine ginkgo and an enormous *Pterocarya fraxinifolia*.

All on edges of old city **Open** Daily dawn–dusk **Owner** City of Vienna
P ➤ ⛨ WC ♿

Vienna has many musical statues; this is Strauss's *Donauweibchen* in the Stadtpark.

Schloßpark Belvedere stretches from the lower palace to the upper, and beyond.

19. Schloßpark Belvedere
Prinz Eugen-Str. 27
1030 Wien

The Belvedere is a spacious baroque garden, first made for the military hero Prince Eugene of Savoy in 1717, and now extending from the Palais Schwarzenberg right up to the city's outer ring-road.

There are two palaces: the *Obere* (Upper) and the *Untere* (Lower) *Belvedere*, and the space between them was laid out by the French architect Dominique Girard. Only a genius could have welded together two such buildings, on different levels, so seamlessly. Ongoing modern restoration is returning the garden to its original format, and the work is of very high quality. A broad walk, lined with neat young cones and obelisks of yew, extravagant white statues and very tall hedges of *Acer campestre*, leads up to a symmetrical display of pools, fountains, cascades and yet more imposing sculptures. The extensive rococo broderies are marked out in box, grass, gravel and crushed brick. The huge pool at the top seems to reflect not only the Obere Belvedere but also the whole sky.

In SE of city ☎ 01 798 41 20 **Open** Daily 6am–dusk (6.30am in winter) **Size** 17ha (42ac) **Owner** The State
🅿 ▣ 🆆🅲 ♿ 🏛
🆆 www.belvedere.at
@ public@belvedere.at

20. Alpinum Wien
Prinz Eugen-Str. 27
1030 Wien

Vienna's alpine garden (also known as *Alpengarten Belvedere*) is one of Europe's best. It was founded in 1803, and moved here in 1865; it can be reached either from the botanic garden or from the Upper Belvedere, but a small admission fee is payable.

The garden's layout is informal, with beds and rockeries to suit as many plant types as possible. The presence of a few alpine trees further increases the opportunities for habitat plantings. Plants come from all over the world, including *Raoulia australis* (the 'vegetable sheep') from New Zealand, bulbs from the East Mediterranean, peat-lovers from North America and a host of native Austrian alpines. The total comes to more than 4000 different taxa, including some 300 sempervivums in a collection on the administration building's roof. All are labelled.

The garden is densely planted and well maintained. It is best to potter around slowly, looking at the beds

Alpinum Wien is a well-established rock-garden with a vast number of interesting plants.

Vienna's botanic garden has some excellent displays of native flowers, including this meadow of East Austrian steppe plants.

22. Schloß Hof
2294 Schloßhof

Schloß Hof was the country palace of Prince Eugene of Savoy. It sits on a spacious plateau high above the river Danube, with magnificent views towards the skyscrapers of suburban Bratislava. It was built in about 1725, and the gardens were laid out by Dominique Girard and Lukas von Hildebrandt. They have very recently been restored, using a painting by Canaletto dated 1760 as documentary evidence for how they appeared in their prime.

Four rococo broderies are tricked out in box, with yew cones and rather widely spaced ornamental plantings around the edges. The infill is of coloured gravel, shells, glass pieces, crushed brick and coal-dust. The design is unbelievably crisp and trim, but will probably lose its neatness as it fills out. There is a small but pretty modern garden in the courtyard of the Mayerhof, an old service area, and a small herb garden nearby.

from all possible angles and wondering at the profusion and beauty of the flowers. The garden also has a good number of bonsai plants, some in a separate display garden.

21. Botanische Garten der Universität Wien
Rennweg 14
1030 Wien

Vienna University's botanic garden was founded in 1754 by Empress Maria Theresa as a medical garden. Its oldest trees, a plane tree and a ginkgo, date from around 1800.

The original baroque layout has given way to an English landscape style, where plants are displayed both systematically and geographically. The systematic beds cover a large area immediately you enter the garden, starting with the graft hybrid + *Laburnocytisus* 'Adamii', magnolias and tulip trees. One surprise in such a cold climate is to find a fair-sized *Nothofagus antarctica* growing well. Other good trees include a three-trunked *Maclura pomifera*, a craggy, burr-encrusted *Populus nigra* subsp. *betulifolia* and a vast *Gymnocladus dioica*.

There is a good display of alpine plants (though the Alpengarten Belvedere is adjacent), including native Austrian plants (with habitat plantings of alpine meadows and the natural steppe communities of east Austria's lowlands). Trial displays of bedding are also chosen to show visitors what they can grow in their own gardens.

The garden's 9000 taxa include extensive glasshouse collections of gesneriads, bromeliads and orchids, but the only house open to the public is an all-purpose simulated tropical rainforest.

The parterres at Schloß Hof have been recently restored, using a Canaletto painting of 1760.

40km E of Vienna 📞 0228 52 00 00
Open Mid-Apr–Oct daily 10am–
6pm **Size** 30ha (74ac) **Owner**
Marchfeldschlösser Revitalisierungs-
und Betriebsgesellschaft
🅿 ♿ 🍴 🚾 ♿ 🚼 🎁 🖼
Ⓦ www.schlosshof.at
@ office@schlosshof.at

23. Rosarium Baden bei Wien

Doblhoffgasse
2500 Baden bei Wien

The rosarium in Baden bei
Wien is a fine example of
an Austrian civic garden. It
once formed part of the landscaped park of a large estate
called Schloß Weikersdorf but
now boasts the largest collection
of roses in the country.

The central point of the
design is the old orangery,
around which the garden was
laid out in the late 1960s.
The design is of that period,
currently unfashionable, but
intended to display roses as
individual blocks of colour.
Pools and fountains add a
sense of space, while height
comes from shrub roses and
a pergola for climbers. Most
of the roses are modern and
brightly coloured, but there are
also sections devoted to old
roses, including a collection
bred by the Hungarian Rudolf
Geschwind. The garden boasts
some 600 cultivars and 20 000
bushes in all.

Nagycenk's present gardens, though criticised by purists, are an imaginative reinterpretation of the original baroque layout.

Just W of town centre **Open** Daily
dawn–dusk **Size** 9ha (22ac)
Owner Town of Baden bei Wien
🅿 ♿ 🍴 🚾 ♿

HUNGARY

24. Nagycenk

Kiscenki u. 3
9485 Nagycenk

The palace and estate of
the Széchenyi family at
Nagycenk have now been
divided into innumerable
attractions: a stud farm,
a coach museum, a hotel,
a restaurant and the István
Széchenyi Memorial Museum.
The palace dates from the

1750s – pretty, baroque and
almost completely rebuilt
after World War II.

The original garden was
laid out in the 1760s, but
what we see today is a 1950s
reinterpretation rather than
an historical reconstruction.
Nevertheless, its box broderies,
clipped yews and hornbeam
hedges are pleasing. Beyond
the central fountain, an
ancient lime avenue, planted
in 1773, marches away for
2.6 km to the Széchenyi
mausoleum. In the 19th-
century park are large
plane trees, pterocaryas,
wellingtonias, liriodendrons,
purple beeches and a noisy
rookery.

25km E of Sopron 📞 99 360 061
Open Daily dawn–dusk **Size** 20ha
(50ac) 🅿 ♿ 🍴 🚾 ♿ 🖼
Ⓦ www.szechenyikastelyszallo.hu

25. Vácrátóti Botanikuskert

Alkotmány utca 2–4
2163 Vácrátót

The botanic garden at
Vácrátót started life in the
1870s as the private hobby
of its owner, Count Sándor
Vigyázó. Only its adoption
by the Hungarian Academy
of Sciences in 1954 saved
it from the fate of many
aristocratic parks in central
and eastern Europe. The
climate is difficult to work
with – annual rainfall is about

The rosarium at Baden bei Wien is Austria's premier rose garden and extremely popular with visitors in June and July.

50 cm and temperatures vary between 40°C in summer and -30°C in winter – but Vácrátót is now the biggest and best botanic garden in Hungary, with more than 12 000 taxa.

The garden is laid out in the style of an English landscape park around a series of artificial lakes, full of islands, bridges, romantic ruins and peninsulars. Grassy glades and long meadowy views show off the trees. Pterocaryas fringe the lakes, and the characteristic tubercles of a very fine *Taxodium distichum* are surrounded by a natural carpet of lily-of-the-valley (*Convallaria*). Common oaks (*Quercus robur*) grow alongside another native, *Q. frainetto*, and the Hungarian ash (*Fraxinus angustifolia* subsp. *pannonica*). The unusual *Populus simonii* 'Fastigiata', with its colourful bark, is worth seeking out, as is the varnish-tree (*Rhus verniciflua*). The hot summers enable such species as *Akebia quinata* and *Vitex negundo* to ripen their wood and survive the winter.

Recent years have seen much replanting, though many of the original trees have grown too close together and few bear name plates. The well-designed systematic gardens, by contrast, have lots of interesting, well-labelled plants. Prairie plants from the steppes, central Asia and the Rockies flourish alongside Hungarian natives, and there

Martonvásár has an English-style park, with lawns, lakes and some exceptional trees.

are good collections of *Hemerocallis*, paeonies, and herbs. But it is the 2800 different tree types that you will remember best.

35km N of Budapest **☎** 28 360122 **Open** Daily 8am–6pm (but 5pm Oct & 4pm Nov–Mar) **Size** 29ha (72ac) **Owner** Hungarian Academy of Sciences
P ☕ ⑪ WC ♿ ♗
W www.botanika.hu

26. Martonvásári Kastélypark
Brunszvik u. 2
2462 Martonvásár

The park of the Brunswick palace at Martonvásár only survived the communist years because of its importance to the Beethoven industry: the great composer wrote his *Appassionata* sonata here. Concerts are held every July and August in the mosquito-ridden, open-air theatre on the island, reached by a long, graceful wooden bridge.

The house is an 1870s English neo-gothic fantasy, white and elegant; half is now a Beethoven museum, while the rest is the seat of an Agricultural Research Institute. The English-style park is spaciously laid out, though there is little to admire except trees, including an ancient *Quercus × hispanica* 'Ambrozyana' by the house and, down by the lake, the tallest *Platanus × hispanica* 'Suttneri' in the world.

Autumn colour is good; the taxodiums on the island, for example, turn russet-brown in October. The whole park is much better maintained than is usual for relics of Hungarian feudalism – the lawns sweeping down to the lake would do credit to an English garden.

30km SW of Budapest
☎ 22 569 500 **Open** Daily (except Mon) 8am–7pm (6pm in winter) **Size** 68ha (168ac) **Owner** Agricultural Research Institute of the Hungarian Academy of Sciences
P ☕ WC ♿
W www.mgki.hu/

Vácrátót has the leading collection of trees in Hungary, as well as its largest botanic garden.

Gardens of South-east Europe

South-east Europe is a fascinating medley of small nation states, each with its own history and traditions. Many of these countries are small and newly independent, where good gardens are few, or even non-existent. Some experienced a brief period of monarchy, which has left them with a scattering of grand gardens, now in public ownership. Most have at least one botanic garden, but it would be a mistake for visitors to carry the usual Western expectations of well-run, well-stocked, interesting gardens throughout this corner of Europe. In Slovenia the standards are respectable, as befits a country whose culture has for centuries been taken from its Austrian neighbours, but there is less to see as one passes through the rest of old Jugoslavia towards Greece and the eastern Mediterranean. Even the national botanic gardens of the Balkan countries are generally neglected and disappointing. The best gardens are now being made by expatriates from northern Europe (notably from Germany, England and the Netherlands) but these are privately owned and not open to visitors.

Against this dark background, the gardens in this chapter stand out as beacons.

The renaissance garden at Trsteno in Croatia is, by any standards, of major importance and great beauty. The botanic gardens in Romania are well maintained and full of good plants. And the garden run by the Mediterranean Garden Society at Sparoza near Athens is a remarkable example of how to garden in the English style in an unEnglish climate. But for the most part, the Balkans is a wasteland where a peasant culture, foreign rule, civil war and political instability have created little and bequeathed nothing.

The future is brighter. Economic and social conditions are improving rapidly, and foreign investment has brought new lifestyle expectations. Old gardens are beginning to undergo restoration, and standards of financing, management and maintenance are improving. And the native flora of the Balkans is among the richest and most variable in Europe, providing a useful conservation mission for botanic gardens within the region, as well as promoting tourism. No holiday company at present would dream of promoting a tour of Greece or Bulgaria to visit gardens, but the time will come when such themed holidays are possible.

OPPOSITE: The relics of the 19th-century formal garden can still be seen at Arboretum Volčji Potok in Slovenia.

Gardens of South-east Europe

Slovenia
1 Botanični Vrt Univerze v Mariboru
2 Botanični Vrt
3 Arboretum Volčji Potok

Croatia
4 Botanički Vrt Prirodoslovno-matematičkog Fakulteta
5 Arboretum Trsteno
6 Botanički Vrt na Otoku Lokrumu

Serbia
7 Botanička Bašta Jevremovac

Romania
8 Grădina Botanică a Universității 'Babeş-Bolyai'
9 Grădina Botanică a Universității din Bucuresti

Bulgaria
10 Balchik Botanic Garden

Greece
11 Cephalonia Botanica
12 Sparoza
13 National Gardens, Athens

The systematic beds at Maribor's botanic garden include some attractive horticultural varieties.

SLOVENIA

1. Botanični Vrt Univerze v Mariboru

Fakulteta za Kmetijstvo
Vrbanska 30
2000 Maribor

Maribor University Botanic Garden is young and full of promise. Work began in 1994, and the garden opened to the public in 2002. It occupies a spacious site along a broad, gently rising valley. The standard of maintenance is good, and the garden has been laid out with much better taste than usual in south-east Europe.

Many of the plants are principally of horticultural interest rather than botanical, which makes it of particular interest to amateur gardeners. The circuit takes you first through a woodland garden of ancient oaks and alders underplanted with ferns, rhododendrons and hydrangeas. Next comes the systematic garden, in strips cut from the grass – paeonies, irises and dianthus are well represented. The pretty rock-garden has separate areas for plants from acid, karstic and serpentine soils, and here are also areas for aquatics. The rose garden is edged with box,

and fairly formal in design, with an attractive display of mainly modern roses. Although not a great garden, it is nevertheless an appealing one to visit.

At Pivola, S of Maribor, on road between Razvanje & Spodnje Hoče **02 2505800 Open** Daily 3–7pm (but opens 9am at weekends); **closed** in winter **Size** 8ha (20ac) **Owner** University of Maribor **P WC**
W www.uni-mb.si/botvrt
@ fk@uni-mb.si

2. Botanični Vrt

Ižanska cesta 15
Ljubljana

Ljubljana's botanic garden was founded in 1810. A lime tree planted by Marshal Auguste Marmont, governor of the Illyrian Provinces, dates back to Napoleonic times, and the arboretum has some venerable conifers and pterocaryas, too. The systematic beds include a good collection of paeony species, but at least one-third of the 4500 taxa in

Ljubljana's botanic garden dates back to 1810 and has some interesting herbaceous plants.

Today the 19th-century Arboretum Volčji Potok is famous for its colourful horticultural displays.

the garden are of Slovenian native plants. The geographical plantings concentrate on the alpine and karst areas and are largely accounted for by the rock-garden. The numerous alpine primulas are especially attractive here in spring, along with the endemic *Sempervivum wulfenii* var. *juvanii* and *Saxifraga hostii*. Substantial sections are also devoted to moorland, marshland and aquatic plants, including sundews (*Drosera* species) and water scissors (*Stratiotes aloides*).

Plans are afoot to move Ljubljana's Botanični Vrt to a newer, larger site soon, but the existing garden will still enjoy statutory protection as a cultural monument.

Within easy reach by city bus No. 3 (direction Rudnik) ☎ 01 4271280 **Open** Daily 7am–7pm (8pm Jul–Aug; 5pm in winter) **Size** 2ha (5ac) **Owner** University of Ljubljana

🅿 💻 🆆🅲 ♿ 🌱 🏛
🆆 www.bf.uni-lj.si/bi/bgarden
@ botanicni.vrt@siol.net

3. Arboretum Volčji Potok
1235 Radomlje

This arboretum is the most visited garden in Slovenia, largely because it has been

developed as a horticultural spectacle since the country gained its independence in 1992. The trees date back to the 19th century, when the estate belonged to the Souvan family; the baroque mansion was destroyed during World War II and has not been restored.

The layout is full of variety, with meadows and woodland areas, lakes, and lots of family entertainment. Good old trees include purple beeches, limes, liriodendrons and pterocaryas, with taxodiums and alders round the lakes and stream. There are about 2500 different trees and shrubs, including some splendid old Japanese maples and a collection of conifers, cornus and lilacs by the spacious rose garden. The garden is best known for its spring displays of daffodils and tulips, but then a sequence of azaleas, rhododendrons, roses, water lilies, summer bedding and dahlias provide the main floral spectacle. The autumn colour is good, too.

On main road between Radomlje and Kamnik ☎ 01 8312345 **Open** Mid-Mar–mid-Nov daily 8am–8pm (**closes** earlier in spring & autumn) **Size** 80ha (198ac) **Owner** Volčji Potok Foundation

🅿 💻 🍴 🆆🅲 ♿ 🌱 🏛
🆆 www.arboretum-vp.si
@ info@arboretum-vp.si

CROATIA

4. Botanički Vrt Prirodoslovno-matematičkog Fakulteta
Marulićev trg 9a
10000, Zagreb

Zagreb's botanic garden was founded in 1889 and the first plantings were undertaken in 1892. Its dual function, then as now, was to assist the research and teaching work of the university and to operate as a public park.

There are limitations to public access, however: the glasshouses are closed to the public, visitors may not walk on the grass, and many of the displays are grown in closed-off areas.

The garden was designed and constructed in the landscape style and much of it is occupied by the arboretum, planted in the later English landscape style. Some 1000 different trees and shrubs are displayed, mainly systematically. Tender plants like camellias and oranges are grown in pots put out for the summer but kept under glass in winter.

Croatia has an exceptionally rich natural flora, some 5500 taxa of higher plants (compare this with Spain's 5048 taxa,

France's 4630 and Germany's 3203). This diversity is very well displayed in the exceptional series of rock-gardens, where Croatian species are grown in three geographical groups: the karstic, the Mediterranean and the sub-Mediterranean. There are also good displays of roses, annuals, biennials and perennials, mainly to give visitors an idea of what they can grow in their own gardens.

Centre of Zagreb **C** 1 48 44 002 **Open** Apr–Oct daily 9am–6pm (7pm in summer). **Closes** 2.30pm Mon & Thu **Size** 4.7ha (12ac) **Owner** University of Zagreb, Faculty of Science
WC ♿ ♣ ▥
W www.hirc.botanic.hr/vrt/eng/ garden.htm
@ botgarzg@botanic.hr

5. Arboretum Trsteno
20233, Trsteno

Trsteno is an exceptional garden – the only one in Croatia of major historic interest. Its roots go back to the Renaissance: the substantial aqueduct that supplies both house and garden was built in 1492 and rebuilt (like the house) after an earthquake of 1667. It feeds into a spectacular baroque nymphaeum, added in 1736, where Neptune stands proudly and fish spew water into a pool. The flow continues down past the house, through basins and gullies, giving a refreshing cool sound.

The house has a fine position on a bluff above a tiny harbour, with a spacious loggia overlooking the sea. A 19th-century collection of plants surrounds it: cycads at the front, citrus to one side, and many palms, including washingtonias and *Livistona chinensis*. Here, too, are small formal gardens with overgrown box hedges. Irises and agapanthus add colour in season. The outlines of further formal gardens are detectable in the woodland behind the house.

The surrounding arboretum has a ground-thicket of bay

(some 15 m high), bamboo and native *Viburnum tinus*, from which introduced plants like *Phoenix canariensis* and Italian cypresses emerge. Fine trees include a very tall *Cinnamomum camphora* (plus several seedlings) and a vast, rugged *Platanus orientalis*, thought to be 400 years old.

The plant collection is not extensive – no more than 500 taxa – and maintenance is not of the highest standard, but it is well labelled. The joy of Trsteno, however, is that it exists at all, not least because the hillside behind it (but thankfully not the garden itself), was torched in the recent war with Serbia.

On coast, 24km NW of Dubrovnik **C** 385 752 019 **Open** Daily 7am–7pm (8am–3pm in winter) **Size** 25ha (63ac) **Owner** Croatian Academy of Sciences & Arts **P** ▢ WC ♿ ▥
W www.hazu.hr/ arboretum_trsteno.html

6. Botanički Vrt na Otoku Lokrumu
Laboratoriji Dubrovnik
20 000, Dubrovnik

The botanic garden on the island of Lokrum was laid out in the 1960s, neglected in the 1990s, and restored in the 2000s as a scientific station that would also attract trippers from Dubrovnik. Some of the older trees date back to plantings made by Archduke Maximilian of Hapsburg (the owner of Miramare near Trieste) in the 1850s.

The collections are small (500 taxa) but interesting, and combine the local flora of the southern Adriatic (including a magnificent specimen of the rare indigenous *Arbutus andrachne*) with trees and shrubs from parts of the world with similar climates. Plants from Chile, Australia, California and the Cape are especially well represented: the collection of some 70 *Eucalyptus* species was once the largest in Europe.

The layout is basically systematic, with allowances

A pergola runs from the house at Arboretum Trsteno to a shaded loggia high above the sea.

made for special cultivation needs. The plantings of palms, cacti, succulents and puyas are especially attractive. Look out for the rare Mexican *Pinus pseudostrobus* var. *oaxacana* and two large bushes (male and female) of *Daphniphyllum himalaense* var. *macropodum*.

Centre of island, reached by boat from Dubrovnik ☎ 020 323978 **Open** Daily dawn–dusk **Size** 1.6ha (4ac) **Owner** Institute of Oceanography and Fisheries 🚪 🚾 ♿ Ⓦ www.izor.hr/hr/lokrum/index.html @ katija@jadran.labdu.izor.hr

SERBIA

7. Botanička Bašta Jevremovac
43, Takovska Ul.
Beograd

Belgrade's botanic garden was founded by King Milan Obrenović in 1889, and named Jevremovac after his grandfather. Its collections are small – some 250 species of trees and bushes and 300 herbaceous plants – but it is a green lung in the centre of the city and pleasantly laid out in the landscape style.

The glasshouses date from 1892 and are in need of restoration, but they house a number of tropical and subtropical plants, including *Phoenix canariensis*, *Chamaerops humilis* and *Cereus peruvianus*. The Japanese garden is also interesting.

Centre of Beograd ☎ 011 768857 **Open** May–Oct daily 9am–7pm **Size** 5ha (12ac) **Owner** Belgrade University 🚪 🚾 ♿

ROMANIA

8. Grădina Botanică a Universităţii 'Babeş-Bolyai'
Gheorghe Bilascu nr 42
Cluj-Napoca

The botanic garden in Cluj was founded in 1920, shortly after the region of Transylvania passed from Hungary to Romania. Though principally a teaching garden, its ornamental layout has made it the city's leading tourist destination, attractively laid out on rolling hills.

The core of the garden is a 4-ha systematic garden arranged in phylogenetic order. The collection of native Romanian plants is very strong, too, with good displays from Transylvania, Bucovina, Dobrogea, Muntenia, Banat, Crisana and Oltenia. The 10 000 taxa also include displays of ornamental, economic and medicinal plants. The Japanese garden is a good one, and the Roman garden houses archaeological remains from the Roman colony of Napoca (among them a statue of Ceres), alongside vegetables and flowers that date back to ancient Roman times.

Two large glasshouses, split into six main sections, display tropical aquatics (including *Victoria cruziana*), palms, Mediterranean and Australian plants, succulents, bromeliads, ferns and orchids.

1km S of old city centre ☎ 264 597604 **Open** Daily 9am–6pm **Size** 14ha (35ac) **Owner** Universităţii 'Babeş-Bolyai' 🅿 🚪 🚾 ♿ 🏛 Ⓦ www.cjnet.ro/t/ rgradinabotanica.html @ grbot@grbot.ubbcluj.ro

9. Grădina Botanică a Universităţii din Bucuresti
Soseaua Cotrocenti nr 32
Sectorul 6, Of. Postal 15
76258 Bucuresti

Bucharest's botanical garden was laid out on a magnificent city-centre site in 1884 by the Belgian designer Fuchs. The collections extend to more than 10 000 species and the garden is one of the best maintained in south-east Europe. It has several formal areas around the glasshouses, and a flowing 19th-century layout elsewhere. The Italian garden, for example, fills a neat geometrical space between two avenues of chestnuts, while the pinetum is informally laid out on a hill from which a waterfall spills down to the looping lake. There are good collections of plants in the systematic beds, a rose garden with 120 cultivars, an iris garden (70 species and cultivars) and a garden of useful plants divided into sections for medicine, industry and fodder.

But the garden's highlight is the collections of native Romanian plants, arranged geographically to include rare endemics from the Carpathians and the Dobrogea area. One of the surprises is a collection of 200 endemic Mediterranean species.

The glasshouses are unusually comprehensive, with sections for palms (40 species), orchids, tropical ferns, tropical water plants (especially *Victoria amazonica*), succulents, cacti and carnivorous plants.

Centre of city, by Cotroceni Palace ☎ 0212 6700 **Open** Daily 8am–5pm Glasshouses: Daily (except Mon) 9am–1pm **Size** 17ha (42ac) **Owner** Universităţii din Bucuresti 🚪 🚾 ♿ 🏛 @ asarbu@botanic.unibuc.ro

BULGARIA

10. Balchik Botanic Garden
9600 Balchik

Balchik's botanic garden is not really a botanic garden at all, but the summer seaside residence of Queen Marie of Romania, who employed Italian architects and Swiss gardeners to lay out her *Tenha Yuva* (Nest of Quiet) in the 1920s. There are certainly good plants here, including a tall *Ginkgo biloba*, a *Metasequoia glyptostroboides*, a rubber tree (*Hevea brasiliensis*), 200-year-old poplars and an olive grove.

It is the garden's design, however, that pleases most – a series of romantic enclosures

brimful with architectural bric-a-brac collected by the queen: huge earthenware jars from Morocco, gravestones from Moldavia and Bessarabia, and a marble throne from Florence. The garden descends gently over six terraces to a magnificent Romanesque-style cloister in pale limestone, with pools and running water that offer coolness in the heat.

The features include a Cretan labyrinth, a French garden (clipped box cones and geometric beds), a Garden of Allah, a Silver Well and a cactus garden that claims (incorrectly) to be second only to Monaco's in size, but is nevertheless large and impressive.

35km N of Varna ☎ 0579 72559
Open Daily dawn–dusk **Size** 6.5ha (16ac) **Owner** University of Sofia
🅿 ◫ 🆆🅲 🖼 🎫
🆆 ww.balchik.net/palace
@ ubg_balchik@yahoo.com

GREECE

11. Cephalonia Botanica
Argostoli 28100
Kefallinia

Cephalonia Botanica is an attempt to garden with native Ionian plants in a way that is both educational and beautiful. It is the brainchild of English landscape architect Jennifer Gay, and her Cephalonian patrons, the Cosmetatos family.

The garden has been made since 2003 within an ancient olive grove on a gently terraced hillside overlooking the Bay of Argostoli, with a stream running down the middle. Some areas are given to genuine native habitats – the characteristic *phrygana* of Greece (including thyme, sage, rosemary and oregano) and the taller Mediterranean *maquis*, including a 6-m high *Quercus coccifera*. Structure is given by such trees as *Cercis siliquastrum* and *Pinus pinea*, plus evergreen shrubs like *Arbutus unedo*, *Viburnum tinus*

Sparoza is the finest example in the Eastern Mediterranean of the modern English style of gardening.

(a much underestimated plant), *Erica arborea* and *Teucrium fruticans*. The cistus include *C. albidus* and *C. salviifolius*. Flower power comes from asphodels and low-growing *Iris unguicularis* and *Narcissus tazetta*. Cephalonia's two endemic species, *Abies cephalonica* and *Viola cephalonica*, are both represented.

The garden is still young and its future depends upon the support of its foundation, but there is nowhere better in the Ionian islands to experience the idealisation of the Greek flora. It is a place to wonder what gardening would be like if William Robinson and Gertrude Jekyll had been Greek.

Southern edge of Argostólion
☎ 026710 26632 **Open** Daily (except Sun–Mon & pub hols) 10am–2pm & 6–8pm **Size** 0.4ha (1ac) **Owner** Focas-Cosmetatos Foundation
🅿 ♿

12. Sparoza
P.O. Box 14
GR-190 02 Peania

Sparoza was a bare hillside – waterless, alkaline and windswept – when first laid out and planted by a landscape architect, Jackie Tyrwhitt, in the 1960s. She also built the house in the style of an old stone farm. It is now owned by the Goulandris Natural

History Museum and operates as the headquarters of the Mediterranean Garden Society.

Sparoza is a first-rate example of how to garden in the English style in a Mediterranean climate, with maximum use of native plants and minimum use of watering. It is also organic. Structure comes from three narrow stone-backed terraces below the house, which drift into the rocky *phrygana*, and through the judicious planting of trees – native *Cupressus sempervirens* and *Pinus halepensis*, cultivated olives, plus specimens of exotic *Eucalyptus*, *Jacaranda* and *Parkinsonia aculeata*, among others. Great use is made of Greek native plants: *Ptilostemon chamaepeuce, Euphorbia characias*, the pungent-leaved *Vitex agnus-castus, Lamium moschatum*, cerinthes, *Acanthus*, lentisks and *Allium neapolitanum*. On the terraces are collections of native Greek tulips, fritillaries, cyclamen, plus lots of *Iris attica, Ebenus cretica*, and *Styrax officinalis*. Opuntias, agaves and aloes provide an exotic touch by being worked into mixed plantings – this was one of Jackie Tyrwhitt's most original ideas.

As the garden moves way from the house and into the surrounding *phrygana*, so the plantings become wilder and less dependant on exotics, and so, too, the wild plants are less controlled, more encouraged to self-seed. These include not just asphodels and irises (*I. germanica*), but hundreds of native orchids. The garden is maintained by a remarkable number of volunteers, mostly of English origin.

2km from Athinai (Athens) airport ☎ 0210 6643 089
Open By appointment
Size 2ha (5ac)
Owner Mediterranean Garden Society ℗
🔟 www.mediterraneangardensociety.org

13. National Gardens, Athens

Athinai

The National Gardens were once the royal gardens attached to the palace in Syntagma Square, first laid out for Queen Amalia in 1839 by the German architect Friedrich von Gärtner. Apart from a fine straight avenue of wine-palms (*Jubaea chilensis*), the garden was laid out irregularly, as a series of serpentine walks in the landscape style, but adapted for a Mediterranean climate. Plants came as gifts from other royal gardens all over Europe. It is not a botanic collection in any sense, though there is a pretty garden building called the Botanical Museum.

The walks are generally lined with rather gappy hedges of such evergreens as *Ligustrum lucidum* and *Pittosporum tobira* and the shrubberies behind are mostly planted with sweet-scented evergreen trees and shrubs, including many orange trees, laurustinus, Canary Island palms, and some venerable plants of bay-laurel (*Laurus nobilis*).

The standard of maintenance is not of the highest order, but everywhere self-sown acanthus remind us how much Greek architecture owes to this most stately of plants, and the gardens offer an oasis of peace in the hell-hole which is central Athens.

Central Athinai **Open** Daily dawn–dusk **Size** 15.5ha (38ac)
Owner City of Athens
🅿 🚾 ♿
🔟 www.athensinfoguide.com/ wtsgarden.htm

An avenue of tall wine-palms (*Jubaea chilensis*) leads down from the ex-royal palace in the National Gardens, Athens.

PLANT COLLECTIONS GUIDE

Many people visit gardens principally to look at plants. Europe has most of the world's largest and oldest plant collections. The following list is intended to direct readers with particular interests to discover the best gardens for the type of plants they most enjoy.

Alpine Plants
Austria Alpinum Wien **Denmark** Botanisk Have Københavns Universitet **France** Jardin Alpin du Lautaret, Jardin d'Altitude du Haut-Chitelet, Jardin des Plantes de Paris **Germany** Botanischer Garten Göttingen, Botanischer Garten und Botanisches Museum Berlin-Dahlem, Botanischer Garten München-Nymphenburg, Botanischergarten der Friedrich-Schiller-Universität, Botanischergarten der Stadt Köln, Rennsteiggarten **Great Britain** Branklyn Garden, Royal Botanic Garden (Edinburgh), Royal Botanic Gardens (Kew), RHS Garden Wisley **The Netherlands** Botanische Tuinen Utrecht **Sweden** Göteborgs Botaniska Trädgård **Switzerland** Jardin Alpin de Pont de Nant 'La Thomasia'

Bamboos
France Bambouseraie de Prafrance **Germany** Botanischer Garten und Botanisches Museum Berlin-Dahlem

Cacti & Succulents
France Jardin Exotique de Monte Carlo, Jardin Exotique de Roscoff, Villa Ephrussi de Rothschild **Germany** Botanischer Garten und Botanisches Museum Berlin-Dahlem, Botanischer Garten München-Nymphenburg **Great Britain** Royal Botanic Gardens (Kew), RHS Garden Wisley, Tresco Abbey **Italy** Giardino Esotico Pallanca, Orto Botanico di Cagliari, Orto Botanico di Catania, Orto Botanico di Palermo **The Netherlands** Arboretum Trompenburg **Spain** Botanicactus, Jardí Botànic Mar i Murtra, Jardí Botànic 'Pinya de Rosa'

Herbaceous Plants
Czech Republic Pražská Botanická Zahrada **Estonia** Tallinna Botaanikaaed **France** Le Clos du Coudray, Jardin des Plantes de Paris **Germany** Freundschaftsinsel, Grugapark Essen, Hermannshof Schau- und Sichtungsgarten, Planten un Blomen, Weihenstephan Sichtungsgarten, Westpark **Great Britain** Beth Chatto Gardens, Cambridge University Botanic Garden, Longstock Water Gardens, Royal Botanic Gardens (Kew), RHS Garden Wisley **The Netherlands** Botanische Tuin De Dreijen, Mien Ruys Tuinen

Mediterranean Plants
France Jardin Exotique de Roscoff **Great Britain** Abbotsbury Sub-tropical Gardens **Greece** Sparoza **Italy** Giardini Hanbury, La Mortella, Orto Botanico di Cagliari, Orto Botanico di Napoli, Orto Botanico di Palermo **Spain** Jardí Botànic de Barcelona **Ukraine** Nikitsky Botanical Garden

Rhododendrons
Finland Mustila Kotikunnassäätiö **France** Arboretum des Grandes Bruyères, Le Bois des Moutiers, Château de Gaujacq **Germany** Botanischergarten der Stadt Köln, Rhododendronpark **Great Britain** Arduaine Garden, Bodnant Gardens, Exbury Gardens, Leonardslee Lakes & Gardens, Royal Botanic Garden (Edinburgh), RHS Garden Wisley, Savill Garden, Wakehurst Place **Ireland** Mount Stewart, Rowallane Garden **Italy** Isola Madre, Parco Burcina 'Felice Piacenza', Villa Carlotta, Villa Taranto **The Netherlands** Arboretum Trompenburg, Botanische Tuin Belmonte **Sweden** Göteborgs Botaniska Trädgård

Roses
Belgium Kasteelpark Coloma **France** Les Chemins de la Rose, Parc de Bagatelle, Parc de la Tête d'Or, Roseraie du Val-de-Marne **Germany** Europa-Rosarium, Europas Rosengarten, Insel Mainau, Westfalenpark **Great Britain** David Austin Roses, Mottisfont Abbey **Italy** Il Roseto di Cavriglia, Villa Reale (Monza) **Sweden** Trädgårdsföreningen

Trees
Belgium Arboretum Kalmthout, Nationale Plantentuin van Belgie **Czech Republic** Státní Hrad Buchlov **France** Arboretum de Balaine, Arboretum National des Barres, Arboretum National de Chèvreloup, Château de Versailles, Jardins de Valloires **Germany** Botanischer Garten und Botanisches Museum Berlin-Dahlem, Botanischer Garten Göttingen, Späth's Arboretum **Great Britain** Benmore Botanic Garden, Caerhays Castle, Castle Howard, Hergest Croft Gardens, National Pinetum, Royal Botanic Gardens (Kew), RHS Garden Wisley, Savill Garden, Sheffield Park Garden, Sir Harold Hillier Gardens, Westonbirt Arboretum **Ireland** Annesley Gardens & Castlewellan National Arboretum, Mount Usher Gardens **Italy** Giardini e Rovine di Ninfa, Villa Taranto **The Netherlands** Arboretum Trompenburg, Botanische Tuin Belmonte, Von Gimborn Arboretum **Portugal** Jardim Botânico Universidade de Lisboa **Spain** La Concepción, Real Jardín Botánico

Tropical Plants & Orchids
Belgium Nationale Plantentuin van Belgie, Serres Royales **Denmark** Botanisk Have Københavns Universitet **France** Jardin des Plantes de Paris, Les Serres d'Auteuil **Germany** Berggarten, Botanische Gärten der Rheinischen Friedrich-Wilhelms-Universität Bonn, Botanischer Garten und Botanisches Museum Berlin-Dahlem, Palmengarten, Park Wilhelma **Great Britain** Royal Botanic Garden (Edinburgh), Royal Botanic Gardens (Kew), RHS Garden Wisley **Russia** Komarov Botanical Garden **Spain** Jardín Botánico de Puerto de la Cruz

GLOSSARY

allée
An avenue of trees planted at regular intervals and usually connecting a house or its formal garden with the wider countryside beyond.

anglo-chinois
A development of the rococo style that incorporated garden houses, bridges and other structures in the Chinese style within an informal English landscape.

Arts-and-Crafts movement
An aesthetic movement that started in England and inspired practitioners of the decorative arts to adopt rustic styles and local diversity. It influenced the cottagey garden designs of William Robinson and Gertrude Jekyll and spread throughout Europe in the years 1880–1915.

azulejos
Ornamental ceramic tiles, usually glazed and coloured, used to make garden tableaux in Spain and, especially, Portugal.

baroque
A style applied to all the arts and characterised by drama, movement, confidence and intricacy, but usually employed as a statement of power. It is particularly associated with the Counter-Reformation and the French monarchy in the period 1600–1750.

basin
A pool of water, typically surrounding a fountain and contained by low walls of stone, but also applied to describe larger, formal stretches of still water.

Bauerngarten
(lit. 'cottage garden') A German kitchen garden, often shaped as a quincunx.

berceaux
Raised flower beds, contained within metal strapwork or wooden canes, resembling a child's cradle and planted with colourful flowers and tender plants.

bosquet
A dense plantation of trees and/or shrubs held within clipped hedges.

broderie
A type of baroque parterre based on embroidery, with elaborate, flowing, curving patterns that resemble ribbons, and often made in clipped box with a background of gravel, grass or crushed brick.

caisses de Versailles
Large planters, usually cube-shaped, with short legs and round finials at the four upper corners, originally developed at Versailles to display large citrus plants in summer.

cottage ornée
A picturesque, excessively rustic cottage, often with gothic windows and a thatched roof, and incorporated into a landscape scheme (*c.*1790–1860).

cour d'honneur
The main courtyard in front of a French château.

cromlech
A prehistoric Celtic stone structure, consisting of a single, round, low chamber and originally used for burials. Imitation cromlechs were a fashionable garden accessory between 1780 and 1840.

fijnbos
The dense native vegetation of the coastal regions of Cape Province in South Africa, similar to the Mediterranean *maquis* and including an exceptionally rich mixture of *Erica*, *Restio* and *Protea* species.

garrigue
The native vegetation of the central and western Mediterranean coast and low-lying areas inland. Strictly speaking, it differs from *maquis* by occurring on alkaline soils, typically with *Quercus ilex*, *Q. coccifera*, rosemary, pistachio, lentisks and *Cistus albidus*, but the two are often used interchangeably.

giardino segreto
(lit. 'secret garden') An Italian phrase for a secluded, enclosed private garden within a larger garden or series of gardens.

giochi d'acqua
(lit. 'water games') Hidden spouts that allow a garden owner to soak his unsuspecting guests with jets of water.

herm
An ancient Greek sculpture with a bearded human head and shoulders emerging from a plain, rectangular pillar, so-called because they were sacred to Hermes, the messenger of the gods.

holotype
The original plant (or part of a plant) from which a species or subspecies was first described and named.

jardin anglais
An English-style landscaped park, typically with 'natural' plantations of trees in grass.

jardin français
A garden in the French baroque style, typically with strong axes, parterres, fountains and terraces.

landscape movement
An English style developed by 'Capability' Brown and Humphry Repton, of laying out large areas of amenity land as parkland, with trees and shrubs arranged in a natural manner surrounded by grass or pasture.

maquis
The native vegetation of the central and western Mediterranean coast and low-lying areas inland. Strictly speaking, it differs from *garrigue* by occurring on acid

soils, typically with *Arbutus unedo*, *Spartium junceum*, *Clematis flammula* and *Rosa sempervirens*.

millefleurs
A method of embellishing parterres, taken from embroidery, which involves planting several different plants (usually annuals) in an agreeable combination; this is then repeated around the edge.

monopteros
A classical building, consisting of an open circle of columns supporting a dome.

mosaïculture
A 19th-century French word for highly coloured bedding schemes, often using large quantities of small plants to create complex patterns or representational scenes.

mudéjar
A Moorish style of architectural decoration based on Islamic precedents in Spain.

patte-d'oie
(lit. 'goose's foot') An arrangement of three walks or avenues radiating out at an angle of 60° from a single point.

phrygana
The native vegetation of the eastern Mediterranean coast and low-lying areas inland. Botanists subdivide *phrygana* into several types according to the geology of the soil and the plant species it supports.

potager
A kitchen garden in the French style, usually formally laid out.

Pulhamite
An artificial stone invented by James Pulham and Son in the 1840s and widely used in Britain to make grottos and large rock-gardens up until 1940.

quincunx
A formal and symmetrical garden with five segments, typically consisting of four rectangular parterres surrounding a central circular bed or pool.

quinta
A Portuguese country estate.

Renaissance
A period in the history of culture that started in Italy *c.*1450 but spread throughout Europe and is characterised by a revival of classical learning.

Robinsonian
A style of wild or woodland gardening developed by William Robinson (1838–1935) in Britain and Ireland.

rocaille
Ornamental rockwork that incorporates tufa, shells or pebbles; a popular feature of the rococo

rococo
A frivolous and amusing style of building and decorating, eventually applied to all the arts, that developed from the baroque and often has oriental elements. It is particularly associated with Catholic parts of Germany in the period 1730–80.

sacro bosco
(lit. 'sacred wood') A woodland imbued with a spiritual quality, often pantheistic, based on classical precedents.

taxon
(pl. 'taxa') A plant identified by a distinguishing name, or a group of plants sharing that name, including genera, species and cultivars.

tesserae
Small, glazed tiles, usually coloured – the basic unit for making mosaic.

tufa
A soft, porous, lightweight limestone rock much used for growing alpine plants and the ornamentation of stonework.

PICTORIAL CREDITS

All photographs by Charles Quest Ritson, except for the following:

Teija Alanko, p. 316 (Helsinki University's botanic garden); **Chistopher Blair**, p. 234 (Haddon Hall, Chatsworth); **Kathryn Bond & Lelde Pfafrode**, p. 327 (Latvijas Nacionālais Botāniskais Dārzs); **Mike Clements**, p. 326 (Palangos Botanikos Parkas); **Tony Fawcett**, p. 128 (Parc Floral d'Apremont); **David Hardy & Judith Davies**, p. 236 (National Botanic Garden of Wales); **Jerry Harpur**, p. 90 (Bagatelle), p. 108 (Jardin du Luxembourg); **Sarah Harris**, p. 250 (Helmingham Hall); **Shauna Hay**, p. 227 (Royal Botanic Garden, Edinburgh); **Peter Hayden**, p. xii (Pavlovsk), pp. 324, 326 (Komarov Botanical Garden), p. 337 (Pavlovsk), p. 338 (Tsarskoe Selo), p. 339 (Gatchina Palace); **Moira Hughes**, p. 222 (Inverewe); **Tessa Knott**, p. 228 (Glenwhan); **Andrew Lawson**, p. viii (Villandry), pp. xvi–vii (Great Dixter), p. 26 (Giardini Boboli), p. 37 (Giardini e Rovine di Ninfa), p. 40 (Villa d'Este); **Robin Llywelyn**, p. 236 (Portmeirion); **Steve McNamara & The National Trust for Scotland**, p. 224 (Branklyn); **Piet Oudolf**, p. xiv (Kwekerij Piet Oudalf), p. 296 (Kwekerij Piet Oudalf); **John Patrick**, p. 139 (Manoir d'Eyrignac); **Guillaume Pellerin**, p. 101 (Jardins du Château de Vauville); **Brigid Quest-Riston**, p. 140 (Bambouseraie de Prafrance), p. 142 (Jardin Méditerranéen de Roquebrun); **Isabelle, Comtesse de Quinsonas-Oudinot**, p. 138 (Château de Touvet); **Jukka Reinikainen**, p. 316 (Mustilan Kotikunnassäätiö); **Martyn & Alison Rix**, p. 301 (Kasteel Hex); **Camilla Roberts & Ruslanas Iržikevičius**, p. 326 (Botanikos Sodas, Vilnius); **Peter Valder**, p. 109 (Les Serres d'Auteuil, Jardins des Tuileries), p. 110 (Parc des Buttes-Chaumont, Parc Floral de Paris), p. 111 (Parc Monceau); **Helen Walch & the Sandringham Estate Office**, p. 247 (Sandringham House); **Charles Williams & Cheryl Kufel**, p. 254 (Caerhays Castle)

The author is indebted to the following for their help with picture research: the de Cossé-Brissac family & Société Hôtelière d'Apremont; Anne James & Fingal County Council; Mairi McVey & The National Trust for Scotland; Eileen O'Rourke, Pauline Dowling & the Office of Public Works; and Patrick Sermadiras de Pouzols de Lile & Shophie Maynard.

INDEX